OXFORD EC L

General Editor: F. G. Jacobs
Advocate General, The Court of Justice
of the European Communities

EC COMPETITION LAW

WITHDRAWN

UTSA LIBRARIES

OXFORD EC LAW LIBRARY

The aim of this series is to publish important and original studies of the various branches of European Community Law. Each work will provide a clear, concise, and critical exposition of the law in its social, economic, and political context, at a level which will interest the advanced student, the practitioner, the academic, and government and Community officials.

Other Titles in the Library

The European Union and its Court of Justice
Anthony Arnull

The General Principles of EC Law
Takis Tridimas

EC Company Law
Vanessa Edwards

EC Sex Equality Law
Second edition
Evelyn Ellis

European Community Law of State Aid
Andrew Evans

External Relations of the European Community
I. MacLeod, I. D. Hendry, and Stephen Hyett

Directives in European Community Law
Sacha Prechal

EC Securities Regulation
Niamh Moloney

EC Tax Law
Paul Farmer and Richard Lyal

The European Internal Market and International Trade
Piet Eeckhout

Trade and Environment in the European Community
Andreas R. Ziegler

EC Employment Law
Second edition
Catherine Barnard

EC Customs Law
Timothy Lyons

The Law of Money and Financial Services in the EC
Second edition
J. A. Usher

EC Agricultural Law
Second edition
J. A. Usher

EC COMPETITION LAW

Fourth Edition

D. G. GOYDER

Solicitor; Visiting Professor in Law at King's College London

OXFORD
UNIVERSITY PRESS

OXFORD
UNIVERSITY PRESS

Great Clarendon Street, Oxford OX2 6DP

Oxford University Press is a department of the University of Oxford.
It furthers the University's objective of excellence in research, scholarship,
and education by publishing worldwide in

Oxford New York

Auckland Bangkok Buenos Aires Cape Town Chennai
Dar es Salaam Delhi Hong Kong Istanbul Karachi Kolkata
Kuala Lumpur Madrid Melbourne Mexico City Mumbai Nairobi
São Paulo Shanghai Taipei Tokyo Toronto

Oxford is a registered trade mark of Oxford University Press
in the UK and in certain other countries

Published in the United States
by Oxford University Press Inc., New York

First published 1988
Second edition 1993
Third edition 1998
Fourth edition 2003

British Library Cataloguing in Publication Data

Data available

ISBN 0–19–925788–4 (pbk.)
ISBN 0–19–926145–8 (hbk.)

1 3 5 7 9 10 8 6 4 2

Typeset in Adobe Minion
by RefineCatch Limited, Bungay, Suffolk
Printed in Great Britain by
TJ International Ltd, Padstow, Cornwall

Dedicated to
Sir Arthur fforde
(1900–1985)
Lawyer, Headmaster, and Poet

GENERAL EDITOR'S FOREWORD

The fourth edition of this book brings up to date once again a work which has established itself, not least by the directness and originality of its approach, as one of the leading works in the field.

But this new edition has a special topicality. The entire machinery for the enforcement of competition law in the European Union is being re-cast, and its provisions are likely to be more fully operational and in many ways more effective than hitherto. With effect from 1 May 2004—which is also the date set for the great enlargement of the European Union—responsibility for enforcing the competition rules in Articles 81 and 82 of the Treaty will lie largely with the national authorities of the Member States. Perhaps most significantly, national authorities and national courts will have the power to apply the exemption provisions of Article 81(3) of the Treaty—a power hitherto reserved to the European Commission—and thus effectively to apply for the first time Articles 81 and 82 in their entirety.

In addition, provisions closely modelled on Articles 81 and 82, and requiring to be interpreted and applied in the same way as the Treaty provisions, are now in force as domestic law in the Member States, and are effectively enforced by national authorities and by national courts—in the United Kingdom, for example, by the Competition Commission and the Competition Appeal Tribunal, as well as by the ordinary Courts. Provisions have been introduced in the UK (and there are parallels in other Member States) for claims for damages by individuals or consumer organizations, and for criminal 'cartel' offences.

Alongside these dramatic reforms in the system of enforcement, substantive competition law itself has radically evolved on many fronts—not only under the central cartel provisions of Article 81 but in such areas as collective dominance, essential facilities, and merger control.

Despite the ever more rapid developments in the subject, the author retains a fresh palette, and still succeeds in providing, within a reasonable compass, a comprehensive work which covers the whole field of EC competition law and policy.

The book not only remains up to date, but also looks to the future. Yet it maintains the virtues of the previous editions: the elucidation of the interconnections between law and economics; the historical perspective which enables the current law to be properly understood; and the concern to look at the subject not only from the viewpoint of the lawyer and the corporate adviser, but also from the perspective of those who administer the system.

The book will be of interest therefore to the student, practitioner, and administrator alike, and especially to those who seek not merely to look up particular points or to discover the rules, but to understand the system of which they form a part.

April 2003   Francis G. Jacobs

AUTHOR'S PREFACE TO THE FOURTH EDITION

New editions of this work have appeared every five years since its first publication in 1988. The period between the third edition in 1998 and this fourth edition has, however, seen far more change and development in the subject than any of the previous equivalent periods. It has made the task of preparing this new edition both unusually demanding and rewarding. EC competition policy in its early days was a small stream whose features could be quite easily and briefly described; over the last forty-five years, however, this stream has grown into a mighty river with an impact far beyond the surrounding European landscape, at times running smoothly but at other moments disturbed by sudden squalls and fierce currents.

In the last five years, for example, the European Commission has altered its techniques for handling cartel cases through a Leniency Programme that has achieved considerable success. It has adopted a new Block Exemption No. 2790/99 for vertical agreements that places far more emphasis on the economic effects of such agreements than its largely form-based predecessors. It has under both internal and external pressures proposed major changes to the Merger Regulation in both procedural and substantive aspects. Moreover, it has been successful in persuading Member States to accept, through the modernization programme, a radical reform under which both national competition authorities and national courts accept from May 2004 a major share in responsibility for enforcing Articles 81 and 82.

For its part, the United Kingdom, after over two decades of relative stagnation in legislative terms, has adopted two major competition statutes: The Competition Act 1998 and The Enterprise Act 2002. These have brought UK competition law effectively into line with Articles 81 and 82 whilst at the same time retaining its well established procedures for merger and market investigation and reducing political involvement in competition matters. These changes have also led to the strengthening of new or reconstituted independent institutions including the Competition Appeal Tribunal (formerly the Competition Commission Appeal Tribunal), chaired by Sir Christopher Bellamy, whose judgments applying EC law in respect of Competition Act appeals in accordance with section 60 of the 1998 Act have been of a consistently high standard. Another important advance at both EC and national level has been the availability of so many decisions and policy documents of both administrative bodies and courts on their websites, an important step forward in transparency and one of major value to both lawyers and law students.

Against this background there has been a temptation to replace much of the older case-law and material with references to recent cases and current developments. I have however tried to keep a balance between recording the past, interpreting the present, and trying to anticipate the course of future developments. Given that the book could not be extended in length by more than a few pages I have tried to make room for new material (especially in Chapters 15, 17, 18, and 20) by pruning minor cases and some historical material of relatively transient interest. However I have tried to retain historical material which relates to the earlier development of individual topics because often this has had a significant impact on later developments. I have continued to describe important cases in some detail because my teaching experience leads me to think that this is helpful to students and lawyers required to seek an understanding of the subject, faced by what is now a formidable number of decided cases, often complex in their factual and legal detail, from which it is not always easy to acquire the salient points at first reading without some guidance.

In referring to Articles of the Treaty of Rome whose numbering was altered by the Treaty of Amsterdam in 1997, I have adopted the practice of referring only to the new number, e.g. Articles 81 and 82 rather than '81(ex. 85) or 82 (ex. 86)'. The only exception is where a court judgment has referred to an Article under its old number; here I have changed the reference to the current numbering but left it in square brackets so as to indicate the change. Likewise for consistency I have described the Directorate General for Competition throughout as 'DG Comp', though strictly speaking the change of name from 'DG IV' occurred only in 1999; merger decisions prior to that change have been left under the reference of IV/M with only cases post-September 1999 as Comp/M.

Towards the end of the period during which this edition was being prepared Regulation No. 1/2003 was published, which will replace Regulation No. 17/62 from 1 May 2004. This Regulation is of major importance, and I have given it coverage both in Chapter 20 (as it affects national competition authorities) and Chapter 21 (as it affects national courts). Moreover in Chapter 25 dealing with the future of European competition policy I have looked at a number of problems which may arise in its implementation both by the Commission and Member States. I have also in Chapters 18 and 25 looked at changes likely in 2004 in the terms of the Merger Regulation, in response both to public criticisms by the Court of First Instance of the Commission's handling of second phase cases and the Commission's own perception of its need to improve substantive and procedural aspects of these important assessments.

In previous editions I have written the entire text, but on this occasion I have been grateful to be able to call in outside assistance, though this phrase may not be a strictly accurate one to describe the help received from my daughter Joanna, Barrister at Law, with Freshfields Bruckhaus Deringer in Brussels, who contributed Chapters 10 and 11 on distribution. She is the author of *Distribution Law* (3rd edn.) published by Palladian Law Publishing in 2000. Chapter 23 on the international aspects of EC competition law was contributed by Philip Marsden who is the author of *A Competition Policy for the WTO* (published in 2003 by Cameron May); he has practised as a trade and competition lawyer in Tokyo and London and as a competition official in Ottawa.

As before, I have had the opportunity of discussing current issues with a number of Commission officials in Brussels including on this occasion the Director General, Alexander Schaub, shortly before his period of office terminated at the end of August 2002, and I am grateful for the help they generously provided. Karen Williams, now a Hearing Officer for competition cases, kindly made all the necessary arrangements for these interviews. Notwithstanding the amount of criticism which some divisions of DG Comp have recently received, notably the Merger Task Force (in spite of the fact that it originally was the most highly praised directorate), the activities and achievements of DG Comp since 1958 have been remarkable; not least has been the ability of its senior officials to think radically about the priorities of competition policy for the early years of the twenty-first century and successfully to obtain enactment of this new Regulation No. 1/2003 to replace Regulation No. 17/62 without major political opposition. Whilst there are a number of aspects of the new régime which will undoubtedly take time to settle down (and upon which I make comment in Chapter 25), the direction of the reforms is undoubtedly essential for the health of Community competition policy and the year 2004 will mark the start of a new era.

My debt to other lawyers is substantial and should be recorded. Over the last five years I have continued to teach as a part-time academic at the Centre of European Law at King's College and have had the privilege of working with Professor Richard Whish, both on the LLM Programme and on the Informa/King's College Distance Learning Course on EC Competition Law, which he introduced and is very successful. I am conscious of having learned much from him as well as from the excellent students from many countries in our LLM class. Since 1999 I have also taught an LLM class in Competition Law at Cambridge University Law School where I have shared its teaching with Dr Albertina Albors-Llorens, Fellow of Girton College, always a most supportive colleague. Professor Claus Dieter Ehlermann has been kind enough to invite me on two occasions to the seminars held annually on major EC Competition Law topics at the European University Institute, Florence. These were excellent occasions for developing an understanding of likely future trends in Community competition law. John Temple Lang, now no longer a Commission official, but still in practice in Brussels, was again generous with both his time and his scholarly offprints.

I also have to acknowledge the very real encouragement received from my colleagues in the Competition Law Group at the London and Brussels offices of Linklaters. In particular, I would mention Bill Allan for allowing me generous leave of absence to make possible the preparation of the new edition against a tight timetable. I am also grateful to those who read over particular chapters and made valuable comments and suggestions; Bill Allan, Christian Ahlborn, Eamonn Doran, Louis Van Lennep (all of Linklaters), Christopher Stothers (formerly of Linklaters), and Daniel Beard, Barrister at Law of Monckton Chambers. Fiona Bain and Emily Cox provided research assistance, and my secretary, Esmee Banville, was always a tower of strength.

Helen Adams and her colleagues at Oxford University Press gave me all the help needed to ensure that the book appeared on time. Once again, secretarial help of high quality was provided by Maureen Watts and Janet Fenton at Capel Typing Services, who had obviously benefited from their experience with the previous edition!

Notwithstanding all the help received and acknowledged I am responsible for the contents of the book and any errors contained in it; all views expressed are personal unless otherwise indicated in the text.

The law is stated as at 31 March 2003.

D.G.G.

One Silk Street
London EC2Y 8HQ   April 2003

AUTHOR'S PREFACE TO THE FIRST EDITION

The actual process of writing a book is necessarily solitary: in spite of Voltaire's belief that 'the happiest of all lives is a busy solitude', there are moments when one could wish for a more gregarious task. Fortunately, however, there are other stages (both at the beginning and the end of the process) which cannot be completed without the help of many others, and that has been especially true on this occasion.

Before writing a general account of the European Community's competition law, it seemed to me important to interview a number of the officials of Directorate-General IV of the Commission, which is responsible for the administration of Community competition policy, particularly as some of the more senior among them would shortly be reaching retirement. I am grateful to all those officials who allowed me to share their memories of the pioneer days of DG IV, as well as their views of past and present events and policy issues. Some of them also later read and commented on individual chapters. As those who helped me in this way were numerous, I have elected not to name them individually, with but two exceptions. The first is Aurelio Pappalardo, now retired from the Commission, who made it possible for me to spend time in DG IV and conduct these interviews; the second is Karen Williams, formerly a colleague at the University of Essex, who after her move to Brussels to join DG IV continued to give me enthusiastic encouragement and practical help on many aspects of the work.

I was also fortunate to be able to spend time in Brussels in the offices of Cleary, Gottlieb, Steen & Hamilton, where Don Holley and his colleagues made me welcome, allowed me the use of their excellent library, and kept me going with copious cups of black coffee. I am also grateful to Don for reading the drafts of several chapters and for his wise comments upon them. Professor Arved Deringer allowed me on a visit to Cologne to benefit from his unrivalled knowledge of the historical roots both of the Treaties of Paris and Rome, and also of the circumstances in which Regulation 17 was enacted in 1962. The Leverhulme Trust awarded me a research grant to help meet part of the travelling and other expenses involved in the writing of the book, and I am pleased to acknowledge their help.

I must also express my thanks to Byron and Eleanor Fox, Barry Hawk, Sir Alan Neale, Noel Ing, Philippa Watson, Francis B. Jacobs (of the European Parliament's Secretariat), and Chris Docksey, all of whom gave me help, in a variety of different ways, during the writing of the book. Most of this writing was done in the Library of the University of Essex at Colchester where Peter Luther ensured that I had all the relevant authorities. I must also express my appreciation to my colleagues, both in Ipswich and at the University Law Department, for their tolerance of my preoccupation with this project at times when they must have wished it was less time-consuming.

All the typing of the manuscript has been done by my former secretary, Elaine Golledge, whom I was fortunately able to persuade to return from premature domestic retirement; she and her husband Brian have tolerated the presence of a word processor in their dining room for eighteen months, which has enabled her to produce a series of consistently accurate typescripts to a succession of increasingly unreasonable deadlines.

My relationship with Oxford University Press has been pleasant, and I would like to thank Richard Hart for ensuring a smooth production process. My final expressions of thanks must, however, be directed towards three people in particular; to my Consulting Editor, Professor Francis Jacobs of London University, for cheerful and admirably constructive advice throughout; to my daughter Joanna, Barrister, for her help, especially with French language material; and finally to my wife Jean, without whose unfailing support this book could certainly not have been written.

This book is dedicated, with the approval of Lady fforde, to Sir Arthur fforde, who died in 1985. After a distinguished career as a City of London solicitor and wartime civil servant, he came as headmaster to Rugby School from 1948 to 1957. Many of us who were in the school during that time remember him with particular respect and affection. I am glad to have this opportunity to acknowledge my own debt of gratitude to him; his inquiring and subtle mind would, I like to think, have enabled him to enjoy the intricacies of EC competition law.

I have finally to issue the customary disclaimers. Though I have received help from many sources, responsibility for the contents of the book and for any errors within it are exclusively mine. Neither the contents nor the errors are to be attributed in any way to any of the persons or organizations referred to in this Preface, nor to any other body with which I am, or have been, associated.

The law is stated as at 31 March 1988.

D.G.G.

20–26 Museum Street
Ipswich, Suffolk   April 1988

CONTENTS

PART II: THE SUBSTANTIVE LAW OF THE EUROPEAN COMMUNITY

CONTENTS

TABLE OF CASES FROM THE EUROPEAN COURT OF JUSTICE AND COURT OF FIRST INSTANCE

TABLE OF EUROPEAN
COMMISSION DECISIONS

TABLE OF CASES FROM
OTHER JURISDICTIONS

UNITED KINGDOM MONOPOLIES AND MERGERS COMMISSION REPORTS

TABLE OF EUROPEAN
COMMUNITY TREATIES

TABLE OF AGREEMENTS
AND CONVENTIONS

TABLE OF EUROPEAN COMMUNITY SECONDARY LEGISLATION

TABLE OF LEGISLATION FROM OTHER JURISDICTIONS

CHRONOLOGICAL TABLE (1951–2003)[1]

Year	Date	Chronological table of events	European Community Council and Commission Regulations	Commission: leading decisions	European Court of Justice leading decisions
1951	18 Apr.	Signature by France, Germany, Italy, and Benelux countries ('the Six') of Treaty of Paris establishing European Coal and Steel Community (ECSC).			
1953	10 Feb.	Common Market in coal comes into force.			
	1 May	Common Market in steel comes into force.			
1957	25 Mar.	Signature of Treaty of Rome establishing European Economic Community by the Six (and establishing EURATOM).			
1958	1 Jan.	Treaty of Rome comes into force.			
1961	7 Sept.	European Parliament report (the Deringer Report) on the draft of Reg. 17 published.			
1962	13 Mar.	First Council Reg. 17 implementing Articles 85 and 86 of the Treaty of Rome comes into force.	COUNCIL Reg. 17/62 Commission's powers and procedures in competition matters.		*Bosch/van Rijn*
	11 May		COUNCIL Reg. 27/26 Notification arrangements.		
	30 July		COUNCIL Reg. 26/62 applying certain competition rules to agriculture.		
	1 Nov.	Deadline for notification of multilateral agreements under Reg. 17/62 (approx. 800 lodged).			
	26 Nov.		COUNCIL Reg. 141/62 retrospectively from 13 Mar. 1962 excluding transport from scope of Reg. 17/62.		

---

[1] For reasons of space, some abbreviations have been used and names are occasionally given in either abbreviated or 'popular' form. Names of cases may change when taken on appeal to the Court from the Commission. Numbers of Treaty articles have not been updated.

Year	Date	Chronological table of events	European Community Council and Commission Regulations	Commission: leading decisions	European Court of Justice leading decisions
1962	24 Dec.	'The Christmas Message' issued by DG IV; Notices on patent licensing and commercial agents.			
1963	31 Jan.	Deadline for registration of bilateral agreements under Reg. 17/62 (approx. 34,000 lodged).			
	24 July	First informal decision by DG IV prohibiting agreement under Article 85(1), the *'Convention Faience'* recommendations.			
	25 July		COMMISSION Reg. 99/63 governing procedures of hearings of individual cases by the Commission.		
1964	13 May	First publication of Notice of proposed decision (the *'Convention Faience'* case) under Article 19(3) of Reg. 17/62.		*Grosfillex–Fillistorf; Grundig–Consten; Bendix–Mertens & Straet; Nicholas–Vitapro*	
1965	2 Mar.	First Council Reg. authorizing the granting of block exemptions by the Commission.	COUNCIL Reg. 19/65 conferring power on Commission to issue block exemptions for Exclusive Distribution and Exclusive Purchasing and Industrial Property Rights licences.	*DRU-Blondel Hummel–Isbecque; Maison Jallate–Voss*	
	8 Apr.	Signature of Treaty on amalgamation of executives of ECSC, EC, and EURATOM.			
1966	13 July	First European Court Justice decision on Art. 85, (*Grundig–Consten/ Commission*)		*Grundig–Consten/ Commission; Italy/Council Commission; STM/Maschinen-bau Ulm*	
1967	1 May	First Commission Reg. granting block exemption comes into force.	COMMISSION Reg. 67/67 block exemptions for specified forms of Exclusive Distribution and Exclusive Purchasing Agreements.	*Transocean Marine Paint (No. 1)*	*Brasserie de Haecht (No. 1)*
	1 July	Effective date for amalgamation of executives of ECSC, EC, and EURATOM.			

Year	Date	Chronological table of events	European Community Council and Commission Regulations	Commission: leading decisions	European Court of Justice leading decisions
1968	1 July		COUNCIL Reg. 1017/68 rules of competition applied by Council to rail, road, and inland waterway transport.	*Eurogypsum; ACEC/Berliet; Cobelaz*	*Parke, Davis/ Probel*
	29 July	Commission issues Notice concerning co-operation between undertakings.			
1969	16 July	First fines imposed by Commission for a substantive violation of Article 85 of the Treaty of Rome (the *Quinine Cartel*).		*Quinine Cartel; Jaz/Peter; Dyestuffs; Christiani– Nielsen*	*Walt Wilhelm/ BKA; Völk/ Vervaecke*
1970	27 May	Commission issues first Notice concerning Agreements of Minor Importance.		*Omega; Kodak; ASBL; German Ceramic Tiles*	*Quinine Cartel*
1971	2 June	First formal decision of Commission on Article 86 (*GEMA*).		*GEMA; Continental Can*	*Sirena/Eda; DGG/Metro*
	7 June	European Parliament first requests the Commission to prepare an Annual Report on Competition Policy.		*VCH; Burroughs– Del-planque; Henkel–Colgate*	*Béguelin/GL Import*
	20 Dec.		COUNCIL Reg. 2821/71 conferring power on Commission to issue block exemptions for specialization agreements; Reg. 2822/71 relieving some specialization agreements from the requirements of notification by amending Reg. 17/62.		
1972		First *Annual Report* on Competition Policy issued.	COMMISSION Reg. 2591/ 72 extending Reg. 67/67 for a further ten years. Reg. 2779/72 group exemption for specialization agreements	*Saviem/MAN; Raymond/ Nagoya; Davidson Rubber; Cimbel; Pittsburgh Corning; Commercial Solvents; WEA–Filipacchi; GISA*	*Dyestuffs*
	19 Dec.		COUNCIL Reg. 2743/72 introducing minor amendments to Reg. 2821/ 71.		

Year	Date	Chronological table of events	European Community Council and Commission Regulations	Commission: leading decisions	European Court of Justice leading decisions
1973	1 Jan.	UK, Ireland, and Denmark enter the Community.		*Sugar Cartel; Kali–Salz; Prym–Beka; Transocean Marine Paint (No. 2)*	*Continental Can; Brasserie de Haecht (No. 2)*
1974			COMMISSION Reg. 2988/74 bringing in rules relating to limitation of actions from 1 Jan. 1975.	*GM Continental; Europair–Duro-dyne; SHV/Chevron; Belgian Wallpapers; FRUBO; Franco-Japanese Ballbearings; BMW*	*BRT/SABAM; Commercial Solvents; Van Zuylen/Hag; Centrafarm; Sterling and Winthrop; French Merchant Seamen*
1975	1 Jan.			*Bayer/Gist–Bro-cades; KEWA/United Processors; United Brands; IFTRA Rules; AOIP/Beyrard; Bomée Stichting*	*Sugar Cartel; GM Continental; Belgian Wallpapers; FRUBO;Kali–Salz*
	15 Dec.	European Patent Convention signed.			
1976				*Vitamins (Hoffman); Pabst–Richarz/BNIA; Junghans; Gerofabriek; Reuter/BASF; Miller International*	*Fonderies Roubaix; EMI/CBS; Terrapin/Terranova*
1977			COMMISSION Reg. 2903/77 amending and extending Reg. 2779/72 on specialization agreements.	*ABG; Hugin/Liptons; Cobelpa/VNP; Campari; GEC/Weir; Vacuum Inter-rupters (No. 1); De Laval/Stork*	*Concordia; Metro/SABA (No. 1); Inno/ATAB*
1977	29 Dec.	Amended Notice concerning Agreements of Minor Importance.		*Spices; Distillers; BMW Belgium*	
1978	7 Feb.	Publication by Commission of new draft Reg. amending 67/67.		*Fedetab; Maize Seed; Black Powder; Zanussi Guarantee*	*Miller International; United Brands; BP Commission; Hoffman-La Roche/Centra-farm;Centrafarm/American Home Products*

Year	Date	Chronological table of events	European Community Council and Commission Regulations	Commission: leading decisions	European Court of Justice leading decisions
1979	3 Mar.	Publication by Commission of new draft Regs. containing block exemption for patent licences.		*Floral Sales; Atka/BP Kemi; Rennet; Pioneer; Beecham, Parke Davies*	*Vitamins (Hoffman); Hugin/Lipton; BMW Belgium; Greenwich/ SACEM*
1980				*Italian Cast Glass; Hennessy– Henkell*	*Fedetab; Perfumes; Camera Care; Distillers; Coditel (No. 1)*
1981	1 Jan.	Greece enters the Community.		*Anseau–Navewa; VBVB–VBBB; Hasselblad; Michelin*	*Coöperative Stremsel; Salonia/ Poidomani; Züchner/Bayer- ische Vereinsbank*
1982	1 Sept.	Post of Hearing Officer for DG IV created.		*AROW/BNIC; Amersham/Buch- ler; AEG/ Telefunken; SSI; Rolled Zinc (CRAM); Toltecs/ Dorcet*	*Maize Seed (Nungesser); Polydor/ Harlequin; Keurkoop/Nancy Kean; Coditel (No. 2)*
1983	1 Jan	New specialization agreement block exemption comes into force.	COMMISSION Reg. 3604/ 82 amended block exemption for specialization agreements replacing Reg. 2779/72, and Regs. 1983/83 and 1984/83 replacing Reg. 67/67 and providing block exemptions for Exclusive Distribution and Exclusive Purchasing Agreements, with special provision for beer and petroleum products.	*Remia–Nutricia; Vimpoltu; Ford; Saba (No. 2); Rockwell/Iveco; Carbon Gas Technology; Int. Energy Authority; Windsurfing International*	*Anseau–Navewa; GVL; Michelin; Pioneer; AEG/ Telefunken; Demo-Studio Schmidt; Kerpen & Kerpen*
1983	1 July	New Exclusive Distribution and Exclusive Purchase block exemption Regs. come into force.			
1984				*Synthetic Fibres; Zinc Cartel; Peroxygen; Woodpulp; Aluminium; IBM Personal Computers; BPCL/ICI; Carlsberg/Grand Met.*	*VBVB–VBBB; Hasselblad; Ford of Europe (interim measures); Rolled Zinc (CRAM); Hydrotherm*

Year	Date	Chronological table of events	European Community Council and Commission Regulations	Commission: leading decisions	European Court of Justice leading decisions
1985	1 Jan.	Commission Reg. granting block exemption for patent licences comes into force.	COMMISSION Reg. 2349/84 block exemption for patent licences.	*Grundig; Villeroy–Boch; Olympic Airways; BP/Kellogg; ECS/AKZO; Ivoclar*	*British Telecom; CBEM–CLT; Toltecs; Ford of Europe (selective distribution system); Leclerc (Books); Leclerc (Petrol); BNIC/Clair (Cognac); Binon; ETA Fabriques; Pharmon v. Hoechst; Remia–Nutricia; SSI*
	1 Mar.	Specialization and R & D block exemptions Regs. come into force.	COMMISSION Reg. 417/85 Specialization Agreements block exemption replacing 3604/82.		
	1 July	Automotive Dealers Distribution Agreements block exemptions Regs. come into force.	COMMISSION Reg. 418/85 R & D block exemption. COMMISSION Reg. 123/85 Automotive Dealers block exemption.		
	5 Aug.		COMMISSION Reg. 2526/85 amending Reg. 27/62 by introducing a new Form A/B for notification purposes.		
1986	1 Jan.	Spain and Portugal enter the Community.		*Polypropylene; Optical Fibres; Meldoc; Fatty Acids; Pronuptia; Yves Rocher; Belasco; Boussois/Interpane Mitchell - Cotts/Sofiltra*	*Nouvelles Frontières; Pronuptia; Windsurfing; International; Metro/SABA (No. 2); British Leyland*
	17 and 28 Feb.	Signature by all Member States of the Single European Act (amending certain provisions of the Treaty of Rome).			
	9 Sept.	Commission Notice on Agreements of Minor Importance issued.			
	22 Dec.		COUNCIL Reg. 4056/86 applying competition rules to maritime transport.		
1987	1 July	Single European Act comes into force.		*Sandoz; Hilti*	*Phillip Morris (merger)*
	1 July	Reg. 4056/86 applying competition rules to maritime transport comes into effect.			
1988	1 Jan.		COUNCIL Regs. 3975–3976/87 applying competition rules to air transport.		
				Bayer/BP Chemicals; VBA; BSC/Napier Brown; Delta Chemie; BPB Industries; PVC/LDPE Cartels; ServiceMaster	*Allen & Hanbury/Generics; Erauw–Jacquery; Bodson; Van Eycke/Aspa Woodpulp (Jurisdiction only) Novasam/Alsatel; Renault/Maxicar; Volvo/Veng*

Year	Date	Chronological table of events	European Community Council and Commission Regulations	Commission: leading decisions	European Court of Justice leading decisions
	30 Nov.	New Commission Regulations adopted for franchising and know-how licensing.			
1989	1 Feb.	Commission Reg. granting block exemption for franchise agreements comes into force.	COMMISSION Reg. 4087/88 block exemption for franchise agreements.	Dutch Banks; Dutch Courier Services; Italian Fire Insurance;	Ahmed Saeed Ottung/Klee Belasco; Hoechst/Dow/Solvay
	1 Apr.	Commission Reg. granting block exemption for know-how licensing agreements comes into force.	COMMISSION Reg. 556/89 block exemption for know-how licensing agreements.	APB; Bayo-n-ox; Welded Steel Mesh; UIP	
	1 Sept.	Establishment of Court of First Instance (CFI) in Luxembourg.			
	21 Dec.	New Council Regulation adopted on control of concentrations (mergers).			
1990	14 Aug.	Commission notices on concentrative/co-operative joint ventures published.		Alcatel/ANT; Elopak/Metal Box (Odin); Moosehead/Whitbread	Sandoz; Tetrapak (CFI); Hag (No. 2)
	21 Sept.	Council Regulation on control of mergers, and Commission Regulation on merger procedures comes into force.	COUNCIL Reg. 4064/89 on control of mergers. COMMISSION Reg. 2367/90 on merger procedures.		
1991	2 Oct.	First Prohibition decision under Merger Regulation (Aerospatiale-Alenia).		Vichy; Ecosystems; Aerospatiale-Alenia (merger)	Delimitis/Henninger Bräu; ECS/AKZO; Magill/RTE (CFI)
1992	23 Dec.	New internal procedures adopted for co-operative joint ventures.	COUNCIL Reg. 479/92. Authorizing Commission to issue block exemptions for liner shipping conferences (amending Reg. 4056/86)	Fiat/Hitachi; Ford/VW; Accor/Wagons Lit (merger); Nestlé/Perrier (merger); du Pont/ICI (merger)	Spanish Banks; Automec (No. 2) (CFI); Italian Flat Glass (CFI); PVC cases (CFI)
1993	1 Jan.	Legislative programme for Single Market completed.	COMMISSION Regs. 1617/93 and 3652/93 amending Reg. 3976/87 by providing block exemption for certain air transport agreements. COMMISSION Reg. 151/93 amending Regs. 417/85 and 418/85.	Sea Containers; Port of Rødby; Kali und Salz (merger)	Woodpulp; Reiff
	1 Nov.	Maastricht Treaty enters into force. Publication of Notice on Co-operation between Commission and national courts in applying Articles 85 and 86			

Year	Date	Chronological table of events	European Community Council and Commission Regulations	Commission: leading decisions	European Court of Justice leading decisions
1994	1 Jan.	European Economic Area EEA comes into existence.	COMMISSION Regs. 3384/ 94 introducing amended Merger Regulation procedures (replacing Reg. 2367/90), 3385/94 introducing amended procedures for Article 85 and 86 (replacing Reg. 27/62).	*Cartonboard, Steel Bar and Cement Cartels;* *Pasteur/Merck; Shell/Montecatini* (merger); *MSG Media* (merger); *Mannesman/ Vallourec/Ilva* (merger); *PG/VP Schickendanz* (merger)	*France v. Commission* (US/ EC Agreement); *IHT/Ideal Standard; Gottrup-Klim; Tetrapak II* (CFI)
	July	EC Competition Newsletter begins publication.			
	12 Dec.	Commission Decision widening terms of reference of Hearing Officer.			
	31 Dec.	Issue of amended Interface Notice on Concentrative/ Co-operative joint ventures			
1995	1 Jan	Austria, Finland, and Sweden join the EU.	MOTOR VEHICLES DISTRIBUTION Reg. 1475/ 95 (replacing 123/85). Reg. 870/95 (block exemption for Liner Shipping Consortia).	*Nordic Satellite* (merger); *Crown Cork* (merger); *RTL/Veronica;* (merger); *Mercedes Benz/ Kässbohrer* (merger)	*Publishers Assoc.; Magill/RTE; Bosman; Langnese/ Schöller* (CFI); *Soda Ash* (CFI)
	1 Jan.	World Trade Organization (WTO) comes into existence.			
	10 Apr.	EC/USA Co-operation Agreement enters into force after ratification by Council.			
1996	1 Apr.	Reg. 240/96 comes into force.	COMMISSION Reg. 240/ 96. Technology Transfer Block Exemption, replacing 2349/84 (patents) and 556/ 89 (know-how).	*Atlas/Phoenix; Gencor/Lonrho* (merger); *Kesko/ Tuko* (merger); *St Gobain/Wacker* (merger); *Kimberley Clark/ Scott* (merger); *Viho Europe*	*Tetrapak II; Eurimpharm; CMB* (CFI); *Metropole* (CFI); *Leclerc/Commis- sion* (perfumes); *Kruidvat/Com- mission* (perfumes)
1997	22 Jan.	Publication of Commission Green Paper on Vertical Restraints.	COUNCIL Reg. 1310/97 amending Merger Reg. 4064/89.	*Boeing/McDon- nell Douglas* (merger); *Irish Sugar; Guinness/ Grand Met* (merger)	*SCK/FNK* (CFI) *Diego Cali* (CFI) *UIC* (ECJ) *Deutsche Bahn* (CFI)
	2 Oct.	Signature of Treaty of Amsterdam (amending Treaty of Rome).	Commission Reg. 1582/97 extending life of Regs. 1983/ 83 and 1984/83 to 31 Dec. 1999.		
	15 Oct.	Publication of Notice on Co-operation between Commission and national competition authorities.			
	9 Dec.	New Notice on Agreements of Minor Importance published.	COMMISSION Reg. 2237/ 97 extending life of Regs. 417/85 and 418/85 to 31 Dec. 2000.		
	9 Dec.	Notice on Market Definition published.			

Year	Date	Chronological table of events	European Community Council and Commission Regulations	Commission: leading decisions	European Court of Justice leading decisions
1998	1 Jan.	Full liberalization of Telecommunications Sector, under Directive 96/19.		*Pre-Insulated District Heating Pipes; VW Audi; TACA; Van der Bergh; Sicasov*	
	14 Jan	Notice on Calculation of Fines published.			*Kali und Salz* (ECJ); *Oscar Bronner* (ECJ); *European Night Services* (CFI)
	1 Mar.	Reg. 1310/97 comes into force	COMMISSION Reg. 1310/97 amending Merger Reg. 4064/89.	*World Com/MCI* (merger)	
	21 Mar.	Reg. 447/98 comes into force.	COMMISSION Reg. 447/98 replacing Reg. No. 3384/94 on Merger Regulation procedures.		
1999	1 Jan.	Euro becomes common currency for 11 Member States.			
	1 Feb	Reg. 2842/98 comes into force.	COMMISSION Reg. 2842/98 comes into force (dealing with procedure at hearings) and replacing Reg. 99/63.	*Seamless Steel Tubes; BA/Virgin; FEG/TU; Airtours* (merger); *Exxon/ Mobil* (merger); *Telia/Telenor* (merger).	*Albany International* (ECJ); *CMB* (ECJ); *Gencor/ Lonrho* (CFI); *Irish Sugar* (CFI)
	28 Apr.	White Paper on Modernization of Article 81 and 82 published			
	1 May	Treaty of Amsterdam came into force (altering numbering of Articles of Treaty of Rome)			
	18 June	Regs. 1215/99 and 1216/99 come into force.	COUNCIL Reg. 1215 and 1216/99 amending Art. 4(2) of Reg. 17/62.		
	22 Dec.	Reg. 2790/99 adopted.			
2000	26 Apr.		COMMISSION Reg. 823/2000 renewing 870/95 (block exemption for liner conferences)	*Volvo/Scania* (merger); *Vodafone/ Mannesman* (merger); *MCI World Com/ Sprint* (merger); *AOL/Time Warner* (merger)	*Masterfoods* (ECJ); *Bayer Adalat* (CFI)
	1 June	Reg. 2790/99 comes into force.	COMMISSION Reg. 2790/99 replacing 1983 and 1984/83 and 4087/88 as block exemptions for vertical restraints.		
	29 Nov.	Regs. 2658 and 2659/00 adopted.			

Year	Date	Chronological table of events	European Community Council and Commission Regulations	Commission: leading decisions	European Court of Justice leading decisions
2001	1 Jan.	Regs. 2658/2000 and 2659/2000 come into force.	COMMISSION Regs. 2658 and 2659/00 replacing 417 and 418/85 respectively as block exemptions for specialization and R&D agreements.	*Vitamins and other major cartel cases; SAS/ Maersk; Michelin (France); Deutsche Post I and II; Volkswagen; UPM Kymmene (merger); GE/Honeywell (merger)*	*Courage/Crehan (ECJ); IMS Health (CFI/ECJ) interim measures*
	23 May	New Mandate for Hearing Officers.			
	11 Dec.	ECMR Green Paper published.			
	22 Dec	New Notice on Agreements of Minor Importance published.			
2002	23 July	Treaty of Paris establishing ECSC expires.			
	1 Oct.	Motor Vehicle Distribution Block Exemption Reg. 1400/202 comes into force.	COMMISSION Reg. 1400/ 2002 replacing 1475/95 as block exemption reg. for motor vehicles.		*Ambulanz Glockner (ECJ); TACA (CFI); Cartonboard Cartel (CFI); Airtours (CFI); Schneider/le Grand (CFI); Tetra/Laval (CFI)*
	9 Dec.	Agreement at Copenhagen by Council and Heads of Member States to admit 10 new Member States from 1 May 2004, subject to ratification.			
	16 Dec.	Modernization Regulation adopted.			
2003			COUNCIL Reg. 1/2003 replacing 17/62 as procedural regulation for Arts. 81 and 82 with effect from 1 May 2004.		
	1 Feb.	Treaty of Nice comes into force.			

ABBREVIATIONS

All ER	All England Law Reports
BCC	British Company Cases
BCLC	Butterworths Company Law Cases
CAT	Competition Appeal Tribunal
CFI	Court of First Instance
CMLR	Common Market law Reports
CML Rev	*Common Market Law Review*
CTM	Community Trade Mark
DG Comp	Directorate-General of the Commission responsible for Competition Policy
EC	European Community
ECJ	European Court of Justice
ECLR	*European Competition Law Review*
ECMR	European Community Merger Regulation
ECR	European Court Reports
ECSC	European Coal and Steel Community
ECU	European Currency unit(s)
EEA	European Economic Area
EEC	European Economic Community
EFTA	European Free Trade Association
EIPR	*European Intellectual Property Review*
EurLR	European Law Reports
EU	European Union
EurLR	European Law Reports
FSR	Fleet Street Reports
IAB	International Advisory Board
IATA	International Air Transport Authority
ICLQ	*International and Comparative Law Quarterly*
ICN	International Competition Network
IEA	International Energy Authority
IIC	*International Review of Industrial Property and Copyright Law*
MLR	*Modern Law Review*
MMC	Monopolies and Mergers Commission
MTF	Merger Task Force
OECD	Organization for Economic Cooperation and Development
OEEC	Organization for European Economic Cooperation
OFT	Office of Fair Trading
OHIM	Office for Harmonisation in the Internal Market
OJ	*Official Journal of the European Communities*
RPM	Resale Price Maintenance
SMEs	Small and Medium sized Companies
US	United States Supreme Court Reports

WLR   Weekly Law reports
WTO   World Trade Organisation
YEL   *Yearbook of European Law*

PART I

THE EARLY YEARS

Contemplation of the actual is succeeded at once by reflection on its implications and possibilities, so men say 'if this is what we have, we can and shall make something different'. We see the process going on all the time. For instance, in politics, governments are always telling us how they will change our world for the better, but when they have brought in their Acts of Parliament, they are very surprised by the consequences, and begin to ask anxiously what exactly is happening, why this new world is behaving in such a strange and unexpected way: and a new crowd of observers set to work to examine the new world, to see what it really is, and to write books and articles about it.

Joyce Cary, *Art and Reality*
(Cambridge University Press, 1958)

1

INTRODUCTION

1. THE SCOPE OF THE BOOK

The aim of this book is to provide in a clear, concise, and critical manner an account of Community competition law and its social, political, and economic context. It is hoped, therefore, that it will be read not only by legal practitioners and students of competition law but equally by administrators and civil servants within the Community and by businessmen and others interested in acquiring a general understanding of its origins, development, current status, and outlook.

Competition law is a complex and often highly technical subject, which does not lend itself to easy summary or concise clarification. In addition to these inherent complexities, further difficulties are caused by the fact that the institutions of the European Community necessarily operate through a number of languages, and the process of translation itself brings the risk of blurring or misunderstanding the point at issue. My objective, therefore, has been to make the understanding of the substantive law easier by explaining its historical origins and early development, and then illustrating the development of the main areas of substantive law arising both from the decisions and policy of the Commission itself and from the many decisions of the European Court of Justice and (since 1989) of the Court of First Instance. The radical proposals of the Commission for the modernization of the system of administering Articles 81(1) and (3), first published in 1999 and taking effect from 2004, are also described, both in connection with the individual chapters on substantive law in Part II and as part of the general overview of the subject contained in Part III. A chronological table is provided to illustrate the sequence of Treaty amendments, Council and Commission Regulations, major cases, and other notable landmarks over the period since 1951.

I have no doubt from my own experience that the study of EC competition law benefits substantially from comparison with other systems of competition law, particularly the wealth of cases found in, and the academic and professional commentary on, United States antitrust[1] law. However, this book is not a study in comparative law, though the reader will discover that I occasionally found it difficult to resist the temptation to draw comparisons, normally confined to footnotes. Moreover, this is a book on substantive, rather than

---

[1] 'Antitrust' is often used as a convenient portmanteau expression referring to US statute, case law, and administrative processes relating to monopoly and competition. The phrase derives from the technical device adopted in the late nineteenth century for vesting shareholdings (held by a number of enterprises) in individual trustees, who then issued trust certificates to those enterprises for whose benefit the pooling of interests had taken place, normally to facilitate the operation of cartels and other restrictive arrangements.

procedural issues, although some reference to important procedural questions is inevitable, particularly in connection with mergers and the modernization programme.

Competition law is a subject of great practical importance. It involves the establishment and development of legal principles and policies for the benefit of the public interest, enforced mainly (but not exclusively) through the work of public authorities; but these principles and policies are applied to a wide range of private agreements and arrangements which commercial undertakings have made for themselves, or with each other, on the basis of existing rights under contract and property law. Whilst the doctrine of restraint of trade has been familiar in the common law for several centuries,[2] the approach of the English courts has largely been that the basis for refusal to enforce the individual restrictive clauses in contractual documents was that they appeared unreasonable in respect of the parties involved, either as employer and employee, or as vendor and purchaser of a business, rather than because they offended against the interests of third parties, let alone those of the State or the public interest generally. Today, however, the justification, both of national and Community competition law, for interfering in such contractual and property rights derives far less from concern for the interests of the parties and far more from the need to protect the economic health of particular markets in individual Member States or the Community as a whole. Moreover, when the Treaty of Rome was first signed no Member State had a competition law of a comprehensive nature and proven effectiveness, whereas all fifteen Member States now have competition law and institutions to enforce it albeit in some cases still limited in both scope and effectiveness of implementation.[3] Moreover the new entrants to the Community in 2004 are also required to have introduced equivalent provisions into their national law.

Community competition law (by which of course is meant competition law that applies to the whole of the European Economic Area (EEA) including Norway, Iceland, and Liechtenstein as well as the fifteen Member States as opposed to the national law of individual Member States) is now of great practical importance, because of its influence upon the everyday conduct of business and industry within the Community of the Fifteen; of course, this alone is not a valid reason why students should study it, especially as the subject provides but few simple answers. On the contrary, after forty-five years of operation it still appears to raise a number of difficult and unsolved questions. Moreover, the active use by the Commission of its powers under Articles 86(3) to issue Directives and Decisions in support of competition law and other Treaty policies have had the effect that Article 82 in particular has been applied through such Directives and Decisions to a number of new and highly important sectors. These have included telecommunications and energy, areas previously not much affected by Community competition policy; this, in turn, has raised fresh problems for the effective application of the Treaty in these sectors. It is therefore a subject eminently worth learning about within the general study of the legal framework of the European Community, and also because of the importance of its substantive rules for both

---

[2] The history of restraint of trade is fully dealt with in J. D. Heydon, *The Restraint of Trade Doctrine* (Butterworths, 1971). See also *Chitty on Contracts*, 28th edn. (Sweet & Maxwell, 1999), Vol. 1. Ch. 17 on 'Illegality and Public Policy', and G. H. Treitel, *The Law of Contracts*, 10th edn. (Sweet & Maxwell, 1999), pp.415–39.

[3] For a contemporary review of the competition laws of the Six in the early days of the Community, see S.A. Riesenfeld, 'Antitrust Laws in the EEC', (1966) 50 *California Law Review* 459. See Ch. 20, for a review of the current state of national competition authorities.

government and business. However, it must be seen as part of the wider sphere of EC law, so that the importance of both the Treaty of Rome and the institutions of the Community can be fully appreciated in their application to many other fields of law as well as to the field of competition law.[4] For freedom of competition is only one of the principles underlying the Treaty of Rome and the Common Market, and may at times have to yield priority to the requirements of other social and political objectives.

2. THE STRUCTURE OF THE BOOK

The book contains three parts. Part I comprises a historical introduction to the subject. After a brief introduction to the economics of competition law in Chapter 2, Chapter 3 examines the early origins of Community competition law by considering the Treaty of Paris which established the European Coal and Steel Community (ECSC) in 1951, but which after a life of fifty years has now in effect been consolidated into the Treaty of Rome.

These events led directly to the negotiations in 1955 and 1956 which culminated in the signature of the Treaty of Rome on 25 March 1957. Reference is made to the influence of the Spaak Report upon whose firm foundations these final negotiations leading to the adoption of Articles 81 to 89 of the Treaty of Rome were based (dealing with various aspects of the subject of monopoly and competition) and to other important influences in establishing the final form of that part of the Treaty.

We next consider in Chapter 4 the early history of how the Commission began its task of implementing the Treaty's provisions on such matters, from its early days to the eventual development of the key procedural regulation known as Regulation 17 of 1962. It is upon this Regulation that all subsequent operations of the Directorate-General of the Commission responsible for competition policy, known as DG Comp,[5] have been based. In view of its subsequent importance to DG Comp and to the Community as a whole, detailed consideration is given to the powers conferred by the Regulation and its influence on later developments in substantive law. Only after over forty years of operation is this Regulation being replaced by a new Regulation (No. 1 of 2003), which forms a key element in the modernization programme for the elimination of notification of individual agreements and the sharing of the administration of Article 81 in its entirety between the Commission and the Member States, as described in Chapters 20 and 21. The early emphasis placed by DG Comp on reviewing vertical agreements concerned with exclusive distribution leads to a description in Chapter 5 of the origins of the first block exemption, applicable to such agreements.

Part II, which comprises some three-quarters of the book, is an account of the current substantive competition law of the European Community, in the context of its development since 1958. Chapters 6 and 7 analyse key features of Article 81(1), including the concept of

---

[4] For the purposes of this book, it is assumed that the reader has at least an outline knowledge of the main provisions of the Treaty of Rome, as amended by the Single European Act and the Treaties of Maastricht (effective 1993), Amsterdam (effective 1999) and Nice (effective 1 February 2003) and of the institutions of the Community. The Bibliography at pp.569–74 lists a number of books to which reference can be made if this assumption proves unfounded, together with some comments on other sources of information about developments in EC competition law.

[5] Previously until 1999 known as 'DG IV' or 'DG 4'.

agreement, concerted practice, and decisions of associations, as well as those of agreements affecting trade between Member States and restricting competition within the common market. Chapter 8 deals in some detail with the conditions for exemption found in Article 81(3), and also with the nullity sanction found in Article 81(2). Chapter 9 considers major case law under Article 81(1) dealing particularly with horizontal agreements relating to price-fixing, market-sharing, and other 'defensive' applications of the Article including 'crisis cartels'.

Chapters 10 and 11 deal with vertical agreements relating mainly to the distribution of goods and in particular with the important Block Exemption Regulation 2790/99. This covers all forms of distribution and has been drafted in a way to accord greater freedom to the parties to include terms appropriate to their commercial relationship, provided that they do not include any of a limited number of prohibited clauses, such as export bans, minimum resale price restrictions, or certain forms of territorial or customer restrictions.

Chapters 12 and 13 address a subject to which the Commission has devoted considerable attention, namely the basis upon which licences for patents and other forms of intellectual property may be approved under Article 81(3) notwithstanding that they combine territorial exclusivity with other restrictions upon the licensee. It also considers the question of reconciling the rights of holders in industrial property (including patents, trade marks, and copyrights) under national law with the overriding needs of the Community for the free movement of goods, as provided by Articles 28 to 30 of the Treaty.

Chapters 14 and 15 are concerned with Article 82, which prohibits abuse by undertakings of a dominant position within the Common Market which affects trade between Member States. Although fewer cases have been dealt with by the Commission and Court under this Article than under Article 81, they have been of major significance both in terms of their effect upon commercial practice and because of the significant size of many of the companies involved. Chapter 16 discusses the relationship between Articles 81 and 82 which has now been considered in a number of cases. Chapters 17 and 18 provide an account of the system of merger control operated by the Community since 1990 under the terms of Council Regulation 4064/89 as subsequently amended by later Regulations. Over two thousand cases have been dealt with under this Regulation; its developing jurisprudence and procedural innovations (including strict time limits) have had an important impact on the administration by the Commission of its longer established responsibilities under Articles 81 and 82. Many joint ventures are also 'concentrations' within the terms of the Merger Regulations and are therefore dealt with in the following Chapter 19.

The final three chapters of Part II attempt to review the operation of the Community competition laws as a system, both in co-operation and occasionally in conflict with a variety of national Member State institutions, administrative, legislative, and judicial, whose actions have considerable effect on the workings and enforceability of Community competition policy. Chapter 20 deals with the relationship between the Commission and Member State competition authorities in their collective enforcement of competition policy, both under the existing rules and as they will develop under the modernization programme. Chapter 21 concerns itself with the application of EC competition rules by national courts. Special attention is given to the approach of UK courts and tribunals. Chapter 22 deals with the extent to which Member States seek on occasion through national legislation to protect local commercial or professional interests against the provisions of Community competition law; it also explains the use by the Commission of its powers under Article 86(3) to bring legislative and case law pressure on Member States to comply both with existing legal requirements under the Treaty and with new Directives introduced to provide suitable rules for new sectors (such as energy and communications) where competition law principles had not previously been implemented. Part II concludes with Chapter 23, which considers the role of competition policy in the context of international trading relationships outside the Community, including the problem of extraterritorial jurisdiction, and the developing role and significance both of bilateral treaties of co-operation between the Community and other jurisdictions, including the USA, and of attempts through the World Trade Organization and other bodies to set up multilateral systems of co-operation.

Part III completes the book with two chapters which reflect on the past achievements of, and the future changes needed by, the Commission and other Community institutions in the field of competition law and policy. Chapter 24 records the Commission's ability to adapt over the years to new challenges and situations: these have included the introduction and effective implementation of the Merger Regulation, the development and continuing revision of block exemptions for both vertical and horizontal agreements, and the influential use of its powers under Article 86(3). Chapter 25 finally assesses the likely future development of the Community's competition policy in the new circumstances in which so much change is taking place, and examines the way in which existing institutions at both Community and national level may have to adapt if effective enforcement is to be ensured.

2

THE NATURE AND
IMPORTANCE OF
COMPETITION POLICY

1. THE DEFINITION OF COMPETITION

1.1 THE BASIC CONCEPT

The competition policy of the European Community is the underlying theme of virtually
every chapter in this book. It may therefore be advisable to consider at this early stage what
is meant in this context by the expression 'competition'. This chapter can attempt only a
brief account of this highly complex topic. However, it may assist those meeting the subject
for the first time to become familiar with some of its basic principles before starting to
grapple with its application to Community competition law. Those already familiar with the
issues can, of course, pass straight to the following chapters.

The Treaty of Rome refers to 'competition' as a concept in both Articles 3(1)(g)[1] and 81,
but perhaps wisely offers no definition. However, it is helpful to have at least a general
understanding of how the word is used, and important to realize that Article 81 has no
application unless the agreement, decision, or practice concerned has either the object or the
effect of preventing, restricting, or distorting competition.

Competition is basically the relationship between a number of undertakings which sell
goods or services of the same kind at the same time to an identifiable group of customers.
Each undertaking having made a commercial decision to place its goods or services on the
market, utilizing its production and distribution facilities, will by that act necessarily bring
itself into a relationship of potential contention and rivalry with the other undertakings in
the same geographical market, whose limits may be a single shopping precinct, a city, a
region, a country, a group of countries, the entire European Community, or even the whole
world. Whilst competition law tends to focus more on the activities of, and relationships
between, sellers it logically applies equally to the like activities and relationships between
buyers, who also find themselves in contention in particular product and geographic markets. Moreover it applies not only to the markets for tangible goods and objects, but also to
the fast-growing range of commercial and personal services available and necessary for the

---

[1] Originally Art. 3(*f*) of the Treaty of Rome referred to the activities of the Community as including 'a
system ensuring that competition in the internal market is not distorted'; under the Treaty of Maastricht this
provision was renumbered Art. 3(*g*) and later under the Treaty of Amsterdam Art. 3(1)(*g*).

smooth operation of a developed modern economy, including banking and financial services, insurance, and the whole range of computer networks and services. There are of
course important differences between on the one hand the operation of competition in
economic theory and on the other its practical workings in real markets.

1.2 THE ADVANTAGES OF COMPETITION

Nevertheless, in spite of its imperfections, the existence of competition within markets is
normally considered by economists to confer real advantages. Among these the following are
often referred to:

(a) the part that it has played in allocating resources in the direction preferred by consumers, generally described as 'allocative efficiency'; this has the benefit of reducing
the risk that goods or services produced will not be wanted, or not wanted at the price
at which they are offered;

(b) the constant process of dynamic adjustment to continual changes in consumer preferences is an incentive for producers to invest in research and development and to
innovate, leading to the survival and growth of those companies which make the
necessary changes in good time, whilst those that fail to do so inevitably fall behind;

(c) the continual pressure on all producers and sellers in the market to keep down costs,
and therefore prices, for fear of losing custom to other sellers who find ways to attract
business either by general price cuts or by special discounts to favoured buyers;

(d) the likelihood that a country whose economy is committed to the competitive process
will enjoy greater advances in productive efficiency and in utilization of its resources
of raw material and human capital.

Though the benefits therefore of competition are great it should not be forgotten that its
effect on the losers in that process may be financially disastrous for them. Nor will those
effects always be without disadvantage even for consumers, as for example when local shops
find themselves put out of business by the very success of the supermarket in the next town.
It is the process of competition, not the preservation of competitors, that is the main
concern of competition and antitrust policy.

2. MONOPOLY, OLIGOPOLY, AND
WORKABLE COMPETITION

2.1 PERFECT MONOPOLY AND PERFECT COMPETITION

The economist illustrates the workings of the competitive process by reference to four
models which are designed, on certain assumptions, to show what would be the rational
behaviour of sellers under two extreme sets of conditions. The two extremes are perfect (or
pure) monopoly and perfect competition: in the real world it is extremely rare to find either,
but they represent the two ends of the spectrum between which markets in the real world
operate. In a perfect monopoly the provider of goods or services has 100 per cent control of
the market and there are no close or even similar products or services to which buyers can

turn. This is normally only possible through State intervention, when a public service or utility is provided either directly by a government department or agency, or through a nationalized body such as the Post Office, although even in these cases some form of competition may exist, such as private delivery courier services. The widespread movement within the Community towards the privatization of those sectors, such as telecommunications, transport, and energy, which were once State monopolies means that such examples are now much less common. Private monopolies controlling 100 per cent of a given market are also rare in their pure form, unless the control is over an essential facility or product which is simply not available elsewhere.[2]

The opposite of pure monopoly is pure (or atomistic) competition, which is also rare. For such a condition to exist, the number of competitors must be so great that the market share of each is tiny, so that none alone has sufficient influence to alter price levels or the balance of supply and demand. In such a market undertakings could, at least in theory, remain totally uninterested in the actions or reactions of their rivals since the market simply responds to the 'invisible hand' whose operations were first explained to us by Adam Smith.[3] Moreover buyers and sellers must be fully aware of the transactions taking place in the market, so that they can make an immediate and appropriate response to ensure that the relevant product remains available at the current market price in both the short and medium term. The type of market most likely to approach this extreme is one consisting of many agricultural producers of the same crop, none of whom has a large enough percentage of total production in the relevant area to be able individually to influence market conditions or prices.

2.2 OLIGOPOLY AND WORKABLE COMPETITION

Far more important for us, however, are the other two principal types of market: oligopoly and workable competition. An oligopoly is a market in which some degree of competition remains but there are only a handful of competitive undertakings (not less than two and probably not more than eight) and the nature of the rivalry between them is substantially affected by this fact. Workable competition is found when there are fewer rivals in the market than are needed for perfect competition, but where the numbers involved and other relevant circumstances mean that there is a sharper degree and different tempo of mutual reaction than in an oligopoly. However, it can on occasion be difficult to distinguish between oligopolistic and workably competitive markets, as the borderline is indistinct.

Some oligopolies are notable for distinct elements of competition among their members, whilst some forms of what appear to be workably competitive markets are necessarily affected significantly by oligopolistic tendencies. In an oligopolistic market there is nearly

---

[2] In US antitrust law, this is often referred to as a 'bottleneck monopoly'. The classic example is the case of *United States* v. *Terminal Railroad Association of St Louis* 224 US 383 (1912), where the Association controlled the only rail approach from the west into St Louis and was ordered by the Supreme Court to make it available to all railroads which desired to serve St Louis, on non-discriminatory terms. See A. Neale and D. Goyder, *The Antitrust Laws of the United States*, 3rd edn. (Cambridge University Press, 1980), pp.128–34. The equivalent phrase under EC law is 'essential facility', discussed in Ch. 15, pp.316–21. For the differences between the US and EC approaches see J. Venit and J. Kallaugher, 'Essential Facilities: a Comparative Law Approach', Fordham Corporate Law Institute (Kluwer, 1995), pp.315–44.

[3] In his famous work, *The Wealth of Nations*, published in 1776.

always a marked degree of interdependence, which is not a recognized feature in markets that enjoy workable competition. The vast majority of the markets which concern us within the Community fall within one of these last two categories. Throughout the remainder of this book references to 'competition' will normally mean 'workable competition', including markets with recognizable features of oligopoly.

Workable competition itself is not easily defined. Its operation may be quite easy to understand if the product is homogeneous, possibly offered for sale in identical form by all competitors within a market, or where product differentiation which suppliers claim to exist is not objectively based, or is merely marginal: for example the differences between various brands of petrol or oil placed on the market by competing oil companies. Other product differences may be tangible or objective, attributable to different physical or chemical formulations or other differences between the relevant ingredients and components of competing products. If the rival products being marketed are substantially identical, with no real or ostensible differentiation being perceived by buyers, then competition is likely to take place largely on the basis of price, and to a lesser extent in terms of the level of service or conditions of sale, or by enabling the simultaneous purchase of a wide variety of other products from the same outlets, as is now possible for example at service stations owned or controlled by major oil companies.

In many markets, however, competition is of a more complex kind, since the products, whilst generally appropriate for the same end uses, have distinct characteristics, perhaps unique to one product. Potential customers are asked to value and assess one of these heterogeneous products as better suited to their needs than any other brand. In this category would fall such popular consumer products as cars, cameras, and television sets. Here the competitive struggle between undertakings is waged on a number of fronts.[4] At one time, the chosen weapon may be price cuts or secret discounts, whilst at other times it may be better warranties or service, changes in product specification, or an increase in the range of models or varieties offered, backed up by widespread advertising and promotion. For some consumer products particular kinds of distribution systems may be thought necessary to promote interbrand competition. With capital goods and other non-capital products which are sold by one industrial concern to another, rather than to individuals, the competitive struggle is usually waged at a more objective level. Such buyers usually have more information about the product which they wish to purchase and will be less susceptible to the blandishments of advertising and the promotional ingenuity of sellers. In the case of consumer goods, however, advertising and sales promotion and the establishment of consumer recognition for the seller's brand may be all-important, and market shares more influenced by the skill of such promotion than by the inherent quality of the product and its pricing, at least in the short term.

2.3 THE DIFFERENCE BETWEEN HORIZONTAL AND VERTICAL AGREEMENTS

If companies seek to eliminate or at least reduce competition between themselves, they will normally try to do so by some form of agreement or concerted practice; these are classified

---

[4] For a full-scale analysis of the competitive process from the viewpoint of the undertaking itself, see M.E. Porter, *Competitive Strategy* (Harvard University Press, 1980) and ibid. *Competitive Advantage* (Harvard University Press, 1985), and *The Competitive Advantage of Nations* (Macmillan Press, 1990).

as 'horizontal' since they are made between undertakings operating at the same level, for example as manufacturers or as retailers. By contrast 'vertical' agreements are those where the relationships of the parties are complementary, for example when a supplier makes a distribution agreement with a dealer or a patent owner enters into a licence agreement with a licensee. Whilst this distinction can normally be made without difficulty, occasionally relationships between undertakings not currently in competition, but with a potential to compete with each other, may pose problems for competition policy; for example, should reciprocal exclusive distributorships be allowed between manufacturers in potential competition with each other? Although it is horizontal agreements that normally offer the greatest danger to competition, vertical agreements containing certain types of restriction can also damage both the Single Market itself and competition within it.

An important consideration for consumer goods markets, involving the distribution of products through retail outlets, is whether manufacturers of such goods can compete fully with each other on an interbrand basis. They can of course choose to sell direct to the public through wholly owned distribution channels: that is, on a vertically integrated basis. However, they will often prefer to sell at arm's length to independent dealers or distributors, who will then sell to consumers.

If each manufacturer has access to sufficient outlets of the required quality in appropriate locations, then even if these vertical agreements contain some degree of restriction, e.g. by requiring exclusivity, interbrand competition should not be seriously affected. On the other hand, if there are not sufficient outlets available to some potential manufacturers then their consequent 'foreclosure' from the market and the subsequent reduction in competition may be damaging to consumer and manufacturer alike.

Foreclosure may occur as a result of excessive concentration in particular markets, leading to domination of wholesale and retail outlets by manufacturers. It can also occur if, although there are enough outlets available, manufacturers so arrange matters that only a few can obtain the goods which consumers actually require. Manufacturers may seek to justify that situation on the ground that too many dealer appointments would deter the best outlets from adequate investment in premises, equipment, staff, and promotional activities. The reason will be the fear that those who make a minimal investment, or enter the market at a later stage, will inherit as 'free riders' the benefit of the larger capital outlay made by the original entrants. Similar arguments can be made by licensees in the context of the terms upon which intellectual property rights are made available. The experience of the Commission over the last forty-five years since the Treaty came into effect has enabled it to simplify its approach towards vertical agreements, to which a succession of block exemptions under Article 81(3) have been applied. Now that the Single Market is well developed, it has proved possible to provide for distribution agreements of various kinds simply a list of prohibited 'black' clauses, without having to spell out a long list of permitted 'white' restrictions; the parties are now free to choose the form of agreement that suits their own requirements, so long as the 'black' clauses are avoided. The only condition imposed on such undertakings is that their market share of the relevant goods or services in the particular market (usually a single Member State) must not exceed 30 per cent. A market share above that level is deemed to confer a degree of market power which renders foreclosure more likely, so that the effect of restrictive clauses in this situation is still for individual assessment. This will be further examined in Chapters 10 and 11.

3. THE ROLE OF COMPETITION POLICY IN THE COMMUNITY

3.1 SINGLE FIRM DOMINANCE

The Treaty of Rome gives prominence to competition policy as one of the main activities of the Community listed in Article 3. The Commission has exercised its responsibilities in this area under three main headings, two conferred by the Treaty itself and the third by a subsequent Regulation. The two original Treaty obligations relate respectively to the control of the content of agreements between undertakings, of both a horizontal and vertical nature, and the control of abuse of dominance, i.e. of market power. The third, is the control of 'concentrations' (mergers) under the authority provided by the Council Regulation 4064/89 (as subsequently amended)

For reasons explained in the following chapters of Part I, the initial emphasis of the Commission was the analysis and treatment of vertical agreements in the context of distribution. For a number of years a lower priority was given to horizontal agreements, partly because of the resources required for, and difficulties encountered in, the establishment of the relevant evidence. Priorities began to change in the last two decades of the twentieth century; from the end of the 1990s improved techniques of handling cases involving major horizontal cartels were adopted and greater resources applied in targeting them. But the greater degree of success in dealing with cases where an agreement or a concerted practice could be clearly identified did not lead to the finding of a solution for the yet more difficult problem, that of the oligopolistic market where the effect of such arrangements could be obtained without the need for any agreement.

By comparison the application of Community competition policy to companies having 'single firm' dominance of particular markets proved at least initially less difficult, though the number of cases taken by the Commission was few and the economic rationale underlying them sometimes doubtful. In almost any market the competitive process itself will probably ensure that some of its participants will sooner or later gain a degree of market power. The acquisition of such market power may in turn enable undertakings to exercise strategic power over prices and levels of output and thus increase their profit margins. This increase in profitability may then allow them, either by taking advantage of economies of scale or by pursuing successful research and development, to gain still further advantage over their competitors. Moreover, such acquisition of market power places the holder in a stronger position to overcome adverse economic trading conditions, including a general economic recession as well as temporary falls in demand. In such circumstances, the likely weakening or demise of some competitors may strengthen its position even further. Competition law can deal with the problem of markets dominated by a single company, by a number of remedies available under anti-monopoly legislation. These include divestiture of assets, regulatory control of prices and profits, and the prohibition of specific trading practices that contribute to a monopolistic position.

3.2 COLLECTIVE DOMINANCE

However, it is far more difficult to find appropriate and effective means of restoring and maintaining competition in an oligopolistic market. Because the number of undertakings in the market is relatively small, it is easier for them to adjust their commercial and pricing policies so as to achieve the effects of a horizontal agreement covering products, prices, conditions of business, and even, to some extent, the pace of technological advance, without actually having to enter into either agreements or concerted practices, even within the broad definition of Article 81. Their mutual interdependence enables an equilibrium to be established between them, at a higher price level than would be possible under conditions of even workable, let alone unrestricted, competition. Each competitor is aware that to cut prices will precipitate a response from the other oligopolists which would render such an initiative futile. The difficulty for competition policy is not only that the oligopolists can achieve these higher prices and profits without agreements or concerted practices, but that the market may at first sight appear to be competitive, in that prices are closely matched, although the process which underpins their proximity (and the level at which they stand) is not one of true competition. For these reasons the concept of 'Joint' or 'Collective' dominance, that enjoyed by more than one company in the same market, has attracted great interest from the European Commission. The concept is considered in leading cases under both Article 82 and the Merger Regulation.[5] An important justification indeed for a strict system of merger control is that it helps to prevent the creation of market structures in which such joint dominance and consequent 'tacit collusion' is possible. Oligopolistic markets however are undoubtedly the most difficult in which to apply an effective competition policy.[6]

3.3 THE ESSENTIAL ELEMENTS OF EFFECTIVE COMPETITION POLICY

The experience both of the Community and of other competition authorities shows that the effectiveness of competition policy depends on the combination of three elements. There has to be a substantive law setting out, not necessarily at great length, the basic rules to be applied. This is found in Article 81 of the Treaty of Rome, which is itself similar to Section 1 of the Sherman Act in the United States, prohibiting agreements in restraint of competition to the extent that they also affect trade between Member States, and in Article 82, prohibiting abuse of a dominant position, equivalent in broad terms to Section 2 of the Sherman Act, to which the merger control rules, found in the EC Merger Regulation and in section 7 of the Clayton Act in the United States are an essential supplement. The second element is the adoption of procedures for ascertaining the relevant facts in each case, from which fair and properly reasoned conclusions can be drawn about the application of the substantive law to the case. A difficult balance has to be struck between the need of the competition authority to have sufficient powers to ascertain these facts, which may be elusive, and the rights of the

---

[5] See Chs 16 (Art. 82), 17, and 18 (mergers) respectively.

[6] The broad terms of the UK Fair Trading Act 1973 (now contained in the Enterprise Act 2002) made possible sectoral inquiries into oligopolistic markets leading to a variety of possible remedies, both of a structural and behavioural character. By contrast Art. 82 with its emphasis on 'punishment' for past abuses is less well adapted for dealing with and providing appropriate remedies for such oligopolistic markets. It is puzzling that the Commission made little use of its investigatory powers into individual sectors of the economy under Art. 12 of Reg. 17/62.

undertakings involved to due process, including access to the allegations made against them[7] and a full right of response. The third element is the maintenance and development of institutions capable of enforcing the substantive rules in a way which is both fair and effective. Here the question of availability of resources is a perennial problem, notwithstanding the major increases in staff numbers for DG Comp over the years. All these three aspects of policy will be considered in the course of Parts II and III.

Over the last few years major changes have taken place in the world and Community economy which have had their impact on the implementation of competition policy. These have included:

— great advances in technology for many markets, such as communications, computers, software, energy, and the Internet revolution, enabling exchange of information between businesses and consumers on a scale previously unimaginable;

— the growth of new markets such as those for sport and the media, to which the Commission had previously been able to pay little attention, but which now needed investigation of their complex activities and networks;

— human rights legislation under the European Convention of Human Rights, impacting on the procedures of the Commission;

— an increase in the number of concentrations with a Community dimension, which has had the effect of making the Commission on occasion act almost as a world merger authority;

— development of increased co-operation with both the United States and other competition authorities outside the Community, leading to increased pressures on the Commission for harmonization of its timetables, rules; and policies in particular with those of the USA;

— adoption by many Member States of national rules of competition law closely based upon both the principles and the language of the Treaty of Rome, including the UK in its Competition Act 1998; and

— the acceptance by twelve out of the fifteen Member States of the euro as their common currency.

The response of the Commission to all these significant changes, and to its own resource problems, has been to alter its approach towards its original monopoly over the application of Article 81(3) in granting individual exemptions, and to propose and obtain Council acceptance for far reaching changes under which Member States would take over far greater responsibility for enforcing Community as well as national competition rules.

---

[7] Often referred to generally as 'access to file'.

3

THE ORIGINS OF EUROPEAN
COMPETITION LAW

1. THE TREATY OF PARIS AND THE FORMATION OF THE EUROPEAN COAL AND STEEL COMMUNITY

1.1 OEEC AND THE COUNCIL OF EUROPE

The original central pillars of the competition law of the European Community were Articles 81 and 82 of the Treaty of Rome, which have been applied in many different situations and to a great variety of agreements and practices. To understand the ideas that underlie the drafting of these particular Articles the events which led up to the signing of the Treaty on 25 March 1957 have first to be considered.

The history of Western Europe during the period from the end of the Second World War up to the actual signature of the Treaty shows a recurring pattern of events.[1] An individual statesman puts forward an idea for European co-operation within a particular area of activity. Then follows acceptance by European nations of that idea as a broad political aim, with later development of that aim itself into a detailed international treaty. Upon the basis of this treaty permanent institutions are then formed in order to implement the broad political aim now established, but which themselves lack the authority or political will to ensure that the co-operation itself develops into any kind of supranational integration. The lack of any real progress in this direction leads other politicians then to propose new ideas, in the hope that these, in spite of the disappointing experience of the past, will have the result of bringing about more than mere co-operation between individual European nations.

The first of these European institutions was the Organization for European Economic Co-operation[2] established in 1948, primarily to allocate Marshall Aid, which was the inspired idea of General George Marshall, then United States Secretary of State. The object of this

---

[1] For a detailed account of the negotiations leading up to the Treaty of Paris 1951 and the Treaty of Rome 1957, see R. Mayne, *The Recovery of Europe* (Weidenfeld & Nicolson, 1970), Chs 8–10, and D. Swann, *The Economics of the Common Market*, 5th edn. (Penguin, 1984), Ch. 1.

[2] This body changed its name in 1960, when joined by the USA and Canada, to that of the Organization for Economic Co-operation and Development (OECD). Among other responsibilities it numbers the International Energy Authority (IEA) which was to feature in an important decision of the Commission referred to in Ch. 8. It plays an important role in co-ordinating the activities of European and a number of other national competition authorities, and publishes influential studies relating for example to cartels and other aspects of competition policy.

plan was the economic rehabilitation of Europe by the provision of much needed financial assistance, not only for its immediate needs of food, fuel, and other necessities, but also the capital investment required for the modernization and re-establishing of much of the industrial capacity destroyed, or allowed to deteriorate, in the course of the Second World War and the depressed days immediately following. Whilst discussions for the implementation of a customs union were held within the framework of OEEC in the late 1940s, the essential political will to convert this organization into one with any elements of supranational integration was lacking. OEEC went on in the following years to play an important role in the liberalization of trade within Western Europe, but its constitution remained that of a permanent conference of sovereign States without any supranational powers. It lacked, therefore, the ability to effect any major changes leading to integration of the economies of the countries of Western Europe.[3]

The second major European institution, created soon afterwards, was the Council of Europe which, however, also lacked any supranational power. Its founders were chiefly Georges Bidault, French Foreign Minister, and Paul-Henri Spaak, the Belgian Foreign Minister, both of whom had attended the famous Congress of Europe at The Hague in May 1948. The original project agreed upon at that Congress had been of a European legislative Assembly to which some sovereign powers, even if of only a limited nature, could be transferred at a future date. British opposition ensured, however, that the Assembly would have a purely consultative rather than a legislative role. The Statute of the Council was signed in May 1949 and the Assembly first met in August that year under the presidency of Paul-Henri Spaak. Its Committee of Ministers could operate only on the basis of unanimity and its Assembly (composed of members of national parliaments) had no legislative powers.

To belittle the achievements of the Council over subsequent decades would be unjust. It was responsible in 1950 and afterwards for the signature by the great majority of European States of the European Convention for the Protection of Human Rights, whose influence has risen steadily over the intervening years. A large number of other conventions have been drafted and negotiated by the staff of the Council, with the support of the Assembly and the Committee of Ministers, covering a wide range of topics including narcotics, terrorism, data protection, enforcement of foreign judgments, family law, and a variety of other social issues. These conventions have had a significant influence on the adoption of related national legislation in the individual member countries participating in the Council. The Council, however, had no influence in the direction of greater co-operation on purely economic and industrial issues. Progress, therefore, towards the economic or political integration of Western Europe during the period prior to 1950 through the creation of new international institutions was limited.

In the meantime, important developments had been taking place in Germany. At the end of the Second World War in 1945 the country was divided up by the Potsdam Agreement into four zones, the Eastern Zone being placed under the control of the USSR and the three Western Zones under the United States, the United Kingdom, and France respectively. As no

---

[3] Richard Mayne records in *The Recovery of Europe* that during the period 1947 to 1950, while France urged that OEEC should be given greater powers, it was the UK which repeatedly opposed all such moves (p.127). Edmund Dell, in *The Schuman Plan and the British Abdication of Leadership in Europe* (Oxford University Press, 1995) emphasizes that while the USA wanted the OEEC to have executive powers so that it could become the primary instrument of European economic integration, the UK insisted on national vetoes and the denying of executive powers, fearing the 'federalistic implications of American ideas' (p.49).

agreement could be reached between the occupying powers as to the basis upon which German industry should be reorganized, each power gradually introduced its own legislative and administrative measures in respect of its zone. The original policy objectives behind these measures had been largely negative (to prevent Germany from again becoming a threat to peace) and restrictive, the 'decartelization' of the existing structures of industry in the various sectors (coal, iron and steel, chemicals, plastics, heavy engineering, banking, etc.) Some of the largest 'Konzerns' were split up; for example IG Farben (the huge chemicals combine) was split into three parts which became Bayer, Hoechst, and BASF respectively, and considerable reorganization took place in some other sectors. As democracy gradually returned, the more positive elements in the programme of the Western powers were given more prominence, in an attempt to ensure that the German economy recovered to a sufficient extent to provide an adequate standard of living for its people. The punitive element in the Allied programmes of reorganization gradually faded, and emphasis switched to the establishment of the most effective and efficient means of ensuring that the German economy could be stabilized and so linked on a non-discriminatory basis with the undertakings of France and other Western European nations. Coal and steel were the industries where the need of this reform was of the greatest urgency.

1.2 THE SCHUMAN PLAN AND THE TREATY OF PARIS

It was at this point that a fresh impetus to change was provided by Jean Monnet, well-known French administrator and civil servant, who throughout his life provided a copious flow of original ideas of economic co-operation between nations both in war and peace.[4] His idea was the bold one of creating a common market for iron, steel, and coal in Western Europe by the removal of all customs duties, tariffs, quotas, and other market restrictions; these rules would be administered by an independent High Authority endowed with supranational powers to which all participating countries would be subject. These ideas were keenly supported and elaborated by Robert Schuman, then French Foreign Minister, and in April 1950 the detailed proposals for the implementation of Monnet's original ideas were put forward as the Schuman Plan.[5]

Not surprisingly, in view of its past negative attitude to the development of other European institutions, the United Kingdom again refused to contemplate participating in any body with powers which could derogate from those of the United Kingdom Parliament. Notwithstanding the fact that the United Kingdom would not join them,[6] the Six (France, Germany, Italy, The Netherlands, Belgium, and Luxembourg) decided to proceed with the Schuman Plan influenced by both the economic and political advantages that the creation of a body with supranational powers could bring to industries so essential to the development of the industrial strength of Western Europe. On 18 April 1951, the Treaty of Paris was

---

[4] Mayne, ibid. p.177. See also Mayne's translation of the Memoirs of Monnet (Collins, 1978). A full account of Monnet's life is contained in 'Jean Monnet, the First Statesman of Interdependence' by François Duchêne (Norton, 1994).

[5] See 'A new idea for Europe: the Schuman declaration – 1950/2000' by Pascal Fontaine, 2nd edn. (European Commission, 2000), for additional background material.

[6] At a later date the UK did enter into a Treaty of Association with the ECSC, but on terms which did not involve the yielding of any parliamentary sovereignty to the new High Authority. See Dell op. cit. for a full assessment of the reasons for the UK's attitude to the Schuman Plan.

signed creating a new legal entity with a status in international law, the European Coal and Steel Community.

The Treaty of Paris was a document of one hundred clauses, three annexes, and a number of protocols. By its terms French and German production of coal and steel was placed under a common High Authority, whose decisions would be binding on the member countries. Its ratification by the governments of the Six was completed by the end of June 1952, and the Common Markets in coal and steel opened on 10 February and 1 May respectively in 1953. It was to have a life of fifty years, coming to an end on 23 July 2002. The objectives of the Treaty were set out in Articles 1 and 2 which defined the task of the Community as: 'to contribute, in harmony with the general economy of the Member States and through the establishment of a Common Market . . . to economic expansion, growth of employment and a rising standard of living in the Member States'. Article 3 set out the duties of the institutions of the Community: to ensure orderly supplies of materials in the Common Market, to promote the expansion and modernization of production and the rational uses of the raw materials avail able within the Community, and to promote international trade in those products. Article 4 continued by listing the following practices as incompatible with the new market and, therefore, to be 'abolished and prohibited', namely:

(a) import and export duties, or charges having equivalent effect, and quantitative restrictions on the movement of products;

(b) measures which discriminate between producers, purchasers, or consumers relating to prices, delivery terms, or transport rates and conditions, or which interfere with the purchaser's free choice of supplier;

(c) subsidies or aids granted by States; and

(d) restrictive practices 'which tend toward the sharing or exploiting of markets'.

Article 5 continued the reference to protection of competition contained in Article 4(d) with a positive obligation placed upon the Community to 'ensure the establishment, maintenance and observance of normal competitive conditions . . .'. Clearly, therefore, an early requirement for the new Community would be that its institutions should take responsibility for identifying any anti-competitive practices and eliminating them. These institutions would include the executive body to be known as the High Authority, which had primary responsibility for carrying out the objectives of the Community.[7] Other relevant institutions created by the Treaty were an Assembly, a Special Council of Ministers, and significantly a Court of Justice required to ensure the implementation and application of the Treaty, to provide interpretation of its terms, and to give rulings binding both on the High Authority and Member States as well as on undertakings within the Community.

At this stage it is appropriate to consider the principal reasons for according so much importance to the value of pro-competitive measures within the framework of the Treaty. The chief element was of course that the absence of, or at least the major imperfections of, competition readily visible in the markets covered by the 1951 Treaty of Paris were felt to be major weaknesses in industries that needed the spur of rivalry in order to achieve a higher

---

[7] The functions of the High Authority are set out in Arts 8 to 19 of the Treaty. The functions of the Assembly (Arts 20 to 25), the Council (Arts 26 to 30), and the Court of Justice (Arts 31 to 45) followed immediately after in the Treaty.

level of performance. Beyond that element, however, lay the known example of the United States, an economy that had apparently reached its position of pre-eminent industrial strength by its reliance over many decades on free competition, the principle that provided the mainspring of antitrust. If the Coal and Steel Community were to avoid the need for a form of supranational control, involving management on a completely centralized basis, then allowing to its undertakings a fuller freedom of exposure to the forces of competition was unavoidable. This conclusion was accepted even though the individual Member States had little tangible evidence from their own national experience to support a wholesale move away from the existing norm of industry regulated by governmental and private agencies towards the uncertainties of a freer and less regulated market.[8]

Nevertheless, the structure of the Treaty of Paris retained certain elements of central control; so long as supplies of coal or steel were in reasonable balance, competitive forces could operate, but if a serious imbalance arose between supply and demand, the Treaty permitted the High Authority to take measures to bring them back into closer accord. This would necessarily involve interference with the operation of the market. Moreover, the High Authority had jurisdiction under the terms of the Treaty to deal with restraints on competition wholly within an individual Member State, as well as those that affected trade between two or more States within the ECSC.[9]

Articles 65 to 66, therefore, provided detailed legislative backing for the enforcement of Article 4(d) Article 65 contained several provisions relating to the preservation of a competitive structure in the Community. First, paragraph (1) of Article 65 stated that agreements between undertakings, decisions by associations of undertakings, and concerted practices were prohibited if they tended directly or indirectly to prevent, restrict, or distort 'normal competition' within the Common Market. Although the prohibition applied to all agreements, decisions, and concerted practices, the attention of the High Authority was drawn in particular to those which tended (a) to fix or determine prices, (b) to restrict or control production, technical development, or investment, or (c) to share markets, products, customers, or sources of supply.

Having laid down the basic rule in paragraph (1), paragraph (2) proceeded with some qualifications; specialization agreements or joint buying or selling agencies could be authorized by the High Authority if it found that the agreement (a) would make for substantial improvement in production or distribution, (b) was also essential to achieve such results and is not more restrictive than necessary for that purpose, and (c) was not liable to give undertakings power to determine prices or restrict production or marketing of a substantial part of the products within the Common Market or shield them against effective competition within the Market. Other agreements found to be 'strictly analogous' and meeting the same requirements were also to be permitted by the High Authority. Authorization of agreements could be both conditional and for a limited period, and could be amended or subsequently revoked if circumstances changed sufficiently.

The sanctions to be applied if agreements were made which did not obtain clearance

---

[8] On the other hand, the Freiburg School, favouring the social market economy as the only means of combining individual liberty with social justice, had substantial influence on the policies of the Christian Democrats under Ludwig Erhard at this time, which in turn led to the enactment of the German Law against Restraints of Competition with effect from January 1958.

[9] A point noted in the editorial preface to the first volume of Common Market Law Reports (1962), a rare example of such comment in the pages of a law report.

under Article 65(2) were twofold. The first (contained in Article 65(4)) was that the relevant agreement, decision, or practice was 'automatically void' and could not be enforced in any Court or Tribunal in the Member States. The second sanction, contained in paragraph (5), was that a fine or penalty could be imposed by the High Authority on an undertaking which entered into or tried to enforce such an agreement. Such fines or penalties could be of a substantial nature rising to 10 per cent of annual turnover in respect of fines for past conduct or 20 per cent daily turnover in the case of penalties imposed to prevent the continuation of an offending agreement.

Article 65, therefore, dealing with agreements, decisions, and concerted practices anticipated in some respects the corresponding Article 81 of the Treaty of Rome. Article 66 by contrast dealt with the problem of future mergers or concentration of undertakings in the coal and steel markets; it is relevant to remember that problems of excessive concentration and oligopolistic structure were always a major issue in these markets which since the ending of the Second World War (and notwithstanding the efforts of the Western powers under their 'decartelization' programmes for Germany) had not enjoyed any period of genuine competition. Consent to such mergers could only be given by the High Authority if it found that the proposed transaction would not give power to the undertakings concerned to determine prices or to control or restrict production or distribution, or to hinder effective competition in a substantial part of the market, or otherwise to evade the rules of competition found in the Treaty so as to give an 'artificially privileged position involving a substantial advantage in access to supplies or markets' to any such undertakings. The High Authority was given authority by paragraph (3) of Article 66 to provide what in effect would be a form of group exemption from the need for prior consent for small undertakings wishing to merge and was also given sweeping powers to impose fines or order divestiture if concentration took place without its consent.

Finally, paragraph (7) dealt with the problem of an undertaking, private or public, which either *de facto* or *de jure* held a dominant position shielding it against effective competition in a substantial part of the Common Market and abused that position for purposes 'contrary to the objectives of the Treaty'. In such a situation, the High Authority could make recommendations to such undertakings to prevent such abuse of its position and in default could 'by decisions taken in consultation with the Government concerned' determine the prices and conditions of sale that that undertaking must apply and draw up mandatory delivery or production programmes with which it must comply. If it failed to comply, substantial fines could be imposed. In this last paragraph (7), we find for the first time the concept of 'abuse of a dominant position' which would appear again in the equivalent Article 82 of the Treaty of Rome.[10]

Article 67 was headed generally 'Interference with conditions of competition' being intended to cover the problem of assistance provided by Member States to undertakings within the coal or steel industry without the approval of the High Authority. The High Authority was itself permitted to allow States to grant aid to individual undertakings but only on terms and for a period which it had laid down. This provision foreshadowed similar clauses found in Articles 87 to 89 of the Treaty of Rome.

To complete the array of powers granted to the High Authority, Article 60 prohibited

---

[10] Duchêne, op. cit. p.213 records that the draftsman of Arts 85 and 86 (now Arts 81 and 82) was a US antitrust lawyer, Robert Bowie.

pricing practices which either involved price reductions of a predatory nature which assisted the acquisition by an undertaking of a monopoly position or, alternatively, discriminatory pricing policies under which sellers applied different conditions to comparable transactions, especially on the ground of the nationality of the buyer. To enable it to cope with any such practices, the High Authority could order that price lists and conditions of sale be made public.

This brief review of the powers conferred on the High Authority of the ECSC shows how the original simple conception contained in the Schuman Plan for unifying the coal, iron, and steel production and sales of the Six was converted through the Treaty of Paris into a set of working rules binding under international law on the Six; it embodied for the first time in an inter-national treaty a set of rules of competition tailored to the special circumstances of particular industrial sectors in a group of sovereign States. The executive authority for implementation of the rules lay firmly with the High Authority, but subject to both the judicial control of an independent Court of Justice and the political control of the Council of Ministers, with whom the High Authority worked in close co-operation. These principles of co-operation, but with legislative powers vested exclusively in the High Authority, and with equality of Member States, provided both an institutional framework and a set of substantive rules which, as we shall see, proved an important model a few years later, when negotiations began which were destined to lead to the extension of the principles of the ECSC into a much wider field.

2. THE TREATY OF ROME AND THE FORMATION OF THE EUROPEAN ECONOMIC COMMUNITY

2.1 THE BENELUX MEMORANDUM

The first real step towards Western European integration in the economic area had now been taken. The success of the Six in agreeing upon a basis for co-operation within such crucial industrial sectors as coal and steel led naturally to further consideration of the possibility of the application of these principles of integration on a broader front. The progress made in establishing the Coal and Steel Community had, however, to some extent been over-shadowed by the subsequent failure of the Six to agree to the terms for a European Defence Community, the French National Assembly having rejected this project at the end of August 1954. Notwithstanding the temporary depression which this setback cast over those who favoured closer industrial and commercial arrangements linking the Six, once again Jean Monnet was ready with proposals for the development of further co-operation, on a wider economic and political level. To his individual contribution further impetus was added by the Benelux Memorandum[11] which was to have long-term significance in the establishment and development of a Common Market on a wider basis even than the Coal and Steel Community. A key extract from this Memorandum reads:

All partial integration tends to solve the difficulties in one sector by measures which harm other

---

[11] Submitted by Spaak on behalf of the Benelux nations to the Foreign Ministers of the Six on 6 May 1955 with a covering note to Monnet 'herewith your child' (Mayne, *Recovery of Europe*, p.232).

sectors or the consumers' interests, and it tends to exclude foreign competition. That is not the way to increase European productivity. Furthermore, sector integration does not help to strengthen the feeling of Europe's solidarity in unity in the same degree as general economic integration. To strengthen this feeling, it is essential that the notion of the European States' joint responsibility for the common good be incorporated in an organization adapted to the pursuit of the general interest and whose executive body is responsible not to Governments but to a supra-national Parliament . . .

That is why it seems opportune for the three Benelux governments to take a well prepared initiative which might usefully be announced at the ECSC Foreign Ministers' meeting. Such an initiative would aim at establishing a supranational community whose task it would be to achieve the economic integration of Europe in the general sense, proceeding by means of a customs union to the establishment of an economic union . . .

A positive response was obtained to this document from the German government, support-ing the need for economic integration, liberalization of trade in goods and services, the elimination of tariffs, and the free movement of persons. The response also significantly emphasized the need for competition rules in order to establish normal market conditions within the integrated market, to protect competition from State intervention and also from private monopoly power.[12]

2.2 THE SPAAK REPORT

The result of this activity was the meeting held at Messina in Sicily on 29 and 30 May 1955 of the Foreign Ministers of the Six, principally to discuss the possibility of extending the principles of the ECSC on a wider front. The resulting Messina Declaration, which was substantially influenced by the Benelux Memorandum, set in motion a series of studies relating to the establishment of a European Common Market to be free from all customs duties and quantitative restrictions between its members. Preparation of treaties to shape these new ideas into detailed political and institutional form was entrusted to a group of senior officials under the presidency of Spaak. The importance of the preservation and promotion of a competitive structure of industry within such a Market was already well understood, and the final resolution of the Messina Conference contained, *inter alia*, the following passage: 'Its [i.e. The Treaty's] application necessitates a study of the following questions . . . *The elaboration of rules to ensure undistorted competition within the Com-munity*, which will in particular exclude any national discrimination'.

The Spaak Report[13] is a seminal document of great importance, which comprises the most important of the various preparatory works (*travaux préparatoires*) upon which the subsequent Treaty of Rome is based. The necessity for freedom of competition within the new Market referred to by the Messina Declaration does not seem to have been in doubt, although the detailed drafting of the rules relating to competition to be contained in the Treaty was to be the subject of keen argument and negotiation between the different Mem-ber States involved, in particular between the French and German representatives.

---

[12] J. Kallaugher, 'The Influence of German Competition Law on the Development of the Competition Law of the European Communities' (unpublished article). The permission of the author to refer to it is gratefully acknowledged.

[13] Kallaugher records in the same article that although the working group responsible for the report was chaired by Spaak, the chief draftsmen were a German, von der Groeben, and a Frenchman, Uri.

The first paragraph of the Spaak Report sets the context within which competition policy will have to operate:

The object of the European Common Market should be to create a vast zone of common economic policy, constituting a powerful unit of production permitting continuous expansion and increased stability and accelerated raising of the standard of living and the development of harmonious relations between its Member States . . . These advantages of a Common Market, however, cannot be obtained unless adequate time is allowed and means are collectively made available to enable the necessary adjustment to be effected, unless practices whereby competition between producers is distorted are put to an end, unless co-operation between states is established, to establish monetary stability, economic expansion, and social progress . . .

At paragraph 55 of the Report, we find reference to the detailed requirements for competition policy in such a market:

In the final period, the elimination of trade barriers will lead to the disappearance of the opportun-ities for discrimination by competing enterprises. The problem only remains because there are enterprises which, owing to their size or specialization or the agreements they have concluded, enjoy a monopoly position. The action against discrimination, therefore, links up with the action that will be necessary to counteract the formation of monopolies within the Common Market. The Treaty will have to lay down basic rules on these points . . . More generally, the Treaty will have to provide means of ensuring that monopoly situations or practices do not stand in the way of the fundamental objectives of the Common Market. To this end, it will be necessary to prevent—

— A division of markets by agreement between enterprises, since this would be tantamount to re-establishing the compartmentalization of the market.

— Agreements to limit production or curb technical progress because they would run counter to progress and productivity.

— The absorption or domination of the market for a product by a single enterprise since this would eliminate one of the essential advantages of a vast market, namely that it reconciles the use of mass production techniques with the maintenance of competition.

Already we can sense here an anticipation of the final wording of Articles 81 and 82, indicating that the new Treaty will go well beyond the more limited objectives of Articles 65 and 66 of the Coal and Steel Community Treaty. The Spaak Report was indeed a document that combined compelling logic with a considerable degree of imagination and was accepted with little amendment by the Foreign Ministers of the Six at the Venice Conference on 29 May 1956. The officials responsible for its preparation resumed work some weeks later at Val Duchesse (just outside Brussels) for the preparation of the Treaty that was to embody the greater part of the content of the Spaak Report, subject to those slight modifications agreed to at the Venice Conference. Preparation of the detailed draft of its Articles then took place continuously over the next ten months prior to the signature of the Treaty of Rome on 27 March 1957.

2.3 NEGOTIATIONS OVER THE TERMS OF ARTICLES 81 AND 82

The minutes and text of the relevant meetings during this period illustrate the ebb and flow of negotiations over the parts of the Treaty which deal with competition and related issues. The section of the Treaty dealing with competition rules is contained in Part III 'Policy of the Community: Title I—Common Rules: Chapter 1—Rules on Competition'. Chapter 1 covers the Articles which were subsequently numbered 81 to 89. Articles 81 and 82 are the main Articles covering the rules of competition applicable to undertakings. The negotiators had, of course, the recent model of Articles 65 and 66 of the Treaty of Paris to follow but the provisions adopted in that Treaty to apply to the mainly oligopolistic market situation for both coal and steel would clearly not be appropriate in their entirety to the far wider range of products, processes, and markets that the new Treaty would have to cover.

One of the earliest points discussed and accepted was that the Treaty should contain a specific prohibition, applicable across the range of industrial activity, against discrimination on grounds of nationality (now found in Article 12). This principle clearly had importance far beyond the rules of competition alone; and was ultimately not included in the later section concerned mainly with rules on competition but earlier in the Treaty, as a 'principle', to emphasize its importance and wide application to all aspects of Community activity rather than just as one of many rules relating to competition.

The more detailed rules contained in the section of the Treaty dealing with competition were in fact drafted before the final form of the agreement was reached on the 'principles' set out in Articles 1 to 7 and in particular before the adoption in its final form of Article $3(1)(f)$. Articles 1 and 2 declared the establishment of the European Economic Community and proclaimed its tasks of establishing a Common Market to bring about, through the progressive approximation of economic policies, a harmonious development of economic activities, a continuous and balanced expansion, an increase in stability, an accelerated raising of the standard of living, and closer relations between States. Article 3 (equivalent to Article 3 of the Treaty of Paris) listed the policies of the Community necessary in order that the purposes set out in Article 2 could be achieved but in accordance with the wider objectives of the Treaty of Rome. They are considerably more comprehensive than in the earlier Treaty and in particular we find (as we do not in the Treaty of Paris) the following original Article relating to competition: '(f) The institution of a system ensuring that competition in the Common Market is not distorted'.[14]

In Article 4 were listed the institutions required to carry out the Community's tasks, namely the Assembly (subsequently known as the European Parliament), the Council, the Commission, and the Court of Justice (and in an advisory capacity only, the Economic and Social Committee); Article 5 laid down a further principle relevant to the maintenance of competition. In this, Member States are required:

To take all appropriate measures, whether general or particular, to ensure fulfilment of the obligations arising out of this Treaty or resulting from actions taken by the institutions of the Community. They shall facilitate the achievement of the Community's tasks. They shall abstain from any measure which could jeopardise the attainment of the objectives of this Treaty.

Under the terms of this Article, it is clear that Member States are required to take measures to ensure that competition in the Common Market is not distorted, this being one of the major objectives of Article 3, and in both a positive and negative sense to contribute to the implementation of competition policy.

We come now to the Articles in the Treaty, numbers 81 to 89, which deal with 'Rules on Competition'. Of these, Articles 81 and 82 contained the main substantive principles of law applicable to undertakings. Article 83 provided for the making of subordinate regulations

---

[14] Now Art. $3(1)(g)$. See fn. 1, Ch. 2.

and directives, and Articles 84 and 85 for the responsibilities of both Member States and the
Commission during the transitional period before such subordinate regulations had been
enacted.

Since it would be unfair if Member States could at the same time effectively reduce the
degree of competitive activity within their own economies by giving privileges to monopolies such as nationalized State bodies or authorities, Articles 86 to 89 inclusive provided
rules governing the activities of Member States in maintaining public undertakings (Article
86), and in providing State aids in any form to undertakings (Articles 87 to 89).

The archives of the Council show that the wording of the Treaty of Rome dealing with the
rules on competition was the subject of lengthy discussion and indeed disagreement
between in particular the French and German officials. The German preference was for an
authorization system, under which agreements which restricted competition would be
automatically void, unless they had received prior authorization from an administrative
body to which the agreement had been notified. The French by contrast preferred a system
normally described as 'control of abuse', under which an agreement containing restrictions
on competition would remain valid unless and until an adverse decision had been rendered
against it.[15]

The final outcome of these negotiations was that wording was adopted for Article 81
which, while clearly rejecting the French proposals in respect of restrictive agreements
(though accepting them in respect of abuses by undertakings of dominant position), did not
accept the German position either. Instead the choice of how the 'prohibition' principle was
to be applied was left over; two methods of implementing it were possible. The strict rule of
prior authorization by an administrative or judicial body, following notification, was one;
the other, less stringent, was that either an entire agreement, or certain clauses found within
it if severable from the rest of the agreement, would be classified under a process of 'exception légale' as either legal or illegal, therefore valid or void. This process would be carried out
by applying together the prohibition in 81(1) and the exemption in 81(3), without any need
for prior notification; the mechanisms however by which such a legal exception rule would
be carried out were left over for the Commission to decide at a later date.[16]

2.4 THE TEXT OF ARTICLES 81 AND 82

Articles 81 and 82 were finally adopted in the following form:

Article 81

1. The following shall be prohibited as incompatible with the common market: all agreements
   between undertakings, decisions by associations of undertakings and concerted practices
   which may affect trade between Member States and which have as their object or effect the

---

[15] Often referred to as the principle of 'exception légale'. The English equivalent of 'legal exception'
though correct, is not in common usage.

[16] The issue of the intention of the draftsmen of Art. 81 became of relevance in the course of the debate
over the modernization proposals of the Commission following their publication in April 1999. See
G. Marenco, at pp.145–96 of European Competition Law Annual 2000: *The Modernization of EC Antitrust
Policy*, ed. C.-D. Ehlermann and I. Atanasiu (Hart Publishing, 2001). See also I. Forrester, at pp.75–122 of the
same volume. Both Marenco and Forrester reach a finding that the legislative history of the drafting of Art. 81
shows that the intention was to leave the Community free to choose at a later date between the two possible
systems for implementing the principle of prohibition contained in that Article.

prevention, restriction or distortion of competition within the common market, and in particular those which:

(*a*) directly or indirectly fix purchase or selling prices or any other trading conditions;

(*b*) limit or control production, markets, technical development, or investment;

(*c*) share markets or sources of supply;

(*d*) apply dissimilar conditions to equivalent transactions with other trading parties, thereby placing them at a competitive disadvantage;

(*e*) make the conclusion of contracts subject to acceptance by the other parties of supplementary obligations which, by their nature or according to commercial usage, have no connection with the subject of such contracts.

2. Any agreements or decisions prohibited pursuant to this Article shall be automatically void.

3. The provisions of paragraph 1 may, however, be declared inapplicable in the case of:

— any agreement or category of agreements between undertakings;

— any decision or category of decisions by associations of undertakings;

— any concerted practice or category of concerted practices;

Which contributes to improving the production or distribution of goods or to promoting technical or economic progress, while allowing consumers a fair share of the resulting benefit, and which does not:

(*a*) impose on the undertakings concerned restrictions which are not indispensable to the attainment of these objectives;

(*b*) afford such undertakings the possibility of eliminating competition in respect of a substantial part of the products in question.

Article 82

Any abuse by one or more undertakings of a dominant position within the common market or in a substantial part of it shall be prohibited as incompatible with the common market in so far as it may affect trade between Member States.

Such abuse may, in particular, consist in:

(*a*) directly or indirectly imposing unfair purchase or selling prices or other unfair trading conditions;

(*b*) limiting production, markets or technical development to the prejudice of consumers;

(*c*) applying dissimilar conditions to equivalent transactions with other trading parties, thereby placing them at a competitive disadvantage;

(*d*) making the conclusion of contracts subject to acceptance by the other parties of supplementary obligations which, by their nature or according to commercial usage have no connection with the subject of such contracts.

2.5 THE TWO SETS OF COMPETITION RULES CONTRASTED

The examples in Article 81(1) were certainly not intended to be exhaustive. They have some common features with, but cover a wider range than, those examples given in Article 65 of the ECSC Treaty, which are limited to agreements which fix prices, restrain production, technical development, or investment, or involve the sharing of markets, products, customers, and sources of supply. Of these provisions in Article 81(1), items (*d*) and (*e*) are unique to it, items (*a*) and (*b*) are more widely drawn than their equivalent in the ECSC

Treaty, and (c) is rather more narrowly drawn. No great significance should, however, be read into these minor differences. Neither the Commission nor the Community Courts have subsequently placed any weight on the fact that any particular type of agreement has been omitted from this list. Whilst inclusion in the list may certainly be of minor relevance, in that it indicates the type of restrictive agreement which the framers of the Treaty may have had in mind, the wide scope remaining for a declaration of inapplicability under paragraph (3) minimizes the significance of even that factor.

The negotiators were well aware of the differences in national competition laws, particularly between French and German law, and were concerned primarily to establish basic principles and to allow the Commission thereafter to deal with the remaining issues. These basic principles corresponding to the three separate paragraphs of Article 81 were:

(1) that a defined category of agreement/concerted practice/decision of an association with anti-competitive objects or effects and the potential to affect trade between Member States would be prohibited; and

(2) that if prohibited, the agreement/concerted practice/decision would be void; and

(3) that the prohibition could nevertheless be declared (in some manner not yet specified) inapplicable, i.e. an exemption could be granted, if the agreement/concerted practice/decision satisfied four conditions.

A major difference between the new Treaty and the Treaty of Paris was clearly to be that the implementation of rules relating to competition would involve the co-operation of the relevant authorities in Member States, since the Commission would not be required nor indeed able (unlike the High Authority under the Treaty of Paris) to deal with the complete range of practices and agreements that would potentially fall under its jurisdiction. The content of Articles 83(2)(e), 84, and 85 soon made clear that in enforcing competition policy a basis for co-operation was required between the Commission and Member States. At this time competition law in the Six was in a primitive state. Neither Italy nor Belgium nor Luxembourg had any such legislation. The Netherlands had only an Economic Competition Act, which required registration of restrictive agreements but granted exemptions on a relatively liberal basis. French competition law was almost entirely concerned with vertical agreements and in particular with preventing refusals to deal. Germany alone had a new and relatively comprehensive competition law and administrative procedures and machinery capable of enforcing it, which came into force on the same date as the Treaty of Rome.

It is the more remarkable, therefore, that whereas the High Authority had exclusive jurisdiction over competition issues under Articles 65 and 66, the Treaty of Rome contained provisions for sharing jurisdiction over the equivalent area of law between the Commission and the Member States. Clearly much work still had to be done after signature of the Treaty to work out how this relationship would be implemented. Article 83(2)(e) stated that the relationship between national and Community laws would have to be dealt with in regulations or directives to be adopted by the Council,[17] acting unanimously on proposals from the Commission and after consultation with the Assembly. Article 84 retained the right for authorities in Member States, until such regulations or directives had been adopted, to rule

---

[17] Dell (op. cit.) notes that the existence of the Council of Ministers as the legislative body under the Treaty of Rome represented the High Authority model under the Treaty of Paris (p.184).

on the status of agreements, decisions, and concerted practices and on abuses of dominant positions within the Common Market in accordance with national law applying, however, the substantive terms of 81(3) and 82. The Commission itself was not allowed to be inactive during the interim period prior to the adoption of such regulations; Article 85 gave it authority to take steps to investigate cases of suspected infringement of the Treaty principles.

The Treaty of Rome came into effect on 1 January 1958. In Part II we shall analyse the substantive content of Articles 81 to 86, but it is already clear from this brief account of their origins that the legal provisions of these Articles, whilst influenced by Articles 65 and 66 of the Treaty of Paris, went considerably beyond them both in width of application and in the specification of the only grounds upon which exemption could be granted. On the other hand, the differences in the relative content of Article 66 of the Treaty of Paris and the new Article 82 appeared to have the result that under the latter Article the Commission lacked any control over concentrations or mergers as such, merely having jurisdiction over abuse of a dominant position by individual undertakings. It seems that those who negotiated Article 82 did not intend that it should provide the Commission with a control mechanism over concentration; had they intended to do so, it might have been expected that they would have made use of wording adapted from that already available in Article 66, paragraphs 1 to 5, rather than the more limited wording using only the terminology of paragraph 7 actually adopted.[18]

In spite of this limitation, it was widely believed that these Articles in the Treaty, and in particular Articles 81 and 82, contained far-reaching and important rules affecting a wide range of agreements and practices that could affect trade between the Member States of the Six. The primary task of that Directorate of the Commission responsible for enforcing competition policy (referred to throughout the rest of the book as 'DG Comp') would be to establish the detailed content of these rules and exemptions, as well as procedural machinery adequate for enforcing them.

[18] See, however, the European Court's judgment in *Europemballage Corporation and Continental Can Co. Inc. v. Commission* Case 6/72 [1973] ECR 215: CMLR 199.

4

THE EARLY YEARS OF
DG COMP

1. THE NEED FOR A PROCEDURAL FRAMEWORK

1.1 THE REQUIREMENTS OF ARTICLE 83

It is a sobering thought that the detailed application of important international treaties and basic constitutional documents, however lofty their inspiration or impressively ceremonial their inauguration, is determined largely by the subsequent thoughts and debates of anxious men and women sitting around a table, blank sheets of paper before them. In other words, the conversion of relatively abstract treaty principles into enforceable procedural and substantive rules adequate to implement the ideals which underlie the constitutional framework can be achieved only through the hard and unromantic task of drafting detailed working documents, and then obtaining sufficient acceptance of their provisions from all interested parties. In this process, the skill involved is to pay enough attention to those parties' special or national interests to obtain their consent without at the same time risking undue compromise over the basic underlying principles of the original Treaty.

The implementation of the Articles of the Treaty of Rome relating to competition itself involved this time-consuming, but inevitable and necessary process. The Treaty had established the Commission as the basic executive body responsible under Article 211 for carrying out the implementation of the Treaty; this Article lays down a four-fold task for the Commission. Of these tasks, two were directly relevant to DG Comp with its particular responsibility for implementing Articles 81 to 89. The first was to ensure that the provisions of the Treaty, as well as measures taken by the Community institutions under its authority, were applied; the second that it should exercise powers, to be conferred on it at a later date by the Council, for the implementation of subordinate legislation which the Council would prescribe. These general obligations were supplemented by the more specific references contained in Article 83. Paragraph (1) provided that the Council was to adopt appropriate regulations and directives to give effect to the principles set out in Articles 81 and 82 'within three years of the entry into force of this Treaty'. If that period elapsed without the regulations being adopted, then the requirement for unanimity ceased, and a qualified majority of the Council could authorize the adoption of regulations; in both cases, however, regulations must be based on a proposal from the Commission, and the Parliament had the right to be consulted.

Such regulations were envisaged by Article 83(2) to deal with five items. These ranged from the general to the highly specific. The general requirements referred to the need to define the outer range of the jurisdiction of the provisions of Articles 81 and 82 so that the extent of their application to transport, agriculture, and other specialized sectors could be clarified. A further general requirement was the need to determine the relationship between national laws and the provisions of the Treaty, and the third general aim was to ensure that the respective functions of the Court of Justice and the Commission were clearly defined.

Two specific objectives were also defined under headings (*a*) and (*b*) of Article 83(2). Compliance with the requirements of these two Articles 81 and 82 could clearly only be enforced if sanctions could be applied by the Commission to undertakings failing to comply with the requirements of the Articles or with decisions made by the Commission in implementing its jurisdiction. It was therefore necessary that fines and periodic penalty payments be provided as sanctions and also that the application of the procedural rules for exemption of agreements contained in Article 81(3) was spelled out. This would require the Commission itself to regulate the proper implementation of these rules, balancing the importance of its effective supervision against the need to keep administrative procedures as simple as possible, in compliance with the requirements of the Treaty.

For this reason, whilst Articles 84 and 85 provided for the temporary enforcement of the rules on competition pending the adoption of the relevant regulations by both Member States and the Commission itself, the preparation of a comprehensive procedural regulation was felt from the earliest days by the officials of DG Comp to be an essential foundation for the exercise of its powers. The initial resources of DG Comp were very small, growing slowly from a handful of senior officials appointed during the first year of its operations, gradually rising to about twenty by the end of the second year, and increasing steadily but slowly to seventy-eight by April 1964 and to just over one hundred by ten years later. To put these figures in proportion, the corresponding figures for 2001 had risen to approximately three hundred 'A' grade staff and a total number of DG Comp employees of between five and six hundred.[1]

1.2 THE NEGOTIATIONS OVER THE DRAFT REGULATION

The first four years of its existence were therefore mainly committed to the preparation of this procedural regulation, later to become familiar as 'Regulation 17', which would need to provide answers to those questions about the application of the competition Rules, for which the Treaty itself either provided no specific answer or one that was plainly inadequate. It had first to conduct a review of the existing national laws of Member States which, as we have seen, varied from the non-existent to the comprehensive but untried. Consultation had to take place on a wide basis with Member States and with numerous experts and organizations: meetings and conferences were held to discuss both the existing systems of law with Member States and the best method of adopting features from them for inclusion in the Regulation. The influence of German lawyers was particularly strong at this time, partly because they had recently seen the introduction of the German competition statute after long and fierce internal debate.[2] The German approach was to favour a system under which specified agreements in restraint of competition were void unless and until exemption was

---

[1] Some of these are engaged however in State aid work rather than in competition matters.
[2] J. Kallaugher, 'The Influence of German Competition Law on the Development of the Competition Law of the European Communities' (unpublished article).

conferred upon them by the constitutive act of the Commission, which alone could have the power of granting exemption from the basic prohibition of the law. In direct contrast, the French preference was for specific exemptions which would be automatically applied if the necessary conditions were satisfied, without the need for any intervention or imprimatur by the Commission. This conflict was eventually resolved by the Council on a basis necessarily involving a compromise between the two approaches.

Those negotiating the wording of Article 81 had, as we have seen in Chapter 3,[3] left over the method of implementation, for resolution at a later date. On the other hand, the terms of the Regulation as finally adopted left open the possibility that agreements in existence at the date of the adoption of the Regulation could be declared invalid following investigation by the Commission, not necessarily with retrospective but simply with prospective effect, and that exemptions could be granted on a retrospective basis rather than merely prospectively. This situation was in due course clarified by the European Court of Justice in *Brasserie de Haecht (No. 2)*[4] when the doctrine of provisional validity for agreements in existence at the implementation date of the Regulation was upheld, and the full rigours of the German preference for total illegality and unenforceability of all agreements pending the granting of the exemption not accepted. Equally however it was felt at that early date, in the absence of national courts or competition authorities experienced in making rulings in competition cases, that the French preference that no prior decision of the Commission was required before a restrictive agreement could be declared void by a national court was unacceptable.

1.3 THE INVOLVEMENT OF THE EUROPEAN PARLIAMENT

Once the draft of the Regulation had been agreed internally within DG Comp, following these protracted negotiations, it had to be approved by the full Commission, and then submitted also to the Economic and Social Committee and the European Parliament. At the instance of the Parliament, whose committee reviewing the Regulation had as rapporteur Professor Arved Deringer, a German lawyer and expert on competition law, some important additional proposals were made. The early paragraphs of the Deringer Report contain a careful analysis of the three possible approaches which the Commission could adopt in its approach to the implementation of Articles 81 and 82 in providing the answers to the essential questions which the Articles themselves for the most part had not dealt with. The first was that adopted in the then current *Dutch* national legislation, under which all restrictive agreements had to be notified, but by notification obtained a presumption of validity until the competition authority was able to prove that any particular agreement constituted an abuse, and then with prospective effect only. The second was the *French* approach, under which undertakings would themselves decide if their agreements were in accordance with the law, but the competition authorities could elect to challenge them and, if successful, declare them unenforceable under the principle of 'legal exception' with retrospective effect. The third was the *German, and ECSC,* approach of preventative control, under which

---

[3] See Ch. 3, fn. 16.

[4] *Brasserie de Haecht* v. *Wilkin-Janssens (No. 2)* Case 48/72 [1973] ECR 77: CMLR 287. This decision of the Court of Justice followed the same general lines as earlier cases decided by it on cases arising under the ECSC rules (*Stork* v. *High Authority* Case 1/58 [1959] ECR 17) and on the interpretation of Art. 1 of Reg. 17 (*de Geus* v. *Robert Bosch* Case 13/61 [1962] ECR 45: CMCR 1). The German view can be said to have prevailed to the extent that the Court's decision excluded the possibility of provisional validity for new agreements.

exemption from the general law prohibiting agreements restraining competition was only effective if notification had been effected and an individual or group exemption then pronounced or applied by the competition authorities.

After discussing the various advantages and disadvantages of these systems, the Parliamentary Committee accepted the third alternative as most consistent with the actual terms of the Treaty, and as the system most likely to give the Commission the widest knowledge of the types of agreement being made by undertakings within the Community. The Committee suggested that Article 82 should also be brought within the procedural framework of the new Regulation, although it had originally been intended to apply only to Article 81, and this was accepted in the final form of the Regulation. Notwithstanding the lesser probability that undertakings would wish to notify to DG Comp the existence of dominant positions held by them in individual markets and possible abuses of which they were guilty, the inclusion of Article 82 within the scope of the Regulation enabled the powers given to the Commission in respect of investigations and the imposition of fines and penalties to be applied likewise to abuses of a dominant position as well as in the control of agreements, decisions, and concerted practices.

It has certainly proved more convenient for the Commission that both Articles are dealt with in the same procedural Regulation. Numerous other suggestions were made by the Parliament's Report, including the introduction of a negative clearance procedure. No such facility existed under German competition law, but this was accepted as part of the procedural machinery of DG Comp, where it has proved its practical usefulness. It enabled the Commission to certify that the relevant Articles of the Treaty did not apply in an individual case because the jurisdictional requirements of Articles 81 or 82 were not satisfied. This might be because of insufficient effect on trade between Member States, or because the sector concerned was not covered by Article 81, or because the agreement was insufficiently restrictive to have any effect detrimental to competition in the Common Market, perhaps having an effect purely within one Member State. A negative clearance, however, would be valid only so long as the facts upon the basis of which it had been granted remained unchanged. If these altered, then the original negative clearance would automatically, and without further decision of the Commission, cease to have effect.

The concept of the 'negative clearance', therefore, had to be contrasted with the effect of granting a formal exemption under the provisions of 81(3). Once the Commission had taken a notified agreement through this procedure and satisfied itself that all four conditions for exemption had been satisfied, the parties were enabled, as with negative clearance, to continue to operate the agreement without fear of fines, penalties, or legal unenforceability in the Courts. Unlike the position with negative clearance, however, DG Comp retained control over the agreement since it would only have been exempted for a specific period of time (not normally exceeding ten years) with a continuing right for the Commission to obtain information from time to time relating to its operation, and subject to renewal at a future date when the renewal conditions might be varied by DG Comp in the light of any change in circumstances since the date of the original exemption.[5] If there were a major

---

[5] Thus, in the well-known *Transocean Marine Paint Association* case, the conditions imposed on renewal of the exemption were considerably more stringent than on the original decision. The two decisions of the Commission can be found at [1967] CMLR D9 and [1974] 1 CMLR D11 respectively, part of the latter being the subject of appeal by the Association to the Court as Case 17/74 [1974] ECR 1063: 2 CMLR 459. The exemption was renewed again in 1980 and 1988.

change in any material circumstances affecting the exemption, or the recipient could be shown to have provided false information to obtain it, then it could be withdrawn at once, if necessary retroactively.

The negotiations over the terms of Regulation 17 were long drawn out, encountering a full measure both of legal and political difficulties. The Commission's attitude to the draft Regulation was understandably ambivalent. On one hand it was alarmed by the sheer size and scope of the jurisdiction which the Treaty provided in this area, so that it welcomed the ability to share it to some extent with Member States and their national authorities. On the other hand, it was concerned not to allow Member States or their national courts to operate the exemption provisions nor to operate a system based on the 'abuse' rather than the 'prohibition' principle, for fear that loss of Commission control over the system would weaken both its effectiveness and its consistency.

1.4 THE ENACTMENT OF REGULATION 17/62

The final text of the Regulation was approved by the Council on 6 February 1962 and published in the Official Journal on 21 February, with the result that it became effective on the following 13 March. For many years it remained in force unaltered save for minor amendments and provided a strong procedural base for the Commission's administration of Community competition policy. It gave the Commission powers which were undoubtedly greater than those granted by the Treaty to any other Directorate General. Not until the very end of the twentieth century would the first significant changes be made to its content, by the widening under Regulation 1216/99 of the categories of agreement to which exemption could be granted without the need for prior notification. Only at the end of April 2004 would it finally be replaced as part of the modernization programme, under which the Commission's monopoly of granting individual exemption under 81(3) would be removed to be shared with national courts and competition authorities, and the process of notification to the Commission abolished.

2. THE PROVISIONS OF REGULATION 17

2.1 RECITALS

Even though Regulation 17/62 has been repealed with effect from 1 May 2004, it is still necessary to be familiar with its content, because of the great influence which it had over the development of Community competition law and policy for over forty years.

It opened with lengthy recitals setting out the background to the adoption of the Regulation by the Council. Under civil law as well as under the practice of the European Court, it is open to courts interpreting such a Regulation to look to the terms of any recitals for assistance in interpreting points of difficulty arising from the construction of individual clauses. The Commission and the Council have both adopted the practice, in regulations governing competition law, of setting out long (some would say overlong) recitals giving the background to the circumstances in which they were adopted and their detailed objectives, apparently in order to assist the European Court of Justice and national courts in their interpretation. Some of the recitals in Regulations were purely precautionary, referring back to relevant Articles of the Treaty of Rome (notably 81, 82, 83, and 229) which establish the powers (*vires*) of the Council or Commission to act and set the framework within which the Regulation has to operate. However, lengthy references are also made, to practical and policy issues which concern the implementation by the Commission through DG Comp of competition policy. Thus Regulation 17 referred to the fact that the number of agreements, decisions, and concerted practices to be investigated would probably be too numerous to be examined at the same time, whilst others may have special features rendering them less prejudicial to the development of a Common Market so that there is a need to provide more flexible arrangements for the treatment of certain categories of agreement. There was also reference to the need for liaison with the competent authorities of the Member States both in acquiring information and in carrying out investigations required to bring to light any agreements prohibited under Article 81 or any abuse of dominant position in breach of Article 82. Reference was also made to the need for procedural requirements to ensure that third parties, whose interests may be affected by a decision, are given the opportunity of submitting their comments before decisions are formally taken. Mention was made of the right of the European Court under Article 229 to exercise its unlimited jurisdiction in respect of any decisions where the Commission imposes fines or periodic penalties.

2.2 ARTICLES 1 TO 9 OF THE REGULATION

After this introduction, Article 1 of Regulation 17 launched immediately into a declaration that agreements, decisions, and concerted practices covered by Article 81(1) and abuses of dominant position covered by Article 82 'shall be prohibited, no prior decision to that effect being required'. The drafting of Article 1 in this way was probably required as a direct consequence of the terms of Articles 81 and 82 in the Treaty. Nevertheless, at least one national court (in The Netherlands) had declared in 1961 that, notwithstanding the terms of Article 81(2), agreements covered by the Article were not invalid until a decision to that effect had been taken by the Commission,[6] so that this Article was required to make clear to Member States and their courts that no Commission decision was required as a necessary condition of invalidity.

It was clearly beneficial to undertakings to be able to obtain confirmation where appropriate that their agreements or practices are not covered by Articles 81 or 82. Article 2 of the Regulation gives authority to the Commission to give such negative clearance. In practice, undertakings did almost invariably apply in the alternative for either negative clearance or an exemption under Article 81(3).

Article 3 covered the important subject of complaints; paragraph (2) states that either Member States or natural or legal persons claiming a legitimate interest in the subject matter of the complaint may make application to the Commission which is then bound to investigate, though of course the volume of complaints and notifications to DG Comp has gradually reached such a level that the Commission could not give priority to all applications and some had to be deferred for a considerable period. If, after investigation, the Commission wished to require the undertakings concerned to bring legal infringements to an end, the

---

[6] The original decision in this case had been given by the District Court of Zutphen in 1958, the decision being upheld by the Arnhem Court of Appeal in 1961.

Article permitted them to do so by way of decision,[7] but paragraph (3) entitled the Commission to attempt to dispose of the complaint by way of informal negotiation and recommendation. In practice, the Commission did dispose of the majority of complaints in this way and indeed, given its limited resources, could not have operated in any other manner.[8]

Articles 4 and 5 set the framework for the notification of both existing agreements and agreements coming into existence after the operative date of the Regulation. New agreements under Article 4(1) had to be notified to the Commission and could not, until after notification, receive the benefit of any exemption under Article 6. The clear intention of the Article was that new agreements should be notified when or immediately after they were made. The only original exception related to three groups of agreement which by their nature are considered less likely to affect competition or trade between Member States, namely:

(1) agreements where the only parties are undertakings from one Member State and the agreements do not relate either to imports or exports between Member States;

(2) where only two undertakings are party to the agreement which itself either

 (a) merely restricts the freedom of one party to the contract in determining prices or conditions of business upon which goods purchased from the other party are to be resold; or

 (b) imposes restrictions on industrial property licensees or persons obtaining know-how under contract or licence relating to the use and applications of industrial processes; or

(3) where the agreements have as their sole object standardization of joint research and development or specialization agreements and where the products the subject of the specialization do not in a substantial part of the Common Market represent more than 15 per cent of the volume of business done in that market so long as the total annual turnover of the participants does not exceed 200 million units of account.[9]

For many years Article 4(2), listing the exceptions to 4(1), remained unchanged apart from a very small extension of the turnover maximum under Regulation 2822/71. Not until the end of the twentieth century did Regulation 1216/99 extend the scope of freedom from notification as a condition precedent to exemption to virtually all distribution agreements, both bilateral and multilateral, and bilateral assignments or licences of intellectual property rights. In all these cases, as notification is voluntary, grant of an exemption at a later stage can be retrospective to the date when the agreement was made rather than, as with all other agreements, simply with effect from the date of notification.

One essential element of this Regulation was to establish a timetable for notification of

---

[7] For an analysis of the Commission procedures in considering complaints including a definition of when a 'decision' is given, see *Automec v. Commission (No. 1)* Case T-64/89 [1991] 4 CMLR 177. See also the *20th Annual Report* (1990), pp.117–18.

[8] DG Comp has gradually developed the practice of negotiating settlements and undertakings from the parties to agreements and practices in order to avoid having to issue formal decisions in every case and also to avoid having to make extensive use of its powers to grant interim measures of relief prior to formal decisions.

[9] Art. 4(2). Amendments to the terms of this clause under Reg. 2822/71 included an increase in the maximum annual turnover permitted to benefit from the Regulation. The Commission's interpretation of the wording of Art. 4(2) tended to be strict. Of course many agreements that might benefit from it come also within the categories covered by block exemption and are freed from the obligation to notify for that reason.

the many existing agreements in force at the date when the Regulation became effective. The Commission elected to receive the forms of agreement required to be notified by two instalments. Multilateral agreements had to be notified to the Commission by 1 November 1962 whilst bilateral agreements (which were to comprise the vast majority of notifications) had to be lodged by the slightly later date of 1 February 1963, other than those, of course, for which exemption from notification had been given under Article 4. These rather short time limits within which agreements had to be notified were the subject of criticism from both United States and European industrial and commercial concerns. They claimed that the volume of agreements to be notified would make it impossible in practice for the Commission to deal with them adequately, given its limited resources. This criticism turned out to be well founded. Originally, the draft of Article 5 dealing with the timetable and supported by the Deringer Report provided also that all agreements notified within the time limit which were not specifically opposed by the Commission within a period of six months from notification should remain provisionally lawful, and therefore enforceable in the Courts of Member States. Opposition procedure is a concept known to German law, under which the German Cartel Authority (the *Bundeskartellamt*) has to object to agreements within a fixed period from receipt of notification if it finds any objectionable features. The Commission had originally suggested that agreements of lesser importance (as listed in Article 4) should be subject to a similar procedure, the time limit being six months, with the consequence that if opposition were not raised by DG Comp the agreements were deemed provisionally (not finally) to be outside the scope of Article 81(1)'s prohibition.

While this proposal certainly had its attractive features (particularly on the score of administrative convenience), it was felt that such a proposal would move too far away from the principle embodied in Article 81 that all restrictive agreements (except those covered by the specified exemptions) were prohibited. For the effect of the opposition procedure being introduced could have been that agreements were allowed to be enforced by national courts, even in cases where no exemption was ultimately given. Another reason why the Commission ultimately declined at this stage to accept the opposition procedure as a basis for reducing its workload was that it was difficult for any administrative body to operate such a procedure without adequate case law experience of the range of restrictive clauses and agreements which it may encounter. At this time, of course, the Commission had had almost no experience of the kind of agreements which would be notified to it for assessment. Opposition procedures did, later on, become more common in block exemptions adopted by the Commission.[10] Not much use of them was made in practice and they are not found in recent block exemptions such as Regulation 2790/99 dealing with vertical restraints.

Articles 6 and 8 dealt with the important subject of exemption under 81(3). It was clear from the combined effect of these Articles that any exemption granted must operate from a specific date, which could be earlier than the date of notification (except for the 'less harmful' agreements referred to in Article 4), for a specified period, and quite possibly upon detailed conditions. No maximum time limit has been attached, though in practice it has rarely exceeded ten years.[11] Conditions and obligations imposed by DG Comp must clearly

---

[10] See, e.g. the 'opposition' procedures to be found in the block exemption regulation covering technology licences (Reg. 240/96).

[11] An exception has been made in some joint venture cases where a fifteen-year exemption has been permitted, e.g. *Optical Fibres* [1986] OJ L236/30, *Brown Boveri/NGK Insulators* [1989] 4 CMLR 610, and see *Electricidade de Portugal, 1993 Annual Report*, pp.139–41.

also be those necessary to ensure compliance with the conditions set out by 81(3) and to make possible supervision of the conditions and general workings of the agreement by DG Comp. Thus, information may be requested as to the names of parties involved in joint buying or selling arrangements or participating in distribution systems exempted on such a basis. Once these Articles entered in force, jurisdiction over the application of Article 81(3) was removed from national authorities of Member States and left entirely in the hands of the Commission (Article 9),[12] although under Article 9(3) until the Commission actually initiated a procedure against an undertaking, the application of Article 81(1) or Article 82 by a Member State could continue.[13]

The combined effect of Articles 1 to 9 was therefore to establish a procedural machinery under which both old and new agreements were to be notified and thereby brought within the knowledge of the Commission; they established both a timetable for notification and a procedure for declaring either that the agreement infringed the Treaty or was entitled to exemption, with or without obligations attached. Breach of such obligations entitled DG Comp to bring action to cancel the exemption.

2.3 ARTICLES 10 TO 14 OF THE REGULATION

Articles 10 to 14 contained powers required by the Commission to carry out its duties effectively. Article 14 is particularly important since it gives authority to the Commission to undertake all necessary investigations, empowering its officials: (*a*) to examine books and other business records, (*b*) to take copies of books or business records, (*c*) to ask for oral explanations on the spot from undertakings investigated, and (*d*) to enter any premises or vehicle or land belonging to undertakings. These powers can be exercised either voluntarily with the consent of the undertaking or compulsorily if a decision of the Commission to such effect is granted.[14] Liaison is required with the competent authority of the Member State in the territory of an undertaking if an 'on-the-spot' search is to be made:[15] a power absent from Article 14 is one to require employees or directors of undertakings to attend a hearing (in Brussels or elsewhere) and to bring relevant documents for that purpose.[16] This

---

[12] This would apply of course only to those sectors covered by Reg. 17 and not to any which were expressly removed by Regulation from its scope, e.g. air and sea transport, where under Art. 84 Member States' existing national authorities would retain jurisdiction to grant exemption until applicable regulations had been made. See the *Nouvelles Frontières* Cases 209–213/84 [1986] ECR 1425: 3 CMLR 173.

[13] The inability of national courts to grant individual exemption to agreements under Art. 81(3) was confirmed by the European Court in *Delimitis* v. *Henninger Bräu*, Case C-234/89 [1991] ECR I-935: [1992] 5 CMLR 210.

[14] The voluntary and compulsory methods of proceeding are found in Art. 14(2) and (3) respectively, and the Commission has complete discretion which to adopt in any particular case. *National Panasonic (UK)* v. *Commission* Case 136/79 [1980] ECR 2033: 3 CMLR 169.

[15] The European Court, in leading cases decided in 1989, laid down important principles controlling the way in which these rights of the Commission are to be carried out. In particular, Commission officials have no right to use force to obtain entry to business premises in order to examine documents, but must obtain appropriate authority from national courts: *Hoechst* v. *Commission* Cases 46/87 and 227/88 [1989] ECR 2859: [1991] 4 CMLR 410. *Dow Benelux* v. *Commission* Case 85/87 and *Dow Chemical Iberica* v. *Commission* Cases 97–99/87 [1989] ECR 3137, 3165 [1991] 4 CMLR 410. *Orkem and Solvay* v. *Commission* Cases 374/87 and 27/88 respectively [1989] ECR 3283, 3355 [1991] 4 CMLR 502. See Ch. 20, pp.439–40.

[16] This would be a power equivalent to that possessed by English Courts to require witnesses to attend with relevant documents (know as a 'subpoena *duces tecum*').

power would have been of considerable use in subsequent cases to the Commission, but it was no doubt felt that Member States would regard its exercise as too great an infringement on the rights and liberties of their nationals.

Considerable emphasis was placed on the obligation of the governments in Member States and their competent authorities[17] to co-operate with the Commission. This obligation was found both in Article 11 (dealing with the right of the Commission to request information from governments and competent authorities of Member States and undertakings in those Member States), and also in the right to require investigation by authorities of Member States under Article 13. Article 10 required Member States to be sent copies of all relevant documents in each case involving an allegation of infringements of Article 81 or 82 or where notification has been made for purposes of obtaining negative clearance or exemption. Article 10(2) provided that all these procedures of DG Comp must be carried out 'in close and constant liaison' with competent authorities, and that 'such authorities shall have the right to express their views upon that procedure'.

Article 10(3) was a clause which caused considerable difficulty during negotiations. It was the wish of France that the Member States would collectively have a veto upon the original decision of DG Comp, before it was sent up for approval by the Commission, by requiring that any decision be supported by the majority of the Advisory Committee. This proposal was strenuously resisted by the Commission officials and by the German negotiators because it was felt that it would both prevent development of competition law criteria applicable uniformly to all Member States and tend to make it far more difficult for the Commission to issue either decisions or exemptions in cases that were politically sensitive. The solution finally adopted was to make the relevant committee, consisting of representatives of Member States, advisory only, without the power of veto, the committee having the right only to express its views, not to pronounce any formal decision. In general the Commissioners called at their meetings to arrive at final decisions in competition cases will attach weight to the opinions expressed by the members of this committee. Nevertheless, some decisions of the Commission have apparently been issued notwithstanding an adverse vote (apparently on occasions even a unanimous vote) in the Advisory Committee, but this is rare. Proceedings of the Advisory Committee are, however, confidential, and it is therefore only possible to speculate how often this has occurred.[18]

2.4 ARTICLES 15 TO 25 OF THE REGULATION

The remaining Articles of the Regulation contained a number of clauses of value to the Commission in its administrative task. Articles 15 and 16 dealt with the ability of the Commission to impose substantial fines and penalties respectively. A fine was imposed for past conduct where undertakings had participated in agreements or practices forbidden

---

[17] The definition of such authorities is referred to in Ch. 20, p.456. Both they and the Commission are limited in the use of information acquired under Arts 11 to 14 for the purposes of the relevant request or investigation (*Spanish Banks* Case C-67/91 [1992] ECR I-4785). Nevertheless in *Zwarteveld* Case 2/88 (1990) ECR II 3365, 4405: 3 CMLR 457 the European Court held that normally the Commission must supply national courts with confidential information in its possession, unless the Court itself directs that the provision of such information would be detrimental to the functioning and independence of the Community.

[18] In contrast, the opinions of the Advisory Committee on draft decisions under the Merger Regulation can be published if the Committee so request, and this has occurred in a number of cases.

under Article 81 or 82, or where incorrect or misleading information had been supplied in the course of investigation. The former type of fine might be of a very substantial amount, not exceeding 10 per cent of the turnover in the preceding business year of each of the undertakings found so to have participated. In fixing the fine, regard was to be had to the duration of the infringement and its seriousness.[19] Fines were not imposed in respect of any period after notification had been made unless a preliminary warning had been given under Article 15(6) that, in the view of the Commission 'after preliminary examination', application of the exemption provisions in 81(3) could not be justified. This procedure has been of value in the course of some investigations where the Commission was satisfied that no exemption would ultimately be available, but where the preparation of the necessary decision required a substantial amount of work, and it was hoped in this way to put pressure upon the undertakings concerned to terminate the agreement or practices, without waiting for the issue of the formal decision. Penalties under Article 16 dealt, not with the past, but with the future, and were payable in respect of each day upon which an undertaking continued to refuse to put an end to an infringement condemned by a decision of the Commission, or to supply information required by a decision of the Commission in the course of its investigation. Proposed fines and penalties were also considered by the Advisory Committee under Article 10, and the Commission's decision was in turn subject to the unlimited jurisdiction of the Court under Article 229, quite apart from the right of an undertaking to seek review of a decision under Article 230. The Court had powers to cancel, reduce, or increase the fine imposed.

Article 19 dealt with the important issue of natural justice. Undertakings were entitled to be heard on matters where the Commission proposes to raise a statement of objections, and rights are also given to other natural or legal persons with a sufficient interest. This concept has been generously interpreted and gave competitors and customers standing to object to decisions by the Commission which are claimed to have prejudiced them.[20] Article 19(3) required the Commission to publish any proposed decisions relating to either negative clearance or exemption in the Official Journal, allowing all interested parties to submit their observations within a time limit of not less than a month. All final decisions, whether for negative clearance exemption or prohibiting the infringement with or without fine, had under Article 21 to be published in detail in the Official Journal, subject only to the requirements of business secrecy.

3. THE IMPLEMENTATION OF REGULATION 17: THE EARLY EXPERIENCE OF DG COMP

The entry into force of this new Regulation was a major psychological boost for DG Comp. At last it had a firm procedural foundation for its inquiries and investigations. The Directorate had previously felt itself inhibited in making inquiries and in carrying out investigations

---

[19] The size of fines imposed has increased substantially in recent years especially in cartel cases. Tables of fines are set out in *EC Competition Law Handbook* (Sweet & Maxwell, published annually), and in practitioners' handbooks. In 1998 the Commission published a Notice setting out the basis on which fines would be calculated: [1998] OJ C9/3 and [1998] 4 CMLR 472. Reductions in or total remission of fines may be possible for undertakings which take advantage of the Commission's Leniency Notice (see Ch. 9, pp.147–9).

[20] See, e.g. *Metro v. Saba (No. 1)* Case 26/76 [1977] ECR 1875: [1978] 2 CMLR 1.

because of its lack of specific powers, notwithstanding the provisions of Article 85. Up to March 1962, therefore, the Commission had investigated only thirty-three cases and had issued no formal decisions, although in some cases it had tried to persuade the parties involved to end particular practices. In one case a boycott of a trader by a producer holding a dominant position was terminated as the result of such pressure, as was also the reservation of one national market to local producers and some preferred foreign producers to the exclusion of other producers within the Community. A magazine taking advertisements from various manufacturers refused to accept advertisements from competing manufacturers in other States; this practice was also brought to an end after intervention by DG Comp.

Whilst in early 1962 officials in DG Comp were therefore generally pleased with the scope of their new powers, they had no doubt that the future pattern of administration would become a great deal more demanding than the comparatively tranquil period that had prevailed since its formation four years previously. Indeed, the Regulation could be (and was) criticized for bringing within coverage for notification too many routine and relatively innocuous agreements, without enabling DG Comp to focus its attention on the kind of horizontal market-sharing and other cartels which are normally considered to have most effect on the health of the competitive process. The mesh of the net for catching notifications was so fine that it was anticipated that the number of agreements likely to be registered, particularly of a vertical nature, would be extremely high, notwithstanding the provisions of Article 4 for exemption from notification of agreements of apparently less immediate threat to competition. The view of the critics was that the Commission, in its natural desire to assert a wide jurisdiction over undertakings within the Common Market, had really attempted 'to bite off more than it could chew'; they claimed that it should have proceeded more gradually in selecting the criteria applicable to notification requirements.

The inherent consequences therefore of the approach adopted by Regulation 17 was to take DG Comp in the direction of having to devote far too much of the energies of its limited staff to vertical agreements relating to distribution of goods and the licensing of intellectual property rights, leaving too few resources to handle horizontal agreements and cartels which might be said to have a 'particularly adverse effect' on the development of the Common Market referred to. The Commission's own response to such criticism at the time would certainly have been that the integration of the Common Market itself positively required an emphasis on vertical agreements relating to distribution and licensing, the very numbers of restrictive agreements of that kind compelling the priority given to them.

The result of the time limits contained in the Regulation was that a total of 920 *multilateral* registrations were filed by the closing date of 1 November 1962, but the much larger and daunting total of 34,500 *bilateral* agreements were filed by 1 February 1963. The 'mass problem' of which the Commission had been warned had indeed arrived: for some months all DG Comp officials had to concentrate simply on giving a preliminary review to as many as possible of the vast number of documents which had arrived and were now piled throughout their offices. The notification form itself (known as 'form A/B') had been prescribed by a Regulation (No. 27 of 1962) made by the Commission under the authority of Council Regulation 17, and a further Regulation (No. 99 of 1963) was shortly afterwards adopted setting out procedures for investigations and oral hearings.

Under Article 2 of this latter Regulation, the Commission was required, when considering a decision against an undertaking, to send a statement of objections raised against it; the undertaking was then entitled to reply, setting out all matters relevant to its defence and attaching any relevant documents. This reply having been considered by the Commission, an oral hearing was called if the undertaking desired it. At the hearing the parties themselves and any other parties with a sufficient interest (in technical terms) might attend and address the Commission. Representatives of the Advisory Committee were also present at this hearing and might question the parties. The procedural frame-work for carrying out investigations was now at last in place,[21] and over the following years decisions of the Commission began to be issued, though initially at a very slow rate.

4. THE *GRUNDIG* CASE AND ITS CONSEQUENCES

4.1 THE FACTS OF *GRUNDIG*

Without question the most important decision to be issued by the Commission in 1964, its first full year of active operation as a decision-making body, was the *Grundig* case. The outcome of this case,[22] following the appeal from the Commission's decision to the European Court of Justice,[23] was to have a major influence on the development of the competition policy of the Commission. The facts of the case are therefore set out in some detail.

The well-known German manufacturer, Grundig, had appointed a firm called Consten as its sole distributor in France, the Saar, and Corsica in respect of a range of products including wireless and television sets, tape recorders, and dictating machines. Consten accepted an obligation to place minimum orders, to set up a repair workshop with an adequate stock of spare parts, and to provide an effective guarantee and after-sales service. It agreed not to sell goods competitive with the Grundig range, and also agreed that it would not make deliveries into other territories, having received an assurance from Grundig that similar restrictions had been placed on Grundig distributors in other countries. Consten was then enabled by Grundig to register under its own name in France the trade mark GINT which was carried on all Grundig appliances including those sold on the German domestic market. However, if Consten ceased to be the sole distributor for France, this trade mark had to be re-assigned to Grundig.

A French competitor of Consten was UNEF, which found itself able to buy Grundig appliances in Germany, for resale to French retailers, at more favourable prices than those available to them in France from Consten. Consten therefore brought an action in the French Courts against UNEF both for unfair competition and for infringement of the trade mark GINT. As the result of a complaint by UNEF to the Commission, an investigation was carried out and a statement of objections filed against Grundig in accordance with the requirements of Regulation 17. The resulting decision of the Commission, issued on 23

---

[21] The leading textbook on the procedural aspects of Community competition law is C.S. Kerse, *EC Antitrust Procedure*, 4th edn. (Sweet & Maxwell, 1998).

[22] *Grundig–Consten* JO [1964] 161/2545: [1964] CMLR 489. On 12 January 1962 the Dutch Supreme Court had already declared an export ban imposed by Grundig on its Dutch distributor to be unenforceable because it violated Art. 81 and had struck down an injunction imposed by a lower court on parallel importers of Grundig products. The Dutch Court had refused to refer the case to the European Court under Art. 234. For a contemporary assessment of the case, see C. Fulda (1965) 65 *Columbia Law Review* 625.

[23] *Consten and Grundig* v. *Commission* Cases 56 and 58/64 [1966] ECR 299: CMLR 418.

September 1964, was that the agreement between Consten and Grundig violated Article 81(1). The Commission ruled that the rights of Consten under both the distribution agreement and the linked trade-mark licence must be limited so that they did not enable Grundig and Consten to prevent parallel imports of these products into France from other Member States. The Commission, therefore, declared the whole agreement between Consten and Grundig to be void and unenforceable.

An appeal was brought against this decision to the European Court. The Court heard the opinion of the Advocate General appointed to the case before considering its own decision. The opinion of Advocate General Roemer was that the numerous complaints of Consten and Grundig against the procedure of DG Comp in investigating the case were justified, as in his view it had not been sufficiently thorough. He believed that it should be reopened to enable the parties to deal more fully with the allegations made. However, the Court disagreed and upheld the Commission's decisions other than on two important points. The points upon which the Court overruled the Commission concerned the Commission's finding that exclusivity alone in a distribution system was sufficient to raise artificial barriers between Member States of the Common Market. It concluded first that such a finding was too sweeping and could not be justified. Nor, in its view, should the Commission have ruled that the clauses of the agreement which did not relate to restrictions on the parallel imports of goods be annulled. Notwithstanding the reference in the wording of Article 81 striking down 'all *agreements* between undertakings . . .', and the like wording in paragraph (2) ('any *agreements* . . . prohibited . . . shall be automatically void') the annulment should apply solely to restrictive clauses and the remainder of the agreement remain fully in force. The remaining findings of the Court, however, wholly supported the approach of the Commission and would have a major influence on future caselaw and competition policy; they can be summarized as follows.

The Court's first ruling was that the expression 'affecting trade' in Article 81(1) meant that the Commission should consider whether the agreement was capable of endangering, directly or indirectly, in fact or potentially, freedom of trade between Member States in a direction which could harm the attainment of the object of a single integrated Market. Such an effect could be found even if the result of the agreement was to favour a large increase in Grundig trade through its appointed distributor, Consten, if at the same time other undertakings (such as UNEF) were prevented from importing Grundig products into France or if Consten itself was prevented from re-exporting. If intrabrand competition between Grundig dealers were weakened by the agreements, then it was no answer for Grundig simply to claim that inter-brand competition between manufacturers would thereby be increased.

Secondly, the Commission was commended for taking into account in its decision the whole 'system' set up in France for absolute territorial protection, including the assignment of the GINT trade mark to Consten. Trade-mark rights should not be used in such a way as to defeat the effectiveness of EC law in this area, nor should the domestic law of Member States relating to unfair competition or intellectual property rights be used for such a purpose. Other Articles of the EC Treaty had been cited in favour of Grundig and Consten to support their use of trade marks to protect the exclusivity of the distribution arrangement; in particular, Article 30 had been referred to in the course of the case because of its reference to the protection of 'industrial and commercial property', and Article 295 because of its statement, as a general principle, that the Treaty was not in any way to 'prejudice the rules of Member States governing the system of property ownership'. Neither Article, however, was adjudged sufficiently far-reaching in its scope to affect the Court's ruling.

4.2 THE CONSEQUENCES OF *GRUNDIG*

The whole Commission had realized that the issues posed by the *Grundig* case were of central importance and that a clear ruling of the Court was needed to provide a sound basis for its future policy, emphasizing the elimination of export bans that would have the effect of segregating national markets, particularly if combined with ancillary restrictions on the use of intellectual property rights such as trade marks. This is but the first of a number of situations in which a clear and authoritative ruling from the Court at a timely moment has enabled the Commission to develop its own policy strengthened by the Court's support on a key issue. In our subsequent review in Part II of various areas of the development of competition policy we shall see how important the role played by the Court has been in assisting the development of the Commission's own confidence in the application of its policies. In particular, the wide interpretation given by the Court to the expression 'which may affect trade between Member States' has enabled the reach of the Commission to be extended more broadly than would have been possible if the Court's interpretation of these words had been more restrictive. It enabled the Commission to exercise jurisdiction in a number of areas where it had previously been thought that the effect on trade between Member States would be insufficient, even when the markets affected were mainly national with comparatively minor effect on imports or exports. Later chapters show that subsequent case law has further developed the principles laid down in the *Grundig* case.[24]

The two points on which the Commission's judgment had been overturned were not damaging to it. The decision that only the restrictive clauses would be struck down and void under 81(2) was not itself limiting to the exercise of the Commission's jurisdiction, although it did appear to run contrary to the apparently categorical wording of Article 81(2). Nor did the refusal of the Court to accept that exclusivity arrangements alone would automatically breach Article 81(1) cause major problems. For DG Comp had already started to develop principles for distinguishing those situations where an element of exclusivity in distribution systems could in fact assist the process of interbrand competition and would eventually enable a large number of the bipartite distribution arrangements notified to it at the beginning of 1963 to receive exemption. To arrange for this to happen, however, would require the introduction of new administrative machinery to permit exemption by category rather than simply on an individual basis.

---

[24] See, e.g. Ch. 13 at pp.249–52 for a discussion of its influence on the distinction between the 'existence' and the 'exercise' of rights.

5

THE ADVENT OF THE
BLOCK EXEMPTION

1. EARLY CASE LAW EXPERIENCE

1.1 THE FIRST CASES ON DISTRIBUTION SYSTEMS

During its first few years of operation DG Comp began to carry out its implementation of Article 81, utilizing its new powers under Regulation 17/62, in a number of minor cases. These included:

Hummel/Isbecque:[1] An agreement between a German manufacturer and a Belgian distributor for the sale of small tractors and other products contained a restriction that the manufacturer, Hummel, could not sell to anyone else in Belgium apart from Isbecque, thereby preventing other Belgian distributors from bypassing Isbecque and buying direct. Individual exemption was granted because the requirements of 81(3) were held to be met. The exclusivity granted to Isbecque was not such as to prevent parallel imports from Germany, and the restrictions imposed on it were limited to those required to ensure that the economic benefits of exclusivity were obtained. There was substantial competition in Belgium for the range of products covered by the agreement. The period of exemption given was six years.

Maison Jallatte/Voss:[2] Here a French manufacturer of safety shoes appointed exclusive distributors for Germany (Voss) and also for Belgium (Vandeputte). Vandeputte had agreed an exclusive purchasing clause under which they consented not to acquire safety shoes from any of Maison Jallatte's competitors, a restriction which had not featured in any previous agreement considered under Article 81. An exemption was granted for an eight-year period, on the basis that the clause would require Vandeputte to exercise its representation of Maison Jallatte in a more vigorous manner, having to make its profit from one range of shoes alone; the range of safety shoes which the distribution agreements would enable customers to buy in these two markets would be considerably wider than those available without the existence of the agreements. Parallel imports remained available for both countries.

Belgian Tiles Cartel:[3] Inevitably the Commission found itself moving on from relatively

---

[1] JO 2581/65: [1965] CMLR 242.   [2] JO 37/66: [1966] CMLR D1.
[3] JO 1167/64: it is also referred to as the 'Convention Faïence' case.

simple bilateral agreements to more complex multilateral agreements. This case involved arrangements between two Belgian trade associations representing tile layers and tile dealers, as well as twenty-nine manufacturers of ceramic tiles throughout the Community. Under the agreements notified, all these manufacturers were required to sell in Belgium only to dealers and tile layers accorded the status under the arrangements of 'recognized customers'. These dealers and layers in turn had a reciprocal obligation to buy their tiles only from manufacturers who were parties to the relevant agreements. General contractors and their agents were barred from membership so that manufacturers could not sell direct to them, nor to other large potential buyers of tiles, such as government departments, hospitals, or factories. The admission of any new manufacturer to the agreements required the unanimous consent of all other manufacturers, and the admission of any new trade associations of tile layers or dealers required the consent of the two existing associations.

As we shall see from later cases decided by the Commission and the European Court, this type of cartel was frequent in the Common Market at the time of the signature of the Treaty of Rome, particularly in Belgium and Holland. The justification claimed for the arrangements, and the basis for requests for exemption under Article 81(3), was that it brought about improvements in the proper use and distribution of ceramic tiles because of the higher standards it was supposed to set for tile layers and dealers. The weakness of this argument was that the rules of the cartel actually contained no reference to minimum technical standards, nor requirements for technical education, so that a manufacturer was actually free to sell tiles to any tile layer or dealer with no control over their end use. The cartel could have achieved its proclaimed objectives by only prescribing minimum technical standards for its distributors and placing other requirements on them for the benefit of their customers, such as the maintenance of a reasonable stock of tiles.

It was clearly impossible for the Commission to find that such a cartel satisfied the four conditions of 81(3). Not only was there no apparent improvement in the distribution of goods, there was certainly no benefit reserved for consumers, and the restrictions imposed on both manufacturers and recognized customers went far beyond the level required for the improvement of technical standards. The conclusive argument against exemption, however, was that with such arrangements in force, the possibility of eliminating competition in the Belgian tile market was not only the aim but the almost certain achievement of the cartel. The association, therefore, had to amend its rules on the definition of customers and on membership.

This important early decision shows that the Commission realized that the established European preference (in certain markets at least) for confining the operation of a national market to a group of approved undertakings (manufacturers and middlemen) which themselves retained a veto on the admission of new members at their respective levels ran completely contrary to the provisions of Article 81. It was a particularly clear case, since the parties to the arrangement included manufacturers not only from Belgium itself but from four other Member States. Later cases extended the principle of this case even to situations where all members of the relevant association were trading within one Member State. The recommendation that entry to the categories of recognized customers should be open to all qualified entrants, assessed on an objective basis, itself had long-term effects on the jurisprudence of the Commission, notably in the area of selective distribution. The case also illustrated the point that horizontal agreements between competitors, especially when combined with restrictions on vertical relationships covering distribution of a product, could also affect the integration of national markets within the Community, as could vertical agreements of the *Grundig* type.[4]

1.2 THE NEXT STEP—THE NEED FOR BLOCK EXEMPTIONS

The way in which the Belgian tile cartel was disposed of, by recommendation rather than formal decision, illustrates that quite early in its operations DG Comp recognized that the volume of cases to be decided made the availability of informal methods of disposal essential. A decision required a number of formal steps, including the preparation of a statement of objections to the parties, probably an oral hearing of the issues, and a presentation of the draft decision to the Advisory Committee, leading up to the Commission's formal decision. All this took considerable time. On the other hand, an informal negotiated settlement could be dealt with far more speedily; it was particularly suitable where only some clauses of an agreement were regarded as contrary to Article 81, which the parties were often willing to remove if it led to a comparatively quick clearance or exemption for the remainder of the agreement.

Neither the mere handful of official decisions in these early years, however, nor even a number of settlements could make substantial inroads into the large number of notified agreements. This problem had weighed heavily, not only in the filing cabinets, but on the minds of the officials in DG Comp from the beginning of 1964 onwards, when for some months all other tasks had to be laid aside whilst an attempt was made to list and assess on a preliminary basis the great numbers of notified agreements. A very substantial proportion of these notifications were exclusive distribution agreements; the next largest category were patent licences.

Clearly, the way forward would have to be the laying down by the Commission of broad criteria under which block exemption[5] could be given to these forms of agreement (particularly in the area of exclusive distribution where the largest number of notifications had occurred) which were regarded as having many pro-competitive features, and restrictions which on the whole fell within the letter and spirit of 81(3). To apply to the Council for a block exemption, however, would be fruitless unless at least some experience of the particular form of agreement for which the exemption was sought could be shown. The experience of the Commission through 1963 and 1964 on the nature and content of exclusive distribution was not extensive, but the experience gained from the *Grundig* case and the other minor cases already referred to had at least begun to show the nature of the distinctions that could be drawn. On one hand, there were relatively straightforward distribution agreements containing mainly the basic clauses essential to any system of exclusive distribution and which would not damage the competitive process so long as parallel imports remained possible; on the other hand there were a variety of more complex and restrictive agreements governing distribution where individual scrutiny of the particular circumstances of the product and the parties' market share would remain necessary before exemption could be allowed. The great advantage of the block exemption, moreover, was that undertakings would have an incentive to frame their new agreements in terms that complied with it. They would thus eliminate all need for notification and thereby reduce further the administrative burden on DG Comp.

---

[4] See in particular cases referred to in Ch. 6 on trade associations.
[5] Specifically referred to in Art. 81(3) as 'exemption by category'.

2. THE ENACTMENT OF COUNCIL REGULATION 19/65

2.1 THE SCOPE OF THE DRAFT BLOCK EXEMPTION

Work had begun as early as the end of 1963 on the preparation of a draft regulation which the Council could adopt under the terms of Article 83, giving the Commission power to grant exemptions on a group or block basis by reference to objective criteria. Under normal consultative arrangements within the Community, once a draft was approved within DG Comp and by the Commission, it had to be circulated by the Council to the Economic and Social Committee and also to the European Parliament. Once their comments had been considered, and any consequential amendments suggested by the Commission, the Council could enact the final version.

Picking up the reference in Article 81(3) to 'any agreement or category of agreements between undertakings' the draft Regulation prepared and circulated for approval referred to two particular types of agreement to which DG Comp wished to be able to declare that Article 81(1) should be inapplicable. These two categories were:

(a) where one party agreed with the other to supply only to that other goods for resale within a defined area of the Common Market; or where one party agreed with the other to purchase only from that other goods for resale; or where two undertakings entered into reciprocal obligations with each other for exclusive supply and purchase of goods for resale; or

(b) where restrictions were imposed on the acquisition or use of industrial property rights (patents, utility models, designs, or trade marks) or on rights arising out of contracts for assignment of or the right to use methods of manufacture or knowledge relating to the use or the application of industrial processes.

The draft made clear that the block exemption to be given by the Commission would only apply to bilateral agreements; each exemption covering a particular category was required to specify both the individual clauses not to be contained in such agreements, and those minimum clauses which had to be contained in the exempted agreements.

With regard to (a), the intention was clearly to cover cases such as those of *Hummel/ Isbecque* and *Maison Jallatte–Voss* of which the Commission had already gained some experience. On the other hand, to issue block exemption for defined categories of patent licences (obviously the main type of agreement covered by (b)), would be more contentious, and considerably more experience would be required before the terms of a published block exemption could be decided upon.[6]

2.2 THE INTRODUCTION OF REGULATION 19/65

The Council recognized the difficulties of DG Comp with regard to the 'mass problem', and authorized relatively quickly the enactment of Regulation 19/65, giving to the Commission

---

[6] The first draft of a block exemption for patent licences was in fact not published until 1979. See Ch. 12 for detailed consideration of this topic.

authority to grant block exemptions for both categories of agreement. The recitals of this Regulation are important. After formal recitals referring to the authority of the Treaty, the proposal made by the Commission and the necessary opinions received from the Parliament and Economic and Social Committee, reference is then made to the large number of notifications received under Regulation 17. It was considered desirable 'in order to facilitate the task of the Commission' that the Commission should be able to declare by way of Regulation that the provisions of Article [81(1)] do not apply to certain categories of agreement. Reference is then made to the importance that the Council should lay down the conditions under which the Commission can grant such exemption 'in close and constant liaison with the competent authorities of the Member States' and also that such exemptions are exercised only 'after sufficient experience has been gained in the light of individual decisions and it becomes possible to define categories of agreements . . . in respect of which the conditions of Article [81(3)] may be considered as being fulfilled'.

This point is often overlooked by subsequent commentators, who have criticized the Commission for not obtaining authority from the Council at an earlier stage for a wide range of block exemptions covering not only vertical but horizontal agreements. This ignores the fact that it was neither possible nor sensible for a body such as DG Comp to issue broad criteria for exemption until they had gained sufficient familiarity with the types of agreement being entered into and the types of restriction which they contain. Only by dealing with a reasonable number of individual requests for negative clearance or exemption could the Commission acquire the necessary experience to publish and implement an effective block exemption, based on criteria that would both make economic and commercial sense and command a broad measure of acceptance and understanding from European commerce and industry.

The Regulation went on to authorize the Commission to make its own Regulation setting out block exemptions in categories (*a*) and (*b*) only, for a specified period of time. Before it could be issued it would have to be considered by the Advisory Committee and published in the Official Journal so that any interested party could submit comments. The Commission was also authorized by Article 7 to withdraw the benefit of the block exemption from any agreement to which it had been applied if it found that the agreement exempted had 'nevertheless certain effects . . . incompatible with the conditions laid down in Article [81(3)] of the Treaty'.

2.3 THE ITALIAN CHALLENGE TO THE REGULATION

The enactment of this Regulation was of course essential for the Commission because it provided the necessary powers for the issue of 'category-type' exemptions which could deal at a stroke with a large number of those bilateral agreements on its books. However, it was not created without challenge. Not long after its enactment on 2 March 1965 Italy brought a case to the European Court of Justice claiming that the Regulation should be annulled.[7] Italy's challenge was based on the ground that the passing of the Regulation by the Council was itself a *détournement de pouvoir* (abuse of power) in that it purported to extend the scope of Article 81 of the Treaty. Amongst other arguments raised by Italy were that the Regulation raised a presumption that those agreements not expressly referred to in it as

---

[7] *Italy v. Council and Commission* Case 32/65 [1966] ECR 389: [1969] CMLR 39.

eligible for group exemption were illegal, and that Article 81 was in any case intended to govern only horizontal relationships between actual competitors, rather than vertical relationships concerning distribution or licensing to which Article 82 alone would apply.

Neither Advocate General Roemer nor the Court had much difficulty in rejecting these arguments. The Advocate General began by pointing out that the case was primarily concerned with a question of principle, not the mere application to a particular case of the Community law of competition. The passing of Regulation 19/65 was the direct result of the large number of notifications received under Regulation 17, and the consequential demand from both DG Comp and European commercial and industrial interests for a speedier treatment of the requests for exemption. The Advocate General continued:

> For anyone who knows the difficulties of the law relating to agreements, it soon becomes clear that this is an area which does not lend itself at all to using legislative means to find a complete and comprehensive solution for all the problems which may occur. Therefore, the institutions empowered to deal with these matters are acting rightly in proceeding by stages. In proceeding thus, they are also acting rightly in directing their attention first to cases, such as exclusive dealing agreements, where relatively harmless restrictions on competition are involved and which, because of their number, call for a set of rules whereby they can be dealt with speedily in the interests of simplifying administration. Although it is not possible to avoid some initial uncertainty as regards various agreements not covered by Regulation 19/65 until decisions about them are taken individually, it must be admitted that difficulties of this sort are inevitable in the very complex matter of the law relating to agreements, particularly at the beginning of its evolution.[8]

He also pointed out that the Treaty was based on a wide concept of competition including not only horizontal but also vertical agreements, of particular economic importance in that the costs of distribution represented an important element in the total costs of consumer goods. He found no distinction in Article 81 between horizontal and vertical agreements, nor any limitation of Article 82 to vertical agreements, and indeed pointed out that the Court in *de Geus/Robert Bosch*[9] had already decided that Article 81 did apply to vertical agreements. He concluded by pointing out the duty of the Commission to make a conscientious examination of all relevant economic factors before granting an exemption under Article 81(3), whether individual or block.[10]

The Court in its judgment emphasized that in adopting Regulation 19/65 the Council had not enlarged the field of application of Article 81. It had merely given the Commission procedural powers to grant exemption to specific categories of agreement and concerted practices, a step clearly contemplated by the drafting of Article 81 with its reference to 'categories'. The definition of a category, however, provided only a framework for the Commission and DG Comp and did not mean that all agreements of that type which failed to comply with the specific obligations laid down for block exemption would be automatically prohibited or ineligible for individual clearance. Moreover, the Court said it would be wrong to read the Regulation as creating any presumption of law about the way in which Article 81(1) was to be interpreted or as limiting the freedom of the Commission to spell out those

---

[8] [1966] ECR 416.

[9] Case 13/61 [1962] ECR 45: CMLR 1.

[10] It is interesting that, in support of his opinion, the Advocate General drew attention to the recent *White Motors* case in the US Supreme Court, which had laid down precisely the same rule for Federal district courts in the USA when examining vertical agreements: 372 US 253 (1963).

conditions which an agreement had to satisfy in order to gain a block exemption. Italy's application for annulment of the Regulation was therefore rejected.

2.4 THE *STM* CASE—A BROAD INTERPRETATION OF ARTICLE 81(1)

This case shows that the Court was fully aware of the administrative difficulties under which DG Comp had been placed by the perhaps over-ambitious scope of Regulation 17, and of the immense task which DG Comp would have in continuing to deal with, and prescribe appropriate criteria for, the large number of notified agreements. For the Court to have rejected the validity of the Council's Regulation would have been to place an impossible weight on the Commission's shoulders, forcing it to proceed solely by way of individual decision. It happened that the decision of the Court was issued on the very same day as its *Grundig* decision, and the combined effect of the two cases was of importance not only in terms of the substantive law but also in raising the morale of the officials in DG Comp. Moreover, only some two weeks earlier,[11] the Court had delivered a preliminary ruling under Article 234 in the case of *Société Technique Minière* v. *Maschinenbau Ulm*[12] on appeal from the Court of Appeal in Paris which would also prove of importance to it. Maschinenbau Ulm had supplied large earth levellers to STM, a French company engaged in the distribution of equipment for public works. STM had difficulties in finding purchasers for all the levellers, of which it had agreed to buy a substantial number over a two-year period. It had also agreed to organize a repair service and a spare parts stock and to meet the whole of the demand for the product in France, promising not to sell any competing products without Maschinenbau Ulm's agreement. In return, Maschinenbau Ulm had granted STM exclusive rights to sell these machines exclusively in both France and certain overseas territories. When Maschinenbau did not receive payment, it sued STM in France; STM defended the claim on the basis that at least some clauses in the agreement were void under Article 81. The Court of Appeal asked the European Court of Justice to decide which, if any, clauses were so affected.

Both the Advocate General and the Court took the view that agreements of this kind could normally be exempt under 81(3). The Advocate General pointed out that it would be impossible in many cases for undertakings of a modest size to risk entering foreign markets if they could not concentrate their distributive efforts in one set of hands, especially if the product were technical, requiring assembly and repair services and supplies of spare parts at short notice to keep the machines working. The offer of exclusivity was in practice, therefore, essential to the setting up of a satisfactory distribution system and would not normally threaten the competitive process because of the same factors seen in the earlier Commission cases such as *Hummel/Isbecque* and *Maison Jallatte–Voss*, namely that it would be difficult for the manufacturers to ensure that only products circulated and distributed through official channels could reach the relevant market.

The Court's view was that one had to look at the severity of the restrictive element in the clauses granting the exclusive right, and decide whether these clauses could have the effect of partitioning the market between the Member States. However, the Court, went on to make an important statement about the interpretation of the words 'agreements . . . which may

---

[11] On 30 June 1966.   [12] Case 56/65 [1966] ECR 234: CMLR 357.

affect trade between Member States' in Article 81(1). The test laid down by the Court was that 'it must be possible to foresee with a sufficient degree of probability on the basis of a set of objective factors of law or of fact that the agreement in question may have an influence, direct or indirect, actual or potential, on the pattern of trade between Member States'.[13] On this basis, the potential jurisdiction of DG Comp was clearly not to be limited to agreements between undertakings in different Member States but could apply equally to agreements operating within one Member State but having wider effects, particularly on imports into or exports from that State.

3. THE FIRST TEN YEARS OF DG COMP: A REVIEW

3.1 THE VALUE OF THE EARLY CASE LAW

The combined effect of these early Court decisions and its own experience in handling individual cases had in 1967 brought DG Comp to a point, some ten years after the signing of the Treaty of Rome, where it could be seen to be applying general principles reached as a result of its own experience and to start operating on a legislative basis, rather than simply applying the Treaty's general rules to the merits of individual notifications. Clearly progress had not been as speedy as might have been hoped, and the achievements of these first ten years were limited, if assessed solely by the number of cases decided either formally or informally. Nevertheless, at the end of its first decade there was no doubt that progress had been made in the establishment of relevant principles which would provide sound foundations for DG Comp and the Commission as a whole in years to come. Apart from a number of informal settlements and recommendations, it had reached formal decisions during this period on four negative clearances and four Article 81(3) exemptions. It had issued Notices relating to commercial agency and patent licences, and carried out a single sectoral investigation under Regulation 17, Article 12 into the margarine industry. In the *Grundig* case it had obtained not only outright support for the disallowing of export bans but also a clarification of the expression 'which have as their object or effect . . .'. The Court had accepted the Commission's argument that it was sufficient to establish that the *purpose* of the restrictive arrangement or agreement was to separate national markets for distribution purposes, and that it was only necessary to consider separately the *effects* of the restrictive clauses in the agreement if no such purpose could be found. It was also clear that the Court would not prevent Community law from having a restrictive influence on the free exercise of industrial property rights under national law, and that rights flowing from such national laws could not be used for purposes contrary to the basic principles of competition law laid down in Articles 81 and 82. The competition which the Court was protecting in dealing with vertical agreements was generally not competition between the parties to that agreement (whose functions would normally complement each other) but competition between those and other parties at both manufacturing and distribution level who desire to compete for that

---

[13] [1966] ECR 249: CMLR 375. As the case was a reference to the Court under Art 234, the Court was not required to decide the issues between the parties but merely to provide a reply to the questions raised by the Paris Court. For further consideration of the words 'may affect trade between Member States', see Ch. 7, Section 1.

particular product. Article 81(1) was, therefore, to be applicable to both horizontal and vertical agreements.

As to the meaning of the phrase 'which may affect trade between Member States', the Court as we have seen in the *STM* case had applied a very broad test, with the effect of maximizing the jurisdiction of the Commission. It is clear from *Grundig*, moreover, that in making this assessment the Court would not operate a 'balancing test'; even if the volume of trade between particular countries had increased as a result of a particular agreement, the restrictive clauses in that same agreement could nevertheless be held to have affected trade in breach of Article 81. What had still to be worked out was the extent to which exclusive distribution agreements would be permitted when they no longer contained an absolute ban on exports but where other restrictions were included which might more indirectly make parallel imports, and therefore intrabrand competition, more difficult. This was indeed one of the problems which faced the Commission when considering the exact phrasing required for the block exemption, on exclusive distribution, shortly to be introduced.

3.2 THE ATTITUDE OF INDUSTRY TO COMPETITION RULES

Of course, many other problems in the interpretation and application of Article 81 remained unsolved. In two major respects, however, the first decade could be said to have achieved important steps forward. The first of these related to the expectation of industrialists and businessmen operating within the original Common Market. In the early years after the Treaty, there had been some expectation, and indeed hope, amongst European businessmen unfamiliar with a totally (or even substantially) competitive environment that the administration of Articles 81 and 82 would be relatively lenient, and that the interpretation given to the application of the exemptions and the interpretation of the phrase 'agreements . . . which may affect trade between Member States and which have as their object or effect the prevention, restriction or distortion of competition within the Common Market . . .' would catch only clear and obvious anti-competitive cartels involving price-fixing or market-sharing between horizontal competitors. This view had been encouraged by the relative weakness of the national competition laws in the Six Member States at that time, with the possible exception of the new German competition law, which was only gradually gathering effectiveness over its first decade of operation in parallel with the growth of the Commission's own jurisdiction. The European tradition had been one which respected close links of loyalty between suppliers and their customers, and such relationships between manufacturers and their dealer or distributor systems were generally thought of greater importance than the free play of competitive influences. Maintenance of associations of manufacturers or dealers with a firm commitment to dealing on a regular basis with each other and excluding undertakings outside the scope of the agreement was considered respectable and normal, rather than as an artificial and objectionable division of national markets into 'insider' and 'outsider' groups. Agreements not to compete or not to export particular categories of product for fear of reprisals by other competitors in neighbouring States had also been considered normal.

Against this traditional fear of an outright rivalry between undertakings, expectation at the outset had been that, though change would be necessary, it would be gradual, even gentle.[14] Although it was some years before the effect of the change in atmosphere was perceived, it had become clear by the middle of the 1960s that Articles 81 and 82, and the Regulations to be made under them, were going to introduce a totally new situation. Undoubtedly, a major influence was that the Commission realized that a system of central-ized planning of industrial and commercial objectives (akin to the centralized planning of agriculture carried out by the Commission to implement the Common Agricultural Policy) was impossible, first because of the size of the bureaucracy needed to enforce such a scheme throughout the Community, and secondly because the ground rules for such common policies could never have been agreed among the Member States in view of their widely differing views on industrial structures and their differing interpretations of national interest.

3.3 RELATIONSHIPS BETWEEN THE COMMISSION AND OTHER COMMUNITY INSTITUTIONS

The second important step was that over this period DG Comp had found it essential to establish working relationships with the other DGs, also with two other Community institu-tions, the Economic and Social Committee and the European Parliament. Although the Parliament had only limited powers at this time (well before the introduction of direct elections) it was able to continue to apply pressure on the Commission as a whole by means of questions tabled for answer by the relevant Commissioner relating to development of competition policy. The questions recorded illustrate the continuing concern of members of the Parliament that DG Comp should continue its forward movement in the development of its policies.[15] The value of the continuing individual questioning of the Commission as a means of ascertaining information about its progress and as a means of goading it on to further efforts should not be underestimated. In later years the Parliament has continued its keen interest in the development of competition law which it exercises on a methodical basis, especially in view of its ability to comment each year on the Annual Report of DG Comp. This Report, which came into existence only as the result of persistent requests from Parliament itself, was first published in 1972 and now appears in early summer with a review of the previous year's activities and developments in competition policy, on which the Parliament enacts.

Relationships between the Commission and the Council had also matured substantially over the period. Whilst the Council is essentially a political body consisting of Ministers for the individual Member States, it had concluded during the early 1960s that substantial powers under Articles 81 and 82 would need to be delegated to the Commission if progress was to be made in enforcing the Articles; it would also be inappropriate for the Council, given its other responsibilities and the technical nature of most of the work to be carried out by DG Comp in implementing Articles 81 and 82, to involve itself in individual cases. Few other Directorates received such wide delegated powers at that stage in the life of the Community as DG Comp with Regulation 17/62. Their existence however enabled DG Comp to continue its progress in enforcing policy both through its administrative (both

---

[14] For an account of the European attitude to competition in the early 1960s, see E. Minoli, 'Industry's View of Trade Regulations in the EEC', *Proceedings of Fordham Corporate Law Institute* (1962).

[15] The questions, and the answers provided by DG Comp, are recorded in the Official Journal.

investigatory and quasi-judicial) and legislative functions, even at times when political dead-lock made it difficult for the Council to reach decisions on many other matters, to the general frustration of those working in other areas of the Commission. To this extent DG Comp has been fortunate in that at a critical stage in its development it did receive these far-reaching delegated powers, not only to investigate but also to make decisions which would be final, subject only to appeal to the Court at Luxembourg[16] on the grounds set out in Article 230 of the Treaty.

It was however, it is, the developing relationship of DG Comp with the European Court of Justice that was the most important single factor in this first ten years of its life. There is no doubt that the support given by the Court to the work of the Commission was of critical importance in enabling its main lines of policy to be established. The outcome of the *Grundig* case was to lay a firm legal foundation supporting the Directorate in its aim to establish market integration as the foremost principle to be considered in applying Article 81(3), to the extent that an export ban found in an agreement imposed on a distributor would alone certainly make it impossible for exemption to be obtained, unless the export ban were simply to countries outside the Common Market itself without any possibility of subsequent re-export of goods into the Market because of the existence of substantial tariff barriers or transport costs.[17] So familiar has this concept become with the passage of time that it is perhaps too easy to overlook the serious consequences had the European Court not firmly supported the Commission on this key issue. The Court's assistance was rendered, of course, through decisions under Article 234 on requests for preliminary rulings from national courts as well as in cases on direct appeal from the Commission's own decisions under Article 230. In the next five years (1967–72), a period when political progress was slow, largely owing to the influence of General De Gaulle, the role of the Court would nevertheless continue to grow in importance in the establishment of further substantive legal doctrine in this area.

3.4 THE FIRST BLOCK EXEMPTION REGULATION 67/67

The end of this first decade was marked by the passage of the first Regulation by the Commission itself, namely Regulation 67/67 setting out the conditions for group exemp-tion of exclusive distribution agreements, to be considered in detail in Chapter 10. At this point the Commission should have been given adequate resources to consider the smaller number of multilateral agreements now notified, many of which involved horizontal agreements having at least an element of market-sharing on a national basis, and therefore representing a greater danger to the competitive process than the mass of bilateral agree-ments, largely relating to exclusive distribution and patent licensing, whose early notifica-tion by 1 February 1963 imposed so heavy a burden on the workings of DG Comp for many years afterwards. It is arguable, though by no means certain, that this could have been done without doing substantial damage to the principle of market integration, usually put for-ward as the essential reason for the early concentration on the bilateral vertical agreement. In the event, not until some years later did the Commission get to grips with some of the

---

[16] Initially to the European Court of Justice, but from 1989 to the Court of First Instance with further appeal to the Court of Justice on points of law only. See Ch. 24, Section 5.

[17] See, e.g. *Javico* v *Yves St Laurent* (Case C-306/96 [1998] ECR I-1983: 5 CMLR 172).

major horizontal cartels that had operated with impunity for some years within the Community.

DG Comp had, however, developed its policies towards vertical agreements far more quickly than towards horizontal agreements and cartels. It is a justifiable criticism of the policy of the Commission during its first ten years that the terms of Regulation 17 inevitably forced this initial concentration on vertical rather than horizontal agreements because of the extent to which the mass notification of the vertical agreements in accordance with the Regulation's requirements limited DG Comp's freedom of action.[18] With hindsight, it might have been better for the Commission to have phased in the notification of such vertical agreements over a longer period of time.

---

[18] This is confirmed by the subsequent figures produced by the Commission itself a decade later. The *9th Annual Report* (1979), pp.15–16, confirms that 40,000 notifications were received by the Commission during the first years of application of Arts 81 and 82, of which as many as 29,500 concerned exclusive dealing agreements, and of which more than 25,000 were eventually disposed of on the basis of Reg. 67/67.

PART II

THE SUBSTANTIVE LAW OF THE EUROPEAN COMMUNITY

Each man's experience starts again from the beginning. Only institutions grow wiser: they accumulate collective experience, and owing to this experience and this wisdom, men subject to the same rules will not see their own nature changing, but their behaviour gradually transformed.

Jean Monnet, quoting the Swiss philosopher Henri-Frédéric Amiel (1821–81),
in the course of a speech to the Common Assembly of the
European Coal and Steel Community in 1955.

6

ARTICLE 81(1): ANALYSIS 1

1. INTRODUCTION

Part I contains a historical account of the early implementation by DG Comp of the policies relating to competition contained in the Treaty of Rome. In retrospect, the first ten years can be seen as a slow-moving, but essential, gestation period for the development of a distinct Community competition policy. The tempo of development begins to increase sharply with the implementation of the block exemption contained in Regulation 67/67 at the end of this first stage. Because of the sheer volume and complexity of substantive law developments since that time, it is not possible to give an account of the substantive law or the development of policy simply by reviewing cases as they occur in successive years. Instead, it is necessary to consider the law under a number of different subject headings, reviewing under each of them relevant major cases and policy developments.

To all these subjects the structure of Article 81 is of central importance. It is therefore logical to begin our examination of the substantive law by analysing its content. Article 81 has not been interpreted by the European Court of Justice, nor by the Court of First Instance, nor indeed by the Commission, in the way that an English Court or administrative agency would interpret an English statute. It has been treated in a far more teleological way, that is in a manner which gives great weight to the particular part that it is considered to play within the general framework of the Treaty,[1] allowing the content of other Articles to influence its interpretation within the general scheme of the Treaty. Correspondingly, whilst keeping this always in mind, less importance is placed on exact analysis of individual words and phrases within the Article. It is probably helpful, nevertheless, to analyse the Article under five separate headings, namely:

(1) the meaning of 'undertaking,' including the concept of 'group economic unit';

(2) the meaning of 'all agreements, decisions by associations of undertakings and concerted practices';

(3) the meaning of 'which may affect trade between Member States';

(4) the meaning of 'which have as their object or effect the prevention, restriction or distortion of competition within the common market'; and

(5) the scope of its coverage, with special reference to sectors partially or totally excepted.

---

[1] The best known example of the teleological approach is an Art. 82 case: *Europemballage Corporation Can Co. Inc.* v. *Commission* Case 6/72 [1973] ECR 215: CMLR 199, but it can be found also in a number of Art. 81 cases. For comment on the general approach of the ECJ in competition cases, see Ch. 24, Section 5 'The Commission and the Comunity Courts'.

The first two items are dealt with in this chapter; the last three are considered in the following chapter.

2. THE CONCEPT OF AN UNDERTAKING

2.1 A BASIC DEFINITION

The definition of an undertaking is the first essential step in the analysis of Article 81(1). An undertaking, of course, must be a body capable of having legal rights and duties and acting in co-operation with other parties. For the purpose of the ECSC the European Court had defined it as 'a single organization of personal, tangible and intangible elements attached to an autonomous legal entity and pursuing a given long-term economic aim'.[2] An examination of the substantial number of cases under the Treaty of Rome in which the term has actually been considered (or held to apply without detailed consideration) illustrates that such a broad definition has been largely accepted, with the exclusion on one hand of activities carried on by a State in the exercise of its sovereign function (as opposed to merely commercial functions) and, at the other extreme, of those that neither involve the conduct of any kind of business nor the coordination of commercial activities to be carried on by others. It can therefore apply to State bodies engaged in commerce, nationalized industries operating as separate legal entities, municipalities, federations, trade associations (regardless of specific function), publicly owned undertakings, and undertakings with special rights granted by the State; it also includes private individuals engaged in any form of business, commerce, or profession, partnerships, co-operatives, companies, and performing rights societies. To be engaged in an economic activity is necessary, but the objective of making a profit is not essential. Identification of an 'undertaking' for the purposes of Article 81 should in the majority of cases thus not present any difficulty, but nevertheless there have been some exceptional cases at the borderline.

From such borderline cases considered by the European Court it is clear that the key element is the nature, not of the body, but of the activities which it carries out. In *Eurocontrol*[3] (European Court 1994) that international organization, responsible for air traffic control over much of Europe, sought to collect charges from a German airline which had claimed that Eurocontrol had been acting in breach of Articles 81 and 82; the Court ruled that this could not be the case since Eurocontrol was not an 'undertaking' to which the Article applied. Whilst the concept of 'undertaking' covered any entity engaged in an economic activity, regardless of legal status and the way it was financed, in this case the function of Eurocontrol was to control and supervise airspace, a task undertaken in the public interest for the safety of air passengers. Collection of route charges could not be separated from the organization's other activities which, taken as a whole, were more like those of a public authority than an economic concern. A similar outcome occurred in the case of *Diego Cali* v. SEPG (European Court 1997).[4] SEPG was a company formed to perform services in the Port of Genoa relating to the prevention and removal of pollution, particularly oil spills. Italian law required that these tasks were performed by the port operator; SEPG acted on behalf of

---

[2] *Mannesman v. High Authority* Case 19/61 [1962] ECR 357, 371.
[3] *SAT v. Eurocontrol* Case C-364/92 [1994] ECR I-43: 5 CMLR 208.
[4] *Diego Cali & Figli v. Servicio Ecologici Porto di Genova* Case C-343/95 [1997] ECR I-1547: 5 CMLR 484.

the port operator and charged users a fee based either on the tonnage of the vessel or the volume of petroleum products being transported. Diego Cali was a shipping company which claimed that it did not require the services of SEPG because it maintained anti-pollution and cleaning-up facilities on its vessels. The Court nevertheless found in favour of SEPG, because its activities involved the performance of a task in the public interest which formed part of the central functions of the State, protecting the marine environment. That the company had been formed under Italian private law did not affect the outcome of the case, which turned on the nature of the activities which it carried out; the fact that a charge was made for those activities, as in *Eurocontrol*, did not render SEPG an undertaking for purposes of the Article. The decisions in these cases appear to suggest that an organization can be an undertaking in respect of some of its activities but not in respect of others, if its first set of activities were essentially commercial but the second involved the performance of functions of a public character equivalent to those carried out by Eurocontrol or SEPG.

In contrast was the finding in *Ambulanz Glockner*[5] heard more recently by the ECJ under Article 234 on a request from a Higher Administrative Court in Germany for a ruling, *inter alia*, on the status of an ambulance service which provided both emergency transport and also routine patient transport. The service received payment for both services both from the Land (Rhineland-Palatinate) and from insurers. The ECJ ruled that, since the provision of goods and services (even emergency services) is an economic activity, *Ambulanz Glockner* was an undertaking, regardless of the source of the payments which it received. A judgment of the new UK Competition Commission Appeal Tribunal (set up by the Competition Act 1998 to hear appeals against decisions of the Office of Fair Trading under provisions of the Act equivalent to Articles 81 and 82) has held that purchases of services from the private sector for the maintenance of old peoples' homes by a public statutory trust are economic activities of an undertaking (*Bettercare*).

2.2 INSURANCE AND SOCIAL SECURITY FUND CASES

A number of the leading cases here involved insurance funds. The first two were a pair of French cases. In the first, *Poucet and Pistre* (European Court 1993),[6] the Court held that a fund running a compulsory social security scheme based on principles of 'solidarity' was not an undertaking. Under its sickness and maternity insurance scheme benefits were paid of an identical size to all recipients but contributions were made proportionate to income. Pension rights paid out under the fund were also not proportionate to contributions. There were also other elements of cross-subsidy which enabled those parts of the fund that were in surplus to assist those parts which were in deficit. By contrast, *Fédération Française des Sociétés d'Assur-ance*[7] concerned a voluntary old-age pension scheme for agricultural workers, supplementing the basic compulsory scheme. Certain private insurers challenged the French law which established this scheme on the basis that it had an effective monopoly. The Court held that the

---

[5] *Ambulanz Glockner* Case C-475/99 [2002] 4 CMLR 726: *Bettercare* [2002] Comp AR 226. Under s. 60 of the Competition Act, the Tribunal and UK Courts are required to apply EC principles and case law in deciding appeals. In Case T-319/99 *Fenin* v. *Commission* (a decision of 4 March 2003) the CFI held, however, that the authority running the Spanish health service was not an undertaking, even though it purchased large quantities of products from commmercial suppliers, as its principle purpose was to carry out functions of a public character.

[6] Cases C-159,160/91 [1993] ECR I-637.

[7] Case C-244/94 [1995] ECR I-4013: [1996] 4 CMLR 536.

insurance company managing the pension scheme was indeed an under-taking. The mere fact that it was non-profit making was irrelevant since it was competing with private insurance companies, and managed according to normal principles of insurance contributions: members received payments linked to the contributions made. Provisions on deferment of contributions because of illness were similar to those found in private insurance schemes, and there was no element of cross-subsidy between different categories of beneficiary.

The *Inail*[8] case from Italy was closer in its facts to *Poucet/Pistre*, since it involved a compulsory scheme covering accidents at work which the managing partner of a firm refused to join, because it had already covered these risks by private insurance and he objected to the monopoly nature of the official scheme. The ECJ ruled that, although the social aims of such a scheme did not rule it out automatically from being classed as an undertaking, the rules of this scheme were strongly redistributive; payments made did not reflect the level of contributions, and were fixed by the State. It was therefore not an undertaking. On the other side of the line fell *Pavlov*,[9] where the consultants at a Dutch hospital had objected to being forced to belong to a pension fund, which had not been set up in the context of collective bargaining, but which was held to be an undertaking because it was carried on in competition with other insurance companies and their equivalent funds. It made no difference, in the view, that the compulsory nature of the fund did restrict competition to a limited extent, as the payments to the fund had only a marginal effect on the cost of the consultants' services.

In a number of Dutch cases involving pension funds these were held on the same grounds to be undertakings, but nevertheless outside the scope of Article 81(1) because of the fact that they had been established as part of collective bargaining arrangements between employers and employees in a particular industry. (See Chapter 7 at pp.104–5).

2.3 EMPLOYEES AND TRADE UNIONS

The position of employees is however clear. They are not undertakings, but 'workers' within the meaning of Article 39, because they perform their duties for and under the direction of the undertaking. In *Becu*[10] a company operating a grain warehousing business in the Ghent port area used registered dockers for loading and unloading grain vessels, but other (less highly paid) workers in its warehouse on other duties. When prosecuted by the Belgian authorities for alleged breach of the Royal Decree giving monopoly rights to registered dockers in respect of dock work, (which included the work carried out in the warehouse), the company claimed that the dockers protected by the Royal Decree were individually acting in breach of Articles 82 and 86. The Court however rejected this argument; the dockers were not undertakings. The status of such employees is moreover unaffected by the fact that they may be linked to other groups of workers employed by the same undertaking by some form of association, so that trade unions are not themselves undertakings (except to the extent that they enter into separate commercial activities involving breaches of Article 81. *FNSEA*: a Commission decision involving French farmers' union engaged in price-fixing agreements with slaughterers).

---

[8] Case C-218/00 [2002] ECR I-6911: 4 CMLR 833.

[9] Case C-180/98 [2001] Cases C-180 and 184/98 [2001] ECRI-6451: 4 CMLR 30.

[10] Case C-22/98 [1999] ECR I-5665: [2001] 4 CMLR 968. See also the opinion of Jacobs A-G in *Albany*, Case C-67/96, [1999] ECR I-5751: [2000] 4 CMLR 446 at para. 227. *FNSEA* was a decision of 3 April 2003.

2.4 AGENTS

The position of agents however depends very much on the extent of their activities. An agent could be classified as an undertaking if the activities in which it is engaged fall outside the normal range of services performed by an agent for its principal, so that to use the language of the Commission Guidelines on Vertical Restraints[11] the agency is no longer a 'genuine' one. When the agency remains genuine then Article 81 is in any case unlikely to have application, since two independent undertakings are required for an agreement or concerted practice to come into being. A genuine agent only accepts a limited amount of risk and does not usually invest its own monies for the benefit of its principal. An agent is normally restricted by its principal as to the territory in which it may operate, the customers to whom it may sell, and the prices and conditions applicable to those sales; an agent without these limitations on his conduct may be at risk of passing over the line into independent status as an undertaking.

Whilst individuals operating their own businesses, alone or in partnership, are undertakings this status will not necessarily be accorded to individuals who are controlling shareholders in companies. On the other hand an individual who controls a number of businesses may be classified as a single undertaking. The issue was raised by a German court under Article 177: a German company, Hydrotherm, claimed that a manufacturing and distribution agreement was void under Article 81(1).[12] The other parties to the agreement were a firm known as Compact and a company called OSA, both owned by an Italian individual, Dr Andreoli. Hydrotherm had agreed to place a substantial order with Compact for the purchase of aluminium alloy radiators; it was claimed that Hydrotherm had not placed an order as large as that required by the contract and the Italian parties sued Hydrotherm for breach of contract before the German court. An issue in the case was whether the agreement could have been covered by the block exemption contained in Regulation 67/67; the Court held that the term 'undertaking' designated an economic unit, even if in law that economic unit consisted of several persons, natural or legal. Regulation 67/67 required that only two undertakings be parties, but the Court held that this condition was satisfied even if one of the parties contracted through the medium of several undertakings with identical interests and controlled by the same natural person. In this case Dr Andreoli controlled all the relevant businesses in his operations, and the Court, adopting the economic analysis suggested by Advocate General Lenz, found that the agreement had been made by only two undertakings, namely Hydrotherm on one side and Andreoli and his businesses on the other.

The issue of agency was considered by the European Court in the *Sugar Cartel*[13] case, where some of the undertakings involved acted as agents for each other in the sugar market, and also as principals on their own account, and were adjudged by the Court to be essentially independent traders to whom Article 81 applied. An element in this decision was clearly the ambiguous relationship between those particular undertakings and their alleged principals; it does not seem to be the Commission's practice to refuse the status of agent to a business simply because it also trades on its own account or for other principals in respect of

---

[11] [2000] OJ C291/1: [2000] 5 CMLR 1074, at paras 12–17.
[12] *Hydrotherm Gerätebau v. Andreoli* Case 170/83 [1984] ECR 2999: [1985] 3 CMLR 224.
[13] *Suiker Unie v. Commission* Case 40/73 [1975] ECR 1663: [1976] 1 CMLR 295.

other products. The actual economic function of the so-called agent must be fully analysed in each case.[14]

It is clear that the mere description of an individual or company as an 'agent' is insufficient to prevent the application of Article 81. In *Pittsburgh Corning Europe*[15] (Commission 1972) certain distributors for Pittsburgh Corning, which supplied cellular glass in Belgium and Holland, were described in relevant documents as agents, although the evidence showed that they were actually distributors. The Commission found that the term 'agent' in the agreement between Pittsburgh Corning and its Belgian representative company was in fact used only for tax reasons.

2.5 A SUMMARY: THE LIMITS TO ITS SCOPE

It may be useful to sum up the situations in which it is unlikely that an individual or other entity will be adjudged to be acting as an undertaking;

— where the nature of the activities carried out, even if they involve the receipt of payment for services rendered, form part of the functions of the State or other public authorities (*Eurocontrol: Diego Cali: Ambulanz Glockner*). An entity performing such functions may nevertheless be classified as an undertaking in respect of other, purely commercial, functions.

— where the function is not one of a commercial nature, since it is a compulsory social security system or insurance fund based on the principles of internal solidarity (*Poucet et Pistre/Inail*) as opposed to being a fund where benefits are paid proportionately to contributions collected from members (*FFSA/Albany International*). Even where the latter situation applies the terms of the fund (though an undertaking) may be outside Article 81(1) if established in the context of a collective bargaining agreement. (*Albany International* and other pension fund cases cited in Chapter 7, pp.104–5).

— where the relevant person is simply an integral part of a larger organization (which itself may well be an undertaking) and had therefore no separate or independent economic role on the market. This will apply to employees (*Becu*) and to genuine agents who do not accept unusual risks on behalf of their principal nor act in practice as principals (*Pittsburgh Corning*).

3. GROUP ECONOMIC UNITS

The second important issue concerning the definition is whether individual corporate bodies comprised within a group are separate undertakings, or whether the group itself constitutes the relevant undertaking. The view usually taken by the Commission and the Court,

---

[14] In December 1986, the first Council Directive on self-employed commercial agents defined them as persons who have a continuing authority to negotiate sales or purchases on behalf of a principal. It laid down certain mandatory clauses applicable to the appointment of such agents relating, *inter alia* to remuneration, termination, and restrictive covenants. [1986] OJ L382/17. The Directive has now been incorporated into the national law of each Member State, in the UK by Statutory Instruments 93/3053 and 3173 and 98/2868.

[15] *Pittsburgh Corning Europe* [1973] CMLR D2. See Ch. 10 p.165 for a fuller description of the case.

(which is consistent also with the approach taken to the status of an agent in relation to its principal) is that each company within a group, either as parent or wholly owned subsidiary, is treated as an undertaking capable of entering into an agreement or concerted practice. On the other hand, the essential condition that both entities concerned must be capable of independent economic policy-making for a relationship between them to be classified as an agreement or concerted practice is not satisfied if the agreement or concerted practice reflects no more than the allocation of functions within a corporate group under the legal and actual control of one company. An early example was the *Kodak* case[16] (Commission 1970). This involved a request for negative clearance by various wholly owned European subsidiaries of the United States company Eastman Kodak, following the introduction of new uniform conditions of sale which permitted export sales by them to other Member State countries at the same price as was charged there by the local Kodak subsidiary, whilst imposing restrictions on sale outside the Community. The Commission took the view that, since these subsidiaries could not act independently of their parent company, their individual agreements within the group were not made between independent economic policy-making units, and therefore no effect on competition was either likely nor possible.

In *Viho Europe* v. *Commission*,[17] (European Court 1996) the Court confirmed that this was the correct interpretation of Article 81. Viho had sought to buy Parker pens direct from that company but Parker had refused to supply direct, though willing that Viho should obtain supplies on less favourable terms from their distributors in Europe, who were all directly owned Parker subsidiaries. It was clear that Parker Pen in Europe traded as a single economic unit, within which subsidiaries did not enjoy autonomy, since their distribution strategies on product ranges, advertising margins, and prices were all centrally controlled. Moreover, the Court made clear that, even if the effect of the internal allocation of functions within a corporate group is 'to contribute to preserving and partitioning the various national markets and in so doing to thwart one of the fundamental objectives to be achieved by the Common Market', it still did not breach Article 81. What would amount to such a breach would be a requirement by the Group that its individual subsidiaries dealt with third parties only on terms which limited price competition or restricted free movement of goods. Thus the Commission was able in the *Interbrew*[18] case to prevent a Belgium brewery group with a dominant position in Belgium from entering into arrangements with its wholly owned subsidiaries under which each of them had to obtain a 'destination clause' from its customers: effectively a promise not to export the beer supplied by the subsidiary. Such an arrangement went far beyond mere 'internal allocation' of duties between subsidiaries of the group.

This approach by the Commission (often referred to as the doctrine of the 'group economic unit') had also been referred to by the Court in its *Centrafarm*[19] and *Ahmed Saeed*[20] cases in 1974 and 1983 respectively, where the Court indicated that Article 81 might well be

---

[16] *Kodak* [1970] CMLR D19.

[17] Case C-73/95P [1996] ECR I-5457: [1997] 4 CMLR 419.

[18] [1996] 5 CMLR 518. Although this informal settlement concerned a company with a dominant position under Art. 82, it nevertheless indicates the Commission's approach under Art. 81 to such arrangements or agreements between the individual subsidiaries of Interbrew and their customers.

[19] *Centrafarm BV* v. *Sterling Drug Inc. and Winthrop BV* Cases 15 and 16/74 [1974] ECR 1147, 1183: 2 CMLR 480.

[20] Case 66/86: [1989] ECR 803: [1990] 4 CMLR 102.

applicable if a company is accorded a measure of independence, either *de facto* or *de jure;* it may well then fall within the scope of the Article, even if the degree of independence is restricted. Difficult issues can also arise in joint venture cases, where the degree of independence of the joint venture company from its parents can present analytical problems for the Commission.

In *Martell-DMP*[21] fines were imposed both on the French cognac producer Martell and on DMP, its 50 per cent-owned subsidiary which distributed the product in France, for conspiracy to prevent parallel exports to Italy (where prices were substantially higher). The parties had acknowledged to the Commission that they regarded themselves as separate, rather than as parts of the same economic unit. Moreover, the other 50 per cent owner of DMP, Piper-Heidsieck, had exactly the same shareholding and representation on the supervisory board of DMP as had Martell. DMP also distributed brands not belonging to its two parent companies and acted independently from them in determining the terms of sales to syndicates in France.

The adoption by the Court of the 'group economic unit' theory has a dual advantage for the Commission. It enables it to apply a test to the relationship between undertakings within a corporate group which gives a realistic degree of emphasis to the actual economic relationship between them, rather than relying on formal tests relating to legal indicia which might more easily be manipulated by the parties. It also enables the Commission (and the Court) to justify the extension of its jurisdiction to parent companies apparently operating from outside the Community, so long as they actively control subsidiary companies resident or doing business within it, an issue discussed further in Chapter 23.

4. AGREEMENTS

4.1 INTRODUCTION: THE BROAD SCOPE OF ARTICLE 81(1)

Article 81(1) was drafted to cover three related, though conceptually distinct, situations. Undertakings can be said to have reached an *agreement* when there can objectively be said to be a sufficient consensus between them as to the bargain to which they have mutually committed themselves. It is clear from cases such as *Asia Motor France (No. 3)*[22] that the parties' lack of autonomy in their choice of commercial arrangements may deprive these of the character of a voluntary 'agreement'. On the other hand, the reasons which induced the making of an agreement need not be identical on all sides. The interests of distributors in being able to supply their principal territory, and also to export product into other territories where higher prices may prevail, may of course be at variance with the interest of the manufacturer in preventing parallel imports.

Identification of such consensus is ultimately a matter for courts of law, not for the undertakings themselves. This task is easier if the contract is written, but a purely verbal, or partly written and partly verbal agreement may exist and be recognized by a court or

---

[21] [1992] 5 CMLR 582. In an Art. 82 case, *Irish Sugar* v. *Commission* Case T-228/97 [1999] ECR II-2969: 5 CMLR 1300. A subsidiary in which Irish Sugar held 51 per cent of the share capital was nevertheless accepted by it as not forming part of a group economic entity.

[22] Case T-387/94 [1996] ECR II-961: 5 CMLR 537.

administrative body, even if the parties claim that, whatever the agreement's outward form, it was not intended to be legally binding but simply a 'gentlemen's agreement'. The case of *Atka A/S* v. BP *Kemi A/S*[23] (Commission 1979) illustrates that even if the relevant document has been neither signed nor dated, it will still be treated as an agreement if it has been acted upon by both parties. In this case, De Danske Spritfabrikker (DDSF) was the only producer in Denmark of synthetic and agricultural ethanol, used in the production of several products including vinegar and cosmetics. About 45 per cent of the total synthetic ethanol production in the Common Market in 1971 was manufactured by BP, and it had begun to supply certain customers in Denmark through its Danish subsidiary (BP Kemi). To protect its market position, DDSF then sought an exclusive purchasing and co-operation agreement with BP and its subsidiaries; a document was drawn up, though never signed nor dated, under which:

(i) DDSF would only buy the product from BP Kemi, up to an agreed maximum, provided that BP Kemi had the opportunity of supplying it also with excess quantities on similar terms; and

(ii) BP Kemi would be entitled to sell yearly in Denmark up to 25 per cent of the combined aggregate sales of the product; but if BP Kemi exceeded this limit, it would pay compensation to DDSF.

There were subsidiary agreements on the pricing of the product (which was to be kept identical by both companies) and on rules for allocating customers within Denmark. Atka, a competitor of DDSF, challenged these arrangements, and the Commission ruled that the mere application by the two parties of identical prices (which continued after the termination of the original agreement) would not necessarily prove the continuing effect of the agreement, but was strong evidence of it if pricing of the product was likely to have been different in normal market competition.

A *decision* by an association is any provision of the rules of a trade association (having members which are either trade associations or, more often, separate undertakings) or any decision or recommendation made under those rules either for or by its members, or arrived at informally within the frame-work which they provide. Again, it is normally quite easy to identify the existence of such decisions. The concept of *concerted practices*, however, is more fluid; it is unquestionably the widest, and the vaguest, of the three expressions, intended to cover any kind of co-operative activity between undertakings which falls short of an actual agreement. For safety's sake, 'concerted practices' are often alleged by the Commission as an alternative even when some kind of 'agreement' probably also exists, as for example in the sales cartel operated in the *Floral* case[24] (Commission 1979). In an early decision, *Brasserie de Haecht* v. *Wilkin-Janssens* (*No. 1*)[25] (European Court 1967) the Court indicated that the three concepts need not be separately distinguished in the Commission's analysis of the situation; the constituent elements of the three forms of relationship could be considered together if they were factually hard to disentangle.

---

[23] [1979] 3 CMLR 684.

[24] *Floral Düngemittelverkaufs* [1980] 2 CMLR 285. In the *Citric Acid* Case [2002] 5 CMLR 1070, the Commission confirmed that the concepts of 'agreement' and 'concerted practice' are fluid and may overlap. See also *Hercules* v. *Commission* Case T-7/89 [1991] ECR II-1711 [1992] 4 CMLR 84.

[25] *Brasserie de Haecht* v. *Wilkin-Janssens* (*No. 1*) Case 23/67 [1967] ECR 407: [1968] CMLR 26.

In this area, Article 81 has again drawn part of its content from Article 65 of the ECSC Treaty, where all three expressions are found. Of these, both 'agreements' and 'concerted practices' require that at least two undertakings be party to the agreement or practice; by contrast, a 'decision' by a trade association could involve the association alone (which may be a single legal person) although in practice it will usually involve the participation of a number of undertakings, almost certainly the members of that association. Although two undertakings must be party to agreements or concerted practices, restrictions need only affect one party.

The Commission and the Court have dealt with numerous cases on both horizontal and vertical agreements. As we have seen, horizontal agreements are those made between undertakings that compete with each other (or at least are believed to do so) because each operates at the same level, whether as manufacturer, wholesaler, distributor, or retailer. On the other hand, vertical agreements are those made between undertakings at different levels in the commercial chain, whose relationship to each other is complementary. The vertical agreement may therefore be between manufacturer and distributor, or wholesaler and retailer, or in another context patentee and licensee. Both types of agreement are covered by Article 81.[26]

4.2 NETWORK AGREEMENTS AND UNILATERAL CONDUCT

Even a document which looks less like an agreement than unilateral instruction may be held to constitute an agreement, if the recipient of the instructions has been required to acknowledge its receipt, even if the recipient was not expressly required to acknowledge its contents. In *WEA-Filipacchi Music* SA[27] (Commission 1972) WEA, a subsidiary of the US corporation Warner Brothers, was engaged in the sale of pop records. It sent a circular to its various French distributors informing them that sales of such records outside France were forbidden. In sending this circular, WEA was influenced by the fact that the French price was considerably lower than the price in Germany, so that sales or distribution by way of 'parallel imports' into Germany could have proved extremely profitable for the French distributors. The distributors were merely asked to affix their official stamp to the circular by way of acknowledgement, without being asked specifically to acknowledge that they were bound by the terms communicated.

In the case of *Sandoz*[28] invoices for the supply of pharmaceuticals used by this producer bore the words 'export prohibited'. In practice that restriction had been accepted by its trade customers. This was held by the European Court (confirming the Commission decision) to represent, not simply a unilateral request, but part of an agreement of which the words endorsed were the documentary evidence.

In the case of *BMW Belgium SA* v. *Commission*[29] (European Court 1979) a circular urging

---

[26] As we have already seen in Ch. 5, pp.49–51, an early attempt by Italy to have vertical agreements read out of the Article failed.

[27] [1973] CMLR D43.

[28] Case 227 [1990] ECR I-45.

[29] Cases 32 and 36–82/78 [1979] ECR 2435: [1980] 1 CMLR 370. It is noteworthy that in this case the BMW subsidiary was fined, but its German parent which had played no part in the arrangements was not even made a defendant, showing that the doctrine of the 'group economic unit' is not, and should not be, applied automatically without analysis of the relevant facts. The rulings of the Commission were upheld by the Court.

dealers to discourage exports of cars to Germany was distributed (without authority from the parent company in Germany) by the Belgian BMW subsidiary. The circular went out after consultation with, and under the signatures of, the BMW Belgium dealers' trade association's executive committee, and a number of Belgian BMW dealers acknowledged its receipt in writing. These were held by the Commission to have acknowledged participation in the arrangements, so that fines were imposed for the attempt which the circular represented to prevent exports of BMW vehicles from Belgium. It is also clear that, once such an agreement has been made, the Commission cannot easily be satisfied that it has been completely terminated: even if the parties claim that this is so, its effect may continue to influence their conduct. In such circumstances it may therefore be held still to exist, or alternatively to have been transformed into concerted practices.[30]

An interesting development of the jurisprudence of the Court on the question of the definition of an 'agreement' has come in cases where a manufacturer has apparently taken unilateral action, but in a way so closely connected to an agreement that it has been interpreted, together with that agreement, as forming part of the general complex of contractual arrangements between the manufacturer and the various distributors or dealers with whom these individual agreements (even if notified or exempted) were made. In *AEG Telefunken* v. *Commission*[31] (European Court 1983) AEG had its selective distribution system for consumer electronic products in Germany and other countries notified to the Commission and exempted under Article 81(3). This distribution agreement contained no right for AEG to lay down resale prices for its dealers. Numerous complaints were received by the Commission from small traders claiming that AEG had sought to discriminate against some of them, especially those who would not maintain resale prices at the level considered appropriate by AEG. The Commission imposed a substantial fine, which was upheld by the Court. The Court ruled that the activities of AEG Telefunken alone in ensuring that at least a substantial proportion of its dealers did not cut prices below the recommended level was not unilateral conduct, but formed an integral part of its contractual nexus with the distributors who, by remaining part of the distribution network, had confirmed their adherence to the AEG policy.

In *Ford* v. *Commission*[32] (European Court 1985) Ford had likewise notified to the Commission its distribution system for Germany. Originally, the products covered by the agreement included both left-hand and right-hand drive cars. By a circular taking effect on 1 May 1982, right-hand drive cars were withdrawn, so that they would not be available for resale to British buyers for import into the United Kingdom at a lower overall price than then prevailed in the UK domestic market. The Commission alleged that exemption should be refused for the distribution system because its effect was to partition national markets, contrary to the well-known *Grundig* principle. Ford claimed that its decision was simply unilateral, having no necessary connection with the main dealer agreement for Germany, and that its distribution system was entitled to exemption under Article 81(3).

The Court upheld the Commission's decision on this substantive issue (although it had

---

[30] Another example is *Binon* v. *Agence et Messageries de la Presse (AMP)* Case 243/83 [1985] ECR 2015: 3 CMLR 800, where the effect of previous arrangements for the distribution of newspapers and periodicals in Belgium was held likely to continue even after a new system had been introduced.

[31] Case 107/82 [1983] ECR 3151: [1984] 3 CMLR 325.

[32] Cases 25–26/84 [1985] ECR 2725: 3 CMLR 528.

earlier granted Ford's appeal against the Commission's order for interim relief[33] which required Ford to continue to supply right-hand drive cars in Germany pending the Court's final ruling) and held that that the decision to change the product covered by the dealer agreement was not simply unilateral. It was rather part of the whole contractual framework between Ford and its dealers; admission to the dealer network in Germany implied acceptance, in the view of the Court, by all parties of the policy pursued by Ford with regard to the choice of models to be delivered to the German market. The Court said that the Commission was entitled, in deciding whether to grant exemption, to take all the relevant facts into account, including the effect which Ford's refusal to supply right-hand drive cars to Germany could have on the partitioning of the Common Market.

In its decision, the Court also laid down an important general finding as to the correct approach to the interpretation of Article 81(1). The Court held that the Commission was not required to rule on each individual element of the agreement, so long as the agreement as a whole fell within the coverage of Article 81(1). Ford had claimed that the Commission must first identify each provision of the agreement in breach of the Article, and then consider that provision in isolation against all the relevant criteria, including the four conditions for exemption contained in Article 81(3). However, the Court, took the view that a more 'broad brush' approach was justified in such circumstances.[34]

4.3 THE *BAYER* CASE

The Commission obviously benefited from these decisions, which characterized the whole distribution network as individually and collectively responsible for both initial policy and subsequent changes of policy decided upon by their supplier. It however suffered a setback on October 2000, when its decision against *Bayer* in the *Adalat* case was annulled by the CFI over the issue of supply quotas. The background to the judgment was the fact that the prices of most Bayer pharmaceuticals sold in France and Spain by its distributors were considerably lower than those prevailing for the same products in the United Kingdom. Adalat was a popular treatment for coronary heart disease, which had to be taken on a regular basis. It is not however the only drug available for this purpose, and Bayer did not have a dominant position for its market in any Member State in terms of Article 82. Bayer's French and Spanish wholesalers were keen to supply not only their regular customers in those countries but also the more lucrative parallel trade in the United Kingdom.

Bayer therefore tried to disrupt this parallel trade by its wholesalers in a number of ways. It reduced the quantities of Adalat supplied to the French and Spanish wholesalers to the level which it believed corresponded to local demand only; it made excuses for being unable to meet the larger orders that the wholesalers continued to place. The key element in the situation, and in the decision of the CFI, was that at no time did the wholesalers acquiesce in Bayer's efforts to reduce their supplies. Bayer did not monitor the levels of parallel trade between the territories involved, so that there was little incentive for the wholesalers to change their commercial strategy, nor were they offered any reward in the hope that they would change their policy. In the absence of such acquiescence, the CFI found no

---

[33] For this aspect of the case, see Cases 228–229/84 [1984] ECR 1129: 1 CMLR 649.
[34] The Court adopted a similar approach in *Windsurfing International* Case 193/83 [1986] ECR 611: 3 CMLR 489, considered in detail in Ch. 12, pp.228–30.

'agreement' between Bayer and the wholesalers could be presumed, and the fine imposed on Bayer for having entered into such an 'agreement' was quashed. The case has now been taken on appeal to the European Court.[35]

In a slightly later Commission decision than that in the *Bayer* case, *Glaxo-Wellcome*,[36] the manufacturer had sought an individual exemption for the terms of its distribution agreement with its Spanish wholesalers, in the same commercial situation as in the *Bayer* case, except that the agreement covered a range of drugs. To discourage diversion of its drugs to the UK market the supplier sought to impose a dual pricing system, drugs purchased for local sale being priced at a lower level than those sold elsewhere. Some of the wholesalers had accepted these new terms, others had refused them.

The main argument raised by Glaxo was that the large scale parallel imports were damaging not only patients generally in Spain, who were not receiving the full quantities of Glaxo products that they needed, but also Glaxo's own business in Europe. It claimed that it had been forced by the parallel imports to scale down its spending on R & D. The Commission however was unimpressed by this argument, pointing out that there was no evidence of any linkage between the volume of parallel imports and the R & D budget. It also stated that under Articles 28 and 30 of the Treaty differences in the treatment of intermediaries in different territories to prevent parallel imports were not allowed, and that Article 81(3) should not be utilized for such purposes.

5. CONCERTED PRACTICES

5.1 THE EARLY CASE LAW

All systems of law which seek to restrain anti-competitive behaviour find that it is difficult to do so unless the prohibitions apply effectively not only to agreements, but also to the many ways which can be used to dispense with the need for actual agreements. Those who originally negotiated the terms of Article 81 would have been well aware of the likelihood that in many sectors of European industry and commerce (particularly where there was a strong oligopolistic element) effective concertation of commercial policy could be arranged without the need for formal agreement, indeed often without creating any external evidence at all. Desired results could often be achieved by far simpler or subtler methods.

The problem for DG Comp as an enforcement authority has been to find evidence of the arrangements made which have the effect of enforcing uniformity of price or other undesirable consequences falling within the range of Article 81. The best evidence, of course, in such cases would be documentation comprising, if not a formal agreement, at least letters, emails, fax copies, minutes of meetings, or other commercial documents: in other words the kind of document which is the routine product of the business office. To enable the Commission through DG Comp to reach these more informal arrangements, the concept of 'concerted practice' was introduced into the Treaty and, thanks to the wide definition given

---

[35] As Cases C-2 and 3/01. There is clearly only a narrow distinction, if any, between the *Ford* and *Bayer* cases. See for critical comment Jephcott, [2001] 22 ECLR 469–476 and Jacobsen and Broberg [2002] 22 ECLR 127–141.

[36] [2002] 4 CMLR 335.

to it by the European Court, has proved vital to the implementation of the Commission's competition policy.

It is noteworthy that at the time of the enactment of the Treaty of Rome in 1957, none of the Member States, even if they had competition legislation in their domestic law, had a concept in their domestic law equivalent to 'concerted action' or 'concerted practice'. Its introduction can undoubtedly be attributed to the influence of US antitrust law, where the concept of 'concerted action' was already familiar in relation to both horizontal and vertical relationships. When parallel conduct by enterprises was found, which arose not because of independent business decisions but as a result of inter-dependent decisions raising the inference that there was a tacit agreement between the parties, then US Federal Courts were entitled, and inclined, to look for 'plus factors' to distinguish the latter situation from the former. Among the factors which they took into account were any actions taken by companies contrary to their own normal business interests. These might include: raising prices at a time when there was a substantial supply available of the relevant product; artificially limiting the supply of products; imposing unusual conditions of sale; refusing to attend sales of goods by auction unless other leading competitors were present; or agreeing to price identical goods to be transported long distance only on identical fixed basing points.[37]

Proof of concerted practices was at issue in the first three major horizontal agreement cases to reach the Court, all being appeals brought against decisions by the Commission to impose fines on groups of manufacturers from a number of separate Member States. The first of these was the *Dyestuffs* case[38] (European Court 1972). Between 1964 and 1967, there were three general and uniform increases in the price of dyestuffs sold by leading European producers. In January 1964, there was a 15 per cent increase for nearly all dyes based on aniline. In January 1965, there was a 10 per cent increase in prices for all dyes and pigments not covered by the increase of the previous year. Major Italian companies did not participate in this increase, so the other European companies did not maintain the price increase for the Italian market even though it had already been announced. In October 1967, the parties uniformly imposed an 8 per cent increase for dyes sold in Germany, The Netherlands, Belgium, and Luxembourg, and a 12 per cent increase in France.

Advocate General Mayras characterized the market for such products as oligopolistic, controlled by a small number of producers with national markets 'walled off' from competition. Customers tended only to have direct contact with producers in their own country, all contact with foreign producers being through their subsidiary companies' representatives or agents. There was therefore no true transparency of price or awareness on a Europe-wide

---

[37] The Supreme Court laid down clear guidelines to prevent the courts from inferring agreements merely from parallel conduct. The *Monsanto* v. *Sprayrite* case, 104 Supreme Court Reports 1551 (1984), finally established that a high degree of collaboration is required between a manufacturer and its distributors if a distributor whose appointment had been ended is to establish the necessary proof of an agreement. The mere fact that complaints have been made by other distributors against that distributor is insufficient, since it is the normal practice of distributors to discuss such matters with their manufacturer, and the mere making of a complaint is not necessarily decisive in the manufacturer's decision to terminate an appointment. Whilst it is not the practice of the European Court of Justice to refer in its decisions to Court decisions or any jurisdiction, let alone those outside the Community, there is no doubt that the US experience has influenced the significant development of the concept of concerted practice through the cases. Advocates General are not so restricted, and examples can be found of cases where their opinions have referred to relevant US cases, e.g. in the *Dyestuffs* case cited in fn. 38.

[38] *ICI and Others* v. *Commission (Dyestuffs)* Cases 48–57/69 [1972] ECR 619: CMLR 557.

basis for the individual customer. The Advocate General felt that in a more competitive market price increases would have followed on a less uniform basis; whereas oligopolistic pressures might account for downward movements of prices on a concerted basis, it would be less likely, without some form of agreement, to have been responsible for such concerted upward moves. He therefore felt sufficiently suspicious about the contacts between the parties to find that the price moves had been coordinated.

The Court agreed that there had been concerted practices by the defendants. There was an element of interconnection between the three separate price increases operating in a virtually simultaneous way. In 1964 the increase had proceeded as planned, but on the two later occasions the advance announcements from major undertakings had allowed each of them to observe the reaction of the others and to eliminate the risk that any one producer's increase might get out of line. Although every producer was legally free in changing its prices to take into account the present or foreseeable conduct of its competitors, it was a breach of Article 81 to co-operate with competitors in a way which enabled a coordinated course of action relating to price increases to be put into effect. It was an even greater breach to ensure the success of that course of action by deliberate prior elimination of all uncertainty about each other's conduct over such matters as percentages of increase, date, place, and exact range of products covered. The term 'concerted practice' was defined by the Court as a 'form of coordination between enterprises, that had not yet reached the point of true contract relationship but which had in practice substituted co-operation for the risks of competition'.[39]

In 1975, a more detailed definition of concerted practices was given by the Court in the *Sugar Cartel* case, as follows:

The concept ... refers to a form of coordination between undertakings which, without having been taken to the stage where an agreement properly so-called has been concluded, knowingly substitutes for the risks of competition practical co-operation between them which leads to conditions of competition which do not correspond to the normal conditions of the market having regard to the nature of the products, the importance and number of the undertakings as well as the size and nature of the said market. Such practical co-operation amounts to a concerted practice, particularly if it enables the persons concerned to consolidate established positions to the detriment of effective freedom of movement of the products in the Common Market and of the freedom of consumers to choose their suppliers.[40]

This complex case[41] involved sugar manufacturers throughout the Community, and required the examination of the market situation in each of the relevant markets. Since sugar came within the scope of the Common Agricultural Policy, there was considerable Member State involvement in the marketing of sugar. In the case of Italy the Court found that the involvement was so substantial as to justify a finding that the restrictive practices of

---

[39] [1972] ECR 655: CMLR 622.

[40] [1975] ECR 1916: [1976] 1 CMLR 405.

[41] The case report in ECR is 491 pages long, and in CMLR 195 pages long. This probably means the report is rarely read in its entirety. It is the kind of case for which the existence of the Court of First Instance would have been invaluable: had it then been in operation, its detailed analysis of the complex facts would have allowed the European Court (if an appeal had been brought) to concentrate on the legal issues involved, rather than having to review so many factual issues individually. On the other hand the *Cement Cartel* Cases 25 to 104/95 [2000]: 5 CMLR 204 were so lengthy that the CMLR report is only a summary—not the full text of the CFI judgment—which in the 2000 ECR report at ECR II, pp.491 to 1,682, amounts to nearly 1,200 pages!

the parties in attempting to preserve the principle of *chacun chez soi* could not of themselves have affected the competitive position, so little room for manoeuvre having been left by the stringent domestic legislation. In other jurisdictions, notably Germany and The Netherlands, the scope for individual agreements and practices was greater and, after a painstaking examination, a number of findings of concerted practices were made, although by no means identical with the findings of the Commission. Some of the fines imposed were therefore reduced.

5.2 THE BURDEN OF PROOF: THE COMMISSION'S TASK

An important element in establishing the existence of concerted practices is contact between the parties, which must involve intentional communication of information between them, either directly or through an intermediary. There must be some positive intention on the part of one party to direct the information to the other, or at least to launch it into the area where the other is likely to receive it. It is also essential for the Commission to show that the party receiving the information is aware of having done so, not accidentally, but as a target. Such giving and receiving of information clearly goes beyond mutual awareness by competitors that the terms which they quote to their customers will subsequently become known to their competitors, who will naturally make use of this knowledge in their own pricing and other competitive strategies. If even awareness of what one's competitor is doing constitutes a sufficient level of contact to justify a claim of concerted practices, independent undertakings would be prevented from adapting intelligently to the conduct of other undertakings. This would be particularly serious in a market whose operations are normally relatively transparent and where there are a substantial number of competitors. The distinction is clearly drawn in the case of *Züchner* v. *Bayerische Vereinsbank*[42] (European Court 1984). Herr Züchner had an account with the Bayerische Vereinsbank at Rosenheim. He challenged the service charge made for the transfer of funds to Italy, on the basis that debiting what appeared to be a uniform charge by a number of banks constituted a concerted practice. The issue was referred under Article 177 to the Court, which confirmed that the banking services were indeed covered by Article 81 and that any such agreement, if proved, would have been in breach of it. The tests which the Court laid down for determining whether the banks had operated sufficiently independently in applying a uniform charge to customers making foreign transfers were:

(*a*) whether contacts between the various banks which had imposed such charges related only to charges made in the past, or also to those to be made in the future;

(*b*) whether in a state of free competition different rates of charge would have applied;

(*c*) the number and importance of the participating banks in the market for monetary transfers between Member States; and

(*d*) the volume of transfers on which a uniform charge was imposed, as compared with the total number of transfers made.

---

[42] Case 172/80 [1981] ECR 2021: [1982] 1 CMLR 313. Contrast the *Eurocheques* Case [1985] OJ L35/43, where uniform charges by banks operating this system were approved because of the substantial advantages that the new system was shown to provide to tourists and other travellers. See J. Faull and A. Nikpay, *The EC Law of Competition* (Oxford University Press 1999), paras 9.10 to 9.62.

In conclusion, the Court said that parallel conduct in debiting uniform charges on transfers by banks from one Member State to another could amount to a concerted practice if it were established not only that the parallel conduct exhibited features of coordination and co-operation characteristic of such a practice, but also that such conduct was capable of having a sufficient effect on competition.

In such cases, the Commission will normally allege that the facts established cannot be explained other than by concerted action. The parties must provide a rational explanation, which the Commission will accept or reject. This is well illustrated by the case of *Compagnie Royal Asturienne des Mines and Rheinzink* v. *Commission*[43] (European Court 1984). These two companies supplied rolled zinc to a Belgian company, Schlitz. Schlitz resold the zinc to a German company, the market price in Germany being higher than that in Belgium. How-ever, Schlitz had obtained its supplies from CRAM and Rheinzink by a false claim that the product would be resold to Egypt; CRAM found out the deceit and refused to make further supplies, and Rheinzink came to a similar conclusion to cut off Schlitz. Evidence showed that there was regular contact between CRAM and Rheinzink.

The Commission found that there was sufficient evidence of concerted practice between the two companies in refusing to continue supplies. The suggested motive was that they wished to continue their own profitable supplies to the German market and to prevent Schlitz from continuing to engage in it. Unfortunately for the Commission, the European Court found, to the contrary, that the reason for the refusal of supplies was in fact the poor credit record of Schlitz, finding sufficient evidence that this was the major ground for the decision to refuse supplies.

5.3 THE *WOODPULP* CASE

In summary, much case law illustrates the great importance of findings of 'concerted prac-tices' from the viewpoint of the Commission as an enforcement agency. The most important case in this area was originally decided by the Commission in December 1984, in *Wood-pulp*.[44] Bleached sulphate pulp, used in the manufacture of many different kinds of paper, can be made from either hardwood or softwood. Many companies were alleged to have concerted prices for this product, either directly or indirectly. The defendants included eleven United States, six Canadian, eleven Swedish, eleven Finnish, one Norwegian, one Portuguese, and one Spanish company who collectively supplied about two-thirds of the EC market. The Commission found that all the companies involved were subject to EC competi-tion law because their conduct had an effect on the EC market, and that the deliberate transparency of prices charged on the European market by such a large number of competi-tors, although in theory making concertation more difficult, might in practice make it easier if carried out in ways which helped anticipation and knowledge of the pricing policy of competitors. Apparently prices were charged on a quarterly basis, the vast majority being quoted in US dollars rather than in the local currency of the company giving the quotation.

The Commission's decision was based on what it characterized as the 'deliberate trans-parency of prices'. It argued that in an open competitive market one would find a variety of approaches to pricing strategy, prices being quoted in different currencies with substantial

---

[43] Cases 29–30/83 [1984] ECR 1679: [1985] 1 CMLR 688.
[44] The Commission decision is reported at [1985] 3 CMLR 474.

reductions for quantities supplied and long-term contracts. It found a suspicious lack of variation between the quoted price levels and the transaction price, and that quoting prices in dollars made any variation from the arrangements easier to identify. Moreover, some of the European agents acted for a number of producers from different countries so as to discover quickly pulp prices and changes. The Commission accepted that the presumption of concerted practices could be displaced if evidence was produced of a genuine equilibrium of price required as the result of independent action by the participants or as a result of the existence of a market leader upon whom other firms had aligned their prices, but said it was not satisfied that these explanations held good.

The European Court's judgment[45] on the appeals raised by the companies ultimately overruled the Commission's findings in most of the cases. At the heart of its judgment was a finding (based on a report by economists appointed by the Court) that there was a convincing explanation for the alleged 'concertation' of announced prices. Concertation was not the only plausible explanation for the parallel conduct of the parties, which the economists said might instead be a rational response to the fact that the pulp market was a long-term one, in which both buyers and sellers sought to limit commercial risk. A system of quarterly price announcements had been established largely at the request of buyers some years before. The price announced was treated as the 'ceiling price' and transaction prices could then be negotiated at lower levels, so the market was characterized by much greater transparency than many other commodity markets, and links between buyers and sellers were close because of the importance of quality. Moreover, the market comprised a 'group of oligopolies' because of the method of manufacturing paper pulp; as each paper is a mixture of several pulps, every paper manufacturer can in practice only deal with a limited number of pulp producers, and conversely each pulp producer could supply only a limited number of customers. For all these reasons, the Commission's original decision was annulled, except in the cases of certain undertakings where there was specific evidence of contact and price agreements between individual producers.

5.4 OTHER EXAMPLES OF CONCERTED PRACTICES BETWEEN COMPETITORS

An example of concerted practices between parties in competition with each other is the *Peroxygen*[46] case (Commission 1984). This involved a limited number of producers in Europe of hydrogen peroxide and its derivatives, which are used as industrial bleaches. There was evidence that major European companies had for some years participated in agreements which had the effect of reserving each national market for supply by its major producer, these arrangements being enforced by regular meetings of the members, at which marginal disputes were resolved, arrangements similar to those found in the *Sugar Cartel* case.[47] Full exchanges were made of information about production, so that each knew the others' general commercial policy. It was held that these arrangements constituted a concerted practice: although the parties had not necessarily agreed a precise or detailed plan in

---

[45] Cases 89, 104, 114, 116–17, and 125–29/81 [1993] ECR I-1307: 4 CMLR 407. For the separate judgment on the issue of jurisdiction, see Ch. 23, pp.50–2, and [1988] ECR 5193: 4 CMLR 901.

[46] *Commission v. Solvay and Laporte* Case 81/74 [1985] 1 CMLR 481.

[47] Though here without the added complications of a common Community policy to give Member States a legitimate opportunity of becoming involved in the market 'arrangements'.

advance, it was sufficient that by their mutual involvement they had departed from the basic requirement that each must determine independently the policy which it intended to adopt on the market.

When the participants in alleged widespread industry arrangements for identical basic products (such as particular chemicals) comprise virtually all the European manufacturers in this industry, the Commission has a major problem in finding evidence to link all the participants sufficiently closely to the arrangements. In cases such as *Polyvinyl Chloride (PVC)* (Commission 1988, annulled on procedural grounds by the European Court)[48] the Commission considered it sufficient to show that all the parties had reached a consensus on a plan which limited, or was likely to limit, their commercial freedom, by determining the general lines of action (or indeed abstention from action) on the market. The fact that some participants attended meetings more assiduously or played a greater role than other companies (a factor possibly relevant in assessing fines) would not absolve the less frequent attenders from being found to have participated in a common enterprise. Responsibility for operating the cartel as a whole would in the view of the Commission apply to 'central' and 'fringe' players alike; this approach seems to be confirmed by the judgment of the Court of First Instance in the *Polypropylene* case in 1991.[49]

The *Cement*[50] cartel case provided the CFI with yet further opportunities to define those undertakings which are deemed to be participators in such practices. It ruled that a concerted practice could be found where there was any direct or indirect contact by an undertaking with participants in the discussions at which their course of conduct was disclosed, either in a formal or informal manner, and as a result of which uncertainty as their future strategy had been removed or at least substantially reduced. Even though concerted practices normally implied reciprocity between the participants, even mere participation at relevant meetings is sufficient unless the undertaking had unequivocally and openly distanced itself from the plan agreed at a particular meeting. The Commission need not prove the exact date on which, or the exact document by which the concerted practice was set in train so long as there is a clear concurrence of wills established on the basis of some documentary evidence.

5.5 CONCERTED PRACTICES IN THE CHAIN OF DISTRIBUTION

We have so far concentrated on the establishment of concerted practices between horizontal competitors. It is also important to define this concept for vertical arrangements. The leading authority is the *Pioneer* case (European Court 1983).[51] Pioneer was a leading Japanese manufacturer of high fidelity equipment and had a number of European distributors in Germany, France, and the United Kingdom. Distribution agreements allowed dealers to export to other countries subject to the usual requirement not actively to solicit business outside their territories. Price levels in the French market were, however, considerably above those in Germany and the UK, so that there was an incentive for parallel importing into

---

[48] Case C-137/92P [1994] ECR I-2555. Problems of proof are considerably reduced if one or more participants confess their involvement to the Commission, in return for a reduction in the fine imposed under the Commission's Leniency Notice. See Ch. 9, pp.147–9.

[49] *Hercules* v. *Commission* Case T-7/89 [1991] ECR II-1711: [1992] 4 CMLR 84.

[50] Cases 25 to 104/95 [2000] 5 CMLR 204. See fn. 41.

[51] *Musique Diffusion Française* v. *Commission* Case 100/80 [1983] ECR 1825: 3 CMLR 221.

France from both those countries. A German distributor was approached for an order for delivery in France. Following pressure from the main distributor in Germany, Melchers, this contract was cancelled. Likewise, the United Kingdom distributor stopped various sub-distributors from exporting to France and Holland.

The parent company, through its Dutch co-ordinating company, Pioneer Electronic Europe NV, became concerned at this activity and called a meeting in Antwerp in January 1976. No records were kept of the meeting, which was attended by all the European distributors, but it was established that various matters were discussed relating to the distribution of Pioneer products, including parallel imports. The Commission obtained evidence that the main complainant was the French distributor, who used the meeting as an opportunity to pass on complaints by other distributors about parallel importing into France. Pioneer Electronic Europe NV then used its influence as co-ordinating Pioneer subsidiary for Europe to damp down the zeal for such sales. The Commission later investigated the arrangements and decided that a reduction in such sales was directly attributable to concerted practices between Pioneer and its distributors. Relationships here were not simply horizontal, since Pioneer Electronic Europe NV had a co-ordinating function to ensure that supplies were available to its various distributors and was not in direct competition with them, whereas in theory all the distributors, although allocated separate territories, were in competition with each other.

The Court naturally referred to its earlier judgments in both *Dyestuffs* and *Sugar Cartel*. In this case, concerted practices had been established by circumstantial as well as direct evidence. The presumption and inference from the facts set out above was that the co-ordinating Pioneer subsidiary had called the relevant meeting in Antwerp to deal with the problem of parallel imports as the result of which the practice had been substantially reduced, at least for a time. It is in the context of parallel imports that coordination between parties in a vertical relationship is most likely; the Commission is therefore alert to the possibility of establishing concerted practices in such situations, though its policy will inevitably be affected by the ultimate outcome of the *Bayer* case.

6. DECISIONS BY ASSOCIATIONS OF UNDERTAKINGS

6.1 THE DEFINITION OF A TRADE ASSOCIATION

Trade associations play an important part in the commercial life of the Community and its Member States. Article 81(1) recognizes this with its prohibition against 'decisions by associations of undertakings' which have the required effect on trade between Member States and on competition within the Common Market.

The normal use of the term 'association' in the Article describes a separate legal entity formed to pursue particular objectives for its members. Since in the context of Article 81 these objectives are almost invariably commercial, it is normal to refer to them as 'trade associations'. It is important, however, when using this term to remember that Article 81 applies to any kind of association which has some form of economic or commercial purpose, and that the association need not have a separate legal personality (or even any formal constitution) to be subject to the prohibitions of Article 81. It may also be a professional organization or association (*Wouters*).[52] The expression 'association' in Article 81 also covers a number of bodies not normally described as trade 'associations', from which they differ in important respects. In particular, co-operatives and other forms of trading association often found in the agricultural sector, which trade actively on behalf of members in both a buying and selling capacity, are subject as associations to the same legal rules under this Article as trade associations proper. This is clear from the *Gottrup-Klim* and *Oude Luttikhuis* cases[53] discussed in Chapter 7. The term also covers an association of which a number of other associations are members, which again may be co-operatives, often in the agricultural sector. If the association is unincorporated, the prohibitions of that Article in effect fall upon its participating members, even though a decision of the Commission may be expressed to cover the association as well. If the association is incorporated the decision will be directed to it and to its participating members.[54]

Not all the bodies loosely referred to by this title necessarily fall within the scope of Article 81 or indeed Article 82. Employers' organizations and Chambers of Commerce or Trade will rarely do so, unless carrying on a particular economic activity, such as an airport, nor will national business organizations such as the Confederation of British Industry.

It is important to emphasize that many, and probably most trade associations raise no problem for authorities such as the Commission, required to enforce competition law. The constitutions of such bodies will be carefully drawn to limit their authorized range of activities so as to avoid any suggestion of facilitating agreements between their members that would offend the provisions of competition law; efforts will also be made to avoid any suggestion that, regardless of its constitution, the association could in practice provide a useful cover for coordination of business activities between competitors. Legal advisers to such associations are aware that the boundary line between the legitimate and the illegitimate in this context, though recognizable, needs careful and regular monitoring.

Nevertheless in some cases the so-called trade association may be actually a cartel seeking to dress itself in respectable clothes. For example, in the *Cement Cartel* case discussed in Chapter 9[55] the role played by Cembureau as the trade association for European cement manufacturers participating in the cartel appeared to fall within this description. It is with such cases, however, that this chapter is primarily concerned. The Commission has in many cases had little difficulty in penetrating the disguise, either because the rules or practices of the association are blatantly restrictive or because they clearly create a market situation where members are encouraged to regard the unity of the industry as more important (as a matter of 'solidarity') than the advantages each might gain from strenuous competitive effort.

---

[52] Case C-309/99 [2002] 4 CMLR 913. See Ch. 7, pp.94–5.

[53] *Gottrup-Klim* v. *DLG* Case C-250/92 [1994] ECR I-5641: [1996] 4 CMLR 191. *Oude Luttikhuis* Case C-399/93 [1995] ECR I-4515: [1996] 5 CMLR 178. See Ch. 7, pp.101–2 and 106–7.

[54] Whatever the legal structure of an 'association' fines levied upon it for breaches of Art 81 or 82 are calculated against the aggregate turnover of its members, in cases at least where its rules are binding on them: in other cases they are calculated against the turnover of the undertaking or association alone. *FNK and SCK* v. *Commission* Cases 213/95 and 18/96 [1997] ECR-II 1739: [1998] 4 CMLR 259.

[55] At pp.158–9.

6.2 DIFFERENT CATEGORIES OF ASSOCIATION

The trade association will normally have a written constitution and relatively predictable rules, which will cover at least:

— the objectives of the association;

— qualifications for membership;

— rules for the conduct of the association, including the appointment of its governing body; and

— rules for the termination of membership.

There may also be by-laws containing detailed rules for the procedural conduct of the affairs of the association.

A trade association, especially in a sector where there is little product differentiation and an oligopolistic market structure, may be tempted to use the association to eliminate as many as possible of the uncertainties inherent in the competitive situation, especially those relating to pricing. This temptation can arise even when the association represents merely a single interest group within the industry, e.g. all manufacturers or wholesalers, or all retailers. If information can be passed to the membership about the way in which each member establishes its costs, sets its prices, obtains its orders, and achieves a particular level of profit and turnover, this will considerably assist the business planning of its fellow members and reduce the uncertainties that will otherwise exist. A member's uncertainty is not simply as to the factual nature of the business of its actual competitors (about which it will normally be fully informed) but also as to the likely reaction of those competitors to any change of policy which the individual member might decide to initiate, a far less easily acquired type of information. The form in which this data is disseminated will, as some recently decided cases illustrate, make a considerable difference to the extent of competition between the members.

However, it has been made very clear by cases decided by both the Commission and the Court that those associations which have the greatest potential for anti-competitive activities are not those where a single interest only is represented in the membership. The potential is greatest where one association includes persons or undertakings with different roles within the same industry, or alternatively, where an association of associations has been created to regulate the basis for a particular industry which almost totally eliminates the element of uncertainty and arm's-length negotiation that would otherwise exist between the different levels. These arrangements, of which particularly notable examples have been found in cases involving Belgian and Dutch trade associations discussed in this chapter, normally provide for 'collective exclusive dealing'; another appropriate description for such entities might be 'closed circuit associations', where a high percentage of the market is insulated from outside entry by rigid and complex rules. On the other hand, trade associations whose membership includes not only producers but also 'consumers' at different levels of the relevant product may enable the 'consumers' to monitor anti-competitive restrictions by the producers.

Having analysed the basic structure of the trade association, it becomes possible to define more exactly what is meant by the expression 'decision' in Article 81. Within the context of such an association, a 'decision' normally means a resolution by the authorized organ of the association (usually a board of management or council with authority delegated by the members under the terms of its constitution) to impose restrictions and obligations on its members, which have the effect of reducing their freedom of action. These obligations and restrictions may prescribe the persons with whom members may deal, and may also control to a greater or lesser extent the terms upon which any business can be carried out. A wide variety of examples can be found among cases decided by the Commission and the Court. It is also clear that the rules of an association can themselves constitute a 'decision' without any form of resolution or recommendation by the board of management. Rules such as those which impose financial penalties on members seeking to leave an association or co-operative, or prohibiting current members from acting in ways believed to be prejudicial to its stability have been the subject of Commission decisions, though such rules have not always been found to breach Article 81. The essential principle set out in *Gottrup-Klim* already mentioned is that the rule must always be proportionate to the needs of the association to carry out its normal function; in particular the interests of those members of the association with relatively limited buying power are treated with respect by both the Commission and the European Court, especially where the price of the products concerned is highly dependent on volumes purchased, as in that case with fertilizers or pesticides. Decisions by associations implemented by agreements between more than one association will, of course, fall within the category of 'agreements'.

6.3 THE DEFINITION OF A DECISION

In *Vimpoltu*,[56] the Dutch trade association was an importer of farm tractors. Sources of purchase here were not restricted, but all members were required to observe decisions of the association. All Dutch tractors were imported from abroad and local demand was gradually declining, although prices remained higher in Holland than in most parts of the Community. For these reasons, the association was anxious to negotiate with the association of dealers in agricultural machinery for a maximum discount by dealers to farmers of 25 per cent. It was agreed that fines would be imposed on any dealer breaking this limit. Importers were required to exchange price lists with each other so that none were able to 'cheat' by importing goods at lower prices than others,[57] and standard terms of business were adopted. In both cases, the rules of the association were found to breach Article 81(1), and the lack of any benefit to consumers from the arrangements meant that no exemption was available under Article 81(3).

However, decisions of a trade association need not formally bind its members for Article 81(1) to apply. An informal decision of a trade association, even one made outside its rules altogether, may be sufficient. However, there must be at least some evidence that the conduct of members has been or might in the future be influenced by information received from the

---

[56] [1983] 3 CMLR 619.

[57] The Commission decision suggested that even the exchange of recommended prices between importers might reduce competition between them, since each would derive from the list a better idea of the likely pricing policy of other importers (para. 38 of the Decision).

association. A clear example was the *IFTRA* case[58] (Commission 1975) where European manufacturers of virgin aluminium had adopted a standard contract which contained fair trading rules, known as the IFTRA rules. The rules purported to set out principles of trading to be adopted by the members to prevent 'unfairness', but in practice gave members an opportunity to take joint action against normal competitive actions and reactions by individual undertakings.

The *Fenex* case[59] (Commission, 1996) illustrates that even non-binding recommendations can be 'decisions'. Here the association of Dutch freight forwarders had for many years authorized a committee to prepare on its behalf a list of suggested charges for various services such as the forwarding of goods and customs clearance. The non-binding tariffs were sent to members each year with a circular which expressed the desirability of compliance in strong terms. Although the Commission was only able to obtain evidence from one member of the association that he had adopted these tariffs, the Commission nevertheless concluded that not only the members of Fenex but also non-member competitors would as a result of the publication of the tariffs in the trade press know considerably more about the structure and movement of such tariffs and would have been influenced in their general approach to pricing by them.

---

[58] [1975] 2 CMLR D20. An unusual feature of the case is that the 'Fair Trading Practice Rules' were written in such appalling English that the editor of Common Market Law Reports was moved (at p.22) to disclaim any responsibility for it. An extract gives the flavour of this remarkable document (p.26): 'Rebates which are granted openly for competitive reasons without any connections to quantities or functions are not unfair as such, but could easily lead to a claim of reactions boomeranging on the instigator'.

[59] [1996] 5 CMLR 332.

7

ARTICLE 81(1): ANALYSIS 2

1. 'WHICH MAY AFFECT TRADE BETWEEN MEMBER STATES'

1.1 EARLY CASES

Agreements, decisions, and concerted practices have no significance under Article 81 unless they are capable of affecting trade between Member States, quite apart from the second and further requirement (considered in the next section of this chapter) that they should have as object or effect the prevention, restriction, or distortion of competition within the Common Market. It is important to remember that the two requirements are both separate and cumulative, and that analysis of the effect of an agreement or concerted practice on interstate trade and on competition should be carried out as two distinct exercises. Both the Community Courts and Commission however have on occasion (for example in all the Notices on Agreements of Minor Importance except the latest in 2001) used language that has blurred, rather than clarified, the difference between these two requirements.

The interpretation of this phrase developed gradually. Initially it was believed that agreements and practices that had effect merely within a single Member State, and upon undertakings whose business was operating only there, could always claim to be outside the scope of the Article. On the other hand, if an agreement contained a transnational element, either because one or more of the undertakings involved was incorporated or resident in a different Member State of the Community, or because the agreements concerned altered the actual or potential flow of goods or services between Member States, then the requirement of the Article was satisfied. This was clearly set out in one of the earliest preliminary rulings given under Article 234 by the European Court, in the *STM*[1] case of 1966 where the phrase was interpreted as follows: 'For this requirement to be fulfilled, it must be possible to foresee with a sufficient degree of probability on the basis of a set of objective factors of law or of fact that the agreement in question may have an influence, direct or indirect, actual or potential, on the pattern of trade between Member States'.

Scarcely two weeks later the European Court supplemented this ruling by its findings in the *Grundig*[2] case: after pointing out that the purpose of this requirement is to establish the

---

[1] *Société Technique Minière* v. *Maschinenbau Ulm* Case 56/65 [1966] ECR 234, 249: CMLR 357, 375.

[2] [1966] ECR 299, 341: CMLR 418, 472. For an account of the development of the meaning attached to this phrase see J. Faull, 'Effect on Trade Between Member States', *Fordham Corporate Law Institute* (1991), pp.481–508.

boundary between Community law and that of Member States in the context of the competition rules, it continued by stating that:

it is only to the extent to which agreement may affect trade between Member States that the deterioration in competition caused by the agreement falls under the prohibition of Community law contained in Article [81]: otherwise it escapes the prohibition. In this connection, what is particularly important is whether the agreement is capable of constituting a threat, either direct or indirect, actual or potential, to freedom of trade between Member States in a manner which might harm the attainment of the objectives of a single market between States. Thus the fact that an agreement encourages an increase, even a large one, in the volume of trade between States is not sufficient to exclude the possibility that the agreement may 'affect' such trade in the above-mentioned manner.

Of course, little difficulty was found in that case in establishing the necessary effects on volume of trade because Consten was clearly restricted from exporting Grundig products to other countries of the Common Market, whilst purchasers of Grundig products in Germany were restrained from exporting Grundig products into France.

At that time, the tests apparently required as the result of these two cases appeared fairly simple to apply. The necessary approach involved imagining a complete overview of trade within the Common Market, as a series of flows and counter-flows crossing and recrossing national boundaries, under the effect of seasonal and other changes in supply and demand, costs, prices, and other external factors. It was necessary to compare this picture, with no restriction on competition, with the picture after the restriction had been introduced; in theory such a comparison should produce a definite answer. It is not necessary however for the agreement at issue actually to have affected trade between Member States so long as it can be shown to be capable of having that effect. This comparatively simple test was later however complicated by further qualifications to the basic rule.

As we have learnt, the Commission was soon faced with a more immediate problem: how to exclude from the coverage of Article 81 a number of agreements considered to be of relatively minor importance, which it was especially anxious to remove from consideration in view of the volume of notified agreements received at the beginning of 1963, whose continuing effect was felt throughout the following years. It received some assistance from the decision of the European Court, under an Article 234 reference from the Munich Oberlandsgericht in the case of *Frans Völk* v. *Vervaecke*.[3] Völk was a small German company that manufactured washing machines and entered into an exclusive distribution agreement for Belgium with Vervaecke, on normal terms including an obligation on the Belgian distributor to take minimum quantities. Subsequently, Vervaecke was sued in Germany by Völk for alleged breach of contract. The question raised by the German Court under Article 234 was whether, in interpreting Article 81, it was entitled to pay attention to the very modest fraction of the relevant geographic market (Belgium) in which the product was sold.

The Court answered that, in principle, insignificant agreements could escape the prohibition of Article 81, since it was essential to be able to show a reasonable expectation that the agreement would exercise an influence direct or indirect, actual or potential, on trade trends between Member States to an extent that would harm the attainment of the objectives of a single market between States. The total market share obtained by Völk in West Germany was about 0.2 and 0.05 per cent in 1963 and 1966 respectively, and the number of machines

---

[3] Case 5/69 [1969] ECR 295: CMLR 273.

annually sold in Belgium and Luxembourg by Vervaecke was about 200. The essence of the decision was that a *de minimis* rule could be applied in such cases. This would mean that in assessing effect on trade flows between Member States, agreements affecting a market share of 1 per cent or below would be most unlikely to have the required effect. However, it should be noted that both parties in this case were small undertakings, and the same generosity of treatment may not be accorded to major public companies even where their market share of the relevant product is less than 1 per cent.[4]

1.2 NOTICES ON AGREEMENTS OF MINOR IMPORTANCE

The Commission followed up this case with its 1970 Notice concerning 'Decisions and concerted practices of minor importance which do not fall under Article [81(1)] of the Treaty'. This stated that agreements whose effects on trade between Member States and on competition are negligible did not fall under the ban of Article 81(1), which only applies if the agreements 'have an appreciable impact on market conditions, that is if they appreciably alter the market position, in other words the sale and supply possibilities, of non-participating firms and of consumers'. This definition followed carefully the approach of the Court in the STM and *Grundig* cases. In this Notice the maximum market share was quantified as five per cent of the relevant market in a substantial part of the Common Market, with a maximum turnover of 20 million units of account for distributors or 15 million units of account for manufacturers; these figures were raised by the later 1986 and 1994 versions of the Notice to 200 and 300 million respectively, whilst the five per cent figure remained unchanged.

By a further Notice in 1997 the maximum aggregate turnover requirement was removed, whilst the percentages remained at five per cent for horizontal and mixed horizontal–vertical agreements but were raised to ten per cent for vertical agreements. The only exceptions were hard core agreements, those whose object was the fixing of prices or the sharing of markets or the setting of production or sales quotas. But the changing priorities of the Commission meant that this Notice too was soon replaced, with effect from 22 December 2001. On this occasion the new Notice[5] stated expressly that it did not deal with the impact of an agreement on interstate trade, but only with a definition of what did not constitute an appreciable restriction of competition. It acknowledged that all earlier Notices on this subject had been 'somewhat ambiguous' on this point, and pointed out that market share percentages were a much better indicator of whether effects on competition were appreciable than in measuring an effect on interstate trade. For the latter, which was an issue directly linked to market integration, a turnover threshold, combined with a much lower market share threshold, would be a better indicator. The new Notice does however emphasize that in any case agreements between SMEs (small and medium sized companies) are rarely capable of appreciably affecting trade between Member States.

Now that the Commission has stated in its latest Notice that it no longer applies to this

---

[4] *Distillers Co.* v. *Commission* Case 30/78 [1980] ECR 2229: 3 CMLR 121. Here the Court stated that Art. 81 would apply and that no exemption would be granted even for a product like Pimm's, which held only a fraction of 1 per cent of the relevant market, if it was only one product of a large company which sold a wide range of products and whose total sales as a percentage of the combined markets exceeded the *de minimis* level. See also the CFI judgment in *European Night Services*, at p.90 in this chapter.

[5] [2001] OJ C368/13.

requirement of Article 81, the natural question that arises is, how is this gap to be filled? The answer lies in the imminent arrival of the modernization programme, described in detail in Chapters 20 and 21. If the application of this Article is to be substantially delegated to national courts and competition authorities, it would have been necessary for the new Regulation No. 1/2003 replacing Regulation 17/62 setting out the ground rules for sharing jurisdiction between the Commission and these bodies itself to have provided guidance (which it does not) or for a new and separate Notice on this subject to be issued (which is likely). The Regulation itself of course will have to operate within the framework of the existing case law jurisprudence of the Community Courts. It was because of these impending developments that the 2001 Notice departed from earlier practice and avoided reference to effects on interstate trade.

1.3 NETWORKS OF AGREEMENTS

Where there is a network of agreements, it is not permissible to treat them individually, ignoring the existence of the network, as the Court emphasized in *Brasserie de Haecht (No. 1)* (European Court 1967).[6] A brewery in Belgium made loans to a married couple called Wilkin-Janssens, proprietors of a café in Esneux. In return, the café owners had agreed to take all their requirements for beer, lemonade, and other drinks exclusively from the brewery for the term of the loan plus a further two years. The brewery subsequently discovered that the agreement had been broken and sued for the return of the loan and damages. The Wilkin-Janssens claimed that the agreement was void under Article 81(1), and the Belgian Court at Liège asked the Court for a ruling whether, in assessing whether 81(1) applied, it was possible to take into account the economic context of the agreement and the surrounding circumstances affecting this particular type of agreement in the Belgian beer market. The Court, closely following in this case the opinion of its Advocate General Roemer, ruled that when assessing whether an individual agreement was in breach of Article 81(1), it was necessary to look not only at the individual agreement but also the context, both economic and legal, in which the agreement had been made. It placed importance on the degree to which the effect of the network would be to foreclose the brewer from finding sufficient outlets for its own products, whether by sales to existing pubs or cafés or through the acquisition of its own chain of outlets. Therefore, if the whole network of similar brewery 'tying' agreements made in Belgium was shown to have an effect on trade between Member States, e.g. if it made it more difficult for breweries in France or Germany to arrange for export of their beers into Belgium, then this fact could be taken into account both in determining whether the original agreement with the Wilkin-Janssens affected trade between Member States, and also with regard to its effect upon competition. The existence of this further qualification upon the rule of *Völk* v. *Vervaecke* likewise served to limit the scope of the application of the Notice on agreements of minor importance.

---

[6] *Brasserie de Haecht* v. *Wilkin-Janssens (No. 1)* Case 23/67 [1967] ECR 407: [1968] CMLR 26. In a subsequent case, however, the Court emphasized that even if an agreement is part of a network of similar agreements the individual contribution of that particular agreement has also to be taken into account: *Delimitis* v. *Henninger Bräu* Case C-234/89 [1991] I-ECR 935: 5 CMLR 210. (See Ch. 10, p. 82).

1.4 LATER DEVELOPMENTS OF ITS INTERPRETATION IN CASE LAW

The subsequent history of the interpretation of this requirement for effect on trade between Member States shows a steady widening of its reach, and the pattern of interpretation accorded to it both by the Commission and the Court has close parallels (although in a totally different environment) with the development by the United States Federal Courts of a constantly expanding definition of 'interstate commerce', for the purpose of interpreting the United States Constitution. In the great majority of cases, however, the effect of the restrictions on trade between Member States is obvious and involves little difficulty for Commission or Court. In the *Windsurfing* case[7] (European Court 1986) the Court gave important assistance to the Commission; it said that in examining an individual agreement it need not look at every clause restricting competition to see if it individually could be shown to have an effect on trade between Member States. Provided that the agreement taken as a whole had such effect, Article 81 would be applicable.[8]

The definitions already adopted were further relied on in a number of cases involving widely based trade associations within a single Member State which draw their members from those engaged at the different levels respectively in manufacturing, wholesaling, importing, and distribution of a specific product in that country, but where the effect of the restrictions was to reduce considerably the attractiveness of that market for imports from other Member States by increasing the difficulties of breaking into the market. This was so even though the relevant trade association rules or related agreements purported to be motivated by other objectives, e.g. protection of quality standards.

Yet further confirmation that even agreements of an apparently domestic nature within a Member State, and without the element of attempting to control the operation of a substantial part of an entire national market, can still affect trade between Member States is seen from *Salonia* v. *Poidomani and Baglieri*[9] (European Court 1981). This was a reference under Article 234 by a Court in Ragusa, Sicily. Salonia was the proprietor of a retail business in Ragusa which dealt in stationery, newspapers, and books. She wanted to be supplied with both newspapers and periodicals by Poidomani and Baglieri from their wholesale warehouse in Ragusa. They refused on the ground that she was not on the list of retailers approved by the Italian publishers' association. Mrs Salonia brought an action in Italy to force the defendants to supply her with newspapers and periodicals, claiming that failure to do so constituted unfair competition.

The European Court was troubled by some uncertainties as to the factual situation in the case, particularly whether the agreement laid down by the publishers' association in Italy was still in existence, and whether the defendants adhered to it. Nevertheless, in dealing with the issues involved, it held that a distribution system operated in accordance with a national trade agreement restricting the supply of relevant products to approved retailers would infringe Article 81, if it were shown that authorized retailers were not chosen by objective criteria, such as their abilities as retailers or their suitability with regard to staff, trading premises, and experience.

---

[7] *Windsurfing International* v. *Commission* Case 193/83 [1986] ECR 611: 3 CMLR 489.

[8] See Ch. 12, pp.228–30.

[9] Case 126/80 [1981] ECR 1563: [1982] I-CMLR 64. Another example of the same principle is *Belasco* v. *Commission* Case 246/82 [1989] ECR 2117: [1991] 4 CMLR 96 involving a cartel of Belgian roof manufacturers.

A number of Commission decisions on this issue have involved the banking sector, in which it has been held that a number of the services provided by banks and related agreements between them in individual Member States (even if involving some foreign banks) did not have a sufficient effect on interstate trade. In particular agreements relating to automatic cash machines, safe custody services, and the conditions governing current accounts have all been treated as primarily domestic. The Commission's approach in this type of case was however challenged by Ruiz-Jarabo Colomer A-G in *Bagnasco (Italian Banks*[10]*)* where debtors of certain Italian banks claimed that the onerous standard form guarantees which they had given had a sufficiently appreciable effect on interstate trade to be subject to Article 81. In support of their arguments he suggested that the existing Single Market in banking across Europe meant that the imposition by a Member State of particular forms of agreement more restrictive than those generally in use in other Member States had a tendency to compartmentalize national markets and damage the provision of financial services on a Community wide basis. The ECJ however did not adopt his opinion, but ruled that the restrictive terms of the guarantees required to support the opening of current accounts with Italian banks did not have an appreciable effect on interstate trade.

It is doubtful if this case by itself indicates any significant shift in the approach of the Court to its definition of agreements having an effect on interstate trade. It is however possible to see the subsequent *Dutch Banks*[11] case as reflecting the Advocate General's opinion in *Bagnasco*. Now that all Member States have national competition laws that can deal with those agreements which have their principal effect in local markets, there is less need for the Commission or the Community Courts to seek to characterize as falling within Article 81 all those categories of relatively routine agreements that may have only a minor impact on interstate trade.

1.5 ARTICLES 81 AND 82 COMPARED

In the light of all these developments, the early debates over the correct interpretation of the word corresponding to 'affect' in the English translation of Article 81 now appear somewhat academic. At a time when there were only the four original authoritative languages for the Treaty of Rome, it was apparent that whilst the Dutch word required an unfavourable influence to be shown on trade between Member States, the equivalent expression in German and Italian was more ambiguous, and the French term 'affecter' had both a neutral and a pejorative sense. The combined effect of the slightly different flavours of these four translations left the impression that an effect upon trade of a purely neutral kind, i.e. having both good and bad consequences, would not necessarily be covered by Article 81(1). Deringer,[12] commenting on these expressions some ten years after signature of the Treaty, indicated that he found the wording alone of the Article insufficient to support a definite conclusion, and that the best means of interpretation was to consider the essential purpose of the expression. This was to promote and protect the free flow of trade within the Common Market, unhampered by private restraints on competition. If the restraint changed the

---

[10] Case C-216/96 [1999] ECR I-135: 4 CMLR 624.

[11] [2000] 4 CMLR 137.

[12] A. Deringer, *The Competition Law of the European Economic Community: A Commentary on the EEC Rules of Competition* (CCH Editions, 1968), pp.22–3.

intensity or the direction of flow of goods, artificially diverting it from its normal and natural course, then the Article would certainly come into play, and the question of whether the effect was adverse or neutral would not normally arise. The Court's approach in *Grundig* v. *Consten* was consistent with this view.

Similar wording is found in Article 82, prohibiting the abuse of dominant positions within the Common Market. The two leading cases in which the European Court has confirmed the interpretation of these words in the context of Article 82 are *Commercial Solvents* v. *Commission*[13] (European Court 1974) and *Hugin* v. *Commission*[14] (European Court 1979). In the former case the Court stated that if an undertaking within the Common Market exploited its position in a way likely to eliminate a competitor, it did not matter whether the conduct complained of related specifically to the exports to be made by the competitor or its general trade within the Common Market, provided it was established that its elimination by the dominant company would have an effect on competitive structures within the Common Market. However, the conduct complained of in the case was a refusal to supply a particular chemical substance essential to the business of the smaller company and for which there was no other source of supply, so that complete elimination from the market would have followed for that smaller company.

By contrast, the *Hugin* case was one of those rarities where the Court decided that there was no sufficient effect on trade between Member States to justify a finding of abuse or breach. The facts were rather unusual, since the product market was of spare parts for cash registers manufactured by Hugin, a large Swedish company, having at the time some 13 per cent of the United Kingdom market for the registers.

Lipton was a company acting in the servicing and maintenance of such machines; following disagreements between the parties further supplies of spare parts were refused, preventing Lipton from carrying on its independent business of servicing them. Lipton claimed that Hugin's refusal to supply spare parts violated Article 82 as, without them, Lipton was unable to carry on its business. No objective reason had been offered for the refusal to supply the parts, now supplied only to Hugin's own subsidiaries. The Court agreed that there was no reason in theory why these facts should not justify a finding of abuse of a dominant position, but found that there was insufficient effect on trade between Member States since Lipton only traded in its capacity as a service company within a 50-mile radius of London and made no exports of any kind. Moreover, the characteristics of the market were that Hugin produced many different models for various countries in Europe which were affected by the different requirements of language and currency, so that the exporting of machines or spare parts from one Member State to another was uneconomic and unlikely. The Court found that an independent undertaking such as Lipton would not benefit from buying spare parts in other Member States rather than from the parent company in Sweden. There was, in the Court's view, no normal pattern of trade in such spare parts between Member States that could be disrupted by the commercial decision made by Hugin not to supply.

---

[13] *Istituto Chemioterapico Italiano and Commercial Solvents Corporation* v. *Commission* Cases 6–7/73 [1974] ECR 223: 1 CMLR 309.

[14] *Hugin* v. *Commission* Case 22/78 [1979] ECR 1869: 3 CMLR 345.

1.6 THE MEANING OF 'TRADE'

'Trade' has received a wide interpretation; it includes not merely the normal industrial and commercial activity of manufacture and distribution, but applies to commercial services of all kinds including not only banking, insurance, and financial services but also to shipping and all forms of transport. A number of important cases have involved transportation, and in particular shipping services. The fact that the routes involved have been to non-Member States has not persuaded the Commission or the Community Courts to refrain from finding an effect on trade between Member States, in particular given the existence and purpose of Regulation 4056/86 to provide shipping lines with a limited measure of exemption from the requirements of Article 81 in view of the well known instability of the business. Another leading case has involved rail services; in *European Night Services*[15] the Court of First Instance overruled a Commission decision that a proposed joint venture between four national rail companies to operate a night sleeper service through the Channel Tunnel affected trade between Member States to the required extent, after determining that the overall market share for passenger traffic held by the participants was no more than four per cent (or slightly more, if a narrower route by route definition was taken). The Court emphasised that, when market shares were so small, it was necessary for the Commission to provide a statement of reasons showing why nevertheless the agreement did have an appreciable effect on interstate trade.

The phrase also applies to a variety of other activities of a commercial nature including, for example, the provision of exhibitions and trade fairs, performing rights societies, television programmes, sport, and cultural activities. Its application is not limited to trade between the fifteen Member States, but extends also to trade with those EFTA countries still outside the Common Market (Iceland, Norway, and Liechtenstein) which form part of the European Economic Area (EEA). It extends also to other countries (such as Switzerland) and associated territories having free trade agreements with the Community, and a number of countries in Eastern Europe with treaties of Association (many of which are likely to become Member States in 2004).

Moreover it is possible for trade between Member States to be affected even if the relevant agreement on its face appears to prohibit such activity. In *Javico v YSL*[16] YSL had appointed Javico as its authorized distributor of luxury cosmetics in Russia, Ukraine, and Slovenia. The contract contained an express prohibition on Javico selling these products outside the authorized territories, either by direct marketing or through re-exports from them. On a reference from a French Court under Article 234 the ECJ held that the national court's decision on whether such a clause could itself be in breach of Article 81 must depend on the information available as to the likely outcome of any such breach. Only if the products intended to be sold in the Community were likely in any case to amount to a very small percentage of the total market for the product then could the Article be held inapplicable without further examination of the economic and legal context of the agreement; in all other cases this would have to be considered before a decision could be reached as to the effect on trade between Member States.

---

[15] Cases T-374–75, 384, 388/94 [1998] ECR II-3141: 5 CMLR 718.

[16] Case C-306/96 [1998] ECR I-1983: 5 CMLR 172. See also *Micro Leader Business* v. *Commission* Case T-198/98 [1999] ER II-3989: [2000] 4 CMLR 886.

2. 'WHICH HAVE AS THEIR OBJECT OR EFFECT THE PREVENTION, RESTRICTION, OR DISTORTION OF COMPETITION WITHIN THE COMMON MARKET'

2.1 A STRICT OR LIBERAL INTERPRETATION?

The difficulties inherent in defining competition were discussed in Chapter 2. If the competition referred to in this Article were to be of that rarely encountered atomistic variety, requiring a very large number of market participants unable by their own policies to influence prices or the level of demand, then to test whether any particular agreement or concerted practice between undertakings would have an effect on the competition within that market would be comparatively simple: its effect would be clearly and immediately perceptible, like the result of throwing a stone into a smooth pond. However, since virtually all the product and service markets encountered within the Community are imperfectly competitive, the task of assessing whether an agreement or practice does cause or have as its object the prevention, restriction, or distortion of competition becomes considerably more problematic.

Another problem is the interpretation of the words 'prevent, restrict, or distort competition within the Common Market'. Too strict a definition might cover almost every agreement for the sale of goods or services. Too liberal a definition would reduce the jurisdiction of the Commission, excluding from its control a substantial number of agreements that may, either individually or cumulatively, have an effect on competitive structures or processes. In determining the correct approach to these words within Article 81(1) it is necessary to decide whether the Article is primarily designed to assert jurisdiction, or whether it seeks to provide an assessment of whether individual agreements can be justified. An Article that seeks to establish initial jurisdiction would normally be expected to be more comprehensively interpreted than one concerned simply with the assessment or substantive justification of the agreements. After all, it is obvious that many more agreements will need scrutiny by the Commission than will ultimately fail to pass whatever substantive criteria are applied to them. This will not necessarily imply, however, that a 'jurisdictional' Article should be read with total adherence to a strictly literal meaning, bringing within its grasp every kind of agreement or concerted practice with the smallest impact on competition. It is clearly sensible for some limit to be placed on the scope even of such a phrase read in a broad sense.

While the European Court has taken the view that Article 81(1) is a jurisdictional clause, there are increasing indications in its decisions that the Court is prepared to accept that there are a number of cogent reasons why Article 81 should not be interpreted literally, so as to bring within its scope such a wide range of commercial agreements and restrictive clauses found within them that the Commission is unable to deal with them effectively. This limit to the scope of Article 81 is sometimes described as 'the rule of reason', although it is misleading to use this phrase because it is not properly to be compared directly with the same phrase used in describing the interpretation by US Federal Courts of Section 1 of the Sherman Act.[17] Section 1 of the Sherman Act is, of course, a combination of both

---

[17] See A.D. Neale and D.G. Goyder, *The Antitrust Laws of the United States*, 3rd edn. (Cambridge University Press, 1981) on this issue, at pp.23–30. See also R. Whish and B. Sufrin, 'Article 81 and the Rule of Reason', *YEL* 1987, pp.1–38.

a 'jurisdictional' and an 'assessment' clause, and the relevant phrase used of 'restraint of trade' necessarily requires a more liberal approach. Over its one hundred years and more of existence the section has seen a variety of different approaches from Courts; the liberal approach to interpretation has been in the ascendant in recent decades, particularly in the treatment of vertical agreements.

The assessment element in Article 81 is found in paragraph (3), and only to a more limited extent in paragraph (1). To discuss the alleged 'rule of reason' in the context of 81(1), especially in the context of the scope of 'prevention, restriction, or distortion of competition', leads to confusion rather than clarity. What is important for a clear understanding of these words is the way in which the Commission and, more importantly, the European Court and the Court of First Instance have interpreted them in a variety of different contexts. Initially interpretation was strict, but in recent years has been more flexible, although never giving an escape from the control of the Article to more than a narrow range of clauses found primarily in joint ventures and certain licensing agreements. Only after the reader has considered the application of this phrase in all the different contexts which decided cases present will it be possible to determine whether there exists under Community Law a single principle to explain all the exceptions to Article 81(1) and to which a general title such as 'rule of reason' could be given, if misleadingly; or whether these examples will remain as relatively limited exceptions to a normally rigorous general interpretation of these words in Article 81(1).

2.2 LEADING CASES ON ITS INTERPRETATION

A good starting point for our review of the way in which this phrase has been interpreted and applied is the recent (2001) Commission Notice on Agreements of Minor Importance, already referred to in the previous section.[18] For the first time the Notice deals only with the meaning of 'prevent, restrict, or distort competition within the Common Market' and not with the effect of the agreement on interstate trade. The 5 per cent and 10 per cent thresholds of the previous Notice are now increased to 10 and 15 per cent respectively; and for the first time a 5 per cent market share threshold is introduced for networks of agreements producing a cumulative anti-competitive effect, which can apply in sectors such as beer and petrol, to which previously the Notice could not apply, because of its specific exclusion of agreements operating in markets where 'competition is restricted by the cumulative effects of parallel networks of similar agreements established by several manufacturers or dealers'.

As before, however, a list of hardcore restrictions incapable of benefiting from the Notice is set out, though in some respects it differs from the list in previous Notices. Those applicable to vertical agreements have deliberately been made identical to those in the Vertical Restraints Block Exemption 2790/99 (discussed in Chapter 10), whilst those relating to horizontal agreements are identical with those in the Horizontal Co-operation Block Exemptions 2658 and 2659/2000 for agreements on specialization and R & D (discussed in Chapter 19). The overall effect of the Notice is to remove a large number of agreements, especially in the area of distribution, from the scope of Article 81(1) altogether; and when this change is added to the more generous terms of these Block Exemptions as compared

---

[18] See fn. 5

with their predecessors, the Article is likely to affect a lower proportion of agreements than before.

Unfortunately the importance of maintaining a clear distinction between the 'jurisdictional' and the 'assessment' element of Article 81 has not always been strictly observed by the ECJ (especially in dealing with cases involving vertical agreements, discussed in Chapter 10, and in *Wouters* (considered in the next section)), which in this respect has not matched the more convincing analytical approach of the Court of First Instance. This was typified by the Court of First Instance's well known *European Night Services* judgment referred to in the previous section,[19] in which it annulled a Commission decision of doubtful validity. The joint venture in question had been granted an exemption by the Commission on onerous terms, including an obligation to supply locomotives and train crews to any potential competitor which sought to offer the same night sleeper service through the Channel Tunnel between the United Kingdom and Europe. The period for the exemption was only eight years, notwithstanding the large capital investment required. The Commission claimed that the agreement would restrict competition:

(i)   between the parties themselves, even though the evidence showed that none of these railway companies, for both financial and operational reasons, could have operated the service on their own, and

(ii)   between the parties and other rail operators, who might have been potential competitors in the provision of the service.

After a full review of the facts and relevant commercial issues, the Court of First Instance ruled that the agreement did not restrict competition on either basis to a sufficiently appreciable extent, so that neither 81(1) nor (3) applied. It made however at paragraph 136 of its judgment an apparently significant statement on the relationship between (1) and (3):

It must be borne in mind that in assessing an agreement under Article [81(1)] of the Treaty, account should be taken of the actual conditions in which it functions, in particular the economic context in which the undertakings operate, the products or services covered by the agreement and the actual structure of the market concerned . . . unless it is an agreement containing obvious restrictions of competition such as price-fixing, market-sharing or the control of outlets . . . in the latter case, such restrictions may be weighed against their claimed pro-competitive effects only in the context of Article [81(3)] of the Treaty, with a view to granting an exemption from the prohibition in Article [81(1)].

Some commentators have suggested that the last of the sentences in this quotation may indicate that the Community Courts may now be more willing to balance the pro- and anti-arguments relating to restraints on competition under 81(1), in all cases except those involving hardcore restrictions. The actual wording of Articles 81(1) and (3) would seem hard to square with such an approach; and the continuing need to preserve the distinction between the two separate paragraphs was underlined by the Court of First Instance in another case some three years later, that of *Metropole* v. *Commission*.[20] Here a group of French television companies had formed a joint venture to challenge in the French pay-TV market the market leader, Canal+. After notification to the Commission this group appealed to the Court of

[19] See fn. 15.   [20] Case T-112/99 [2001] ECR II-2459: 5 CMLR 1236.

First Instance against the conditions imposed by the Commission under 81(3), and in particular that only for a three-year period were restrictions allowed on the use by the joint venture participants of 'general interest' and 'special interest' television channels, other than through the joint venture itself. The joint venture claimed that the Commission should have assessed the restrictions under the 'rule of reason', balancing their pro- and anti-competitive elements under Article 81(1), rather than under 81(3) alone.

In rejecting this claim the Court of First Instance referred to the *European Night Services* judgment but emphasized that it was only in the 'precise framework' of Article 81(3) that the balancing of these issues could be carried out. The fact that some earlier judgments of Community Courts had found certain agreements outside Article 81(1) was not to be explained by the existence of a so-called 'rule of reason' but rather by the characterization of some restraints on the parties as merely restrictions on *conduct* rather than on *competition*. This approach seems correct and preferable in terms of the structure of the Article, even if its application to individual cases still remains difficult.

2.3 THE *WOUTERS* CASE

A more puzzling case is *Wouters*,[21] which involved a dispute between two Dutch lawyers and the Dutch Bar Council. The Bar Council had a rule that its members could only enter into partnerships with members of other professions if the Council's consent had been given. Wouters and another lawyer each wanted to join a firm of well known chartered account-ants, but were refused consent by the Council. On appeal the case was referred to the ECJ; its judgment confirmed that the rule was 'the decision of an association', and therefore subject to Article 81, and moreover that the rule did have an effect on competition in the market for legal services. Nevertheless it held that the rule was not in breach of Article 81(1), because it had been introduced for reasons of 'public interest', not merely in the interests of the Dutch legal profession. It could (said the Court in its Article 234 judgment which contrasted strongly with the opinion of Leger A-G) be regarded as a reasonable exercise of the Bar Council's concern to ensure that lawyers acted for clients with complete independence and without any risk of conflict of interest, which multidisciplinary partnerships might raise.

The problem with this decision is that, while it could well have been taken, had the rule been notified to the Commission (which it had not) under the provisions of Article 81(3), on the basis that the concerns of the Bar Council might have been considered to represent an 'improvement' of legal services in The Netherlands, it was actually taken under Article 81(1), after balancing the acknowledged restriction of competition that it involves against the stated public interest arguments of the Bar Council. It is noteworthy that the judgment does not expressly state that in the context of the varied aims of the Treaty, both social and economic, rules relating to the provision of professional services should be treated as outside Article 81(1), as agreements which were the product of collective bargaining between employers and employees have been (as in *Albany International* and other cases mentioned later in this chapter). What appears to have happened is that the two parts of the Article have been conflated and operated as if they were a single provision (in the same way as under section 1 of the Sherman Act in a case like *California Dental Association* v. *FTC*[22]). This may

---

[21] Case C-309/99 [2002] ECR I-1979: 4 CMLR 913. The first substantive decision of the UK Competition Commission Appeal Tribunal, in *GISC*, raised some similar issues [2001] Comp AR 62.

[22] 119 S. Ct 1604 (1999).

become the usual method of applying Article 81 from 1 May 2004 once the modernization programme has been implemented and after the Commission has surrendered its monopoly of granting individual exemptions. It is certainly not to be regarded as an application of the 'rule of reason'.

2.4 MARKETS WHERE COMPETITION IS INHERENTLY RESTRICTED

The meaning of 'prevent, restrict, or distort' becomes clearer if one considers the normal mental processes of any businessman seeking to enter a specific geographic and product market. If there are no agreements or concerted practices then he will have complete freedom of choice as to the territories in which he can sell, the availability of outlets through whom he can distribute his goods, the prices and conditions of sale at which he can distribute, and a range of choices in other matters such as marketing techniques. However, if there are agreements between other undertakings which have the effect of limiting his freedom of choice so that he is, for example, foreclosed from using his first choice of distributors, or cannot (because of earlier exclusive appointments) be appointed a franchisee for particular goods, cannot be appointed an exclusive dealer himself because there is a quantitative limit on those nominated within a given territory, or if he cannot manufacture successfully in a particular Member State because sole or dominant suppliers have entered into agreements which restrict their ability to sell to him, then in all these cases the restraint of trade is directly responsible for the reduction in freedom imposed on his business by the agreements in existence between others already in the market. The object of Article 81 is to eliminate or reduce the number of such agreements, and to try to distinguish between agreements without sufficient redeeming virtues and those whose effect on competition, or whose purpose of reducing competition, is nevertheless accompanied by substantial advantages of the kind referred to in Article 81(3).

In some cases, the restraint will affect all manufacturers or all wholesalers or retailers of a particular product in a particular Member State: in other cases, the range of undertakings affected will be smaller. An important preliminary point, however, is that fully free competition is not possible in all markets because of government intervention in their workings.

The best known example of this is the *Sugar Cartel*[23] case. The Italian government had laid down complex rules governing the marketing of sugar; the Italian public authority in charge of sugar prices, the CIP, adopted a series of regulations intended mainly to benefit Italian sugar-beet producers and exporters. Aids were financed by a levy applied to both Italian sugar manufacture and imported sugar, but permitting reduction of the levy in a few cases to encourage a certain level of imports so as to fill up the gap between Italian production and the target level of demand. Foreign producers were invited to tender to supply certain quantities of sugar for import, and complicated regulations determined the extent to which the levy was charged in full or only in part. The effect of the regulations together with the risks attaching to the invitations to tender was that foreign manufacturers often agreed to allocate between themselves the right to supply into Italy, because they otherwise risked being individually excluded from the market altogether. Certain imports were permitted outside the formal system of invitations to tender, but only in limited quantities, and further regulations controlled the price that could be obtained by foreign concerns for imports into

---

[23] Case 40/73 [1975] ECR 1663: [1976] 1 CMLR 295.

Italy. The regulations also had the result of concentrating demand in Italy in the hands of the large producers, since they alone were likely to be able to fulfil on a reliable basis the requirements of purchasers. The real consequence of these regulations was to match supply closely to demand, which itself removed a vital element of normal competition, and had a considerable effect on both the buyer's freedom to choose his supplier (and vice versa) and the price at which the goods were supplied. The Court concluded that:

All these considerations show that Italian regulations and the way in which they have been imple-mented had a determinative effect on some of the most important aspects of the course of conduct of the undertakings concerned which the Commission criticises, so that it appears that, had it not been for these regulations and their implementation, the co-operation which is the subject matter of these proceedings, either would not have taken place, or would have assumed a form different from that found by the Commission to have existed.[24]

The Court's ruling in this instance was, therefore, that the sugar producers concerned, who themselves operated restrictive agreements in response to the Italian 'sugar regime', did not prevent, restrict, or distort competition because of the limited scope left for it by the result of the Italian State intervention.[25]

2.5 'OBJECT OR EFFECT' OF RESTRICTING COMPETITION

It was established in the early days of the Court that an agreement could satisfy the require-ments of these words if it had as its object a restriction on competition, or if (whatever its object) the restriction had that effect; it was unnecessary to prove both object and effects in any individual case.[26] This wording is significantly different from the terms of Article 65 of the Treaty of Paris, which referred to agreements 'tending directly or indirectly' to the prevention, restriction, or distortion of competition. The requirement for either an 'object' or 'effect' of such a restriction in the Treaty of Rome is more specific. The agreement must either be intended to have such a result on competition or, regardless of the parties' inten-tions, actually to have such a result. This has over the years proved both a comprehensive and workable definition.

The Court stated that it was first necessary to look at the object or purpose of the agreement by reference to its express provisions, considered in its economic context. Only if it did not appear that the purpose of the agreement was to restrain competition was it necessary to consider its effects. If effects had to be considered, then the issue was whether the agreement restricted competition perceptibly, comparing the results of the agreement with the State of affairs likely to exist in the absence of that restriction. Restrictions had always to be considered in the circumstances of their economic background.

The case law has established that some contractual restrictions are, *prima facie*, so likely to affect competition that this effect will be presumed. Clearly, those categories of agreements which are listed under sections (*a*) to (*e*) of Article 81(1) would probably fall into this category. This despite the fact that these lists are only examples, and in no sense an

---

[24] [1975] ECR 1923: [1976] 1 CMLR 410.

[25] Ch. 22 considers other leading cases where the degree of competition, in particular national markets, was reduced by governmental measures, without necessarily allowing undertakings affected by it to avoid the application of Art. 81(1).

[26] See *STM* (fn. 1 above). A recent case in which this point is emphasized is *TACA* Case T-395/94 [2002] 4 CMLR 1008.

exhaustive list of the kinds of agreement which the Article prohibits. Later chapters consider some individual examples of agreements falling within these categories. The category which has come closest to being called illegal *per se* is the agreement which, like the restrictions in *Grundig*, directly bans parallel imports by imposing export bans on distributors, or which in arrangements between horizontal competitors bans the export of goods to other countries within the Common Market or into territories outside the Market from which they were in practice likely to be re-imported into the Market.

It is necessary however to examine these two concepts separately. Certain types of restrictive clauses and/or agreements are regarded as having an object which is so manifestly anticompetitive that consideration of their effects is unnecessary, for example the hardcore restrictions listed in the 2001 Notice on Agreements of Minor Importance,[27] which may be either horizontal or vertical.

Such horizontal restrictions include:

— price fixing between competitors;

— market sharing agreements (of territory or of customers); and

— quotas or limitations of production or sales.

Vertical restrictions include:

— minimum resale price restrictions; and

— customer allocation clauses (with some exceptions).

The majority of these clauses would be described by a US antitrust lawyer as *per se* breaches of section 1 of the Sherman Act, equivalent to Article 81. Is it ever necessary then to go on to seek to ascertain the subjective intent of the parties? The answer is yes, but only rarely; in the majority of cases the 'object' of the agreement is clear on its face. Occasionally, however, the subjective intent of the parties may need to be sought; for example where the Commission are aware of an industry-wide scheme that purports to have beneficial objectives of, for example, improved standards, but where these may prove after investigation to be cosmetic only.[28] Such cases, however, will be few, compared to the number where the object clearly stands out from the very nature of the agreement itself.

A number of cases illustrate this important feature of the jurisprudence of the Common Market, deriving from the original judgment of the European Court in *Grundig*, which has proved to be so important. Twenty-five years ago, in the *WEA-Filipacchi*[29] case, German manufacturers sought to restrain various French dealers in pop records from reselling the records outside France, particularly in Germany. One of the arguments raised by the manufacturers was that in practice they would not have been able to enforce these restrictions, and that they were therefore without effect. The Commission held, however, that any restriction in an agreement which effectively operated as an export ban was so inherently the type of agreement that would have as its objective the prevention of free movement of goods across national boundaries by way of parallel imports that it was unnecessary to consider the further issue of whether the manufacturer concerned had the actual power to enforce such

---

[27] See fn. 5.
[28] As, e.g. in the *IAZ* cases, Cases 96–102, 104–5, 108, 110/82 [1983] ECR 3369: [1984] 3 CMLR 276.
[29] [1973] CMLR D43.

restrictions. A similar decision was reached by the Court itself in *Miller International* v. *Commission*[30] (European Court 1978). Again a record company had imposed an export ban on its French distributors. On this occasion the Court disregarded the opinion of the Advocate General, who had recommended a cancellation of the fine imposed by the Commission and remission of the case to the Commission on the ground that the undertakings has been misled by advice given by its lawyer. The Court found that the export ban was by its very nature a restriction on competition, whether adopted at the instigation of the supplier or of the customer, since the whole basis of the agreement between the parties was an endeavour to isolate a part of the market.

Export ban cases, perhaps surprisingly, continue to arise and to attract fines from the Commission, despite the relevant principles of law being established and well known to both business and legal communities. For example, in *Parker Pen*[31] (Court of First Instance 1994) Parker had made an agreement with Herlitz, a German dealer, with a clause prohibiting sales of its products outside Germany. Herlitz claimed that it had no interest in any 'export ban' since it was only interested in providing a wide range of stock for independent department stores in Germany and other Member States. It claimed not to have implemented the export ban in a number of cases. The Court ruled, nevertheless, that the mere existence of the 'export ban' in such an agreement had a 'visual and psychological' effect which could contribute to the partitioning of the market. The same point was made by the Commission in *BASF(L+F)—Accinauto*[32] where a dealer in car refinishing paints manufactured by BASF had under his agreement to refer all orders received from outside his contract territory to BASF, so that BASF could allocate them between its official dealers in the relevant territories and prevent parallel importers acquiring goods. It was clear that the dealer had not always complied with this contractual restriction, yet a substantial fine was nevertheless imposed on BASF and a nominal fine on the dealer. Other examples can currently be found, as in the *Bayer* case, where the Commission recognizes that dealers are not always enthusiastic supporters of such clauses.

In many cases however it will still be necessary to examine the economic context of the agreement and the actual effect that the restrictive clauses will have or possibly have already had, if it has been implemented already. The classic authority for this is the well-known *Delimitis*[33] case, whose facts are set out in Chapter 10 at p.183. The contractual restriction on the tenant of a Frankfurt café was that he had to purchase all his supplies of beer from Henniger Brau, the owner of the café, though there were advantages to both the tenant and his landlord in the arrangements. The cumulative effect of the brewery's network had to be assessed, the number of outlets tied by the brewery, and the degree of loyalty of tenants generally to it. The option for the tenant to purchase beer from outside Germany should also be considered. The actual contribution of the individual tenant's agreement to the blocking effect on potential new entry was also relevant.

A more recent case dealt with by the ECJ involved exclusive purchasing agreements by petrol stations in Finland. In *Neste Markinouti* v. *Youtuuli Ky,*[34] Neste was an oil company

[30] Case 19/77 [1978] ECR 131: 2 CMLR 334.
[31] Case T-77/92 [1994] ECR II-549: [1995] 5 CMLR 435.
[32] [1996] 4 CMLR 811, appeal to the CFI dismissed; Cases T-175/176 of 1995 [1999] ECR II-1581, 1635: [2000] 4 CMLR 33, 67.
[33] Case C-234/89 [1991] ECR I-935: [1992] 5 CMLR 210.
[34] Case C-214/99 [2001] 4 CMLR 993.

with a large national chain of petrol stations, and a market share of petrol and diesel fuel sales in that country of 33.5 per cent and 44.2 per cent respectively. Some of these stations had agreements for as long as ten years, others for much shorter periods such as a year. The ECJ held that, in the case of an agreement for a year only, the degree to which such agreements foreclosed the access of rival oil companies to the retail market was too limited to fall within the range of Article 81.

2.6 RESTRICTIONS ON COMPETITION BY NON-RESIDENT PARTIES

To restrict competition within the Common Market, it is not necessary that all parties to the agreement are resident within it. This is illustrated by Commission decisions relating to trade between the Common Market and Japan. In *Siemens/Fanuc*[35] (Commission 1985), a fine was imposed on both a German and a Japanese company which had entered into reciprocal exclusive dealing agreements covering numerical controls for machine tools for Asia and the EC respectively, and under which a substantial range of restrictions was imposed and extremely high prices charged to all customers, who could not obtain the controls from other sources. In *Franco-Japanese Ballbearings*[36] (Commission 1974), it was proved that meetings had taken place between the manufacturers of ballbearings in France and Japan to discuss the sales and pricing policy of Japanese manufacturers with regard to imports into France. Considerable pressure was applied upon the Japanese manufacturers to bring export prices to France into line with French prices, and to inform the French manufacturers of the prices and discounts that the Japanese would grant to purchasers in France. Here the restraint on competition was clear and its result was that customers for the ballbearings would find themselves paying a higher price to Japanese manufacturers than would otherwise have been the case. The flow of trade between Member States within the Common Market would also be affected, since Japanese ballbearings were supplied to other Common Market countries and the likely effects would be a reduction in direct imports from Japan and an increase in parallel imports to France from other Common Market countries, and possibly an overall reduction in the purchase by France from Japanese sources. The Court of Justice in the *Woodpulp*[37] case focused on the place where the agreement was implemented, regardless of where it was made or where its parties were situate.

2.7 SUMMARY OF THE COMMISSION'S TASK

In conclusion the Commission must in nearly all cases conduct a market analysis of the effect of particular restrictions or agreements on the patterns of trade. There will be occasions when it may be excused from doing this in detail, either because the restriction is of the type, e.g. an export ban, so clearly established as having the required effect on competition as not to need substantial proof of its individual effect on the particular market concerned, or because the objective of the agreement is so clearly anti-competitive that the Commission does not need to analyse the effects of the restriction.

---

[35] [1988] 4 CMLR 945.   [36] [1975] 1 CMLR D8.   [37] See Ch. 23, pp.501–2.

3. ANCILLARY RESTRICTIONS ON COMPETITION

3.1 VENDORS AND PURCHASERS

One of the ways in which the Court of First Instance and European Court have been able to restrict the scope of Article 81(1) has been by characterizing a wide range of restrictions on conduct contained in commercial agreements as 'ancillary'. Ancillary restrictions can occur in a wide variety of situations. Their essential characteristic is that without the restriction the proposed transaction would not take place because one party would be unable to prevent the other from acting subsequently so as to deprive the transaction of its main commercial benefit.

Some of these cases involve restrictive covenants on vendors which have sold their businesses, imposed by purchasers acquiring their goodwill as well as their business assets. In *Reuter* v. *BASF*[38] (Commission 1976). Dr Reuter sold to the German chemical company, BASF, a business which involved the manufacture of polyurethanes, synthetic products used in the manufacture of plastics and varnishes. As part of the agreements, Dr Reuter accepted a number of covenants restricting his own future activities, and which he subsequently complained were contrary to Article 81. The principal covenant restrained him for eight years from engaging directly or indirectly either in Germany or elsewhere in research, development, manufacture, use, or distribution of any chemical product required in the production of polyurethanes or related products. He was also prevented for eight years from relating any confidential technical matters known to him before the sale. The Commission ruled that any restrictive covenant on the sale of a business or of know-how must be limited in length and width to an extent proportionate to the goodwill and business sold. In assessing reasonable duration and extent for such a covenant, the factors to be considered included the nature of the know-how, opportunities for its use, and the transferee's own technical knowledge. Such a clause should normally be restricted to the markets in which the vendor was active before the sale or in which he could be regarded as a potential competitor; any clause covering new developments could not be of greater length than those properly inserted to protect existing markets. If clauses were limited in this way they might well not even be caught by the provisions of 81(1), and would not therefore be subject to the individual exemption process.

Applying these principles to Dr Reuter's agreement, the Commission held that the contractual clauses were invalid because they covered non-commercial as well as commercial research and development, and went beyond what was required to safeguard the interests of the purchaser in preserving the value of the goodwill and assets acquired. Moreover, it was felt that the obligation on Dr Reuter to keep information confidential for as long as eight years might be used to prevent him from competing with the purchaser later through his further development of basic know-how not covered by the sale agreement. The Commission also ruled that a competition-restraining agreement between a vendor and a purchaser, even if situate in the same Member State, would be likely to affect trade between Member States if it affected goods or services which if put on sale by the vendor of the business could be the subject of trade between Member States. The Commission ultimately ordered that the

---

[38] [1976] 2 CMLR D44.

agreement should stand for a period of only five years, instead of the eight-year period originally imposed.

A similar intervention occurred in *Remia and Nutricia*[39] (European Court 1984), involving the sale of two businesses in Holland for the production of sauces and pickles. Here the Court upheld a Commission decision that covenants restraining the vendors from competitive activity were reduced from ten to four years in one case, and from five to two years in another, on the basis that even such apparently normal clauses may impose restraints upon trade between Member States which the Commission is required to consider. The Court, however, emphasized that clauses of this kind whose length, scope, or geographical application do no more than is necessary to permit the agreement in which they occur are not caught by 81(1), but are simply ancillary to a necessary and legitimate business transaction.

3.2 OTHER FORMS OF ANCILLARY RESTRICTIONS: *GOTTRUP KLIM*

The concept of the ancillary restraint can also arise in connection with the rules of trade associations or co-operatives. *Gottrup Klim v. DLG* (European Court of Justice 1994)[40] involved the rules of a Danish farmers' co-operative, DLG, which was open to both individuals and associations of farmers, and its treatment under those rules of smaller associations which sought to terminate their membership. The plaintiffs were various smaller associations which remained members of DLG, but had elected to buy the majority of their requirements of fertilizers and pesticides direct from suppliers. The consequent reduction of orders placed through DLG led to discounts for its members on those products being reduced. DLG then decided to change its rules so that membership of any association that competed with it in the purchase of pesticides and fertilizers would lead to expulsion of its members from DLG. Members of such small associations could however continue to buy their individual requirements either direct from suppliers or through DLG.

The small associations expelled as a result of the change of rules brought an action in the Danish courts, and under Article 234 a number of issues relating to the DLG rules were raised with the European Court. The Court ruled that a provision in the statutes of an organization like DLG prohibiting its members from joining competing co-operatives to acquire certain products did not necessarily constitute a restriction of competition within the meaning of Article 81, provided that the rule was restricted to what was necessary to ensure that the co-operative functioned properly and was able to maintain its contractual power in relation to suppliers. Such was the case with the DLG rules, where (*a*) the prohibition only covered products (principally fertilizers and pesticides) where there was a direct relationship between sales volume and price, (*b*) non-members of the co-operative were allowed to buy from it the whole range of products sold on by it on the same terms and at the same prices as its members, and (*c*) members of DLG were allowed to buy those products direct outside DLG provided, as mentioned above, that they did not buy through a competing co-operative. The issue in determining whether 81(1) applied was whether the

---

[39] *Remia and Nutricia v. Commission* Case 42/84 [1985] ECR 2566: [1987] 1 CMLR 1. The Court pointed out that the effect of such sales or businesses is to increase the number of potential competitors in the market. However, a clause of this kind which seeks to protect the *vendor* against the competing activities of the *purchaser* in particular territories is never regarded as ancillary: *Quantel International* v. *Quantel SA* [1993] 5 CMLR 497.

[40] Case C-250/92 [1994] ECR I-5641: [1996] 4 CMLR 191.

rules containing such restrictions were necessary to ensure that the co-operative functioned properly and maintained its contractual power in relation to producers, in the interests of its ordinary individual members.

3.3 OTHER ANCILLARY CLAUSES

Ancillary clauses can however be found in many different types of agreement apart from sales of businesses. In joint ventures the parent companies may quite reasonably impose covenants upon each other not to compete with the business of the joint venture, at least for a period of years, and not to take other action that might prejudice it. Franchisers may normally seek to restrict the business methods adopted by their franchisees so as to protect their business secrets; and suppliers of certain products and services may wish to adopt certain quality standards for their selective distributors. The owners and licensors of some specialized intellectual property rights may also with justification seek to protect themselves during the early years of the commercial development of a particular plant or seed by imposing export bans for a period, with the object of controlling the extent of widespread licensing. Nevertheless the Commission will be unwilling to accept the classification of a restrictive clause as ancillary without clear evidence that its adoption is a *sine qua non* of the transaction of which it forms part.

The question of whether a contractual restriction can be properly described as ancillary also arises under the Merger Regulation, and the detailed contents of the Commission Notice on this subject is to be found at Chapter 18 at pp.385–9. The treatment of such restrictions under this Regulation focuses on whether, in the absence of such a clause, the particular merger could be implemented at all, or only under more uncertain conditions or at substantially higher cost. Whilst some of the ancillary clauses found in merger agreements are similar to those mentioned in this section, the range of clauses included in merger agreements, usually in an attempt to preserve the continuity and stability of the merged undertaking, is wider. The Notice is specific as to the maximum length of non-compete clauses which can be treated as ancillary, two years when goodwill alone is transferred and three years if both goodwill and know-how are conveyed, unless the circumstances are exceptional. The Notice however mentions that, even if a particular clause appears in a merger agreement, this does not prevent it from benefiting from the provisions of Article 81(3) or of a Block Exemption such as Regulation 240/96 or 2790/99.

4. THE WIDTH OF THE COVERAGE OF ARTICLE 81

4.1 INTRODUCTION

The general approach of the Treaty is to provide for only a very limited number of sectoral exceptions to the general application of the competition rules[41] and the Community Court have interpreted these exceptions in a restrictive way. It is therefore sensible to approach a discussion of the coverage of the Article by listing those particular sectors which have been

---

[41] See Jacobs A-G's Opinion in *Albany International* Case C-67/96, [1999] ECR I-5751: [2000] 4 CMLR 446 at paras 120–126.

specifically excluded from its scope rather than by trying to enumerate all those which it covers. In some cases exclusion from its coverage has meant that there is partial or complete exemption from a sector from the competition rule; but in other cases the exclusion from coverage by Article 81 has been comprehensive so as to provide an alternative set of competition rules. Some of the exclusions or exceptions result directly from specific provisions in the Treaty, while others arise from the adoption of Regulations made under the authority of the Treaty.

4.2 DEFENCE

The competition rules may be excluded under Article 296 from applying to any product included in the list of Defence items prepared by the Council of Ministers. This Article gives Member States the right to take necessary measures to protect their essential security interests connected with the production of or trade in arms, munitions, and war materials; the only qualification is that 'such measures shall not adversely affect the conditions of competition in the Common Market regarding products which were not intended for specifically military purposes'. This distinction is presumably drawn so as to ensure that while undertaking they be allowed to enter into agreements otherwise within the scope of Article 81 but for the fact that they relate for example to the supply of rifles or tanks. Similar arrangements made to cover, for example, the supply of boots (potentially suitable for army or civilian use) are not so excluded. The tendency of the Commission in recent years has been to narrow the scope of this exemption. Moreover, under Article 298 the Commission is entitled to intervene if it believes that a Member State is abusing its rights under Article 296 with the effect of distorting conditions of competition within the Common Market.

Perhaps the greatest reliance by Member States on Article 296 has arisen in the context of mergers, where the Commission has accepted their right in several such cases to deal with those cases themselves, without the individual undertaking having to supply the Commission with information relating to their Defence activities. The Commission has in each case so far stated publicly that the measures taken by the Member State in such a case were necessary for the protection of its essential security interests and had little effect on competition or suppliers. It should not be assumed, however, that all Defence cases and notably mergers involving companies in the Defence industry, will be dealt with solely by Member States, as in a number of cases under the Merger Regulation the Commission has nevertheless taken jurisdiction under the Regulation of non-Defence areas of the business being acquired (see Chapter 18, Section 1.4).

4.3 COAL AND STEEL: NUCLEAR ENERGY

Article 305(1) states that the provisions of the Treaty of Rome (including of course Articles 81–89 containing the rules on competition) shall not affect the ECSC Treaty 'and in particular the rules laid down by that Treaty for the functioning of the Common Market in coal and steel'. Articles 65 and 66 of the ECSC Treaty clearly therefore formed part of those rules and were applied by the Commission in parallel with Articles 81 and 82 of the Rome Treaty. As from 23 July 2002, however, the fifty-year life of the ECSC came to an end and a Communication from the Commission set out the transitional arrangements in respect of pending ECSC cases, and also those for the future application of the competition rules of the Treaty of Rome to the coal and steel sector. This change is perhaps less dramatic than might have been expected. Over its fifty-year life the size of the Community Coal and Steel industry has sharply reduced, even while the Community increased from six to fifteen Member States, and the approach of the Commission in its application of the ECSC rules under the Treaty of Paris had for many years been converging with its practices under the Treaty of Rome. In future however national competition authorities and national courts will be competent to deal with coal and steel cases in parallel with the Commission, in the same way as they can deal with cases under Articles 81 and 82.

In its Communication at [2002] OJC152/5 the Commission has explained that it does not intend to initiate procedures under Article 81 or 82 against agreements formally exempted under the ECSC regime provided that no new elements of fact or law appear which put into question the exemptability of those agreements. Under the ECSC Treaty the Commission had jurisdiction over all concentrations and joint ventures covering the relevant products whether or not they were full-function, but in the future it will only take jurisdiction over those concentrations which meet the world and Community's turnover thresholds set out in the Regulation (see Chapter 17, Section 2.1).

By contrast the Nuclear Energy Industry continues to retain its separate regime under Article 305(2) which states that the Treaty of Rome shall not derogate from the provisions of the Treaty establishing the European Atomic Energy Community, which in practice means that Articles 81 (and 82) are applied to this sector if required. The relationship between the two treaties was considered by the Court of First Instance in *ENU* v. *Commission*[42] and by the European Court in its *Ruling on the Physical Protection of Nuclear Materials.*[43]

4.4 COLLECTIVE BARGAINING

No specific exemption is found in the Treaty for agreements that form part of the collective bargaining process within the Community, but on social policy grounds the ECJ has ruled in several cases that such agreements fall outside the scope of Article 81. The leading case is *Albany International.*[44] Companies in the Dutch textile industry were required to provide supplementary pensions for their employees. Albany already had its own such scheme (which it claimed was more generous than the compulsory scheme) and claimed also that the compulsory scheme was in breach of Article 81 so that it could not be required to participate in it. The ECJ however rejected Albany's claim; whilst Article 81 was applicable to the scheme because of its compulsory nature the scheme was justified under the terms of Article 86(2) of the Treaty because of the social policy objectives which the Treaty embodied. For the same reason, however, Article 81 did not apply to the collective agreement between employers and employees for the establishment and maintenance of the scheme. The Court followed the strong lead given by Jacobs A-G, whose opinion laid down conditions for holding such agreements outside the scope of Article 81. These were that the agreement was made as part of normal collective bargaining, that it was made in good faith rather than to conceal restrictions of competition and that it dealt with the core subjects of collective bargaining, such as wages or other conditions of work, and did not affect third parties.

---

[42] Case T-458 and 523/93 [1995] ECR II-2459.   [43] Case C-1/78 [1978] ECR 2151.
[44] Case C-67/96 [1999] ECR I-5751: [2000] 4 CMLR 446.

There have been a number of other cases, also mainly from The Netherlands, in which similar conclusions have been reached by the courts. Whether the actual agreement established a trust fund or a Social Security scheme against industrial accidents is covered by the competition rules is of course a different question from whether the fund itself is an undertaking; the answer in several of the cases has been that the trust fund or scheme created by collective agreement was itself an undertaking but that nevertheless for the reasons of social policy mentioned above, Article 81 had no application to it. Thus on the same day as the *Albany* case was decided, the Court reached a similar finding in *Brentjens* v. *SBVHB*[45] where the appellant was a wholesaler in the buildings material sector. It likewise wished to withdraw from the industry compulsory scheme on the grounds that it had already provided a scheme of equivalent value for its employees. Funds that are not the outcome of a collective bargaining process may well however fall within the scope of Article 81 as in the *Pavlov* case discussed above (in Chapter 6 at p.62).

4.5 AGRICULTURE

The position of agricultural products is covered by Article 36 of the Treaty. This declares that the competition rules shall only apply to agriculture to the extent that the Council determines, within the framework of and subject to the requirements of the Common Agricultural Policy, which is set out in outline in Article 37. The detailed objectives of Article 33 are to be taken into account in framing these Regulations. The objectives set out in Article 33 for the Common Agricultural Policy include:

- (*a*) increasing agricultural productivity by promoting technical progress, and by ensuring the rational development of agricultural production and the optimum utilization of the factors of production, in particular labour;
- (*b*) ensuring a fair standard of living for the agricultural community;
- (*c*) stabilization of markets;
- (*d*) assurance of the availability of supplies; and
- (*e*) ensuring that supplies reach consumers at reasonable prices.

In working out these policies account is to be taken of the particular nature of agricultural activity, including: its social functions and the disparities between different regions, the need to effect the appropriate adjustments gradually, and its close links with the rest of the economy of Member States. Some of these objectives, especially (*c*) and (*d*), appear inevitably to require substantial intervention in free markets, and indeed the terms of the Common Agricultural Policy at present in force illustrate this. Accordingly, Regulation 26/62 was adopted by the Council, which in substance permits the competition rules to apply (Article 1) subject to two substantial exceptions. The first of these is any agreement which forms an integral part of a national market organization. Such organizations are now rare since the marketing rules for agricultural products have, for a number of years, been dealt with on a Community wide basis. Occasionally however such organizations are still created. The

---

[45] Cases C-115 to 117/97 [1999] ECR I-6025: [2000] 4 CMLR 566. Other similar Dutch cases were *MDB* v. *SPVH* Case C-219/97 [1999] ECR I-6121: [2000] 4 CMLR 599 and *Van der Woude* Case C-222/98 [2000] ECR I-7111: [2001] 4 CMLR 93.

second exception is any agreement which 'is necessary for the attainment of the objectives set out in Article [83] of the Treaty' as set out above. The Commission's interpretation of this ground of exemption has invariably been strict.

An example of the attitude taken by the Commission and Court towards the interpretation of Regulation 26 is the *FRUBO* case.[46] This involved an agreement between a trade association of Dutch fruit importers and another association of Dutch fruit wholesalers. Under the agreement, wholesalers were not allowed to seek alternative sources of supply into the Common Market of fruit and vegetables originating from outside the Community, other than through the Rotterdam fruit auctions. As a result, of all the apples, pears, and citrus fruit imported into Holland, at least 75 per cent usually came in through the Rotterdam auctions, making it extremely difficult for Dutch importers to seek long-term import agreements with other parties within the Common Market. A rather half-hearted argument was put forward by the associations that, under Dutch law, the practices of the associations did not constitute contractual relationships between their members, comprising only a 'gentlemen's agreement'; even if this argument had been successful, such an agreement would in any case be caught by the provisions of Article 81. The contractual nature of these rules was emphasized that the fact that they contained penalties for their breach with the possibility of the exclusion of defaulters from participation in the Rotterdam fruit auction, a serious detriment for the importers.

Both the Commission and the European Court of Justice rejected the argument that these arrangements were an integral part of a national market organization or necessary for the attainment of the objectives of Article 33. The Court concluded that the agreements might possibly improve the distribution of fruit in Holland, and even that consumers might receive the benefit of price reduction as a result, though it remained sceptical on this issue. Nevertheless, the exemption under Article 81(3) was unavailable, for the restrictions placed on the parties were not indispensable to the agreements' claimed purpose: the improvement of fruit distribution throughout Holland.

The restrictions also, of course, contravened the 'integration' principle laid down in *Grundig*, under which the wholesalers should have been left free to search for alternative sources of supply outside their own country rather than being kept effectively 'segmented' from the rest of the Common Market. The effect of the restriction was substantial: in practice it meant that a Dutch wholesaler could not act as an importer and that importers established in the other Member States could not, without joining the association and participating in the fruit auction, deliver fruit to Dutch wholesalers. At least in the area of marketing agricultural products, Article 81 clearly has considerable application, and has also been utilized, for example, in the sugar, vegetable, and dairy products sectors.[47]

Subsequent cases have explained the role of national courts in determining whether the exemption found in Article 2 is applicable. In the *Dijkstra, Van Roesell*, and *Luttikhuis* cases[48] the European Court had to deal with a number of issues on this Article raised by Dutch courts under Article 234. In each case, farmers had left milk producers' co-operatives and

---

[46] *FRUBO* v. *Commission* Case 71/74 [1975] ECR 563: 2 CMLR 123. See also *VBA/Florimex* Case C-265/97P [1999] ECR I-2061.

[47] The marketing of Dutch milk was the subject of the *Meldoc* decision [1989] 4 CMLR 813.

[48] *Dijkstra and Van Roesell* Cases C-319/93, 40/94, and 224/94 [1995] ECR I-4471: [1996] 5 CMLR 178. *Oude Luttikhuis* Case C-399/93 [1995] ECR I-4515: [1996] 5 CMLR 178.

argued that rules which required them to pay money to the co-operative on withdrawal were void as being in breach of Article 81(1). The Court's ruling was that national courts were competent to determine whether the payment obligation on the withdrawing member comprised an infringement of Article 81(1) (and was therefore void under Article 81(2)) if it was clear to that court that the terms of Article 2(1) of Regulation 26/62 could not be met. However, if it had any doubt on the matter it should suspend proceedings in order to enable the Commission to make its own decision under Regulation 26. In any case, the restrictions imposed by agricultural co-operatives on their members must be limited to those necessary to ensure that the co-operatives function properly with a sufficiently wide commercial base and a reasonable degree of stability.

4.6 AIR TRANSPORT

As a mark of its importance to the economy of the Common Market the transport sector was given special mention within the treaty in Articles 70 to 80. Article 80(1) states that the provisions of this title apply to road, rail, and inland waterway transport and paragraph (2) states that the Council may decide whether appropriate provisions may also be laid down for sea and air transport, for which a qualified majority has been required since the Single European Act.

The position of air transport has always been special. There were a number of international treaties and conventions setting out the basis upon which such services were to be carried out, going back to the Chicago Convention, entered into as long ago as 1944 which had led to the creation of the International Air Transport Authority (IATA) to play a leading role in the worldwide coordination of fixing both its services and fares. The perceived need to support national airlines had naturally led Member States to themselves become much involved in the fixing of details relating to the revision of air services. For a considerable period therefore no competition rules applied to air transport. Numerous references were found in the early Annual Competition Reports to Commission proposals for the introduction of regulation in the sector. Owing to strong opposition by some Member States, the Commission then sought alternative means of opening up the sector to a greater degree of competition and the position was firmly clarified by the *Nouvelles Frontières*[49] case. This to some extent strengthened the position of the Commission, although it did not give it the full authority for which it had hoped to impose the complete range of competition rules on Member States and air undertakings within them. The case arose after the Tribunal de Police in Paris asked the Court for a ruling under Article 234 on whether it was contrary to the Treaty for Member States to require Courts to apply the criminal law to undertakings which had failed to comply with mandatory tariffs for air transport 'if it were established that those tariffs were the result of an agreement, decision or concerted practice between undertakings contrary to Article [81]'.

The Court, noting that no regulation had been made for air and sea transport under Article 83, nevertheless concluded that Articles 84 and 85 remained applicable. Article 84 required authorities in the Member States to apply Article 81, including paragraph (3), and Article 82 until relevant regulations had been adopted. However the authorities referred to in Article 84 did not include criminal courts (whose task was simply to punish infringement

---

[49] *Ministère Public* v. *Asjes* Cases C-209–213/84 [1986] ECR 1425: 3 CMLR 173.

of the law) but merely administrative bodies charged with administering competition law and civil courts having jurisdiction over such authorities or to apply such laws. Neither the French authorities nor the Commission had in fact exercised any of their powers under Articles 84 and 85 with regard to the air transport tariff agreements which had allegedly been broken by the defendant travel agents in the criminal proceedings before the Tribunal de Police.

The Court, following earlier cases, held that the two Articles were 'not of such a nature as to ensure a complete and consistent application of Article 81' so as to permit the assumption that Article 81 had been fully effective from the date of entry into force of the Treaty. The principle of legal certainty, to which the Court had always attached great importance, therefore meant that these agreements remained provisionally valid unless and until the Member State, or the Commission, took action under those Articles (84 and 85 respectively) which gave transitional powers to them. Only when such a ruling had been given could the French courts be required to hold, as a matter of Treaty obligation, that no criminal liability could be imposed for breach of the relevant requirement of the French Code of Civil Aviation, which required sales of air tickets to be at official approved prices.

As a result of *Nouvelles Frontières*, it became clear that, until the Council adopted a regulation dealing with air transport, the Commission would be able to make progress only by implementing Article 81. The Commission subsequently gave notice during the summer of 1982 that it would be implementing Article 81 against ten airline undertakings in Member States with regard to certain forms of agreement, although it would prefer the Council to adopt a group of measures under which the rules of competition would be introduced initially to a limited extent only, applying first to fare and capacity agreements between airlines, and then gradually to the full range of agreements between them. The Commission prepared separate reasoned decisions against three leading European airlines under Article 85, requiring them to end agreements on setting fares and sharing route capacity and revenues. This had the desired effect of persuading those airlines to modify their agreements to the extent required by the Commission. In December 1987 the Council adopted a package of measures applying Articles 81 and 82, including two Regulations (3975 and 3976/87), two Directives and a Decision. The collective effect of these was to place some limits on the terms of route- and capacity-sharing agreements between airlines, to enable some new discount fares to be offered, and to authorize the Commission to issue block exemptions for some categories of agreement whose effect on competition is only minor. The minor block exemption is available under Regulation 1617/93 (whose life has been extended by Regulation 1105/2002 until 30 June 2005) covering passenger transit consultations and slot allocations at airports. Other Regulations have been issued dealing with computer reservation systems and ground handling services.

Regulations 3975 and 3976/87 apply only to domestic and international air transport between Community airports, and Article 81 also applies only to such routes, and not to international routes to or from non-Member States. By contrast, under the Merger Regulation 4064/89 the Commission has intervened in a number of proposed mergers involving such routes where it has perceived potentially anti-competitive effects. It is very conscious of the need to extend the scope of its jurisdiction under Article 81 to such important international routes. The Commissioner for Competition therefore introduced proposals in May 1997 under which Regulation 3975/87 would be extended to cover such routes, so that the

Commission could apply Article 81 to them without the need to use the cumbersome and transitional regime of Article 85.

The Commission has however not yet been able to obtain the specific agreement of Member States that Article 81 should apply to international routes to and from the Community; it has however made some progress as a result of the judgment of the ECJ in the *Open Skies*[50] case. Here the Commission had challenged a number of Member States, which had signed bilateral aviation service agreements with the USA, claiming that they had acted in breach of the Treaty. The Court's judgment was partially in favour of the Commission. It accepted its claim that the 'nationality' clauses in the agreements deprived other Community airlines of their Treaty rights not to be discriminated against on the grounds of nationality; it also agreed that in respect of those matters, e.g. airport slots and computer reservation systems, where the Council had authorized the Commission to act for the Community as a whole, Member States no longer retained jurisdiction. But until the adoption of an appropriate resolution by the Council giving jurisdiction over the remaining aspects of international air transport to the Commission, Member States still retained the right to deal with them, subject however to the obligation not to discriminate on grounds of nationality against other Member States. Further negotiations are now in process between the Commission and Member States on these issues.

4.7 MARITIME TRANSPORT

Article 84(2) of the Treaty had provided that it was for the Council to decide whether appropriate provisions should be laid down for sea transport and for some years, as with air transport, the Commission were unsuccessful in introducing any Community legislation where a permanent exemption for sea transport was unacceptable given its importance to the economies of Member States. Nonetheless, some Member States were prepared to argue that the rules of competition did not apply to this sector at all, at least until an appropriate regulation had been adopted by the Council. Originally, the only case that appeared relevant to this issue was that of the *French Merchant Seaman*.[51] This case, which came before the European Court of Justice, had considered whether the French government was in breach of Article 39 prohibiting discrimination based on nationality between workers of individual Member States affecting their rights to employment and conditions of work. The French Code du Travail Maritime had laid down that French merchant ships should be manned by not less than three Frenchmen to each seaman of other nationality. The French government claimed that instructions had been given to the naval authorities to treat other EC nationals as if they were French, but that such instruction was a matter for unilateral French discretion rather than Treaty compulsion.

The Court ruled, to the contrary, that as the Treaty was in principle applicable to the whole range of economic activities; these Treaty rules could be rendered inapplicable only as a result of an express clause in the Treaty to that effect. The Court also said that the reference to the 'objectives' of the Treaty in Article 70 meant those set out in Articles 2 and 3. So far as air and sea transport was concerned, both remained subject to the general rules of the Treaty

---

[50] *Commission v. UK, Germany, and others.* Cases C-466, 476/98 [2003] 1CMLR 143, 217.
[51] *Commission v. France* Case 167/73 [1974] ECR 359: 2 CMLR 216.

until the provision of a transport policy under Article 80(2); in the interim period, the other Treaty provisions continued to apply, unless an express exception was granted, including the principle of freedom of movement for workers contained in Article 39. The Court therefore ruled that the French legislation was discriminatory against foreign seamen in breach of this Article.

The Council eventually adopted the detailed Regulation 4056/86, applying to regular international maritime transport services from or to a Community port, but not to tramp vessel services. It included both procedural rules under which the Commission could carry out its duties under Articles 81 and 82, with powers largely equivalent to those conferred upon it under Regulation 17, and special substantive provisions applicable to liner conferences. These provisions included block exemptions for certain categories of agreement (notably those laying down technical standards and coordinating timetables, the frequency of sailing, and carrying capacity) provided that safeguards of publicity, non-discrimination in rates and Commission supervisory rights were observed. A further block exemption, Regulation 870/95, was later adopted for a five-year period, to exempt liner shipping consortia. Such consortia are agreements between shipping companies which relate to co-operation in a technical and operational area, applicable to regular international cargo services principally by container to or from Community ports. The fixing of prices or rates however is not protected by the Regulation. It has now been succeeded by a new Regulation 823/2000, introducing some changes to its operation.

It will become clear from later chapters of this book that the provisions of the block exemption for the sea transport sector does not provide any exemption for shipping lines or liner conferences (association of shipping lines on a particular route) from Articles 81 or 82. In fact the very existence of the block exemption has appeared to provide some incentive to Members of liner conferences (as evidenced by a number of cases) to build a web of anti-competitive practices around the limited technical exemption which Regulation 4056/86 provides. The practices condemned in subsequent cases brought by the Commission have included attempts to fix prices for the entire door-to-door conveyance of containers (whereas the Regulation provides an exemption only for the sea portion of the journey) and a variety of other practices designed deliberately to exclude competitors from particular routes, through the introduction of 'fighting ships' subsidized by members of the liner conferences and by the provision of quotas upon which given routes were shared between members of that conference (see Chapter 9 pp.149–51 for a description of recent cases in this sector).

4.8 ROAD AND RAIL TRANSPORT AND INLAND WATERWAYS

This was the first of the transport sectors to receive its own specialized Regulation 1017/68 which confirmed that Articles 81 and 82 were to apply to undertakings dealing with road, rail and inland waterway traffic, with the following qualifications:

(a) Article 5 provided for a declaration of non-applicability (equivalent to that contained in Article 81(3)) for agreements which furthered technical and economic progress or improved the quality of transport services, or promoted greater continuity and stability in satisfaction of transport needs in those markets, where supply and demand fluctuated widely.

(*b*) Article 3 exempted agreements for standardization of equipment or other technical matters, including the coordination of timetables and routes, and organization of combined transport operations.

(*c*) Article 4 provided special exemptions for small and medium-sized undertakings subject to some maximum carrying capacities (10,000 metric tons for road transport, 500,000 metric tons for inland waterways). The exemption would not apply if effects were found by the Commission to be incompatible with the requirements of Article 5 and to constitute an abuse of the exemption.

(*d*) The Commission might also provide specific exemption if there were disturbances amounting to 'a state of crisis' in a transport market; even here no special exemption could be given unless the restriction imposed was indispensable to reduce these disturbances and did not make it possible for competition to be eliminated for a substantial part of the market concerned.

As a result of this Regulation, Articles 81 and 82 apply only marginally less to the field of road, rail, and inland waterways than to industry in general, though the Commission must be careful to proceed under the appropriate Regulation if challenging agreements claimed to be restrictive of competition. This was confirmed in *Commission* v. *UIC* (European Court 1997).[52] UIC was an international association of national railway organizations which had laid down rules about selling tickets for international journeys. These included a ten per cent standard-rate commission on ticket sales, an obligation on agents to sell tickets only at the official rate, and other restrictions on the activities of travel agents engaged in the sale of these tickets. After the Commission had imposed a fine in respect of this agreement under Article 81, UIC appealed successfully to the Court of First Instance (whose decision was upheld by the European Court) claiming that the Commission should have proceeded, not under Article 81, but under Regulation 1017/68. The Court of First Instance had stressed that the key criterion for deciding whether 1017/68 applied was whether the agreement had the object or effect of fixing transport rates or limiting the control of the supply of transport; this does not necessarily mean that all activities related to rail transport would necessarily fall outside Article 81. Articles 81 and 82 have indeed been applied to a number of important agreements, including joint ventures for major trans-European networks and key transport links such as the gas inter-connector pipeline across the North Sea, and other major rail and road projects. The Court of Justice has for example applied the Regulation to prevent the application in France of a levy on barge operators which effectively discriminated against non-French operators.[53]

There have also been more recently leading cases in this sector notable among which has been the *European Night Services*[54] case in which the Commission's grant of individual exemption to a proposal to provide night sleeper services through the Channel Tunnel between the United Kingdom and Europe was quashed by the Court of First Instance on grounds that its effects on restriction of competition were insufficient to breach Article 81.

---

[52] Case C-264/95P [1997] 5 CMLR 49.
[53] *ANTIB* v. *Commission* Case 272/85 [1987] ECR 2201: [1988] 4 CMLR 677.
[54] See fn. 15.

8

ARTICLE 81(3): CONDITIONS FOR EXEMPTION

1. THE ROLE OF THE COMMISSION

1.1 INTRODUCTION

The main task of the Commission in the area of competition policy has been to apply and enforce the two balanced paragraphs 81(1) and 81(3), the former setting out the prohibition, and the latter limiting its application. They are linked by the provision in paragraph (2) setting out the legal consequences of the applicability of the Article to a specific agreement, if the relief given by paragraph (3) is unavailable. The effect of this sanction of voidness in paragraph (2) is considered at the end of this chapter. Before we reach it, however, it is necessary to understand how the Commission goes about the task of applying this Article and in particular how it has operated the exempting provisions of Article 81(3).

The main features of the exemption process have been as follows:

— The Commission has always had the monopoly over its exercise in individual cases,[1] under the provisions of Regulation 17/62, Article 9(1).

— In practice the Commission has only granted a few formal exemptions each year, dealing with most requests through a system of 'comfort letters'.

— Of more practical importance in most cases than the grant of individual exemptions have been the legislative provisions under which Council and Commission have promulgated block exemptions which apply to particular categories of agreements.

— These relate primarily to vertical agreements, such as exclusive distribution and purchasing arrangements and other forms of distribution and to technology transfer licences.

— A few deal with horizontal agreements, including research and development and specialization agreements.

The Commission exercises its powers through a number of Directorates-General,[2] which in turn are divided into directorates. Each Directorate-General has, under Article 211 and subsequent regulations made by the Council, some policy-making functions. In some areas,

---

[1] The removal of this monopoly and of the requirement of notification are of course the main elements in the modernization programme to take effect from 1 May 2004.

[2] Normally abbreviated to DG both orally and in writing.

e.g. the harmonization of corporate and tax laws of Member States or environmental pollution control within the Community, little can be achieved by an individual Directorate-General without active support on issues of policy from the Council of Ministers and increasingly the European Parliament. This is so even if all twenty Commissioners are supportive of the proposals put forward. This means that the staff of a directorate within a Directorate-General may consult widely and work up proposals over a long period, only to find that their draft suggestions (negotiated in detail over many months with individual Member States and relevant organizations) are ultimately ignored or rejected or, at the least, postponed because of political difficulties arising at the Council or at the Parliament.

It is notable that DG Comp, as the Directorate-General responsible for competition matters, has managed to avoid some, if not all, of this frustration and in many respects operates differently from other DGs. The reason is mainly that, through Council Regulation 17/62, it obtained early a procedural statute delegating considerable powers from the Council to the Commission itself, including complete monopoly over the grant of individual exemption to agreements under Article 81(3). The Commission normally[3] acts on the advice and recommendation of the Commissioner having special responsibility for competition. He in turn will normally be guided by the advice of his officials, thoroughly discussed in advance with the Commissioner's 'cabinet', the group of individual officials operating as his private office, and having been the subject of prior consideration by the Advisory Committee, which comprises official representatives of Member States entitled to comment both on proposed individual decisions and on proposed Community legislation on competition issues.[4]

So far as competition issues are concerned, the Council will now normally become involved only if new legislation is needed for which authority has not already been given to the Commission.[5] In general, therefore, the Commission conducts its regular decision-making function without political intervention. All decisions taken by the Commission are, however, subject to a right of review for interested parties under Article 230 of the Treaty and in respect of alleged failure by the Commission to act under Article 232. Article 230 may be invoked by any person challenging a procedural or substantive error by the Commission, including a failure to provide economic analysis into the factual background to any decision, and may lead to that decision being quashed on one of the following grounds:

(*a*) lack of competence (or authority);

(*b*) infringement of an essential procedural requirement;

(*c*) infringement of the terms of the Treaty (or any rule of law relating to its application); or

(*d*) misuse of powers.[6]

---

[3] Though there have been some cases of concentrations under the Merger Regulation 4064/89 where the Commissioners have not accepted the original draft decision of DG Comp.

[4] Under the terms of Art. 10(3) of Reg. 17.

[5] For example in adopting the Merger Regulation 4064/89 after many years of negotiation.

[6] This phrase represents the expression *détournement de pouvoir* used in French constitutional and administrative law.

1.2 THE ORGANIZATION OF DG COMP

DG Comp, acting on behalf of the Commission in the application and enforcement of Articles 81 and 82, has functions which can conveniently be divided into administrative, legislative, and decision-making. The administrative function includes both the investigation process and all areas of executive control, including the recording and review of notifications, and the correspondence, meetings, and negotiations necessarily involved with undertakings involved in notifications or complaints which may lead to the preparation of a draft decision. DG Comp is divided into eight operating divisions under the Director General and his staff:

— Directorate A is responsible for general competition policy internal affairs and relationships with other institutions and for co-ordinating the work of the various directorates.

– Directorate B comprises the Merger Task Force whose responsibility is the operation of the Merger Regulation, discussed in detail in Chapters 18 and 19.

Directorates C–F deal with particular sectors:

— Directorate C deals with information, communication, and multimedia.

— Directorate D deals with services including financial services, transport, and distributive trades.

— Directorate E deals with basic industries such as steel, construction, chemicals, and energy, and cartels generally.

— Directorate F deals with capital and consumer goods industries such as mechanical and electrical engineering, motor vehicles, food, pharmaceutical products, textiles, and other consumer goods.

— Directorates G and H deal with State Aids.

The whole staff of DG Comp operates from its headquarters in rue Joseph II in the heart of Brussels. Its current organizational structures are likely to be the subject of considerable change, in connection with the radical reforms taking effect from 2004.[7]

2. BLOCK EXEMPTIONS

2.1 MAJOR CURRENT EXAMPLES

These have increased in both number and importance over the years, and are made either by the Council under the authority of Article 83 or by the Commission under delegated authority from by the Council. The principal substantive Regulations adopted as block exemptions by the Council and still in force include:

---

[7] Including the enlargement of the Community to include new Member States, the Merger Regulation reforms, and the modernization programme.

Reg. No.	Year	Subject Matter
26	1962	Application of competition rules to the agriculture sector
141 & 1017	1962	Application of competition rules to road, rail, and inland
	1968	waterways sectors
4056	1982	A block exemption for maritime transport
3975 & 3976	1987	Application of competition rules and powers to publish block exemptions for air transport (certain aspects only)

Regulations made by the Commission providing block exemptions are more numerous; the principal ones in force are as follows:

Reg. No.	Year	Subject Matter
1617	1993	Agreements for air services
240	1996	Transfer of technology agreements
2790	1999	Vertical restrictions in distribution agreements (goods and services)
823	2000	Liner shipping agreements for maritime transport
2658	2000	Specialization agreements
2659	2000	Research and development agreements
1400	2002	Motor vehicle distribution agreements
358	2003	Insurance agreements

The Commission has also made a number of Regulations dealing with procedural matters such as notification of agreements, completion of the relevant forms of notification, and timetables.

2.2 THE PREPARATION OF BLOCK EXEMPTIONS

Finalizing the terms of any regulation is a lengthy process. It involves a great deal of consultation with interested parties including the authorities of all Member States (through the Advisory Committee) and relevant commercial and industrial interests. If the Regulation is to be made by the Council, it is originally drafted by the staff of DG Comp (with specialist advice from the Legal Service of the Commission) who themselves consult widely with Member States and other interested bodies before sending a draft to the Commissioner. Once the Commissioner has given his approval, it reaches the agenda of the full Commission and once approved goes on to the Council. As we have seen when discussing Regulation 17, the draft then goes from the Council for approval by the European Parliament, who return it with their comments for reconsideration by the Commission. Though the Commission is not legally bound to accept comments or suggestions made by these other bodies, it normally pays close attention to them, and the final draft sent forward to the Council for approval will normally be in a revised form.[8]

On the other hand, if the Regulation is to be made by the Commission under delegated powers, it does not go to the Council but to the Advisory Committee of representatives of

---

[8] This is a simplified account of the normal legislative process. For a fuller account see Hartley, *The Foundations of European Community Law*, 4th edn. (Oxford University Press, 1998) pp.37–48.

Member States as established under Article 10 of Regulation 17, usually both before and after its publication in the Official Journal. The Economic and Social Committee and the European Parliament are also shown the draft on a consultative basis. It is important for DG Comp to obtain approval from the Advisory Committee for any draft regulation it puts forward, because when it later comes before the Commission it can be shown to confirm that the national interests of individual Member States have been taken into consideration.[9]

Both Council and Commission members are aware that the adoption of a new block exemption or the revision of an existing one is a protracted process, involving the need to establish consensus with the many interests concerned. Sufficient interest has to be paid to the preferences, susceptibilities, and suspicions of individual Member States. Moreover, commercial, industrial, and professional interests must also be sought and the benefit of their experience gained. Obtaining agreement on the form of the block exemption can be a laborious process; the rules must not only meet the policy needs of the Commission but also comply with the requirements of the many interested regional, national, and sectoral pressure groups which have a voice in the process. The introduction of the block exemption on transfer technology (240/96) showed the importance which the Commission places on gaining the assent of these interest groups, particularly in respect of the more technical block exemptions. The final version of this exemption showed many and important differences from earlier drafts, as the description of its legislative process records.[10]

2.3 THE FORM OF BLOCK EXEMPTIONS

Block exemptions once had a clearly recognizable form. After extensive recitals setting out the policy considerations which led to the introduction of the measure, there followed a statement of the basic scope of the exemption. Next would come a list of restrictions permitted to be included in the exempted agreements (popularly called 'the white list'),[11] matched immediately afterwards by a list of those restrictions whose inclusion would prevent the block exemption from applying ('the black list'). Some but not all block exemptions also contained a provision for 'opposition'. This means that the parties to the agreement might put forward clauses restraining competition which are found in neither the 'white' nor the 'black list', and which therefore might be described as 'grey'. Since the enactment of Regulation 2790/99 however the normal form of a block exemption no longer includes a 'white list' nor an opposition procedure. They do still contain a 'black list' of clauses whose inclusion will either totally prevent the block exemption from applying, or would at least be themselves void (even if the validity of the rest of the agreement is unaffected).[12] They are likely also to include a wider provision for the withdrawal of the block exemption from particular agreements, if either the Commission or even individual Member States believe that the exemption is no longer appropriate. It is also now more likely that a condition precedent for undertaking seeking to benefit from the block exemption is that their market

---

[9] The recitals to Reg. 19/65 refer specifically to the need for the Commission to prepare its block exemption regulations in close and constant liaison with the competent authorities of Member States.

[10] See Ch. 12, pp.233–4.

[11] The number of clauses contained in the 'white lists' grew substantially in the block exemptions, up to and including the transfer of technology block exemptions (240/96).

[12] Note, e.g. the difference in treatment of 'black' clauses listed respectively under Arts 4 and 5 of Reg. 2790/99.

share for the relevant market does not exceed a given percentage, normally in the range of between 20–30 per cent, though this will vary between different block exemptions.

It is normal for all block exemptions to be subject to certain general conditions which continue to apply throughout their life. These conditions normally relate to the free movement of goods between Member States and the continuing existence of competition to those goods protected by the exemption. For example, in the case of exclusive distribution agreements the exemption can in principle be withdrawn if the exclusive distributor, without objectively valid reasons, refuses to supply within his contract territory certain categories of purchaser who are unable to obtain the goods elsewhere. If any of these conditions are not satisfied, the Commission has the right to withdraw the benefit of the block exemption from an individual agreement. To do so, it must go through the normal procedure laid down by Regulation 17 for making any decision, and in practice the Commission has scarcely used this 'safety-valve' power.[13]

It should also be noted that block exemptions must have a time limit. This is normally for ten years, or at most fifteen.[14] Review occurs as the expiration date approaches, and changes to the terms of the regulation are normally proposed. The experience of its operation may in some cases lead to pressure for change or even, in extreme cases, for non-renewal of the regulation as a whole. If the Commission has difficulty in completing its consultation, negotiation, and drafting process before the date on which the Regulation should expire, an extension of one or even two years is often given to the existing Regulation. An example was the extension of both the Exclusive Distribution and Exclusive Purchasing block exemptions (Nos 1983 and 1984 of 1983) from the end of 1997 to the end of 1999,[15] pending the implementation of Regulation 2790/99 from the start of 2000.

One final point should be made about block exemptions. They are not interpreted with the same liberality as Article 81. The European Court has made it very clear that it expects them to be interpreted strictly and, unless a particular agreement complies exactly with the precise terms of the relevant legislation, it cannot have the benefit which that legislation provides. This was established in *Delimitis*:[16] concerning an exclusive purchasing arrangement between a brewery and a cafe owner, where the principle of strict interpretation was laid down.

3. INDIVIDUAL APPLICATION FOR EXEMPTION UNDER ARTICLE 81(3): THE FOUR CONDITIONS

3.1 THE COMMISSION'S GENERAL APPROACH

One of the chief administrative functions of DG Comp has been to deal with notifications of individual agreements. From the adoption of Regulation 17/62 the Commission has held the monopoly of granting such individual exemptions under Article 9(1). Under the

---

[13] A rare example of its use occurred in the *Langnese and Schöller* cases [1994] 4 CMLR 51, a Commission decision varied slightly on appeal by the Court of First Instance: Cases T-7 and 9/93 [1995] ECR II-1533, 1611: 5 CMLR 602.

[14] In exceptional cases longer periods have been allowed, though often with special conditions: see Ch. 4, fn. 11.

[15] By Reg. 1582/97.   [16] See Ch. 10, p.183 for a full account of this case.

modernization proposals which are planned to take effect from the start of 2004 which are discussed in detail in Chapters 20 and 21 and Part III, responsibility for applying Article 81 as a whole will be shared by the Commission with national courts and with national competition authorities which previously had legal power to apply only Article 81(1) and not 81(3). Moreover, the mechanism of individual notification of agreements containing clauses that may be in breach of Article 81(1), and the requesting in the alternative of negative clearance or individual exemption for them, will no longer operate. It is nevertheless essential to understand how the system of notification of agreements has been operated for so many years and the reasons why it is now being brought to an end.

The basic framework of Regulation 17/62 has already been described in Chapter 4; it gave the Commission extensive powers to carry out its responsibilities under both Article 81 and 82, in particular under Article 11 to send out requests for information to Member States and to authorities and to commercial undertakings of all kinds, and by Article 14 to carry out 'dawn raids' at the premises of undertakings. In addition Article 12 gave the Commission powers to carry out general enquiries into any economic sector where it believed that competition was being restricted; the powers under this last Article had been little used for many years though there had been signs in recent times that the Commission is now at last more willing to make such enquiries[17] (for which purpose it has also its existing powers under Article 11 and 14).

The original intention behind the Regulation was, as we have seen, that notification of all relevant agreements would be made to the Commission by undertakings which had entered into them, and that the granting of an exemption under Article 81(3) could only apply to actually notified agreements (Article 4(1)). The only exception to this principle, set out in Article 4(2) was a very limited list of bilateral agreements, essentially with either the distribution of goods or the licensing of technology. This position however has changed radically with the adoption of Regulation 1216/99 whose effect was to extend Article 4(2) of Regulation 17/62 to all categories of vertical agreements (bilateral or multilateral) concerned with the production or distribution chain and to virtually all bilateral licences for the transfer of technology. This means that all such vertical agreements could be exempted retrospectively back to the date when they were first made (even if prior to the implementation of Regulation 1216/99), rather than simply from the date of notification to the Commission. The effect has been to protect the Commission from possible mass notification of vertical agreements, following the introduction of the new block exemption for vertical agreements 2790/99, and, moreover, prepares the way for the introduction of the new system under modernization which will eliminate the need for notification of any agreement to the Commission.

To understand the way in which DG Comp operates it is essential to realize that the process which it sets in hand usually involves negotiated settlement, such that formal or informal clearance can be given to an agreement or concerted practice after removal of those features which appear unacceptable under the terms of Article 81(1) and 81(3). As the European Court itself put it in the 1984 *Dutch Books*[18] case: 'The purpose of the preliminary administrative procedure is to prepare the way for the Commission's decision on the

---

[17] The 1999 *Annual Report* recorded that a sectoral inquiry had been opened into three areas of telecommunications (leased lines, the 'local loop' and mobile 'roaming' services), paras 74–76.

[18] *VBVB and VBBB v. Commission* Cases 43 and 63/82 [1984] ECR 19, 68: [1981] 1 CMLR 27, 95.

infringement of the rules on competition, but ... also presents the opportunity for the undertakings concerned to adapt the practices at issue to the rules of the Treaty'. Only exceptionally will an agreement, not covered by a block exemption and individually notified, be found either so harmless that it can be approved in its entirety, or so restrictive and anti-competitive that it will have to be rejected by a formal decision to that effect. The majority of agreements notified individually fall between those two extremes and are therefore suitable to form the subject for negotiation.

The range of choices for DG Comp when considering an individual agreement is therefore as follows. First, it may decide that the agreement falls outside Article 81(1) altogether, and thus entitled to what is described in Article 2, Regulation 17/62 as a 'negative clearance'. There may sometimes be insufficient evidence of an agreement or concerted practice between undertakings, or that the relevant trade association made a decision or recommendation; sometimes it is not possible to show a sufficient effect on trade between Member States or on competition within the Common Market. The parties to the agreement may be small and their agreement covered by the *de minimis* rule of the current Notice on Minor Agreements; or they may be covered by one of the other Commission Notices interpreting the application of Article 81(1) to particular types of agreement. If the agreement does fall within the scope of Article 81(1), the next question is whether it is covered by an existing block exemption. If so, its restrictions can be disregarded because Article 81(1) has by that block exemption been determined as inapplicable; indeed there is no need for an agreement falling within that category to be notified at all. Only if it is decided that the agreement is within Article 81(1), but is not covered by the terms of an existing block exemption, will the availability of individual exemption be relevant at least until 18 May 2004.

Regulation 17, Article 9(1) gave DG Comp authority to grant individual exemption, subject to the right of the European Court to review any such decision on appeal under Article 230. Once a procedure had officially been started by the Commission, the jurisdiction of a Member State to pronounce such an agreement, even to be within or without Article 81(1), ceased.

3.2 THE APPLICATION OF THE FOUR CONDITIONS

The first question is whether the agreement is entitled to negative clearance because it falls outside the terms of Article 81(1) for one of the reasons already stated. If not, DG Comp must apply the four conditions in Article 81(3) which are the only criteria for assessing whether exemption can be applied, with or without amendments to the agreement. The conditions for exemption set out in Article 81(3) are essentially four separate conditions. In each case, four separate questions have to be asked and answered: exemption can be available only if the Commission answers 'Yes' to the first pair and 'No' to the second pair. *Positive condition 1* is: 'Does the agreement, decision, or concerted practice improve the production or distribution of goods or promote technical economic progress?' *Positive condition 2* is: 'If so, does it also allow consumers a fair share of the resulting benefit?' *Negative condition 1* is: 'Does the agreement impose restrictions on the undertakings not indispensable to the attainment of the objectives already referred to?' Finally, *negative condition 2* asks: 'Does the agreement afford the undertakings the possibility of eliminating competition in respect of a substantial part of the products?'.

If Article 81 were a United Kingdom statute, we would have to conduct a textual analysis of each of these conditions and examine how they have been applied by the Commission and Community Courts. However, this is not a useful or productive way of understanding how they are dealt with by either the Commission or the Courts. The four conditions are treated more like provisions in a civil code, as broad statements of principle to be read in the context of the remainder of Article 81 and the other Treaty provisions, as well as in the light of the many cases in which they have already been applied. On the other hand, there is no principle of *stare decisis* binding on all subsequent cases. In theory (though not always in practice), the Commission is free to look at each case individually; it will, however, apply well established principles of interpretation, based on the underlying objectives of Article 81 as a whole, to the particular restrictive clauses encountered.

There is some ambivalence in the way in which DG Comp addresses the analysis of individual agreements. Its general approach, which would appear to be required by the terms of Article 81, is to take each condition separately and to consider logically whether an appropriate answer can be given to each of the four questions. Only if the appropriate answer can be given in each case will the question of non-applicability of 81(1) arise. On the other hand, one frequently obtains the impression from the terms of Commission decisions that the positive question 1, and to a lesser extent question 2, demand priority of attention; if a satisfactory answer can be given to those questions from analysis of the factual background, then lesser difficulties will be raised in many cases by negative questions 1 and 2. Again, reports of decisions some-times give the impression that the Commission deliberately chose the phrasing of its answers to the first two questions in order to make it easier to give an appropriate answer to the two following negative questions.

In practice, the Commission first analyses the agreement to see if it is outside the terms of any block exemption and therefore liable to individual notification, and if so whether it contains any of those restrictive clauses which have, as the result of analysis in earlier cases, become almost automatically deemed to lead to the splitting up or segmentation of geographical markets. This may be caused either by a specific clause to that effect between parties in competition with each other, or as the result of export bans contained in vertical agreements, perhaps patent licences or distribution agreements, which prevent the free movement of goods at a lower level of the distribution stage from country to country within the Single Market by way of parallel imports. If any such clause is found in the agreement, then it is unlikely that the requirements of even the first positive question can be satisfied.

Only if no such presumptively illegal clause appears will DG Comp proceed to the next stage of the inquiry, to analyse the main objectives and effects of the agreement, and to carry out the balancing test of whether the anti-competitive restraints are outweighed by the advantages claimed as likely to result from them. In carrying out this process, the four questions may be approached in order. If, after a first review, the agreement does not seem tainted by any restrictions or restraints on competition within it, an attempt is made to save it by removing undesirable features. This process is not a court hearing but a review by an administrative body seeking to apply the provisions of paragraph (3) in a flexible way, in the light of the objectives of the Treaty and the Regulations made under it, also taking into account the considerable case law that now exists as the result of both Court and Commission decisions.

3.3 THE INDIVIDUAL CONDITIONS

Positive Condition 1: 'Which contributes to improving the production or distribution of goods or to promoting technical or economic progress'

Of the four conditions, this is normally considered first and is probably the most important in the eyes of DG Comp. It is essential that the economic benefit is clearly identified, and balanced against the detriment which the various restrictions will or may place on the competitive process. The Commission is required to examine the objective behind the agreements and to use its resources sensibly to establish the relevant facts and circumstances.[19] Nevertheless, though the Commission must be constructive in its approach to the investigation, the burden of proof of all these conditions is upon the parties to the agreement. The 'improvements' or 'progress' may arise either immediately following the production by the undertakings, or at a later date, following processes in which value has been added or distribution has taken place. In other words, the 'improvement' or 'progress' need not be at the same level, e.g. manufacturing, as that in which the parties to the agreement are involved. 'Improvement' can include almost any kind of beneficial alteration to the operation of industry or commerce, including the elimination of barriers to entry, increased output from a given number of inputs, better quality in production, greater speed or quality control in manufacturing output, a greater range of products produced from the same inputs, or the possibility of making a wider range of products on the same plant or range of machine tools. As we saw in early Commission cases, distribution systems likely to improve the service of local markets with their particular features also qualify.

Whilst such improvements are fairly tangible, the assessment of the alternative benefit, 'technical' or 'economic' progress, is a good deal more shadowy. It is an expression familiar in French law, requiring a reasonable conjecture to be made about the likely outcome of an agreement. However, it does not involve a broad social balancing of economic advantages and disadvantages. This was illustrated by *Fedetab* (European Court 1980).[20] This case involved the majority of those engaged in the tobacco trade in Belgium, including manufacturers, wholesalers, and retailers, where Belgian legislation relating to excise tax and price controls made it virtually impossible for undertakings selling cigarettes and tobacco retail to compete with each other on selling prices. Nevertheless, the Commission found, and the Court agreed, that the legislation did not prevent competition entirely, since this was still possible on terms of payment, profit margins for both wholesalers and retailers, and on rebates payable. The rules of Fedetab for classification of wholesalers and retailers into a number of categories, fixing discounts for each category, and laying down in great detail the terms of business between each level of distribution, brought rigidity even to those areas which had been left unaffected by the government regulations. A justification put forward for the restrictive systems involved was that it enabled a very large number (approximately 80,000) of retail outlets to be preserved, and it was argued that this enabled the retailer to offer customers a much larger number of brands of cigarettes and cigars than would otherwise have been the case, as well as improving the freshness of products for the customer. The

---

[19] This was laid down in the early case of *Grundig–Consten*, discussed in Ch. 4. The Commission cannot therefore insist that it can adopt a passive 'wait-and-see' attitude until the parties to the agreement have produced sufficient evidence.

[20] Cases 209–215, 218/78 [1980] ECR 3125, 3278: [1981] 3 CMLR 134, 247.

Commission took the view that if the services which specialized wholesalers and retailers offered were as valuable as the association maintained, customers and retailers would ensure by their buying practices that wholesalers and retailers of this specialized nature survived, and that it was therefore unnecessary for the association to give them more favourable treatment to ensure their survival (especially if there was no guarantee that in return for this special treatment they would actually provide services of the desired standard).

It had been hoped that the European Court would confirm in the *Fedetab* case whether 'social' arguments relating to the protection of small businessmen and shopkeepers in the tobacco trade were relevant considerations properly to be taken into account by the Commission in applying Article 81(3). The Commission obtained no clear answer, because the Court avoided the question. The same question arose in the *Publishers Association* case (European Court 1995)[21] and the tone, if not the precise terms, of the judgment seemed to indicate that social objectives, including the decrease in the number of stockholding book-sellers and book sales, leading to smaller print runs and higher prices, could be taken into account, as they had been in UK proceedings by the Restrictive Practices Court at an earlier date.[22] The European Court also stated that the benefits from the agreement under scrutiny occurred not only in the territories of the parties to the agreement, and could be taken into account even if taking place in other Member States. In *Fedetab*, however the Court was divided and unable to reach a clear-cut decision upon it, though such indications as it gave were that it would not allow such an argument to be adopted under 81(3). Of some significance was the statement that 'the number of intermediaries and brands is not necessarily an essential criterion for approving distribution within the meaning of Article 81(3) which has above all to be judged by its commercial flexibility and capacity to react to stimuli from both manufacturers and consumers'. The Court preferred to decide the case on the fact that restrictions gave the parties the possibility of almost entirely eliminating competition on the Belgian cigarette market, so that there was no need in upholding the Commission's decision to decide whether any of the other three conditions were specifically satisfied.

In recent years the Commission's decisions have indicated a rather more expansive approach to this condition. Thus in *Ford/Volkswagen*[23] the social benefits to be expected from increased employment likely to be generated by the proposed joint venture for the construction of a multipurpose vehicle in Northern Portugal was referred to as a positive element in the favourable exemption decision granted; and the Court of First Instance, in dealing with an appeal by a third party contesting against that exemption decision (*Matra Hachette* v. *Commission*), did not criticize the Commission's approach in this respect.[24] In a number of the 'crisis cartel' cases reviewed at Chapter 9, pp.151–3, the Commission likewise has given weight to agreement which would enable structural changes to take place in an orderly and socially acceptable manner. Environmental issues will also on occasion be taken into account, as is illustrated by the *CECED* and related cases considered in detail in the next section of this chapter.

In conclusion: this condition has generally been given a broad interpretation, extending to a wide variety of situations and responsive to many different types of economic progress and

---

[21] Case 360/92P [1995] ECR I-23: 5 CMLR 33.

[22] For an account of the previous proceedings in the Restrictive Practices Court, see in particular paras 2 to 31 of the ECJ's judgment.

[23] [1993] 5 CMLR 617.   [24] Case T-17/93 [1994] ECR II-595.

technical advance. In particular this condition has recently been generously interpreted in a large number of proposed joint ventures in advanced technological areas, such as telecommunications, computers, and multi-media, and to major transport network proposals within the Community. However, the most radical application, was that in the *Phoenix-Atlas* joint venture decision (see Chapter 19), where an application by the French and German governments for a joint venture in telecommunications on both a domestic and a worldwide basis was exempted only when new conditions were included, which not only changed the terms of the agreement but required liberalization of the French and German telecommunications markets in accordance with the 'Full Competition' Directive of the Commission (96/19) issued under Article 86(3). Environmental benefits are also acknowledged by the Commission in a number of *Annual Reports* as constituting important 'technical and economic progress' for the purposes of this condition.

Positive Condition 2: 'While allowing consumers a fair share of the resulting benefit'

At one time there was considerable debate as to whether it was strictly 'consumers' or 'users' who were entitled to benefit, in the light of the language used in the four original versions of the Treaty. It soon became clear, however, that the word was to be interpreted broadly and would not be limited to final consumers or retail purchasers. The use in the French text of the expression *utilisateurs* was always a cogent indication that the class of 'consumers' was wide enough to cover those who acquired the goods at any stage of the distribution process, whether in order to add value or merely to make use of the product for any purpose. This was later confirmed by the Commission.[25] Again, a broad definition of 'benefit' is taken, not limited to reductions in purchase price, but including any other economic advantage which a consumer may enjoy, such as an increase in the number or quality of outlets from which the goods can be purchased, better guarantee and service facilities, quicker delivery, greater range of goods, or more responsive distribution systems. The agreement need only be capable of producing some or all of these advantages in the course of normal trade; proof it has done so is not required, provided that there is some connection between the agreement and the subsequent 'benefit' to users of the relevant goods or services.

The 'improvement' or 'progress' required must not simply benefit the parties themselves. This is clearly laid down in the case involving exchanges of information between the Dutch Paper Industry Federation (VNP) and its Belgian counterpart (Cobelpa).[26] Nearly all the important manufacturers of stationery were members, accounting for approximately 80 to 90 per cent of domestic output in both countries. The Commission found a clear breach of Article 81(1) and refused exemption under paragraph (3). The extent of the information exchanged between the association and its members was so detailed and so readily identifiable to the transactions of specific companies that it had become more than simply the provision of an information service for a trade association. It had become rather so detailed a source of information as to provide artificial market stability, which in turn eliminated a large number of the competitive risks involved for members of both associations. This was particularly so as the benefit of the information accrued solely to sellers of paper, not to buyers, so that transparency of prices and terms of trading were still absent from one side of the market.

---

[25] In, e.g. *Kabel und Metallwerke Neumeyer/Luchaire* [1975] 2 CMLR D40.

[26] *VNP/Cobelpa* [1977] 2 CMLR D28.

Both associations claimed that their arrangements meant that progress and improvements were available to members of the association, who were able to plan output and investment on a more stable basis because of the information in their possession about future trends in the market and prices being charged by their competitors. The Commission ruled that such benefit could not be taken into account since, to be treated as an improvement or as progress, a benefit must have the potential at least to help third parties, whether the benefit was short-term or one whose results would take longer to become apparent. The fact that the improvement of production or distribution or the promotion of economic or technical progress was only one of the effects of the agreement is not necessarily fatal to an exemption, however, provided that the overall balance of detriment and benefit is sufficiently favourable to have some recognizable value for such third parties.

Negative Condition 1: 'Which does not impose on the undertakings concerned restrictions which are not indispensable to the attainment of these objectives'

The first negative condition deals with the effect of the restrictions on the undertakings. The objectives referred to in the condition are those set out as justification for the exemption under the first positive condition. It is essential for undertakings to show that the individual restrictions, individually and collectively, are tailored strictly to the valid purposes of the agreement, and that subsequent damage to the competitive process does not spill over to wider effect. The concept of necessity is very closely related to the principle of proportionality, familiar as a general principle of law which plays an important part in the jurisprudence of the European Court of Justice.[27] In this more limited context too, proportionality is highly relevant. Often, agreements able to satisfy the two positive conditions fail to clear the hurdle of this condition, sometimes because the effect of the restrictions has not been carefully enough analysed by the parties to the agreement.

A case where the two positive conditions were satisfied, but where the agreement failed on this first negative condition was *Rennet* (European Court 1981).[28] A co-operative at Leeuwaden produced animal rennet and colouring agents for cheese. It accounted for 100 per cent of the Dutch national output of rennet and 90 per cent of colouring agents; of this production, 94 per cent of the rennet and 80 per cent of the colouring agents went to its members, who between them accounted for over 90 per cent of the total output of Dutch dairy products. The members were obliged to purchase all their requirements from the co-operative, and on breach of this obligation were fined heavily. Members who resigned from the co-operative were subject to a financial penalty, calculated on the average quantity of rennet which they had purchased in each of their last five years' membership. Resignation was therefore made extremely expensive, whether its purpose was because the member wanted to obtain supplies from another source, or to produce his own rennet in competition with the co-operative. Although the Commission agreed that the first two conditions were satisfied by the restrictive clauses, which promoted greater efficiency in rennet production within Holland and some benefit in terms of price to purchasers, it considered that the two

---

[27] See Hartley, op. cit. pp.148–9.
[28] *Cöoperative Stremsel-en Kleurselfabriek* v. *Commission* Case 61/80 [1981] ECR 851: [1982] 1 CMLR 240. In other cases involving farmers' co-operatives some restrictions in their rules have been held to fall outside Art. 81(1) altogether. See cases cited at Ch. 7, fn. 48.

negative conditions (including the issue of indispensability) were not satisfied. The economic advantages could be obtained by less sweeping restrictions on the members: for example, an obligation to take a smaller percentage of its requirements, or to give reasonable notice of intention to withdraw, would have been adequate to protect the interests of the co-operative, without the infliction of a large fine. The Commission's decision was upheld by the Court.

Another well-known example is the early *Grundig*[29] case where, although the distribution contract under which Consten was entitled to distribute *Grundig* products on an exclusive basis in France was found likely to lead to an improvement in distribution, the use of trade mark law to ensure absolute territorial protection constituted unnecessarily broad restrictions of competition for the benefit of the distributor. It was felt that Consten could have derived sufficient strength simply from its exclusive appointment, without the additional protection conferred and the attempted use of French unfair competition law to keep out all parallel imports from Germany and other Member States.

In *Bayo-n-ox* (Commission 1990)[30] Bayer had manufactured a growth-promoting product for piglets, which was normally added to their feed. The relevant patents had expired and Bayer was concerned that parallel imports of the product were increasing. It therefore sought to sell it to feed manufacturers subject to the express condition that they should only use it in the preparation of their own mixes, and not sell it on separately. Bayer's claimed justification for this restrictive clause was that it was necessary to prevent the mixing of the products with other products of lower quality, with possible ill effects to the piglets. The Commission refused an individual exemption, pointing out that the restriction was actually so wide as to have prevented feed manufacturers from supplying the product even to reputable undertakings in Germany and elsewhere in Europe, to whom Bayer would have had no reason to refuse direct supplies. The restriction was therefore too widely drawn to allow an individual exemption to be granted, even if Bayer's original objective of limiting parallel imports of the product had been considered valid (itself most unlikely).

A totally different type of agreement was presented to the Commission in *BT/SES/Astra* (Commission 1992).[31] BT had proposed a joint venture with SES, the Luxembourg operator of the Astra satellite, to sell space for programmes on the satellite and to provide an 'up-link' for television programmes produced in the United Knigdom. SES could have approached potential UK customers direct, but under the agreement all marketing was done by BT; BT was not allowed to offer more favourable terms on other satellites at its disposal to those customers who were signed up to Astra. Moreover, SES was prevented by the arrangement from negotiating direct with customers on 'up-link' terms in respect of non-UK territories. The Commission ruled that there was no distinct advantage to the customers from these arrangements to justify the restrictions, as in its view SES could well have provided its 'up-link' service in the United Kingdom without BT's involvement in this manner and the consequent restrictions. By contrast, in *Publishers Association* (European Court 1995)[32] the Commission, and indeed the Court of First Instance, were held by the European Court to have failed to show that a collective system of fixed prices for books was not indispensable, especially as earlier rulings by the Restrictive Practices Court in the United Kingdom had

[29] Cases 56 and 58/64 [1966] ECR 299: CMLR 418.
[30] [1990] 4 CMLR 905.   [31] [1994] 5 CMLR 226.   [32] See fn. 21.

held that such an agreement was indispensable on public interest grounds for the book trade in the United Kingdom.

Negative Condition 2: 'And which do not afford such undertakings the possibility of eliminating competition in respect of a substantial part of the product in question'

This final condition relates to the external effect of the agreement and clearly indicates that, as with the application of Article 81(1), there is a need for market analysis by the Commission on both the product range and the geographic range of that market. In spite of the volume of economic and legal writings on the subject, analysis of markets is far from an exact science,[33] and the Court has made it clear that it will only interfere if the Commission abuses the wide discretion given to it for the purposes of paragraph (3). It is probably primarily the result of this condition (as well as under the first positive condition) that specific market-sharing arrangements between competitors, as well as export bans in vertical arrangements, will fail to obtain exemption because of the priority given rightly by DG Comp to retaining the possibility of parallel imports as a controlling influence upon price levels. Similar considerations apply in respect of dual pricing, under which goods for export are priced at a level different from those for home consumption, since DG Comp normally regards these also as likely to discourage exports.[34]

The Commission looks at the nature of the market involved, which could be the entire Common Market, one or more Member States, or simply a substantial region of a Member State. The absolute size of the enterprises concerned, and their market shares in the relevant product, are then considered; and the structural condition of that market will be taken into account; DG Comp is always interested in knowing whether the market trends are procompetitive or in the opposite direction. It will be necessary to ask whether particular forms of competition exist, possibly in promotion or product innovation, which may be especially damaged by the agreement. The Commission here is normally concerned with interbrand competition; reductions in intrabrand competition, i.e. between rival distributors of the same brand of goods, will not normally weigh heavily so long as there is still reasonable competition between the different brands and the possibility of these brands crossing national boundaries.

It is insufficient for the Commission, however, simply to allege that some degree of competition will be eliminated by the restrictions, in a case where the parties account collectively for a substantial part of the market already. Nor are the terms of this condition intended to be equivalent to a statement that parties to an agreement who collectively could be said to have a dominant position in a market can never satisfy it. This was illustrated by the judgment on the *TACA35*[35] appeal from an adverse decision of the Commission refusing individual exemption to an agreement between a number of shipping companies involved in container transport on the North Atlantic routes. Although these companies had some 75 per cent of the container transport on these routes the Court examined in detail the way in

---

[33] The Commission has published its own Notice on market definition: [1997] OJ C372/5 (9 December 1997). See also Ch. 14, Section 2, and Ch. 17, Sections 6 and 7.

[34] *Distillers v. Commission* Case 30/78 [1980] ECR 2229: [1978] 3 CMLR 121: *Glaxo Wellcome* [2002] 4 CMLR 335.

[35] Case T-395/94 [2002] 4 CMLR 1008, 1091. ('The prohibition on eliminating competition is a narrower concept than that of the existence or acquisition of a dominant position'.)

which the Commission had itself investigated the extent to which there was both actual and potential competition on the route; the Court only found against the TACA on this point because none of the independent shipping companies were shown to have sufficient power on the market to exert 'real pressure' on it.

3.4 THE RULE OF REASON

It is often asked whether the implementation of Article 81(3) by the Commission amounts to the equivalent of the 'rule of reason', for many years applied by Federal Courts in the United States to a wide variety of agreements not covered by the *per se* rule. If the US rule of reason is relevant at all it is (as already explained in Chapter 7) more appropriate to compare it with Article 81(3) than with 81(1). A superficial answer is that the broad effect of the decisions rendered over the years since DG Comp was first established has been similar to that of the case law jurisprudence of these US courts; the restrictions to which Article 81(1) has been applied have been analysed in the context of their particular markets, product and geographic, and in their function and consequences (trivial or weighty) within the framework of the relevant agreement. The Commission, like the United States Courts, has in applying Article 81(3) been aware of the importance of distinguishing between restrictions which are merely ancillary to a legitimate commercial purpose, and those others which provide a measure of relief for the participants from the rigours of competitive struggle.

Nevertheless, at a deeper level, the difference between the two jurisdictions remains pronounced. The US courts may take into account all the positive and negative features of the restraint, as well as the context in which it is applied, remaining as free from statutory restriction as the courts of common law in assessing the real validity of contractual restraints between vendor and purchaser or employer and employee. By comparison, the Commission must operate within a rigid conceptual framework which allows less freedom of manoeuvre and requires the restriction to pass, not one single balancing test, but a cumulative series of four separate tests. Credit obtained by a restraint for passing any particular condition by a considerable margin cannot be taken advantage of at a later stage (at least in theory) if the restraint fails to satisfy a subsequent condition for exemption. There cannot be an 'overall' balancing of debits and credits under the system laid down by Article 81(3). If the consumer does not receive a fair benefit from the improved production or distribution of goods, or if the restrictions appear to outweigh the benefits obtained, even if shared fairly with consumers, then in principle in principle no 'rule of reason' can prevail to exempt the restriction.[36]

3.5 INDIVIDUAL EXEMPTIONS UNDER THE MODERNIZATION PROPOSALS

Under the modernization proposals which are to take effect from May 2004 both the Commission and national courts and national competition authorities will be considering the provisions of Articles 81(1) and 81(3) together rather than having to deal with them separately. This however should not mean that the outcome of the examination of any individual

---

[36] See e.g. the CFI judgment in *TACA* at p.1078 citing in this context the ECJ judgment in *SPO* v. *Commission* Case C-137/95 P [1996] ECR I-1611.

agreement will be different, because the national court or authority will still need to apply each of the four conditions in the way explained above. Failure by the parties to show that they can satisfy each of the cumulative conditions should even under such a new system lead to the same outcome as under the well understood existing arrangements operating for many years under Regulation 17/62. Whether national courts in particular will nevertheless find it difficult to apply the provisions of Article 81(3) to individual agreements is an issue which will be discussed in Chapter 25.

4. THE APPLICATION OF ARTICLE 81(3) IN INDIVIDUAL CASES: SOME EXAMPLES

4.1 IN MULTIPARTY AGREEMENTS

To understand how the Commission and Community Courts had interpreted these conditions it is useful to consider the application of Article 81(3) in a number of different individual cases, in some of which exemption was granted, some refused or subject to onerous conditions. A straightforward example of an agreement which failed to satisfy any of the four conditions was *Floral Sales*[37] (Commission 1980); here, exemption was refused to an agreement between the three leading French manufacturers of fertilizer who co-operated to form a German subsidiary company to carry out their export to Germany of compound fertilizer. Although these three French undertakings sold to their German subsidiary at varying prices, the product was resold in Germany at a uniform price and on uniform terms and conditions.

The parties argued that the formation of the joint sales subsidiary was necessary to improve the efficiency of their export sales, but it was not an argument accepted by the Commission. They were the largest producers of these fertilizers in France, with excess production capacity, and as the market in France was itself oligopolistic the effect of their joining together was an appreciable limitation of competition *inter se*. The joint selling arrangements had not only no compelling commercial justification, but also no beneficial effects on either production or distribution to offset the competitive disadvantages. Use could have been made of the normal wholesale and retail distribution facilities provided for the sale of the straight compound nitrogenous fertilizers which they sold, and no reduction in buying price resulted for customers in Germany which could be regarded as a consequent benefit to 'consumers'.

Clearly, the market strength and share of these companies weighed heavily against them; the case may therefore be contrasted with the weak market position and small size of the companies involved in *Transocean Marine Paint*[38] often cited as a good example of the flexible use of Article 81(3) in allowing joint sales arrangements between small companies with a weak market position, even where these amount to a horizontal market-sharing agreement. However, the restrictions imposed must be the minimum essential for carrying out effective marketing, and only for products where there are technical reasons for allowing

---

[37] *Floral Düngemittelverkaufs* [1980] 2 CMLR 285.
[38] *Transocean Marine Paint Association v. Commission* Case 17/74 [1974] ECR 1063: 2 CMLR 459. See also Ch. 4, n. 5.

allocation of territories, as in the case of *Transocean Marine Paint*, when customers would be travelling from port to port and would need a range of standard quality paints available at a number of ports of call. The Commission in that case accepted that such an arrangement would not be possible for small companies without this kind of market-sharing agreement. On renewal of an individual exemption, however, restrictions exempted on an earlier occasion may be considered to have become unnecessary for the achievement of the original objectives of the agreement.

The approach of the Commission to the application of these four conditions can be further illustrated by a unique and complex example, the 1983 decision relating to the Energy Programme of the International Energy Authority (IEA).[39] The OECD had established a separate agency known as the International Energy Authority which carried out this International Energy Programme. Its objectives were to take common measures effective to meet any oil supply emergency by providing a plan for self-sufficiency that would restrain demand and allocate available oil on an equitable basis between the members. It was agreed that, since each country's supply position was slightly different, any crisis leading to shortages would affect them differently. Some would have a large refining capacity and would normally import mainly crude oil, whilst others would normally import only refined products. Some countries would have oil provided from only one source, others from many, and others again might be largely self-sufficient, having their own production. Supply rights were established by IEA for each country; in the event of disruption in any part of the world the rights of each country would be compared with the overall supplies available in the world. If it was determined that the country had more than its equitable share, it would be deemed to have an 'allocation obligation', if less, an 'allocation right'. Those with allocation obligations would yield up excess supplies to those with allocation rights.

To make this system function, an International Advisory Board (IAB) had to be established from the oil industry to assist the IEA in providing effective emergency measures. On the IAB were represented sixteen oil companies and two oil company trade associations; altogether forty-six oil companies were reporting regular information relating to imports, exports, levels of production, refining, etc. to both the IEA and national governments during any crisis period. Other non-reporting companies were also asked to submit data to their national governments, who would then pass the aggregated information on to the IEA.

A group of expert oil company employees coordinated these arrangements on a monthly cycle in the event of a crisis. Transactions were placed in three categories. Type 1 was a voluntary rearrangement of supply between a reporting and a non-reporting company. A type 2 transaction was the rearrangement of supplies by reporting companies in response to a specific request from the IEA. It could be effected either by special arrangements between two companies or by the company receiving the request making an open offer to provide supplies capable of acceptance by any company having an allocation right. Type 3, the rarest transaction, was required to supplement the voluntary system, if the situation was sufficiently serious that participating countries had to meet and discuss further allocations, if and only if type 1 and type 2 arrangements could not meet the deficit.

---

[39] [1984] 2 CMLR 186. The members of the IEA were the then twenty-one members of OECD, including all the Member States of the Community other than France. The Community itself had observer status at the IEA. The exemption was renewed for a further ten years in February 1994: [1994] 4 CMLR 506.

These arrangements came into force only when the overall shortfall to all countries within the plan was at least 7 per cent; when this level of supply was reached again, the allocation process ceased. Nevertheless, members of the oil industry, because of their knowledge of the market, were involved in the scheme before it was activated and remained involved after it had been laid to rest. It was clear that the International Energy Programme could not operate satisfactorily without the assistance of the oil companies in carrying out the emergency oil allocation system. The oil companies' agreement to participate in the system was at least a concerted practice, if not an agreement *stricto sensu*, even though the rules had been laid down by the IEA on an inter-governmental basis. The involvement of the major oil companies had a specific objective, namely the redistribution of oil products that would enable the allocation rights and obligations to be met and ensure that no company and no country was unfairly treated. To achieve this result, extensive information would be needed as to sources of oil, both in general and as to particular cargoes, with supporting detail on its quality, the location of tankers, refinery capacity, and storage capacity. This exchange of information would inevitably provide company representatives with much data from their rivals which would normally have remained confidential.

Clearly, such concerted practices could have had the effect of distorting competition. Oil under type 2 and 3 arrangements would be sent to destinations it would not have gone to in a free market, and the sharing of information with many companies who would not normally know it might cause oil companies to behave otherwise than would have been the case if the scheme had not existed. If fully implemented, an International Energy Programme would probably involve redistribution of about 10 to 15 million tonnes of oil every month out of a total monthly supply to IEA members of approximately 120 million tonnes.

Not surprisingly, many of the oil companies, notably those from the United States, were unwilling to participate in such arrangements unless a specific clearance under Article 81(3) was obtained. The oil industry has a long history of cartel arrangements, and the size and power of many of the participants in the industry was substantial by any standard. Nevertheless, after complex negotiations an exemption was granted by DG Comp. It was tailored as carefully as possible to the precise needs of the International Energy Programme. Some of the conditions imposed to ensure that the agreement did not contain any unnecessary broad restraints were the following:

(*a*) The programme did not apply to any exchange of price information except in so far as it was absolutely necessary for negotiating a specific bilateral transaction, e.g. the price of a single cargo available in a tanker at a particular port on a particular date. More general price information could not be exchanged.

(*b*) These arrangements could only be put into effect while the emergency oil allocation system was operating, except that consultation was allowed in preparation for the commencement of an actual allocation period. Test runs to ensure the efficiency of the system could also be dealt with on this basis.

(*c*) To ensure that discussions on oil prices and other sensitive commercial information did not stray beyond the permitted limits, the Commission was itself entitled to attend meetings of the International Advisory Board and to be shown copies of relevant documentation.

With these restrictions a decision was ultimately issued that the requirements of Article

81(3) were satisfied. The concerted practices were said to contribute to improving oil distribution throughout Western Europe, and thereby promoting economic progress and substantially reducing the inconvenience (possibly even major economic distress) that would be caused if supplies to any one participating country were substantially interfered with. Consumers would benefit because they knew that their own country would receive proportionately equal supplies in any such crisis, and the agreement would minimize the impact of shortages on the general economy of each country involved. Great care had been taken to ensure that the restrictions imposed were limited to those indispensable to the scheme, and that competition in respect of 90 per cent of oil supplies would remain on the same basis as before. In fact, with the majority of type 1 and type 2 transactions the companies themselves would still establish the commercial terms for supply of the product. The negotiation of this agreement represents a considerable achievement for the Commission and the other participants. To adjust an agreement of such importance to the members of OECD within the 'four conditions' without either compromising the integrity of those conditions or imposing impossible requirements upon the oil companies and governments participating was no small task.

However, it would be wrong to assume from the IEA case that the Commission's interpretation of paragraph (3) is such that any programme of mutual assistance will be upheld. In *Rheinzink*[40] (European Court 1984) a reciprocal supply agreement between three large suppliers of rolled zinc was not given an exemption. The arrangement was that if the companies suffered disruption which caused a loss of supply of 20 tonnes per day, or a total of 200 tonnes, each of the other parties would make good the shortfall up to a total of 1,500 tonnes so long as its own production was not disrupted. This agreement would be for a contract year and automatically renewed for another year.

The Court in assessing the arrangements concluded that the agreement would deprive the parties of their independence of action, their ability to adapt individually to circumstances, and the possibility of benefiting by increasing direct sales to customers, from production stoppages or reductions in output sustained by other undertakings. The contract could also compel the parties to supply each other with considerable tonnages.

The Court concluded that a contract of such general scope and of such long duration 'institutionalizes mutual aid in place of competition and was likely to prevent any change in the respective market position'.[41] However, it indicated that it would not necessarily have disallowed a mutual supply agreement applicable simply to cases of *force majeure*, that is, loss of supplies directly attributable to an external natural disaster or act outside the control of the parties. Here it was fearful that the agreement in question could be implemented otherwise than in the limited circumstances which the parties claimed to have envisaged.

It is in this perhaps that the agreement differs from the *IEA* case, even though the extent of assistance to be provided in the latter case was also substantial. Nevertheless, some points of difference can be seen. First, the involvement of national governments in the *IEA* case made it unlikely that the agreement could be used as a cover for market-sharing arrangements wider than those specifically referred to in the actual agreement. Second, the threshold of a 7 per cent reduction in supplies before the crisis arrangement came into force meant

---

[40] *Compagnie Royal Austurienne des Mines and Rheinzink v. Commission* Cases 29 and 30/83 [1984] ECR 1679: [1981] 1 CMLR 688.

[41] Para. 33 of the Court's decision.

that circumstances had to be at least moderately critical before the co-operation arrangements were triggered. Finally, the external factors causing the intervention were more clearly defined in the IEA case, as being an interruption of supplies in circumstances falling normally within the *force majeure* situation.

4.2 IN INSURANCE CASES

In agreements relating to services the Commission has to go through precisely the same analytical process as with those relating to goods. This is illustrated by the *Concordato Italiano*[42] case. This involved an agreement between twenty-eight Italian insurance companies setting up a non-profit association in order to coordinate some aspects of their activities in the industrial fire insurance sector, which controlled about 50 per cent of the Italian industrial fire insurance market. Originally members who did not use a standard form of agreement had to notify the association, but this obligation was removed at the request of the Commission. The association's responsibilities include the definition of various key terms relevant to the policy, the preparation of relevant statistics required for the calculation of premiums, the updating of the required premium rates in the light of the risks shown, and a study of preventive measures to reduce risks. Membership of the association was open to all insurance undertakings in Italy, initially for a term of two years.

The Commission had no difficulty in concluding that the agreement fell within Article 81(1); its effect would undoubtedly be to limit competition between members, which would tend to standardize premiums, and in general to use the recommended terms and conditions. There would be an effect on trade between Member States because of the existence of foreign insurers operating in these markets in Italy, as well as the fact that some of the property insured by members of the association would be owned by undertakings outside Italy. In reviewing the application of the four conditions the Commission stated that the acquisition of specialized knowledge by the association was a means of improving the services provided, and that the statistical and other assistance which the association could provide could make it easier for new entry to the market to quote sensible premiums for industrial fire cover. Consumers would therefore have a wider choice of insurance cover. The existence of standard conditions would also make it easier for them to compare the policies offered by different insurers, both in terms of extent of cover and premium paid. No part of the agreement permitted the different insurance companies to agree the final premium to be quoted to potential customers.

The Commission took the view that the restrictions on competition contained in the agreement were indispensable to the attainment of the association's objectives. Only by establishing certain common practices with regard to the premiums and conditions would the insurers and their clients have a proper basis for evaluating the quality of management and of service offered by the individual companies. This should lead to higher standards within the fire insurance industry in Italy. The Commission did not feel that the agreement would afford the members the possibility of eliminating competition for a substantial part of the services. Members were free to fix their own premium rates and could vary the terms

---

[42] [1991] 4 CMLR 199. The facts were different in *Verband des Sachversicheres* v. *Commission* Case 45/81 [1987] ECR 405: [1988] 4 CMLR 264, where recommendations on actual percentage increases were made to association members.

of the standard policies to suit particular cases. In addition a number of powerful insurance companies outside the agreement were in active competition with members of the association. Exemption for a period of ten years from the date of notification was therefore granted.

Another example of the application of Article 81(3) to the insurance sector was the renewal by the Commission in 1999 of the earlier exemption granted to *P & I Clubs*.[43] Mutual non-profit making insurers offered pooled cover on a worldwide basis to ship owners for a wide variety of risks. Shipowners join individual clubs which belong to the International Group, whose rules allocate the basis upon which claims would be met. At certain levels the claims were shared equally between the clubs whilst claims at a higher level were shared according to the percentage of each club in claims, tonnage, and total calls. At higher levels still reinsurance cover was applicable. Some amendments to the rules were made by the Commission in view of complaints that the minimum cover required by the clubs to be taken out by each member was too high. Moreover, the exemption granted by the Commission can be withdrawn if the members of the International Group collectively come to hold a market share larger than twice the minimum scale economically required to provide the level of cover agreed to at the time with that Group.

4.3 IN TELEVISION RIGHTS CASES

The saga of the European Broadcasting Union (EBU) rules[44] illustrates the application of the four conditions in a complex and multilateral context. In 1993 the Commission had granted the EBU an individual exemption for five years for its Eurovision rules for sports broadcasting. At the time of the decision EBU had sixty-seven members from forty-seven countries, mainly public sector broadcasters, and a few private companies. Only from 1988 had its membership criteria included a requirement that the member provide a broadcasting service of 'national character and national importance'. Their members agreed that through Eurovision they would share on an exclusive basis major sports and other programmes, though limited contractual access would be given to non-members of the Union. Screensport, a television company, was refused access to these programmes and complained to the Commission of non-admission to membership as well as the refusal to license these programmes unless exemption had been given from the rule. The Commission in reaching this decision had apparently used as its main criterion the question of whether the EBU was fulfilling a particular 'public mission' within the concept of Article 86(2), but had failed sufficiently to examine other relevant aspects of the case. These included whether the exclusivity required under its rules was indispensable to allow members a fair return on their investment, and whether it was possible to introduce a system of financial compensation for the burdens and obligations imposed on its members as a result of the 'public mission' aspects of their business.

The Court of First Instance found that EBU members were not required by its statutes to comply with a 'public mission' requirement, and referred in particular to Canal Plus in France. In the Court's view, the Commission had failed to examine whether the rules were objective and sufficiently determinate to be applied uniformly and in a non-discriminatory way to potential members of EBU. The criteria in EBU's own statutes were too vague for

[43] [1999] OJ L125/12: 5 CMLR 646.
[44] Cases T-528, 542, 543 and 546/93 [1996] ECR II-649: 5 CMLR 386 (*Métropole* v. *Commission*).

application to ensure non-discrimination. Moreover, the voluntary acceptance by some members of the different obligations of a public nature was insufficient as a basis for the grant of an individual exemption. For these reasons the restrictions in the rules were held not to be indispensable to the essential function of EBU. In granting an exemption the Commission had wrongly given priority to Article 86(2) over Article 81(3), even though it was agreed that Article 86(2) had no application to this particular organization. The pursuit of public interest goals was not irrelevant to Article 81(3) but could not outweigh the importance of the indispensability requirements.

The EBU had therefore to redraft its rules so as to meet the terms of the Court of First Instance judgment and duly notified these amended rules to the Commission. Since the original decision of the Court of First Instance the EBU had suffered a substantial loss of market share in Europe at the hands of commercial television companies against a back-ground of sharply rising prices paid for major sports on television such as football. These factors were taken into account by the Commission in assessing the fourth condition. In a number of respects, however, the revised rules offered better opportunities to non-members of the EBU to have access to broadcasts of major sporting events. Although the EBU would still submit bids for major events on behalf of all its members there would now be greater opportunities for small member companies, often in small countries, to have access to such transmissions. Competition between the members and non-members of the EBU was not eliminated because of this sub-licensing arrangements for non EBU members; the technical rules covered the use of the Eurovision signal had been amended to improve distribution and coverage for major events throughout Europe. Moreover non-members could also acquire the right to broadcast on their individual pay TV channels identical or comparable for competition to those presented on the EBU's members channel. The period of the exemption[45] granted was until 2005 but the EBU were required as a condition of the exemption to provide the Commission regularly with information about the application of its rules to particular major sporting events. Unfortunately not all of the European free-to-air television companies were happy with the revised sub-licensing arrangements: French, Spanish and Portuguese companies appealed to the CFI against this second decision on the grounds that the sub-licensing rules gave insufficient access to transmission rights for sport-ing events to non-members of EBU. The rights were generally sold on an exclusive basis and were not freely available to third parties; whilst the restrictions imposed were at their most severe for live transmissions, even deferred coverage was subject to editing and embargo time limitations. Ruling in favour of the complainants, the second grant of exemption by the Commission was also struck down by the CFI.[46]

4.4 IN FINANCIAL CASES

It is noticeable that in recent years many of the leading decisions in respect of individual exemptions under Article 81(3) have involved multilateral networks operating across Europe, where the need to establish stable relationships and deal with inevitable technical problems have had to be balanced against the inherent risk that such networks will incorporate an unreasonable degree of exclusivity and also have some prejudice to consumer

---

[45] [2000] 5 CMLR 650 (The Commission's second decision).
[46] Case T-206/99: [2001] 4 CMLR 1423. Cases T-185, 216, 299/300–00: [2003] 4 CMLR 707.

choice. The *VISA* rules for Multilateral Interchange Fees (MIF) illustrate that even agreements that provide for the fixing of prices to be charged by undertakings and competition with each other can in exceptional cases be exempted. The banks from numerous Member States participating in the VISA debit and credit card systems would not normally have been able, without a breach of Article 81(1), to make these arrangements, but the ability to be able to fix a standard fee applicable to all costs-border payment transactions at retail outlets meant that many more banks were in fact able to join the network without incurring substantial transaction costs of negotiated fees with all other banks participating. An important element in the granting of the exemption, however, was the placing by the Commission of a 'cap' on the amount of the MIF, which related to the audited costs of services which the banks would be rendering to the retailers and their own customers.[47]

4.5 IN ENVIRONMENTAL CASES

A group of recent related decisions underlines the importance which the Commission will attach to environmental benefits even on agreements that have an industry wide basis. In the *CECED Washing Machines* case[48] the agreement was made between members of a trade association of washing machine manufacturers who covered some 90 per cent of the manufacturing market in the EEA. The members of this association included nearly all the major manufacturers of such machines; and the purpose of the agreement was to discontinue the manufacture and import of certain makes and models that had only a low energy efficiency, and to set a new target under which all machines produced in future would reach a particular level of efficiency through improved technology. The new more efficient models would also reduce the amount of water required in each washing cycle. It was accepted that the agreement would in some ways narrow down consumer choice and restrict competition. But it imposed no rules as to manufacturer's pricing in future (indeed as costs might be increased by the arrangement, prices too might increase) nor for reduction of their output; but the agreement would have the benefit both of reducing customers' electricity bills and overall electricity demand.

In weighing the benefits of the agreement the following matters were taken into account:

— Energy consumption of the new models would be at least 15–20 per cent lower and would cause less pollution.

— The additional costs of machines would be recouped by the average domestic user between nine and fourteen months after purchase.

— All the restrictions were indispensable for the fulfilment of the objective benefits and it would not have been adequate simply to agree a target for the industry without the accompanying detailed restrictions.

— There was no elimination of competition, which was active in this market.

The period of exemption granted was four and a quarter years. This case proved a precedent for other related agreements relating to water heaters, household dishwashers and low

---

[47] [2002] OJ L318/17: [2003] 4 CMLR 283. The remaining elements of its credit card system had already received negative clearance from the Commission [2002] OJ L293/24: 4 CMLR 168.

[48] [2000] 5 CMLR 635. Certain restrictions, e.g. as to exchange of information were held to fall outside Art. 81(1) altogether. See also *EACM* in 1998 AR p.152: (1999) 4 CMLR 508.

voltage motors used in a range of pumps and ventilators.[49] In each case the members of the association agreed to phase out production of the least efficient categories of machine, and thereby reduce overall electricity and water consumption by users.

4.6 IN BEER SUPPLY CASES

A large number of exemption decisions have also been rendered in respect of bilateral agreements between United Kingdom brewers and their tenants, these having been notified in considerable numbers to the Commission during the 1990s. It was the argument of the tenants that many of such agreements (drawn up in almost entirely standard form) did not meet the requirements of the existing block exemption (No. 1984/83) and were therefore void. After considerable delays the Commission did eventually issue formal decisions providing individual exemptions for certain standard tenancy agreements of a number of British breweries. Following the start of litigation in which tenants claimed that the standard leases which they had signed with the breweries were void because they infringed Article 81(1), Whitbread, Bass, and Scottish & Newcastle notified their agreements to the Commission with a view to obtaining negative clearance or individual exemption.

The Commission first considered whether the agreements infringed Article 81. The principal restrictions were found to be the exclusive purchasing obligation and the 'beer tie' or non-compete clause, and these were found to have a considerable effect on the opportunities for other breweries to gain access to the retail market, given that such restrictions applied to about half the market by volume. The Commission went on to find that the agreements of each brewery made a significant contribution to this foreclosure effect, as the most recent UK retail market share figures showed shares of 6.12 per cent, 13.7 per cent, and 9.44 per cent respectively. Therefore both limbs of the *Delimitis* test were satisfied and there was an infringement of Article 81(1).

Because the agreements did not fit precisely within the terms of the block exemption in force at the time the Commission had to decide whether the conditions of Article 81(3) were satisfied. It held that although the tenants (with 'tied houses') paid higher prices for their beer than the so-called 'free houses', they benefited from compensating measures such as subsidized rents, bulk buying and procurement services and other forms of financial and operational support. An individual exemption was granted to each brewery.[50]

4.7 IN HORTICULTURAL CASES

In recent years the Commission has also shown itself noticeably more willing to reach a finding that the effect of a notified agreement on competition has been insufficiently appreciable to bring Article 81(3) into play at all. The Commission has been willing in such cases to give a formal or informal confirmation of a negative clearance, in some cases to the entire agreement, in others to important features of it. This for example was the outcome in

---

[49] [2001] 5 CMLR 1401, 1405.

[50] [1999] 5 CMLR 118, 782, 831. See also *Shaw and Falla* v. *Commission* Case T-131/99 [2002] 5 CMLR 81 and *Joynson* v. *Commission* Case T-231/99 [2002] 5 CMLR 123. Not all notified beer supply agreements, however, met the requirements of Art. 81(3), and a number of such notifications were withdrawn. See *Crehan* v. *Courage* Case C-453/99 [2001] 5 CMLR 1058.

Sicasov,[51] an application by an organization of French breeders of plant varieties and seeds for negative clearance or exemption for their standard form agreements. Both Regulations and Directives had been made by the Community giving protection for individual plant varieties (broadly equivalent to patent protection) which laid down conditions for the production and marketing of seeds. Seeds had to be certified as to their identity and purity and could only be marketed if this had been done. A distinction was made between 'basic seed' used only for producing additional seed of a later generation and 'certified seed' (commercial seed intended for sale to farmers for sowing which could not normally however be used for the production of further seeds). The role of Sicasov in France was to manage its members' rights by granting licences for the reproduction and sale of plant breeders' rights and the marketing of seeds.

The standard agreement contained restrictions on 'multipliers' who purchased basic seed from members of Sicasov preventing them from reselling such seeds to third parties outside France. This was a safeguard against possible technical mishandling of the seed. The restriction applied also to purchasers within France of basic seed from the original multiplier/purchaser; the multiplier was required to prevent purchasers of certified seed from using it as a 'basic seed' in their own country whose propagation rules may not have been as strict as those in France.

The export of 'certified seeds' from France could be banned under these agreements for four years from the date of original registration, though foreign purchasers could acquire them indirectly through intermediaries established in France; this export was held to be covered by Article 81(1) but nevertheless exemption was granted for a ten-year period. The benefit which the overall agreement provided was that it facilitated the dissemination of new varieties from France to other Member States by encouraging undertakings in those countries to accept the risks involved in marketing new varieties selected by French breeders, without having the concurrent risk of contending with the competition of direct exports from France by multipliers during the first years of trial. The four-year restriction on the sales of basic seed by such multipliers forced the multipliers to concentrate on the French market, but, nevertheless, purchasers from such multipliers were able to acquire seed indirectly. The period of four years before the export ban was lifted was regarded by the Commission as a reasonable one to allow the establishment or dissemination of new varieties. It was noted that parallel imports from France through purchasers having branches or subsidiaries established in that country remained possible.

4.8 THE USE OF CONDITIONS

It is important to note, however, that a decision granting an exemption need not be absolute, but may be subject to a number of conditions. These may relate to the period of exemption, to supervision by the Commission, or to reporting and even attendance conditions. The exemption is normally for a fixed period, usually a minimum of three years and up to twelve or fifteen years. The supervision required by DG Comp will vary according to the circumstances and may in some cases be limited to the simple provision of annual accounts by undertakings, or of lists of members in or persons refused membership of an association, ranging up to detailed review by the Commission of individual contracts or the business

---

[51] [1999] 4 CMLR 192.

dealings of the parties exempted. Reporting requirements may be imposed on the working of particular aspects of an agreement and, as in the *IEA* case, the attendance of representatives of the Commission may be made a specific term of approval. In at least one case, IBM,[52] it was a condition of the settlement that the operation of the relevant business transactions of IBM were reported annually to the Commission, which enabled close contact to be maintained between the company's senior executives and those supervising officials of the Commission.

5. NULLITY: THE EFFECT OF ARTICLE 81(2)

5.1 THE SCOPE OF THE BASIC RULE

Between the basic rule of prohibition found in Article 81(1) and the exemption or 'non-applicability' provision of Article 81(3) lies the short and deceptively simple paragraph (2) which states that any 'agreements or decisions prohibited pursuant to this Article shall be automatically void'. For a considerable period neither the ECJ nor the CFI had, in spite of its importance as a matter of both national and Community law, thrown light in any judgment on the correct approach to the interpretation of this paragraph. Finally however in *Crehan* v. *Courage*[53] the ECJ in an Article 234 reference from the English Court of Appeal has now confirmed the effect of this paragraph. The effect of the automatic nullity of an agreement which falls within the prohibition of Article 81(1), without benefiting from 81(3), is that the agreement has no effect as between the parties to it, nor can it be set up as a defence to a claim by third parties. This principle has of course to be understood in the light of the earlier ruling in *Grundig* that, if severance of the clauses held void is possible under relevant national law, then only those clauses themselves rather than the entire agreement are unenforceable.

It is of course possible to conclude from the bare words of the text of Article 81(2) that the quality of voidness should apply to the entire agreement containing prohibited clauses, and this was the original attitude adopted by the Commission in the *Grundig* case. The Court however adopted a different interpretation, finding that those clauses of the agreement which did not contain restraints in breach of Article 81(1) were not rendered void either by the terms of Article 81(2) or Regulation 17.

It is however for the national court to rule on each individual case whether it is possible for the contract to remain in being after removal, i.e. severance of the clauses held in breach of Article 81(1). Authority from the UK cases is limited but it appears that judges are often unwilling to make a finding that the inclusion in a contract of clauses of breach of Article 81(1) necessarily renders the whole agreement unenforceable. To reach such an unpalatable conclusion from the viewpoint of the parties seems to require a finding by the Court that as a result of the removal of the offending clauses the parties have been left with a contract so different from that with which they began their relationship it would be unconscionable to hold them to it. The main finding in *Crehan*, however, was that the automatic invalidity

---

[52] See Ch. 15, pp.301–4, and the *14th Annual Report* (1984), pp.77–9, and for a more recent assessment of these arrangements, DG Comp Competition Policy Newsletter (1998) No. 3, pp.7–11.

[53] Case C-453/99 [2001] 5 CMLR 1058.

imposed by paragraph (2) could not itself prevent an undertaking or person which is a party to such a contract from relying upon the contract and its illegal clauses in order to claim damages in the appropriate national court from the other party. Further discussion of this important case is found in Chapter 21 (pp.468–70). An important question is what is the legal position if the parties to an agreement fail to raise in court the question of the application of Article 81 to contractual restrictions. The European Court has held in *Van Schijndel*[54] that the court hearing the case must of its own initiative raise the issue. Moreover, in *ECO Swiss* v. *Benetton*[55] the Court confirmed that, as Article 81 has direct application in national courts as a rule of public policy, an arbitrator must apply Article 81(2) so as to render an agreement or restriction prohibited by it unenforceable; and an award of damages made under such an agreement would therefore be a nullity, even if the issue was not raised by the party at the arbitration hearing or on appeal.

5.2 THE 'SHIMMERING' NATURE OF THE PROHIBITION

The effect therefore of *Crehan* has been to overrule a number of Court of Appeal and High Court decisions in the UK where claims for damages have been made by parties to contracts containing restrictive clauses, many of which involved the brewers and their tenants. It does not however affect the outcome of another judgment given by the UK Court of Appeal as to the application of Article 81(2). In *Passmore* v. *Morland*,[56] Passmore had been a tenant of Inntrepreneur a large national pub owning company which entered into a long lease of the pub with Passmore containing the usual requirements that he purchase all his beer exclusively from Inntrepreneur. At some point in the tenancy Inntrepreneur transferred it to a much smaller brewery company with a de minimis share of the national beer market. Passmore sought to argue that the tie fell within Article 81(2) and therefore could not be enforced against him. The response of the new brewery landlord, Morland, was to argue that the prohibition in Article 81(2) is not a 'once for all' consequence but simply a provisional 'shimmering' prohibition, effective only so long as the economic circumstances of the agreement remain unchanged. Since the effect of the restrictive clause on the beer market once the tenancy was in the hands of Morland was not appreciable, Morland claimed that the enforceability of the contract was no longer an issue, even if this had been void under Article 81(1) at the time when it was originally granted.

The Court of Appeal agreed with the argument of Morland and logically it seems hard to fault. It raises however the possibility of difficult issues having to be resolved in future cases, where, for example, either the relevant agreement has been transferred from one party to another, as in the *Passmore* case, or even when the agreement was made between the original parties but where their relative bargaining position and other economic circumstances changed, so that the Court may find itself imposing the finding of nullity at a later stage in the performance of the contract, even though, at the time it was made, no finding of nullity would have been appropriate. The Court of Appeal was considerably influenced by the fact that Article 81 is essentially dealing with the 'effects' of particular contracts that may restrict competition, which may later change, rather than with their legal form which remains unaltered.

---

[54] Case C-430/93 [1995] ECR I-4705: [1996] 1 CMLR 801.
[55] Case C-126/97 [1999] ECR I-3055: [2000] 5 CMLR 816.   [56] [1999] 1 CMLR 1129.

9

HORIZONTAL AGREEMENTS: CARTELS

1. INTRODUCTION

1.1 CATEGORIES OF HORIZONTAL AGREEMENTS

At first sight any horizontal agreement between undertakings which are actual, or at least, potential competitors to each other would seem less likely to escape prohibition under Article 81(1) than those agreements which are vertical, where the function of the parties are complementary to each other.[1] Nevertheless, there is an important distinction to be drawn at the outset between two principal categories of horizontal agreements.

The first of these categories is where the agreement has a primary objective which is not substantially anti-competitive, even though its detailed terms may include restrictions possibly falling within the range covered by Article 81(1). It includes: co-operation agreements and specialization agreements, agreements for sharing research and development or for establishing industry standards and also some types of joint venture. The task for DG Comp with this category, if the requirements of a particular block exemption are not met, is to analyse the alleged benefits arising from the agreement and the extent to which they are in turn likely to be passed on to consumers, while at the same time considering whether the anti-competitive restrictions are no more widely drawn than necessary for its objectives to be obtained.

The second category is the agreement whose primary objective is the object of the reduction or elimination of competition between the parties, or it may be simply to protect existing market positions, or to prevent a feared deterioration. It may be brought on by other causes such as shortages, lack of demand, or simply lack of confidence in the future of the industry in a competitive environment. Cartels and market sharing agreements are often found here, sometimes as a response to over-capacity in a sector where demand has fallen substantially and is unlikely to revive. Often the enforcement of this kind of agreement is marked by machinery for tight control with sanctions to ensure that all participants stay in line. External and internal influences on individual members of the cartel may mean that they are fragile and in time either collapse completely or become only partially effective. Sometimes a cartel arises largely from corporate greed in an attempt to extract more from the customers of the industry than would be paid under competitive conditions.

---

[1] Chapters 10 and 11 deal with vertical agreements for distribution; Ch. 12 with vertical agreements involving licensing of intellectual property rights.

1.2 THE APPROACH OF THE COMMISSION TO CARTELS

Cartels are most often found in respect of products which are standard commodities, such as sugar, cement, steel, and basic chemicals, where price is the principal criterion for competition, though the recent experience of the Commission shows that they can spring up in an almost infinitely wide variety of markets. The OECD has played a leading role in co-ordinating the activities of the competition authorities in its Member States in combating such arrangements. Although there were important cartel cases in the early years of the Treaty of Rome, it has been during the 1990s that investigation by the Commission has been substantially increased and accompanied by an important change in strategy. One of the principal problems in establishing the existence of cartels has always been that of obtaining the necessary evidence against the participants, who will normally have taken careful steps to conceal their activities even if these have not always been totally successful. Although additional resources had been allocated by the Commission to pursue cartels as early as the 1980s, the need to establish sufficient evidence in respect of such concerted practices and agreements led to a major change of strategy in the 1990s, which has considerably improved the record of the Commission in successfully finding and punishing such arrangements.

Of course, many types of horizontal agreements contain clauses embodying restraints of trade, to which Article 81(1) may apply. Sometimes, as discussed in Chapter 7, a restraint of trade is merely a minor (indeed a normal) element in a routine contract: for example, the sale of an existing business including its goodwill. The covenant restraining the subsequent trading activities of the vendor may be strictly ancillary to the need of the purchaser to protect the goodwill sold under the agreement. However, in most cases coming before the Commission for individual exemption the anti-competitive restraint plays a more significant part. The analysis of such restraints has to be thorough and probing, sensitive to the nuances and special circumstances of particular industries. The parties may seek to conceal a naked cartel in the fine clothes of what appears to be a legitimate trade association or creative joint venture: the officials of DG Comp have to be ready and able to distinguish substance from surface. This chapter examines next some examples from the first category of agreements, those having a primarily defensive quality, and then considers some of the leading cases where Article 81(1) has been applied by the Commission and the Courts. The Commission has since the end of the 1980s taken a more vigorous approach towards major cartels. It has found additional resources for conducting such cases, often difficult to complete with their many defendants and a complex web of evidence spanning a number of years. It has established a unit within DG Comp to specialize in this kind of case and this has achieved some notable successes in identifying breaches of Article 81 and imposing heavy fines in a number of such cases.

The Article itself provides examples of the kind of agreement which will normally fall within its prohibition; however, they provide little assistance as to the basis upon which the benefits and burdens of the restraints are to be assessed, referring simply to certain general types of agreement. Whilst it is sometimes possible to allocate notified agreements neatly within these headings, there is little value in trying to do so in every case since many agreements fall within more than one category.

2. PRICE-FIXING AND MARKET-SHARING AGREEMENTS

2.1 EARLY CASES

The first category (*a*) in Article 81(1) refers to agreements which 'directly or indirectly fix purchase or selling prices or any other trading condition'. We know from *Italy* v. *Council and Commission*[2] (European Court 1966) that both horizontal and vertical agreements fall within the prohibition. Clearly, however, (*a*) deals primarily with agreements or concerted practices made between horizontally related competitors on prices to be charged, markets to be allocated, or conditions of sale to be applied. It could also apply to such agreements between rival manufacturers to enforce resale price maintenance within a particular sector, or even to an agreement between a manufacturer and a distributor or dealer requiring resale price maintenance over sales by the latter. One of the earliest cases on horizontal cartels within category (*a*) dealt with by the Commission (whose decision was later upheld by the Court) was that of the *Quinine Cartel*.[3]

The participants in this cartel were companies in France, Germany, and Holland. The companies were engaged in the sale of quinine, used for making medicines to treat malaria, and also in synthetic quinidine, an ingredient for making other medicines. Both products are obtained from cinchoma bark, which grows in a number of third-world countries. Co-operation between the companies in the European industry dated back to 1913 when agreements were made in an attempt to stabilize market conditions for the supply of the raw material. After the Second World War, new plantations of cinchoma were established in Congo and Indonesia; supplies of the bark then rose steadily, with the result that by 1958 prices had reached a lower level than had prevailed twenty years before. At the same time the US government elected to dispose of surplus held by the General Services Administration (GSA) at auction, having accumulated very large stocks over the previous year. In the face of this unstable market situation, the defendant companies decided in 1958 to put together a defensive cartel, involving collaboration on the prices to be paid for the bark, the allocation of purchases of the GSA stockpile, and the protection of individual national markets for their respective national producers. It was also decided that particular export markets would be reserved for particular companies, and that quotas would be allocated in respect of those markets when they were permitted to 'compete' there.

The original agreement was for a period of five years and, in order that compliance with the agreement could be policed, members had to notify each other of their quarterly sales and prices. If a company was unable to reach its quota for export sales, compensating sales would then have to be made to other members which would be supervised by the Dutch company (Nedchem) which took prime responsibility for administration of the cartel and for the enforcement of restrictions on the manufacture of quinidine by companies other than the German and Dutch participants.

---

[2] Case 32/65 [1966] ECR 389: [1969] CMLR 39.

[3] *Boehringer Mannheim* v. *Commission* Case 45/69 [1970] ECR 769. UK companies were mentioned in the report as participating in the agreement, but were not proceeded against by the Commission. The Commission's decision is reported at [1969] CMLR D41.

Some of these arrangements were contained in so-called 'export agreements' and others in so-called 'gentlemen's agreements'. Although the Common Market was excluded from the scope of the export agreement, in practice all companies set their Common Market prices on the basis of those charged for exports outside the Market so that, as a result of the arrangements, pricing effects were felt within Europe. Market prices within Europe at the time were generally higher than those in world markets. Later in 1961 a buying pool was set up to stabilize the cost of the cinchoma bark and quotas were allocated. The evidence in the case deals interestingly with the reaction of the participants to the entry into force of the Treaty of Rome. They had to decide whether to notify the agreements, terminate them, or keep them in existence secretly. They determined to amend the agreements slightly, but to keep them in force without notification to the Commission. Subsequently market conditions changed sharply as bark supplies were reduced, and the prices charged by all companies rose substantially. A contributing factor was the demand by the United States Defence Department for use in Vietnam during the early 1960s. The arrangement eventually came to an end in 1965.

The Commission had imposed substantial fines on the participants, and these were only slightly reduced on appeal to the European Court, on the basis of a finding as to the period during which the principal agreement had affected the market price within the industry. The Court made it clear, however, that it would not accept any legalistic distinctions between the effects of the export agreement and those of the gentlemen's agreement, and stated that it regarded both as a single set of concerted practices.

We saw in Chapter 6 that the definition of 'concerted practices' lay at the heart of the next important horizontal cartel case decided by the Court: the *Dyestuffs*[4] case (European Court 1972). Undoubtedly, the evidence was more circumstantial than in the *Quinine Cartel* case, and in particular the proof of concerted practices between the dyestuffs manufacturers depended largely on inferences drawn from the similarities of price increases and subsequent retraction of individual increases as a response to withdrawals of the increases by other parties to the agreement. As with quinine, the dyestuffs agreement was intended both to protect national markets from outside intervention and to maintain price levels generally. The number of companies engaged in the Common Market in the dyestuffs business was relatively small (approximately ten) but all were of a very substantial size, and the nature of the market was distinctly oligopolistic. Whereas *Quinine* had dealt with a small number of related medicinal products, dyestuffs manufacturers produced between them several thousand different dyes, with a large variety of different customers having slightly different needs. The manufacturers considered it essential to maintain control of their local markets by ensuring that local national producers maintained direct contact with all their large national customers, being attentive to their needs and having natural advantages of location and nationality over foreign producers, who were likely to be represented locally only by subsidiaries, representatives, or agents who could not give the same complete service as the local manufacturers. The price of dye is only a small element in the total price of clothing and other items to which it is applied; therefore the market was not very price elastic, quality of service counting for much in the competitive process. Each leading manufacturer within its own country tended to behave as a price leader, but always faced the risk that undertakings from outside the country would make a positive effort to penetrate the

---

[4] Cases 48, 49, 51–57/69 [1972] ECR 619: CMLR 557 (*ICI and Others* v. *Commission*).

national market by selective price cutting. The purpose of the cartel was to remove this risk.

In its judgment, the Court considered the need for competition in such markets against the perceived needs and wishes of the producers for stability. With regard to the former, it stated that:

the function of competition in relation to prices is to maintain prices at the lowest possible level, and to encourage the movement of products between member-States so as to permit an optimum sharing out of activities on the basis of productivity and the adaptive capacity of undertakings. The variation of price rates encourages the pursuit of one of the essential aims of the Treaty, namely the inter-penetration of national markets, and hence the direct access of consumers to the sources of production of the whole Community.

However, the purpose of the cartel was deliberately designed to counter these aims:

in these circumstances, having regard to the characteristics of the market in these products, the behaviour of the applicant, in conjunction with other undertakings . . . was designed to substitute for the risks of competition, and the hazards of their spontaneous reactions, a co-operation which amounts to a concerted practice prohibited by Article 81(1) of the Treaty.

The manufacturers argued that uniform price changes in 1964, 1965, and 1967 were the result of price leadership by different undertakings making their choice of pricing policies, which in turn produced a response required to maintain the equilibrium between the major manufacturers. The weakness in this explanation of the conduct of the parties was pointed out by Advocate General Mayras, namely that while such equilibrium could perhaps have explained a downward adjustment of price to keep in line with the price leadership, it was less probable that substantial parallel increases would be explained in this way, especially when there were so many different varieties of dyestuffs at such a range of prices.

Elimination of the risks of competition lies at the heart of many horizontal cartels. It was central to the *Sugar Cartel*[5] case, though here the factual complexities were compounded by the Commission's decision to proceed under both Articles 81 and 82, because some European sugar producers had engaged in unilateral action to protect or extend dominance within specific Member States (or important regions of Member States), quite apart from the concerted practices adopted by the parties with a view to protecting national markets and price levels. The European Court judgment considered each of these geographical markets in turn and (as in the *Dyestuffs* case) found that the principle of *chacun chez soi* (to each his own) dominated the attitude of the participants. The lengthy judgment takes us through a variety of individual national or regional markets, examining the evidence to an extent, at the time, unique for the European Court. Italy had proved a special case, where the degree of government intervention meant that the residual element left for restraints of competition by arrangement between the sugar companies was so limited that it was not sufficient to affect competition to an extent that would constitute a breach of Article 81.[6] In the remaining jurisdictions, the position was that whilst Common Market agricultural policy, including the intervention and target prices set for producers, provided the background to the arrangements, there was still considerable scope for competition between them. There

---

[5] *Suiker Unie* v. *Commission* Cases 40–48, 50, 54, 56, 111, 113, 114/73 [1975] ECR 1663: [1976] 1 CMLR 295.

[6] See Ch. 7, pp.95–6.

was indeed a considerable surplus of sugar production over demand within the Common Market. France and Belgium in particular had surplus capacity, and in a freer market would have been able to sell substantial quantities to major end-users and sugar brokers or wholesalers within the Community; there were also collusive arrangements for obtaining tenders for sales into export where export refunds were available from the Commission to cover the difference between world prices and Community prices. The purpose and the effect of the cartel was to restrain the degree to which sugar was bought and sold across national boundaries within the Common Market and to allocate the export sales between the participants.

In giving strong support to most of the Commission's findings in these important cases early in the history of the Community's competition policy, the Court gave an important boost to the confidence of the Commission in preparing and bringing substantial cartel cases. The wide definition which the Court was prepared to give to concerted practices, and its willingness to take a broad view of the exercise of the Commission's discretion in reaching conclusions from the evidence available, encouraged the Commission to bring other cases of similar magnitude in following years. Such cases often require several years' investigation and preparation before decisions can be issued.

2.2 LEADING CASES OF THE 1980s

The 1980s brought several important cases. In the *Peroxygen*[7] case, a number of European producers of hydrogen peroxide and its derivatives, used as industrial bleaches, were found to have participated for several years in an allocation of markets which (as in *Sugar* and *Dyestuffs*) gave preference to home producers on their own national markets. As a result prices for these products were kept at a higher level than would have prevailed under competitive conditions. There were arrangements for meetings between the companies to settle any disputes about the allocation of territories or about sales made over quota. Production and sales details were also freely exchanged between companies so that the operation of the cartel could be easily controlled. The Commission pointed out in its decision that if the parties were prepared to take such trouble to enter into and maintain such arrangements, and to concert their policies and practices so as to produce such convenient results, it could be presumed that they believed it gave them an actual trading benefit. Therefore, the mere fact that the end result in terms of prices might be much the same as could have been expected from an oligopolistic market without the exchange of information would not itself provide any defence to a claim under Article 81(1).

The *Aluminium Cartel*[8] was a particularly long-lived arrangement between several European and North American producers between 1963 and 1976. The object here was not to protect individual home markets for specific companies but to protect Western markets generally from supplies of aluminium ingot produced in Eastern Europe, which could have undercut Western producers on a price basis and force world prices down if released onto the market without control. To prevent this, Western producers arranged through a broker, Brandeis Goldschmidt and Co. Ltd. and its Swiss subsidiary, that all the Eastern European production would be purchased by this broker, who would then allocate it to the participants in the cartel, in a ratio corresponding to the share of each in Western European sales. Each manufacturer within the cartel would allow both its own allocated quota and those of

[7] [1985] 1 CMLR 481.
[8] [1987] 3 CMLR 813. See also the *14th Annual Report* (1984), pp.58–9 and Ch. 22, pp.482.

other members. To disguise the source of the metal, and in order to check whether the Eastern Bloc countries still managed to export any metal direct to the West, all participants agreed that the Eastern metal purchased through Brandeis Goldschmidt would not be resold outside the cartel until it had been melted down.[9]

Many aluminium producers are also engaged in the production of semi-manufactured items such as aluminium plates, sheets, strips, and foil (known generally as rolled products) as well as rods and sections, tubes, and wire (known as extruded or drawn products). Those remaining manufacturers of aluminium products without access to the raw material of aluminium ingot, and who wished to produce semi-manufactured or manufactured items (rolled or extruded) in aluminium, were heavily dependent upon the integrated producers for their supplies; this control enabled the integrated producers within the cartel to increase substantially the prices they charged for semi-manufactured products. Moreover, the parties in the cartel did all they could to prevent aluminium being traded freely or quoted on the London Metal Exchange, since this again could have weakened the effect of the main agreement by introducing greater volatility to prices. The agreement had a substantial impact on competition in Western Europe, directly affecting the price of between 13 and 20 per cent of the total consumption in that territory. No fines were imposed by the Commission, allegedly for technical reasons relating to the age of the agreement, and this no doubt influenced the decision of the participants not to appeal.

In the late 1980s there were several important cases involving the great majority of large chemical producers in Western Europe, where it was alleged that price cartels had existed and that important production information had been exchanged by the manufacturers of polypropylene, polyvinylchloride (PVC), and low density polyethylene (LDPE) respectively. In each of these cases[10] the Commission imposed substantial fines on participants; regular meetings of the leading producers were proved, though clearly there were both 'leaders' and 'followers' in respect of each product, and not all producers were always as closely involved in the industry's continuing efforts to protect its price levels against the background of oversupply and excessive production capacity. Uniform price increases and closely matching list prices appeared to be the outcome of these arrangements. The individual cases were taken on appeal to the Court of First Instance,[11] and subsequently on legal issues to the European Court itself. It would be wrong, though understandable, to assume that agreements affecting the price to be paid for raw materials will always be struck down under Article 81(1) by the Commission. Exemption can be given under paragraph (3) if there are any compensating advantages which relate to improvement of production or distribution and where consequent benefits arise not only for the participants but also for purchasers and consumers. The *National Sulphuric Acid Association* case[12] (Commission 1980) is an

---

[9] Technical arguments were raised by the participants that the metal from Eastern Bloc sources had to be mixed with other aluminium of a higher grade before commercial use.

[10] The original Commission decisions were *PVC Cartel* [1990] 4 CMLR 345; *LDPE Cartel* [1990] 4 CMLR 382; and *Polypropylene Cartel* [1988] 4 CMLR 347.

[11] e.g. *Hercules v. Commission (Polypropylene)* Case C-51/92P [1999] ECR I-4235: 5 CMLR 976. The *PVC Cartel (No. 1)* decision of the Commission was later annulled by the ECJ on procedural grounds, but a subsequent Commission decision (*PVC Cartel No. 2*) was upheld by the CFI in *Limburgse Vinyl v. Commission* Cases T-305–7, 313–16, 318, 325, 328–9, and 335/94 [1999] ECR II-931: 5 CMLR 303: (2003) 4 CMLR 397.

[12] [1980] 3 CMLR 429. The UK 'buying pool' had been upheld by the UK Restrictive Practices Court under the Restrictive Practices Acts. See *National Sulphuric Acid Association's Agreement* [1963] 3 All ER 73: LR 4 RP 169 and [1966] LR 6 RP 210.

example. Sulphur in solid form is heavy and expensive to transport from the United States, where almost all of it is produced. Manufacturers of sulphuric acid in the United Kingdom had formed a buying pool for sulphur, which nearly all the producers within the United Kingdom had joined. The existence of the buying pool had made it much easier for substantial dock installations to be built in England enabling sulphur to be imported by tankers in liquid form, enabling the smaller undertakings within the pool to receive small loads at convenient ports; the agreement also enabled the price of sulphuric acid to be reduced and continuity of supplies protected. However, the Commission successfully objected to restrictions in the original agreement imposed on resales to non-members and against use being made of the sulphur for other than acid-making purposes. Moreover, the members of the pool were not obliged under the amended agreement to take more than 25 per cent of their total needs from the pool, whereas this figure had originally been 100 per cent. In practice some 30 per cent of the sulphuric acid produced by pool members was sold to third parties and competition between members of the pool was thus maintained. The terms of the final agreement, whilst maintaining the essential advantages of the pool, limited the restrictions contained in it to those which the Commission found to be necessary for its objects to be achieved. The result might have been different had the buying pool given the buyers disproportionate market power over the sellers.

2.3 A NEW COMMISSION APPROACH—THE LENIENCY NOTICES

It is however during the second half of the 1990s that the campaign on cartels began to achieve a succession of important victories and in which a change of strategy by the Commission has played an ever-increasing role, starting with the *Cartonboard*[13] case. Cartonboard is manufactured in large mills and sold to converters who transform it into folding cartons for use in food and other industries. Over the period 1982 to 1991 some twenty-three companies in Scandinavia and Western Europe had met regularly as 'the Product Group Paper Board' to discuss market shares and production quotas. Regular price rises were implemented every six months and confidential information exchanged. The results of this concertation was that the parties' market shares remained stable and prices, following annual rises of between 6 and 10 per cent, stayed well above those that would have existed if true competition had prevailed, even at times when raw material prices were falling. The minutes of the Product Group Paper Board and its various sub-committees which enforced the cartel provided convincing evidence of the existence of the agreements and concerted practices, both by their contents and significant omissions.

The Commission's ability to acquire relevant evidence in this case was substantially assisted by the fact that one of the participants, Stora, co-operated with them from an early stage. Stora none the less received a substantial fine at the conclusion of the case, though it would have been still higher absent its co-operation. Following this case the Commission issued a Notice in July 1996 making official its policy towards 'whistle-blowers' in this type of case, previously dealt with only unofficially. Three levels of co-operation with the Commission were officially identified:

— An undertaking which is the first to provide full and documentary evidence of a cartel

---

[13] [1994] 5 CMLR 547.

before DG Comp has started its own investigation and which immediately ceases participation in it could benefit by a reduction of between 75 to 100 per cent of the potential fine.

— An undertaking which acted in this way after the Commission's investigation has begun could benefit by between 50 to 75 per cent of the potential fine.

— Other undertakings providing co-operation at a later stage could benefit from between 10 to 50 per cent of the potential fine.[14]

The number of cartels involving major companies discovered and against whom decisions were reached under Article 81 rose sharply towards the end of the twentieth century. Such decisions were given in a wide variety of sectors including lysine and amino acids, graphite electrodes, vitamins, citric acid, sodium gluconate, zinc phosphate, heating pipes, banking, breweries, carbonless paper, sugar and airlines. A number of these cases were not merely European in their scope but arose after successful investigations by the Department of Justice or Federal Trade Commission in the United States. Once the proceedings had been completed in the United States the information available in the public domain was normally sufficient that the parties did not seek to contest cases brought consequentially under Article 81, even if in some cases they refused to waive rights of confidentiality in respect of all matters uncovered in the US investigations. An influential part of the practice of the US authorities was the application of the principles of immunity and leniency offered to those undertakings prepared to break ranks with their fellow members and disclose details of the restrictive agreement at a sufficiently early stage in the enquiries.

But it soon became apparent that the original 1996 Notice required revision. It is true that in statistical terms the Notice had proved successful. It had been applied in some sixteen cases and over eighty companies had sought to benefit from its terms. Reductions in fines on undertakings found to have been engaged in cartels had amounted to some 1,400 million euros with reductions ranging from 100 per cent in certain cases to 10 per cent in cases where the information was provided only at a late stage and after pressure from the Commission. The exercise by the Commission of its discretion under the Notice, in respect of the contribution made to the resolution of the case by the disclosures of individual undertakings in this way, was upheld by the Court of First Instance in more than one case.

Nevertheless in spite of this degree of success the Commission learnt from experience that the Notice did not always produce results as satisfactory as might have been hoped. Undertakings apparently felt that the degree to which their co-operation with the Commission would secure a substantial reduction in those fines was uncertain; the evidence provided had to be decisive and supplied with the time before any other undertaking within the cartel had revealed it. Nor was the full benefit of the Notice available to any company which had been a ring-leader, i.e. had played a determining role within it. These uncertainties meant that much of the information provided to the Commission came too late in the case to have much 'added value'.

For these reasons the revised Notice of 2002[15] gave, by way of incentive, yet larger rewards

---

[14] For a description of how fines are calculated, see C.S. Kerse, *EC Antitrust Procedure*, 4th edn. (Sweet & Maxwell, 1998), Ch. 7, and the guidelines published by the Commission [1998] OJ C9/3: 4 CMLR 472. Price cartels are divided for this purpose into three categories: minor, serious, and very serious.

[15] [2002] OJ C45/3. An explanatory article can be found in DG Comp Competition Policy Newsletter [2002] No. 2, pp.15–22.

to the undertaking which first brought the existence of the cartel to the attention of the Commission. The Notice also tried to make the reduction in fines obtainable by other participants more closely related to the value of their co-operation. Immunity for fines was made available only to the first company to approach the Commission in respect of the particular cartel. The evidence which this company had to bring had either to enable the Commission:

(i)   to carry out an investigation under Article 14(3) of Regulation 17/62; or

(ii) to find an infringement of Article 81(1).

Two different situations therefore may lead to the grant of immunity. The Commission may be totally unaware of the existence of a cartel and the information provided to it under (i), while insufficient to enable it to make a finding of a breach of the Article, may yet be reliable enough for it to launch a successful 'dawn raid'. On the other hand under (ii), the Commission may have already carried out a 'dawn raid' without finding sufficient incriminating material, but is then enabled by the information provided to move to a finding under Article 81. Immunity can however only be given to the first company to contact the Commission and the company must continue with its co-operation throughout the course of the case. The mere fact of being a 'ring-leader' does not automatically block a claim for immunity, so long as no coercion was used to induce other companies to take part in the arrangements (though the establishment of such matters will always be a difficult question of proof). A decision to grant immunity will normally be available from the Commission within a few weeks of receipt of the original disclosure.

For those companies which do not qualify for immunity, which are of course necessarily the majority of participants in the cartel, a revised leniency tariff is still available. The criterion applied by the Commission is whether the information provided had significant 'added value', and the greater reductions go to those first to reach the Commission with their evidence. Tariffs are from a 30–50 per cent reduction in fine for the first company in this category, 20–30 per cent for the next and only up to 20 per cent for any subsequent providers of such information.

3. CARTELS INVOLVING SHIPPING LINES

In Chapter 7 (at p.110) reference was made to a block exemption from Article 81(1) found in Council Regulation 4056/86. This block exemption applied only however to certain categories of agreements between ship-owners operating as a liner conference on specific routes under which the same tariff is applied to each freight shipper. It had no application if there was discrimination in rates charged, nor to passenger services. A number of shipping conferences were subsequently found to have been operating cartels as to prices and capacities on particular routes which did not comply with the block exemption. The Commission therefore brought proceedings against a number of them. In 1992 fines were imposed against members of the *French/West African Ship Owners Conference*[16] for activities falling outside those permitted by the Regulation. Under arrangements between members of these Conferences, all commodities travelling between France and the eleven West and Central

---

[16] [1993] 5 CMLR 446.

African States involved were allocated; 40 per cent to French companies, which had a fixed percentage of that amount, 40 per cent to African companies, and 20 per cent to others. Any cargo for which a line had insufficient capacity could be transferred only to other members of the Conferences. The effect of these arrangements was that the French companies were able to carry the majority of the cargoes on these routes, against the intention of the UNCTAD Code of Conduct for Liner Conferences which sought to guarantee for carriers from developing countries a greater percentage of the markets previously dominated by carriers from the developed world; such arrangements were not within the scope of the exemption in Regulation 4056/82. None of the requirements for individual exemption under Article 81(3) were satisfied.

The Commission has also taken action against multimodal price-fixing by such Conferences. This practice arises because shippers of goods prefer to obtain a single quotation for the cost of sending goods from A to B, covering the overland journeys as well as the sea voyage itself. Liner conferences have therefore been giving quotations, and agreeing rates with other members of Conferences for covering the entire route, not simply the sea voyage. Later in 1994 the Commission reached its first decision in this area, against the *Far Eastern Freight Conference*,[17] imposing a nominal fine on fourteen undertakings for breaches of Regulation 1017/68 relating to price fixing for road and rail transport routes. The Commission claimed that exemption could not apply to such an arrangements because the existence of such land tariffs limited competition between the shipping lines to provide the best and cheapest service on those routes; the more competitive shipping companies were, because of the arrangements, unable to offer better terms to shippers, which in turn affected the trade carried on at particular Community ports. No member of a Conference was contractually obliged to quote only the rates set by the Conference but in practice it would normally follow the tariff recommendation of the Conference. An appeal to the Court of First Instance[18] was unsuccessful. The Court held that there was no evidence that the fixing of rates for inland transport would actually improve the stability of the shipping business, and the restrictions on competition of which the agreement imposed were not indispensable in any case and its ostensible objectives.

A similar case was brought against the Transatlantic Agreement operated by members of the relevant shipping Conferences leading to a further decision in October 1994.[19] The Association here provided rules for establishing freight rates on services contracts under which customers undertook to ship a minimum quantity over a given period in exchange for a discounted freight rate and on a capacity management program, designed to limit the supply of transport in order to stabilize the market; these freight rates related to inter-modal transport as well as to maritime freight. Following the decision the members of the Conference applied to the Court of First Instance[20] for interim measures pending the hearing of a full appeal; the Conference members claimed that their inability to fix jointly through inter-modal rates as in the past would lead to a collapse in maritime transport rates generally, which could affect the regularity of service so that some carriers would actually have to terminate operating their lines. On this occasion the Court ruled that the immediate application of the Commission decision risked such serious and irreparable damage to the shipping lines that the balance of interest required that its operation be suspended, insofar

---

[17] [1994] OJ L378/17.   [18] Case T-86/95 [2002] 4 CMLR 1115.   [19] (1994) OJ L367/1.
[20] Cases T-395/94R and C-149/95P [1995] ECR II-595, 2893: [1997] 5 CMLR 167, 181, 195.

as it prohibited them from jointly exercising rate-making authority for the inland portions of intermodal transport services. The substantive appeal was eventually heard by the CFI, where the Commission's findings were upheld, save in one minor respect.

4. CRISIS CARTELS

The effect of many of the agreements referred to so far could have been to 'limit or control production', within the terms of Article 81(1)(b). Perhaps the clearest example of agreements that have this effect directly are so-called 'crisis cartels' whose participants agree to close down part of their productive capacity in the event that demand falls so far that normal competition is thought to be impossible. This arises because of the disparity between the total productive capacity of the industry and the actual demand for output of those factories. Without some form of industry-wide agreement the weaker units in the sector may close down altogether, leaving only a small number of active undertakings, leading inevitably to a sharp increase in unemployment and social dislocation.

Under normal economic theory, the productive capacity of such an industry would have to decline to the point where it matched available demand, notwithstanding the painful nature of that transition period. The Treaty of Rome came into being at a time when economic expansion seemed set to continue indefinitely, and no qualifying clauses limit the operation of Article 81 in the event of such crises arising. The agreement entered into to mitigate the effect of such substantial falls in demand would be essentially 'defensive', rather than creative, and therefore open to suspicion. Moreover, it was not immediately apparent how the four conditions could be applied without considerable strain upon their language. In particular, it was difficult to see how a crisis cartel could be shown to 'improve the production or distribution of goods' or 'promote technical or economic progress' if consumers had to receive a fair share of the resulting benefit. The furthest that the Commission went during the first years of its operation was to reduce or dispense with fines in cases where proven agreements or concerted practices were made during crises in various industries affected by major recession in demand, such as iron and steel, lead, glass, and cement.

The continuation of the recession through the late 1970s eventually led to a reconsideration of policy which surfaced officially in the *12th Annual Report*,[21] in which the Commission gave guidance on how far solutions for restructuring individual industries were compatible with Article 81. The Commission defined the situation in which it would tolerate restructuring agreements, but not in the form of official notices, of the kind issued in respect of commercial agencies and sub-contracting on earlier occasions, nor in the form of a block exemption, as this would have required preparation of a draft whose content would have posed particular difficulties and which would in any case have been subject to the usual extended consultation. The announcement in the *12th Annual Report* was on a more informal basis, indicating that the Commission's approach was to treat such agreements more generously, and providing guidelines to alert those preparing such agreements to the limitations the Commission would impose upon them.

The minimum requirement laid down by the Commission for this kind of agreement was

---

[21] (1982), pp.43–5, where the issues that such cases place before the Commission are well stated. A more recent statement of the Commission's attitude is found in the *23rd Annual Report* (1993), pp.47–50.

that a structural overcapacity must be shown to exist which had caused all the undertakings concerned, over a prolonged period, a significant reduction in their rate of capacity utilization leading to a drop in output accompanied by substantial operating losses with no expectation of lasting improvement in the medium term. The conditions upon which the Commission would insist before granting exemption for an agreement containing mutual reductions in capacity and output would include the following:

(a) the reduction in overcapacity must be permanent and irreversible and of an amount which would enable the existing participants in the industry to compete at this lower level of capacity;[22]

(b) the cutback must facilitate moves to specialization by individual companies; and

(c) the timing of the reduction in capacity must be carried out so as to minimize the social dislocation caused by the inevitable loss of employment.

Since the first announcement of the policy change, there have been a number of decisions by the Commission permitting agreements in this category. A leading example is the *Synthetic Fibres* case[23] (Commission 1985). The companies involved manufactured synthetic fibres, principally polyester and polyamide. The factories owned by the undertakings had been operating for the period 1981 to 1983, with between 54.7 and 77.6 per cent of the various markets for the different fibres, and comprised 81 per cent of the installed products capacity for the EC. As a result of a serious imbalance between this capacity and existing demand, they had tried in 1978 to implement a 13 per cent reduction in capacity, but clearance had been refused by the Commission because of the extent to which production and delivery quotas were an integral part of the scheme. The scheme, although refused clearance, had nevertheless been provisionally implemented. The subject of the new Commission decision was a supplementary agreement signed in 1982 which had also already been partly implemented. Under this each company would commit itself to achieving its own reduction in capacity by a given date and would agree not to increase this until the end of 1985. All the figures would be checked by independent experts and the overall target for the period would be a reduction of 18 per cent of the capacity originally scheduled to remain in existence at the end of the operation of the 1978 agreement.

In its decision approving the exemption, the Commission referred to the definition given in the *12th Annual Report* of continuing over-capacity, and to the fact that market forces had tried but failed to achieve the reduction necessary to re-establish and maintain in a longer term an effective competitive structure. In these circumstances, the need to organize on a collective basis an adjustment to the new levels of demand could, taking a longer view, be argued to be in the benefit of consumers: the industry that would emerge from the restructuring would, at least in theory, have potential for fresh competition, the capacity remaining could be more intensively operated, and trends to specialization encouraged once profitability had returned, since the least profitable plants were those which were likely to be scheduled for closure under the scheme. There was little possibility that the parties would increase prices as the result of approval of the plan because they operated in what was a very competitive market under pressure from available substitute products. Unlike the earlier

---

[22] So that it would not simply become an allocation of existing production levels between them.
[23] [1985] 1 CMLR 787.

1978 agreement, there were no restrictions on the parties' level of production from the reduced capacity or the total deliveries which they could make. Whilst the number of decisions of this kind has remained small in recent years it would be wise to remember that economic circumstances can change and that the principles applied in cases like *Synthetic Fibres* may well become relevant once again. That this area of the law remains far from a dead letter. is shown by *Stichting Baksteen*[24] in 1995. Here the Dutch brick industry found itself in crisis at the beginning of the 1990s with a considerable surplus of brick production capacity which had led to large stock piles. The surplus had been caused by a combination of larger plants producing bricks at a higher rate and a fall in demand owing to recession in the building industry in The Netherlands. The high capital cost of brickworks means that they are only economic if run close to full capacity; to bring supply and demand into balance through price adjustments was impossible because of the inelasticity of demand. The only rational solution was the closure of the oldest and least efficient brick plants. This could only be achieved by an agreement between all the Dutch producers, under which a levy was paid by each of them in order to compensate those producers whose plants had to be permanently closed down under the industry plan.

The Commission had objected to the industry original plan which involved the implementation of production quotas backed by a system of fines in order to support the permanent closure of some works. The later revised plan was however approved and it was agreed that no new capacity would be brought onstream for a period of at least five years.

The history of the alteration of Commission policy towards crisis cartels shows the flexibility inherent in Article 81(3) and in particular that the results of its application may vary at different times against differing economic backgrounds. These cases, however, do pose major difficulties in DG Comp and the Commission generally, because of the substantial political pressures which inevitably accompany such cases. Such pressures may come not only from national and industrial sources, but also from other DGs within the Commission, whose differing responsibilities may result in them urging policy arguments which in their view should take precedence over normal application of Article 81(1).

5. CARTELS CONTROLLING NATIONAL MARKETS

The Commission has struck down numerous horizontal agreements which have attempted to provide either exclusive purchasing arrangements or exclusive selling agreements between manufacturers in competition with each other. By contrast, bilateral arrangements made for the distribution of goods in particular territories have generally been regarded in a more favourable light by the Commission. A case however of exclusive purchasing unfavourably received by the Commission was *Atka A/S v. BP Kemi A/S and Danske Spritfabrikker.*[25] Here, the element in the agreement to which the Commission objected was the fact that DDSF was required to purchase all its requirements of synthetic ethanol from BP Kemi up to a maximum amount, and BP Kemi had the opportunity of supplying excess quantities on similar terms. This would give BP Kemi a substantial advantage over all other competitors in the market, especially because in return for its assurance of supplies, BP Kemi was guaranteed

---

[24] [1995] 4 CMLR 646.   [25] Discussed in Ch. 6, p.67.

by DDSF at least one-quarter of the combined sales of ethanol in Denmark; if these exceeded certain percentages, compensating payments had to be made to DDSF in return. In effect this was a market-sharing agreement which assured supplies to DDSF for a period of six years and would in practice relieve it from having to seek supplies from any other foreign source.

Restrictive agreements of a horizontal nature affecting national sales are commonly found in the cement industry. In *Netherlands Cement*[26] (Commission 1972) a sales agency was formed by a number of German cement manufacturers to handle the sale of their cement in that country. These manufacturers bound themselves to sell only through this company, at the price fixed by the trade association of Dutch cement traders. Quotas were granted to individual German suppliers, and detailed provisions governing the conditions of sale, quality guarantees, freight charges, and many other contractual details were imposed, with penalties to be paid if a member deviated from the rules. The manufacturers retained no freedom as to the prices to be charged and had to follow the decision of the Dutch cement traders. The application for exemption under Article 81(3) was refused because the obliga- tion of the manufacturers in Germany to sell only on these conditions restrained their freedom substantially, whereas each was perfectly capable of selling direct into Holland. The buyers, rather than having a number of suppliers, would have to deal with only a single supplier, and the volume of business was again controlled not by the individual manufactur- ers responding to demand but by a single agency working in close association with the traders' association. Even if the arrangements did make the distribution process more effi- cient, there was little evidence that it would benefit buyers.

By contrast, the case of *Société de Vente de Ciments et Bétons de l'Est (SVCB)* v. *Kerpen and Kerpen*[27] (European Court 1985) involved a bilateral agreement. The French plaintiff com- pany (which later went into liquidation) agreed to supply 40,000 tonnes of cement annually to Kerpens in Germany annually for the next five years. The German company agreed as a condition of the contract that it would not resell the cement in Saarland and would also pay attention to the interests of the works partly owned by the supplier at Karlsruhe if asked to make deliveries in that area. When the liquidator of SVCB claimed payment for the cement, the defendant argued that the contract was void under Article 81. In a preliminary ruling under Article 234, the Court held that the agreement was indeed void since it had as its object the reduction of competition in a part of the Common Market; moreover as the total quantity on an annual basis amounted to between 10 and 15 per cent of all exports of cement by France to Germany, this was adjudged sufficient to have an appreciable effect on trade between Member States.

However, not all such arrangements necessarily fall within the prohibition of the Art- icle. In the *Kali und Salz* cases[28] (European Court 1975) the Commission had ruled that Article 81(1) applied to an agreement under which Kali-Chemi sold its surplus potash production, which it did not require for the manufacture of compound fertilizer, to a much larger company, Kali und Salz. This was the only other German potash manu- facturer, having approximately 90 per cent of the total production, Kali-Chemi having the

---

[26] *Cementregeling voor Nederland* [1973] CMLR D149. See also *Cimbel* [1973] CMLR D167 and *Neder- landse Cement-Handelsmaatshappij* [1973] CMLR D257.

[27] Case 319/82 [1983] ECR 4173: [1985] 1 CMLR 511.

[28] Cases 19–20/74 [1975] ECR 499: 2 CMLR 154.

other 10 per cent. There had been a gradual decline in the surplus quantities made available by Kali-Chemi to Kali und Salz, and in defending the agreement Kali-Chemi argued that it could not have disposed of the potash in any other way because of the expense involved in setting up a separate sales organization solely for the sale of potash. The Court ruled that the Commission's decision had failed to give sufficient weight, neither to the fact that the surplus supplies which Kali-Chemi had agreed that Kali und Salz should dispose of were gradually reducing nor to the expense involved for Kali-Chemi in establishing a separate sales organization. For this reason the decision was annulled.

In other sectors, the benefit to purchasers may be held sufficient to justify the grant of exemption to joint selling arrangements, notwithstanding the Commission's normal long-standing objection to such arrangements. In *United International Pictures*[29] (Commission 1989) three major US film producers (Paramount, MGM, and MCA) with a total market share of 25 per cent in the Common Market had formed a joint sales company for distributing their films. Each shareholder/producer had to give the sales company a right of first refusal for the distribution of its films, and could require it to distribute particular films if it chose. The Commission found that the agreement had not eliminated all competition between the three producers since each retained considerable control over distribution in certain Member States; however, it did enable more effective distribution through the Community as a whole so that consumers in each Member State could enjoy a wider range of films.

The flexibility of Article 81(3) in its application to horizontal agreements relating to national markets is shown by subsequent developments in this case. Originally the Commission had intimated to the parties that it would be unwilling to continue the individual exemption after its expiration in 1993. Subsequent investigations, however, indicated to the Commission that competition in the film exhibition business in the Member States of the Community had substantially improved, with a number of new cinemas having been opened. The balance of power between the European and the US films had apparently not been affected by the horizontal agreement between the major producers approved in the original decision, and indeed the market share of the UIP consortium had fallen over the 1990s. It had not been used to coordinate release dates in an anti-competitive way; the renewal of the arrangements was actually supported by a large number of the industry players including independent producers and exhibitors. A comfort letter was therefore issued in this case continuing the exemption subject to certain changes in the agreement under which for example UIP's right of first refusal in respect of the films made by the three participants had to be applied on a national basis rather than for the entire Community as one territory. The filmmakers for their part gave an undertaking to maintain the highest possible degree of independence in the conduct of their filming businesses. It appears, nevertheless, from press comment at the start of 2003 that the Commission now has renewed concerns about the restrictive quality of distribution agreements in this industry which affect the EC, and a further investigation has been launched.

[29] [1990] 4 CMLR 749.

6. CARTELS OPERATED BY OR THROUGH TRADE ASSOCIATIONS

6.1 DUTCH TRADE ASSOCIATION CASES

The experience of competition authorities in both the EC and the United States has led to the conclusion that often trade associations are very closely associated with agreements or concerted practice in breach of Article 81(1) or its US equivalent, section 1 of the Sherman Act. In cases such as the *Cement* case, mentioned below,[30] a trade association has often been created primarily to provide the necessary administrative links for the operation of the cartel and may indeed have no other real reason for existence. In other cases, however, the trade association does have a valid primary purpose, of representing the interests of its members and of providing facilities of value to their business. Many of such agreements have not involved necessarily a background of recession or fall in demand but have been maintained simply on a basis of protectionism.

The absence until more recently of a Dutch national law dealing with cartels has meant that the Commission has had to intervene in a number of national cartels in that Member State. The *SPO*[31] case involved the Dutch building industry association, on which large fines were imposed by the Commission which were confirmed by the Court of First Instance in early 1995. The rules of this Association provided that when its members tendered for a building contract a meeting of the tenderers should be held to determine which undertaking would deliver the lowest competitive bid. The tenderer chosen would then be protected in various ways from competition by the other members and would also have to add certain sums to the tendered price to cover reimbursement by it to the other tenderers of their own unsuccessful tender costs. The Court confirmed the finding of the Commission that this exchange of information was unlawful since it limited the party's freedom to negotiate and increased the price payable by the building customer. Benefits from the arrangements were enjoyed by the members of the association, not by the customers. The restrictions of competition were also held not to be indispensable to achieve their alleged aims, namely improvement of the market balance between demand and supply; limiting transaction costs for tenderers would ruin competition between them. In particular, the Court believed that contract awarders who knew their requirements best were effectively excluded from the system:

The *FEG/TU*[32] case concerned the Dutch Association of Wholesalers for Electrical Fittings such as cables, switches, switchgear equipment and trunking (FEG) and its largest and most influential member TU. A British company found difficulties in obtaining supplies on the Dutch market because it was not a member of the FEG and was refused membership (on the grounds that its turnover in The Netherlands was insufficiently high!) as the rules of FEG prohibited supply to non-members. FEG and TU had combined their market leverage to engage in collective exclusive dealing agreements both with individual suppliers and with NAVEG (the importer' association) for such

---

[30] At pp.158–9.

[31] Case T-29/92 [1995] ECR II-289. The new Dutch competition law adopting the provisions equivalent to Arts 81 and 82, came into force on 1 January 1998, too late to be applicable here.

[32] [2000] 4 CMLR 1208.

fittings so as to prevent non-members of FEG entering the market. Moreover in relation to its own wholesale members FEG fixed increases in retail prices and regulated discounts prohibiting loss leader advertisements. All these practices had the single aim of improving the profit margins of the FEG members. The Commission found the practices a clear breach of Article 81(1) and imposed fines on both FEG and TU.

6.2 CARTELS OPERATING THROUGH THE EXCHANGE OF INFORMATION

One of the most effective ways of reducing competition within an industry is by the detailed exchange of confidential information between its members, and trade associations are often involved in such activities.

Nevertheless, it is important to realize that such agreements may exist between undertakings without any form of common membership in an organization, while an organization may have only a tenuous existence as a trade association if dominated by a few large producers in an oligopolistic setting. The *Fatty Acids*[33] decision shows that the Commission is capable of sophisticated analysis of this type of arrangement and is able to distinguish the 'pure exchange' of information from that which is linked to anti-competitive involvement in the details of a competitor's trading arrangements, including market shares, pricing, and order book. In the *Fatty Acids* case, three leading European manufacturers of oleine and stearine were fined for information exchanges which allowed them to adjust their production and marketing policies with knowledge of each other's plans and thereby avoid 'destructive' competition.

The case of *VNP/Cobelpa*[34] raised new issues relating to the exchange of financial information between associations. Important manufacturers in two countries belonged to the relevant federations, and the information exchanged between them and their individual members included notification of relevant prices, naming individual companies, their general terms of supply, sales, and payments, including discounts granted to particular customers, rebates, and changes in price levels. The original object of their coordination was claimed to have been to align prices with those of manufacturers in countries to which they exported, but it gradually developed into a widespread collection, analysis, and distribution of virtually all the data that would have been required by undertakings within the two countries so as to anticipate the trading and pricing policies of their rivals.

The Commission's view was that the collection and analysis of figures from individual members of the association, with the object of preparing output and sales statistics, was itself a legitimate purpose for a trade association,[35] nor could there be objection to national associations or federations exchanging the same type of statistical information giving a general picture of the output and sales of the individual federation. Real objections, however, arise when individual undertakings within the body are identified, or where the simple exchange of aggregated information about the collective fortunes of the industry is replaced

---

[33] [1989] 4 CMLR 445. See Ch. 8, pp.123–4.

[34] [1977] 2 CMLR D28. The federations were of paper manufacturers in Belgium and The Netherlands.

[35] This view had been cautiously expressed by the Commission as long ago as the 1968 Notice on Co-Operation between Enterprises, where the distinction was drawn between the provisions of aggregated data on the one hand and 'conclusions given in a form that they induce at least some of the participating enterprises to behave in an identical manner on the market' on the other.

by a supply of information about the trading of individual members of the associations. In this case, the exchange was so detailed that it allowed members to plan export sales policy with exact knowledge of the prices charged by the local manufacturers in that market for various grades of paper. Even if some of the pricing information could have been obtained from other sources, the convenient form in which it was provided saved the parties a considerable amount of time. Whilst there was some price legislation in effect, the exchange of information went far beyond mere exchange of those prices subject to control.

More recently the UK *Agricultural Tractor Registration Exchange* decision[36] (Commission 1992, upheld by the CFI in 1995 and the ECJ in 1998) emphasized the importance of the extent to which, in the context of a national market, the exchange of information identifies individual undertakings. The seven manufacturers or sole importers of agricultural tractors into the United Kingdom between 1975 and 1988 had systematically exchanged information through their association about their individual sales. This information was extremely detailed, broken down into sales at national, regional, county, dealer territory, and post code level. This meant not only that manufacturers' sales performance could be measured but even the performance of individual dealers in their territories. The information included the exact number of particular models sold by each member, as well as the volume of retail sales and market share held by each for particular horse-power groups. These facts were passed by each manufacturer to all its own dealers, creating a market with almost complete transparency.

In a fully competitive market it could of course be argued that such transparency would aid competition. The UK tractor market, however, was oligopolistic, the four largest suppliers holding some 80 per cent, and the remaining three members of the association only 2 or 3 per cent each, whilst non-members held no more than 13 per cent (a figure that had not increased since the information exchange began in 1975). Moreover, in some areas the smaller suppliers were not represented at all. Barriers to entry were high, because of the need for suppliers to provide a large network of dealers to carry out repairs and service quickly for farmer customers. Sales volumes were quite low (about 20,000 tractors per annum) and brand loyalty had made it hard even for existing members, let alone new entrants, to increase their market share.

In its decision upholding the Commission decision terminating the exchange, the Court of First Instance found that there was an effective agreement between the members of the association that each would organize their sales territories in a way that facilitated this exchange, and that this knowledge enabled them to reduce competition between members and between their dealers, the element of uncertainty in respect of sales strategy and performance having been almost completely eliminated.

The value of the exchange of relevant information can be equally important at an international level. In the *Cement Cartel*[37] case Cembureau had compiled for its members, cement producers and associations of producers across Western Europe, a wide range of information on prices prevailing for cement in different markets as well as the supply and demand balance at different times. In some cases this information would not have been

---

[36] *Fiatagri UK and Others v. Commission* Cases T-34 and 35/92 [1994] ECR II-905. The Commission decision is reported at [1993] 4 CMLR 358. The ECJ decision (Cases 7 and 8/95) is at [1998] ECR I-3111, 3175, and 5 CMLR 311, 362.

[37] Cases 25–104/95 [2000] ECR II-491: 5 CMLR 204.

available at all to the members, in others only as a result of considerable expenditure of time and money. Nevertheless the Commission has shown itself willing to give individual exemption or even negative clearance to information exchanges when these are limited to associations of relatively weak undertakings which may be purchasers in a oligopolistic market, especially if the exchange does not include the most sensitive categories of data such as current sales information or identification of customers. In *Eudim*[38] (Commission 1996) a group of wholesalers supplying plumbing, heating, and sanitary equipment exchanged information on general market conditions in various Member States where they operated and especially about prices being charged by their suppliers, mainly large companies. It was agreed, however, as part of the exemption of the agreement by the Commission that a restriction preventing members from trading outside their own national territories would be eliminated.

It is possible from these decided cases to identify those elements in an information exchange scheme which are most likely to damage the competitive structure of individual markets. First, the extent to which the information provided is aggregated by taking a large number of individual companies, and producing global figures for individual regions or countries, by contrast with information provided about individual undertakings so that their costs, turnover, and even profits can be calculated with some accuracy by rivals. The second relevant factor is the extent to which information as to relevant products are split into their individual grades or classes, or are aggregated so as to make calculation of individual statistics more difficult. The third element is the extent to which this information is made available to the public, and in particular to end-users and consumers; the more widely disseminated the information, the less likely that it will provide the basis for anti-competitive coordination. The fourth, and perhaps most important issue, is the time-scale and the extent to which information is provided on a current basis or in arrears. The more current the basis upon which the information is provided, the more valuable it is as an aid in eliminating the uncertainty of competitive reaction in planning pricing policy. Other relevant factors are whether restrictions are placed on the identity of those to whom it may be communicated and the purpose to which it may be put. Significant also would be whether current conditions of sale are notified as well as lists of discounts, rebates, and other special deals, and whether the association includes interpretative comments with the figures. Probably of minor importance only is whether the research has been carried out by the association itself, through its own staff or on information provided by members, or whether a third party such as a market research organization or firm of independent chartered accountants carried out the research and provided it on an arm's-length basis. An effective anti-competitive price information scheme could, however, be implemented on either basis, although members of the association will be able to place greater reliance on the accuracy of the figures if certified by such an independent agency.

6.3 CARTELS OPERATED BY TRADE ASSOCIATIONS CONTROLLING STANDARDS AND CERTIFICATION

Another way in which trade associations may seek to reduce competition and raise barriers to new entry is by controlling standards and certification. Standards and certification rights

---

[38] [1996] 4 CMLR 871.

are often originally linked with objective standards of health and safety whose enforcement is delegated to the associations by national government or authorities. Such privileges, however, can be abused.

In the case of *Community* v. *Anseau-Navewa*[39] (European Court 1982) fines were imposed by the Commission, and upheld by the Court of Justice, on associations of manufacturers, importers, and distributors of washing machines and dishwashers in Belgium, as well as an association of water supply companies in that country which had statutory duties to approve appliances to be connected to the public water supply. Under these arrangements machines could only be installed if they had a certificate of conformity, available only from particular associations. These in turn restricted their membership to manufacturers and sole importers, so that general importers and dealers found themselves unable to obtain the necessary certificates. It was clear that the intention of these arrangements was to make it more difficult for parallel imports of such appliances to occur, and exemption under Article 81(3) was therefore refused. The Commission and Court both held that where a trade association is a party to a restrictive agreement of this kind but does not have formal power to order its members to conform, if its recommendations are in practice followed because of the grave practical problems which the manufacturers and dealers will other-wise encounter, then the agreement will be regarded as binding on the members and treated as a 'decision' under Article 81. The grave practical disadvantage in this case was that foreign manufacturers of washing machines were forced to use sole agents to handle imports into Belgium; any other kind of importer, e.g. a distributor of a variety of such machines, would not be eligible to obtain the necessary certificate.

Difficulties in certifying the safety of cranes which foreign mobile crane operators wished to introduce to The Netherlands were raised in *van Marwijk* v. *FNK* and *SCK* (Commission 1995).[40] Here the trade association of Dutch mobile crane operators (FNK) also controlled the certification agency, SCK. Both national and Community rules required safety checks to be made on mobile cranes and certification that these had been met. Participation in certification by SCK was much cheaper for national members of the local trade association FNK than for non-members including foreign operators. The certification procedure by SCK was not totally open and transparent and gave no weight to equivalent guarantees produced by certification systems in other Member States. Under the system of *inhuurverbod* firms were not allowed to hire mobile cranes from undertakings not affiliated to SCK. The rules of the certification scheme were adjudged to breach Article 81(1), and fines were imposed.

6.4 OTHER FORMS OF TRADE ASSOCIATION RESTRICTIONS ON COMPETITION

Where the membership of a trade association consists largely of producers of the same goods or services, its rules may seek to limit the competition between them. *The Danish Fur Breeders' Association* provided a number of facilities for its members who sold fox and mink

---

[39] Cases 96–102, 104–5, 108, 110/82 [1983] ECR 3369: [1984] 3 CMLR 276, reported at the European Court level as *IAZ International Belgium* v. *Commission*.

[40] [1996] 4 CMLR 565, a Commission decision upheld by the CFI as Cases T-213/95 and 18/96 [1997] ECR II-1739: [1998] 4 CMLR 259.

furs, including a production centre for pelts and an auction house. Use of the facilities was conditional upon the observation of a number of rules limiting the use by members of other auction houses for disposal of their pelts, and their ability to act as collecting agents for competing sales organizations. Each member also had to agree to a certain percentage of its production being sold at one of five auctions held annually by the Association. These rules were not surprisingly found to be in breach of Article 81 and a fine was imposed.[41]

Particular problems are also caused when members of trade associations combine in connection with exports. The law of individual States often permits export associations to make agreements that would normally be illegal if carried out purely for domestic markets. The oldest and best known example is the United States Webb-Pomerene Export Trade Act 1918, which provides that nothing in the Sherman Act shall make illegal 'an association entered into for the sole purpose of engaging in export trade and actually engaged solely in such export trade'. The *Woodpulp*[42] decision of the European Court in 1988 had to consider the status of such an agreement, by the Kraft Export Association, to which several pulp manufacturers in the United States belonged and who were accused by the Commission of having agreed prices for sulphate pulp.

The Court's finding was that this Association could not be held responsible for any agreements on pricing made between its members since it made no separate recommendations to them but simply announced the terms of pricing agreements made by them in a number of separate meetings. The Association had also always distanced itself from the implementation of those agreements.

In considering the effect of restrictions that trade associations may seek to impose on their members, the degree of their influence and their power of exclusion from national or regional markets will be closely considered by DG Comp. Therefore, if an association is able to control public markets or 'bottle neck' facilities, any restrictive provisions which cause detriment to members, non-member traders, or consumers are likely to be in breach of Article 81(1). The *FRUBO*[43] case is a clear example. Here, the associations of fruit importers and wholesalers between them controlled 75 per cent of the sales of apples, pears, and citrus fruits in The Netherlands. The associations were able to impose the sanction of total exclusion from such auction on any importer or wholesaler who dared to break the associations' rules, which with very limited exceptions provided that the Rotterdam auctions should be the only route for importing fruit into The Netherlands. The object and the likely effect of these restrictions, if unchecked, would have been to give Rotterdam a virtual monopoly over the import of fruit into The Netherlands and to prevent wholesalers from using alternative sources of supply of fruit originating from outside the Community.

Trade associations also frequently attempt to make rules for their members covering the holding of international trade fairs and exhibitions, since they claim that an absence of guidelines applied to the organization of and attendance by exhibitors at such occasions could seriously affect the reputation of individual major events by limiting the full range of products displayed, reducing the special impact which the exhibition may have on its market. The Commission has attempted to apply Article 81(3) to such restrictions in a

---

[41] *Hudson's Bay and Annings* v. *Danish Fur Breeders' Association (No. 1)* [1989] 4 CMLR 340; on appeal some of the Commission's findings were overruled and the fine reduced. (Case T-61/89 [1992] ECR II-1931.)

[42] Cases 89, 104, 114, 116–17, 125–9/85: [1988] ECR 5193: 4 CMLR 901.

[43] Case 71/74 [1975] ECR 563: 2 CMLR 123. The facts were considered in Ch. 7, p.106.

reasonable way, in order to provide in effect a 'rule of reason' for their assessment, distinguishing between, on one hand, those ancillary to the need for some limitation on the 'free for all' that could exist if no restrictions were allowed, and on the other hand, restrictions which are unduly and unnecessarily onerous. Examples from a number of industries, including motor cars, exhibitions, engineering, and dental products, can be found in various Annual Reports: a common thread running through the cases is the importance of preventing discrimination in the relevant rules on a national basis. Commission decisions which illustrate the way in which it applies this principle include those in *British Dental Trade Association*[44] and *CECIMO (No. 3).*[45]

The reader may be surprised that the cases cited in this chapter are invariably dealt with under Article 81 rather than Article 82.[46] The main reason is that the wide definitions given by the Court and Commission to 'decision' and to 'concerted practices' makes the use of Article 82 unnecessary in the great majority of cases, since the structure and rules of the association will usually ensure that any practices which it authorizes, or rules which it enforces or suggests, will come within one or more of these definitions. There will be no need for the Commission to perform the possibly more difficult task of showing that the association is 'dominant' in some particular market and that it is abusing its dominance.

---

[44] [1989] 4 CMLR 1021.   [45] [1990] 4 CMLR 231.

[46] Chapter 15, Section 8, considers the use made by the Commission of Article 82 against a particular form of trade association; namely, collective owners of intellectual property rights.

10

DISTRIBUTION AGREEMENTS AND PRACTICES

1. INTRODUCTION

The development of any product for sale involves a substantial investment of both time and money. This may be wasted if an appropriate system is not available for distributing the product to the point of sale. This is particularly true of consumer goods, e.g. lawn-mowers, clothing, or cutlery, sold in large numbers primarily through wholesalers, then to a variety of retail establishments including specialist shops, department stores, cash-and-carry outlets, supermarkets, and discount houses. The same applies to goods for industrial use, whether sold for use or consumption by industrial concerns or for incorporation by purchasers in their own manufacturing operation, e.g. screws, valves, or iron bars. In every case, commercial success depends largely on the choice of an appropriate distribution system.

Any manufacturer considering how to distribute products in the European Union or any of its Member States has a wide range of choice. The main decision is how far its distribution system should be integrated with the rest of its organization. The greatest degree of control is generally obtained by making its own employees (whether based at home or abroad) responsible for ensuring distribution of its goods to the chosen form of outlet in the relevant geographical markets within the Community. Reliance on one's own employees for sales can, of course, be combined with other means of promotion such as exhibiting at trade fairs, maintaining a local showroom or warehouse, and mailing catalogues and other sales information to prospective customers.

In many cases, however, direct representation may not be the best method of ensuring effective distribution in a foreign country. The advantages of organizing distribution through those familiar with local markets, languages, and conditions may well mean that a local representative is chosen, either an agent or a distributor. A manufacturer's relationship with an agent is quite different from that with a distributor; an agent is a person or company with the task of bringing its principal (the manufacturer) into contractual relationships with customers. Agents are normally paid by a percentage commission on the sales which they effect. By contrast, the distributor stands at arm's length from the manufacturer, purchasing goods from it on agreed terms, normally at its own risk, and reselling either direct to the public or indirectly through its choice of wholesalers and dealers.

2. DISTRIBUTION THROUGH AN AGENT

2.1 ARTICLE 81 AND AGENCY

Although competition policy in the Community has been far more concerned with the relationship between manufacturers and their distributors, particularly exclusive distributors, a review of the law relating to distribution of goods must begin with a brief consideration of the legal position of the commercial agent. There are, of course, many varieties of commercial agent. These include the simple commission agent, who does not hold stocks of the product but merely passes orders back to the manufacturer, who delivers goods direct to the customer. Another is the 'stocking agent' who, in addition to his selling function, provides warehousing facilities for a certain amount of the manufacturer's stock, for which he receives a fixed payment, but without acquiring ownership of the goods. An agent may also give other kinds of help to the manufacturer, such as the provision of service facilities for which he will often have to carry a stock of spare parts purchased from the manufacturer. The agent may also take on a *del credere* responsibility, under which he will accept liability for payment of accounts by those customers whom he introduced to the manufacturer, relieving the manufacturer of the risk of non-payment, for the cost of an additional commission percentage.

The mere appointment of an agent, however, does not itself bring in Article 81 unless it involves some express or implied restriction upon either the agent or his principal. If an agent is appointed simply to act as an agent for a product in a particular territory, Article 81 has no application, since the essential restriction upon competition is lacking. Whilst manufacturers do sometimes retain the right to appoint a number of agents in parallel in one territory, competing with each other, and agents are sometimes under no restriction as to the supply of competing products to customers, this is comparatively rare. It is far more usual in the European Union to find that either manufacturer or agent, or both, accept restrictions on their commercial freedom. The restriction on the manufacturer may be that having appointed an agent for a given territory, say France, it agrees to appoint no other agent for that territory; for its part, the agent may agree that within France it will represent no other manufacturer selling identical or competing products.

2.2 THE 1962 NOTICE

It is with this latter kind of agency agreement that the 1962 Commission Notice on exclusive agency contracts made with commercial agents was concerned. This stated that the decisive criterion which in the view of the Commission distinguished an agent from the independent trader was the extent of the agent's responsibility for the financial risks connected with the performance of his obligations. If the agent undertook any element of risk on his own account, then his function became more similar to that of an independent trader and, for the purposes of the competition rules, he was to be treated as an independent undertaking. On the other hand, if the agent simply performed the basic role of seeking customers for its principal, the agent's restriction to the goods of its principal was acceptable as the inherent consequence of the agency relationship.

The timing of the 1962 announcement was significant: it appeared only five weeks before the deadline for notification of bilateral agreements under Regulation 17/62 (1 February 1963). It was the first of a number of Notices issued by the Commission providing guidance to enable undertakings to decide their legal position under Article 81(1) and to discourage them from filing unnecessary and purely precautionary notifications. The legal basis for the Notice had already been challenged by the Italian government in proceedings at the European Court in the *Consten-Grundig*[1] case in 1966. The Court, rejecting the suggestion that Article 81 applied only to arrangements between parties in direct competition with each other, ruled to the contrary that this Article referred generally to all agreements which distorted competition within the Community. The Article made no distinction at all between agreements between undertakings competing at the same level of production and those between non-competing undertakings operating at different levels. The Court went on to say that a distortion of competition could occur within the meaning of Article 81(1) not only where agreements limited competition between the parties but also where agreements prevented competition between one of them and third parties.

It was also established early that the Commission will always look at the economic reality of a commercial relationship, rather than the legal description applied by the parties to their agreements. This principle is highlighted by the decision in *Pittsburg Corning Europe*.[2] In this case, a Belgian subsidiary of a United States corporation manufactured cellular glass and distributed it in Belgium, Holland, and Germany. The prices which it was able to obtain for this product in Germany were some 40 per cent higher than those which could be obtained in Belgium and Holland. It therefore tried to insist that orders from its Belgian and Dutch distributors always indicated the ultimate country of destination of the goods ordered (the glass normally being used in the construction of a new building), so as to deter distributors from sending goods by way of parallel imports into Germany and undercutting the prices being obtained by its German distributors. Because parallel imports into Germany had occurred, the system of control was later tightened still further by increasing prices for glass sold into Belgium and Holland substantially, subject to a reduction if it could be shown later that the glass had actually been installed in a site in Belgium or Holland rather than Germany.

The arrangement, if made between independent undertakings, clearly represented a concerted practice under which a single territory with a high price level for this product was separated from other territories with a lower price level. The argument raised by Pittsburg Corning Europe was that the Belgian distributor, Formica Belgium, was merely an agent; the written agreement described Formica Belgium in this way. After examining the facts, the Commission concluded that the designation 'agent' in this agreement was accorded merely for tax reasons and did not reflect the actual relationship. For this reason, the agency concession contained in the Notice was inapplicable, and a fine was imposed on Pittsburg Corning Europe for breach of the provisions of Article 81 by its arrangements for differential pricing between the separate national markets.

The question also arose as to whether the benefit of the Notice could apply to agents who act for more than one principal. The argument has been made that a principal cannot claim to have integrated an agent into its own sales network (as the Notice appears to

---

[1] Cases 56 and 58/64 [1966] ECR 299: CMLR 418. See also *Italy* v. *Council and Commission*, discussed in Ch. 5, pp.49–51.

[2] [1973] CMLR D2. This case was briefly referred to in Ch. 6, at p.64.

contemplate) if that agent devotes only part of its time and effort to promoting the products of that principal, reserving a substantial commitment also to competing manufacturers. The approach taken by the Court in the complex *Sugar Cartel*[3] case suggests that so long as the agent only undertakes a limited function, it does not matter whether it takes this function solely for a single principal (with whom it normally becomes closely associated in the course of dealing) or whether it spreads its efforts over a number of principals for each of which it will remain only partially involved, provided only that it accepts no risk in any of them. If, however, the appointment is accepted by the agent, not as its sole occupation, but while it is also engaged as a broker or manufacturer, then this split status would tend to weaken the likelihood that the Notice could benefit it.[4] Also the Notice probably did not apply if the company claiming to act as agent was so large and powerful that in practice it was suf-ficiently independent not simply to obey the requirements of the principal but to have substantial influence on the distribution policy of the principal. It was also essential that the appointment of an agent did not involve the appointment of an actual or potential competi-tor, since the required integration of function clearly was not possible if the economic interests of the two undertakings were opposed to each other.

2.3 THE POLICY DILEMMA

After some years it became clear that the Notice no longer reflected the later Court decisions already mentioned, nor certain changes in the Commission's own approach. Over the years following the publication of the Notice, Court decisions and Commission practice had diverged appreciably from it, perhaps most noticeably over the significance of an 'agent' working for more than one principal[5] and it became clear that a revised Notice was needed. In fact it was not until 2000 that the Commission published official revised guidelines.

While a principal reason for the lack of progress in this area was the low priority accorded by the Commission to agency matters, as compared with issues of exclusive distribution and purchasing, mergers, and joint ventures, there was also a clear policy dilemma.

The problem was reflected in the opinion of Advocate General Tesauro in the *BKA/VW* case[6] (European Court 1996). This Article 234 case concerned the issue of whether the requirement by VW on its German dealers to develop their activities as agents for leasing out VW cars exclusively through VW's own leasing subsidiary (VAG Leasing) was caught by Article 81(1). VW argued that the German VAG dealers, as agents for VAG Leasing, formed a 'single economic unit' with both VW and VAG Leasing. The Court rejected this argument, principally on the basis that the commercial risks taken by the dealers were greater than under the normal form of agency; the agency was not voluntary but an obligatory adjunct to their status as selective distributors of VW cars for sale. No VW dealer had the alternative available to it of running its own leasing company.

---

[3] Case 40/73 [1975] ECR 1663: [1976] 1 CMLR 295. See also Ch. 6, pp.95/96.

[4] See also the Commission's decision in *ARG/Unipart* [1988] 4 CMLR 513, a case where the agent's role varied according to the category of product (various kinds of spare parts for cars) in which it dealt. Art. 81(1) was held to apply to all the relationships except that where the agent accepted no risk at all. However, an individual exemption for seven years was granted to all the arrangements, which included wholesaling functions for some products as well as agency relationships for others.

[5] In particular in *Flemish Travel Agents* Case 311/85 [1987] ECR 3801: [1989] 4 CMLR 213.

[6] Case C-266/93 [1995] ECR I-3477: [1996] 4 CMLR 505, 514.

The Advocate General's opinion also dealt with issues that went to the heart of the Commission's dilemma in framing general principles on agency issues. It summarized the Commission's attitude to agency as having identified three situations where Article 81 would apply to such a relationship. First when the agent bore, at least in part, the financial risks involved; second when the agent competed on its own account directly against its principal in the same market; and third when the agent acted for a number of competing principals in the same market. The Commission's problem is that it was the restrictive clauses which the agent entered into in its Volkswagen contract which actually prevented it from taking part in activities under the second and third categories, which Volkswagen argued made it more of an 'integrated agent'; but these very restrictions were themselves anti-competitive. For this reason Tesauro A-G rightly concluded that the concept of the 'economic unit' by itself provided no general solution to the problem of deciding which agency contracts fall under Article 81; he stated that 'search for universal parameters capable of providing a general answer to all agency contracts . . . is doomed to fail'.

2.4 CURRENT POLICY ON AGENCY AGREEMENTS

Review of the 1962 Notice was repeatedly postponed, and it is perhaps a measure of the difficulty of this issue that even in its 1996 Green Paper[7] in which it proposed radical reform of the competition rules on distribution agreements, the Commission chose not to discuss agency at all. But presumably the consultations following its publication convinced the Commission that the issue was too important to be postponed yet again, because the resulting Guidelines, though primarily focused on distribution by independent distributors, did deal with it. However, the relevant parts of the Guidelines were clearly drafted relatively late in the day and are not entirely satisfactory.

Current official guidance on the Commission's approach to agency agreements is contained in paragraphs 12 to 20 of its Guidelines on Vertical Restraints.[8] Despite Tesauro A-G's scepticism as to the appropriateness of making special provision for agency agreements, this is what has again been done by the Commission. But because the Guidelines do not accord in all respects with the Court's case law, which is of higher legal authority, the law remains uncertain, and this is an area of law where it is crucial to read the Guidelines in conjunction with the relevant judgments.

The Guidelines make clear that, as under the 1962 Notice, the crucial criterion for the more favourable treatment under Article 81 is that of financial and commercial risk. The relevant types of risk which will prevent an agent being regarded as a 'genuine agent' are categorised as either relating to the contracts negotiated or concluded, such as financing of stocks, or relating to market-specific investments which are required to enable the agent to negotiate of conclude the type of contract concerned, and which are unlikely to be recouped if he leaves that field of activity, and a non-exhaustive list of both kinds of risk is given. Where an agent bears any significant risk of either type he is regarded as an independent dealer who must be free to determine his own marketing strategy and Article 81 applies in full to arrangements made between him and his principal, just as it would to any other distribution arrangement. On the other hand, the kind of risks borne by anyone in business,

---

[7] Green Paper on Vertical Restraints in EC Competition Policy COM(96)721.
[8] [2000] OJ C291/1 [2000] 5 CMLR 1074.

such as those inherent in leasing premises, or related to his degree of success as an agent, are not relevant.

The Guidelines are silent in respect of other criteria of agency that have been applied by the Court. For example, in a number of cases the Commission has referred to 'independence of action' of the agent as precluding genuine agency. This may be because of the size or economic strength of the agent, or the fact that it has a number of other profitable businesses, and particularly businesses which compete with the principal, which prevent it from being economically dependent on the principal. More recently the Court in *BKA/VW* mentioned as a factor precluding genuine agency the fact that the agents' 'principal business of sales and after-sales services is carried on, largely independently, in their own name and for their own account'.

Even more difficult to interpret is the fact that the Guidelines do not refer explicitly to the requirement that the agent be 'integrated' into the principal's business, which was a key factor in the Court's rejection of arguments based on agency in the *Sugar Cartel* and *Flemish Travel Agents* cases. As recently as 1995 the Court reiterated in *BKA/VW* that agents had to act as 'auxiliary organs forming an integrated part of the principal's undertaking'. All the Guidelines say, and this in direct contradiction to the Court in these cases, is that it is irrelevant whether the agent acts for one or several principals.

Even in the case of genuine agency, the Guidelines do not allow all aspects of the contract between agent and principal to escape the application of Article 81. They state that in such cases, Article 81 does not apply to 'obligations imposed on the agent as to the contracts negotiated and/or concluded on behalf of the principal'. These include limitations on the area in which or the customers to whom the agent may sell goods or services, and the prices and conditions which the agent is required to apply.

Other restrictive terms in the agency agreement, such as territorial or customer exclusivity, or a prohibition on the agent acting as agent for competing goods, are in principle subject to Article 81, even in the case of genuine agency. The Commission considers that the former do not normally have anti-competitive effects. As to the latter, it says that non-compete clauses may infringe Article 81(1) if they foreclose the market to competing products. This is consistent with the position that an agent may act for several principals, because if agents were required to work for one principal only, then a non-compete clause, or at least the absence of such competition, would be a requirement of 'genuine agency'. However, it contradicts the Court cases referred to above, which suggest that Article 81 does not apply at all to a genuine agency agreement.

The divergence between the Court's case law and the Commission's Guidelines is perhaps explained by the fact that the case law, in particular on the need for integration and the restriction of the agent to one principal, has itself been the subject of criticism, not least by Tesauro A-G. However, given that the Court in *BKA/VW* chose not to follow his approach, it is not at all clear why the Commission now feels justified in taking a similar approach.

3. DISTRIBUTION AGREEMENTS: THE EARLY YEARS

3.1 EXCLUSIVE DISTRIBUTION

Before considering current law and policy relating to distribution it is useful to summarize events leading up to it. The present state of the law is more easily understood once the development of the subject during the early years has been explained.

The number of bilateral distribution agreements filed after the coming into force of Regulation 17 was so large that the Commission's priority was to prepare a block exemption eliminating the need to review too many individual agreements. It chose exclusive distribution as the subject of its first block exemption, Regulation 67/67, in part because early on it had recognized the advantages of exclusivity agreements for both manufacturer and distributor. Some of these advantages were set out by the Commission in the recitals to the original block exemption which it issued in 1967:

The entrepreneur is able to consolidate his sales activities . . . he is not obliged to maintain numerous business contracts with a large number of dealers, and the . . . fact of maintaining contacts with only one dealer makes it easier to overcome sales difficulties resulting from linguistic, legal and other differences; . . . exclusive dealing agreements facilitate the promotion of the sale of a product and make it possible to carry out more intensive marketing and to ensure continuity of supplies, while at the same time rationalising distribution; moreover the appointment of an exclusive distributor . . . who will take over, in place of the manufacturer, sales promotion, after-sales service and carrying of stocks, is often the sole means whereby small and medium-sized undertakings can compete in the market . . .[9]

Another important factor was that such agreements amounted to nearly three-quarters of all bilateral agreements notified. Of course, the Commission had already issued a certain number of decisions on exclusive distribution agreements. The primary influence on the content of the Regulation was *Consten-Grundig*, which provided a clear model for future patterns of distribution by exclusive distributors. The principles laid down by the Commission in its decision, approved with only minor adjustments by the Court, formed the foundation for the original block exemption Regulation.

It is important to note that the European Court had established very early on, before Regulation 67/67 was adopted, that not all distribution arrangements, nor even all exclusive distribution arrangements, fall within Article 81(1). In the 1966 case of *Société Technique Minière (STM)* v. *Maschinenbau Ulm*,[10] the Court had ruled that some exclusive distribution agreements did not contain the elements necessary to bring them within Article 81(1), and that in determining this issue the following should be considered:

(1) the nature of the products covered, and whether the supply was of limited or unlimited amount;

(2) the importance of both the supplier and the distributor with respect to the relevant markets;

(3) whether the agreement was isolated or one of a network of agreements covering at least a substantial area or region of a Member State; and

---

[9] Recital 10 of Reg. 67/67, which came into force on 1 May 1967.

[10] Case 56/65 [1966] ECR 234: CMLR 357.

(4) the degree of territorial protection afforded by the agreement, in particular whether the agreement aimed to give absolute territorial protection, and whether parallel imports could be brought into the territory by third parties.

If, after applying these tests, it appears that there is either no effect on trade between Member States or no object or effect of imposing any restriction on competition within the Community, then the Commission's interest should cease. If, however, as is often the case, there is significant impact in both these respects, then Article 81(1) applies and exemption, either through a block exemption or individual Commission decision, is needed.

Regulation 67/67 exempted agreements:

(i)   between one supplier (S) and one distributor (D);

(ii)   under which S agreed to supply only D with the relevant defined goods (G) for resale within a specific territory (T) forming part or all of the Community;

(iii) if D agreed to purchase such goods for resale in T only from S, and not to sell competing goods during the term of the agreement or for one year afterwards. (D could not be restricted as to unrelated types of goods);

(iv)   if S could place no restriction on D as to prices or customers but could subject D to certain obligations, namely to purchase complete ranges of goods or minimum quantities, to sell goods under S's trade marks and packaging, and to take promotional measures including provision of an adequate sales network, stock, guarantee services and adequate trained staff;

(v)   it was essential that S remain free to supply other dealers or users outside T, even if he knew they intended to use or resell them in T, and

(vi)   D had to be free to sell G outside T provided that it received the orders passively, not advertising or having branches or depots outside T. Finally,

(vii) S and D could not be competing manufacturers granting each other reciprocal distribution rights;

(viii) nor could they exercise industrial property rights or otherwise act so as to make it difficult for dealers or consumers to obtain G from elsewhere.

These eight elements comprised the original model for automatically permitted exclusive distribution; they were subsequently interpreted and developed by both Commission and Court decisions[11] during the period between the first implementation of the Regulations in 1967 and their replacement in 1983.

After 1967 a large proportion of notified exclusive distribution agreements were brought under the terms of the block exemption, enabling DG Comp to turn to the other individual notifications already made: many other distribution agreements that could not benefit from the exemption remained for consideration. Some kinds of clauses could make individual exemption difficult or impossible. The central importance of the integration of the national markets into a single market meant that the existence within such an agreement of any form

[11] For example, the Commission originally assumed that exclusive distribution agreements affecting only one Member State, and made between parties solely from that State, would fall outside Art. 81 because of the lack of effect on trade between Member States; however, the European Court took a different view in *Fonderies Roubaix-Wattrelos* v. *Fonderies Roux* Case 63/75 [1976] ECR 111: 1 CMLR 538.

of ban on exports, direct or indirect, was fatal to a claim for individual exemption. The strong line adopted from the outset by the Commission in this area was fully supported by the Court. This, of course, runs directly contrary to the immediate interests of the distributor, who would prefer to have absolute territorial protection for his own area so that neither the manufacturer nor any other distributor appointed for another Member State could enter it. This had been precisely the hope of Consten in the *Grundig* case, in which such protection had been sought deliberately both by the use of the 'GINT' trade mark coupled with French unfair competition law and by the contractual export restriction on distributors in Germany. Even now, any absolute ban on exports in an exclusive distribution agreement will almost certainly have to be deleted if exemption is to be available. This has been laid down in a number of cases before the Commission and by several European Court rulings.[12]

Distribution could also be hindered indirectly rather than directly by clauses creating a disincentive to export. If consumer goods were sold within one Member State, the Commission regarded it as essential that there be no restriction on their resale which discouraged their export to other Member States. For example, in the case of consumer goods, this resale was less easy if a purchaser in another Member State was unable to rely on the original guarantee.[13]

3.2 EXCLUSIVE PURCHASING

One of the issues arising under Regulation 67/67 was the extent to which it covered exclusive purchasing (that is, a requirement on D to purchase all of his supplies of G from S) and non-compete clauses (that is, where D is prohibited from selling within T goods which compete with G), in the absence of exclusive distribution: in other words whether (ii) above was essential if an agreement was to benefit from automatic exemption.

An exclusive distribution agreement will normally include a promise by the distributor to its manufacturer not to distribute or manufacture competing goods made by other manufacturers. It may in addition be required to purchase all its needs for contract goods from the other party, and not, say, from other distributors. In the exclusive distribution agreement, this exclusivity relates to a specific territorial area. In the true exclusive purchasing agreement, no territorial area is named, and the purchaser remains in competition with all other parties entering into similar agreements, though of course the manufacturer will normally take care to ensure that the number of distributors granted this concession is not unrealistically high, so that all can enjoy a reasonable level of turnover. Undoubtedly, such agreements offer potential economic advantages to both parties. The manufacturer is enabled to calculate the likely demand for his product over the period of the agreement. The distributor, in return for committing himself for a reasonable length of time, often receives special prices, preference in supply if shortages occur, and perhaps the provision of technical

---

[12] *Miller International* v. *Commission* Case 19/77 [1978] ECR 131: 2 CMLR 334. See Ch. 7, p.98.

[13] *Zanussi* [1979] 1 CMLR 81. See also *ETA Fabriques d'Ebauches* v. *DK Investment SA* Case 31/85 [1985] ECR 3933: [1986] 2 CMLR 674, an Art. 234 case involving cheap Swiss watches. On the other hand, it is not a breach of Art. 81 for a retailer to provide a special service for goods acquired through official distributors so long as the standard manufacturer's guarantee is available to all purchasers. *Hasselblad* v. *Commission* Case 86/82 [1984] ECR 883: 1 CMLR 559. Nor are manufacturers of goods sold through selective distributorships obliged to provide guarantees on their products that have been sold to the public other than through their official dealer network: *Metro* v. *Cartier*, Case C-376/92 [1994] ECR I-15: 5 CMLR 331. See Ch. 11, p.195.

and financial assistance. In particular, the acceptance of an exclusive purchase arrangement is often the principal condition for making loans on favourable terms to individual businesses which cannot easily acquire these funds on comparable terms from other sources.

At an early stage in the development of competition policy, the European Court had taken a relatively relaxed attitude to non-compete agreements. In *Brasserie de Haecht* v. *Wilkin-Janssens (No. 1)*[14] (European Court 1967) the Court of Justice stated that:

agreements whereby an undertaking agrees to obtain its supplies from one undertaking to the exclusion of all others do not by their very nature necessarily include all the elements constituting incompatibility with the Common Market as referred to in Article 81(1) of the Treaty. Such agreements may, however, exhibit such elements, where taken either in isolation or together with others, and in the economic and legal context in which they are made on the basis of a set of objective factors of law or of fact, they may affect trade between Member States and where they have either as their object or effect the prevention, restriction or distortion of competition.

In this case a Belgian brewery brought a claim against its tenants for breach of their agreement to sell only beers produced by the brewery; the tenants claimed that the agreement was null and void under Article 81 because it prevented them from selling other beers and thereby restricted trade between Member States, since it limited the outlets in Belgium for foreign breweries. Although the effects would be trivial for an agreement affecting a single café or inn, the Court of Justice held, on this reference for a preliminary ruling under Article 234, that the effects of such a tying agreement must not be considered in isolation but in the light of the fact that it formed part of a network of similar agreements. On the other hand, if one or more parties to the agreement were powerful in their particular markets, and had important market shares, their agreement considered in isolation might be caught under 81(1) so that the issue of exemption under the four conditions of 81(3) would become relevant. If additional restrictions were placed upon the dealer, particularly those affecting the terms and conditions upon which he could resell or his choice of customers, these were likely to weigh against the validity of the agreement. However, if market entry by manufacturers through the opening up of new outlets (or finding alternative forms of distribution such as hyper-markets) was in practice available, then clearly the exclusionary effect of the purchasing arrangements would be less pronounced.

Whilst Commission consideration of the amendments to be introduced to Regulation 67/67 was still in progress, the Court held in the *Concordia* case[15] that the Regulation could apply even when there was no specific geographical area referred to in the contract within which resale of the product was permitted.

3.3 THE 1983 BLOCK EXEMPTIONS

In fact Regulation 67/67 was replaced in 1983 by two separate block exemption Regulations. Regulation 1983/83, like its predecessor, exempted certain types of exclusive distribution agreements, while Regulation 1984/83 exempted certain exclusive purchasing agreements. The new Regulations aimed to reflect the Commission's experience of distribution agreements and the Court's judgments, but they proved controversial and went through a

---

[14] Case 23/67 [1967] ECR 407: [1968] CMLR 26; discussed in Ch. 7, p.86.
[15] *De Norre* v. *Brouwerij Concordia* Case 47/76 [1977] ECR 65: 1 CMLR 378.

number of drafts, the first dated February 1978, and only finally entered into effect on 1 July 1983.

Regulation 1983/83 retained the same basic thrust as Regulation 67/67, but there were a number of detailed amendments to the rules. Regulation 1984/83 covered both exclusive purchasing and non-compete obligations (that is, both the requirement on D to obtain all his supplies of G from S, and not to manufacture or distribute goods competing with G) but imposed a maximum duration of five years. It also included special rules applicable to beer and petrol distribution, which presented particular problems in the light of the cumulative effect of the many large exclusive purchase networks in these sectors.

In addition, for the first time, at the request of numerous industrial and commercial organizations and trade associations, the Commission issued guidelines on its interpretation of the individual clauses of the Regulations. Though these did not prevent a national court interpreting the Regulations independently, and still less did they stop the European Court from making its own, legally binding, interpretation, they were extremely useful to any lawyer or businessman seeking to interpret the Regulations, and usually had at least persuasive influence. Not least, they were also an invaluable aid to the DG Comp officials applying the rules. The practice of issuing Guidelines in support of new Block Exemption Regulations is now well established.

In general, these block exemptions worked well, and for many sectors they were adopted as the operating model. The extensive use of the legislation, however, had the effect of placing the legal structure of distribution in a 'strait-jacket', which was not commercially desirable, especially as distribution methods continue to change in the light of advancing technology. The European Court had already made clear in the *Delimitis* case[16] that even a minor or technical departure from the permitted model of the block exemption in the form of an additional obligation or restriction on the distributor or supplier made the benefit of the exemption totally unavailable. Support therefore gradually grew for a more flexible, economics-based approach, which was officially discussed for the first time in the Commission's 1996 Green Paper.

4. THE 1996 COMMISSION GREEN PAPER ON VERTICAL RESTRAINTS

The question of the approach to be adopted towards vertical agreements for the distribution of goods was a principal concern within DG Comp throughout the second half of the 1990s. The discussion ranged much more widely than exclusive distribution and purchasing, encompassing also franchising and selective distribution,[17] both of which were by then very popular forms of distribution. The process of reform of the block exemption for licences for technology transfer, as described in Chapter 12, had shown the Commission the importance of substantive and far-reaching consultation with all interested groups before making formal proposals for amendment of existing legislation. It was found necessary in that case to take into account not only the wishes and views of industry, of the professions, and of Member States, in the light of the experience of how the block exemption for technology

---

[16] Case C-234/89 [1991] ECR I-935: [1992] 5 CMLR 210. [17] Discussed in Ch. 11 at pp.199–203.

transfer had worked over a number of years, but also to consider the ability of the Commission to operate an effective system while it remained unable to deal promptly with individual notification of agreements because of lack of resources. For this reason it was decided that a Green Paper should be published setting out the options for the future shape of such block exemptions; after some delay, caused by disagreements within the Commission, this was published in 1996.[18]

The Green Paper set out its aim of providing a detailed consultation process on the approach to be adopted by the Commission to distribution in the light of three major factors, namely:

— that the existing block exemption covering forms of distribution would expire shortly and that review was necessary to prepare for its renewal, with any changes considered necessary;

— that the Single Market legislation was now largely in place so that in future private barriers, that is arrangements between undertakings, might gain in importance relative to public barriers as a cause of partition of the Single Market; and

— that there had been major changes in both the structure of final distribution and the organization of distribution logistics, largely due to the application of information technology.

Of the Green Paper's eight chapters, Nos 1 and 7 provided an interesting account of the changing patterns of the distribution of goods, reflecting evidence submitted from a number of sources. The distinction between manufacturing, wholesaling, and retail functions was now less clearly defined than before: increasingly the chain of supply is treated as indivisible, without clear demarcation points; suppliers often provide wholesaling services whilst retailers are often integrated backwards into wholesaling or even manufacture. Distribution is a major activity within the Community: at the beginning of the 1990s there were over 4 million undertakings involved in it, of which some three-quarters were retailing businesses.

The Commission acknowledged that it is not always easy to define what wholesaling means under modern circumstances. The central concept, however, is that of a 'bridge' between the supplier and the retailer which brings about the necessary conversion from the goods leaving the production line in one form into the quantities to be supplied through location, timing, and price in a form acceptable to retailers. The existence of wholesalers in any market plays an important role in maintaining its competitive nature. Technological change has operated against the maintenance of wholesalers as a separate form of undertaking; in particular the point of sale information now available to retail chains enables them to forecast demand with great accuracy and thus to exercise precise control over their stock levels and delivery requirements. The principles of delivery 'just in time' which in recent years has meant that factories have been requiring component deliveries for production lines merely hours, in some cases even minutes, prior to actual use has for this reason spread to the distribution market. This forces very close co-operation between all parties in the chain of supply.

Undertakings specializing in warehousing and physical distribution for a number of larger manufacturers have also come into existence, and can now provide some of the services previously offered by wholesalers, without necessarily acquiring title to the goods

---

[18] See fn. 7.

which they handle. Small buyers, for example local grocery shops, have often formed buying groups or co-operatives under which a single trading style is applied to all its members to enable bulk purchases and keener pricing. Alternatively, such retail outlets may obtain much of their stock, not by delivery from manufacturers or wholesalers, but by themselves visiting local cash and carry warehouses. Retailing itself has become more specialized for products such as garden and recreational equipment, furniture, clothing, and toys. On the other hand, it was clear that many retailers remained hesitant about obtaining goods from parallel import sources because of the lack of certainty of continuity of supply and fear of retaliatory action by manufacturers.

Chapter 2 of the Green Paper contained an economic analysis of the way in which a variety of contractual restraints contained in distribution contracts have affected the growth of the Single Market. It was clear that the process of integration still had some way to go and that it was still possible to find significant price differences between Member States. The statistics produced did show some convergence in consumer goods and services, though considerably less in sectors such as energy and construction where the Single Market has developed more slowly. The Paper stated that vertical restraints, e.g. exclusivity of territory, may in many circumstances have had a beneficial effect on relationships between suppliers and distributors, enabling distributors to focus their efforts on the products of particular manufacturers and to minimize 'free riding' by other dealers at the expense of those dealers who do make the required investment. On the other hand, the structure of exclusive distribution itself can make intrabrand competition less lively than may be desirable. Competing manufacturers seeking to come into such a market at a later date may not in such circumstances be able to find sufficient competent distributors in strategic locations.

The rest of the Green Paper described existing law and practice at Community and national level, and finally set out possible options for change, ranging from maintaining the existing system more or less unchanged, to the replacement of the existing rules by a generally applicable block exemption available where the parties' market shares fell below 40 per cent.

In November 1998 this discussion text was followed by the Commission's 'Follow-up to the Green Paper on Vertical Restraints,'[19] which set out the Commission's intention to adopt a single, broadly applicable block exemption Regulation, to include market share limits on its application. Though the detail of this proposal was somewhat changed by the time it was adopted, the broad framework proposed by the Commission remained. The details of the new Regulation will be discussed in the following sections.

5. DISTRIBUTION AGREEMENTS: POLICY SINCE 1999

Some three years after the Green Paper was published, the solution finally adopted was the replacement of the block exemptions on exclusive distribution, exclusive purchasing, and franchising with a single block exemption Regulation[20] intended to cover these three

---

[19] [1998] OJ C365/3 [1999] 4 CMLR 281.

[20] Regulation 2790/99 on the application of Art. 81(3) of the Treaty to categories of vertical agreements and concerted practices [1999] OJ L336/21 [2000] 4 CMLR 398. Although the title of the Regulation refers to vertical agreements, in fact it is only intended to deal with supply and distribution, and not with other types of vertical agreements such as intellectual property licences.

types of agreement, as well as selective distribution agreements, which had not previously benefited from any block exemption.[21] It entered into force on 1 June 2000. The Regulation was accompanied by very detailed Guidelines[22] on the application of the Regulation, and on the treatment of distribution agreements falling outside the scope of the Regulation.

The current policy on vertical restraints is still of course governed by Article 81 and the Court's jurisprudence. However, while the Commission still works within the bounds of this framework, its general approach is now clearly grounded more firmly in economics than in the past, and a generally more relaxed attitude to such restraints is in evidence.[23] This can be seen in the policy statements in the Guidelines, and in the new block exemption, which provides a much greater degree of freedom for firms without market power than did the earlier block exemptions. As a result, the number of notifications to the Commission of vertical agreements has dropped substantially.

Firms above the 30 per cent market threshold laid down by the Regulation, on the other hand, are now in a worse position than before, as they can never benefit from a block exemption. If they enjoy over 40 per cent and are dominant in their market their situation is even worse: not only can they no longer benefit from any block exemption, but the Commission has said in its Guidelines that such firms are unlikely to receive individual exemption for their vertical restraints.

The following discussion will deal with distribution agreements in general, and much of what is said here applies to selective distribution and franchising agreements. However, as there is much to be said in addition which specifically relates to these particular types of distribution arrangement, they will also be discussed separately in the next chapter.

5.1 WHEN WILL A DISTRIBUTION AGREEMENT INFRINGE ARTICLE 81(1)?

For obvious practical reasons there is a tendency to approach distribution law issues as block exemption issues: that is, to start by seeing whether the arrangement in question fits within the scope of the applicable block exemption. However, as the European Court established in 1966 in *STM* v. *Maschinenbau Ulm*,[24] distribution agreements, even exclusive ones, do not necessarily infringe Article 81(1). In the case of many agreements no exemption is therefore necessary. As DG Comp's practice has evolved, particularly in recent years, to look increasingly at the economic effects and less at the contractual wording of agreements, it has become confirmed in its view that most distribution agreements deserve generous treatment.

Economics classifies distribution agreements as 'vertical' (because they concern parties acting, at least for the purposes of the agreement, at different levels in the supply chain) and

---

[21] Before the Commission could adopt such a broad block exemption the Council enabling Reg. 19/65 had to be amended to give it the necessary powers: Reg. 1215/99, [1999] OJ L148/1.

[22] Guidelines on Vertical Restraints [2000] OJ C291/1 [2000] 5 CMLR 1074.

[23] Though some have argued that the reform should have been more radical, e.g. 'The Reform of the European Competition Policy concerning Vertical Restraints', R. Subiotto and F. Amato (2000), 69 *Antitrust Law Journal* 147–193. See also J. Lever and S. Neubauer, 'Vertical Restraints: Their Motivation and Justification' [2000] 21 ECLR 7–23.

[24] Case 56/65 (1966) ECR 235: CMLR 357.

as a general rule, from an economic point of view, these pose less of a threat to competition than do 'horizontal' agreements (between competing firms).

The Commission's approach, stated expressly in the Guidelines, is that restrictions in distribution agreements are frequently economically beneficial as long as interbrand competition remains strong.[25] Most restrictive clauses need to be looked at in their market and economic context in order to establish whether they do in fact constitute an appreciable restriction on competition. Relevant factors include market shares and market structure, product differentiation, barriers to entry, the existence of potential competition, collusion or oligopolistic behaviour between competing firms, buyer power, and the cumulative effects of a number of similar networks.

Restrictions on interbrand competition are normally viewed with more concern than restrictions on intrabrand competition. Where a supplier has a strong market presence then exclusive purchase and non-compete clauses will raise issues, because of the risk to interbrand competition where competing suppliers cannot find distributors for their products. Foreclosure of other buyers may occur where a powerful distributor operates an exclusive distribution system, but because the effects will be felt on intrabrand competition, they are less likely to raise concerns, unless interbrand competition is weak.

Only maximum resale price maintenance and absolute export prohibitions are treated as infringing Article 81(1) *per se*. These, and various other clauses which are judged on the basis of their economic effects, will now be considered in turn.

5.2 RESALE PRICE MAINTENANCE (RPM)

Resale price maintenance is expressly prohibited by Article 81(1)(*a*) and is treated by the Commission at Court as *a per se* infringement of Article 81(1), though it is a practice whose effects are variously regarded by economists.[26] It may be horizontal, where it is agreed between suppliers, or vertical where a supplier imposes it on his distributor. A whole range of justifications for the practice have been claimed. The manufacturer or supplier may argue that if prices are cut, the prestige or luxury connotations of the product, e.g. perfume, may suggest to consumers that it is of less value.[27] A related argument is that without resale price maintenance, dealers may sell popular brands at unreasonably low prices as loss leaders, even below cost (thereby in the manufacturer's view 'devaluing the brand') in order to attract to its premises customers who will then buy other goods at high prices. It is suggested that without resale price maintenance, the more aggressive retailer will drive smaller dealers out of business, depriving smaller communities of competition at the retail level and permitting the remaining dealers to raise their prices to unreasonable levels.

Another argument in support of the practice is that resale price maintenance is necessary to guarantee dealers a generous profit margin, so that services can be provided which are of value to both customers and the cultural life of the community. In this category could be placed the profit required for electronic consumer goods, where extensive demonstration and advice from the dealer involves substantial expense, which may be incurred without any

---

[25] Paras 5 and 100–102.

[26] The literature on this topic is extensive. For citations see n. 7 of the opinion of Advocate General VerLoren van Themaat in *Dutch Books (VBVB-VBBB)* Cases 43–63/82 [1984] ECR 19: [1985] 1 CMLR 27.

[27] The same argument has been used to justify certain forms of selective distribution, as described in Ch. 11 at pp.195–8.

return if the customer then purchases the goods from a discount store or department store not offering such services but merely the same goods at a lower price. This is an example of the 'free rider' argument often raised as justification for exclusive or selective distribution systems. Alternatively, the manufacturer may claim that a large number of outlets are required for the best distribution of its product, which can only be obtained by offering guaranteed margins. Resale price maintenance may be of value in helping new entrants in a particular trade to obtain dealers who will be encouraged to promote their products if the margins are generous. Of course, contrary arguments are available to most of these grounds for supporting resale price maintenance. The most important is that legalizing the practice prevents retailers from competing with each other on price, and hence tends to raise the overall level of prices that consumers are required to pay. It tends also to have the effect that, if as its consequence inefficient dealers are protected against their inefficiency, efficient dealers are thereby prevented from taking the advantage to which they are entitled from their superior performance.

In its early years DG Comp spent much energy establishing the principle that, even where resale price maintenance was legal at national level, Article 81 applied whenever a system prevented consumers or intermediaries from obtaining products wherever they chose within the Community. But the general trend of recent decades in Member States of the Community and beyond has been to reduce the extent to which resale price maintenance is an acceptable economic practice. By 1997 RPM was generally prohibited in almost all OECD countries, subject only to certain exceptions for books, newspapers, and medicines[28] This means that retail price maintenance is now rare in the Community.

However, in the publishing sector, arguments based on the cultural imperatives of protecting small bookshops unable to afford to discount 'bestseller' titles, and to encourage the continued publishing of books with a small print run have to some extent prevailed.[29] These arguments have strong political support in particular in Germany, where it has been argued in some quarters that this is a cultural issue falling outside the Commission's jurisdiction. Where the system is imposed by law then the Community free movement rules are relevant, but where it is composed of agreements between publishers and retailers Article 81 is potentially applicable.

In 2000 the Commission concluded lengthy negotiations on the legality of German and Austrian RPM systems for German-language books.[30] The version of the agreement eventually accepted by the Commission as not infringing Article 81 applied only within national borders, and could not be applied to exported and re-imported goods. However, it did apply to such goods where they had been exported solely for the purpose of avoiding the national RPM arrangements, a result unlikely to be reached in any other product sector. Such is the political sensitivity of this topic, that the Parliament has called, most recently in May 2002, for the Commission to propose a directive to safeguard national retail price fixing systems

---

[28] OECD Report: Resale Price Maintenance, OCDE/GD(97)229.

[29] Even in the book sector RPM is becoming rarer. In the UK, RPM for books formally came to an end in 1997, when the publishers' agreement known as the Net Book Agreement was declared illegal by the Restrictive Practices Court. However, in practice it had been abandoned in 1995 when several major publishers had withdrawn from it.

[30] *Sammelrevers and Einzelrevers,* [2002] 4 CMLR 1278. A relevant earlier case is *Leclerc Books,* Case 229/83 [1985] ECR I: 2 CMLR 286.

for books. So far the Commission has resisted, saying that there is no need for such legislation.[31]

The Commission's current Guidelines repeat the general rule that RPM affecting trade between Member States is prohibited by Article 81, and express considerable reserve with regard even to recommended or fixed maximum prices where a supplier has a strong market position.[32] It considers that in such circumstances these practices may result in most distributors charging the same price (that is, *de facto* RPM), and also that they may facilitate collusion between suppliers. Interestingly, an earlier draft of the Regulation had proposed exempting recommended and fixed maximum price clauses without any market share limit.

5.3 EXCLUSIVE DISTRIBUTION AND TERRITORIAL PROTECTION

Despite its acknowledged benefits, in practice the granting of an exclusive territory to the distributor also is generally treated by the Commission as infringing Article 81, and the greater the degree of territorial protection granted, the more serious is the infringement. Absolute protection, so that a distributor is completely protected from competition from other distributors, even those based outside his territory, is normally treated as a *per se* infringement of Article 81(1) and is unlikely to be exempted. Lesser degrees of protection will also infringe Article 81(1), though they may benefit from exemption. This is partly because of the potential for intrabrand competition to be limited, but more importantly because of the danger it is perceived as posing to creation of a single European market.

As we have already seen, the aim of Community market integration has meant that vertical restraints which divide up territories have been severely treated, and this has tended to obscure the general principle that vertical restrictions are frequently benign. As already discussed, both the Commission and the Court have been severe in their treatment of clauses which either directly or indirectly tend to divide up markets along national frontiers. A recent example illustrating the zeal with which the Commission will pursue any kind of disincentive to distributors to sell outside their own territory is the *Bayer* case[33] (CFI 2000).

Like all pharmaceuticals producers, Bayer has to contend with the existence of different national health policies in different Member States, and in particular with the differing extents to which national governments intervene to set pharmaceutical prices at lower than market rate. In the case of the heart disease drug Adalat, the prices fixed by the Spanish and French health services were, on average, 40 per cent lower than in the United Kingdom.

As a result, Spanish and French wholesalers exported to the United Kingdom, causing Bayer's direct sales there to fall dramatically. To combat this parallel importing, Bayer ceased fulfilling the increasingly large orders which these wholesalers were placing with its Spanish

[31] The special and sensitive nature of this market is underlined by a 1999 Council Resolution which called on the Commission 'whilst applying European competition rules to agreements in cross-border linguistic areas, to take account of the provisions and implications of Art. 128(4) of the Treaty, of the special cultural role of the book market and of the specific value of the book as a cultural object, as well as of relevant national cultural policies', and a similar Resolution in 2001.

[32] Paras 111–112.

[33] Case T-41/96 [2000] ECR II-3383:[2001] 4 CMLR 126, discussed in Ch. 6, pp.70–1. The case is on appeal to the ECJ, Cases C-2 and 3/01P, the Commission arguing that the judgment raises the standard of proof required for a finding of an 'agreement' between undertakings.

and French subsidiaries. Wholesalers complained, and the Commission held that Bayer's conduct amounted to an export prohibition and infringed Article 81(1). It fined Bayer €3 million and ordered it to inform its wholesalers that exports within the Community were not restricted and would not be penalized.

The Court of First Instance took the unusual step of suspending operation of the decision pending the appeal, and eventually annulled the Commission's decision on the grounds that there was no agreement or concerted practice, which is an essential element of Article 81(1), and this aspect of the case is discussed in Chapter 6. In reaching its decision, the Court examined the conduct of Bayer, its national subsidiaries, and its wholesalers in minute detail, before finding that there was not in fact the necessary concurrence of wills for an agreement. But the detail in which the facts are examined suggests that, had they been slightly different, for example had Bayer put an exports monitoring system in place, or had threatened uncooperative wholesalers with sanctions, it might well have lost the case. This is because such conduct could have indicated the existence of an export ban which the wholesalers had implicitly accepted by continuing to deal with Bayer, rather than only a unilateral reduction by Bayer of quantities supplied.

Amongst the many Commission arguments that the Court rejected was the contention that a distribution system operated with the aim of hindering parallel imports necessarily infringes Article 81. While this judgment shows that this is not the case, that there are limits to the Commission's ability to promote parallel imports using Article 81, and that the Court will uphold those limits, it also shows the lengths to which DG Comp is prepared to go in pursuit of the market integration aim. In its 2001 *Annual Report*[34] it stresses the importance it attaches to its pending appeal in this case to the Court of Justice, in the context of its policy of preserving parallel trade.

In a more recent decision the Commission prohibited a dual pricing scheme put in place by *Glaxo*[35] to deal with a similar parallel import problem between Spain and the United Kingdom. The written sales conditions notified to and accepted by wholesalers gave different prices according to the market for which the products were intended, so there was clearly an agreement in this case. Glaxo argued that it was in fact only setting one price, and that the second lower price was imposed on it by Spanish legislation, so that it could not be said to be setting two different prices, and it said that its policy did no more than compensate for a distortion of competition resulting from Spain's national pricing rules and an absence of Community-wide harmonization.

The Commission rejected these arguments, holding that Glaxo does in fact negotiate prices with the Spanish government (though one can question what scope there is for genuine negotiation with a monopoly purchaser), and that the main reason for parallel trade is currency fluctuations. The *Glaxo* decision is currently also on appeal.[36]

It is noteworthy that, even in the absence of a single market for the product concerned, and in the presence of national price controls, there is no scope under Article 81 for manufacturers to take measures to maintain market prices in countries where there is a free market. Essentially, pharmaceutical companies are required to behave as if there were a freely competitive single market for pharmaceuticals throughout the European Union,

---

[34] Para. 231.
[35] [2001] OJ L302/1: [2002] 4 CMLR 335. This case is discussed in Ch. 6, p.71.
[36] Case T-168/01.

whereas in reality national governments keep prices artificially low in some Member States. The Court has been clear that such problems 'must be remedied by measures taken by the Community authorities' rather than by non-application of the competition rules. It can be argued that a company is free to choose not to supply its products in Spain at all. While this is undoubtedly true, it will hardly further the Single Market, or the consumer, cause if companies simply stay out of certain national markets.

In its Vertical Agreement Guidelines the Commission makes particular mention of the importance it attaches to consumers' freedom to purchase in any Member State,[37] and it has imposed extremely high fines in cases where this freedom has been restricted. Despite the benevolence with which DG Comp generally regards distribution agreements, one of the highest fines it has ever imposed on a single company was the €149 million fine on *Nintendo* in 2002 for colluding to prevent exports from the UK to Germany, The Netherlands,[38] and other European countries. Another example is the €102 million fine imposed on *Volkswagen* for hindering parallel imports between Germany and Italy.[39] Indeed, it has been particularly active in rooting out such practices in the car market, and this will be discussed in more detail in the next chapter.

A recently introduced exception to the *per se* prohibition of absolute territorial protection mentioned in the Guidelines occurs when it is used temporarily to launch a new product or penetrate a new area of the Community. The Commission states that such restrictions, provided that they do not last more than two years from the first marketing of the product, will not generally infringe Article 81(1) at all.[40]

5.4 EXCLUSIVE PURCHASE AND NON-COMPETE CLAUSES

As already discussed, a combination of exclusive purchase and non-compete clauses have recognized economic benefits. However, the Commission is well aware that in certain market conditions they pose the risk of foreclosure of the market to competing and potential suppliers, facilitation of supplier collusion, and reduction in interbrand competition.

An 'English clause', which requires the distributor to report any better offer to his supplier, and giving the supplier the opportunity to match that offer, will often have a similar, if perhaps weaker, effect. So will 'quantity forcing', which refers to incentives agreed between the parties which tend to make the distributor concentrate his purchases with that supplier, such as minimum purchase requirements and loyalty rebate schemes.

In deciding whether Article 81 is infringed, the Commission will look at the usual factors such as the market strength of the supplier, but also in particular at the duration of the restriction. The Guidelines give the rule of thumb that non-compete obligations shorter than one year entered into by non-dominant companies can normally be assumed not to infringe Article 81, but that they may do so if concluded for longer than this, depending on other factors.[41]

The *Ice Cream* cases[42] illustrate the kind of situation in which exclusive purchasing

---

[37] Para. 103.   [38] IP/02/1584 of 30 October 2002.

[39] [1998] OJ L124/60. The fine was reduced to €90 million on appeal. See fn. 45, Ch. 11.

[40] Para. 119.

[41] Para. 141.

[42] Case T-7/93 *Langnese-Iglo* v. *Commission* [1995] II ECR 1533: 5 CMLR 602 upheld in Case C-279/95 [1998] I ECR 5609 and Case T-9/93 *Schöller Lebensmittel* v. *Commission* [1995] ECR II-1611: 5 CMLR 602.

arrangements will infringe Article 81(1). Schöller Lebensmittel and Langnese-Iglo had substantial shares in the German market for 'impulse' ice cream. Each operated through a large number of exclusive purchase agreements with retail outlets under which these would buy all their ice cream requirements exclusively from their supplier. For their part both Schöller and Langnese provided freezer cabinets to the retailers without charge provided they were only used for the suppliers' own product and not for those of rival manufacturers. These arrangements were challenged by Mars, which had a very small share of the German 'impulse' ice cream market and sought to win additional market share, *inter alia*, by offering an original range of products under the trade names of well known chocolate bars. The Court of First Instance upheld the Commission's decision in Mars' favour, and ruled that the existing exclusive purchase arrangements operated by Schöller and Langnese not only breached Article 81(1) but were also ineligible for block exemption under Reg. 1984/83 and individual exemption.

In reaching its decision the Court of First Instance referred to the important earlier case of *Delimitis*,[43] which principally concerned the legality of beer supply under ties. In that case, however, the European Court had laid down the principles for the assessment of exclusive purchase agreements generally against Article 81(1). It stressed the importance of looking in a realistic way at the anti-competitive effect of an individual agreement, taking into account both its own terms against the background of the retail market and the circumstances in which the agreements operated generally as part of an overall network.

The relevant factors in the *Ice Cream* cases were the percentage of the market controlled by the tied supplies from the manufacturers in question, and the length of the exclusive purchase obligations agreed to by which trade between Member States was affected. The Court found that there was an appreciable effect on competition as a result of these exclusive purchase arrangements leading to foreclosure of Mars from access to the German market, an effect to which the provision of freezers for exclusive use by retailers for those two suppliers' ice cream made a major contribution. Trade between Member States was affected in that imports from the French subsidiary of Mars were considerably reduced as a result of the exclusive purchase arrangements operated by the two German suppliers.

5.5 OTHER RESTRICTIONS ON DISTRIBUTORS

Article 81 may be infringed where a supplier imposes other restrictions on the way in which his distributors market his goods. The Commission's concerns will be similar to those raised by exclusive distribution and territorial protection though they will be less when there is healthy competition in the relevant market from suppliers of competing goods. Such restrictions might include exclusive customer allocation, where a distributor may only distribute to a restricted group of customers (though this will not necessarily infringe Article 81 in the context of selective distribution, as explained in the next chapter).

Another example is the practice of 'tying' whereby the supplier makes the supply of one product to the distributor conditional upon the purchase of another product, where the second is one that customers do not normally want or expect always to purchase together. The Commission's main concern here is about possible foreclosure of the market for the

---

[43] *Delimitis v. Henninger* Case C-234/89 [1991] ECR I-935: [1992] 5 CMLR 210.

tied product, in particular where tying is combined with a non-compete clause.[44] It will look in particular at factors such as the supplier's strength on the market for the tying product, and the existence of buyer power, to establish whether Article 81(1) is infringed.

5.6 PARALLEL NETWORKS

The leading case on the effect of parallel networks is *Delimitis* v. *Henninger Bräu*[45] (Court of Justice 1991). A dispute had arisen between Delimitis, a former tenant of a café in Frankfurt, and Henninger Bräu, the brewery which owned the premises, as to the sums owing between the parties. Delimitis claimed before the Oberlandesgericht that the exclusive purchase agreements which his agreement with Henninger Bräu contained were not protected by the block exemption and were therefore void under Article 81(1). A number of important issues were raised in the resulting Article 234 reference.

As far as the parallel networks were concerned, the judgment first stated that there were advantages to both brewery and its tenant in having an exclusive distribution agreement, provided that it was neither intended to make nor made it difficult for competitors to enter the beer market in competition with the brewery. The cumulative effect of the brewery's network was, as earlier case law had established, one factor to take into account, looking at the number of the outlets so tied, the duration of that tie, and the degree of loyalty of tenants to the breweries. In addition, however, the actual contribution of the disputed contract to the blocking effect on potential new entry had also to be weighed up. This had perhaps not been sufficiently emphasized in the earlier cases.

6. THE 1999 BLOCK EXEMPTION REGULATION 2790/99

6.1 ELIMINATION OF THE 'WHITE LIST'

Perhaps the single most liberating change in approach in the current block exemption Regulation as compared with earlier block exemptions is the fact that Regulation 2790/99 operates on the basis that everything which is not expressly prohibited is permitted. In other words there are no 'white' and 'grey' lists of clauses to which the parties must limit themselves.

The new rules, involving as they do concepts such as market share, are less clear-cut than those in the previous block exemptions which focused more on the wording of clauses, but the Guidelines offer substantial and detailed assistance to those applying them.

To a large extent the new Regulation removed the 'strait-jacket' effect for which the earlier regimes had been repeatedly criticized, but the unavoidable concomitant of this was a lower level of legal certainty. During consultations, the aim of only subjecting agreements between parties with significant power to individual examination by the Commission was not controversial, but the uncertainty inherent in the economic concepts necessary to achieve this were the subject of much argument.

The impact of this uncertainty is reduced to some extent by a change in the procedural

---

[44] Guidelines, paras 215–224.   [45] See fn. 43.

rules of Regulation 17/62 which, since June 1999, has allowed retrospective exemption of vertical agreements.[46] Previously the Commission could not (except in a very few cases) grant exemption in respect of any period prior to the date of notification of the agreement to the Commission. This means that now, in particular where there is genuine doubt as to whether the block exemption applies, parties need no longer make a preventive filing to protect themselves in the event of future national court litigation. However, while the possibility of retrospective exemption does now exist, in practice, once litigation is threatened or underway, third parties may well object and it may not be as easy to obtain an exemption as it would have been at an earlier stage.

6.2 THE 30 PER CENT MARKET SHARE CAP

In line with its aim of treating distribution in an economics-based, rather than a formalistic, manner, Regulation 2790/99 is intended to grant exemption to distribution agreements between parties without substantial market power. Market power being difficult to measure, market share is taken as an approximate indicator of market power. So the block exemption incorporates for the first time a market share threshold above which automatic exemption is unavailable, and the Regulation is available only where the supplier (or, in the case of exclusive distribution where the exclusive territory covers the whole of the Community, the distributor) does not have a relevant market share exceeding 30 per cent (Article 3).

The introduction of a market share cap was one of the most hotly contested aspects of the Regulation. Industry and its lawyers argued long and vigorously that such a rule would be unworkable, since it is so difficult to establish market shares with any degree of precision, particularly in rapidly developing markets. However, the Commission insisted that there was no better means of ensuring that the benefit of the new, more generous, block exemption, did not go to firms with too much market power, and the market share cap stayed, albeit in the form of a single threshold of 30 per cent, rather than two of 20 per cent and of 40 per cent which had been proposed in an earlier draft. One factor which may have assisted the Commission in prevailing was the fact that while discussions on the block exemption were going on, it published its White Paper on procedural modernization in the application of Articles 81 and 82, which proposed the abolition of the notification system altogether. This may have led some to feel less strongly about the content of the block exemption.

The Guidelines[47] deal in considerable detail with the theoretical question of how to establish market share, and further assistance is available from the Commission's Notice on Market Definition.[48] The question can be particularly difficult in innovative markets involving new technologies, where market definitions and shares shift rapidly with each new technological development. On the one hand, the first to market a new product may, at least for a short time, hold a 100 per cent market share. On the other hand, the phenomenon of 'convergence' whereby it becomes possible to receive phone messages or watch films on a personal computer, means that product market definitions change rapidly. However, in most markets the difficulty often lies not so much in theoretical market definition, as in the absence of the kind of statistics and information required, since companies frequently do not have records broken down in a suitable way, and even where they do, the information for

---

[46] Effected by Reg. 1216/99, [1999] OJ L148/5.   [47] Paras 88–99.
[48] [1997] OJ C372/5: [1998] 4 CMLR 177.

different product and geographical markets is often scattered in different places and hard to track down.

Where a company has a market share above the threshold for some of its products and below the threshold for others, the question arises as to whether they need to be split up into different agreements in order to benefit from the Regulation in respect of some products. In practice the Commission is quite relaxed about this, and allows the Regulation to apply in respect of those goods or services for which the conditions of application are fulfilled, even where other goods and services are also covered by the same agreement.

In fact, during the first two years of operation of the Regulation, the Commission has received very few queries in connection with the market share rule. Nor has the flood of notifications from parties with large market shares, predicted by some during the consultations which led up to adoption of the Regulation, materialized. This may be partly due to the fact that, since 1999, vertical distribution agreements have been eligible for retroactive exemption,[49] so that in borderline cases firms may well decide not to notify their agreements. The lengthy consultations leading up to adoption of Regulation seem generally to have resulted in a very reasonable compromise, and one which does not appear to have given rise to any major problems during its first two years of operation.

6.3 WIDER SCOPE OF AGREEMENTS COVERED

Block exemption Regulation 2790/99 is fundamentally different from its predecessors in other ways too. There is no list of permitted restrictions, and so everything which is not expressly prohibited is permitted. This creates a radically different environment from that of earlier exemptions. Parties and their advisers used to have to draft agreements to fit in with the framework provided by a block exemption, and to ensure that no restrictions beyond those expressly permitted were included, failing which the benefit of the block exemption was lost entirely. Now, their situation depends on whether they are below or above the 30 per cent threshold: if below, they are reasonably free to draft as they wish, provided they bear in mind certain forbidden 'hard core' restrictions; if above they cannot benefit from the block exemption at all.

If the market share requirement is satisfied, Article 2(1) provides a broad general exemption where 'two or more undertakings each of which operates, for the purposes of the agreement,[50] at a different level of the production or distribution chain, and relating to the conditions under which the parties may purchase, sell, or resell certain goods or services'.

This means that many types of agreement which previously did not fall within the scope of any of the narrowly drafted previous block exemptions can now enjoy such automatic exemption. The definition cited above includes, for example, agency agreements, agreements for the supply of services and intermediate goods, industrial supply agreements, customer allocation agreements, and many forms of selective distribution. On the other hand, it does not cover motor vehicle distribution agreements[51] nor technology transfer agreements such as intellectual property licences. Nor does it cover rental or leasing contracts, and this can

---

[49] See fn. 46.

[50] Though agreements between competitors may fall within this general definition, the extent to which these can benefit from the Regulation is circumscribed by the additional requirements of Art. 2(4).

[51] These are covered by a sector-specific Reg. 1400/2002 described in the next chapter.

lead to difficulties of interpretation where, for example, access to a telecommunications network is granted, as this can be seen as leasing of the lines, or as supply of a service.

Though the exemption is broadly drawn, the presence of clauses dealing with intellectual property rights can preclude its application altogether, because the agreement is within its scope only where the rights concerned are 'directly related to the use, sale or resale' of the goods or services being supplied to the buyer and are not the 'primary object' of the agreement (Article 2(3)). One consequence of this is that the Commission considers software distribution to fall outside the scope of the Regulation where the distributor is licensed to reproduce the software, but within it if he resells diskettes or CD-Roms containing the software. On the other hand, where software is incorporated in hardware being sold, even where the software is protected by copyright, the Regulation will normally apply.[52] This limitation is also of particular importance in the context of franchising and so will be discussed in the next chapter.

6.4 PROHIBITED OR 'BLACK-LISTED' CLAUSES

As in previous block exemptions, Article 4 sets out a list of elements whose presence in an agreement will make the benefit of the block exemption unavailable to the whole agreement. This is in contrast to the types of clause set out in Article 5, which only entail lack of enforceability of the specific clause, and not of the whole agreement. Interestingly, all the black clauses concern limitations on intrabrand competition, which the Commission has said are usually less detrimental to competition than limitations on competition between different brands. In fact it is not just such express clauses which are caught, but any means which 'directly or indirectly, in isolation or in combination with other factors under the control of the parties', have the same object, which means that companies and their advisers will need to look further than the bare wording of the agreement, even in the context of black clauses. Taking this together with the fact that, although shorter than some of its predecessors, the black list is fairly complex in its wording, it is perhaps not surprising that, of all the aspects of the new policy, it is the black list that has been the subject of the most unofficial queries to DG Comp. The five types of 'black-listed clauses' or 'hard core restraints' covered by Article 4 are discussed below.

(i) Fixed or minimum resale prices (Article 4(a))

The first prohibition mentioned is that on fixed or minimum resale prices, whether these are directly or indirectly enforced. As we have already seen, resale price maintenance has always been treated as a *per se* infringement of Article 81(1), so it was bound to be excluded from any block exemption. The Guidelines mention as an example of possible indirect price-fixing the pre-printing of recommended prices on the packaging of goods.[53]

(ii) Restrictions on the buyer as to where or to whom he may sell (Article 4(b))

The second prohibition, on restrictions on the buyer as to where or to whom he may sell, is the most complex, as it encompasses a rule against such restrictions and four exceptions to that rule. As a first exception, there may be a ban on active sales into an exclusive territory allocated to another buyer or exclusively reserved to the supplier, or on active sales to

---

[52] Guidelines, paras 39–41.   [53] Para. 7.

certain customer categories reserved to another buyer or to the supplier. Exemption of such customer restrictions is a new feature which has not before appeared in block exemptions.

It can be difficult to assess whether a given restriction is, or has the effect of, an active sales ban,[54] in particular where modern electronic forms of distribution are involved. Use of a website to reach customers is not normally considered active selling, and this applies regardless of the language used. This means that, for example, although it is clear that placing advertising in a German newspaper or on a billboard in Germany constitutes active selling, the Guidelines[55] seem to indicate, for example, that the placing of German language advertising on the Internet site of a French company that can be accessed in Germany does not constitute active selling into Germany. This is perhaps surprising, for the main reason for including the German language advertising will almost certainly be to reach customers in Germany.

Second, wholesalers may be stopped from supplying end-users. The third exception relates only to selective distribution and will be discussed in the next chapter, and the fourth allows the buyer to be banned from reselling components, which have been sold to him for incorporation into another product, to competing manufacturers.

(iii) Prohibition on selective distribution retailers making active or passive sales to any end-users (Article 4(c))

Selective distribution cannot therefore be combined with an exclusive distribution obligation on the buyer, except to the extent that the use of location clauses can be used to limit the buyer's freedom of action.[56]

(iv) Prohibition on cross-supplies between members of a selective distribution network (Article 4(d))

(v) Restrictions on the sale of parts to end-users and independent repairers by suppliers to OEM manufacturers (Article 4(e))

The fifth hard-core restriction listed in Article 4 means that OEM manufacturers cannot prevent suppliers selling parts to end-users and independent repairers who are not part of the manufacturer's network. Note that this is the only type of hard-core restriction listed in Article 4 which involves a restriction on the supplier rather than the buyer.

6.5 SINGLE-BRANDING (NON-COMPETE) CLAUSES

The rules on non-compete[57] and related clauses are contained in Article 5 and have in one respect been tightened up in comparison with the previous block exemptions. In the context of exclusive distribution and franchising an exemption was available under them irrespective of the duration of such a clause, but now its duration must be limited to five years, whatever the type of agreement.

---

[54] See Guidelines, paras 49–52.   [55] Para. 51.

[56] This is discussed in Ch. 11 at p.201, with other issues relating to selective distribution.

[57] In Art. 1, 'non-compete' is defined for the purposes of the Regulation so as to include non-compete and requirements clauses which bind a buyer to sourcing over 80 per cent of the type of product in question from the supplier.

On the other hand, such clauses have a special status as compared with other types of prohibited restriction in that they are severable for the purposes of the Regulation, and so their inclusion does not mean that the whole agreement is ineligible for exemption under it. Furthermore, the way in which 'non-compete' is defined would appear to mean that pure exclusive purchase clauses (relating only to where the buyer should source his stocks of the supplier's product, and not mentioning competing products) are not mentioned in the Regulation at all, and so are exempted regardless of duration or the percentage of supplies concerned.

6.6 PARALLEL NETWORKS

In Article 8, a novel provision which caused unease at the time of its proposal and adoption, the Commission is given the power, where 'parallel networks' account for over 50 per cent of a market, to exclude, by means of a specific exemption, its application to certain types of agreement in that market.[58] Six months' notice of such an intended withdrawal, which may apply to specific product and geographic markets as well as to particular types of clause, has to be given. Though it was claimed that this provision amounted to permission for the Commission to rewrite the block exemption at will, and to reintroduce sector-specific rules, to date it has not been used at all.

6.7 BEER AND PETROL

There are, of course, several features common to these two sectors. Both involve liquid products, widely regarded as essential to the maintenance of normal life, which are consumed or utilized on a regular basis in relatively small quantities by individual consumers, but which have to be provided on a wide geographical basis from a large number of outlets. Brand preference is an important factor, so that heavy promotional expenditure is incurred in order to ensure brand loyalty from customers and to attract support for new products; product differentiation is a major element in the competitive struggle between manufacturers. In both cases outlets have to be regularly visited by the supplier's vehicles carrying fresh supplies, and tanks, pumps, and equipment have to be provided. Any interruption in these supplies (as the result of strikes or other cause) may be commercially disastrous, particularly if local competitors are able to take advantage.

The cost of acquiring sites for retail outlets and of rendering them attractive to customers is substantial and often beyond the financial resources of those who will run them. Therefore, it is necessary for suppliers to ensure that these outlets can be let to tenants at rents ultimately linked with the level of turnover they can obtain, or alternatively run by managers employed to run them effectively. Substantial financial assistance to tenants of the outlets is often needed for fitting out the premises to an appropriate standard. This assistance is also made available on favourable terms to owners of premises who are prepared to accept a partial or total tie to the lender's products in return for such loans.

---

[58] The motor vehicle block exemption Regulation (discussed in the next chapter) is a good example of a sector which the Commission sees as requiring extra legal safeguards in the light of the cumulative effect of the high number of near-identical distribution networks.

These factors have led to the development in both industries of many large exclusive purchasing and non-compete agreements, and when it was drafting Regulation 1984/83 the Commission decided that specific provisions were needed to cover these special sectors with their own particular problems. Since then market developments have persuaded the Commission that there is no longer any need for this, and when that Regulation was replaced by Regulation 2790/99 the beer and petrol industries more or less lost their special regimes and were brought within the general rules.

The only remaining vestiges of these sector-specific regimes appear in Article 5 of the vertical restraints block exemption. Article 5(a) provides that the usual limit on exemptable exclusive purchase and non-compete clauses of five years' duration does not apply 'where the contract goods or services are sold by the buyer from premises and land owned by the supplier or leased by the supplier from third parties not connected with the buyer, provided that the duration of the ... obligation does not exceed the period of occupancy of the premises and land by the buyer'. In practice this exception is most likely to apply in the beer and petrol markets.

6.8 WITHDRAWAL BY NATIONAL AUTHORITIES

At the procedural level a major change is that, in any specific case, Article 7 allows withdrawal of the benefit of exemption in respect of all or part of a Member State can be made by the relevant national authorities.[59] Previously, this could only be done by the Commission, and this change anticipates the procedural modernization measures which will apply as from 1 May 2004, and which devolve certain enforcement responsibilities from the Commission to national courts and competition authorities.

6.9 PROVISION OF INDIVIDUAL EXEMPTIONS UNDER ARTICLE 81(3)

The application of Article 81(3) has been considered in detail in Chapter 8. In its Guidelines, the Commission stresses that there is no presumption of infringement of Article 81(3) where the relevant market share is over 30 per cent.[60] The Guidelines refer to benefits arising from restrictions in distribution arrangements including increased interbrand competition, more efficient market penetration, and the streamlining of distribution logistics.[61] The Commission also summarizes what it sees as the four main negative effects of vertical restraints:[62]

(i) 'foreclosure of other suppliers or other buyers by raising barriers to entry';

(ii) 'reduction of interbrand competition between the companies operating on the market, including facilitation of collusion amongst suppliers or buyers';

(iii) 'reduction of intrabrand competition between distributors of the same brand'; and

(iv) 'the creation of obstacles to market integration, including, above all, the freedom of consumers to purchase goods or services in any Member State they choose'.

---

[59] In order to allow the Commission to include this clause the Council enabling Reg. 19/65 had to be amended to give it the necessary powers: Reg. 1215/99, [1999] OJ L148/1.

[60] Para. 62.   [61] Paras 115–117.   [62] Guidelines, para. 103.

7. DISTRIBUTION AND ABUSE OF A DOMINANT POSITION

We have seen that firms with market shares exceeding 30 per cent face a more stringent legal regime than those below the 30 per cent threshold, and that this is a change introduced for the first time by the 1999 block exemption Regulation.

Firms with market shares exceeding around 40 per cent may, depending on the market situation, be regarded as having a dominant position. Article 82 prohibits firms with a dominant market position from abusing that position, and that applies to their distribution practices just as it does to their behaviour in other areas of their business. A number of the potentially abusive practices dealt with in Chapter 15 relate to distribution, including refusal to deal, discriminatory pricing, excessive and predatory pricing, operating discount, and rebate systems and tying.

11

DISTRIBUTION: SELECTIVE DISTRIBUTION AND FRANCHISING

Selective distribution and franchising are forms of distribution. Moreover, since 2000 they have been covered by the same Regulation 2790/99 and its accompanying Guidelines which apply to distribution agreements generally, so that much of the previous chapter is relevant to such systems. However, both the Regulation and Guidelines also include rules and guidance referring specifically to selective distribution and franchising, and these will be discussed in this chapter, together with the relevant Commission decisions and European Court judgments. There is also a section on motor vehicle distribution agreements, which normally involve selective distribution, and which have long been subject to a sector-specific regime.

1. SELECTIVE DISTRIBUTION SYSTEMS

1.1 INTRODUCTION

Selective distribution systems differ from both open and exclusive distribution systems in that, whilst no specific territorial area is allocated to the dealer, a unique restriction is placed upon him, namely a prohibition on the resale of contract goods to other dealers unless these other dealers have themselves already been admitted to the selective system. The essence of selectivity, therefore, is not simply that the supplier selects its main distributors or wholesalers, for if this were the only restrictive element, it would be hard to see how Article 81 could apply at all to such a unilateral act of commercial policy. It is rather that the supplier limits the distribution of goods only to those wholesalers and retailers which satisfy appropriate criteria and as a result have been allowed to join the system. Wholesalers will normally sell to any wholesaler or retailer within the system, whereas retailers may sell to consumers or users, and also, sometimes, to dealers within the approved list.

The establishment of a distribution system utilizing such restrictions might appear at first sight to raise problems under Article 81(1), if the other requirements of the Article were also present. In fact, both Commission and Court have taken a tolerant view of such systems, which provide perhaps the only example of an important group of commercial agreements with specifically restrictive provisions being allowed to remain outside the scope of Article 81(1), for the sake of the advantages which they are said to confer for the distribution of certain types of product. However, this is conditional upon the systems being operated in accordance with limits placed upon them to minimize their overall effect on competition.

1.2 SELECTIVE DISTRIBUTION: THE EARLY YEARS — *METRO/SABA (NO. 1)* AND OTHER CASES

Selective distribution developed particularly in respect of products that fell into one of two categories. The first category, and the most important, was consumer products requiring a high degree of after-sales service because of their inherent complexity and the purchaser's reasonable requirements for both initial guarantee and later sales and service coverage. In this category came motor cars, electric and electronic equipment (such as high-fidelity equipment and personal computers), and (perhaps unexpectedly) false teeth. The second category comprised goods which were not necessarily highly complex but which were expensive and sold under prestige brand names which had been extensively promoted; their manufacturers believe that continuing control over the environment in which the goods are sold is important to their goodwill and continuing success. Into this latter category come watches and clocks, jewellery, perfume, and some borderline items such as porcelain and possibly even newspapers. (As will be discussed later, the fact that the borders of this second category have been extended so far means that under the 1999 block exemption and related Guidelines the categorization has now become of limited relevance.)

The Commission first began to give active consideration to the legal basis for the assessment of such systems of distribution for both technical and luxury products in the early 1970s. The earliest cases arose in the perfume, automobile, and electrical goods markets. The most important early decision was *Metro/Saba (No. 1)*[1] (European Court 1977). Saba was a German company specializing in electrical and electronic equipment including high-fidelity equipment and television sets. It had established a distribution network in Germany which involved the appointment of wholesalers who would purchase the Saba products and resell them to approved specialist dealers, whose turnover had to be obtained mainly from the sale of electric and electronic equipment of this kind. Department and discount stores would therefore normally have difficulties in obtaining appointment. Other qualifications related to the premises, the acceptance of substantial minimum supply figures, and the stocking of a full range of products, whilst distributors' employees had to have a suitable level of technical expertise. In other EC countries, sales by Saba were made direct to its sole distributor, dealing also only with approved specialist dealers, who in turn served the public.

In the original forms of agreement, there were numerous prohibitions on the sole distributors (and wholesalers) and the specialist dealers. These included prohibition against export to other EC countries, prohibition against 'cross-supplies' (wholesaler to wholesaler or retailer to retailer), 'return supplies' (retailer to wholesaler), and direct supplies by wholesalers or sole distributors to consumers. The Commission rejected all these restrictions except the last, which was accepted on the ground that a separation of the function of wholesalers from those of retailers was appropriate to the multilevel distribution system that Saba operated.

The Commission's decision was challenged by Metro, a self-service wholesaler, running a cash and carry business for retailers which had been unable to obtain admission to the Saba

---

[1] Case 26/76 [1977] ECR 1875: [1978] 2 CMLR 1.

system.[2] Metro challenged the decision of the Commission, claiming that the prohibition on making supplies available to private customers should not be permitted under the exemption afforded by Article 81(3). It also challenged the requirement imposed by Saba that the turnover of wholesalers engaged in a number of different sectors and having a special department for such electrical goods must be on a level comparable with that of a specialized wholesaler. The decision of the Court, given in October 1977, provided the first authoritative judicial pronouncement on the criteria which the Commission had applied to selective distribution systems. The Court held that Metro, whilst entitled to challenge the ruling of the Commission, had failed to adduce sufficient evidence to overturn it. Pointing out that Saba's market share in relation to the various products concerned was in no case greater than approximately 10 per cent (and in some cases less) the Court stated that the nature and intensiveness of competition in such markets would vary to an extent dictated by the nature of the products as well as by the structure of the relevant market itself.

The Court emphasized that price competition was not the only form of competition for specialist wholesalers and retailers. The acceptance of a certain level of prices consistent with consumers' interests in retaining a network of specialist dealers alongside a parallel system of wholesalers operating self-service and other methods of 'low price, no frills' distribution formed a rational objective for the Commission. The availability of this choice for the consumer was considered appropriate especially in sectors covering the production of high quality and technically advanced consumer durable goods, where a relatively small number of large and medium-sized sale producers offered a varied range of readily interchangeable items. While the Commission exempted the various restrictions of the selective distribution system under Article 81(3), the Court took a slightly different approach and ruled that some of those restrictions did not fall under Article 81(1) at all, being normal requirements in the distribution of the sale of consumer durables. Any marketing system based on the selection of outlets necessarily involved the obligation on wholesalers to supply only appointed resellers; therefore, the right for Saba to verify that the wholesalers had carried out these obligations fell outside 81(1), as also the restriction on the sale only to dealers already approved as members of the system.[3]

This decision seemed to give a green light to the approval of such systems, provided that the choice of dealers within the system was based on the qualitative grounds adopted by Saba. On the other hand, the terms of the judgment suggested that a system based on other grounds, e.g. on limiting the total number of distributors within a given Member State or particular area, could only be justified by way of individual exemption, if at all. To keep the agreement outside Article 81(1), the criteria applied had to relate to the technical qualifications of the retailer and its staff and the suitability of its trading premises. Moreover, all conditions had to be laid down uniformly for all potential dealers and not in a discriminatory way, as subsequently confirmed by the Court both in an Article 234 reference in the *Perfumes* cases[4] (European Court 1980) and in the later *AEG/Telefunken* case[5] (European Court 1983), where the Court said:

[2] Metro was later admitted to the system on condition it complied with the restrictions applicable to wholesalers, which included a ban on sales to both private customers and to institutional customers such as schools and hospitals.

[3] Separation of functions as a part of the system also entitled Saba to prohibit wholesalers from selling direct to the large institutional customers which Metro had wished to serve.

[4] E.g. *Lancôme* v. *Etos* Case 99/79 [1980] ECR 2511: [1981] 2 CMLR 164.

[5] Case 107/82 [1983] ECR 3151: [1984] 3 CMLR 325.

It is common ground that agreements constituting a selective system necessarily affect competition in the Common Market. However, it has always been recognised in the case law of the Court that there are legitimate requirements, such as the maintenance of a specialist trade capable of providing specific services as regards high-quality and high-technology products, which may justify a reduction of price competition in favour of competition relating to factors other than price. Systems of selective distribution, in so far as they aim at the attainment of a legitimate goal capable of improving competition in relation to factors other than price, therefore constitute an element of competition which is in conformity with Article [81(1)]. The limitations inherent in a selective distribution system are, however, acceptable only on condition that their aim is in fact an improvement in competition in the sense above mentioned. Otherwise they would have no justification inasmuch as their sole effect would be to reduce price competition.[6]

The application of these principles can be well illustrated by the subsequent 1984 decision of the Commission in the *IBM Personal Computers*[7] case. IBM had created a selective distribution system for which it wished to recruit a large number of dealers capable of offering skilled pre- and post-sales service acting as independent undertakings to sell personal computers in direct competition with IBM's own sales force. Criteria had been published for such appointment and IBM had publicly announced that it would appoint any applicant who satisfied them. The distribution system would then consist of all these authorized dealers who would be required to sell the goods only to each other or to consumers, not to unauthorized dealers. IBM had also appointed wholesale distributors to operate alongside and in competition with its own wholesale subsidiary company. It stated that it would also appoint other wholesalers in such a capacity as long as they could also provide a service of the required standard. Given the high level of skill required from dealers, the criteria laid down for their appointment being matched appropriately to the nature of the product, and IBM's commitment to its uniform application without discrimination, the Commission gave negative clearance to the system.

The essential element in this system was that, although the restriction on selling to unauthorized dealers was retained, entry to the system was 'open' for any qualified dealer, so that any restriction on competition flowing from the restrictions on resale outside the approved circle was kept to a minimum. If such agreements are to remain outside Article 81(1), it is essential that the obligations imposed on the retailer do not exceed those absolutely necessary to maintain the quality of the goods or to ensure they are sold under proper conditions. Obligations that go beyond this, e.g. to purchase complete ranges of the product or prescribing substantial minimum turnover figures over a particular period of time, would be regarded as 'quantitative' restrictions of competition meaning that, if they were to be included, individual application for exemption under Article 81(3) would be necessary. Likewise, no discrimination can be practised by a manufacturer between, on one hand, specialized retailers and, on the other, department and discount stores, provided that each is able to meet the criterion of ability to sell the relevant products at the required standard. Nor may the manufacturer exercise its power of selection on the basis that a particular dealer has either exported or imported the goods outside official channels or has failed to comply with any particular pricing policy.[8]

---

[6] Paras 33, 34.

[7] [1984] 2 CMLR 342. See also the *14th Annual Report* (1984), pp.60–1.

[8] However, such agreements might escape the reach of Art. 81(1) altogether if the market share of the producers operating the system is very small.

1.3 REFUSAL TO HONOUR GUARANTEES

A particular issue which has come up in the context of selective distribution concerns selective dealers who find themselves in competition with others selling identical goods purchased from the manufacturer in another country (normally at lower prices) which have been brought in as parallel imports. The question before the European Court in *Metro* v. *Cartier*[9] was whether Cartier, a manufacturer of luxury watches sold throughout the Community by selective distribution, was entitled to refuse to honour guarantees on its watches obtained in non-Community countries such as Switzerland where there were gaps in the selective distribution system. Since 1984 Cartier had refused to provide a guarantee for watches not obtained from its authorized dealers within the selective system, and Metro had applied for a declaration that Cartier was nonetheless under an obligation to give this guarantee because there would otherwise be a breach of Article 81(1). The issue was raised under Article 234 by the German Bundesgerichtshof; the European Court ruled that, if the goods in question were appropriate for a selective distribution system, manufacturers were able to prevent trade sales to unauthorized dealers and were logically, therefore, entitled also to limit the benefit of guarantee on the product to those sold through such dealers. Moreover, whether or not the particular distribution system was 'impervious', i.e. had no gaps in it, enabling products to be sold outside the officially authorized sales network was irrelevant to the issue under Article 81, though treated as essential to validity of the system under German law. This rule in *Metro* v. *Cartier* does not apply to cars because of the terms of the block exemption 1400/2002 (Article 4(1)(*b*) and recital 17) which requires authorized repairers to honour guarantees for any motor vehicle acquired within the Community, regardless of the Member State in which it was bought and whether it has passed through the hands of dealers not part of the official chain.

1.4 SELECTIVE DISTRIBUTION OF PERFUME AND COSMETICS

A common link between many of the sectors where selective distribution systems have been approved is that the goods are expensive, technically complex, and require sales and service facilities of sufficient standard to ensure that customers obtain satisfaction from their purchases. To find that selective distribution is also used for perfume and cosmetics comes initially as a surprise, and the legal basis for using selective distribution for goods which, although expensive, lack complexity or the need for after-sales service or repair requires explanation. The requirement for selectivity in retail outlets for such products is based on a claim by manufacturers that their products can only be satisfactorily sold in a suitable atmosphere or ambience, where the luxurious quality of the products is not spoilt by association with more mundane and less expensive goods.

The Commission's 1974 *Annual Report*[10] refers to the examination by DG Comp of the distribution systems adopted by Christian Dior and Lancôme, which organized the sale of

---

[9] Case C-376/92 [1994] ECR I-15: 5 CMLR 331. The issue of whether the system was 'impervious' may nevertheless under Community law be relevant to the issue of whether a trade-mark owner in the Community can be deemed to have made it impossible for sales within the EEA to have taken place outside official distribution channels. See Ch. 13, p.260.

[10] Pp.60–1.

perfume and other beauty and toiletry goods through a selective distribution network limited to a restricted number of approved retailers supervised by their general agent in each Member State. The Commission[11] insisted on the deletion from the agreement of several clauses imposing, in its view, severe restraints on competition. These included, for example, restrictions on resale prices to be charged by Dior and Lancôme dealers when supplying any other retail outlet, either inside or outside their own country. The retailers were also prevented from obtaining supplies from any source other than their national general agent. If such clauses had not been removed, the individual national market would have been partitioned securely; their removal meant that the retailers were enabled within their trade network to sell or purchase to or from any approved agent or retailer in any EC country, and obtained freedom as to the resale prices charged on goods obtained from any source. The Commission commented that it expected this to lead to an alignment of prices for such products in the different Member States, and also that the market for these products is characterized by the existence of a fairly large number of competing firms, none of which held much more than 5 per cent of the market.

In the following year, the *5th Annual Report* referred to further consideration of these distribution arrangements. A large number of other companies in the industry had been involved in negotiations with the Commission seeking approval of similar distribution terms. We find the Commission here complimenting itself for having been able to apply a 'uniform general arrangement throughout an entire industry, the perfume industry, without having to issue formal decisions'.[12]

However, litigation over the selective distribution system did arise, and was ultimately referred by French courts to the European Court for an Article 234 ruling. The case arose in the French courts because the Commission, though having approved the arrangements for the industry, had done so merely by a 'comfort letter' confirming that the system was not considered to be in breach of Article 81(1). Various perfume shops which had tried unsuccessfully to obtain supplies from Lancôme, Guerlain, and other leading suppliers brought action under the French law, which forbids refusal to supply. The perfume manufacturers argued that the existence of the 'comfort letter' provided a complete defence to this claim, but the European Court rejected this argument.[13] It held that national courts are quite free to reach their own findings on the standing of such agreements. National courts may, of course, act on the basis of all information available to them, and are therefore not bound by the 'comfort letter', although they may take its contents into account.

In principle, a system which relies, as did the perfume manufacturers, not merely on qualitative criteria for admission to the system but upon a quantitative selection of retailers would fall within the prohibition of Article 81(1). Nevertheless, in considering whether either an individual agreement or a set of agreements distorted competition, the Court ruled that it was necessary to consider the context within which they were established. Relevant factors here were the nature and quantity of the product, the position and importance of the parties on the market, and whether the retail outlet was isolated or formed part of a large network. The judgment of the Court contains an interesting explanation of the rationale for

---

[11] The Commission in this case granted negative clearance from Art. 81(1) by informal settlement rather than by formal decision. Given the high prices charged, and the apparent lack of consumer benefit from the systems, granting formal exemption under 81(3) might well have presented difficulties to the Commission.

[12] P.51.

[13] The *Perfume* Cases 253/78, 37, 99/79 [1980] ECR 2327, 2481, 2511: [1981] 2 CMLR 99, 143, 164.

allowing selective criteria in the choice of outlets for luxury goods. The Court indicated that a selective system could be accepted provided it was laid down uniformly for all potential resellers, and that the objective criteria for selection were not applied in a discriminatory fashion. It was also necessary to examine whether the product required 'for the purpose of preserving its quality and ensuring that it is used correctly' such a system. National courts should also take into account whether national legislation already covered such requirements by specifying conditions of sale or qualifications for entry into the occupation of such a reseller.

Another case raised the issue of whether the sale of cosmetics, often found in the same retail outlets as perfumes, can be limited to those shops where a qualified pharmacist is present. In its 1991 *Vichy* decision[14] the Commission found that the basis on which the French company operated lacked consistency. In France it supplied cosmetics through a variety of outlets, but outside France only to retail pharmacies run by a qualified pharmacist. Vichy argued that this requirement was objective, necessary, and proportionate, that it improved quality control and the services given to customers, and enhanced interbrand competition with other cosmetic manufacturers. The Commission rejected these arguments. Its finding was clearly assisted by the difference between the distribution systems adopted by Vichy in France and in other Member States, and based principally on the ground that the benefits claimed could be obtained by less restrictive means.

In this decision it followed the pattern established in the slightly earlier case of the *Association Pharmaceutique Belge* (APB) (Commission 1990).[15] Here the national association of pharmacists in Belgium, who were legally responsible for the products which they sold in their retail shops, gave manufacturers the right to affix the APB mark of guaranteed quality to their parapharmaceutical products[16] in return for the manufacturer's agreement to sell these products only through members of the association. The manufacturers had originally agreed not to sell the goods (with or without the stamp) to other retail outlets, but this clause had to be deleted; it would have not only limited the manufacturer's freedom of choice as to outlet, but would also have restricted competition between the members of the APB and other distributors of such products. Negative clearance was granted to the agreement in its amended form: manufacturers could still supply such products to other outlets, but without the quality stamp.

Important also was the Court of First Instance decision in *Leclerc* at the end of 1996.[17] On this occasion, the Leclerc group, a frequent litigator in competition cases, challenged a 1991 negative clearance provided to the distribution system of Yves St Laurent (much as Metro had challenged Saba's exemption for electrical goods). Its principal argument was that the criteria applied by the Commission in their decision would preclude the sale of Yves St Laurent cosmetics by retail outlets in the Leclerc group. The outcome of the case, however, was as unsatisfactory for Leclerc as Metro's experience had been. The Court upheld the Commission's decisions in all but one respect: its approval of a clause that Yves St Laurent would treat applications from retailers less favourably if their total sale of

---

[14] Upheld by the CFI in Case T-19/91 [1992] ECR II-415.   [15] [1990] 4 CMLR 619.

[16] These include such non-medicinal products as cosmetics, dietary products, and baby foods. In the view of the Commission they did not need to be sold by a qualified pharmacist.

[17] Case T-19/92 [1997] 4 CMLR 995.

perfumes was less than 60 per cent of their overall sales. Such a ruling was held to be unnecessarily discriminatory, since it favoured applications by specialist perfumeries at the expense of multiproduct shops, even if the latter had specialized areas laid out so as to meet all the criteria specified by Yves St Laurent for the sale of their luxury cosmetics. In all other respects the Commission confirmed the earlier case law to the effect that such systems were outside Article 81(1) so long as the criteria specified were objective, uniform, and non-discriminatory. It emphasized that it was for national courts and competition authorities to decide if the criteria were being properly applied to particular markets, and indicated that any subjective or discriminatory application of the criteria would lead to restrictions being held within Article 81(1) but without the possibility of individual exemption under 81(3).[18]

1.5 REFUSAL TO DEAL

Refusals by a supplier to deal with or supply a distributor are normally purely unilateral and so fall outside Article 81.[19] Selective distribution by its nature requires that members of the network be in a position to refuse to supply non-authorized distributors, and this will be reflected in the agreements concerned. Nevertheless, since selective distribution systems are outside the range of Article 81 if they comply with the requirements set out in the *Metro/ Saba (No. 1)* case, involving qualitative criteria only in the selection of their dealers, the inherent nature of selectivity means that some refusals to deal are acceptable and will not invalidate the system so as to bring it back within the range of the Article. It is inherent in the system that a manufacturer or wholesaler or retailer cannot refuse to deal with qualified applicants and that the criteria must be applied without discrimination to all qualified applicants. Moreover, as we have seen, the criteria need often not be applied by the manufacturer itself but can be applied by a wholesaler or sole distributor, normally within a short time limit as in the *IBM Personal Computers*[20] and *Grundig*[21] cases.

An interesting and not finally decided issue is the effect of a refusal to deal with a qualified applicant who has been admitted to the distribution system. If the refusal to deal is part of a deliberate policy by a manufacturer to introduce into the distribution system a discouragement to certain outlets (perhaps because it feels that they are too inclined to cut prices) or in other ways to depart from the manufacturer's policy, then if it is likely that the refusal to deal is more than an isolated incident the Commission may be justified in withdrawing any negative clearance or exemption given, as in *AEG/Telefunken*.

The case of *Demo-Studio Schmidt* v. *Commission*[22] (European Court 1983) deals by contract with the rights of applicants to be appointed as selective distributors. Schmidt, a designer in a German machinery factory, decided to set up his own electronic equipment business as a sideline to his salaried activities. He opened a small shop in Wiesbaden with opening hours of a limited nature, selling a variety of consumer electronics made by Revox.

---

[18] It is clear that the Commission will carefully scrutinize the procedures and criteria by which applicants in this sector are assessed and will expect arbitration to be available for unsuccessful applicants. See Commission *Press Release* IP/95/736 of 11 July 1995. The Commission prefers that the supply chain incorporates wholesalers as well as retailers. Arbitration procedures are also recommended in the *Fine Fragrances Report* of the MMC, 1993 (Cm. 2380), Ch 8, para. 188.

[19] Article 82 may apply if the supplier is dominant in the relevant market.

[20] [1984] 2 CMLR 342.

[21] *15th Annual Report* (1985), pp.66–7.   [22] Case 210/81 [1983] ECR 3045: [1984] 1 CMLR 63.

Revox later discussed Schmidt's request to be supplied with its Series B products, which were its more expensive items and afforded a higher profit margin, and made it clear to him that supply would be conditional on his sales premises remaining open for the whole of the working day. Schmidt said he would take a salesman on for this purpose. Later, however, Revox told Schmidt they had decided he could not be appointed a specialist retailer entitled to deal in Series B equipment because he did not satisfy the conditions laid down by them relating to the technical qualifications of staff and the design of sales area, as well as the observance of normal opening hours.

Revox having refused supplies of Series B equipment to him, Schmidt complained to the Commission, who rejected his claim saying that it had no grounds under Article 81 to order Revox to supply him with products. Schmidt asked the European Court to annul this decision, but it also rejected his claim. Their view was that if a selective distribution system was properly adopted for highly technical electronic goods, it was reasonable for a manufacturer to require retailers to be open for normal shopping hours, and that supplies could be refused to a part-time establishment. Even if the selective distribution system had elements which made it incompatible with Article 81(1), this would not of itself entitle Schmidt to be appointed a dealer by Revox, nor to force Revox to supply any particular range of products to him. The case therefore does not seem to give a broad right to a manufacturer not to deal with any particular applicant (whether or not he satisfies the necessary criteria laid down for the relevant distribution system) but places a duty on the manufacturer (or distributor with delegated responsibility) fairly to assess the criteria in the case of each applicant, taking the facts as they were at the time when the application was made.

1.6 SELECTIVE DISTRIBUTION: THE 1999 BLOCK EXEMPTION

During all this time selective distribution had remained the only common type of distribution arrangement not covered by a block exemption, and there was discussion as to whether a new block Regulation should be adopted for the benefit of such systems. Though there was some support for this, some considered that it was not necessary, given that, according to the Court's case law, many such systems fall outside the scope of Article 81(1) anyway. Others were against it on the grounds that selective distribution arrangements vary so widely that one block exemption could not take into account all the necessary possibilities and types of goods without becoming unwieldy. But both objections could be countered by pointing to other block exemptions in place at the time. The Court has said in the case of both exclusive distribution and franchising many agreements fall outside Article 81(1), but block exemptions existed for such agreements. As to the varied nature of selective distribution agreements, the motor vehicle block exemption covers, amongst other things, selective distribution.[23]

1.6.1 Qualitative and Quantitative Criteria

Early drafts of what became the block exemption on vertical agreements, Regulation 2790/99, included selective distribution within its scope, but proposed different market share thresholds depending on whether the system was based on qualitative or quantitative criteria. These categories were based on the case law discussed above.

[23] See pp.207–8. Though admittedly this Regulation is particularly complex and detailed.

As we have seen, the first category involves products whose suppliers impose selectivity upon outlets which can be restrained from trading freely with non-approved outlets so long as entry to this 'family circle' is open to all suitably qualified undertakings. These tests for suitability relate to objective factors such as technical expertise, suitability of premises, adequacy of staff, and financial stability. The Commission tends now to require that these tests be applied quickly, i.e. within a few weeks, and not simply by the manufacturer but at a delegated level, i.e. that of the wholesaler or sole distributor, so as to prevent a supplier from finding excuses to exclude undertakings more inclined to aggressive promotional innovation or even price cutting.

The second category involves products where the technical requirements for pre- and post-sales services and guarantee work justify additional restrictions being imposed by the supplier, namely quantitative limits on the number of appointed dealers within a Member State.[24]

It was initially proposed that the latter could benefit from automatic exemption only below a 20 per cent threshold, with the former being subject only to a 40 per cent threshold. But in the Regulation as finally adopted no distinction of this sort was made, and the same 30 per cent threshold was applied to all selective distribution as to other types of distribution agreement.[25]

1.6.2 Product Type

There had also been speculation that any block exemption covering selective distribution would be restricted to certain product types, as early cases had stressed that selective distribution was appropriate only for certain classes of goods. But over the years exemption had been granted in such a wide variety of different sectors, starting with watches and clocks in the *Omega Watches* case[26] (Commission 1970) that the distinction no longer seemed sustainable.

The principal reason for the blurring of the distinction is probably the Commission's acceptance, based on the judgment of the European Court in the *Perfume* cases, of the principle that selectivity can be justified by the circumstances in which goods are thought to have to be sold, as much as by their actual technical requirements. Thus, as we have seen, the privilege of classification as a selective distribution system has been accorded to a variety of products, not simply because of the nature of the product, justification being also drawn from other extraneous circumstances and alleged commercial needs, which many commentators feel lack validity. In this category, for example, are claims by newspapers, as in *Salonia* v. *Poidomani*[27] (European Court 1981) and *Binon*[28] (European Court

---

[24] Though the dividing line between the two permitted classes is itself indistinct: close examination of the case law shows considerable ambiguity as to what is 'qualitative' and what is 'quantitative'. Thus, in *Grundig* (*15th Annual Report* (1985), pp.66–7), exemption was granted to the Grundig selective distribution system for consumer electronic goods, where a number of restrictions were described by the Commission as quantitative which could as well have been classified as qualitative, and vice versa. It is in fact difficult to find a totally consistent thread of principle throughout the cases.

[25] But in the motor vehicles block exemption qualitative and quantitative systems are subject to different market share thresholds (see p.207).

[26] [1970] CMLR D49.

[27] Case 126/80 [1981] ECR 1563: [1982] 1 CMLR 64.

[28] Case 243/83 [1985] ECR 2105: 3 CMLR 800.

1985) where it seemed that the justification for permitting selectivity turned largely on the problems of financing the return of unsold newspapers.[29] Whilst the Commission appears to have heeded the requirement imposed by the European Court in the *Perfume* cases that consideration should be given to whether national law provides sufficient safeguards so that selectivity of distribution outlets is unnecessary, and applied it in the *Grohe/Ideal Standard*[30] cases relating to bathroom fittings (and refused to accept that the sale of normal household furniture requires the setting up of such systems[31]), the criteria still appear unpredictable.

In practice therefore product type has now ceased to be a criterion for clearance or exemption of a selective distribution system. Rather, it has come to be required only that the selection criteria applied be appropriate to the goods or services concerned. This is reflected in the treatment of selective distribution under the vertical restraints block exemption, which makes no mention of product type as a criteria of exemption.

1.6.3 Black-listed Clauses

In order to benefit from automatic exemption under the vertical restraints block exemption selective distribution agreements have to satisfy all the general requirements of the Regulation, such as the 30 per cent market share threshold, and the prohibition on fixed or minimum resale prices. The particular nature of selective distribution, however, means that in this context a restriction on sales to unauthorized distributors is not black-listed as it is in the context of other types of distribution system (Article 4(b)).

However, the Regulation also lays down some specific requirements in the case of selective distribution, which it defines as 'a distribution system where the supplier undertakes to sell the contract goods or services, either directly or indirectly, only to distributors selected on the basis of specified criteria and where these distributors undertake not to sell such goods or services to unauthorized distributors' (Article 1(d)). As we have seen, for the purposes of the application of the block exemption no distinction is made on the basis either of the type of product being distributed, or of whether the criteria applied are qualitative or quantitative.

There is no prohibition in the exemption preventing selective distribution being combined with the allocation of an exclusive territory. However, where both are combined Article 4(c) prohibits any ban on either passive or active sales to users outside the allotted territory; and such a restriction prevents an agreement from benefiting from the Regulation. This means that the distributor must be free, for example to advertise in all ways and to seek custom by using an Internet site[32] (which may however be subject to quality standards). The exclusivity in such a case is an obligation on the supplier only, and not on the distributor: the supplier can agree not to supply anyone else at any level of trade within that territory. However, the dealer may be prohibited from opening additional sales outlets without his supplier's permission.

---

[29] Another questionable example is the *Villeroy-Boch* case, where a selective distribution system relating to the sale of high-class porcelain was approved: *15th Annual Report* (1985), p.66, [1985] OJ L376/15.

[30] *14th Annual Report* (1984), p.61.

[31] *15th Annual Report* (1985), p.66.

[32] In May 2001, the Commission issued a press release confirming that Yves Saint Laurent's selective distribution was exempted by the Regulation, making special mention of the fact that approved retailers already operating a physical sales outlet were authorized to sell also via the Internet IP/01/713.

According to the Guidelines,[33] a prohibition on selling through an Internet site will count as a hard-core restriction and take the system outside the ambit of the exemption, in the absence of 'an objective justification' for such a clause. In the context of selective distribution the Guidelines recognize that it may well be appropriate for a supplier to establish quality requirements in respect of the site, but it will be rare that there is objective justification for prohibiting use of an Internet site outright.

Nor can there be any ban on cross supplies between authorized distributors at any level in the network (Article 4(d)), or on supply even to non-authorized dealers in territories where the supplier does not operate a selective distribution system.[34]

1.6.4 Non-Compete Clauses

As we have seen, certain non-compete clauses will not benefit from exemption under the Regulation, but they are regarded as severable and so do not compromise the exempted status of the rest of the agreement. In the case of selective distribution Article 5(c) gives an additional non-exempted clause: suppliers may not stop dealers from selling the brands of particular competing suppliers, though they may impose an absolute non-compete provision. The Commission believes that selective non-compete clauses can facilitate horizontal cooperation between competing suppliers using the same network of outlets, so as to foreclose specific competitors from the market.[35]

1.6.5 Parallel Networks

As we have seen, the Commission is on the look out for any undesirable 'network effect', by which is meant the combined restrictive effect of a number of similar networks in a market, and Article 6 the Regulation gives the Commission the power to withdraw the benefit of the Regulation where particular agreements, despite falling within the scope of the Regulation, do not in fact satisfy the requirements of Article 81(3).[36] Further, Article 8 allows the Commission to enact Regulations declaring the block exemption inapplicable to vertical agreements containing specific restraints relating to the market where such networks account for over 50 per cent of the relevant market.

1.7 INDIVIDUAL EXEMPTION FOR SELECTIVE DISTRIBUTION: THE CURRENT POLICY

As already discussed, many selective distribution systems of course do not infringe Article 81 at all and so do not require any kind of exemption. The Guidelines state that, as case law has established, qualitative selective distribution falls outside Article 81 altogether, provided that certain conditions (necessity of the system to preserve the quality and proper use of product, and necessary, objective, qualitative, non-discriminatory criteria) are satisfied.[37] Acceptable

---

[33] Paras 50–51.

[34] This is the Commission's interpretation of Art. 4(b): Guidelines, para. 52.

[35] Guidelines, para. 61.

[36] The Regulation does not confine the application of Art. 6 to selective distribution systems, but the 13th recital to the Regulation states explicitly that such concerns may arise in connection with such systems.

[37] Para. 185.

clauses in this context include the application of the qualitative criteria themselves, as well as those connected with their application. They mention that the Commission's main concerns in the context of selective distribution are the risk of a reduction in competition between competing brands of goods, and a reduction in competition as a result of the cumulative effects of a number of similar networks operating on the same market, either because of foreclosure of distributors from entering or remaining on the market, or because collusion between suppliers or buyers is facilitated.

Systems involving quantitative or other types of restriction, and which for some reason do not fall within the scope of Regulation 2970/99 may qualify for individual exemption. The overriding consideration will be the market position of the supplier, as the Guidelines state explicitly that a loss of competition within the same brand is only problematic if competition between brands is limited.[38] Much importance will also be placed on the presence on the market of a number of similar distribution networks, and in such cases the risk of foreclosure will be closely examined, especially if non-compete or similar clauses are present.

As to the relevance of product type, the Guidelines refer to the need to combat 'free-riding' and to create brand image, and say that the argument for exemption is strongest for new products, complex products, products which are difficult to judge before consumption ('experience products') and products difficult to judge even after consumption ('credence products').[39] Though this is quite a different formulation from the older product categories, it clearly has its roots in the same reasoning. It also shows why product type is not a criterion included in the Regulation: concepts such as 'complex products' are too difficult to define clearly to be appropriate for use in a block exemption.

2. MOTOR VEHICLE DISTRIBUTION AND SERVICING NETWORKS

2.1 THE HISTORICAL BACKGROUND

The motor car is probably the most complex consumer product of all, as well as being the most expensive purchase that many consumers ever make. These unique characteristics have been put forward by motor manufacturers as justifying special rules on the distribution of cars. The issue first reached the Commission in the *BMW* case. The importance of the Commission's decision is shown by the fact that some two and a half pages are devoted to it in the *4th Annual Report*.[40] The most notable feature of the exemption granted is that it permits a restriction on the number of dealers allowed in Germany, which is a quantitative, not a qualitative, criterion. The Commission justified its decision by saying that 'Motor vehicles, being products of limited life, high cost and complex technology, require regular maintenance by specially equipped garages or service depots because their use can be dangerous to life, health and property and can have a harmful effect on the environment'. It described the required co-operation between BMW and its dealers as going beyond the mere marketing of products and involving co-operation which not only promoted economic

---

[38] Para. 187.   [39] Para. 195.
[40] [1975] 1 CMLR D44, 56. The comments are found at pp.57–9.

progress and the distribution of the vehicles but also gave benefits to consumers in the form of improved service. The Commission felt that this close co-operation and specialization by the dealers would not be possible if BMW were required to admit to the system, without limit of numbers, any dealer required merely to show he had adequate premises, staff, and other qualitative attributes.

The first official draft of a block exemption for car distribution was published in June 1983, and met strong opposition from the motor industry. Amongst their complaints were that it sought to bring about an artificial realignment of vehicle prices within the EC, sought to interfere without justification in the detailed relationship between manufacturer and dealer, and failed to provide sufficient legal certainty for both. The content of the original draft actually owed a considerable amount to the principles already laid down in the *BMW* case. The Commission acknowledged that in the motor vehicle sector (covering cars, buses, and vans) many of the restrictions of competition approved in the *BMW* case fulfilled the requirements of 81(3). In particular, the benefit to the public claimed for a system of authorized dealers was that it provided more satisfactory maintenance and repair services; the degree of competition of an interbrand nature between the major car manufacturers made competition on an intrabrand basis between their dealers rather less important. The Regulation would grant exemption for the placing of restrictions on the motor dealer against:

(1) selling another manufacturer's vehicles or parts;

(2) actively seeking customers outside its allotted territory;

(3) sub-contracting distribution, servicing, or repairs without the manufacturer's consent; and

(4) selling the vehicles or parts to dealers outside the distribution network.

In return, the manufacturer would agree not to appoint other dealers in the allotted territory during the period of the contract.

Considerable concern, especially by consumers' organizations, had been expressed about difficulties placed in the way of purchasers desiring to make parallel imports of vehicles from Member States where cars could be purchased more cheaply, and the draft contained clauses designed to give some protection to the consumer. Thus, consumers were entitled to have servicing or repairs done under a manufacturer's warranty anywhere in the Community, and were entitled to order cars to the specifications required at the place where they are to be registered from a dealer in another Member State, provided that the manufacturer or his importer sold the relevant model through the official distribution network at both places. Spare parts supplied by third parties, matching the quality of those supplied by the manufacturer, could also be purchased by dealers in the official network without breach of their agreement with the manufacturer.

The original draft dealt specifically with this sensitive issue of the freeing of parallel imports, providing that if the difference between retail prices recommended in any two countries exceeded 12 per cent over a six-month period, the authorized dealers would be free to sell to dealers outside the network in that second country. This freedom would not apply if prices were artificially held at different levels as the result of very high Member State tax rates, or where there was a temporary legislative freeze on the fixing of prices or profit margins. Fierce debate continued right up to the last moment as to whether the overall terms of the Regulation were unduly onerous upon the car manufacturers or upon dealers.

2.2 THE FIRST MOTOR VEHICLE DISTRIBUTION BLOCK EXEMPTIONS: REGULATIONS 123/85 AND 1475/95

When Regulation 123/85 was finally issued at the end of 1984, some important changes had been made to the original draft. Dealers were now entitled to a minimum period of four years' appointment in order that they would not be made over-dependent on the manufacturer or importer. Additional safeguards were included to make it difficult for manufacturers or importers to prevent sales in the United Kingdom of right-hand-drive versions of cars bought through official channels on the Continent. The Commission, however, had removed the reference to the original price differential of 12 per cent from the Regulation and transferred it to an accompanying Notice[41] issued by way of interpretation of the Commission's attitude to the Regulation.

The Regulation preserved the right for dealers to sell to intermediaries, as agents for individual customers; this was the subject of the Court of First Instance decision in *Peugeot* v. *Ecosystems*.[42] This decision in favour of the intermediary's right to act on behalf of customers was accompanied by a Notice[43] from the Commission limiting the number of vehicles which an individual dealer is entitled to dispose of annually in this way to 10 per cent of its total sales. The great majority of any dealer's sales still had to be made direct to individual purchasers; intermediary sales could constitute only a relatively minor part of its business.

Regulation 123/85 turned out to be unsuccessful in accommodating the conflicting interests of the different parties, and when it was replaced ten years later by Regulation 1475/95 the principal aim was to redress the balance in favour of dealers so as to give them more independence from their suppliers and to increase competition between them. Numerous changes to this end were made to the rules, including provisions allowing dealers to sell competing brands and giving them more freedom to sell outside their allotted territory, and granting better protection of independent suppliers of spare parts.

2.3 THE NEW BLOCK EXEMPTION: REGULATION 1400/2002: THE DEBATE OVER ITS ADOPTION

But when, five years on, the time approached to review the Regulation again, the Commission admitted that these aims had again not been achieved. It was dissatisfied with the situation on two main counts. First, its twice-yearly statistics-gathering exercises showed that the tightening up of the Regulation in 1995 had not brought about significant price convergence: prices for some models still varied by up to 50 per cent between Member States. Second, despite the special privileges accorded to the industry by the block exemption, a number of large manufacturers were found to be flouting the competition rules and, in particular, to be hindering parallel imports between Member States.

---

[41] [1985] OJ C17/4.   [42] Case T-9/92 [1993] ECR II-493: [1995] 5 CMLR 696.
[43] [1991] OJ C329/20. This remained applicable under Reg. 1475/95, though not now under Reg. 1400/2002.

Volkswagen was the first of a number of manufacturers to be investigated and heavily fined for such behaviour. The Commission found that dealers in Italy had been discouraged by a number of means from exporting cars to Germany and Austria, where higher retail prices made importing from Italy an attractive proposition. Their means included tying dealer bonuses to the subsequent registration of vehicles in Italy, restricting supplies and penalizing exporting distributors.[44] The €102 million fine imposed on Volkswagen in 1998 was at the time the highest ever imposed by the Commission for breach of Article 81. This underlines the fact that although vertical restraints are generally less serious from a competition point of view than agreements between competitors, when they divide markets along national borders they will be regarded as extremely serious infringements. The Court of First Instance later reduced the fine to €90 million, but itself emphasized the gravity of the infringement.[45]

After Volkswagen, large fines were also imposed on Opel (€43 million in 2000), JCB (€39.6 million in 2000), DaimlerChrysler (€71.825 million in 2001) and Volkswagen again (€30.96 million in 2001) for similar behaviour. Though it is not logically linked, such widespread conduct in the industry clearly influenced the Commission's thinking.

As required by Regulation 1475/95, in November 2000 the Commission made a report on its operation: this identified a number of specific drawbacks to the existing regime, and confirmed the Commission's impression that it had not achieved some of the aims it had set out in 1995. First, the fact that exclusive dealer territories could be combined with both quantitative and qualitative selective distribution meant that sales networks were closed to many potential distributors and too tightly controlled by manufacturers. Consumers had no alternative source of supply outside the networks, and still found it difficult to buy cars outside their home country. Furthermore, the development of new types of distribution channel such as supermarkets and Internet sites was being hampered.

At this point the Commission had three basic options to consider: extending the application of the existing Regulation, allowing the Regulation to lapse so that the motor vehicle sector became covered by the general rules on vertical restraints, or drafting a new motor vehicles block exemption.

The first option was rejected because of the failures identified by the Commission in its report. The second was also rejected, in part for similar reasons, since the application of Regulation 2790/99 would have allowed most networks to continue to function more or less unchanged, and would therefore not have alleviated these problems. Moreover, it would not have helped to open up the after-sales service market, nor would it have ensured the use of the so-called 'availability clause' which allows, for example, a British motorist to purchase a right-hand drive model in Belgium.

The two years leading up to the adoption of the new Regulation 1400/2002 in July 2002 saw some of the fiercest lobbying of the Commission and Parliament since the abolition of duty-free sales. Manufacturers rehearsed the usual arguments, in particular that increased competition would threaten quality and safety standards as well as the viability of small dealerships. They argued especially strongly that, if a combination of exclusive and selective distribution were no longer permitted, manufacturers relying on selective distribution still

---

[44] [1998] OJ L124/60, [1998] 5 CMLR 33.
[45] Case T-62/98, ECR II-2707: [2000] 5 CMLR 853; an appeal is pending in the Court of Justice, Case C-338/00.

needed to be able to impose a 'location clause' on dealers, preventing them from establishing a sales outlet or depot away from their main outlet. The Commission for its part saw the outlawing of location clauses as key to encouraging parallel imports.

2.4 DETAILS OF REGULATION 1400/2002

Regulation 1400/2002[46] as finally adopted in July 2002 to some extent follows the general trend towards more flexible and economics-based block exemptions. It does not exempt a combination of exclusive and selective distribution, but leaves manufacturers free to choose to use one or the other. Nor does it contain 'white' and 'grey' lists of permitted clauses: as under the vertical restraints block exemption, the principle is that anything not expressly prohibited is exempted. It also introduces market share thresholds above which certain types of agreement are not exempted (Article 3(1)). However, the 'black list' of prohibited, hard core restrictions, is extremely detailed, and there are many additional clauses mentioning characteristics which the distribution systems are required to have or not to have in order to qualify for exemption. This means that the 'strait-jacket' effect, for which older generations of block exemptions have often been criticized, is in many ways still a feature of this new Regulation.

The Commission explains in the second recital to the new block exemption that stricter rules are needed in this sector than those provided for in Regulation 2790/99, and it is true that many more requirements are laid down by the motor vehicle Regulation.[47] For example, a choice has to be made between exclusive and selective distribution, and the limits of this choice vary depending on whether the agreements concern motor vehicles, spare parts or repair and maintenance, or a combination of the three. The rules also vary according to whether they cover passenger cars or light commercial vehicles, or heavier vehicles.

However, in some respects the rules are more generous than those of Regulation 2790/99. Although Article 3(1) states that the exemption is generally available in respect of sale of new vehicles and spare parts, and repair services, as under the vertical restraints block exemption, up to a market share threshold of 30 per cent, it adds that quantitative selective distribution for new vehicle sales is exempted up to a 40 per cent threshold. Qualitative selective distribution is exempted irrespective of market share.

If exclusive distribution is the option chosen, dealers have to be left free to make passive supplies to anyone in any territory (and active sales into any territories where selective distribution is used), including supermarkets and Internet-based operators. It is not expected that many manufacturers will take this route. More popular is likely to be selective distribution, which may be both quantitative and qualitative. However, even here, it will not be possible to discriminate against supermarkets if they satisfy the manufacturer's selection criteria. These criteria may be established so as to exclude operators working purely through the Internet, but not those with outlets which satisfy the criteria but which also deal via the Internet. Selective distribution dealers must be allowed to make even active sales to any

---

[46] [2002] OJ L203/30. See also the Explanatory Brochure on the Regulation, an 83-page document available on DG Comp's website (www.europa.eu.int/comm/competition/publications/).

[47] It is ironic that whereas the first block exemptions overall provided car manufacturers with a more generous regime than was available in other markets, the latest more imposes more restrictions on them than would be the case under the Regulation (2790/99) generally applicable to distribution agreements. Being regarded as a 'special case' has become a burden rather than a privilege!

end-user in any part of the Community, except exclusive distributorship territories, in respect of which only passive sales have to be permitted.

Manufacturers are required to allow dealers to stock competing vehicles in the same showroom and may no longer require that competing products be sold in separate premises, under separate management, and by a separate legal entity. More freedom is also ensured for operators purchasing as intermediaries, who can no longer be refused supplies in volumes beyond 10 per cent of their total sales, as was the case under the previous block exemption (see fn. 43). There are also detailed requirements regarding the length and means of termination of agreements and settling of disputes, and transfer of dealerships, all designed to prevent manufacturers from exerting illicit pressure on dealers.

Distributors will no longer be able to be forced to provide repair and maintenance services as well as distributing new motor vehicles, and they must be allowed to source components from the same producers that supply the manufacturer. Manufacturers have to make available to independent service providers the necessary spare parts, technical information, training and tools, and a number of other detailed rules aim to free up the market for servicing and spare parts.

The new Regulation thus significantly tightens the rules for manufacturers, and contains only one significant concession to the powerful industry and political lobbying: manufacturers have won the right to continue to use a location clause in respect of cars and light commercial vehicles until October 2005, whereas the rest of the Regulation became applicable on 1 October 2002.

Though manufacturers are not legally required to operate through agreements that follow these requirements, if they choose to work outside them they will almost certainly need to apply for an individual exemption decision from the Commission. In practice, therefore, the scheme laid down by the new Regulation will, like its predecessors, be widely followed by the industry. Market shares in new vehicle sales will rarely exceed 30 per cent, and even more rarely will they exceed 40 per cent, which in practice is likely to be the threshold of interest to most producers, so there will be little incentive to seek individual exemption for a different scheme. (The thresholds are more likely to be exceeded in the case of spare parts and repair services.) The Commission and consumer groups are optimistic that price differences across the European Union will decrease, as will prices themselves. Some producers however are predicting that prices will rise, with prices across the Union becoming more closely aligned with the highest existing prices. In any case the Commission will be watching market developments carefully, and is required to publish an evaluation report by 31 May 2008.

3. FRANCHISING

3.1 FRANCHISE SYSTEMS: THE EARLY YEARS

Another method available for the large-scale distribution of goods or services is franchising. The basic idea is that, instead of appointing an independent distributor who takes on the risk of reselling the supplier's product within a particular area and is responsible for determining sales policy within the territory, the manufacturer (franchisor) appoints an independent undertaking (franchisee) to operate in a manner far more closely integrated with the franchisor; the franchisor supplies the franchisee not just with a product or service for sale, but with a standardized and highly detailed promotional framework within which the franchisee has to operate. This will probably include the following elements:

(*a*) a right for the franchisee to sell the relevant product or service from a location in a particular contract territory;

(*b*) the provision of trade-mark and know-how licences to ensure that the presentation of the brand image of the product is identical to that of the franchisor and all other franchised outlets;

(*c*) a requirement that the required products or services are obtained through or from the franchisor, and if from some third party then in accordance with detailed specifications;

(*d*) an obligation on the franchisee to pay both a lump sum for the know-how provided and royalties in respect of all sales made, as well as to adhere strictly to the terms of the franchisor's package (in terms of the layout of his retail premises and in all respects in which the business is conducted); and

(*e*) a network of other franchise holders operating on an identical basis.

Franchises came into common use in the Community in the early 1970s, developing out of business models adopted from the United States. By May 1982, there were 200 franchise systems in the Federal Republic of Germany involving 120,000 franchisees; in France there were nearly 400 franchise systems at that time; in The Netherlands, 280 franchise systems in 1983. Similar developments took place in other Member States.[48]

There are three main varieties of business format franchising which apply to the retail distribution of goods and services. The first, which most concerns us here, is a *distribution franchise* where the function of the trade mark is to assist the effective distribution of the franchisor's goods in a recognizable way. Other varieties of the same concept of 'business format franchising' are *service* franchising, which is similar to the distribution franchise except that any goods provided are only ancillary to the service offered, and *production* franchising, where the producer/franchisor arranges for the manufacture of the particular range of brand goods to be carried out by his franchisee. Within normal categories of service franchising are found restaurants and hotels, car hire, accounting bureaux, and data-processing services; in the field of production franchising are found clothes, cosmetics, footwear, and other mass production items.

Distribution franchising, however, can apply to almost every type of product. A normal franchise agreement for the distribution of goods is a lengthy document of up to 100 pages, presenting in great detail the way in which the parties are to carry out their mutual obligations. Inherent in most franchising arrangements are a number of clauses which restrict competition; and the issue immediately arises whether any of these clauses fall under Article 81(1) and if so whether exemption will be available. Since the essence of a franchise system, like that of exclusive distribution, is a network of agreements conferring partial or total

---

[48] These figures are taken from the opinion of Advocate General VerLoren van Themaat in the *Pronuptia* case (see fn. 50) which itself provides a full account of the economic role and development of the system of franchising.

territorial exclusivity on the franchisee in return for substantial payments by the franchisee, the franchisor may be asked to accept some or all of the following restrictions:

(1) not to appoint another franchisee in the territory allocated;

(2) not to be involved in the sale of the franchise goods within the territory, e.g. by opening a rival shop; and

(3) not to sell, directly or indirectly, contract goods to persons who will resell them in the contract territory.

The franchisee may have to accept a large number of restrictions, including:

(1) the obligation to sell franchise goods only to customers of his specified shops at named locations, which have to be fitted out exactly in accordance with the franchisor's requirements;

(2) not to change the location of these shops nor to assign the agreement to third parties without the consent of the franchisor;

(3) not to sell franchise goods to dealers outside the franchise network;

(4) not to sell except at the prices (maximum or minimum) laid down or recommended by the franchisor;

(5) not to deal in any competing goods, or possibly to deal with them only to a limited extent; and

(6) not for a period after the end of the franchise agreement to enter into competition with the franchisor in respect of the contract product.

The Commission originally had some difficulty in deciding how to classify franchise agreements, since they exhibited in varying degrees features commonly found in no less than three other categories of agreement with which DG Comp was familiar and for which it had, with the assistance of the European Court, developed detailed ground rules. These were: exclusive dealing agreements, selective dealing agreements, and patent and trade-mark licensing.

Although there were similarities between each of these three classes of agreement and franchising, franchising remained inherently distinct from each of them by virtue of the close control maintained over the manner in which the franchisee conducts his business. In the case of exclusive dealing agreements, by contrast, though the dealer could be required to sell goods under the supplier's trade mark and packaging under the terms of the block exemption then in force, the dealer retained considerable independence in its marketing policy and was normally free to sell from whatever outlets and in whatever way it chose. Moreover, also under the terms of the block exemption, it had to be free to respond to orders outside its territory so long as it did not promote sales actively there itself, and the supplier remained free to sell to other distributors or dealers outside the territory even if they would subsequently resell into the contract territory. Any licensing of know-how or trade marks was ancillary to these distribution rights.

The selective distribution systems discussed earlier in this chapter also showed considerable differences from franchising. Here again, the dealer normally remained free to sell competing goods in addition to the contract goods, and agreements did not normally prescribe specific territories beyond allocating territorial areas of primary responsibility.

Nor did the Patent Licence Regulation or case law on trade-mark or know-how licences provide much assistance to the Commission. In such licences, the primary subject is the transfer of, for example, know-how, whereas in franchising these licences are often merely ancillary to the whole 'business package', which the franchisee usually acquires for a substantial payment.

It was argued that the Commission should adopt a tolerant attitude towards franchise agreements, and a strong case can indeed be made for claiming that it has some beneficial and pro-competitive aspects.[49] The close support received from the franchisor enables new retail outlets to compete strongly and immediately with other outlets, and it is also claimed that it contributes to the reduction of prices for manufacturers' goods without any sacrifice of quality. It can be argued to have a significant ability in the creation of an EC mass market and in breaking down frontiers, by allowing the coverage of large territories in a number of Member States without having to produce substantial product differentiation on a national level. The promotion of the 'brand image' enables recognition of the product to spread faster than would otherwise be the case, and thereby enables unit costs to be kept lower and prices possibly reduced. Whilst not all these arguments would necessarily be accepted, it was widely expected that the European Court would take a relatively positive attitude towards this form of distribution.

3.2 THE *PRONUPTIA* CASE

The opportunity arose in the well-known *Pronuptia* case[50] (European Court 1986). Mrs Schillgalis had entered into a franchise agreement in Germany several years previously to sell wedding dresses and other wedding items under the trade mark 'Pronuptia de Paris'. Her appointment covered three separate areas (Hamburg, Oldenburg, and Hanover) and contained restrictions on both her and Pronuptia. The main restrictions on Pronuptia were:

(1) that it would grant Mrs Schillgalis the exclusive right to use the trade name for the marketing of the contract goods in a specific territory;

(2) that it would not open any other Pronuptia shop in that territory or provide goods or services to third parties in the territory; and

(3) that it would assist Mrs Schillgalis with regard to all commercial aspects of her business, including advertizing, staff training, fashion purchasing, marketing, and any other help needed to improve her turnover and profitability.

In return, Mrs Schillgalis accepted a large number of restrictions, which included the following:

(*a*) to sell wedding gowns under the trade mark 'Pronuptia de Paris' only in the shops specified, which had to be equipped and decorated exactly as the franchisor required

---

[49] A useful early source of information on franchising, written from a US viewpoint before the Court delivered its *Pronuptia* judgment, and urging its liberal treatment on the ground that it has a significant ability to make retail markets more competitive, is R.J. Goebel, 'The Uneasy Fate of Franchising Under EEC Antitrust Laws' (1985) 10 *EurLR* 87–118.

[50] Case 161/84 [1986] ECR 353: 1 CMLR 414. When the relevant agreements were entered into Reg. 67/67 was still in force.

and could not be transferred to another location or altered without the franchisor's agreement;

(b) to purchase 80 per cent of wedding dresses and accessories to be sold from Pronuptia direct, and to purchase at least a proportion of other dresses from the franchisor or from suppliers approved by the franchisor, and to make the sale of bridal fashions her main concern;

(c) to pay an entry fee for the know-how of DM 15,000 and thereafter a royalty of 10 per cent on the total sales of Pronuptia products;

(d) to advertise only in a manner approved by the franchisor and in general to use the business methods prescribed by the franchisor, save that the fact that prices were recommended by Pronuptia did not affect her ultimate freedom to fix her own prices; and

(e) to refrain during the contract and for one year afterwards from competing in any way with Pronuptia outside her own contract territory.

When later sued for substantial arrears of royalty by Pronuptia, she claimed that the agreement was void under Article 81(2) and that she was therefore not required to pay. Her argument succeeded before the Frankfurt Court of Appeal (Oberlandgericht); the German Supreme Court (the Bundesgerichthof) referred to the European Court under Article 234 the issue of whether Article 81 applied to franchise agreements, and if so whether Block Exemption 67/67 could also have applied to it.

In such Article 234 references the European Court does not review the case as a whole but merely answers the specific questions asked by the national court. It is, therefore, less likely in such cases that the European Court will find it possible to pronounce in general terms on the legal principles involved than, say, when a review from a DG Comp decision is brought under Article 234. Nevertheless, there have been occasions, such as the *Perfumes* case, when the Court took the opportunity of an Article 234 reference to state or restate basic principles relating to competition law, and it was hoped that it would take this opportunity to provide assistance to the Commission in dealing with the increasing numbers and types of franchise agreements now being notified to it.

Advocate General VerLoren van Themaat took a relatively relaxed view of such agreements; after careful review of the earlier Court jurisprudence on related areas (such as exclusive distribution agreements and licence agreements) he reached the general conclusion that franchising as a method of distribution had major advantages for both the franchisor and the franchisee, and in general should not fall within Article 81(1) unless:

(a) the agreement was made between a franchisor from one Member State or its subsidiary on one hand and one or more franchisees in one or more other Member States on the other hand; and

(b) the franchisor had through its subsidiaries and franchisees in one or more of those Member States or a significant part of their territory a substantial share of the market for that product; and

(c) the agreement had the effect or intention of restricting either parallel imports of the product into the contract territory or exports of those products by the franchisee to other Member States; or

(d) the agreement resulted in the establishment of unreasonably high resale prices, that is prices which could not be charged if effective competition existed for them.

The Advocate General also considered that Regulation 67/67 did not apply to the Pronuptia franchises at issue, since no consideration had been given to the question of franchising when the Regulation was drawn up, and since in any case the issues of exclusive supply and exclusive purchasing covered by that Regulation are only minor factors in the normal franchise agreement.

The European Court, whilst agreeing that Regulation 67/67 was inapplicable, declined to give broad approval to franchise agreements in the way that the Advocate General had suggested. It accepted that such agreements gave substantial advantages to both franchisors and franchisees and allowed the franchisor to derive financial benefit from its expertise without having to invest its own capital. The franchisee benefited because it could receive, even without any past experience of the trade, access to trading methods which the franchisor had successfully utilized, and for which it had gained a reputation. In order for such a system to work, therefore, protecting the legitimate expectations of the franchisor, restrictive conditions could be accepted as falling outside Article 81(1) if they contributed to satisfying one of two conditions.

The first condition was that the franchisor must be able to pass on its know-how to franchisees and provide them with the necessary promotional and other assistance without running a risk that this might benefit its competitors. Under this heading, a clause preventing the franchisee both during and for a reasonable period after the agreement from opening a shop of the same or similar nature in another area (where he might compete with another member of the franchise network) was acceptable and outside 81(1), as also was any restriction on proposed transfer of the shop to another party without the franchisor's approval.

The second condition was that the franchisor must be allowed to take the necessary measures to maintain the identity and reputation of the franchise network, to the extent that it had to exercise control over it. This would cover obligations on the franchisee to apply the franchisor's business method and sell the goods covered by the contract only in premises laid out and decorated according to the franchisor's instructions, which were intended to ensure uniform presentation. Likewise, the franchisor could impose requirements as to the location of the shop and its subsequent transfer and prohibit the transfer by the franchisee of its rights and obligations without the franchisor's approval. In order that the goods supplied by each franchisee should be of the same quality, it was reasonable for the franchisor to require that the franchisee sell only products supplied by the franchisor or a supplier selected by it. The franchisee must be allowed to purchase such goods from other franchisees.

However, the judgment did indicate clearly that Article 81(1) would apply to a clause obliging the franchisee to sell goods covered by the contract only in specified premises, e.g. preventing him or her from opening up a second shop in his own territory when the franchisor is obliged to ensure the franchisee exclusivity in that territory. For if such a restriction were applied throughout the network, it would mean that a Member State would be divided up by the franchisor into a number of closed territories. If it was shown nevertheless by the franchisor that franchisees would not risk entering the network and investing substantial sums on the purchase of the franchise without such an assured exclusive territory, then these matters should be considered on an individual application under Article 81(3). The Court ruled that provisions which shared markets between the franchisor and franchisee or between the franchisees themselves were likely to affect trade between Member

States, even if entered into solely by undertakings established in one Member State, because of their ability to prevent franchisees in one Member State from establishing themselves also in another Member State.

Finally, on the question of control over resale prices by the franchisor, the Court took a more severe view than the Advocate General. He had indicated that resale price maintenance should not be illegal unless one party has a position of economic strength on the local market concerned where price maintenance was also applied by competitors or where the franchisor is in a position of a price leader on that particular market. The Court said that only recommendations on price were permissible, but failed to distinguish between maximum and minimum price recommendation, and indicated that price recommendations would only be acceptable so long as there was no concerted practice between the parties as to their application.

3.3 THE ADOPTION OF THE BLOCK EXEMPTION 4087/88

Pressure was now growing for the adoption of a draft block exemption, which was finally published in August 1987. Drawing substantially on the *Pronuptia* judgment, it adopted a generally favourable approach to the concept of both distribution and service franchises, without seeking to cover industrial or manufacturing franchising. Regulation 4087/88 came into force on 1 February 1989.

Its general shape followed the traditional pattern for block exemptions, with a definition of its coverage and lists of exempted and prohibited restrictions, the 'white' and 'black' lists, a list of relevant conditions that had to continue to apply throughout the duration of the exemption, an opposition procedure, and grounds for withdrawal of the exemption. Article 2 contained a particularly long list of restrictions exempted, including the exclusive right of the franchisee to operate his franchise in a particular territory from his contract premises only and without seeking to solicit customers outside that territory. The franchisee could be prohibited from selling competing goods or services. The 'white' list also included two main categories of clause which the Court had referred to in *Pronuptia*: first, those permitted in so far as they were needed to protect the franchisor's intellectual property rights, and second, those that maintained the common identity and reputation of the particular franchise network.

The 'black' list of clauses was comparatively brief. It naturally included any restriction on the franchisee's freedom to determine sale prices, no-challenge clauses against intellectual property rights, and any attempt to limit competition between franchisees or to impose restrictions on sources of supply for contract products. An opposition clause was included to enable additional restrictions not found in the lists to be presented to the Commission; and the 'safety valve' Article 8 provided a number of situations in which the Commission would be entitled to withdraw the benefit of the exemption from individual agreements, including any where franchisees engaged in horizontal price-fixing or obstruction to parallel imports, where goods or services faced no effective competition in the Common Market, or where the franchisor used its contractual rights and considerable influence over the franchisee for purposes wider than the proper protection of its identity and reputation within the framework of the contract.

During the time that the block exemption was being drafted, the Commission adopted a few individual exemptions.[51] In *Servicemaster*[52] the franchise covered the supply of house-keeping, cleaning, and maintenance services for both commercial and domestic customers. The Commission pointed out that, although the Regulation only referred to the distribution of goods, franchises dealing with services alone should be treated similarly. Characteristic features of service franchises include the relative importance of the know-how provided to the franchisee, and the fact that his services were normally provided at the customer's premises creating a personal relationship with him. Individual exemption was granted both here and in case on the *Charles Jourdan*[53] franchise for the sale of a brand of French shoes and other leather goods. Charles Jourdan as franchisor reserved the right to approve individual managers who had been selected for the franchised shops and an exact territory was allocated to each franchisee. Franchisees all had to pay an entry fee, either to run the business from particular premises within the territory, or for being granted a 'franchise-corner', an area within a shop but with no exterior sign. The effect of the close control maintained by the franchisor was to give each franchisee relatively strong protection from competition within its territory against other franchisees. The Commission ruled, however, in granting the exemption that unless territorial exclusivity were given few prospective franchisees would be willing to make the necessary investment in this franchise. The product itself only had 10 per cent of the French market for medium and top-quality shoes, and as little as 2 per cent of the whole Community market for such products. The decision illustrates that individual exemptions may be available for such arrangements even if the goods have no great technical complexity and are sold alongside similar products not the subject of a franchise.

 The comparatively liberal terms of the Regulation led to their widespread use as a model by companies throughout the Community, in some cases to replace use of the exclusive dealing Block Exemption Regulation 1983/83 with its far more limited list of permitted restrictions. In fact, during the whole eleven years that Regulation 4087/88 remained in force, there were no further Commission decisions or Court judgments on franchising agreements, nor have there been since. This meant that, when the Commission was drafting its 1997 Green Paper and later adopting the Vertical Restraints Block Exemption Regulation and accompanying Guidelines, franchising was expected to be one of the least controversial aspects of the exercise. Once it emerged that a block exemption applicable to vertical restraints generally was being drafted, it was assumed that franchise agreements would be covered, and would continue to enjoy the generous treatment they had so far received.

3.4 FRANCHISE SYSTEMS: THE 1999 BLOCK EXEMPTION 2790/1999

Franchise businesses were therefore disturbed to see the way that the scope of the new Regulation was defined. The general definition in Article 2(1) of 'vertical agreements' is broad enough to include many franchising agreements, including those involving agency or

---

[51] Cynics have suggested that the franchising systems in question did not require exemption, but that exemption decisions were taken to prove that the Commission had the necessary 'experience' of franchise agreements to justify the adoption of a block exemption.

[52] [1989] 4 CMLR 581.

[53] [1989] 4 CMLR 591. The lesser restrictions placed on the 'franchise-corner' retailer were actually held to fall outside Art. 81(1) altogether.

based on selective distribution. However, Article 2(3) provides that where vertical agreements contain provisions relating to the assignment to the buyer or use by him of intellectual property rights (IPRs), they would only be within the scope of the block exemption 'provided that those provisions do not constitute the primary object of such agreements and are directly related to the use, sale or resale of goods or services' by the buyer or his customers.

Some have argued that Article 2(3) is not a limitation on the general scope of the exemption, but rather an extension of it.[54] However, the more widely held view, and certainly the Commission's intention as expressed in its Guidelines,[55] is that it is an additional requirement which agreements must satisfy if they are to benefit from block exemption. On this view, it is true that at least on the face of the Regulation it would appear that some types of distribution and service franchises which were exempted by the old franchising block exemption are no longer exempted by the new Regulation.

The concept of the IPR provisions in an agreement being the 'primary object' of the agreement, rather than 'ancillary'[56] is far from clear and is nowhere defined. Moreover, the Commission itself stated in the recitals to the old franchising block exemption that 'franchising agreements consist essentially of licences of industrial or intellectual property rights relating to trade marks or signs and know-how', which suggests that such agreements should not generally be covered by the new Regulation. Certainly it seems hard to argue that service or distribution franchises involving IPRs, and where the franchisor does not himself supply goods or materials to the franchisee, have anything other than IPRs as their 'primary object'. In this context franchisors may be concerned by the Commission's decision in *Moosehead/Whitbread*,[57] where it found an exclusive licence for a little known trade mark not to be 'ancillary' to a grant of know-how covering the production and promotion of a brand of beer.

On the other hand, if the franchise consists mainly of a business method which can be characterized as 'know-how' rather than IPRs, then it should be covered by the Regulation. The Regulation defines both IPRs and know-how separately and the limitation in Article 2(3) only mentions IPRs and so does not extend to know-how.

So, depending on the nature of the product or service franchise concerned, it may well include a substantial intellectual property element and it is feared that many distribution and service agreements previously covered by the franchising block exemption no longer benefit from any block exemption. Production franchising, on the other hand, is almost certainly not covered by the new Regulation, because there the focus of the agreement is normally the IPRs, but nor was it under the old block exemption.

3.5 FRANCHISE SYSTEMS: THE 2000 GUIDELINES

So far we have considered the text of the Regulation itself, and we now turn to the Commission's Guidelines.[58] These make clear the Commission's intention to include most

---

[54] E.g. V.L. Korah and D. O'Sullivan, *Vertical Agreements: Distribution Agreements under the EC Competition Rules* (Hart Publishing, 2002), pp.141ff.

[55] Paras 30–36.

[56] This is the word used in recital 3 of the Regulation.

[57] [1990] OJ L100/32 [1991] 4 CMLR 391. See Ch. 12, p.241.

[58] [2000] OJ C291/1: 5 CMLR 1074.

distribution and service franchises within the scope of the Regulation and Community law requires legislation to be interpreted in the light of the intention of the legislator.[59] Neverthe-less, it is unfortunate that these intentions are not clearly reflected in the wording of the Regulation.

Paragraph 44 of the Guidelines lists seven types of restrictions generally considered neces-sary to protect the franchisor's IPRs, but which the Regulation is intended to exempt if for any reason they do infringe Article 81(1). Paragraph 119 also indirectly indicates the Com-mission's continuing support for franchising as a generally desirable distribution method justifying a number of restrictive contractual provisions where these are linked to the transfer of know-how, saying that the more a vertical restraint is linked to the transfer of know-how, the less likely it is to infringe Article 81.

The Guidelines also make it clear that distribution and service franchising is intended to be covered, though not 'industrial franchise agreements'. Paragraph 31 explains that the intention is to include agreements featuring IPRs where these allow the more effective distribution of goods or services. Paragraph 43 says that intellectual property right (IPR) licensing contained in franchise agreements escapes the application of Article 2(3) and remains within the scope of the Regulation if it satisfies the conditions listed in paragraph 30:

— The IPR provisions must be part of a vertical agreement, i.e. an agreement with conditions under which the parties may purchase, sell or resell certain goods or services.

— The IPRs must be assigned to, or for use by, the buyer.

— The IPR provisions must not constitue the primary object of the agreement.

— The IPR provisions must be directly related to the use, sale or resale of goods or services by the buyer or his customers. In the case of franchising where marketing forms the object of the exploitation of the IPRs, the goods or services are distributed by the master franchisee or the franchisees.

— The IPR provisions, in relation to the contract goods or services, must not contain restrictions of competition having the same object or effect as vertical restraints which are not exempted under the Block Exemption Regulation.

The Guidelines do recognize, however, that the block exemption will not apply to franchise agreements where the franchisor does not supply goods or services (including not only services passed on to consumers, but also commercial and technical assistance services to the franchisee) to his franchisees, and the franchise consists mainly or entirely of IPR licensing. It says that such franchises 'will be treated in a way similar to those franchise agreements which are covered' by the Regulation. Though this sounds comforting, presumably it means no more than that such franchisors are likely to receive a sympathetic hearing if they request exemption or a comfort letter.

The same rules apply in respect of non-compete and exclusive purchasing agreements in franchising agreements as apply to other distribution agreements, indeed non-compete clauses in the context of franchising do not infringe Article 81(1) at all when they are necessary to maintain the common identity and reputation of a franchised network.

[59] For another example of this principle, see Case T-102/96 *Gencor* v. *Commission* [1999] ECR II-753, [1999] 4 CMLR 971 at para. 148, where the Court of First Instance had to decide whether the EC Merger Regulation could be applied to situations of collective dominance. See Ch. 17, pp. 366–7.

Furthermore, Article 5(b), while not explicitly mentioning franchising, will frequently be to the benefit of franchisors. It is the rule which says that normally any restriction on the buyer making, purchasing, selling or reselling goods or services after the agreement has come to an end is not exempted, but that there is an exception where the obligation:

— relates to competing goods or services;
— is limited to premises and land from which the buyer operated during the contract period; and
— is indispensable to protect know-how transferred by the supplier to the buyer.

Even where these conditions are satisfied, the non-compete clause must apply for no longer than a year, unless the obligation relates to use and disclosure of know-how which has not entered the public domain.

So far franchise agreements have apparently not caused significant problems which have been brought to the attention of the Commission. But franchisors may remain concerned, despite the comforting words of the Guidelines. If their agreements fall to be considered by a national court or authority rather than the Commission, as will happen more frequently once the new modernization rules enter into force, there must be a risk that these bodies reject the interpretation given in the Guidelines, and refuse the application of the Regulation to franchise agreements which the Commission appears to have intended it to cover.

12

INTELLECTUAL PROPERTY RIGHTS: LICENSING

1. INTRODUCTION

1.1 THE NATURE OF INTELLECTUAL PROPERTY RIGHTS

The protection by national law of different types of intellectual property is common to all Member States. The range of that legislation, however, and the classification of the rights thus protected, vary considerably between them. These rights include patents, registered and unregistered designs, trade marks, and copyright together with various other minor or specialized categories such as plant breeders' rights. The methods of protection adopted themselves differ; some can be protected only by registration, after a more or less rigorous process of screening for acceptance, as with patents, trade marks, and registered designs. In other cases, rights can simply be acquired as the result of publication, as with artistic or literary copyright protected by Community Directives, by national legislation, and by a number of international conventions. Such proprietary rights can protect technical information of importance and value for commercial and industrial activities, or they may simply protect the identity and commercial individuality of an undertaking, as in the case of business names and trade marks.

There is an inherent conflict between, on one hand, the existence and exercise of any such rights, which will necessarily give a degree of exclusivity and protection to their owners, and on the other the general aims of competition policy as embodied in Articles 81 and 82. In this chapter we review the way in which the Commission, in applying these Articles and Regulations made under the Treaty, has dealt with agreements that relate to the use and exploitation of industrial property rights, in particular patents and know-how, to which most of its attention in this area has been devoted. There is a further limitation to the exploitation and enjoyment of industrial property rights, arising from the very nature of the European Community as described in the Treaty. This is the restraint placed upon owners of such rights in Member States to prevent their use in a way that hinders the free movement of goods and services within the Community. Articles 28 and 29 of the Treaty set out the basic prohibitions on quantitative restrictions on imports and exports, and all measures having equivalent effect (a number of which arise as a direct consequence of the protection of industrial and commercial property), whilst Article 30, *inter alia*, preserves the right of a Member State nevertheless to impose prohibitions or restrictions on imports and exports required to protect industrial and commercial property, so long as those restrictions or prohibitions are neither a means of arbitrary discrimination nor a disguised restriction on trade between Member States. The exact interpretation of these concepts, which have been considered by the European Court in many cases, are considered in the next chapter.

1.2 THE EXPLOITATION OF SUCH RIGHTS

The owner of intellectual property rights naturally desires the greatest possible freedom to negotiate the basis upon which their exploitation can be arranged. However, whilst, the manufacturer of goods will select a particular system of distribution through which its sales can be maximized, in the exploitation of intellectual property the owner normally finds that it is best to part with only a limited interest in the asset, giving a licence to a third party for its use, whilst still retaining ownership of the asset. Assignment of the owner's rights to a third party by assignment always remains a possible alternative.

The owner of an intellectual property right has a wide choice over the exploitation of its asset. A patent can, of course, be used simply to assist the owner's own manufacturing activities, a defensive shield preventing others from making use of the data comprised within its protection. Provided that the owner itself is making adequate use in its own processes of the information, then it is highly unlikely that licences for use of that right will be compulsorily issued under any national legislation, since this procedure can normally only be adopted when a patent owner conspicuously fails to make adequate use of its patent.[1] On many occasions, however, mere defensive use of the right will prove insufficiently profitable to its owner, who may wish to obtain additional revenue by licensing one or more other undertakings who will pay to utilize the information or process for their own purposes.

Three kinds of licence are found. The simplest is the *non-exclusive* licence, where no licensee receives any guarantee from the licensor as to the exclusivity of the rights provided, which the owner remains free to grant also to other undertakings. Clearly, the value of each such licence is thereby reduced and the percentage payable by way of royalty is normally less than for an equivalent exclusive licence. The *exclusive* licence, an equally common method of exploitation of industrial property, contains the same two-way bargain found in exclusive distribution arrangements. The owner agrees that it will not itself license any undertaking within the particular territory apart from the chosen exclusive licensee, and agrees that it will itself not exploit that particular right in that territory. An exclusive licence where the owner of the right reserves for itself the right to compete in the licensed territory, but must refrain from licensing any third parties situate there, is known as a *sole* licence.

In the earlier editions of this work the development of Community policy towards the licensing of intellectual property was treated in detail and on a historical basis, setting out the various stages through which the thinking of the Community and its Member States have passed. Now that more that forty years have passed since the 'Christmas Message' first announced its initial attitude towards patent licensing, it seems appropriate to treat the earlier developments of the subject more briefly, and to focus on the present and likely future developments in the licensing not only of patents, but of know-how, trade marks, copyright and software.

---

[1] For the legal position in the UK, see the Patents Act 1977, ss.48–59. Compulsory licensing of registered design rights and copyright may now also be required in certain circumstances. See *Terrell on the Law of Patents*, 15th edn. (Sweet & Maxwell, 2000), Ch. 11, and the Copyright Designs and Patents Act 1988, ss.144 and 237–9. Sections 44 and 45 of the Patents Act 1977 declaring certain practices by patentees illegal have been repealed by the 1998 Competition Act, which now governs such practices.

2. EARLY COMMISSION ATTITUDES TO PATENT LICENSING

2.1 THE 1962 CHRISTMAS MESSAGE

In spite of predictions from some sources that national patent systems in Europe would become obsolete as a result of the ever quickening pace of new technical developments, arriving at both their high point of value and subsequent obsolescence more quickly than could be adequately coped with by relatively cumbersome national patent systems, a large number of patents have continued to be granted both in Member States and, since 1975, by the European Patent Office in Munich on behalf of the individual Member States. From the viewpoint of DG Comp, therefore, a method of controlling and dealing with the large number of patent licences became an important element in early competition policy. Many of the problems which it faced were similar to those which arose as the result of the very large number of exclusive distribution arrangements notified. A substantial number of such individual agreements might fall within the terms of Article 81(1) and would therefore need consideration for exemption under Article 81(3). This in turn would mean a demand from industrial sources for an early block exemption in order to avoid the delay inherent in individual consideration of a very large number of patent licence agreements.

Just as with exclusive distribution, block exemptions could only be provided, both as a matter of good administration and under the express terms of Regulation 19/65,[2] when sufficient experience had been gained of individual case law. This meant in practice that first block exemption covering patents was not issued until well over twenty years after the adoption of Regulation 17. However, it would be unfair to DG Comp not to point out that, by comparison with exclusive distribution and purchasing, patents and other intellectual property rights and their licensing present considerably more complex issues. This is not only because of their individual protection under national legislation but also because they normally involve a greater degree of exclusivity, which in turn requires the consideration of a larger variety of restrictions upon licensees.[3] Given the inherent tension between the provisions of national laws on one hand and the requirements of Articles 81 and 82 on the other, it was not surprising that the problem of reconciliation took a considerable time.[4]

Amongst the very large number of agreements notified to the Commission at the end of 1962 and the beginning of 1963 under the provisions of Regulation 17 were many thousands of such licences. Considerable prior discussion had already taken place in DG Comp as to

---

[2] The relevant recital reads 'Whereas it should be laid down under what conditions the Commission . . . may exercise such powers after sufficient experience has been gained in the light of individual decisions and it becomes possible to define categories of agreement and concerted practices in respect of which the conditions of Article 81(3) may be considered as being fulfilled'.

[3] This is clearly illustrated by the considerably greater detail and complexity of the Patent Block Exemption Reg. 2349/84 compared with those on Exclusive Distribution (Reg. 1983/83) or Exclusive Purchasing (Reg. 1984/83).

[4] This does not mean, however, that the block exemption need ultimately have taken as long as it actually did, namely, some eight years (1977–84) from the publication of the first draft to the implementation of the exemption.

the basis upon which patent licences would be dealt with. It was accepted from the start that a certain number of restrictions would inevitably be imposed by licensors on their licensees as the direct result of the inherent nature of patents, and of the fact that, in granting a licence, the licensor is not disposing of its entire asset but only a limited interest whose bounds have to be carefully delineated. A difficult policy choice, which the Commission could not avoid, was the need to distinguish between those restrictions which merely reflected this right of the patentee to spell out the extent of the licence, and other restrictions which would actually restrict competition between the licensee and other licensees in respect of specific territories, and in particular would interfere with the basic principle of the need for integration of the Common Market itself by the free movement of goods across national boundaries.

A few weeks before the closing date for the notification of bilateral agreements under Regulation 17 came the publication of the 'Christmas Message' on 24 December 1962, the first public statement by the Commission of the approach that it would adopt to patent licences. This Notice contained four sections. The first set out the list of clauses which it regarded as falling outside Article 81(1). These were:

— obligations imposed on the licensee having as their objects either limitation of the exploitation of the invention to manufacture, use, or sale, and limitations to certain fields of use;

— limitations imposed also to the quantity of products to be manufactured, the period and territorial area for which they were permitted to be used, and limitations on the licensee's powers of disposal, e.g. on sub-licensing;

— obligations as to marking of the product with a patent number and the observance of quality standards necessary for the technically perfect exploitation of the patent, also non-exclusive improvement undertakings on a reciprocal basis between licensor and licensee; and

— undertakings to ensure that the exclusivity of the grant to the licensee was protected.

The second section confirmed that all other clauses would be looked at on their individual merits, and that in any case a general 'appraisal' was not possible for agreements relating to joint ownership of patents, reciprocal licensing, or multiple parallel licensing, or to any clauses which purported to extend beyond the period of validity of the relevant patent. The third section of the Notice confirmed that patent licences containing only those clauses referred to in the first part of the Notice did not require to be notified. The fourth stated that the basis of the Notice was that the clauses referred to 'entail only the partial maintenance of the right of prohibition contained in the patentee's exclusive right in relation to the licensee who in other respects is authorized to exploit the invention. The list . . . is not an exhaustive definition of the rights conferred by the patent'.

This Notice initially received little adverse comment, especially as the approach which it had adopted corresponded generally to current attitudes in Member States. The acceptance of the principle of exclusive licensing of patents was strongly influenced by the attitude of German law, whose statute against restraints of competition had adopted a relatively mild approach to such exclusivity. Moreover, the Commission had at that time only very limited case law experience and was chiefly occupied with notifications relating to exclusive distribution agreements.

2.2 THE COMMISSION'S CHANGING ATTITUDE TO EXCLUSIVITY

A distinct change of policy occurred over the latter part of the 1960s. By the end of the decade, DG Comp no longer regarded an exclusive patent licence as *prima facie* outside the scope of Article 81(1) and was already starting to take a stricter view, namely that exclusivity had to be justified by the particular circumstances of the licensing arrangements. A number of suggestions have been made as to the reason for this change in policy, including the influence of *Grundig-Consten*[5] decided by the European Court in 1966. Under this argument, the distinction drawn in that case between the *existence* of a right of intellectual property, protected by Article 30 of the Treaty, as opposed to the exercise of that right, which is subject not only to Article 28 but also to Article 81, led inevitably to a more rigorous examination of the justification for exclusivity of licensing. The alternative explanation for the change in policy was that the Commission was influenced by cases decided by the European Court relating to the interpretation of Articles 28 to 30, as applied to the free movement of goods, and the broad interpretation by the Court of Article 28, as compared with the narrower approach adopted to the limitations and exceptions set out in Article 30.[6]

Neither of those two suggestions is completely convincing. Whilst the *Grundig-Consten* case, as the leading influence on policy within DG Comp during the 1960s, undoubtedly influenced the thinking of officials and ensured the pre-eminence of the principle of market integration, more than this would have been necessary to effect the major shift apparent from the original Christmas Message of late 1962 to the position adopted in the cases decided in 1971. Moreover, nothing in the judgment leads inevitably to a conclusion that exclusive patent licences fall inherently within the scope of Article 81(1); the strictures of the Court apply specifically to such uses of those rights as may defeat the effectiveness of the Community law on agreements that are restrictive of competition. It can be argued that the limitation placed by the *Grundig* decision on the use of intellectual property rights, in this case trade-mark rights, to make it hard for distributors to effect parallel imports was indeed covered by the terms of the Christmas Message, and that the case alone could not be the foundation for such a complete change of attitude to exclusivity in patent licences.[7]

We therefore need to find other explanations for the change of policy. It would surely be reasonable to conclude that it occurred primarily because of the weight of experience accumulating within DG Comp as the result of examining a large number of patent agreement notifications during the six or seven years following Regulation 17's implementation at the start of 1963. Some evidence of this is the very full treatment given to this topic in the *First Annual Report* of the Commission.[8] It was clearly felt at that time that an explanation was needed of the course of development of policy relating to patent licences since the Christmas Message, and an account is given of the examination of some 500 such licences. The Commission explained that these agreements were analysed in order to determine which clauses most often occurred, also to ascertain which of the restrictions imposed were

---

[5] Cases 56 and 58/64 [1966] ECR 299: CMLR 418. For the facts of the case see pp.42–4.

[6] See L. Gormley, *Prohibiting Restrictions on Trade within the EEC* (North-Holland, 1985), esp. pp.184–9 and 230–3.

[7] While the subsequent European Court decision in *Parke, Davis* v. *Probel* Case 24/67 [1968] ECR 55: CMLR 47, confirmed the application of *Grundig-Consten* to patents, it took the issue of exclusivity no further. See Ch. 13, p.251.

[8] This appeared in 1972 and covered the work of DG Comp to the end of 1971. See pp.65–74 of the Report.

made essential either by the inherent nature of national patent rights, or to maintain the secrecy of related know-how, or which for other reasons did not have the effect of restricting competition. The Report stated that the analysis was being used in the preparation of a draft block exemption covering two-party agreements such as patent licences, which was permitted by the terms of Council Regulation 19/65, which also gave the Commission powers to introduce the existing block exemption for exclusive distribution agreements.

The growing awareness of the Commission of the scope for application of Article 81(1) to exclusive patent licensing is perhaps most clearly shown by its decision in *AOIP* v. *Beyrard*.[9] Beyrard was a French inventor resident in Paris who granted an exclusive patent licence to AOIP to manufacture and market in France and in certain foreign French territories rheostats and speed changers for electric motors. In the decision, the principle of exclusivity itself was challenged. The clauses struck down by the Commission as being in breach of 81(1), and not capable of exemption under Article 81(3), included the exclusivity of the rights granted, and an export prohibition applying to any country where Beyrard had either licensed his patent or assigned his rights to third parties. Among other clauses struck down were a no-challenge clause and an obligation to pay royalties during the lifetime of the most recent original or improvement patent, whether or not the patent was being exploited by the licensee. Finally, there was an obligation on the licensee to refrain from any kind of competition with the licensor in the field covered by the agreement. If the licensor invested new processes or devices in the field (even if based on different principles but which could be used for the same purpose) such processes and devices automatically fell within the scope of the agreement. On the other hand, if the licensee made any such devices by processes other than those of the licensor, he still had to pay royalties on them. All these restrictions were treated as inherently incapable of exemption.

3. THE EVOLUTION OF THE PATENT BLOCK EXEMPTION

3.1 TRAVAUX PRÉPARATOIRES AND THE *MAIZE SEED* CASE

Commission policy had now travelled so far from the 1962 Christmas Message that some official clarification of the content of patent licences acceptable to the Commission was clearly necessary. The principal point of difficulty was the extent to which the licensor could establish a group of exclusive licensees within the Common Market with territorial protection from each other, and whether this territorial protection could be made complete, or would be invalid to the extent that it impeded the movement of parallel imports under the *Grundig-Consten* principle. In the view of the Commission, all such arrangements involving any degree of exclusivity had to be considered under Article 81(3), thus raising the possibility in every case that a claim for exemption would be rejected.[10]

---

[9] [1976] 1 CMLR D14.

[10] A problem raised for the Commission was that the 1975 Luxembourg Patent Convention included an express provision (Art. 43, para. 2) that the exclusive territorial licence for a part of the Community formed part of the Community's patent regime, and was therefore immune from Arts. 81 and 82. The Commission never accepted that this was a correct statement of the legal position. See Ch. 13, pp.246–7.

This uncertainty about the status of exclusive licences could not continue indefinitely. A draft Regulation was submitted at the end of that year for consideration by the Member States, and made public for consultative purposes. In this early draft it was indicated that the inclusion of any of the following clauses, amongst others, would be likely to prevent the grant of a block exemption:

(1) no-challenge clauses, debarring the licensee from challenging the patent;

(2) non-competition clauses between licensor and licensee in respect of matters not directly covered by the relevant patents and know-how;

(3) extension of agreements beyond the life of the most recent patents covered by the agreement unless the agreement is terminable by the parties on reasonably short notice; also forbidden are requirements to pay royalties after the expiry of the last patent;

(4) agreements requiring purchase of unpatented supplies for use with the patented process;

(5) restrictions on the manner in which the product made with the licensed patent is sold, e.g. in small tubes or large bottles and in what kinds of packaging; and

(6) exclusivity of sales and export restrictions exceeding the period necessary for a new product having to penetrate its market. The amended draft introduced the condition that the combined licensed territory for individual licensees (or licensees within the same group) have a maximum population of one hundred million.

Criticism that the draft was too stringent continued from industrial sources; objection was taken to the limit on the extent to which field of use restrictions can be imposed, which would, it was claimed, make the proposed Regulation unattractive to most potential licensors. The restriction of one hundred million population for a territory within which exclusive licensing would be allowed incurred particular criticism as unnecessarily arbitrary;[11] in response the Commission indicated that it was prepared to consider replacing it by a more generous qualification.

Further indications of the views of the Commission on the preferred content of the draft Regulation were shown by its decision in the *Maize Seed*[12] case. This case arose out of the assignment by a French State agency for agricultural research (Inra) of plant breeders' rights in a variety of maize seed to Eisele, a German resident, who proceeded to register them in Germany. Eisele and Inra also later concluded an arrangement under which Eisele received the exclusive right to distribute Inra's maize seed varieties in Germany, and under which Inra accepted an obligation to prevent other imports of its own maize seed into Germany. Subsequently Inra assigned to a French company, Frasema, an exclusive licence for commercial exploitation of its maize seed and vested all its own rights in that company. Meanwhile, Eisele agreed to purchase two-thirds of the maize seed which he sold in Germany from Inra, whilst in respect of the remaining third he was free either to produce

[11] Similar objections had also been raised to the proposed application of such limitation on the areas for which exclusive distribution agreements could be permitted.

[12] The report of the original Commission decision is at [1978] 3 CMLR 434. The European Court reports referring to *Nungesser* v. *Commission* Case 258/78 are at [1982] ECR 2015 and [1983] 1 CMLR 278. The rights originally granted to Eisele were later transferred to Nungesser KG, a business controlled by him.

it or to arrange for its production under his supervision. Eisele also agreed not to sell competing seeds and to set prices in agreement with Inra, although in practice this last arrangement was apparently not enforced. Eisele had enforced his rights in the German Court against at least one parallel importer and had obtained a settlement under which the importer agreed not to sell Inra's maize seed in Germany without Eisele's permission.

The decision of the Commission in 1978 was that all the restrictive terms referred to above and those incorporated in the settlement in the German Court were in violation of Article 81(1). The claim for exemption under Article 81(3) was rejected. Eisele appealed to the Court of Justice against all the findings of the Commission except those relating to the requirements clause, the non-competition clause, and the resale price maintenance requirement. The Commission's viewpoint is summed up by the following extract from the subsequent Court decision:

The Commission considered that, as in the case of a patent, exclusive propagation rights granted by the owner of breeders' rights to a licensee within the Common Market are, in principle, capable of being considered to have satisfied the tests for exemption under Article [81(3)]. There are even circumstances in which exclusive selling rights linked with prohibitions against exporting might also be exempted, for example when the exclusivity is needed to protect small or medium-sized undertakings in their attempt to penetrate a new market or promoting a new product provided that parallel imports are not restricted at the same time.[13]

In *Maize Seed*, however, the Commission felt that the absolute territorial protection afforded to Eisele did not satisfy these tests, especially as the prices paid for the seed in Germany were as much as 70 per cent higher than were paid in France.

The first official publication of the Patent Licensing block exemption, already considerably revised since the draft was first shown to the Advisory Committee, appeared in 1979. In spite of its publication, further progress was apparently blocked by the need for the Commission's procedures to be under-pinned by the Court's judgment on the appeal pending from the Commission's *Maize Seed* decision. Moreover, the complexity of the subject and the different interests involved inevitably caused some delay in its resolution; this was exacerbated by procedural difficulties encountered by the European Court of Justice in finalizing the hearings on the case, where its final decision was not rendered until summer 1982. The Court's ultimate decision reversed some parts of the Commission's 1978 decision, ruling that the following restrictions did not *per se* amount to a violation of Article 81(1):

(*a*) the obligation upon Inra (or those deriving rights through it) to refrain from producing or selling relevant seeds in Germany to other licensees; and

(*b*) the obligation upon Inra (or those deriving rights through it) to refrain from producing or selling the relevant seeds in Germany themselves.

The Court upheld the remainder of the Commission's decision, namely that a violation of 81(1) was involved by the obligation upon Inra or those deriving rights from it to prevent third parties from exporting the relevant seeds into Germany without Eisele's authorization, as also by Eisele's concurrent use of his own contractual and proprietary rights to prevent all imports into Germany of the seed. These violations resulted from the fact that the licensee had obtained absolute territorial protection not only from the licensor, but from fellow

---

[13] [1982] ECR 2023–4.

licensees in other territories, as a result of the combined effect of the licensor's undertaking to prevent exports by third parties into Germany and by Eisele's own use of his exclusive rights to challenge parallel imports in the German Courts. The Court also confirmed that an agreement which permitted such 'blanket' protection would not receive exemption under 81(3). The Court also indicated that a German Court had previously approved settlement between the licensee and David, a parallel importer, requiring David to obtain Eisele's consent before marketing seed in Germany, which settlement itself violated Article 81(1).

The Court drew an important distinction between, on one hand, an 'open' exclusive licence in which the licensor only agreed not to grant rights to other licensees for the same territories without affecting the ability of third parties, such as parallel importers and licensees for other territories, to compete and, on the other hand, exclusive licences accompanied by absolute territorial protection aimed at eliminating competition from third parties, especially parallel importers. Whilst absolute territorial protection could never receive negative clearance under Article 81(1), the grant of exclusivity under an open licence had to be considered in the light of a number of factors, including the nature of the product, the novelty and importance of the relevant technology, the investment risks assumed by the licensee, and the development of inter-brand competition. These last two factors deserved to carry most weight. It is, however, unlikely that the Court intended this definition of an open exclusive licence outside the reach of Article 81 to include licences containing clauses protecting the licensee for even limited periods from competition from other licensees of the same technologies in other territories. Such restrictions would surely have had to be assessed in each case under the terms of Article 81(3), where under the terms of the relevant Block Exemption or by way of individual exemption.

Commentators on the case felt that its effect would be very considerably to widen the scope for argument by the owners of intellectual property rights, and that the Commission should thereafter show a more generous attitude towards restrictive clauses necessary to protect the interests of licensors and licensees in exclusivity. The Court had after all made it clear that it regarded its decision as relevant, not only to the narrower field of plant breeders' rights, but to the more general application of patent licences. In late 1983 a further draft of the block exemption appeared, incorporating a number of amendments, followed by a 1984 version containing still more alterations, mainly extending the number of restrictions that could be imposed. It also introduced the concept, already familiar in the block exemption of exclusive distribution, that a licensee could be prevented from active sales outside the territory although able to satisfy unsolicited sales orders from outside its territory.

3.2 THE BLOCK EXEMPTION REGULATION (REG NO. 2349/84)

The major features of the new Block Exemption included the following:

(1) It applied only to bilateral agreements (for which alone the Council Regulation 19/65 had given authority to the Commission to adopt such category exemption).

(2) Its coverage was for patent licences only, but including those which also had a licence of secret know-how which enabled better exploitation of the licenced patent.

(3) The licensor could grant the licensee exclusive rights to make themselves items covered by the patent throughout its duration.

(4) The licensee could be given absolute territorial protection for five years from the date when the patented product was first marketed in the Community.

(5) A long list of 'black' clauses was set out which could not be included, as well as an even longer list of permitted 'white' clauses containing restrictions which were allowed, though in some cases subject to qualification. The 'white' list included a number of clauses deemed permissible by the ECJ in the *Maize Seed* case.

(6) Any restrictions found in neither the 'black' nor 'white' list could be notified to the Commission as 'grey' clauses under a procedure known as 'opposition'; if the Commission failed to object to such a clause within six months after notification, the block exemption was deemed to apply to it.

(7) It applied only where the licensee was actually manufacturing the products, directly or through subcontractors, not if it was engaged only in distribution.

(8) Benefit of the block exemption could be withdrawn if the licensee refused without any objectively valid reason to meet unsolicited demands from users or resellers in the territory of other licensees, or made it difficult for users or resellers to obtain products from other resellers in the Community.

3.3 THE *WINDSURFING* CASE

After the implementation of the Patent Regulation, the number of notifications of individual agreements substantially reduced, as DG Comp had hoped, though there remained a number of patent licences which for one reason or another did not fall within the framework of the block exemption. An indication of the likely treatment of such agreements was given by the Court decision in *Windsurfing International* v. *Commission*[14] (ECJ 1986). The importance of this case was that it was the first occasion since the introduction of the block exemption when the Court had an opportunity of laying down rules for the assessment of individual patent licences. The Commission had imposed a fine, albeit a small one, on a patent licensor, Windsurfing International. The licences under challenge were those between Windsurfing International and its German licensees. The Court accepted the Commission's finding that the coverage of the German patent obtained by Windsurfing International was not for a complete sailboard but only for the rig (mast, sail, and spars) attached to the board. There was a market for the rig alone, though usually boards and rigs were sold as an integrated unit. Several restrictions in the licence were stated by the Commission to be in breach of Article 81(1), as follows:

(1) the licensed product having been specified as a complete sailboard, the licensor's approval was nevertheless needed for any type of board on which the licensee intended to place the rig;

(2) an obligation on the licensee to sell only complete sailboards, i.e. the patented rig and an approved board;

(3) the licensee's obligation to pay royalties on the entire selling price of the complete sailboard (rather than solely on that of the patented rig);

---

[14] Case 193/83 [1986] ECR 611: 3 CMLR 489. The founder of the company, Mr Hoyle Schweitzer, was one of the leading figures in the development of the sailboard.

(4) a requirement on the licensee to fix a notice on the board stating that it was 'licensed' by the licensor;

(5) no-challenge clauses with respect to the licensor's trade mark and patent;[15] and

(6) a restriction against the licensee manufacturing the sailboard except at certain factories in Germany.

Advocate General Lenz disagreed with a number of findings made by the Commission and himself undertook a very thorough investigation of the facts. In his lengthy opinion, he concluded that only three of the restrictions could be held to be in breach of Article 81(1), numbers (1), (2), and (3) above. With regard to the others his opinion was either that the restrictions could not have any effect on competition or that they would in practice have insufficient effect on trade between Member States. He therefore recommended that the fine be reduced.

The Court took a stricter view, concurring with the views of the Commission on all except item (3) above, and reduced the fine slightly. The reasons given by the Court were important for the future. With regard to restriction (1), the Court found that Windsurfing International had failed to show that their control over the manufacture of non-patented components, such as boards, related to any objective criteria to do with the patented rig as no technical method of verifying the quality of the board was provided by the agreement. The Court found that its real interest lay 'in ensuring that there was sufficient product differentiation between its licensee's sailboards to cover the widest possible spectrum of market demand'. If any passing off of other boards as Windsurfing International boards by the licensees was found, this could have been dealt with by an action in the national Courts. The distinction drawn by the Court in respect of item (3) was that the method of calculating royalties on the entire sailboard might have a small effect in restricting competition with regard to the board, but would have no effect on the sale of rigs, especially as the royalties levied on the sale of complete sailboards proved to have been no higher than that laid down for the sale of separate rigs.[16] With regard to restriction (6), the Court rejected the argument by Windsurfing International that the restriction of manufacturers to one location was required by quality control. The Commission's argument to the contrary was accepted, that in fact numerous licensees throughout Germany were manufacturing components for the rig, and that Windsurfing International in any case would have had no say in the quality control of such manufacturers. The Court also gave an important general ruling on the interpretation of Article 81(1): it said that the Commission need not examine each clause restricting competition to see if each could be shown to have an effect on trade between Member States. Provided that the agreement taken as a whole had such an effect, Article 81(1) would be applicable to it. The Court appears to have found the necessary effect on trade from the levels of imports into the Community of both complete sailboards (about 20 per cent of national markets) and of their individual components (where the corresponding figure was about 10 per cent).

---

[15] On the other hand, the Court subsequently held that a no-challenge clause cannot restrict competition if the licence itself is free, since the licensee then suffers no competitive disadvantage by any payment of royalties: *Bayer* v. *Sülhöfer* Case 65/86 [1988] ECR 5249: [1990] 4 CMLR 182.

[16] The licensee acknowledged that it would be equitable to accept a higher rate of royalty if it were calculated on the price of the rig alone.

This case also importantly illustrates that the Court will generally support the Commission in its analysis of restrictions imposed by the holders of an intellectual property right (here a patent, but equally applicable to other forms of such rights). It will divide them into those (comparatively limited in number) which flow from the inherent subject matter of the right (and can, therefore, be said to form part of the right itself) and those which represent an attempt to extend the holder's rights beyond, even if only marginally. It will also respect the Commission's findings as to the scope of the right (provided that the findings appear reasonable in the light of all the evidence presented); crucial in this case was its finding that the patent covered only the rig and not the complete sailboard, a factor that influenced most of the adverse rulings against Windsurfing International.

4. KNOW-HOW LICENCES AND THE KNOW-HOW BLOCK EXEMPTION REGULATION 556/89

4.1 THE SUB-CONTRACTING NOTICE

Much technical information exists that is essential, or at least of substantial importance, to manufacturing operations or other industrial activities. Although undoubtedly a form of industrial property, it cannot be protected by registration, notification, or symbol; it either exists alone or forms part of a 'package' of technical information which includes patents and other intellectual property rights. It is well defined by Hawk as 'a catch-all expression embracing a broad and ill-defined spectrum of unpatented and unpatentable inventions, techniques, processes, formulae, devices, blueprints, technical and production skills, etc'.[17] Since no time limit applies to the protection, it has been argued that it should be more strictly treated by the Commission than patents. It could also be argued that a great deal of what starts as technical know-how will reach the public domain relatively quickly, so that in practice its commercial value for exploitation will last for a considerably shorter period than patents, trade marks, or copyright. These factors could be put forward in support of a shorter period of protection for know-how than for such other rights.

Light was shed on the Commission's attitude to the related topic of know-how after the termination of a licence for its use by the publication in December 1978 of a Notice on subcontracting agreements. This topic had been under discussion for four or five years with interested industrial groups, trade associations, and Member States. Under such agreements, a main contractor, often but not necessarily as the result of an order it had received from a third party, would order from a subcontractor goods or services that had to be integrated closely with its own manufacturing or service operations. A typical example is the supply by a subcontractor of components for assembly and incorporation in complex mechanical and electrical machinery or apparatus such as aircraft, motor cars, or computers. Similarities exist between such subcontracts and patent/know-how licences, although subcontracts normally last for a shorter time than patent licences, so that the main contractor would be particularly concerned to restrict future use by the subcontractor of the patented or unpatented information provided to him for the purposes of the subcontract. It is also

---

[17] B.E. Hawk, *United States, Common Market and International Antitrust: A Comparative Guide*, 2nd edn., Vol. ii (Harcourt Brace Jovanovitch, 1994 Supplement), p.691.

important to ensure the close integration of the subcontractors' manufacturing processes with those of the main contractor. Article 81 is relevant to the restrictions under which the main contractor seeks to protect his interests by limiting the use of this information by the subcontractor once the contract has been terminated.

The solution eventually adopted was a compromise: the publication in December 1978 of a Notice.[18] This, of course, had less value in terms of legal certainty than a block exemption. However, it did at least indicate DG Comp's views on the restrictions available for placing within a subcontract and enabled greater scope to be given to the main contractor's wish to restrict the subsequent use of know-how by its previous subcontractors. The Notice can be summarized as follows:

(1) Article [81] would not apply to a sub-contracting agreement where the subcontractor received either industrial property rights or unpatented secret data (know-how) or documents, dies, or tools belonging to the contractor and which permitted the manufacture of goods in a manner which differed in form, function, or composition from other goods on the market, unless the subcontractor was able to obtain access to the relevant technology and equipment needed to produce the relevant goods from sources in the public domain.

(2) If the relevant conditions were satisfied, then Article [81] would not apply to a clause whereby the technology or equipment provided by the contractor, and necessary for the subcontractor to carry out its obligations, could not be used except for the purposes of the subcontracting agreement or made available to third parties, and whereby goods or services resulting from its use should be supplied only to the contractor.

(3) Further ancillary restrictions would be permitted, namely that during the period of the subcontract the parties would not disclose confidential information, and that the subcontractor might enter into an obligation not to reveal the relevant know-how of a secret nature even after the expiration of the agreement, and to pass on to the main contractor improvements which the subcontractor has discovered, on a non-exclusive basis. On the other hand, the mere previous existence of a subcontracting agreement should not be allowed to displace the subcontractor's ability to compete in the future with the main contractor, utilizing independently its own technical information and know-how even if this had developed from experience gained during the main contract.

The Notice attempted to strike a fair balance between the interests of the main contractor in preventing unfair activity at a subsequent date by the subcontractor in utilizing the main contractor's information, whilst relieving the subcontractor from onerous restrictions placed upon it after the termination of the contract, that would restrict it from utilizing the benefits of the research and development which it may have carried out, and which may in turn have substantially contributed to its own specialized input to the contract. The difficulty of balancing these equally legitimate interests in the sub-contracting area well illustrated the difficulties that faced the Commission in preparing the framework of model agreements acceptable as block exemptions for both patented and unpatented material.

---

[18] [1979] OJ C1/2.

4.2 THE KNOW-HOW REGULATION 556/89

It was by now clear that the model of the Patent Licence Block Exemption 2349/84 would not be wholly suitable for the many licences whose principal subject matter was non-patented know-how. At this time the Commission did obtain some experience from individual applications for exemption in respect of know-how licences in a variety of different markets, whose outcome suggested that it would be quite liberal in the level of protection it would give to licensees of know-how against the sole's activities of other licensees in different territories.

The Know-how Block Exemption Regulation came into force on 1 April 1989. Its main features were as follows:

(1) It applied both to pure know-how agreements and also to mixed agreements covering both know-how and patents, which did not come within the Patent Licence Block Exemption.

(2) It applied only to bilateral agreements.

(3) The agreement had to contain at least one of eight restrictions which included an obligation on the licensor itself not to exploit know-how in the licensed territory nor to license other undertakings to do so and an obligation on the licensee not to actively market the know-how in territories licensed to others.

(4) A list of 'black' clauses included were largely modelled on those contained in Regulation 2349/84, included no-challenge and non-competition clauses, and restrictions on the customers should be supplied, maximum production quantities and price restrictions.

(5) A long list of 'white' clauses included those making the licence exclusive to the licensee, but prohibiting sub-licensing and limiting the use of know-how to the particular fields of use, while the licensee could enjoy the benefit of a 'most favoured licensee' clause to ensure that no other licensee received better terms.

(6) the periods of protection allowed were shorter than those in the Patent Licence Block Exemption; ten years for the licensor against his licensee and vice versa and for the licensee against the active selling by other licensees into its territory, calculated from the date when the first licence was granted by the licensor in any Member State; five years by contrast for the licensee against passive selling into its territory.

The recitals followed the normal pattern, setting out at great length the policy considerations underlying its introduction. After emphasizing the growing importance of know-how within the Community, they stress the need of limiting with precision what is to be properly covered by this very general phrase. Not all useful information is to be benefited; it must be secret, substantial, and identified. It originally included the requirement that it must be of 'decisive importance' to the technology involved, but this was later discarded. None of the three definitions is totally straightforward. 'Secret' means not that all the information is totally unknown (save to the licensor), but that, taken as a whole, it is not generally known or easily accessible so that its use can give the licensee lead time once communicated to it. 'Substantial' means that it has important value for the whole or a significant part of a manufacturing process or a product or service or its development. In practical terms it must be useful to the licensee in its commercial operations. 'Identified' means that the package of information is described or recorded in sufficient detail for the other obligations of substantiality and secrecy to be verified and to clarify for the licensee where its existing knowledge stops and the new know-how package begins. The exemption did not cover licences connected to franchising or distribution (as opposed to production technology).[19]

5. THE 1996 BLOCK EXEMPTION FOR TECHNOLOGY TRANSFER REGULATION 240/96

5.1 THE TRAVAUX PRÉPARATOIRES

By the end of the 1980s, therefore, the would-be licensor in intellectual property, patented or unpatented, had block exemptions to provide a model for licences so long as they were relatively straightforward and did not fall into the awkward no-man's-land where the know-how involved was neither ancillary to the licence patent (so covered by the Patent Regulation) nor more than ancillary to them (covered by the Know-how Regulation), even if by concession the Commission did not take this particular point in the great majority of cases. The licensor had also however to consider whether any of the other intellectual property rights covered by a licence were commercially more important than either the patents or know-how which it licensed, as for example in the *Moosehead/Whitbread* case considered in Section 7, below. If these other rights were more significant than either the patents or know-how concerned, then individual exemption would be necessary.

A desire to eliminate these other awkward points covering both groups of licence led the Commission in 1993 to consider how to amalgamate the two block exemptions into a single instrument. The fact that the block exemption for patent licences was due to expire on 31 December 1994 was an incentive for action, and the fact that the Know-how Regulation was not due to expire until the end of 1999 seemed no obstacle to an amalgamation. The original target date for the adoption of the new joint Regulation was 1 January 1995, but difficulties were encountered in obtaining final approval to the draft referred to below, so that this was postponed on several occasions, ultimately to 1 April 1996.

The main problem in drafting the Regulation was the Commission's concern that it should not benefit either licensors or licensees with a particularly substantial market share in a particular product or service market in a given geographical area (normally that of a single Member State). The Commission suggested in early drafts for this reason that no exclusivity should be allowed if the licensee alone had more than 40 per cent of that relevant market, nor if, holding at least 10 per cent itself, was one of a number of oligopolists or if three or less had 50 per cent of the market, or if five or less had two-thirds of that market. Moreover, territorial restrictions on both licensor and licensee against selling their output arising from the licence into competing markets were limited to cases where they had less than 20 per cent of the market share. What the Commission failed to take sufficiently into account in making these proposals was that, as case law under Article 82 and the Merger Regulation had already made clear, the establishment of definite market shares for either licensors or licensees in particular geographical markets is more than a matter of quantitative analysis. The

---

[19] Apart from transitional arrangements when a licensee acts temporarily as a distributor prior to commencing manufacture with the aid of the know-how.

Commission's 1997 Notice on defining relevant markets illustrates that the task involves judgment, not merely statistical calculations, taking account of both demand and supply side substitutability in assessing actual and potential competition, and very detailed consideration of relevant price changes. The product to be licensed might be new, for example, a new drug with characteristics not possessed by existing products, or it might have multiple uses, again not paralleled by its existing competitors. For such reasons, it is turnover, a relatively objective measure, that can be calculated reasonably quickly without so many delicate judgments, which is normally preferable as a jurisdictional test in merger control cases, even though market shares might be thought to have far more connection with the issues of dominance which Article 2 of the Merger Regulation contains, and upon which the examination of the merger will concentrate.

For these reasons there was almost total opposition from industry, commerce, and professional advisers to these 'market share' proposals, expressed in particular at the public hearing on the Commission's proposals, just as for Regulation 2349/84 previously. The original proposals were watered down, and the calculation of the 40 per cent market share was elaborated as follows:

(a) by altogether ignoring the licensor's market share (if any) in the relevant territory;

(b) by giving no attribution of market share to the products actually to be manufactured under the terms of the licence agreement;

(c) by measuring the licensee's market share only at the moment when the agreement was made, before any licenced technology had been used;

(d) by taking into account only those products substitutable for those to be produced by the licence technology; and

(e) if the licensee's market share so calculated was less than 40 per cent, then territorial exclusivity would be permitted (i.e. the original 20 per cent restriction was removed).

Despite these proposed changes, there was still considerable opposition and finally, at the end of 1995, the Commission drew back from confrontation; in its final draft it withdrew all references to market share except one. Article 7 lists circumstances in which the Commission is entitled to withdraw the benefit of the exemption, and states that this will happen if:

the effect of the agreement is to prevent the licensed products from being exposed to effective competition in the licensed territory from identical goods or services, or from goods or services considered by users as interchangeable or substitutable in view of their characteristic, price and intended use, which may, in particular, occur when a licensee's market share exceeds 40 per cent.

In the past the Commission has only on extremely rare occasions gone through the full procedure for withdrawing the benefit of a block exemption.[20] It remains to be seen whether it will be more willing to do so against the background of this specific provision.

5.2 THE BLOCK EXEMPTION IN DETAIL (NO. 240/96)

As it finally emerged, the Regulation reflects a less doctrinaire approach to licensing by the Commission and a greater willingness to accept that the block exemption must contain

---

[20] *Langnese Iglo and Schöller* ('the German ice-cream cases') are a rare example: Cases T-7 and 9/93 [1995] ECR II-1533, 1611: 5 CMLR 602.

sufficient incentives for licensors to grant licences as well as a reduction of the restrictions which they can be allowed to place on licensees, which could have limited the ability of licensees to compete. The recitals reflect many provisions of the two predecessor Regulations, but make clear that they apply to licences of patents (national, Community, and European) as well to know-how licences and mixed agreements which combine both forms of property. The principal elements of this Regulation are as follows:

(1) It applies primarily to exclusive licences but in practice will also have within its scope a large number of non-exclusive licences, since these will inevitably tend to contain a number of restrictions included in the eight listed in Article 1(1) which will bring the licence within the scope of the block exemption, for example an obligation on the licensee not to exploit the licence technology in the territory of the licensor or of other licensees. It applies also to assignments which require the assignee to pay the assignor by reference to a formula based on the assignee's success in exploiting the technology for example on its turnover.

(2) It still applies only to bilateral agreements, not for example to patent pools or multiple-cross licensing.

(3) It covers patent licences, know-how licences, mixed patent/know-how licences; licences for other intellectual property rights, such as trade marks, design rights, and copyright are covered only if ancillary to the principal licence.

(4) It provides a substantial measure of territorial protection to the licensee, potentially longer in duration for the patent licensee than the know-how licensee, against both the licensor and other licensees of the same licensor.

(5) It permits field of use restriction, provision for minimum royalties and minimum quantities, as well as tying where this is needed to ensure technically proper exploitation in technology.

(6) It does not however permit customer allocation nor price restrictions on the licensee nor, subject to certain qualifications, no-challenge clauses nor non-compete obligations.

Article 2 contains the 'white list', which is rather longer than either of the predecessor Regulations. There are a large number of drafting and presentational changes but the substantive content does not differ greatly from the earlier Regulations. Changes tend to give greater freedom to the parties. The main changes are as follows:

(i) Under Article 2(1)(4) the parties have greater freedom with regard to licensing back improvements. Now the licensor is entitled to require the licensee to grant back his improvements or new application of the licence technology on two conditions, namely that the licensor agrees to grant either an exclusive or a non-exclusive licence of his own improvements to the licensee, and that the licensee can in the case of 'severable' improvements insist on a non-exclusive licence, so that he remains free to license them to third parties provided no disclosure of original know-how is concerned that has been obtained from the licensor.

(ii) Under Article 2(1)(12), reflecting earlier recital 24, the licensee may still not use the know-how other than for its own purposes, e.g. it could not utilize it to build factories for third parties. It may, however, set up additional facilities of its own 'on normal commercial terms', including payment of additional royalties. Problems may arise if licensors are unwilling to commit themselves when the licence is first drawn up to a specific rate of royalties. This is not surprising since when the original licence is drawn up the circumstances in which subsequent additional sites are to be built may be unknown, and the ability of the parties to anticipate the future will be limited. One of the omissions from the Regulation is clear provision with regard to the extent to which site licences are permitted. In 1997 the Commission opened proceedings in a case, where the original licence limited to a particular factory site in Spain stated that the parties should negotiate mutually acceptable terms for future site licences, on the basis that, since the licence did not guarantee the licensee the right to utilize the technology at a new site, the licence was in breach of Article 81(1) and possibly outside the rather ambiguous terms of the block exemption. After the parties, ARCO and Repsol, had compromised their dispute, the Commission abandoned the case, unfortunately leaving the basic issues unresolved.[21]

(iii) Under Article 2(1)(13) the normal prohibition against limiting the number of licensed products to be made by the licensee does not apply if the licence was granted so that the customer in question was able to have a second source of supply inside the licence territory, nor does the prohibition apply if the customer is the licensee and has the licence provided in order to give a second source of supply, provided that the customer manufactures the licensed products or has them manufactured by a subcontractor.

(iv) Under Article 2(1)(15) the licensor has a specific right to terminate the agreement in the event of challenge by the licensee to the secret or substantial nature of the know-how or the validity of licence.

Article 3 contains the 'black list', now rather shorter than in the earlier block exemptions. These include the following clauses:

(i)   restrictions on the determination of prices for the licensed products.

(ii) a restriction of one party from competing with the other in respect of products that compete with the licensed product, though this prohibition is qualified by the licensor's right to include a clause obliging the licensee to use his best endeavours to promote the licensed products and to convert an exclusive licence to non-exclusive if the licensee starts to compete with him in this way.

(iii) a restriction that requires a party without any objectively justified reason to refuse to meet orders from users or resellers in their respective territories who would market products in other territories within the Common Market, or makes it difficult for such users or resellers to obtain products from such other resellers within the Common Market.

(iv) restrictions between competing manufacturers on categories of customer to be supplied, with prohibitions on employing certain forms of distribution.

(v)   unqualified restrictions on the quantity of licensed products produced (same as permitted specifically by the 'white list', as mentioned above) or unqualified

---

[21] See M. Dolman and M. Odriosola, 'Site Licences under EC Competition Law' [1998] 19 ECLR 493–500 and in reply J. Townend, 'The Case for Site Licences' [1999] 20 ECLR 168–174.

obligations of the licensee to assign the benefit of improvements to the licensed technology to the licensor save as permitted under Article 2(1)(4), mentioned above.

Article 4 provides an opposition clause; certain restrictions not falling within either the 'white' or the 'black list' can be put forward to the Commission for approval, with a time limit for objections to be raised, now in a more streamlined form. The time limit within which the Commission must object to proposed clauses is reduced from six to four months. Moreover, Article 4(2) expressly provides that the two clauses no longer 'black listed' ('no challenge' and 'tying' clauses) can be submitted under this procedure supported by a statement of the reasons for their inclusion. The Commission always has the option to oppose or to accept the clause in question, though as before it must oppose the claim if requested to do so by Member States. On the other hand, the procedural innovation suggested for such clauses on severability were not retained in the final version. This would have allowed an agreement to retain the benefit of the block exemption even if it contained such a 'grey' clause, merely by ignoring the clause as if it did not appear in the agreement at all, without affecting the validity of the remainder of the agreement. The lack of such a provision means that a licence agreement which contains a single 'grey' clause which has not been accepted by the Commission through the opposition procedure will remain totally ineffective, even if in all other respects it meets the requirements of the new Regulation. Perhaps the novelty of such a provision appeared less attractive to the Commission in comparison with the familiar opposition procedure.

Article 5 lists five categories of licence to which the block exemption does not apply, including patent or know-how pools, joint ventures between competitors or agreements between competitors involving reciprocal rights, sales licences and licences of intellectual property rights other than patents. Article 5(2), however, states that the benefit of the Regulation does apply to licences granted by a parent to the joint venture provided that the licensed products do not have, in the case of production licences, more than a 20 per cent market share, and in the case of a production and distribution licence, a more than 10 per cent share of the relevant market for the licensed products and substitutable or interchangeable goods.

6. THE FUTURE OF THE 1996 BLOCK EXEMPTION FOR TECHNOLOGY TRANSFER

Since the adoption of this Regulation the original timetable under which it would have remained in force until 2006 has begun to look unrealistic, because of three important developments relevant to its future.

The first is that the approach of the Commission to block exemptions in general has changed, so as to become less prescriptive and to focus much more on setting out the restrictive clauses which are *not* allowed without seeking to list in detail other restrictive clauses which the parties may wish to include, provided that the market share of the licensor is below the threshold at which substantial market power or even dominance can be assumed to exist. Regulation 2790/99 is a new model for this, as described in Chapter 10, in which there is neither a 'white' nor 'grey' list but simply a relatively short 'black' list. The concern of the Commission is much more with the effects of the restriction, rather than with its legal form; for this reason it seeks to place more reliance on both the market share threshold and the publication of extensive guidelines to accompany the Regulation that on seeking to control in detail the precise content of the agreement in a way that places a straightjacket on the parties. It also seeks to place more emphasis on the encouragement of inter-brand competition rather than intra-brand competition, through the liberalization of the whole process of providing block exemptions.

The second change is that new block exemptions introduced after Regulation 240/96 had been adopted have themselves introduced provisions which have impacted on its present content. In the area of vertical agreements covering distribution, Regulation 2790/99 has included within the scope of the block exemption the assignment or licence of intellectual property rights which are ancillary to the distribution arrangements for goods or services and are directly related to the use for sales of goods by the distributor. In the area of horizontal agreements, Regulations 2658/2000 and 2659/2000 also provide new rules for ancillary rights in intellectual property which form part of a principal agreement covered by these measures on specialization and R and D respectively (see Chapter 19).

The third, and perhaps the most important, change is that the modernization programme of the Commission and the replacement after some forty years of Regulation 17/62 will bring with it in 2004 the end of the granting by the Commission of individual exemption to licences and intellectual property rights, even though the block exemptions themselves will remain of essential importance. The rules for implementing Article 81(1) and (3) will in the future be applied by national courts and national competition authorities. This will in turn mean that considerable clarification and simplification of the rules applied to transfers of technology of all kinds will be needed.

In the light of these changing circumstances the Commission at the end of 2001 produced a comprehensive report on the operation of Regulation 240/96 and the changes that might be needed to it. The Report called for full consultation on the issues; it is clear from the responses received (to be found on the Commission website) that any replacement block exemption in this area will have to incorporate radical changes if the challenge already raised by these major shifts in Commission policy are to be satisfactorily met. The Commission itself in the closing section of the Report suggested some of the principal changes that might be needed, namely:

— a broader range of licensing agreements to be covered, including copyright licences;

— an extension of its scope to include multi-party agreements;

— the elimination of the concept of 'white' and 'grey' clauses for restrictions and the further simplification of the list of 'black' clauses;

— a distinction between licences between non-competitors, where a number of the present 'black list' restrictions could be eliminated, and those between competitors, where they would need to be maintained; and

— a market share threshold to determine which licensors would be entitled to benefit from the block exemptions, which might be set at a higher level, say 30 per cent for non-competitors or say 25 per cent for undertakings in competition with each other.

7. TRADE MARK LICENCES

7.1 EARLY CASES ON TRADE MARKS

Both trade marks and copyright are familiar types of intellectual property rights which often carry considerable commercial value: their development and protection are justified by the time, effort, and expenditure that their owners have incurred in their creation. Both, of course, have potentially much longer lives than patents; indeed while the legal protection of copyright does ultimately expire,[22] the use of trade marks can continue indefinitely. In early European Court jurisprudence a feeling can be detected (notably in *Sirena* v. *Eda* discussed below) that trade marks are perhaps not as worthy of protection as other forms of intellectual property. In more recent cases, however, notably *Hag (No. 2)*,[23] a firm basis has been provided for treating trade marks as no less important than any other form of intellectual property. Their chief importance is that they enable a manufacturer who consistently produces high quality goods to extend his reputation from one market to another without having to start from scratch in every case. Earlier suggestions by the Commission that it was considering the issue of a draft block exemption for trade marks have not, however, been followed up.

Early European Court cases were concerned mainly with horizontal agreements relating to trade-mark rights. The early case of *Sirena* v. *Eda*[24] (European Court of Justice 1971) shows the width of application of Article 81 in this context. In this case, an Italian Court sought, by an Article 177 reference, to know whether Articles 81 and 82 prevented an Italian company (Sirena) from asserting its registered trade mark, 'Prep', so as to prevent the sale in Italy under the same trade mark of similar hairdressing products made in Germany by another manufacturer. Both the Italian and the German undertaking claimed to have rights to the use of this trade mark, by assignments from an American company as long as thirty years previously. The problem had arisen because the German product had been imported into Italy for resale at prices lower than those at which the Italian product was sold, and Sirena wished to prevent these imports by relying on its registration of the mark in Italy. The Italian importer of the German product naturally contested the action on the basis that such a finding would be in breach of Article 81, claiming that the previous assignment of the two licences constituted an agreement between the United States owner and the licensees in their two separate markets, even though these assignments had taken place a considerable number of years previously.

As in all Article 234 cases, the Court was not required to rule on the merits of the case between the parties, only to answer questions on legal issues submitted to it by the national Court responsible for deciding the case. The terms of the opinion given, however, were substantially in favour of the importer of the German product. The Court agreed with its

---

[22] The duration of copyright protection in the Community has been harmonized (and for many Member States extended) by Directive 93/98.

[23] [1990] 3 CMLR 571. See Ch. 14. pp.261–3 for a detailed description of this case.

[24] Case 40/70 [1971] ECR 69: CMLR 260. Had the case reached the European Court at a later date, after the development of the extensive case law considered in Ch. 14 relating to the effect upon national intellectual property rights of Arts 28–30, it would probably have been decided (with much the same ultimate result) by reference to those Articles, rather than to Art. 81.

argument that the effect of licences or assignments relating to trade marks can be that of preventing imports, notably through allocating particular watertight areas to individual undertakings, and that it would be a breach of Article 81 if such arrangements actually had such an effect, even if not intended to do so. The result of *Sirena* v. *Eda* initially caused some alarm, since Article 81 seemed to be applicable without reference to the length of time that had passed since the original trade mark rights had been allocated. However, the potentially wide effects of the decision were substantially reduced by *EMI Records Ltd.* v. *CBS United Kingdom Ltd.*[25] (also considered in the next Chapter) where the Court confirmed that, to bring Article 81 into play, the original allocation of trade marks had to be accompanied by a continuing relationship between the original owner of the trade mark and its licensees or assignees.

A case which reached the European Court in 1985[26] related to a trade-mark agreement between BAT (the German subsidiary of the multinational British-American Tobacco Ltd.) and a small Dutch tobacco manufacturer, Segers. This limited the use of trade marks which were alleged, rather unconvincingly, to be of a confusingly close nature. BAT owned a German trade mark, 'Dorcet', which had never been utilized for any particular tobacco product; Segers owned a mark in Holland 'Toltecs Special' in respect of fine cut tobacco. Segers had applied to have its trade mark registered in Germany (as well as in some other countries); BAT opposed this on the ground of potential confusion. The compromise set out in the relevant agreement involved withdrawal of opposition by BAT, if Segers restricted the application of 'Toltecs' to the sale of its fine cut tobacco and agreed not to market its tobacco under the Toltecs mark in Germany except through BAT's approved importers. Moreover, Segers was not to exercise his trade-mark rights against BAT even if the Dorcet mark remained unused for a period of over five years. The Commission had found that in reality there was no serious risk of confusion between the two trade marks, and imposed a fine on BAT for agreeing the no-challenge clause, even though a five-year period of non-use had already expired. The Court annulled the fine on technical grounds, ruling that the restriction on Segers limited only the use of the mark, not trade in goods or services, but confirmed that BAT had, by attempting to control the distribution of Segers's products in this way, misused their trade-mark rights available under national German law. Not all settlements of trade-mark disputes involving the allocation of territories between competitors will be in breach of Article 81(1)[27]

7.2 TRADE MARK LICENCES UNDER REGULATION 240/96

The more liberal terms of the block exemption 240/96 encompass a broader range of agreements covering both patented and unpatented material and other intellectual property rights. Provided that the principal purpose of the licence is the licensing of patents or unpatented know-how, or a mixture of the two, the inclusion within the licence of other rights (such as trade marks) does not prejudice the granting of exemption provided that these other rights can properly be defined as ancillary (Article 5(1)(4)). In many cases this

[25] Case 51/75 [1976] ECR 811: 2 CMLR 235.
[26] BAT *Cigaretten-Fabrieken* v. *Commission* Case 35/83 [1985] ECR 363: 2 CMLR 470. The original Commission decision is reported as *Toltecs-Dorcet Trade Marks* [1983] 1 CMLR 412.
[27] See, e.g. *Penney's Trade Mark* [1978] 2 CMLR 100.

will mean that trade-mark licences will be covered by the Regulation when part of a package of rights granted to the licensee, just as with Regulation 2790/99 in its treatment of ancillary intellectual property rights.[28]

In determining whether individual exemption can be granted to trade-mark licences under Article 81(3), the same principles are likely to be applied as under Regulation 240/96. In particular, the equivalent clauses to those contained in the 'black list' of the block exemption are unlikely to be acceptable, for example, where the licensee is placed under restrictions as to price, customer, or quantity. On the other hand it seems clear from the *Moosehead*[29] case that 'no challenge' clauses as to ownership will be acceptable since the issue of trade-mark ownership lies only between licensor and licensee, not between third parties. Any 'no challenge' clause as to the general validity of the mark would fall however within Article 81(1), since it could affect third parties, but it might nevertheless obtain exemption unless it was believed to be potentially damaging to competitors. In the *Moosehead* case, Moosehead, a Canadian brewery, wished to sell its beer in the United Kingdom but could not justify the capital costs of setting up its own production and distribution facilities there. By entering into a licence with Whitbread, a well established UK public company with its own brewing and distribution facilities, Moosehead could obtain access to the UK market. Under the arrangements, know-how was to be provided to Whitbread to enable them to produce and sell Moosehead beer. The principal object of the agreement, however, was the exploitation of the Moosehead trade mark, rather than this know-how, so that the block exemption then in force, 556/89 could not apply. The Commission, however, granted individual exemption to a number of restrictive clauses, including the exclusive use of the trade mark in the United Kingdom and prohibitions on Whitbread against actively selling the product outside the UK or dealing in competing brands of lager.[30]

8. COPYRIGHT AND SOFTWARE LICENCES

8.1 COPYRIGHT LICENCES

The importance of copyright in protecting a wide variety of commercial rights continues to grow. It applies to books, magazines, and other printed matter, and the varied products of the entertainment and music industry, such as compact discs, DVDs, videos, cassettes, CD-ROMs, films, programs, and the diverse new digital products created by advanced technology. Community legislation reflecting its importance is described in the next chapter. The willingness of the European Court to look at the special characteristics of copyright was

---

[28] In *Campari* [1978] 2 CMLR 397, a network of exclusive licences to a variety of undertakings from the original manufacturers of that well known aperitif was granted individual exemption once tying and export ban clauses had been removed.

[29] [1991] 4 CMLR 391.

[30] The Commission also ruled that a 'no challenge' clause to the validity of a trade mark may constitute a restriction of competition within the terms of 81(1), as a successful challenge could bring the mark into the public domain for use by everyone, but only if the mark were already well known (not the case with Moosehead in the UK) and its use an important advantage to a company competing in a particular market, so that its unavailability would be a barrier to entry.

illustrated early by the *Coditel* cases. In *Coditel (No. 1)*[31] the European Court ruled that Article 59, protecting the freedom to provide services, did not prevent the granting of a seven-year exclusive copyright licence in a film by the French producer to a Belgian distributor (Cine Vog) thus entitling Cine Vog to prevent Coditel, a Belgian cable television company, from intercepting the transmission of the film and reshowing it to its subscribers, even with the consent of the original French producer. In the sequel case (in this context more important), *Coditel (No. 2)*,[32] the Court went on to rule that an exclusive grant of copyright in a film did not automatically bring the licence within Article 81(1) since there were many special circumstances relating to the film industry; the difficulties in obtaining a return on investment in a film, which did not apply to other goods and services, entitled the Court to make a full economic analysis of the effects of the particular agreements before reaching a conclusion.

The Court stated that the exercise of exclusive rights would fall within Article 81(1) only if economic analysis showed that it gave the parties to the licence the opportunity either to create artificial barriers to the market, or to charge fees exceeding a fair return on the investment, to provide exclusivity for a disproportionate period of time or, on a more general note, that it enabled the parties in a particular Member State to prevent or restrict competition in that country. The Court seemed to accept, reflecting its earlier conclusions in the *Maize Seed* case referred to above,[33] that original investment in films is far more likely if accompanied by the possibility of an exclusive licence being granted. Given also the comparatively short life of many films, it seems reasonable to accord them greater protection for that short period than is reasonable for other products, for example, those protected by plant breeders' rights in the *Maize Seed* case.

Again no block exemption has been provided by the Commission but in analysing licences of this kind the Commission and the Court will take into account not only the geographic and product markets concerned but also the duration of the licence granted and the particular characteristics of the industry involved. In the German TV films case *Commission v. Degeto Film*,[34] the proposed licence related to a large number of feature films owned by MGM/United Artists Corporation. The original intention was to license these exclusively to Degeto, a subsidiary of the association of public broadcasting companies in Germany. The exclusivity apparently covered some 1,350 of the 3,000 films owned by MGM/UAC and would have lasted for terms of approximately fifteen years starting on different dates. During these exclusive periods, third parties would have no access to the films. Degeto would also have rights over new films produced by MGM/UAC during the period of the agreement. The Commission found that feature films played an important part in television programming, as they were very popular with audiences and often of a higher artistic standard than films produced specifically for television. The licence period of fifteen years, however, was at least five years longer than the normal permitted period for such agreements, and the total number of films covered extremely large; both these factors caused concern to the Commission.

The licence was eventually given Article 81(3) exemption following substantial

---

[31] *Coditel* v. *Cine Vog Films (No. 1)* Case 62/79 [1980] ECR 881: [1981] 2 CMLR 362, discussed in more detail in Ch. 13, pp.260–1.

[32] *Coditel* v. *Cine Vog Films (No. 2)* Case 262/81 [1982] ECR 3381: [1983] 1 CMLR 49.

[33] At pp.225–7.

[34] [1990] 4 CMLR 841.

amendments to it; 'windows' were introduced to the agreement, permitting the licensing of the films to third parties for particular periods during its lifetime. These 'windows' would last for periods of two to six years, considerably reducing the degree of exclusivity. Exemption was granted because with these amendments some advantages could be obtained for German viewers who would have greater access to a larger number of films. The package deal provided would reduce the price per film licensed, and thus also the operating costs of public broadcasting organizations. The remaining degree of exclusivity was accepted as necessary in order to allow MGM/UAC a fair return for their original investment.

8.2 SOFTWARE LICENCES

The protection of computer software raises special issues. In some cases aspects of software may be protected by patent and the source code protected as know-how of a confidential nature. Licences of such patents and know-how would presumably be eligible for protection under the transfer of technology block exemption equally if the software were merely ancillary to other patents or unpatented know-how. On the other hand, the existence of Software Directive 91/250, adopted on 4 May 1991, which required Member States to adopt national laws implementing the Directive by 1 January 1993, makes clear that the basic form of intellectual property for protection of software is to be copyright.[35] The Directive itself specifies the rights of the software owners. First the right on an exclusive basis to prevent copying, both permanent and temporary, and against translation, alteration, and distribution. The only exception to these rights is where the work carried out by the licensee in this way is necessary for the use of the programme in its intended purpose. Moreover, subject to certain limits set out in the Directive, the licensee is entitled to decompile and reverse engineer in order to obtain sufficient information to create other programmes to interface with the licensed programmes. Of course, the provisions of a Directive cannot change the terms of Articles 81 or 82. However, it would be reasonable to expect the Commission, in assessing such licences, to recognize and follow the policy contained in the Directive, which recognizes the particular characteristics of this form of property, including its necessary exclusivity and the vital need for the control of copying, often reinforced by licensing of particular work sites rather than in general terms. It is perhaps surprising that no individual case on individual licensing of software has yet apparently been dealt with, at least by way of formal decision.

In assessing the range of restrictions which might be imposed on a license for the use of software, for which individual exemption might be available under Article 81(3), the Commission would undoubtedly take into account its special features, which in some respects make it more difficult to safeguard than other forms of intellectual property. The licensor of software might properly define the field of use in which a particular programme or group of programmes is to be used, since if the licensee were to make a broader application than the licensor intended, the licensor might lose substantially in terms of the royalties to be obtained.

---

[35] Nevertheless, in February 2002, the Commission published a proposal that, under Community law, patent protection should be granted to a limited category of software; mainly computer-implemented inventions (Com. (2002) 92 final).

On the other hand, although decompilers will normally seek to rely on the rights given to them by the Directive, they may well find situations in which these rights do not apply, but they believe they should be entitled to decompile, for example, whether the decompiling right extends to obtaining and using interface information to enable the designing of hardware to interface with the relevant software. The recitals of the software Directive do say that the Directive does not prejudice the application of Article 82 'if a dominant supplier refuses to make information available which is necessary for inter-operability'.

One final general point needs to be made which applies to all forms of licensing of intellectual property. The terms of the licence cannot be used to extend the inherent right of the owner of the particular form of intellectual property or his period of ownership. The Commission has in recent years been attempting to harmonize these rights, and the software Directive referred to above is one attempt to lay down common standards, not only for these rights but also for the terms upon which software licences may be granted. The duration of copyright has itself been determined for all EC countries by a Directive. The Council's first Directive[36] on Trade Mark Licences (dated 21 December 1988) also sought to specify the rights which the owner of a trade mark may regard as his under Community principles. This includes a definition of trade marks, enumerates when they cannot be accepted for registration, and defines the rights which they are capable of conferring. They also provide that non-use for a five-year period after registration can lead to revocation of a proprietor's rights.

8.3 OTHER FORMS OF INTELLECTUAL PROPERTY RIGHTS

Special rights exist for other types of property. For example, it is clear from *Erauw-Jacquery* v. *La Hesbignonne* (European Court 1988)[37] that the rights of the owners of basic seeds may well include protection against improper handling and the control of propagation by those establishments regarded as suitable. For this reason, and to this extent, a clause prohibiting a licensee from selling or exporting basic seeds would not come within the prohibition of Article 81(1), even though an equivalent clause would not be permitted in a copyright or know-how licence. The Court pointed out that the breeder of basic seeds is in some respects similar to a franchisor, rather than the owner of a copyright, and that the breeder's control over use of the seeds was essential to prevent its know-how becoming too easily available to its competitors. The same products were the subject of a more recent *Sicasov* case, the facts of which are discussed in Chapter 8 (p.137). Here the rights of the French plant breeders to control the use made of their basic seeds (used only for propagating new seed) were held outside Article 81(1), whilst restrictions on the export of certified seeds (available for use in sowing by growers and farmers) fell within Article 81, even though on the facts an individual exemption under Article 81(3) was granted. The validity of licence terms in types of intellectual property yet to be developed may well also be influenced substantially by the nature of the right being licensed, and the benefits to both licensors and consumers from the restrictions to be imposed.

[36] Directive 89/104 [1989] OJ L40/1.   [37] Case 27/87 [1988] ECR 1919: 4 CMLR 576.

13

INTELLECTUAL PROPERTY RIGHTS: THE PURPOSES AND EFFECTS OF ARTICLES 28 TO 30

1. THE PURPOSES OF ARTICLES 28 TO 30

It is not only under the terms of Articles 81 and 82 that intellectual property rights fall to be considered. Articles 28 and 30 of the Treaty contain basic rules protecting the free movement of goods: Article 28 provides the central principle, and Article 30 sets out the limited exceptions. The wording of Article 28 is concise: 'Quantitative restrictions on imports and all measures having equivalent effect shall, without prejudice to the following provisions, be prohibited between Member States'. Article 29 sets out similar provisions applying to exports. Article 30 contains the qualifications to those basic rules, as follows:

The provisions of Articles 28 to 30 shall not preclude prohibitions or restrictions on imports, exports or goods in transit justified on grounds of public morality, public policy or public security; protection of health and life of humans, animals or plants; the protection of national treasures possessing artistic, historic or archaeological value; or the *protection of industrial and commercial property*. Such prohibitions or restrictions shall not, however, constitute a means of arbitrary discrimination or a disguised restriction on trade between Member States.

This chapter considers the relationship between, on one hand, Articles 81 and 82 with their prohibition against agreements and concerted practices between undertakings (the 'competition rules') and, on the other hand, Articles 28 to 30 addressed to Member States, including their legislative, judicial, and administrative authorities responsible for implementation and enforcement of national intellectual property rights (the 'free movement rules').

It is first essential however to understand the place of Articles 28 to 30 within the framework of the Treaty. Within any common market, one of the essential freedoms is the free movement of goods. The removal of internal tariff barriers and of straightforward and quantitative limits, such as quotas, on the import and export of goods between Member States occurred at an early stage in the development of the Common Market. However, non-tariff barriers, including national legislation and administrative practices relating to the regulation of prices, indications of national origin and other labelling requirements, public health, and consumer legislation have presented, and still provide, far greater difficulties, notwithstanding the near completion of the Single Market legislation programme in the early 1990s. As a result, the expression 'all measures having equivalent effect' in Article 28 has been considered in many cases since 1974 by the European Court of Justice. The vast majority of these cases were references by national Courts to the European Court of Justice for preliminary rulings under Article 234, rather than appeals against specific decisions of the Commission under Article 230. A considerable body of case law has built up on the interpretation of Articles 28 and 30 since the landmark decisions of *Dassonville* and *Cassis de Dijon* and much of this has had an important influence on the competition law relating to intellectual property.[1] In many of these cases provisions of national law containing either directly discriminatory provisions against imported goods or other provisions which indirectly discriminated in this way have been struck down. In a later line of cases, however, beginning with the 'Sunday Trading' cases and *Keck*,[2] the European Court also made it clear that it will not normally interfere in national marketing rules which simply lay down selling arrangements applicable to all goods.

2. HARMONIZATION OF MEMBER STATE LAW BY COMMUNITY MEASURES

2.1 PATENT LAW

The national laws of Member States protecting intellectual property rights vary substantially from each other in their classification and substantive content. This diversity has caused major problems for the development of Community principles to cover both free movement of goods and market integration. With hindsight the founders of the Community should perhaps have laid down, at the outset, at least some basic principles to govern the harmonization of such laws.

While Article 30 includes the 'protection of industrial and commercial property' as one of the exceptions to the basic principle of free movement of goods, there is no doubt that the attainment of a fully integrated market will remain difficult, if not impossible, so long as such diversity remains. The harmonization, therefore, of the law relating to intellectual property within the Community, relating in particular to patents and trade marks, as well as the gradual harmonization of the classification and definition of all the other various intellectual property rights found to exist within Member States, and covering rights as varied as copyright, registered and unregistered designs, and the protection of computer software and databases, remains an objective of great importance.

Progress has been especially slow towards the provision of uniform rules for the Community in the case of patents. The 1973 European Patent Convention (often referred to as the 'Munich Convention') has for some time enabled applicants to the European Patent Office in Munich to obtain a set of patents in respect of each of those States which have so far ratified the Convention, currently the fifteen Member States and Switzerland,

---

[1] See L. Gormley, *Prohibiting Restrictions on Trade within the EEC* (North-Holland, 1985), *passim*: *Procureur du Roi* v. *B & G Dassonville* Case 8/74 [1974] ECR 837: 2 CMLR 436: *Rewe-Zentral* v. *Bundesmonopolverwaltung für Branntwein* Case 120/78 [1979] ECR 649: 3 CMLR 494 (the *Cassis de Dijon* case).

[2] See, e.g. *Stoke on Trent BC* v. *B&Q* Case C169/91 [1992] ECR 6635: [1993] 1 CMLR 426: 2 CMLR 509. *Keck and Mithouard* Cases C-267 and 268/91 [1993] ECR I-6097: [1995] 1 CMLR 101. See also J. Steiner and L. Woods, *Textbook on EC Law*, 7th edn. (Blackstone Press, 2000), Ch. 11, pp.171–91.

Liechtenstein, Monaco, Cyprus, and Turkey. The Luxembourg Patent Convention by contrast, though signed as long ago as 1975, and providing for the grant of a Community patent has never actually entered into force because of insufficient ratification. In recent years both the Commission and Presidents of the Council have tried hard to secure agreement between Member States on the terms of a new Convention that would create a Community patent, emphasizing its importance to the scientific and technological development of Europe. But a number of issues proved difficult to resolve. These included the number of languages into which the patent application had to be translated by the European Patent Office, the nature and jurisdiction of any Community Patent Court and its relationship with national patent courts, and the future involvement of such national courts as well as of national patent offices (some of which raise considerable revenue for Member States). However, under the agreement reached between Member States in March 2003 a Community Patent will exist from 2007; a Community Patent Court will be established in Luxembourg from 2010, but until that date national patent courts will retain jurisdiction over patent disputes.

2.2 OTHER CATEGORIES OF INTELLECTUAL PROPERTY

Better progress has been made towards the harmonization of other intellectual property rules. As a result of the enactment of the Trade Mark Regulation 40/94 and its supporting procedural Regulation 2868/95, it became possible from the beginning of 1996 to file an application for registration of a Community Trade Mark (CTM) with the Office for Harmonization in the Internal Market (OHIM) in Alicante, Spain. Unlike the European Patent Office, the Community Trade Mark Office is already able to issue a Community trade mark, which is defined in Article 1(2) of Regulation 40/94 as having 'a unitary character. It shall have equal effect throughout the Community; it shall not be registered, transferred or surrendered, or be the subject of a decision revoking the rights of the proprietor or declaring it invalid, nor shall its use be prohibited, save in respect of the whole Community'. The definition of such a Community mark is therefore very similar to that of trade marks in the United Kingdom under the 1994 Trade Marks Act. However, a number of important differences remain between rules governing the alteration of Community trade marks and national rules in Member States. Failure to put the mark to genuine use within the Community for a continuous period of five years will lead to its revocation in the absence of proper reasons for non-use. The success of the OHIM office in attracting applications has already led to great delays in dealing with the applications for the Community mark, but this emphasizes the need for the Community approach towards harmonization of such rights.

The Trade Mark Directive (89/104) setting out the basic rules for trade marks throughout the Community has led to substantial harmonization of Member State law.[3] It incorporates a number of rules and principles laid down in the case law of the European Court, as discussed in this chapter, including the important principle of exhaustion of rights. The 1994 UK Trade Marks Act incorporates the provisions of the Directive. A number of other Directives have recently been adopted to cover other forms of intellectual property and

---

[3] It has also had the result of increasing substantially the number of trade mark cases referred to the ECJ under Art. 234.

neighbouring rights. These have included: Directive 91/250 on the legal protection of computer program; a directive on rental and lending rights and other copyright provisions (Directive 92/100); the coordination of rules on satellite and cable re-transmission (Directive 93/83); a Directive (93/98) harmonizing the term of protection of copyright, now extended to life and seventy years in all Member States; and the Database Directive (96/9) which took effect on 1 January 1998 providing protection from copying for commercial databases; and most recently the Digital Copyright Directive (2001/29) applying certain copyright principles to the on-line content in electronic commerce. Moreover, the Designs Directive (98/71) and the subsequent Community Design Regulation (2002/6) have brought about the creation of two categories of design rights protected by Community law. The registered design right applies to new designs with an aesthetic element, capable of industrial application for which the OHIM office may provide a five-year period of protection renewable up to a total period of twenty-five years. Also protected would be design rights that are not registered if they comprise an original design for a three-dimensional item. Protection in such cases is obtained for fifteen years from the date of creation or ten years from the date from which the design was placed on the market.

The European Court has in a number of cases given attention both to the core content of individual property rights under national law, in order to ascertain their boundaries, and to the criteria by which the exercise of those rights are to be judged. These rights and criteria are usually referred to respectively as the 'specific subject matter' and the 'essential function' of particular forms of intellectual property under national laws. In principle the excessive use even of a right falling within the specific subject matter can be restricted under Community law, if it would lead to an artificial discrimination or disguised restriction on trade between Member States, or would in exceptional circumstances enable abuse of a dominant position.

In spite of its progress in this direction, however, the European Court has been notably cautious in its treatment of national law provisions which give extended or unusually generous scope to individual property rights. Thus we find, for example in the *Renault* case, unwillingness to interfere in the extent of protection given by design copyrights under Italian law following the Court's earlier decision in *Keurkoop* v. *Nancy Kean*.[4] Even more extreme, perhaps, was the refusal of the Court in the *Thetford* v. *Fiamma*[5] to interfere with the UK patent rule that patents could be issued for inventions which had not been exploited for more than fifty years. Such a patent had been granted in Britain for a form of portable toilet and was used to oppose the import of toilets of a similar type manufactured in Italy. The Court said it was satisfied that the rule did not give rise to arbitrary discrimination or disguised restriction on trade, and therefore refused to rule that the unusual provision of UK law should be disregarded.

Finally, the *Magill*[6] case showed that a form of copyright in schedules for radio and television under Irish law, which under national law was classified as copyright although it arose not as a result of creative endeavour but ancillary to the provision of programmes, was nevertheless entitled to acceptance under Article 30. This despite the fact that in most other

---

[4] *Keurkoop* Case 144/81 [1982] ECR 2853: [1983] 2 CMLR 47; *Renault* Case 53/87 [1988] ECR 6211: [1990] 4 CMLR 265.

[5] Case 35/87 [1988] ECR 3585: [1988] 3 CMLR 549.

[6] *Magill/RTE* Case C-241/91P [1995] ECR I-797: 4 CMLR 718.

Member States, apart from the United Kingdom and Ireland, such programme information would not have been protected by copyright. The Court was clearly influenced in its approach to the application of Article 82 in *Magill* by its belief that this form of copyright was questionable. Its decision, however, did not actually refuse the benefit of Article 30 to Irish law's broad definition of copyright. The unwillingness of the European Court to seek to harmonize even such doubtful elements of intellectual property law through its cases underlines the importance of harmonization through legislative means by the issue of directives and regulations, processes given further urgency by the very rapid technological advances in computing, telecommunications, biotechnology, and other scientific fields.[7]

3. THE DEVELOPMENT OF ARTICLES 28 TO 30 BY CASE LAW: THE 'EXHAUSTION OF RIGHTS' PRINCIPLE

3.1 EARLY CASES

The primary issue for the Court has been whether to give a narrow or a broad interpretation of the words of qualification in Article 30. If the interpretation given had been broad, the effect might have been that individual national intellectual property rights could be asserted, even where they might have the effect or purpose of preventing free movement of goods, so long as they did not conflict with the express prohibition in that Article of being either 'a means of arbitrary discrimination' or 'a disguised restriction on trade' between Member States.

Fortunately, from the viewpoint of those concerned with the effectiveness of competition law (and in particular the officials of DG Comp), the choice of the Court has been, with very few exceptions, to confine claims based on Article 30 under the reference to 'the protection of industrial and commercial property' to a narrow range; in striking a balance between the requirements of Community law and national legislation, the needs of the Community have been given priority. The often repeated (and criticized) distinction which the Court has made between the 'existence' and 'exercise' of such rights is no more than the necessary application of the express provisions of the Treaty.[8] The 'existence' of the rights is apparently protected by Article 295 ('The Treaty shall in no way prejudice the rules in Member States governing the system of property ownership'),[9] but any existing rights, to have any commercial value, must also be capable of being exercised. The issue that has concerned the Court primarily is how far that exercise can be allowed, while preserving the freedom of movement of goods between Member States, including the freedom of parallel imports. Whilst debate about how the Court may have chosen to interpret the effect of national legislation in any particular case is essential, to criticize (as some commentators have done)

---

[7] W.R. Cornish, *Intellectual Property*, 4th edn. (Sweet & Maxwell, 1999), Ch. 1, pp.22–5.

[8] See *Hag (No. 2)* Case C-10/89 [1990] ECRI 3711: 3 CMLR 571, especially Jacobs A-G at pp.581–2, though the Court in its judgment appeared to lay less stress on the existence/exercise dichotomy.

[9] It is often claimed that it is wrong to attach too much importance in this context to the general words of this Article, which does little more than preserve the right of Member States to nationalize or denationalize individual sectors.

the Court's distinction between 'existence' and 'exercise' is to miss the point that this distinction is part of the framework of the Treaty itself. The distinction is not simply a 'gloss' read into the Treaty by the Court. More crucial, however, than that distinction is the issue of how the Court would define those special rights regarded as so essential to and inherent in the existence of a national intellectual property right that they had to be protected under the terms of Article 30, even where their effect on trade between Member States could be measured.

The term 'industrial and commercial property' is not necessarily the exact equivalent to 'intellectual property rights' or 'industrial property rights'. From the Court's case law, there is certainly a wide area of overlap between the two concepts; industrial and commercial property cover patents, registered designs, trade marks, copyrights, and plant breeders' rights. The Court tends in borderline cases to look for an analogy between special types of intellectual property for which protection is claimed and the well established categories, by seeing if there are common features, for example rights of exclusivity following registration or prior use, and also by examining the provisions of relevant international conventions to see which definition they accord in the particular area. On the wrong side of the borderline have fallen a number of cases such as *Prantl Bocksbeutel*[10] (European Court of Justice 1983) where the Court refused the protection requested by the German government to the producers of wine from Franconia for a bottle of distinctive shape against imports of a different variety of wine in similar bottles from Italy. The decision was, however, taken not on the basis that legislation conferring rights relating to certificates of national origin could never constitute industrial and commercial property, but because the Court felt that the particular German legislation was too general in its application to qualify under such a heading, since it protected descriptions even of a very general or generic nature. The honest concurrent use of similar bottles by Italian producers could be permitted without damage to consumer interests, simply by requiring adequate labelling indicating national origin.

The prohibition of Article 28 applies to a wide range of actions. It goes far beyond coverage of formal governmental action or legislative acts, and applies to government agencies, nationalized bodies, and any public bodies wholly or partially financed by government or as a result of charges levied under legislative authority, whether direct or by way of secondary legislation, as well as to acts of regional or local government by way of administrative action or bylaws, and to judicial decisions. The acts involved may be formal or informal, including practices and customs as well as legal rules or administrative systems having the required effect on trade. Even if the effect on trade is slight, Article 28 will apply: the principle of *de minimis* established by *Völk* v. *Vervaecke*[11] has no application since this Article has no reference to 'having an effect on trade between Member States'.

Grundig-Consten provided early evidence of the approach that the Court would adopt to the potential conflict between Article 30 and Article 81. After confirming that Article 30 cannot limit the field of application of Article 81, the Court continued:

Article [295] confines itself to stating that 'the Treaty shall in no way prejudice the rules in Member States governing the system of property ownership'. The injunction in . . . the contested decision to refrain from using rights under national trade-mark law in order to set an obstacle in the way of parallel imports, does not affect the grant of those rights, but only limits their exercise to the extent

---

[10] Case 16/83 [1984] ECR 1299: [1985] 2 CMLR 238.
[11] Case 5/69 [1969] ECR 295: CMLR 273. See Ch. 7, pp.84–5.

necessary to give effect to the prohibition under Article [81(1)]. The power of the Commission to issue an injunction, for which provision is made in Article 3 of Regulation 17 . . . is in harmony with the nature of the Community rules on competition, which have immediate effect and are directly binding on individuals. Such a body of rules . . . does not allow the improper use of rights under any national trade-mark law in order to frustrate the Community's law on cartels.[12]

Two years later the Court confirmed that similar principles apply to patents. In *Parke, Davis* v. *Probel*[13] the Court held that normal use of a patent cannot be treated as abuse of a dominant position under Article 82, whereas its use for some other purpose could constitute such an abuse, for example if used like the 'GINT' trade mark in the *Grundig* case. The Court here ruled that a patent holder, the owner of a Dutch patent for an antibiotic process, was entitled to prevent the marketing of this product in Holland by the defendant, who obtained it from a third party who had manufactured it in Italy, where patent protection was at that time totally unavailable for drugs. The Court held that the use of the Dutch patent to prevent importation of the unpatented Italian product was a normal use of the right of exclusivity under the patent, since the patent holder had not itself placed the product on the Italian market, nor indeed could it have had its own product patented in that country. This principle applied whether or not the price charged in Holland exceeded that payable for the drug as imported by Centrafarm.

This case was, of course, not concerned with parallel imports from Member States where the products had originally been placed on the market either by the plaintiff or by its own licensee; it therefore revolved around the interpretation of Article 82 rather than Articles 28 to 30. The terms of the judgment, however, gave a clear indication that once a case was referred to the Court involving an alleged abuse of an intellectual property right in order to prevent parallel imports, the Court was likely to look sympathetically on a defendant who relied on the argument that marketing of the patented product acquired in the normal course of business from the plaintiff would be protected by Article 28. In the early 1970s, cases were referred to the Court dealing with copyright, patents, and trade marks raising this very point, and decisions followed lines predictable from earlier case law. The first case was *Deutsche Grammophon* v. *Metro*,[14] a reference from a German Court under Article 234, also significant in relation to the development of law on resale price maintenance. The Court, affirming Advocate General Roemer, also held that the right of the holder of exclusive rights, namely copyrights, in sound recordings to prohibit the import into its own country of records which have been marketed by its owner in another country is not any part of the 'industrial and commercial property' for which protection is available under Article 30. The owners of the right to the copyright are limited to protection afforded to enable the first sale to be made either in its own country or in a foreign country. Once the goods have been placed on the market, however, it is a 'measure having equivalent effect' for the Court of the country where the original copyright was granted to seek to prevent the import by a purchaser in the normal course of trade from seeking to market the goods, as parallel imports, in Germany.

---

[12] Cases 56 and 58/64 [1966] ECR 299, 345: CMLR 418.
[13] Case 24/67 [1968] ECR 55: CMLR 47.
[14] Case 78/70 [1971] ECR 487: CMLR 631.

3.2 THE *CENTRAFARM* CASES

The application of the same principles to patent and trade mark cases was dealt with in the well-known *Centrafarm* cases of 1974 at the Court which involved the Sterling-Winthrop group, a drug manufacturer in the United Kingdom, and Centrafarm, whose business involved the reselling of drugs purchased in the United Kingdom and Germany in The Netherlands, where for a variety of reasons a higher price level prevailed. In the first case, *Centrafarm* v. *Sterling Drug Inc.*,[15] Centrafarm had bought various drugs from subsidiaries of Sterling-Winthrop under the trade name of 'Negram' in both the United Kingdom and Germany for resale in Holland. Sterling tried to prevent Centrafarm from selling the drugs at a profit in Holland, claiming exclusivity under Dutch patent law. The same basic facts applied in the second case, *Centrafarm* v. *Winthrop BV*,[16] when Centrafarm marketed in Holland under the trade mark Negram drugs previously purchased in the United Kingdom. Winthrop relied on the fact that it was the proprietary owner in Holland of the trade mark, Negram, covering this particular drug, to stop Centrafarm from selling in the Dutch market. The Court was able to apply precisely the same principles in both cases. It held that the effect of Article 30 is to permit exceptions to the principle of free movement of goods only when the restrictions can be justified for the purpose of safeguarding rights constituting the specific object of the intellectual property right. This phrase had been used by the European Court in the *Metro* case; but now it is defined in its application to patents and trade marks. Dealing with patents, the Court identified the characteristics specific to them: first, the right to exploit an invention for the purpose of making and then selling a product and, second, the corresponding right to prevent an 'infringement' by a third party seeking either to make or to sell the product without the patent owner's consent. What the phrase did not include was any right to prevent imported products from coming into its territory, which had been marketed in another Member State by it or by a third party with its consent, merely because it thereby sustained economic loss, possibly because of Member State intervention in pricing levels. Applying the same criteria to trade marks, the Court suggested that the 'specific object' covered the protection of the owner against competitors by the exclusive use of the mark for the purpose of first putting the product into circulation, but did not extend as far as preventing the import of goods bearing the mark which legitimately have been marketed into or in another Member State.

The limitation thus placed on the holders of both patents and trade marks was necessary because of the express words of Articles 28 to 30, which were incompatible with any wider view of their rights, regardless of the differences in prices between the respective countries. Sterling-Winthrop was therefore unable to prevent Centrafarm from marketing drugs purchased in a conventional manner on the United Kingdom market and reselling them in Holland. By reason of the first sale in the United Kingdom, the rights of the holder of the intellectual property were 'exhausted', and thereafter the purchaser of the products which are the subject of the intellectual property rights was free to market them as it saw fit.

Some four years later, Centrafarm was involved in a further pair of cases involving similar facts except that the product, a tranquillizer, was not resold exactly as originally purchased in

---

[15] Case 15/74 [1974] ECR 1147: 2 CMLR 480.

[16] Case 16/74 [1974] ECR 1183: 2 CMLR 480. Other characteristics of the 'specific object' of intellectual property rights are considered in *Parke, Davis* v. *Probel* and *Hag (No. 2)*. Whilst the French word used in this context is '*objet*', a more exact English equivalent may be 'subject matter'.

the United Kingdom but in a repackaged form. The issue presented under Article 234 to the European Court in the case of *Hoffmann-La Roche* v. *Centrafarm*[17] was whether this slight change of circumstances gave the owner of the relevant trade mark the right to prevent the sale, unless the goods had been purchased from the original patent holder, as in the earlier cases. The Court ruled once again that Centrafarm was free to sell the product, even after repackaging, provided that certain simple conditions were satisfied. Thus, the repackaging itself must not adversely affect the original condition of the product, and prior notice had to be given to the owners of the trade mark of the proposed marketing of the repackaged product; the repackaging must state by whom it had been carried out. The final requirement was that it must be shown that enforcement of the trade mark rights against the proposed repackager would contribute to the artificial partitioning of the Common Market. The national court must be satisfied that each of these conditions has been met before it can conclude that the enforcement of the trade mark right amounts to a disguised restriction on trade within the meaning of the second sentence of Article 30.

In the second case *Centrafarm* v. *American Home Products* there was a further difference in the factual situation, namely that the products were sold under different brand names in the United Kingdom and The Netherlands. This meant that the mark fixed by the parallel importers into The Netherlands was different from that fixed in the United Kingdom by the original suppliers. The court ruled that the importer could be sued for infringement in The Netherlands unless the owner of the mark could be shown to have adapted the dual marks with the express object of artificially partitioning the Common Market, a test essentially subjective.

A similar approach to the *Hoffman* case was adopted by the Court in *Pfizer* v. *Eurim-Pharm*[18] (European Court 1981). Here an antibiotic 'Vibramycin' had been purchased by the defendants in the United Kingdom and repackaged for resale in Germany. The original blister strips containing the capsules had been removed from Pfizer's original external packaging and placed in a new box designed by Eurim-Pharm, but without altering either the strip or its contents. On the front of the new box there was an opening covered with transparent material through which the original trade mark appeared on a sheet incorporated with the blister strips. The back of the box contained a statement that the goods had been manufactured by Pfizer in the United Kingdom, but imported and repackaged by Eurim-Pharm; a leaflet in German, containing the required information about the product, prepared by Eurim-Pharm, was included. The Court refused to allow Pfizer to prevent the marketing of the antibiotics repackaged in this way, because the product had not been interfered with in any prejudicial manner and the consumer would not be confused by the packaging or instructions about the fact that they had been repackaged before sale in Germany.

3.3 LATER REPACKAGING CASES

Some fifteen years later the issue of repackaging again came before the Court in a large group of similar cases[19] involving packets of tablets and pills for the treatment of a wide

---

[17] Case 102/77 [1978] ECR 1139: 3 CMLR 217.
[18] Case 1/81 [1981] ECR 2913: [1982] 1 CMLR 406.
[19] Cases C-427, 429, 436/93. *Bristol-Myers Squibb* v. *Paranova;* Cases C-71–73/94 *Eurim-Pharm* v. *Beiersdorf;* Case C-232/94 *MPA Pharma* v. *Rhône-Poulenc* all reported at [1996] ECR I-3457: [1997] 1 CMLR 1151.

range of ailments including cancer, high blood pressure, asthma, and mouth infections. In these cases parallel importers had imported products in large quantities to Denmark and Germany, Member States where price levels for a number of reasons were high. The products had been imported from other Member States with lower price levels. National legislation in both Denmark and Germany forced repackaging upon the parallel importer; sometimes only putting the blister strips of pills into new external packaging was required, but in some cases the size of packs had to be reduced, and in other cases parts of the original packaging had to be removed, for example a spray. Moreover, instructions for use had to be included in the language appropriate in the country of final sale to replace the original instructions in other languages.

In its answer to the numerous questions raised under Article 234 the European Court was considerably assisted by the lengthy opinion of Advocate General Jacobs whose views were largely adopted. It accepted that repackaging was not, in principle, an interference with goods which would prevent the principle of 'exhaustion of rights' applying, but imposed nevertheless on the importer of such goods more demanding conditions than in the earlier *Hoffmann* v. *Centrafarm* case. The requirements set out in that case were repeated but two new conditions were imposed on the importer. First was a substantive general requirement that the presentation of the product after repackaging must not be such as to damage the reputation of the trade mark owner. Thus the packaging must be of good quality and not defective or untidy. The second requirement was procedural: that on demand the proprietor of the trade mark is not only given notice of the repackaging but also supplied with a specimen of the repackaged product to enable him to assess whether the requirements of Community law have been fully observed.

The Court in this case was able to rely not only on principles established in earlier case law, but also on the fact that these had been incorporated in Trade Mark Directive 89/104, which states that:

the trade mark shall not entitle the proprietor to prohibit its use in relation to goods which have been put on to the market in the Community under that trade mark by the proprietor or with his consent; (2) Paragraph 1 shall not apply when there exist legitimate reasons for the proprietor to oppose further commercialization of the goods especially where the condition of the goods is changed or impaired after they have been put on the market.

In a further case shortly afterwards a new issue was raised; were the rights of the importer affected by the fact that it had applied to the goods a different[20] trade mark from those under which they had been sold by the original supplier? In this case, *Pharmacia & Upjohn* v. *Paranova*,[21] the parallel importer, had brought antibiotics in Greece and France under the trade marks 'Dalacin C' and 'Dalacine' respectively but sought to resell them in Denmark under Upjohn's Danish trade mark 'Dalacin'. The Court departing from the subjective test applied in *Centrafarm* v. *American Home Products* as to the intentions of the trade mark proprietor now laid down a new test which focused on whether the parallel importer had an objective need to change the trade mark applied to the goods, for

[20] The importer will be able to use the supplier's own trade mark to promote his sales, unless the supplier can show it will seriously damage the value of his trade mark. *Dior* v. *Evora* Case C-337/95 [1997] ECR I-6013 [1998]: 1 CMLR 737.
[21] Case C-379/97 [1997] ECR I-6927: [2000] 1 CMLR 51, S. Kon and P. Schaeffer, 'Parallel Imports of Pharmaceutical Products' 1997 *ECLR* 123–144.

example, because of national laws of the Member State into which they were being imported, prohibiting their sale unless the local trade mark was affixed. If the reason for this change was however simply the commercial advantage of the importer then the rights of the trade mark owner would nevertheless prevail. In other words the European Court had now linked the outcome of such cases to the objective motives of the importer rather than the subjective intention of the trade mark owner in having dual marks in separate countries.

But the European Court had not yet finished with the subject of repackaging and a batch of further cases had to be decided in 2002. In *Merck, Sharp & Dohme* v. *Paranova*[22] the parallel import of a product used for the treatment of prostate conditions, originally purchased in Spain, was challenged by the Austrian trade mark owner, because it was proposed to give the product on sale in Austria a new outer packaging rather than merely affixing stickers to the outside of the original box in which the Spanish sale had been made. The Court, recognizing the commercial realities of the situation, confirmed the principle already established in the earlier cases, that trade mark owner's opposition to repackaging is unjustified if it blocks effective access of the imported product to the local market.[23] The Court cited as examples local rules relating to the packaging of pharmaceuticals, well established prescription practices based on standard box sizes, and also consumer resistance to the relabelling or 'over-sticking' of such products. It was however in all cases for the national court to decide whether any of these conditions existed so as to justify the repackaging by the importer. Moreover, in a group of cases[24] referred under Article 234 by the Chancery Division of the English High Court further clarification of the repackaging issues was sought by Laddie J, who was clearly concerned that the obligations placed on parallel importers as a condition for importation were too stringent. Nevertheless, the European Court maintained its previous stance, confirming that parallel importers must strictly observe the cumulative requirements which previous case law had laid down. The effect of this decision is that in all cases the parallel importer must comply strictly with the following four conditions if it is to be able successfully to withstand the local trade mark owner's claim for infringement:

First there must be an objective necessity for repackaging without which effective marketing cannot take place, whether this is based on local legal requirements or strong consumer preferences, not merely commercial advantage to the importer.

Second, the repackaging chosen must not have an adverse effect on the original condition of the product nor mislead the purchaser as to its origin.

Thirdly, the quality of the repackaging must not be such as to damage the reputation of the trade mark holder;

And fourth, reasonable prior notice of the importation (to be assessed by the national Court), together with samples, must be given to the manufacturer by the parallel importer prior to proposed commencement of sale.

It is clear that at least some judges in the United Kingdom feel that such rules are unduly restrictive for parallel importers; but given the consistent approach both of Jacobs A-G and other Advocates General and the European Court in the cases referred to, it seems unlikely

---

[22] Case C-443/99 (case decided 23 April 2002).

[23] *Loendersloot* v. *Ballantine* Case C-349/95 [1997] ECR I-6227.

[24] *Boehringer Ingelheim and Others* v. *Dowelhurst Ltd and Swingward Ltd* Case 143/00 [2002] 2 CMLR 623.

that these will now be varied though there may well be further cases reaching the Court on the precise application of these conditions.

4. THE EXCEPTIONS TO THE PRINCIPLE OF 'EXHAUSTION OF RIGHTS'

4.1 EXHAUSTION OF COMMUNITY RIGHTS

The broad principles behind the Court's interpretation of Article 30 had now been clarified, but later cases were to graft several important exceptions onto them. In the 1976 case of *EMI Records* v. *CBS United Kingdom*,[25] the issue was whether the principle of exhaustion of rights of trade marks would enable EMI, which owned the relevant mark 'Columbia' throughout the EC, to prevent CBS from manufacturing records under that trade mark through subsidiaries established in the various Member States. The original trade mark had been owned solely by US companies. By a series of agreements over a period of thirty years to the end of the Second World War, ownership was divided so that CBS owned the mark in the United States, whilst EMI owned it in other parts of the world, including the whole of the European Community. Although there had been some co-operation between the parties after the end of the Second World War, ownership of the trade-mark rights had been clearly divided for a substantial period. The Court held that the Treaty did not prevent EMI, as proprietor of a trade mark throughout the Community, from exercising its right to prevent the import of similar products carrying the same mark from a third country outside the EC. The rationale of this decision was that the exercise of such rights could not affect trade between Member States, even if it were classifiable as a measure equivalent to a quantitative restriction under Article 28, and thus it could not pose any threat to the integration of trading within the Common Market which that Article was designed to bring about. However, in the light of the decision in *Hag (No. 2)*,[26] discussed below, it is unclear whether EMI would have been in the same fortunate position had CBS owned the trade mark rights in even one of the Member States.

A similar result was achieved in *Polydor Records* v. *Harlequin Record Shops*,[27] a case referred under Article 234 to the European Court by the English High Court. Polydor owned the copyright in a recording of songs by the Bee Gees pop group. The defendants imported copies of the records from Portugal where they had been manufactured by a licensee of the plaintiff. Both the importation into and sale in the United Kingdom were effected without the consent of the plaintiff. When sued for copyright infringement, the defendants referred to the Free Trade Agreement between the Community and Portugal, which contained clauses equivalent to those set out in Articles 28 and 30 of the Treaty. Although the Court agreed that the language was similar, it declined to allow the defendant the benefit of the principle of exhaustion of rights. Its explanation for this decision was that the Free Trade Area provisions relating to free movement of goods did not have the same purpose as the Treaty of Rome. The Free Trade Area agreement between the Community and a

---

[25] Case 51/75 [1976] ECR 811: 2 CMLR 235.   [26] See below at pp.261–3.

[27] Case 270/80 [1982] ECR 329: 1 CMLR 677. At the relevant date Portugal was not a member of the Community.

non-Member State did not purport to create a single market reproducing as closely as possible the conditions of a domestic market, because the instruments which the Community had at its disposal to achieve uniform application of Community law and the progressive abolition of legislative disparities had no equivalent in the context of a relationship simply between the EC and Portugal. The principle of strict territoriality for copyright items no longer existed between each of the Member States, but could still exist in the relationship between the Community and non-member countries, even those with whom it had a free trade agreement.

The second important exception to the basic rule of exhaustion of rights is derived from *Parke, Davis* v. *Probel*.[28] In that early case the Court had held that the exhaustion principle did not apply where goods had originally been placed on the market in a country where no patent protection was available, and without the consent of Parke, Davis who held the patent protection in The Netherlands where the defendants sought to sell the goods. This decision was based on the argument that the principle of exhaustion could not apply because Parke, Davis had not had the opportunity of obtaining a reward for the investment in the invention of the relevant drug, because of the failure of Italian law to provide patent protection. In the more recent case of *Merck* v. *Stephar*,[29] the facts were similar to Parke, Davis except that Merck had them-selves marketed the drug known as 'Moduretic' in Italy, even though unable to obtain a patent either for the drug or the manufacturing process. Merck had obtained some return for their investment through their sales in Italy, even though the lack of patent protection possibly reduced the price which they were able to obtain; the Court felt that the goods had been placed in commerce within the Common Market. Merck could not expect, simply by placing the product on the market, to guarantee that the full reward potentially available for patented products would be available for all its non-patented products.

The principle in this case has remained unpopular with the manufacturers of pharmaceutical products which have been the subject of extensive parallel importing. It was challenged again in the European Court by Merck and Beecham in the *Primecrown*[30] cases. Here the products concerned were drugs for treating hypertension and glaucoma and from Spain and Portugal where at the relevant dates (though not now) patent protection could not be obtained. The manufacturers sought in the Chancery Division of the English High Court to prevent these imported drugs from being sold in the United Kingdom on the ground that the manufacturers had both legal and ethical obligations to sell the drugs in Spain and Portugal without the patent protection and could not damage the interests of their patients in those countries, once marketing had begun, by later withdrawing them from sale. In other words they claimed that their 'consent' to the marketing was conditional rather than absolute. Mr Justice Jacob referred the issues to the European Court under Article 234. However, the European Court, partially overruling Fennelly A-G, distinguished between the situation where plaintiffs had an ethical or moral obligation to supply a drug, and that where they were under a legal obligation; only in the latter case would 'consent' be deemed not to have been given, since the position of the proprietors of a trade mark in those situations would be little different from an owner obliged to give a licence of right. No sufficient legal obligation to market the products could be found under the laws of Spain and Portugal. By contrast, if

---

[28] Case 24/67 [1968] ECR 55: CMLR 47.   [29] Case 187/80 [1981] ECR 2063: 3 CMLR 463.
[30] Cases C-267 and 268/95. [1996] ECR I-6285: [1997] 1 CMLR 83.

ethical obligations were to be relied on, these were far harder to measure and to apply to the issue of whether consent had been given in the case of any particular drug. The existence of price controls in the country of first sale was, as in earlier cases, held to be irrelevant.

However, the original placing on the market of a patented process, not by the voluntary act of its proprietor but because a mandatory licence has been granted under the provisions of national patent law, to a licensee, would lack the essential element of the proprietor's consent, and the patentee would be entitled to invoke his patent against parallel imports into a second Member State where its patent protection existed.[31] Similar principles would apply in the case of licences of right also available under the national patent law of certain Member States.

However, the proprietor cannot prevent the actual import of products subject to the licence of right provided that the importer undertakes to pay the licence fee laid down by agreement or, in default of agreement, as determined by the national patent authorities. The importer has to be treated in the same way as the domestic manufacturer of such products under the licence of right. This means that the importer cannot, for example, be required to give security in advance for royalties payable or to delay distribution of the product pending satisfactory health and safety clearance. The fact that the relevant product was a pharmaceutical product imported from a Member State where patenting of such products is not possible again did not affect the principles involved.[32]

4.2 INTERNATIONAL EXHAUSTION OF RIGHTS

The most important exception however to the principle is undoubtedly that which applies when the original sale has been made, not within any Member State but elsewhere, and a parallel importer then seeks to bring such products into the Community for resale. The first occasion on which the European Court considered this issue was the 1998 *Silhouette*[33] case. This Austrian company produced fashion spectacles and sunglasses and had disposed of some old stock to a Bulgarian company on condition that the products were resold only in Bulgaria and some other East European countries. The defendant, however, another Austrian company, purchased the products from the Bulgarian company and then sought to market them back in Austria. The European Court found in favour of Silhouette upon an Article 234 reference on the basis that Article 7 of the Trade Mark Directive limited the rights of Member States to apply the 'exhaustion of rights' principle to sales made originally in the Community, so that an individual Member State was not entitled to extend the principle to other sales. This approach was also adopted in the subsequent *Sebago* v. *GB-Unic*[34] where the argument of the parallel importer was that shoes similar to those which it

---

[31] This principle was established in *Pharmon* v. *Hoechst* Case 19/84 [1985] ECR 2281: 3 CMLR 775. In *EMI Electrola* v. *Patricia* (European Court 1989) Case 341/87 [1989] ECR 79: [1989] 2 CMLR 413, the same principle was applied in the context of copyright. The owner of a Cliff Richard record, for which copyright in Denmark had expired, was allowed to continue to make use of its copyright in Germany so as to exclude imports from Denmark. It had given no consent to the manufacture of the record in Denmark and therefore, by analogy with *Pharmon* v. *Hoechst*, Art. 28 had no application.

[32] *Allen and Hanburys Ltd.* v. *Generic (UK) Ltd.* Case 434/85 [1988] ECR 1245: 1 CMLR 701: [1989] 2 CMLR 325.

[33] Case C-355/96 [1998] ECR I-4799: 2 CMLR 953.

[34] Case C-173/98 [1999] ECR I-4103: 2 CMLR 1317.

was seeking to import into the Community (from El Salvador) had already been sold by the plaintiff trade mark owner within the Community. The Court, following again the opinion of Jacobs A-G, ruled that exhaustion as a principle applies to individual goods or batches, not to product lines as a whole. Subsequently in June 2000, Commissioner Bolkestein announced, following detailed consultations with Member States and other interested parties, that the Commission would not extend the geographic area in which European registered trade marks were deemed exhausted, by amendment of the Trade Mark Directive. The debate leading up to this decision had been fiercely contested with scope for compromise limited. On the one hand trade mark owners supported the status quo, on the ground that their ownership of intellectual property rights, including trade marks, entitled them to determine, in respect of non EC sales, the market in which their products could be sold and that it was an unreasonable limitation of their rights to permit parallel importers to seek to exploit price differences between different markets throughout the world. In contrast, parallel importers argued that to introduce 'international exhaustion' permitting parallel imports into Europe wherever the goods had originally been sold, would bring down prices within the Community and reduce the exploitation by trade-mark owners of captive markets within the Community.

It was foreseeable that such a controversial question would be brought back to the European Court and this came to pass in two linked cases *Zino Davidoff* v. *A & G Imports*[35] and *Levi Strauss* v. *Tesco* and *Costco*.[36] In the first case Davidoff had sold toiletries under its trade mark 'Cool Water' which was registered in the United Kingdom, and in other jurisdictions. A-G Imports acquired stock originally sold in Singapore by Davidoff and began importing it into the United Kingdom. In the second case, Tesco and Costco both purchased '501 Levi' jeans from Levi Strauss outside the Community and were sued for infringement by Levi. In both cases the product imported into the United Kingdom was made available to the public there by the importers at considerably lower prices than the normal prices charged in the UK by the authorized distributors for Zino Davidoff and Levi Strauss.

The trade mark proprietors therefore brought an action in the United Kingdom to prevent these parallel imports, on the legal basis that they had not given any consent to the importation of these goods nor could their consent be implied from the mere act of placing them on markets *outside* the European Community. The parallel importers, encouraged doubtless by the sympathy with which their arguments had been met by Laddie J.[37] at the original hearing of the claim before the Chancery Division of the High Court, argued that once the trade mark proprietor had obtained a profit from his original sale, it could not then utilize its intellectual property rights to prevent a purchaser of goods from reselling them in any market that it might choose (a right described by Laddie J in the proceedings as 'a parasitic right to interfere with the distribution of goods which bears little or no relationship to the proper function of the trade mark right'); even if the right to import could be excluded by an express contract clause passed down the entire chain of purchasers, no such restriction should be implied. The absence of such express restriction, they argued, meant that the importer could claim implied consent by the trade-mark proprietor.

The judgment of the European Court however, was at all points in favour of the trade mark owners. It stated that importation would only be permitted if the proprietor of the

---

[35] Case C-414/99 [2002] 1 CMLR 1.

[36] Cases C-415 and 416/99 [2002] 1 CMLR 1. Subsequent UK proceedings are reported at [2002] 3 CMLR 281.

[37] [1999] 3 All ER 711: 2 CMLR 1317.

trade mark had given express consent in respect of the particular goods concerned. The burden of proof that consent had been given was on the importer and could not be assumed either from the proprietor's silence nor from the absence of any warning placed on the goods or their packaging nor upon the absence of any communication by the owner to subsequent purchasers of its products, stating objection to their marketing within the Community. The existence of national laws containing restrictions on the enforcement of intellectual property rights against third parties not involved in the original sale was held irrelevant to this issue of consent. Although these important cases dealt only with trade marks, the underlying reasoning of the Court can be seen as equally applicable to all other intellectual property rights. An important aspect of these cases is the location of the burden of proof; should it be entirely on the importer to show the express consent of the trade mark owner? It may be that in practice this places an impossible task on the importer. Sympathy for this argument is found in the Judgment of the ECJ in *Van Doren* v. *Lifestyle Sports*,[38] which lays down that the burden of proof be shared. Initially it is suggested that the trade-mark owner must prove that there are no 'gaps' in its distribution system within the EEA, that is no source from which the imported goods may originally have come other than from its official distribution channels. If this can be done, then the burden of proving express consent to marketing in the EEA passes fully to the importer. In the meantime Member States remain divided in their approach to international exhaustion, though it is believed that by a small majority they would prefer it to be permitted and the effect of the Court judgments to the contrary overruled by a change in the Trade Mark Directive and Regulation.

4.3 THE POSITION OF SERVICES

Another exception to the rule of exhaustion is where the property right concerned relates, not to goods, but to services covered by the provisions of Articles 49 to 55. The Belgian court made two successive references for preliminary rulings under Article 234 in the *Coditel* cases.[39] In the first case the European Court held that the provisions of Article 59 did not prevent the owner of copyright in a film under national law from invoking its rights against cable TV companies. The facts of *Coditel (No. 1)* (European Court 1980) were that Cine Vog had acquired the exclusive right to show the film *Le Boucher* in Belgium for a period of seven years, provided that it did not show it on television for a minimum of forty months after the first screening in Belgium. The film was sold by the owners for screening on German television, but when shown the transmission was picked up by Coditel which operated the cable television service in Belgium and then distributed to its own cable subscribers in Belgium. Cine Vog then claimed that Coditel had breached the copyright vested in it under the original seven-year agreement.

In the second reference *Coditel (No. 2)* the issue before the Court was whether an exclusive licence to show a film was subject to the prohibitions of Article 81. In the course of its judgment the Court indicated that the distinction drawn in the earlier cases between the

---

[38] Case C-244/00, decided on 8 April 2003. The issue of whether a distribution system is 'impervious' also arose in *Metro* v. *Cartier* Case C-376/92 [1994] ECR I-15: 5 CMLR 331, in connection with the question of the enforceability of guarantees for products sold other than by the suppliers' authorized dealers. See Ch. 11, fn. 9.

[39] *Coditel* v. *Cine Vog Films (No. 1)* Case 62/79 [1980] ECR 881: [1981] 2 CMLR 362. *Coditel* v. *Cine Vog Films (No. 2)* Case 262/81 [1982] ECR 3381: [1983] 1 CMLR 49.

existence and the exercise of industrial property rights under Article 30 could also apply when such rights were exercised in the framework of the provision of services. In both cases it held that cinema films were made available to the public by performances capable of being repeated without limit, so that copyright owners had legitimate interests in calculating the fees due in respect of an authorization to show the film 'on the basis of the actual or probable number of performances and in authorising a television broadcast of the film only after it had been exhibited in cinemas for a certain period of time'. In other words, it treated the nature of copyright in a film as inherently different from that in either a book or gramophone record. It is noteworthy that, in his opinion in the first *Coditel* case, Advocate General Warner indicated that in his view the omission from Articles 49 to 55 of the Treaty dealing with services of any provision for the protection of industrial property was probably the result of oversight rather than deliberate intention. Given the opportunist nature of the action of Coditel, the Court's decision has commanded general support, and especially the finding after appropriate economic analysis that an exclusive copyright licence does not necessarily violate Article 81.

4.4 THE 'COMMON ORIGIN' EXCEPTION

For a long time it was believed that the fact that a particular trade mark came from a 'common origin' or 'common source' also protected it from challenge by the proprietor of a related mark. This belief arose from the 1974 case of *Van Zuylen Freres v. Hag*[40] where identical trade marks had come from a common source. Van Zuylen was the assignee of the Benelux trade mark in 'Hag' coffee, having acquired it by purchase from the Custodian of Enemy Property following the confiscation of the assets of the former Belgian subsidiary of Hag AG of Germany at the end of the Second World War. The trade mark was registered in Benelux, and Van Zuylen sold coffee at the retail level. In the meantime, the original German company, Hag AG of Bremen, had recommenced marketing coffee in the Benelux area under its own identical trade mark, and Van Zuylen tried to stop Hag AG from importing coffee into Luxembourg, claiming it to be an infringement of the mark owned and registered by it. The Court rejected the claim by Van Zuylen, repeating the distinction made in earlier cases between the existence and the exercise of rights. It held that it could not allow the holder of a trade mark effective in one Member State to prohibit the marketing in that Member State of goods legally produced in another Member State under an identical trade mark that had the same origins.

This decision was overruled in *Hag (No. 2)*[41] towards the end of 1990. In his opinion Attorney General Jacobs convincingly argued that the original Hag decision was flawed in that the consent of the owners of the Benelux mark to the use of the similar German trade mark in Benelux had been wrongly presumed, from the mere fact of the original common source. The facts of *Hag (No. 2)* presented the reverse situation from the earlier case, as it was now the German Hag company (which in the first case had successfully defended its right to sell coffee in Benelux under its German trade mark) which sought to prevent the owner of the Benelux trade mark (successor in title to Van Zuylen) from selling its coffee in Germany.

---

[40] Case 192/73 [1974] ECR 731: 2 CMLR 127.
[41] Case C-10/89 [1990] ECR I-3711: 3 CMLR 571.

In upholding the right of the German company to prevent the Belgian company from selling its coffee in Germany, Jacobs A-G pointed out that the doctrine of common origin is nowhere referred to in the Treaty and had no rational basis. The earlier judgment had failed to analyse satisfactorily the inherent subject matter of trade marks, and therefore under-estimated their importance as property rights. They were necessary to protect the manu-facturer who consistently produced high quality goods and should not be regarded as a secondary form of intellectual property rights since they enable existing quality to be recog-nized in the new markets. To remove the exclusive right to the mark from a manufacturer takes from him the power to influence and capitalize on the goodwill associated with it. The specific subject matter of the trade mark is the guarantee given by its owner that it has the exclusive right to use it in order to put into production and circulation a quality product, which can be protected against competitors who later seek to acquire unfairly the benefit of the original manufacturer's goodwill.

Any doubts that remained after the *Hag (No. 2)* decision as to the breadth of its applica-tion were removed by the *Ideal-Standard*[42] case. Until 1984 a US company held the rights to sell both sanitary and heating equipment under the mark 'Ideal-Standard' in France and Germany through its subsidiary companies. The French subsidiary then became insolvent and in realizing its assets so as to meet its obligations to creditors had voluntarily sold its heating installation business (including its goodwill and related trade marks) to SGF, which in turn transferred them to CIC, an independent company. CIC tried after manufacturing the heaters to export them to Germany under the Ideal-Standard trade mark through a German distributor IHT. The German subsidiary of Ideal-Standard claimed that it had the sole right to use the Ideal-Standard mark in Germany even though since 1976 it had not produced heaters or heating installations but only sanitary ware. Under the doctrine of common origin as originally set out in *Hag (No. 1)* the argument by the German subsidiary would have failed because of the original common origin of the marks owned by the French and German subsidiaries of Ideal-Standard.

However, the Court made clear that *Hag (No. 1)* was no longer good law, even in cases where ownership of the trade marks had been separated on a voluntary basis rather than under a compulsory process of sequestration. The Court pointed out that, in the circum-stances in which the assignment had occurred, Ideal-Standard had been unable to control the quality of goods that would be produced under its French trade mark; therefore differ-ences in quality between goods produced under the French trade mark 'Ideal-Standard' and under the same mark in other jurisdictions could not be controlled. This was quite different from the situation where Ideal-Standard had deliberately licensed the use of the market in another jurisdiction but failed to maintain adequate quality controls of the kind normal in licensing agreements. If imports under the French trade mark were allowed, consumers would no longer be able to identify with confidence the origin of marked goods, and Ideal-Standard as the proprietor of the original trade marks could be held responsible for any deficiencies in them without any control over their specification. The issue of whether a genuine risk of confusion existed was a matter for national courts; it did not matter whether the goods were identical or merely sufficiently similar, and the European Court could not substitute its own finding on that issue. The mere fact that the German subsidiary had not

---

[42] Case C-9/93 [1994] ECR I-2789: 3 CMLR 857.

for a number of years sold heating installations under the Ideal-Standard trade mark did not affect its rights.

Hag (No. 2) seems therefore to apply to any voluntary division of trade marks within the Community. The basis for this principle is the same as that set out by Jacobs A-G in *Hag (No. 2)*, namely the importance for the owner of the mark to be able to exercise control over the quality of goods produced under it in another Member State. If a trade mark owner decides to split ownership between itself and another company in another Member State it has, of course, to accept responsibility for the quality of the goods to be produced by their assignee; it will normally exercise that control by making obtainment of quality standards a primary term of the assignment. In that case the reimport of goods into the territory of the assignor is still one which the assignor can control. However, where the terms of the assignment prevent the national owner of the trade mark from exercising control (as in the rather special circumstances of the *Ideal-Standard* case) the assignor should be entitled to prevent the risk of damage to its own reputation as well as confusion about the source of the goods by relying on its national rights. This will allow it to prevent importation of the goods by the assignees; in other words, to consent to an assignment of the mark without retention of control over its use, in cases where such control is not commercially possible, is not 'consent' for purposes of the exhaustion rule.

4.5 SIMILARITY OF SEPARATE TRADE MARKS

Concern had been expressed as a result of *Hag (No. 1)* that the European Court would also look unfavourably on attempts by trade mark owners in one Member State to prevent the use in that Member State of another trade mark originating from a second Member State which might be considered confusingly identical, even where there was no element of common origin and the parties were at arm's length. This fear, however, was laid to rest by the *Terrapin (Overseas)* v. *Terranova*[43] case two years later. Terranova was a German company which had manufactured plaster for buildings façades for a considerable period of time, and which was the registered proprietor in Germany of a number of trade marks including the words 'Terra', 'Terranova', and 'Terra-fabrikate' in respect of various building materials. Terrapin was an English company which manufactured prefabricated houses and components under the trade mark 'Terrapin'. The English company operated in Germany directly and through a subsidiary and had applied to register their trade mark there. A number of legal actions arose between the parties because of the similarity of their respective trade marks. The German Supreme Court finally referred the issue to the European Court under Article 234: the issue was whether the registration of the United Kingdom mark in Germany would give rise to confusion with the mark owned by the German company, a legitimate proprietor of its own trade mark in its own country; and if so, whether the German company could then legitimately within the terms of Article 30 oppose use of the name 'Terrapin' to describe the English product in Germany.

Had the Court taken an excessively purist view of intellectual property rights in the Community under the regime of Articles 28 to 30, one might have expected that the doctrine of honest concurrent use which the Court did apply in other cases might have prevailed. Nevertheless, the Court, clearly feeling that the risk of confusion was genuine

---

[43] Case 119/75 [1976] ECR 1039: 2 CMLR 482.

owing to the similarity of the respective companies' business and trade marks, found that a refusal by German authorities to register 'Terrapin' in Germany would not breach Article 28. The situation was very different from that in the *Hag (No. 1)* case; the trade mark had arisen quite separately under the laws of different Member States and there were no legal or economic links between the companies. The desirability of the free movement of goods and the legitimate interest of the proprietor of the threatened trade mark had to be reconciled in such a way as would both protect legitimate use of trade mark rights and prevent their abuse in a manner enabling segmentation of the territories within the Common Market. The Court concluded, therefore, that the German Court could restrain the use of the imported mark, since otherwise, if the principle of free movement of goods was nevertheless to prevail in such a case, even a specific and important object of the system of industrial and com-mercial property rights, the differentiation of competing products, would be seriously undermined. However, in such circumstances it was essential that the national Court be satisfied both that there were no links between the respective companies and that the origins of the marks were completely independent. Such questions are now, of course, governed by Community law and the application of the Trade Mark Directive 89/104.[44]

5. THE RELATIONSHIP OF FREE MOVEMENT RULES TO COMPETITION RULES

5.1 DIFFERENCES BETWEEN THE TWO SETS OF RULES

In the previous sections of this chapter we have examined how the Community Courts have in a number of cases sought to establish definite limits on the extent to which the Article 30 exceptions for 'industrial and commercial property' to the free movement rules can be allowed to weaken their effect. The next step is to understand how in these circumstances the relationship between the competition rules and the free movement rules has been handled by the Courts and the Commission. As noted above, the principal differences between the scope of the two groups of rules must be borne in mind. Although their objectives are not necessarily in conflict, there is equally no inherent harmony between them since each group of rules operates in its own way, largely without overlap. Articles 28 and 30, as we have seen, are addressed to Member States and their executive, legislative, and judicial authorities at all levels, to prevent the use of legislation, judicial decision, or administrative practice from maintaining non-tariff barriers, save to the limited extent allowed by the narrow interpret-ation placed by the European Court of Justice on Article 30. By contrast, Articles 81 and 82 apply only to undertakings, and Article 86 to public undertakings and those to which Member States grant special or exclusive rights. They require either an agreement or a concerted practice between at least two undertakings, or the abuse of a dominant position. A sanction for entering into an agreement in contravention of Article 81 is that an undertaking may incur fines and penalties from the Commission; no such sanction is available if a government or its agency breaches Article 28. On the other hand, Article 81(2) provides that

---

[44] See P. Oliver, *Free Movement of Goods in the EC,* 4th edn., pp.335–8, which refers to the attempt by Jacobs A-G in *Hag (No. 2)* to prevent an unduly broad view of the concept of confusion being adapted by national Courts, and also by *SABEL* v. *Puma*, Case C-251/95 [1997].

the offending clauses of such an agreement are void and without legal effect. By contrast a court in which an Article 28 defence is raised, by a defendant accused for example of infringing the patent or trade mark rights of a plaintiff seeking to exercise such rights in a situation where the European Court has ruled it would be in breach of Article 28, is required to uphold its defence. It must, moreover, reject the plaintiff's claim so as to ensure that neither civil nor criminal sanctions are imposed upon the defendant.

In general terms, competition and free market rules have similar objectives: the freeing of trade between Member States from restraints imposed by either private or public sources. However, the European Court has made it clear in a number of cases that it will not allow one set of rules to be used to justify freedom from the other. Thus, as far back as the *Grundig*[45] case in 1966, these provisions later being embodied in Regulation 67/67, the European Court laid down that the protection given by Article 30 to industrial and commercial property should not enable those rights to be used in a way which supported a distribution system that sought to exclude the possibility of parallel imports. The same principle underlies the subsequent Court decisions of *Sirena* v. *Eda*[46] and *DGG* v. *Metro*[47] referring to copyright, and the several *Centrafarm*[48] cases in the years immediately following. On the other hand, since the free movement rules protect the existence of industrial and commercial property, the mere exercise of rights under national law which do not conflict with the principle of exhaustion of rights would not breach Article 82, a principle established by both the *Probel* and *Terrapin* cases.

5.2 RECONCILIATION OF THE TWO SETS OF RULES

A similarity between the two sets of rules is, of course, that Member States are under a duty not to introduce legislation which would cause a breach of them. This obligation is specifically expressed in Articles 28 and 29, and has been stated also to apply to the competition rules: see *Inno* v. *ATAB*[49] (European Court 1977). In that case the Court spelled out the duties of Member States not to enact measures enabling private undertakings to evade the constraints of the rules against competition even if in practice such measures might well also offend Articles 28 or 29.

Whilst only Articles 81 and 82 have a *de minimis* provision which is inherent from the wording of the Article ('. . . and which may affect trade between Member States . . .'), it is arguable that Articles 28/29 are to be interpreted as if containing an inherent 'rule of reason'. In *IDG* v. *Beele*[50] (European Court 1982), the Court concluded that, in a straightforward case of 'passing off' involving exact imitations of cable ducts, Article 28 should be interpreted so as not to prevent a rule of national law (applying to domestic and imported products alike) from allowing one trader to obtain an injunction preventing another from continuing to

---

[45] Cases 56 and 58/64 [1966] ECR 299: CMLR 418. See also Ch. 5, pp.43–4.

[46] Case 40/70 [1971] ECR 69: CMLR 260.

[47] Case 78/70 [1971] ECR 487: CMLR 631.

[48] See fnn. 15 and 16.

[49] Case 13/77 [1977] ECR 2115: [1978] 1 CMLR 283. The case involved a Belgian statute requiring all tobacco products sold at retail to have a label affixed showing the maximum price. This was claimed by the Belgian government to have as its purpose the prevention of fraud on the tax authorities, but the Court ruled that it had been introduced mainly to protect a resale price maintenance system. The case is further considered in Ch. 22, pp.475–6.

[50] Case 6/81 [1982] ECR 707: 3 CMLR 102.

market a product lawfully marketed, but which 'for no compelling reason' was sold in a form almost identical to the first named product, causing needless confusion between the two.

Exceptions to the prohibitions against restrictions of competition contained in or effected by agreements and concerted practices are based on grounds that are mainly economic, namely the two negative and the two positive conditions of Article 81(3), whereas the better view in relation to Article 30 appears to be that arguments of an essentially economic nature cannot be used to justify claims for exemption; on the other hand, the mere fact that governmental measures introduced on other grounds referred to in Article 30, e.g. national security, may also have some economic advantages will not automatically mean that the measure will violate Article 28. However, the precise relief which such measures may be permitted to give to government will be strictly limited to those proportionate to the national security interest required to be protected.[51]

The development by DG Comp of competition policy in respect of patent licences, discussed in Chapter 12, might cause difficulties in the future under Article 28. While case law has made clear that intellectual property rights cannot be used to prevent or restrict parallel imports, i.e. goods imported by persons who have obtained them lawfully, directly or indirectly, from licensees in other Member States, the position is less clear with regard to the exercise of such rights, directly or indirectly, either by the original licensor against his own licensee or by one licensee against another licensee of the same licensor. Under the terms of the technology transfer block exemption contained in Regulation 240/96, the restrictions that can be placed on licensees include a total ban on 'active' sales by licensees outside their area, and even a five-year ban on responding to unsolicited requests for sale from outside the area. If, in infringement of such agreements, sales of patented products were made by one licensee into the territory of another, an action to restrain the licensee from doing so might be met by a claim that Article 28 itself prevented courts from approving it. The established precedents of *Centrafarm* could be quoted in support of this view, notwithstanding that the patent licence terms were clearly covered by Article 81 and the block exemption, so that the rights were not being abused so as to avoid Article 81, as in the *Grundig* case.

In other words, while it has long been clear that the application of Article 81(1) to an agreement will not be restricted because the agreement might also involve a breach of Article 28, it is far less clear whether the fact that Article 81(1) will not be held to apply to a particular agreement, e.g. as a result of a block exemption, means that Article 28 cannot then be raised by a defendant against whom the agreement is pleaded.[52]

The European Court of Justice might well seek, as a matter of policy, to limit the application of Article 28 to situations other than those where the Commission itself had, after protracted consultations and negotiations, established a model for technology transfer within the Community which would not in its view restrain competition within the terms of

---

[51] This is illustrated by *Campus Oil* v. *Ministry of Industry and Energy* Case 72/83 [1984] ECR 2727: 3 CMLR 544, where the Irish government had introduced measures obliging various oil companies to acquire a minimum quantity of oil from its only State refinery. The Court ruled that the national Court had the jurisdiction to approve such measures to the extent that they applied only to the minimum supply requirements, without which the State's public security would be affected, or at which the level of production had to be maintained to ensure the refinery's production capacity in the event of a crisis.

[52] For a detailed discussion of this complex question, see Oliver, op. cit., pp.73–84.

Article 81. The fact that the restriction permitted went beyond the reach of that open exclusive licence permitted in *Maize Seed* (though far from comprising absolute territorial protection of a kind clearly unacceptable under Article 81) should not of itself permit Article 28 to be successfully raised as a defence by a licensee sued in these circumstances.

Both free movement and competition rules have now been developed and defined over a considerable period and by a wealth of case law, allowing their central consistency to become apparent. Identical concepts and expressions have been relied upon both in cases under Sections 28 to 30 and under Articles 81 and 82. Case law does not appear to have raised any inconsistencies between the operation of the two sets of rules; if in future a case did arise which threatened to arrange a clash between them, the Court would be likely to seek a solution which harmonized the approaches of the two sets of rules rather than emphasizing any differences between them.[53]

---

[53] K. Mortelmans, 'Towards Convergence on the application of the Rules in Free Movement and Competition' [2001] 38 *CMLR* 613–649.

14

ARTICLE 82: THE CONCEPT OF DOMINANCE

1. THE DEFINITION OF DOMINANCE

1.1 *UNITED BRANDS* AND *HOFFMANN-LA ROCHE*

Preceding chapters have dealt almost exclusively with the development of the law relating to Article 81, and its application to both horizontal and vertical agreements and concerted practices. Although the resources devoted by DG Comp to the administration of Article 81 have far exceeded those spent on Article 82, this second of the twin pillars of the competition policy established under the Treaty has nevertheless given rise to decisions of great significance, from both the Commission and the Community Courts. Article 82 is increasingly important to the Commission in its continuing enforcement of competition policy; it has potential for further development and application by way of control, in a great variety of circumstances, of the problem of the abuse by undertakings of dominant positions in specific markets. It has proved particularly valuable to the Commission as it has through its powers under Article 86(3) issued directives bringing more competition to key Community markets, including energy, telecommunications, transport, and postal services.

Article 82 is itself brief. It states that abuse by one or more undertakings of a dominant position within the Common Market (or a substantial part of it) should be prohibited, in so far as it may affect trade between Member States. This chapter examines the concept of dominance which necessarily leads on to a consideration of the process of market definition, of both products (goods and services) and the geographical areas in which they are sold or provided. Chapter 15 then deals with the various categories of abuse and abusive conduct.

Dominance is an abstract word, but used in a commercial context it refers to a position of substantial power for an undertaking in relation to a specific product market and within a relevant geographical market, both of which must be defined. Fortunately dominance was considered in detail by the European Court in one of its early cases arising out of this Article, *United Brands*.[1] The market power of this company (engaged in the large-scale international fruit business) derived principally from the degree to which it had integrated its various

---

[1] Case 27/76 [1978] ECR 207: 1 CMLR 429. This chapter deals with dominance by a single undertaking or corporate group. Joint dominance by two or more undertakings is dealt with in Ch. 16. A comprehensive account of the significant differences between Art. 82 and Section 2 of the Sherman Act is found in P. Jebsen and R. Stevens, 'Assumptions, Goals, and Dominant Undertakings: the Regulation of Competition under Article [82] of the EU', 64 *ALJ*, issue 3, (1996), 443–516.

activities. Although it also had a market share in the four relevant Member States of between 40 and 45 per cent, its strength and dominance derived from the fact that at each stage of the production and distribution process it was able from its own resources to accept and react to variations in demand. It alone was capable of carrying over two-thirds of its production in its own fleet of specially designed ships. It alone was able to advertise the 'Chiquita' brand name and to revolutionize the commercial exploitation of the banana. Its large capital investment in purchasing and equipping its plantations allowed it to increase its source of supply, so as to overcome any effects from disease or bad weather. It was enabled by the scale of its capital investment to introduce a distribution system for a highly perishable commodity through the extensive use of refrigeration facilities, giving it a strategic advantage over all its competitors. In particular, the ability to control the timing of the ripening process close to the ultimate retail market within the Community gave it an important element of strategic leverage, placing all its competitors at a disadvantage. The combined effect of these measures led the Court to characterize the concept of dominance as follows: 'The position of economic strength enjoyed by an undertaking enabling it . . . to behave to an appreciable extent independently of its competitors and customers and ultimately of its consumers. In general, it derives from a combination of several factors which taken separately are not determinative'.[2]

Not long after in the *Hoffmann-La Roche* case, the Court gave a rather more extended definition to the concept of dominance:

The dominant position . . . relates to a position of economic strength enjoyed by an undertaking which enables it to prevent effective competition being maintained on the relevant market by affording it the power to behave to an appreciable extent independently of its competitors, its customers and ultimately of the consumers. Such a position does not preclude some competition which it does where there is a monopoly or quasi-monopoly but enables the undertaking which profits by it, if not to determine, at least to have an appreciable influence on the conditions under which that competition will develop, and in any case to act largely in disregard of it so long as such conduct does not operate to its detriment.

. . . The existence of a dominant position may derive from several factors which taken separately are not necessarily determinative but among these factors a highly important one is the existence of very large market shares.[3]

Such comments by the Court need to be illustrated by reference to specific markets in cases decided by it. In *Hoffmann-La Roche*, the Court found that La Roche held the following market shares within the Community:

Vitamin A — 47 per cent

Vitamin B$_2$ — 86 per cent

Vitamin B$_3$ — 64 per cent

Vitamin B$_6$ — 95 per cent

Vitamin C — 68 per cent

Vitamin E — 70 per cent

Vitamin H — 95 per cent

---

[2] [1978] 1 CMLR 486, 487.
[3] Case 85/76 [1979] ECR 461, 520: 3 CMLR 211, 274, often called the *Vitamins* case.

In 1974, the turnover of the company in the Common Market comprised 60 per cent of the total sale of vitamins worldwide. The group had altogether some 5,000 customers, many of whom were large multinational companies who purchased in large orders the entire range of vitamins produced, particularly under pressure of the fidelity rebate scheme already discussed. On the basis of these figures, for all except Vitamin A there was an overwhelming presumption of dominance from the market share alone, which gave Hoffman-La Roche a position of strength, allowing it freedom of action in responding to changes in market conditions. In the case of Vitamin A, where the market share was lower, the factors upon which the Court placed heavy reliance were the great disparity between its market share and that of its next largest competitors, and the wide technological lead which it enjoyed over them. The absence of real challenge in many of the markets, and the extent to which the Roche sales network was more highly developed than any of its competitors, were also factors that could be taken into account.

On the other hand, whilst the Commission had placed weight on the size of the company and the volume of turnover it provided, the Court itself did not accept that size and turnover alone could establish dominance. The Court also placed far less reliance than the Commission on both the range of products produced by Roche and the fact that it had retained market share over a continuous period of time, pointing out that this could be explained by a large number of other factors, including simply its ability to compete effectively in a normal manner.

1.2 ITS APPLICABILITY TO SMALL MARKETS AS WELL AS LARGE

However, the concept of dominance is not limited to large-scale markets but is also found in markets that are narrow, where one undertaking has, through legislation or other circumstances, obtained a monopoly or a very strong position which completely or substantially reduces competition. The earliest example was *General Motors Continental*.[4] This involved granting type approval for GM cars manufactured in Germany but which required certification before import into Belgium; the cars in question were parallel imports for whose certification GM Continental had charged excessive prices. After the complaints had been raised, GM reduced their charges to actual cost and refunded the excess, before the Commission's investigation had even begun. On appeal from the Commission's decision, the European Court of Justice annulled the decision, indicating that it felt the Commission had been unjustified in raising under the Article what appeared to be so trivial a case, especially as General Motors had corrected the overcharge made. Nevertheless, the case had a certain value as a precedent, though actually more relevant to market integration then to excessive pricing.[5]

Any undertaking which holds an exclusive legal right for the performance of a statutory duty, delegated by a State or public authority, must in carrying out its duties not abuse the powers conferred so as to enhance its other objectives, such as rendering less attractive the

---

[4] Case 26/75 [1975] ECR 1367: [1976] 1 CMLR 95.

[5] A direct descendant of *General Motors Continental* is *British Leyland* v. *Commission* Case 226/84 [1986] ECR 3263: [1987] 1 CMLR 185, where the Commission's fine on British Leyland was upheld. The actions of which the Commission complained were BL's refusal to issue national type approval certificates for Leyland cars imported into the United Kingdom other than through official channels, and for charging £150 for certificates of conformity to those national type approvals for those dealers and individuals who sought to import Metros with left-hand drive from the Continent.

possibility of parallel imports. In *Hilti* v. *Commission*[6] the Court of First Instance ruled that it was an abuse of dominant position for a company owning a patent, required by national legislation to grant a licence of right, to demand a fee six times higher than that ultimately awarded by the Comptroller of Patents, thereby prolonging the proceedings needlessly. *Hugin* v. *Commission*[7] (European Court 1979) shows that dominance can occur even in a market for spare parts. In this case, the product market was Hugin cash registers, although the European Court of Justice ruled that no effect on trade between Member States had been shown by its practices. An example of narrow geographical markets in which dominance is shown are the 'essential facilities' cases discussed in the next chapter, where even a single harbour or airport within the Community may be held to be a market of sufficient significance for Article 82 to be applicable.

The ownership of intellectual property rights sometimes provides a dominant position in a product covered by the relevant rights. In *Volvo* v. *Eric Veng (UK)* the car makers Volvo sued Veng for breach of its registered designs covering a front wing panel for a particular Volvo model. The prime issue in the case (an Article 234 reference from the High Court) was whether Volvo's refusal to grant a licence to Veng to manufacture such panels was an abuse by Volvo of its undoubted dominant position with regard to that part; in a parallel case decided on the same day the Court also rendered its opinion under an Article 234 reference in the *Renault* case.[8] Renault had claimed monopoly rights under Italian law for its ornamental body panels. It was accepted by the Court in these cases that, although under national law Volvo or Renault could validly secure the exclusive right to manufacture these panels and thereby obtain complete dominance of that product, this alone did not justify an adverse finding under Article 82. Dominance alone, even as to 100 per cent, is insufficient as it is not the monopoly or quasi-monopoly that can be challenged but its abuse.[9]

One hundred per cent control of a particular product or service market may arise under other national legislation; in the *Magill* case, finally decided by the European Court in 1995,[10] the law of copyright gave RTE in the Republic of Ireland complete control of the compilation of programme schedules for radio and television, which were therefore not available (absent the grant of an appropriate licence by their owners) to those entrepreneurs who wished to publish weekly magazines including such details. National legislation conferring a monopoly may also place a business in such a position of dominance; an example was the granting of sole rights in The Netherlands and Spain for certain categories of letter delivery to the national postal authorities to the exclusion of commercial organizations who wished to compete for this business.[11]

---

[6] Case T-30/89 [1991] ECR II-1439: [1992] 4 CMLR 16.

[7] Case 22/78 [1979] ECR 1869: 3 CMLR 345.

[8] *Maxicar and Others* v. *Renault* Case 53/87 [1988] ECR 6039: [1990] 4 CMLR 265: *Volvo* v. *Veng* Case 238/87 [1988] ECR 6211: [1989] 4 CMLR 122.

[9] For an example of the same principle applied by the English High Court, see *Pitney Bowes* v. *Francotype* [1990] 3 CMLR 466.

[10] Case C-241/91P [1995] ECR I-743: 4 CMLR 718. At earlier stages there had been similar Community cases involving the BBC and ITP in the United Kingdom. See Cases T-69 and 70/89 [1991] ECR II-535, 575: 4 CMLR 669, 745.

[11] *Dutch Courier Services* [1990] 4 CMLR 947. The Commission decision was however annulled by the European Court on procedural grounds. Cases C-48 and 66/90 [1992] ECR I-565: [1993] 5 CMLR 316. See also *Spanish Courier Services* [1991] 4 CMLR 560.

1.3 SUPER DOMINANT COMPANIES: THEIR 'SPECIAL RESPONSIBILITY'

The wording of Article 82 appears to state that an undertaking will either be in a dominant position in relation to a given market or will not, and no mention is made of any separate categories of dominance. Nevertheless there have been some cases where the market share of the defendant undertaking has been so large, amounting to a percentage in excess of 90 per cent, that the 'special responsibility' of dominant companies with very high market shares referred to by the ECJ in *Tetrapak (No. 2)*[12] has apparently led to a more onerous or comprehensive obligation being placed on them not to engage in particular practices, such as predatory or excessive pricing or refusal to deal. A recent example of this approach is found in *Compagnie Maritime Belge* v. *Commission*[13] which involved selective price cutting and use of 'fighting ships' by members of a shipping conference holding between them more than 90 per cent of the relevant market, in order to drive out a particular rival which had sought to compete with them. Fennelly A-G made this point with particular clarity: 'Article 82 cannot be interpreted as permitting monopolists or quasi-monopolists *to exploit the very significant power which their super dominance confers* so as to preclude the emergence of either a new or additional competitor'. Though the European Court itself did not make use of precisely the same language, it nevertheless placed emphasis in its judgment on the significance of the market share of the conference members being more than 90 per cent.

1.4 COMPANIES WITH LOWER MARKET SHARES

At the other end of the scale, the Court in *Metro (No. 2)*[14] made it clear that no question of dominance could arise when a supermarket chain had less than 10 per cent of the general electronic equipment market for leisure purposes and less than 7 per cent of the colour television market. In practice, it seems unlikely that any undertaking having a market share of less than 25 per cent will be held to have a dominant position. Whilst neither the Court nor the Commission has made a firm statement to this effect, it is noteworthy that recital 15 to the Merger Regulation 4064/89 sets out a presumption that a concentration significantly impeding competition cannot be created if the parties' joint market shares do not exceed 25 per cent. Over that percentage dominance can become an issue: then the larger the percentage share, the more difficult to avoid the presumption that the undertaking benefits from a lesser degree of control from normal competitive pressures. Notwithstanding the lesser emphasis placed by the Court than the Commission on levels of market share in *United Brands*, the Commission continues to place great emphasis on such percentages, and once these can be shown to reach 45 per cent it becomes almost impossible to claim that an undertaking lacks power unless there is another undertaking in the same market with a share of equivalent size.[15]

In *British Airways/Virgin*[16] the market share held by British Airways of 39.7 per cent of air

---

[12] Case C-333/94 P [1996] ECR I-5951 [1997] 4 CMLR 662.

[13] Cases C-395/96 P [2000] ECR I-1365: 4 CMLR 1076.

[14] Case 75/84 [1986] ECR 3021: [1987] 1 CMLR 118.

[15] In *AKZO* v. *Commission* (see pp.286–7 below) AKZO's share of the relevant product market was found to be about 50 per cent, regarded as sufficient to justify a presumption of dominant position.

[16] [2000] 4 CMLR 999: on appeal to the CFI as Case T-219/99. See Ch. 15, p. 295.

ticket sales in the United Kingdom, when the next largest competitor airline had sales of only 5.5 per cent, was held sufficient to confer dominance when coupled with other market factors such as the number of routes operated to and from the United Kingdom, its large holding of slots at major UK airports, and other factors.

1.5 FACTORS INVOLVED IN ASSESSING DOMINANCE

The identification however of a dominant position is never solely a quantitative task. The Commission and courts have also to take into account that 'combination of several factors' which is the qualitative nature of the relevant market. The number and strength of competitors will always be important; if there is a wide gap between the market share and resources of the principal company in the market compared with the next largest companies, this will be significant. Also relevant will be the ability of competitors as the result of unused productive capacity to respond promptly to output reduction or expansion or price increases by the principal company or market leader. The likelihood of new entry will depend on the barriers that exist; these may be inherent in the nature of the market or have been brought about rather by the actions of the dominant company.

Barriers inherent in the nature of the market will include Community or Member State regulations, for example, those dealing with health and safety, economies of scale or scope, and the risk of having to make large capital investments to enter the market that may turn out to be irrecoverable (referred to as 'sunk costs'). Barriers caused by the dominant company itself might involve the use of intellectual property rights such as patents and copyrights, the need for vertical integration for purposes of distribution, and the need (especially with consumer products) for heavy expenditure on marketing and brand promotion, and in some cases access to scarce raw materials. Sometimes dominance is alleged by the Commission to have been enhanced by the very acts which have been complained about since potential new entrants may fear to enter a market where incumbents are known to react vigorously against new entrants, for example, by predatory pricing as indeed was well illustrated in the shipping conference cases such as *Compagnie Maritime Belge*.

2. THE DEFINITIONS OF RELEVANT GEOGRAPHIC AND PRODUCT MARKETS

2.1 THE GEOGRAPHIC MARKET

Market share percentages only have meaning when the market to which they relate has been defined. The search for the relevant geographic market begins with the words of the Article: '. . . within the Common Market or in a substantial part of it . . .' A Member State's territory will often provide a natural geographic setting equivalent to the commercial area in which competition is taking place; in early cases the assumption was readily made that geographic markets would be, if not the entire area of the Community, then no smaller than an individual Member State. This tendency was first challenged in the *Sugar Cartel* case[17] when

---

[17] The Court here accepted Southern Germany as a geographic market for sales of sugar. Cases 40–48, 50, 54, 56, 111, 113, 114/73 [1975] ECR 1991–4: [1976] 1 CMLR 463–5.

the Court accepted the Commission's contention that a substantial part or region of a Member State could also constitute a market given a sufficient volume of sales.

In each case the parties concerned and the Commission will advance economic arguments to justify their contention, including any existing barriers to the free movement of goods, consumer buying habits, and costs of transporting goods in from neighbouring areas. The easier it is to bring goods in from a distance, using the improved transport systems now found in many parts of the Community, the wider the likely market will be. It is usually in the interests of the undertakings to suggest that a market is a relatively wide area so that their individual shares are reduced. The Commission in contrast will normally argue that narrower areas form natural individual markets. The Commission will often reach a conclusion that, since undertakings organize their distribution arrangements on a national basis, this implies that they regard such national territories as separate markets, an approach adopted, for example, in both *United Brands* and *Michelin*. If national legislation also creates different market conditions in individual Member States, this too will tend to establish them as separate markets.

The Court has shown in at least one Article 234 opinion that in this context it is prepared to look beyond the geographical focus of the immediate case and to define the geographic market more broadly if circumstances require. In *Alsatel* v. *Novasam*[18] (European Court 1988) the original dispute arose when the Alsace Telephone Authority tried to enforce payment from Novasam, an employment agency, as compensation for Novasam's early termination of a long-term telephone rental installation. Under the terms of an admittedly onerous contract, Novasam as the price of early cancellation had to pay some three-quarters of the remaining payments for the original duration of the agreement. Moreover, the agreement stated that if the equipment provided was at any time supplemented so as to increase Novasam's annual rental by more than 25 per cent, then this automatically extended the contract for a further fifteen years. Alsatel alone was entitled to make any extension or modification to the equipment. The making and enforcement of such an onerous contract was found by the Court to be potentially abusive but the relevant geographic market was considered to be not simply Alsace (with which the immediate case was concerned) but the whole of France. Businesses such as Novasam were not limited to obtaining telephone equipment from Alsatel but could purchase or rent it from any part of France. In this wider market Alsatel had a market share well below that required to constitute dominance.

Another French case referred to the Court under Article 234 on this type of issue was the *Bodson* v. *Pompes Funèbres* case[19] (European Court 1988). The Court did not reach a finding on the facts as to whether Pompes Funèbres had a dominant position, this being left for the national Court to decide. Nevertheless, it pointed out that Pompes Funèbres held the exclusive concession for conducting funerals (apart from the provision of church services, flowers, and monuments) for some 2,800 of those 5,000 local communes in France in which the performance of external aspects of conducting funerals had been delegated exclusively to one specified private firm. These 5,000 communes covered 45 per cent of the entire French population. The contrast between this and the *Alsatel* case is that the individual purchaser of funeral services could in practice clearly not choose from a wide variety of enterprises but was obliged to use the firm or firms authorized by the local commune. The Court stressed

---

[18] Case 247/86 [1988] ECR 5987: [1990] 4 CMLR 434.
[19] Case 30/87 [1988] ECR 2479: [1989] 4 CMLR 984.

that in assessing dominance (as well as the effect on trade between Member States) it was the share of the population affected by the exclusive allocation that was crucial, rather than simply the total percentage of communes affected, though in this case, this factor was not crucial to market definition.

2.2 THE PRODUCT OR SERVICE MARKET

The definition of product markets is, if anything, even more elusive. There are few products for which there are not substitutes of some kind, and the interrelationship of quality, price, and availability is in nearly all cases difficult to analyse with precision. Cross-elasticity of demand between substitute products has been at issue in a number of cases, notably *United Brands*, in which the banana's unique characteristics were considered in meticulous detail in the context of an ultimately unsuccessful argument that it should be considered as part of a wider product market including fruit of different kinds. The Court upheld the Commission's view that in terms of year-round avail-ability, price, suitability for particular types of consumer, notably the very young and very old, and other characteristics, the product market could not be said to include any other kind of fruit, a decision whose effect increased the market shares held by United Brands. This part of the decision has however been attacked by a number of commentators on the grounds that the analysis by the Court of substitutability of different fruits for bananas was based on inadequate economic data or surveys to show accurately the cross-elasticity of demand between the banana and such other fruits. The interchangeability of products was also considered by the Court in *Hoffmann-La Roche*, where the Court found, *inter alia*, that a simple product could be considered as belonging to separate product markets if applied for more than one end use. Generally, however, the more emphasis placed on the degree of market power possessed by the defendant, the clearer the process of identifying the relevant market.

3. LEADING JUDGMENTS OF THE EUROPEAN COURT ON MARKET DEFINITION

3.1 *AHMED SAAED*

One of the leading cases on market definition arose on an Article 234 reference from a German court. In *Ahmed Saaed*,[20] two travel firms in West Germany had sold airline tickets at prices which substantially undercut the official Federal government approved tariffs, exploiting anomalies in the pricing system. The tickets they purchased were for a journey from Portugal via a German airport to a third country at rates cheaper than the shorter journey from that German airport to the same foreign destination. Under German law, such opportunism is not encouraged, but is a criminal offence. On the appeal by the travel firm against their convictions for such ticket sales, the Court ruled that the product market in Article 82 cases was not limited to different forms of air travel, namely charter and scheduled flights, but included all other means of travelling between the same points, including rail and coach services. It emphasized, however, that every case would turn on its own facts.

[20] Case 66/86 [1989] ECR 803: [1990] 4 CMLR 102.

3.2 *HILTI*

In two important later cases the market assessment of the Commission was directly in issue. In *Hilti* v. *Commission*[21] the Commission's definition was challenged before the Court of First Instance and the European Court, being regarded as crucial to the eventual outcome of the case. Hilti, a Luxembourg company, had patent protection for both its nail guns and the cartridge strips inserted into the guns, but not for the individual nails which the gun fired from that strip. Hilti argued that the product market here could not be limited to powder-actuated fastening systems (the technical description of the particular type of nail gun) but covered a variety of other fastening methods used on building sites. It pointed out that such fastenings could also be created in certain circumstances with hand or power drills, spot welding, screws, bolts, and nuts. The choice of method would depend on a variety of factors, including the technical problems of the particular materials to be fastened, the load it would need to bear, the skill of the operators, and the time available for carrying out work, quite apart from the cost of the fixing materials.

The Commission had regarded powder-actuated fastening systems in certain situations as giving builders particular advantages. These included versatility of use, easy portability, and speed of operations, even if there were some materials which these systems could not fix and some loads which such fixings could not sustain. Moreover, the nails and cartridges used were often considerably more expensive than alternatives, such as screws and bolts. Nevertheless, in its view powder-actuated fastening systems could be properly regarded as a product market separate from that of the alternatives because the cost of fixing represented only a very small element in the total cost of building; the relatively minor variation in cost attributable to the use of that system made it unlikely that a small change in the price of Hilti's own guns, cartridge strips, or nails would cause a shift by customers to an alternative product. The Court of First Instance upheld the Commission's decision and its fine of six million ECUs. Hilti's share in the UK market for nails was found to be between 70 and 80 per cent. The Court also confirmed that not only were guns, cartridge strips, and nails all separate product markets, but also that the powder-actuated fastening system which they comprised was sufficiently different from other fastening systems to justify a finding that the degree of substitutability between them was relatively low. In rejecting the appeal from the Court of First Instance the European Court emphasized that it would not normally disturb findings of fact by the lower court unless it had a clear sense that the evidence had become distorted, which was not the case here. Moreover, the Court ruled that if the Commission defines a product market on the basis of factual evidence, as opposed to supposition, the Court may require the appellant to prove that his different version of the market is correct and cannot merely rely on showing that the facts on which the Commission relied could be interpreted in a different way.

3.3 *TETRAPAK (NO. 2)*

An even more complex case on market definition was *Tetrapak (No. 2)*[22] in 1996. Tetrapak were alleged to have had a dominant position in four related markets. Those for carton

---

[21] See n. 6. The ECJ report is Case C-53/92P [1994] ECR I-667: 4 CMLR 614.

[22] The ECJ report is Case C-333/94P [1996] ECR I-5951: [1997] 4 CMLR 662. The CFI report is Case T-83/91 [1994] ECR II-755: [1997] 4 CMLR 726.

machinery and cartons for UHT (aseptic) milk, and carton machinery and cartons for ordinary milk. It is, of course, sold in glass and plastic bottles as well as in cartons, and market shares for these different types of container had varied over the fifteen years to 1991 with which the Commission had been concerned. The Commission found that each of the four markets was separate because the technology of carton manufacturing for aseptic and for ordinary milk was quite different. Under other forms of packaging, aseptic products presented little competitive threat to aseptic milk cartons. Tetrapak's argument that it provided an 'integrated' packaging system combining machinery and cartons with consequent public health advantages was not accepted, on the basis that in the absence of mandatory consumer protection rules any undertaking should be free to manufacture consumable items, such as cartons, intended for use in equipment being manufactured by others.

The share held by Tetrapak in the four markets varied; in the two aseptic markets it had unquestioned dominance, with over 90 per cent of the markets for both cartons and machinery. In the two markets related to ordinary milk its market share was lower, about 55 per cent, giving it an overall market of some 78 per cent for cartons of all kinds. Rather than relying, however, on the lower market share for a finding of dominance separately in the non-aseptic markets, the European Court chose to uphold the Court of First Instance and the Commission in their finding that the aseptic and non-aseptic markets were so closely associated that, taking them together, 'Tetrapak's practices on the non-aseptic markets are liable to be caught by Article 82 of the Treaty without its being necessary to establish the existence for a dominant position on those markets taken in isolation, since that undertaking's leading position on the non-aseptic markets, combined with the close associative links between those markets and the aseptic markets, gave Tetrapak freedom of conduct compared with the other economic operators on the non-aseptic market, such as to impose on it a special responsibility under Article 82 to maintain genuine undistorted competition on those markets'.

It is only fair to record that some leading commentators, including Korah,[23] have criticized this ruling on the basis that the finding of dominance in the second market as a result of its close association with a primary market is a dangerously wide doctrine, which could be used to support findings of dominance in secondary markets where the company really had relatively little market power. The facts in the *Tetrapak (No. 2)* case, however, were unusual and particularly strong. The products being packaged in the two markets were similar and many of the same companies acquired product from Tetrapak in both markets, even though only 35 per cent of Tetrapak's customers purchased both types of equipment. Tetrapak's control of the aseptic market was almost a complete monopoly, enabling it to do business on very favourable terms in the ordinary milk market. It is possible, however, that there would be few other cases where the links between the two relevant markets are so strong as to justify such a finding.

---

[23] '*Tetrapak (No. 2)*—Lack of Reasoning in Court's Judgment' (1997) 18 ECLR 98–102.

4. THE INFLUENCE OF THE MERGER REGULATION ON MARKET DEFINITION BY THE COMMISSION

4.1 THE 1997 NOTICE ON MARKET DEFINITION

Market definition plays a key role not only in Article 82 cases, but also in cases brought under the Merger Regulation which are considerably more numerous. The need to carry out a large number of market definition analyses from 1990 onwards under the Merger Regulation (with its strict time limits) has alerted the Commission to the importance of a methodical and consistent approach to market definition in all cases. There is truth in the suggestion that in its early Article 82 cases the nature and scope of the abusive conduct identified was sometimes allowed to play too important a role in the identification of the geographic market in which the dominance was sought to be established. The Commission Notice on Market Definition in 1997 was not therefore primarily intended to announce any revolutionary new approach to the process of analysis, but to provide reassurance that the Commission would seek a consistent methodology in both Article 82 and merger cases. It does, however, point out the significant difference between market definition in the two situations. In merger cases the focus is inevitably on the future consequences of the concentration and the probability, or even possibility, of important changes in the future, for example as a result of changes in distribution, patent, or technological advances. In Article 82 cases the focus has to be on the past conduct of the particular undertaking and the Commission must be at least primarily concerned with the way markets have worked over that period. However, in many cases the decision as to the relevant market, in both product and geographical terms, will ultimately be reached on the same basis in both merger and Article 82 cases.

In its Notice[24] the Commission sets out the basis upon which it defines both product and geographic markets. Relevant product markets are defined as comprising 'all those products and/or services which are regarded as interchangeable or substitutable by the consumer, by reason of the product's characteristics, their prices and their intended use.' Relevant geographic markets are defined as '. . . the area in which the undertakings concerned are involved in the supply and demand of products or services, in which the conditions of competition are sufficiently homogeneous and which can be distinguished from neighbouring areas because the conditions of competition are appreciably different in those areas'. The Commission begins by pointing out that this concept of relevant market is closely related to the particular objectives with which the individual case is concerned. In an Article 82 case, its focus is on whether the undertaking in question can behave, to an appreciable extent, independently of competitors and its customers; and this ability will often, though not invariably, follow from its possession of a large market share in the supply of products or services. The assessment inevitably has to work backwards in time since the determination of whether a breach of Article 82 has occurred is not made in the abstract but in respect of a particular past period, which may only cover a few months, but is more frequently a period of some years.

The Notice goes on to identify three main competitive constraints from which relevant

---

24 [1997] OJ C372/5: [1998] 4 CMLR 177.

product markets can be identified: demand substitutability, supply substitutability, and potential competition. Of these, demand substitution, with its focus on consumer preferences, is considered the most relevant and important. This follows the precedent of the United States Department of Justice Antitrust Division Merger Guidelines and of the practices of other leading antitrust authorities throughout the world. The key test is the natural reaction of customers to a small (5 to 10 per cent) but permanent rise in prices;[25] if its effect is to cause customers to switch to readily available substitutes, or to suppliers located elsewhere, to the point that the original price rise becomes unprofitable owing to the loss of sales incurred, then these additional suppliers will be included in the scope of the relevant market. However, if there is little or no such switching by customers, then the existing market patterns are likely to be adopted as the relevant market. In the case of a dominant company already charging particularly high prices, it is possible that the prevailing price may already have been substantially increased above market levels and this will be taken into account (often referred to as the 'Cellophane fallacy').[26]

By contrast, 'supply side' substitutability is a measurement of the degree to which suppliers can switch production to a new product quickly and market it without incurring significant additional costs or risks, in response to small and permanent changes in the relative prices of existing suppliers. When this occurs it will naturally have some 'disciplinary' effect on the pricing behaviour of the original suppliers in respect of all products with which the 'switchers' can compete. This form of competition may be adequate even if the new suppliers can only provide part of the range of products sourced from the original suppliers. By contrast, if the would-be new suppliers would not be able to enter the market without first building new factories or making other substantial investments over time, then these will not be regarded as part of the relevant product market. Examples are given of products where branding is important, such as soft drinks, where the value of the brand can only be built up by substantial advertising over time. For the same reason potential, rather than actual, competition for supplies is not given great weight, unless there is some real evidence of a company with both the ability and the intention to enter the market in the foreseeable future.

The Commission goes on to list a number of factors which it regards as important in the assessment both of demand and supply. In some cases the issue will be relatively straightforward and narrow; if a particular product is not substitutable for another, then the required market shares will fall short of the necessary level and no further enquiries will be needed. In other cases a precise market definition will be required before the issue of dominance can be decided. Information will then be sought from the principal companies as to their activities, the range of prices they pay, and the increases they would be prepared to accept from existing suppliers. Consumer preferences may be relevant and existing data from market research studies can be utilized, though ad hoc surveys in response to a particular case are treated with more reserve. Evidence of past price changes in response to market 'shocks' will also be taken into account. There are particular barriers or costs associated with switching from one product to another. These will also be considered; they may include regulatory barriers or simply substantial capital cost incurred for the provision of the manufacturing capacity or promotional expenditure required.

---

[25] Often referred to as the 'SSNIP' test, standing for 'Small but significant non-transitory increase in price'.
[26] *US v. du Pont* (the 'Cellophane' case) 351 US 377: 76 S. Ct 994 (1956).

4.2 SOME PROBLEMS IN ASSESSING DOMINANCE

There is thus no lack of both Court and Commission case law on the interpretation and application of the concept of dominance. It would, however, be misleading to give the impression that the ascertainment in individual cases of whether dominance exists is necessarily straightforward. Whilst in some cases its existence is clear and indisputable, especially where market shares represent a very high percentage and there are barriers to entry, there are other cases where the basis on which dominance has been alleged by the Commission has given rise to strong criticism by both economists and legal commentators.

These difficulties begin with the initial definition provided by the ECJ in *Hoffmann-La Roche*, with its emphasis on 'economic strength . . . affording [the dominant company] power to behave to an appreciable extent independently of its competitors. . . .' It is clear that a large market share is important but not necessarily determinative. In other words, this definition embodies not only quantitative but also qualitative elements and the balance between them has to be worked out on a case by case basis. In presenting such a formula the Court seems to suggest that it will be possible to decide in each case whether an undertaking is or is not dominant.

In recent years however the approach of the ECJ and CFI has changed; 'the special responsibility' of all dominant companies not to abuse their position has been supplemented by a new requirement on the 'super dominant' as already mentioned and as has been pointed out by Whish in the latest edition of his 'Competition Law'.[27] The cases (*Tetrapak No. 2* and *Compagnie Maritime Belge*) in which this special obligation has been referred to, have all been in the 90–95 per cent market share range; the concept is clearly to be applied with restraint, not simply to all companies with a market share well above the 50 per cent level. But this development, however desirable in its application to the particular facts of those cases, goes far beyond the *ECS/Akzo* presumption of dominance at the much lower level of 50 per cent and appears to contain the following message to undertakings. 'We can tell you in broad terms at what market share you may start to be dominant but your responsibility as a dominant company is not simply to refrain from particular activities; it is to refrain from all activities inappropriate to your individual market share considered in the context of all other circumstances'. As applied, for example in *Compagnie Maritime Belge*, this means that price cuts not actually below average variable costs but made for the purpose of excluding a competitor from the market might still for this reason be abusive, even if equivalent reductions made by a dominant company with a smaller market share would not have been.

While we have always known that undertakings with non-dominant positions are free to indulge in pricing or marketing strategies that a dominant company may not adopt, for example in the framing of discount or rebate schemes, it appears that it is the degree of dominance which may now determine the exact classifications of those actions or strategies that will be characterized as abusive; in other words a 'sliding scale' approach to dominance.

A further difficulty in the application of the concept of dominance is that the definition found in *Hoffmann-La Roche* is itself hard to apply to individual cases. This is because it does not analyse the way in which economic markets actually work, which is that even dominant companies find that their pricing strategy is to some extent controlled by consumers; the

---

[27] R. Whish, *Competition Law*, 4th edn. (Butterworths, 2001), pp.162–3.

demand curve for their products in that market imposes a discipline or restraint upon even the company with a very large market share.[28] Competitors, even if considerably weaker than the dominant company, will themselves sometimes be able to force the dominant company to change its pricing strategy if they themselves reduce prices, and if the dominant company wishes to remain at a profit maximizing level. If it was possible in each market to determine what was the 'competitive price level' then it might also be possible to decide if at any particular time in that market whether the alleged dominant company was pricing above it; but in practice economists are unanimous in saying that the competitive price level in a given market is usually impossible to measure accurately. It may be possible to have a 'hunch' about it but legal prohibitions should have a firmer basis. A better test, which at least stays closer to the *Hoffmann-La Roche* definition, may be that the probability of the dominant company being able to act independently of the market is to be measured by its ability to restrict current output in the market, which may give it in turn power over price and ability thereby to hurt consumers. In conclusion therefore the problem with dominance as a concept is that it is often too complex to serve as a satisfactory criterion for determining jurisdiction; it may be difficult indeed to know if it exists until after completing a detailed examination of the market including the nature and effects of the alleged abusive acts. Clearly this is not always the problem as there are some situations where the existence of dominance is obvious. Nevertheless clearer guidelines are needed for the many situations where the answer is far from obvious and where present Court jurisprudence provides inadequate assistance for the guidance of companies with a reasonable degree of market power and their advisers

It should also be noted that the Commission has now proposed, in its suggested amendments to the Merger Regulation put forward in December 2002,[29] that the definition of 'dominance' in Article 2 should (for the purposes of the Regulation) be expanded so as to cover all forms of unilateral effects which the concentration may bring about. This proposed amendment to the Regulation (which has not yet been accepted by Member States) would have the effect of separating the concept of dominance under the Regulation from that established by case law of the Community Courts in relation to Article 82.

---

[28] See D. Ridyard, 'Exclusionary Pricing and Price Discrimination Abuses under Art. 82—An Economic Analysis' [2002] 23 ECLR 286–303.

[29] See Ch. 18, pp.394–7. The possible effect of the jurisprudence of the Community Courts Under Art. 82 on the application of Art. 2 of the Merger Regulation is sometimes referred to as the risk of 'cross-contamination'.

15
ARTICLE 82: ABUSE

1. INTRODUCTION

1.1 THE NATURE OF ABUSE

Article 82 does not attempt to provide a definition of abuse, but does give a number of examples, namely:

(*a*) directly or indirectly imposing unfair purchase or selling prices or other unfair trading conditions;

(*b*) limiting production, markets, or technical development to the prejudice of consumers;

(*c*) applying dissimilar conditions to equivalent transactions with other trading parties, thereby placing them at a competitive disadvantage; and

(*d*) making the conclusion of contracts subject to acceptance by the other parties of supplementary obligations which, by their nature or according to commercial usage, have no connection with the subject of such contracts.

The fundamental nature of the concept of abuse was addressed quite early by the European Court in *Hoffmann-La Roche*[1] and described as:

an objective concept relating to the behaviour of an undertaking in a dominant position which is such as to influence the structure of a market where, as the result of the very presence of the undertaking in question, the degree of competition is weakened and which, through recourse to methods different from those which condition normal competition in products or services on the basis of the transactions of commercial operators, has the effect of hindering the maintenance of the degree of competition still existing in the market or the growth of that competition.

This definition covers not only the illustrations of abuse set out in the text of the Article, but also a large number of other practices not specifically mentioned, but which have been considered in the case law of the Community Courts. The majority of these cases in which such practices have been defined and analysed have been appeals from decisions of the Commission, under Article 230, which have often involved the imposition of a fine on the dominant undertaking. There have also been a small number of such cases brought to the ECJ under Article 234 from national courts, which have required the opinion of the ECJ on such issues.

---

[1] *Hoffmann-La Roche* Case 85/76 [1979] ECR 461, 541: 3 CMLR 211, 290.

Abuses are often classified as either exclusionary or exploitative, though the Commission regards the distinction as not of great importance. An exclusionary abuse is one of those of the kind referred to in the quotation above from *Hoffman-La Roche*, where its effects are primarily on the structure of the market, for example by weakening competitors through raising their costs, refusing to deal with them or denying access to essential facilities. By contrast exploitative abuses are aimed directly at consumers, for example by imposing excessive prices or unreasonable terms and conditions; of course a successful use of exclusionary abuses may well lead on to subsequent use of exploitative ones, or they may be used simultaneously and in combination. Under Section 2 of the Sherman Act, however, mere exploitation abuses would not normally be prohibited.

1.2 CATEGORIES OF ABUSE

In reviewing the extensive case law relating to abuse, it is helpful to deal in turn with the principal categories, as follows:

(i)   those connected with pricing, including excessive and predatory pricing, discriminatory and cross-subsidized pricing, and rebate and discount schemes with anti-competitive features;

(ii) those involving a refusal to deal by the dominant company in respect of goods or services, either absolutely or except on unreasonable terms (such as a 'tying' obligation);

(iii) those involving a refusal either by an individual proprietor or collective societies to grant licences of intellectual property rights (or otherwise to abuse their exploitation);

(iv) those involving a refusal to grant access to essential facilities; and

(v)   other miscellaneous acts, including abuse of legal proceedings or insisting upon unreasonable terms and conditions with contractual partners.

The Commission's ability to issue directives to Member States under Article 86(3) is of particular relevance here since it is able to identify aspects of conduct which it regards as likely to interfere with competition in markets where previous dominance by the national monopoly supplier, such as a national telephone company or other dominant undertaking, can now be challenged in such sectors as communications, energy, and transport. An example is the Notice[2] from the Commission on the application of the competition rules to 'access agreements in the telecommunications sector'. The Notice not only summarizes the access principles derived from a large number of Commission decisions, some of which are considered below, but also explains how Article 82 should be applied consistently across various sectors involved in the provision of new multimedia communication services, especially in the principle of access to system 'gateways'. Many of the particular abuses referred to, including refusal to provide access to competitors, withdrawal of existing access, exclusionary practices within networks, tying, excessive or predatory pricing, and discrimination, reflect the case law under Article 82 from other sectors, discussed below.

It is also important to emphasize that many of the leading decisions of the Commission

---

[2] Press Release IP/98/309 of 31 March 1998 announced the adoption of the final text of the Notice, which is found at [1998] OJ C265/2 and [1998] 5 CMLR 821.

and judgment of the Community Courts in respect of this Article have been controversial and subject to criticism by both lawyers and economists, principally in respect of alleged failure to analyse in sufficient depth the various types of abusive conduct, in particular those dealing with price and with access to essential facilities. It has been alleged that some of the practices characterized as abusive reflect normal competitive practice for larger companies.

2. EXCESSIVE PRICING

2.1 EARLY CASES

The wording of Article 82(*a*) refers to the imposition of 'unfair' purchase or selling prices. The charging of excessive prices clearly falls within this description. The criteria by which prices can be assessed as 'excessive' are however in practice often difficult to establish and there is less authority from either the Commission or from Community Court cases to rely upon than might have been expected.

The Court first dealt with this issue in the rather unusual case of *General Motors Continental*[3] discussed in Chapter 14 (p.270) but the circumstances of the case meant that its value as a precedent was limited. The charge made by General Motors for the approval certificates required by importers of its cars into Belgium (made only over a relatively short period) was accepted as being excessive by all parties and had been refunded by General Motors to those customers before the Commission's investigation had begun. In overruling therefore the finding of the Commission that on these facts a breach of Article 82 had occurred, the Court did not need to go into depth into the concept of an 'excessive' price. The decision was nevertheless valuable to the Commission in showing that in an appropriate case the use of the pricing mechanism by undertakings to interfere in the process of integrating national markets (by making parallel imports more difficult) would be treated as a breach of the competition rules.

Shortly afterwards the issue arose for the first time in a major case in *United Brands*, where one of the allegations made by the Commission was that the prices charged for bananas in some national markets were excessive. Here the Commission had relied on the prices charged for Ireland, which were the lowest, as a base line from which to claim that the higher prices in the other countries were demonstrably excessive. As in *Continental Can*[4] and other cases, the Court refused to accept the Commission's economic analysis on the basis that it lacked the depth and adequacy to substantiate the claims made. In particular, it indicated that it felt that the basis for the Irish prices had not been sufficiently investigated, to see if in fact they were loss-making prices. The Court confirmed that Article 82 could apply when the dominant undertaking directly or indirectly applied unfair prices to its customers. The Court stated that prices are excessive when they have no reasonable relation to the economic value of the product supplied, and that Article 82 could be breached if the consumer suffered as the result of such pricing policies, even if no effect on competition could be shown. It would perhaps have been too much to expect that the Court would indicate exactly how an individual price or range of prices could be assessed as excessive, a problem only too familiar to economists. The Court did, however, indicate that a detailed cost

---

[3] Case 26/75 [1975] ECR 1367: [1976] 1 CMLR 95.   [4] See Ch. 17, pp.327–8.

analysis was an essential preliminary in every case, and that the next step was to compare the prices charged with those charged by competitors for the same product. The finding of the Court on this issue was that the difference between the Chiquita bananas and those of its principal competitors was only 7 per cent, which evidence alone was insufficient to justify a finding of excessive prices. Hence, on this aspect of the case, United Brands were not adjudged to have acted in breach of Article 82. Other examples of excessive pricing are referred to in Section 8.2.

2.2 RECENT EC AND UK CASES

There are of course a number of benchmarks against which prices can be examined to see if they are so far above the competitive price level for the relevant market as to be classified as 'unfair'. One approach is to examine the profit margin made by the seller over and above its costs (of all kinds), another to compare prices against those charged for the same goods or services in other markets (as for example in *Bodson*).[5] The issues may arise in the context of another alleged abuse such as a refusal to allow access to an essential facility (see pp.316–21) or in connection with the calculation of royalties to be paid under collective licensing schemes (see pp.314–16).

One of the recent few cases in which cost and price analysis was carried out in detail both by the Commission and on appeal to the Court of First Instance was *Industrie des Poudres Spheriques (IPS)* v. *Commission*.[6] IPS wished to purchase supplies of primary calcium metal from Pechiney, in order to manufacture spherical balls of calcium metal through its own atomisation process. Pechiney offered supplies at a price which IPS rejected as excessive; IPS then made a complaint to the Commission that Pechiney was in breach of Article 82 both because of the pricing policy and because of its participation in anti-dumping procedures aimed at preventing imports of primary calcium metal into the Common Market from third countries. Both the Commission and Court of First Instance, having examined the detailed costing of the Pechiney operations, came to the conclusion that the IPS allegations should be rejected.

There is still, however, a singular lack of case law on this subject which is perhaps surprising in view of its importance. For this reason it was welcome that the first major decision of the Competition Commission Appeal Tribunal established by the 1998 Competition Act in the United Kingdom was on this topic, namely *Napp Pharmaceuticals* v. *Director General of Fair Trading*.[7] It dealt, *inter alia*, with issues of excessive pricing over a number of years for morphine supplied to the National Health Service. Section 60 of the Competition Act 1998 requires the Tribunal and the Director General to apply EC law in cases under both Chapter 1 of the Act (equivalent to Article 81) or Chapter 2 of the Act (equivalent to Article 82). Napp had been found by the DGFT to have abused its dominant position in the market for sustained release morphine, a painkiller used widely both in hospitals and in community medicine (sales by pharmacists). Napp was fined £3.21M for predatory pricing in regard to

---

[5] Ch. 14, pp.274–5.   [6] Case T-5/97 [2001] 4 CMLR 1020.

[7] [2002] Comp AR 13: European Commercial Cases 177. The predatory pricing allegations were the main issue in the case, and the excessive pricing claims might well not have been pursued apart from them. It can be argued that predatory pricing may have more serious effects, by driving out competitors, than excessive pricing, which may attract new entry.

hospital sales which represented some ten per cent of its overall sales by volume and for excessive pricing in sales to the community (which represented the other 90 per cent of its sales). Its position of dominance with over 90 per cent of the relevant market in the United Kingdom for some twenty years was not in issue. The main ground of Napp's appeal from the Director General's decision related rather to whether its pricing practices were abusive; the issue of predatory pricing is dealt with in the next section of this Chapter. On the issue of whether the prices charged in the community were excessive, the Tribunal reached the conclusion on several grounds that they were indeed such. These grounds included:

— that the profit margin made on the product by Napp compared to other of its products was excessive (especially as its relevant patents had expired several years ago);

— that its prices for community sales were some 33–67 per cent higher than for similar drugs sold by its competitors;

— that the prices for such sales by Napp to the community outlets were on average 1400 per cent higher than average corresponding prices in the hospital market and indeed on some products even higher;

— that the gross profit realized by Napp on this product was over 80 per cent whilst on other products it made no more than half that amount; and

— that such prices exceeded substantially the prices charged by Napp for export sales of the same product in competitive markets.

On the other hand the Tribunal did not adopt the DGFT's suggestion that Napp's cost of capital should be analysed and compared with the weighted average cost of capital regarded as normal for undertakings in the pharmaceutical sector, possibly perhaps because the evidence on the costs and profit side of the analysis was already so convincing. If a similar case were to reach the Commission or the Court of First Instance, it is to be hoped that it will also be able to carry out a detailed analysis of this kind, which is necessary if the outcome of the decision is to be regarded as authoritative.

3. PREDATORY PRICING

3.1 THE *AKZO* CASE

Predatory pricing is the pricing of goods and services at a very low level with the object of driving out competitors from the market who are unable to compete at that price level, with the likely consequence that price levels in that market will rise again after such competitors have been forced out. It is the dominant company in such a market which is likely to have both the inclination and the resources to finance such a strategy and such pricing can be as equally 'unfair' to competitors as excessive pricing.

The leading case in this area is *AKZO* (European Court 1991).[8] This concerned an appeal by AKZO against a decision of the Commission taken as long ago as 1985 following a dispute with the original complainant, ECS, which was a small producer of benzoyl peroxide in the United Kingdom. ECS originally supplied its product for use as an additive to flour, a small market found only in the United Kingdom and Eire. It planned to expand its sales

---

[8] Case C-62/86 [1991] ECR I-3359: [1993] 5 CMLR 215.

within the Community by marketing its product also to the plastics industry, a much larger potential market, and AKZO became unhappy about the prospect of this competition in Europe from ECS. According to the complaint by ECS, AKZO had threatened over a period of several years to take reprisals against it by way of selected price cuts unless ECS abandoned its intention of selling to the plastics market. AKZO was a much larger company, whose trade in the flour additive field was of little importance compared to its trade with the chemical companies, and who could afford to undercut ECS substantially in the flour additives field, even to the extent of putting it out of business. It appeared prepared to do so to protect its position in the more important market.

Interim measures were applied for and granted to protect ECS, and the Commission issued a decision that AKZO's predatory pricing and use of threats to induce ECS to withdraw from the plastics market were breaches of Article 82. A substantial fine of 10 million ECUs was imposed on AKZO. However, the Commission refused to prescribe any specific pricing rules linked to costs, or to define the precise stage at which price cutting by a dominant firm became abusive. It concentrated rather on the objectives of a dominant company which were shown (from the evidence obtained by the Commission through the use of its investigatory powers under Regulation 17) to have been intended to eliminate or damage ECS as a competitor in the relevant markets.

The Court's decision, however, went into considerable detail about the basis upon which the finding of abuse was to be confirmed. It stated in its judgment that, in applying the *Hoffmann-La Roche* principles to AKZO's pricing, it was to be presumed that prices charged that were lower than average variable costs alone were intended to eliminate competitors since they would be necessarily loss-making.[9] Moreover, even at a higher level above average variable cost, pricing would still be presumed abusive if it did not succeed in recovering average total costs and was part of a deliberate plan to eliminate a competitor with fewer financial resources.

The Court also confirmed the Commission's findings about the use of threats against ECS and that offers of both benzoyl peroxide and other related chemicals had been made (at prices below average total costs) by AKZO to customers which normally dealt with ECS. AKZO was also found to have sold its products cheaply in the flour market to some major customers in return for exclusivity of purchase by them. However, the fine was reduced to 7.5 million ECUs, mainly because of the novelty of the pricing issues and because ECS had not actually lost substantial market share as the result of AKZO's conduct.

It is also clear from the European Court judgment in *Tetrapak (No. 2)*[10] that the Commission need not prove that the dominant company will actually succeed in subsequently raising its prices following the elimination or weakening of its competitor. It is sufficient for the Commission to show that the pricing practices were sufficiently below cost to be likely to eliminate competitors; a further test that the ability to recoup the losses in the future must be shown is not a requirement for a finding of abuse.

3.2 THE *COMPAGNIE MARITIME BELGE* CASE

The case of *Compagnie Maritime Belge*[11] (ECJ 2000) involved allegations of predatory pricing by members of the Central and West African shipping conference (CEWAL). CEWAL was a

---

[9] I.e. those which remained constant regardless of the quantities produced.
[10] See Ch. 14 at pp.276–7.   [11] Ch. 14, fn. 13.

liner conference whose members benefited from the provisions of Regulation 4056/86 giving block exemption to such conferences which were permitted to fix shipping rates and sched-ules for particular services. When a non-member line sought to compete with them, members of the conference agreed to designate certain sailings to the ports covered by the conference as 'fighting ships' for which lower, though not loss-making, rates would be quoted to shippers. The challenger would thus be prevented from gaining freight business from the other mem-bers of the conference. The losses incurred for the fighting ships' lower charges would then be shared between all members of the conference. This targeted use of a pricing strategy to eliminate a competitor, even if the rates charged were not below cost but simply reduced earnings of the conference members, was held abusive. The analysis by Fennelly A-G of the application of Article 82 in these circumstances is essential reading for an understanding of the issues that can arise in such cases, where the object of price cutting strategy is clearly exclusionary even if the participants can show that they are not thereby actually making a loss.

3.3 THE *DEUTSCHE POST* CASE

It is however clear that the rules stated in the *AKZO* case by the ECJ are by themselves inadequate for application in all kinds of predatory pricing cases. A welcome further deci-sion in this area was therefore the *UPS/Deutsche Post*[12] case. Here Deutsche Post, in addition to its letter post monopoly in Germany, operated a business parcel service in competition with private operators. One of these private operators, United Parcel Services, complained to the Commission that Deutsche Post was cross-subsidizing its business parcel services from its monopoly letter mail revenues and thereby abusing its dominant position in both mar-kets. The Commission's investigations established that for five years Deutsche Post had not covered the long-run incremental costs incurred in providing the business parcel service. No fine was imposed for this breach of Article 82 although a fine was imposed for a separate breach of the Article involving the granting of fidelity rebates to mail order customers. Deutsche Post was however required to reorganize its business so as to make its postal services' finances transparent. The parcels business would provide its services either from its own resources or through entering into a contract at full market prices with Deutsche Post or third parties. Deutsche Post for its part had to agree to supply any services provided to the parcels business at the same terms and prices as to third party competitors. It was not however required to cease to make use of its existing infrastructure of freight centres and delivery offices so that any existing economies of scope arising from the joint provision of several services from these could continue to benefit customers.

The main principle which this case establishes was that a dominant company, especially one with a statutory monopoly, which then sets up a new business must cover the entire incremental cost incurred by the new venture entirely from its revenues from that new business. With this case however should be contrasted the ruling of the CFI in *UPS Europe* v. *Commission*[13] that the mere possession by a dominant company of the funds enabling it to make acquisition of a competitor is not itself evidence of abuse, provided that the funds obtained are not then used for excessive pricing or predatory pricing in breach of Article 82.

In the United Kingdom guidelines produced by the DGFT and sectoral regulators have also adopted a similar approach and to varying degrees explained that such 'avoidable costs'

---

12 [2001] OJ L125/27: 5 CMLR 99.   13 Case T-175/99 [2002] 5 CMLR 67.

should be the approach to be adopted, taking into account marginal long-run or incremental costs of the particular service, including the necessary capital investment in fixed assets. The most contentious issue is the period over which these costs should be calculated, which will tend to vary from sector to sector according to the anticipated life of assets.

The *Napp* case referred to in the previous section also placed emphasis on two elements in determining whether predatory pricing is abusive. The first is the importance of the evidence of exclusionary intent, a factor also present in both *AKZO* and *Compagnie Maritime Belge*. The Tribunal found that over a period of years after Napp's patents for slow release morphine had expired it had methodically lowered its hospital prices to match those of its much smaller competitors, at least one of which was forced to leave the market. The second was the element of discretion enjoyed by the dominant company, in that the losses incurred by Napp on its sales to the hospital market (whereas some 10 per cent of sales were made) were more than balanced by the very high prices charged to general practitioners and pharmacies in the community making up the other 90 per cent of its sales.

4. DISCRIMINATORY PRICING

4.1 *UNITED BRANDS*

Discriminatory pricing is closely related to predatory pricing and is itself an example of the third illustrative example in Article 82(c) 'applying dissimilar conditions to equivalent transactions with other trading parties thereby placing them at a competitive disadvantage'.

The first case involving such practices was *United Brands*.[14] The charge against United Brands was that it had charged discriminatory prices to its distributors in different Member States. It was shown that there were substantial differences in prices between, on one hand, Denmark and Germany where prices were relatively high, and, on the other hand, the Benelux countries and Ireland where they were much lower. It was apparently the practice of the Rotterdam management of United Brands to fix scale prices to the distributor so as to reflect as closely as possible the anticipated price obtainable in its territory for ripe (yellow) bananas in the following week. The ability of United Brands to obtain such prices from its different distributors, and therefore to disadvantage those distributors who purchased at the higher prices, served to underline the strength of the company in Western Europe. All the bananas were sold 'free on rail' (f.o.r.) from Rotterdam and costs were virtually identical in each case. United Brands claimed that the difference in the pricing resulted from a commercial decision as to what each part of the market could bear, but the Commission and the Court concluded that this was not an objective justification for the differences imposed.

It is not clear from the terms of the Court's decision to what degree such a company when determining its prices may take into account market forces of supply and demand. It appeared to suggest that this would be permitted only in cases where the seller takes a substantial risk, having involved itself in local production and distribution to such an extent that market movements in that country are likely to affect it directly. The facts in this case were different, United Brands not being involved in the local markets as it was selling to all the distributors at Rotterdam, and in practice it was the distributors who bore the risks of

---

[14] Case 27/76 [1978] ECR 207: 1 CMLR 429.

the individual national markets. The Court's judgment left uncertain what was meant by 'involvement' in local markets, but gave the impression that United Brands might have had a stronger case, had the discrimination in pricing reflected pressures resulting from market conditions in the individual countries, i.e. 'market lead pressures', rather than appearing to arise from United Brands' own ability to impose higher prices on its distributors in those markets because of the absence of effective competition. Had United Brands itself been carrying out the distribution function in the Member States, then it would have been taking a greater risk and having a closer involvement with the national markets; to that extent its freedom to adjust its prices to local dealers would have been greater.

4.2 A PRICE SQUEEZE

Another category of price discrimination involves a 'price squeeze', as in *Napier Brown* v. *British Sugar*[15] (1988, Commission). In this case British Sugar was fined three million units of account for abuse of dominant position for refusing to supply industrial sugar to Napier Brown. It gave the excuse that it had insufficient supplies but the true commercial reason was that it wished to make it more difficult for Napier Brown to compete with it in the market for retail consumers purchasing one- kilogram bags. British Sugar was also found to have engaged in other practices to make life difficult for Napier Brown, for example maintaining a margin between the price it charged Napier Brown for raw materials supplied and the charge which it made for its own consumer sales such that Napier Brown were unable profitably to transform the industrial sugar into consumer retail packets. Moreover, it prevented customers from collecting industrial sugar from its factory and denied supplies of raw material of particular types and origin to Napier Brown, whilst still willing to supply these to other companies. It also offered rebates to other buyers on condition that they bought from it exclusively in future.

4.3 *TETRAPAK (NO. 2)* AND *IRISH SUGAR*

Similar practices were found in *Tetrapak (No. 2)*.[16] Here there were substantial variations in the prices charged for milk cartons and the machines for manufacturing them as between Member States; customers in particular in Italy were charged prices substantially lower than those in other countries in Western Europe, at a time when Tetrapak's main competitor, Elopak, was providing particularly fierce competition to it in that country. Another complex case in this area was *Irish Sugar*[17] (European Court 2001). This company held over 90 per cent of the Irish market for both industrial and retail sugar and was the sole producer of sugar beet in that country. Its pricing strategies were held abusive in three separate respects. The first was by way of discriminatory prices offered to those industrial customers who agreed to export their sugar purchases rather than reselling on the Irish market in competition with the defendant. The second was by the offering of discriminatory prices (whether by special rebates or other means) to rival packers depending again upon whether they agreed to resell sugar in retail packs otherwise than in competition with Irish Sugar's own

---

[15] [1990] 4 CMLR 196. The particular 'squeeze' in this case was easy to calculate. The same principle may however prove considerably more difficult to apply in the more complex markets, such as telecommunication services. See also *National Carbonizing Co.* v. *Commission and NCB* Case 109/75R [1975] ECR 1193: 2 CMLR 457.

[16] Ch. 14, fn. 12.   [17] Case C-497/99R [2001] 5 CMLR 1082.

retail business. The third was a case of geographical discrimination under which retail purchasers in the border area of Ireland were given special rebates in order to make it difficult for cheaper supplies in Northern Ireland to enter the Irish market and thereby insulate it from this competition. The Court of First Instance upheld the Commission's decision and its judgment which was in turn upheld by the European Court.

4.4 DISCRIMINATION IN AIRPORT CHARGES

A number of price discrimination cases also relate to charges for airport services made in several Member States, including Belgium, Finland, Spain, and Portugal. The normal situation to be found in these cases was that landing charges were calculated by the airport managers on a basis that favoured the national incumbent airline which would normally have the largest number of flights, disadvantaging all other airlines which would have a lower number, even if by the offering of substantial discounts at the higher level of flights. Community Courts have twice had to review Commission decisions in this area and on both occasions have fully supported its reasoning.

In the case of *Commission* v. *Portugal* (European Court 2001)[18] the discount structure at several Portuguese airports was held abusive partly because of the fact that the airport could show no economies of scale arising as a result of the greater number of flights made by Portuguese airlines. In *Alpha Flight Services* v. *Commission*[19] (European Court 2002 upholding CFI's earlier decision) this discrimination was not in landing charges but in different charges made to the companies who provided catering and ground-handling services. Preferential terms were offered to a French company which disadvantaged its rival, Alpha, a subsidiary of a British public company. The Court held that dominant undertakings managing international airports must justify any different rates charged by establishing the existence of either objectively different situations or circumstances to justify the discrimination.

5. DISCOUNTS AND REBATES

5.1 EARLY CASES: *HOFFMANN* AND *MICHELIN*

The granting of discounts and rebates by suppliers is closely linked with price discrimination, and indeed the discrimination itself may be effected through the terms of the discount or rebate scheme. A discount is normally a percentage reduction in the price of goods or services which appears on or closely associated with a supply invoice. A rebate, although sometimes offered in addition to a discount, is in effect an aggregation of discounts seeking to attract and bind customers to a particular supplier over a longer period. Its normal function is to encourage a customer to do business with a supplier on a regular basis by offering it a retrospective cash payment calculated on its purchases over the year or other fixed period. It has however the same commercial purpose over a longer period as does the offer of an individual discount on a single particular transaction: to encourage the buyer to do business with that seller rather than with its competitors.

[18] Case C-163/99 [2002] 4 CMLR 319.
[19] Case T-128/98 [2000] ECR II-3929. Case C-02/01 [2003] 4 CMLR 609.

Rebates are often used quite legitimately, even by dominant undertakings, particularly in markets where there is active price competition, and in cases where the seller can reasonably claim that its costs are lower if customers show loyalty by placing regular orders with it. Rebates can also however be used by a dominant company so as to make it difficult for customers without substantial countervailing market power to switch purchases between suppliers, to take advantage either of price fluctuations, or other changes in market conditions, or because some of the products of other suppliers are considered of better quality or suitability. The use of the rebate by a dominant company is often, therefore, linked with its desire to ensure 'fidelity' from its buyers, using the leverage of one product to compel buyers to acquire the remainder of their needs from it, involving a form of 'tying' on the buyer.

In a notice of a settlement made with the Coca Cola Export Company in 1988,[20] the Commission recorded that the use of fidelity rebates by a Coca Cola subsidiary having a dominant position on the Italian Cola market had been discontinued, it being accepted that the fidelity rebates were an abuse of its position in that market. In the text of the settlement, however, a distinction was drawn between certain types of unacceptable rebate, namely those conditional on targets linked to volume of purchases in the previous year, or linked to targets which relate to a group of products in different markets, as contrasted with rebates conditional on the purchase of a series of different sizes of product, or participation in advertising promotions, which were acceptable.

The treatment of such practices under Article 82 is shown by two European Court cases, *Hoffmann-La Roche* (1979)[21] and *Michelin* (1983).[22] Hoffmann-La Roche is a multinational group whose parent company is based in Switzerland. As already discussed in Chapter 14, the Commission had decided that this company had abused its dominant position for seven categories of vitamins. One abuse was committed by entering into exclusive or preferential supply contracts with major industrial purchasers, containing 'fidelity rebates' which placed considerable pressure on the buyers to obtain virtually all their vitamin requirements from Roche. A large fine had been imposed and, although the Court reduced the fine by one-third, it substantially upheld the main elements in the Commission's decision. The Court for the first time took the opportunity to give a general definition of 'abusive conduct'; it stated that this was the conduct of an undertaking which, having a dominant position and thereby able to influence market structure to the point whereby the degree of competition was weakened, as mentioned in the Introduction (paragraph 1.1) to this chapter. The definition has of course since then been applied in a wide variety of other situations.

Pressure thus applied by a dominant undertaking to its purchasers to obtain all or most of their requirements from itself is an abuse, whether or not accompanied by a rebate payable to the customer so long as the customer remains loyal for all (or at least a large proportion of) its requirements. The Court held that the application of such pressure is itself incompatible with the normal working of competition, since it has the effect that orders are placed not because the buyer has made a simple commercial choice in its own interests, but because the buyer, given his dependence on the dominant supplier, simply cannot afford to spread

---

[20] Dated 13 October 1988: IP (88) 615. In *British Plasterboard (BPB)* v. *Commission* Case 310/93 [1995] ECR I-865: [1997] 4 CMLR 238, the abuse was found to consist of the payment of rebates in return for dealers agreeing not to handle plasterboard supplied by Spanish importers.

[21] See fn. 1, above.

[22] Case 322/81 [1983] ECR 3461: [1985] 1 CMLR 282.

his orders over a variety of suppliers and thus risk losing the rebate offered by the dominant company.

Roche had placed considerable reliance in their argument on the price alignment clause included in its agreements, widely known as the 'English clause'. Under this, a customer who obtained a better price quotation from another producer was entitled to ask Roche to align its prices to those prices. If Roche failed to do so, the customer could then buy from the other producers without losing the benefit of the fidelity rebate. The Court felt that this clause, rather than enabling competitive pressure to work effectively for the benefit of the buyer, actually had the effect of providing Roche with a great deal of information about the State of the relevant vitamin markets, and the pricing and marketing strategies open to it in the light of actions being adopted by its competitors. The information which it received in this way further enhanced its ability to dominate; the effect of the 'English clause' therefore was to weaken still further the competitive structure of the market, which the Court regarded as an important factor.

The *Michelin* case had also concerned itself largely with fidelity rebates. Again the initial decision of the Commission was upheld by the Court, although the fine was reduced in this case by more than half. Michelin held a strong position in the Dutch replacement tyre market for heavy vehicles including trucks and buses. The Commission's decision had been based on a number of grounds and had focused particularly on the fact that the rebates fixed by Michelin in return for the achievement of sales targets of individual distributors were not sufficiently objective, and the rebate schemes characterized by a general lack of transparency. There were also findings that the relevant targets and rebates given for 1977 had linked two different tyre markets (heavy vehicle and light vehicle markets respectively) and then used Michelin's market dominance for heavy vehicle tyres to promote sales of light vehicle tyres. The Commission had ruled that, for the use of rebates to be acceptable as normal commercial practice for the purpose of Article 82, they must be both clearly known to the purchaser and defined on an objective basis, the sums payable to dealers being commensurate with the task they performed and the services which they actually provided.

Following the Commission's decision fears were expressed by manufacturers that its effect would be to reduce considerably the extent to which manufacturers with a strong market position would feel able to use any form of rebate or bonus scheme. The terms of the subsequent Court decision to some extent reduced that concern. The Court did, however, concur with the Commission's view that the system adopted by Michelin for variable discounts linked to the attainment of individual sales targets, and the method of administering the scheme through frequent personal visits by Michelin representatives applying pressure to its distributors to attain those targets (particularly towards the end of the sales year) constituted an abuse, in view of the undue pressure placed on dealers. Michelin set out neither the rebate scale nor sales targets in writing; this would increase the disinclination of the dealers to deal with Michelin's competitors particularly towards the end of that relevant year. All these factors contributed to strengthening Michelin's market position and increasing the barriers to entry in the Dutch tyre market by its competitors.

These findings alone were sufficient to justify confirmation by the Court of the Commission's finding of abuse, even though some of the factual findings of the Commission were rejected. The Court did not, for example, accept that resellers of tyres would have hesitated to complain about the lack of written confirmation of sales targets, and also rejected allegations that both targets and rebates were related to the percentage that Michelin sales made by the client bore to the total sales of all makes by it, a formula known as 'temperature Michelin'. It also rejected the finding by the Commission that different rates of rebate, representing differences in treatment between dealers, were the result of the application of unequal criteria and had no basis in ordinary commercial practice.

5.2 RECENT CASES: *BA*/VIRGIN AND OTHERS

Michelin were in 2001 again involved in a decision[23] of the Commission which related to the French market for retread and new replacement tyres for heavy vehicles where its market share in France was over 50 per cent. It operated a complex system of quantitative bonuses (linked to rebate schemes) for both products, which had the effect of discouraging dealers from choosing between Michelin and other manufacturers on their merits. Each Michelin dealer was allocated a 'base', that is the minimum number of tyres which it was expected to order in a year and rebates were awarded under a number of steeply graded 'steps' above the base level. In 1995 and 1996 the rebate was changed by reducing the number of steps within the scheme and by the retrospective application of the rebates to all tyres ordered over the whole period not merely any excess over the base.

In return for these schemes the dealers were obliged to provide Michelin with much information about their businesses and to remain faithful to it. There was little wholesaler activity in France nor evidence of parallel importing. The strength of the Michelin brand was such that it was an 'unavoidable partner' on the French market for tyre dealers and garages. The period of these rebate schemes was normally one year, far longer than the maximum of three months recommended by the Commission as reasonable. Profit margins on tyres were low and thus for the dealers the rebate was essential to their financial health. The fact that the loyalty element of the rebate scheme was implicit in its structure other than explicit did not lessen its practical effect in keeping the dealers loyal. One element in the scheme was progress-related, in that it depended on the actual sales target of the tyres reached as a percentage above the level reached in the previous year, an important element in the *BA/Virgin* case discussed below.

Overall, the result of the *Michelin* and *Hoffmann-La Roche* cases seems to be that the use of rebates by dominant companies, although not prohibited outright, requires very careful analysis of the services for which they are granted. It is not permitted to tie them simply to exclusive purchasing obligations, but they can be linked to the achievement of objective sales targets provided that the operation of the system is sufficiently objective and transparent so as not to impose undue pressure on dealers, and does not discriminate between different categories of dealers on a basis that does not reflect cost savings to the supplier. The supplier will also be in a stronger position to withstand proceedings under Article 82 if its rebate system corresponds to those generally adopted by its non-dominant competitors in the same markets, though in *BA/Virgin*, this argument was not accepted by the Commission.

In *UPS/Deutsche Post*,[24] Deutsche Post had made contracts with its customers for both mail order and bulky parcels under which the contract prices offered were conditional on those customers providing exclusivity to Deutsche Post for all parcels in those categories, or in some cases linked to a very high percentage of their total requirements. This had the effect

---

[23] [2002] 5 CMLR 388. See B. Sher, 'Price Discounts and Michelin 2' [2002] 23 ECLR 482–489.

[24] See fn. 12.

of preventing large mail order companies from establishing their own postal arrangements which in time might have developed also into the provision of services for third parties in direct competition with Deutsche Post. A substantial fine was levied on Deutsche Post for imposing this scheme.

The extent to which 'fidelity' as a forbidden element in such schemes is now being imputed by the Commission from the inherent structure of those schemes rather than by express obligation of the customers is well illustrated by *BA/Virgin*.[25] Virgin had complained to the Commission that the British Airways commission scheme (equivalent to a discount scheme) provided a 'performance reward' to its travel agents, which the Commission regarded as making them sell an increasing number of BA tickets every year, thereby giving BA an unfair advantage against other airlines. A flat commission of 7 per cent was paid by BA to its agents for ticket sales but under the 'performance reward' additional commission payments of up to 3 per cent on international flights and 1 per cent on domestic flights could be earned, by matching the agent's total sales in a given month against its sales in the corresponding month of the previous year. The increased commission was retrospective and applied to all sales within the relevant period, not merely for the excess after the previous year's level had been reached.

In its defence BA pointed out to the Commission that there were other similar commission schemes operated by major airlines in Europe and that there were cost savings and efficiencies which the performance reward scheme brought about; moreover there was little evidence that the scheme had a damaging effect on competing airlines. These arguments were not however accepted by the Commission, which ruled that the scheme was abusive in its calculation of commission on sales in the current year by reference to levels of performance in the previous year. Following the decision general guidelines were issued by the Commission[26] in respect of such schemes. This required commissions to be differentiated only to the extent that:

– there are variations in distribution costs through different agents or in the differing value of their services to airlines;

– commissions are to increase only in respect of these factors, not in relation to sales in any previous period, and are to an increase in a straightline basis from any base line set out in the agreement: and

– the period for calculation of commission is not to exceed six months.

It is clear from these guidelines that the Commission has moved well beyond the point of prohibiting merely schemes that expressly require fidelity or exclusivity as the price of the rebate or discount. The effect of this decision will be to prohibit in addition schemes that by their terms encourage loyalty and are not strictly cost related. Its more rigid approach comes close to saying that only cost-based schemes can avoid breaching Article 82, and that the use of a number of different incentives by dominant companies in a particular sector cannot by definition be a part of normal competition. The guidelines may, however, require adjustment in the light of the terms of the judgment of the CFI expected in 2003, especially if it is adverse to the Commission.

---

[25] [2000] 4 CMLR 999, on appeal to the CFI as Case T-219/99.   [26] IP/99/504 14 July 1999.

6. REFUSAL TO DEAL (IN GOODS OR SERVICES)

6.1 *COMMERCIAL SOLVENTS*

The first European Court case involving a refusal to deal was *Commercial Solvents*[27] in 1974. Nitropropane is a compound that results from the nitration of paraffin and is the base product for the industrial production of a substance called aminobutanol. This in turn is the base product for the industrial production of ethambutol, a compound used in the treatment of pulmonary tuberculosis. Commercial Solvents Corporation (CSC) had a world monopoly in the manufacture of products derived from the nitration of paraffin, including both nitropropane and aminobutanol. Although the relevant patents had largely expired, it was difficult for other enterprises to enter the market because of the difficulty of finding outlets for other products that could also be derived from the nitration of paraffin, and because of the high cost of research and development. The necessary manufacturing installations were also of considerable complexity and cost.

CSC had originally been willing to supply ethambutol to a smaller Italian company, Zoja, through its Italian subsidiary, Istituto Chemioterapico Italiano (ICI) over which it exercised complete control. After merger talks between ICI and Zoja had broken down, ICI on the instructions of CSC raised its prices for ethambutol to Zoja and sought gradually to reduce the level of its supplies. Originally, aminobutanol remained available from other sources, but these gradually dried up. By the start of 1971 Zoja was unable to manufacture any further ethambutol and complained to DG IV that CSC and ICI were abusing their dominant position as world leaders in production both of nitropropane and aminobutanol. It claimed the object of this conduct was to eliminate Zoja from the market place in Europe as a producer of ethambutol. Ethambutol was important for the treatment of tuberculosis in conjunction with other drugs, and there was no valid reason why Zoja could not be supplied by CSC, which had adequate supplies. On the basis of these facts, the Commission imposed a fine of 200,000 units of account on CSC and ordered an immediate resumption of supplies by it to Zoja at a price no higher than the maximum price which it had previously charged for both nitropropane and aminobutanol.

The Advocate General, although finding that the facts established by the Commission were largely correct, would have cancelled the fine because prior to its decision CSC had offered to resume sufficient supplies to Zoja to carry on business within the Community. The Court, however, upheld the imposition of a fine, though reduced to 100,000 units of account, and in other respects upheld the findings of the Commission.

In particular, the Court agreed with the Commission that CSC and ICI between them held a dominant position in the relevant market of nitro-propane and aminobutanol. By abusing their dominant position in these markets, they were able to restrict competition in the market for the derivative obtained from those products, namely ethambutol. Such effect must be taken into account in considering the effect of CSC's action, even if the market for the derivatives was not self-contained but could be met from other sources. The refusal to supply Zoja involved an abuse of its market power, particularly as it had previously supplied

---

[27] *Istituto Chemioterapico Italiano and Commercial Solvents Corporation v. Commission* Cases 6–7/73 [1974] ECR 223: 1 CMLR 309.

it and then discontinued supply without adequate commercial reason. The case would, of course, have been less clear had CSC never supplied Zoja, and even more so if Zoja had been merely a potential entrant to the market rather than an actual competitor; in those circumstances it is doubtful if CSC would have had an obligation to supply.[28] Finally, the Court ruled that any undertaking that abuses its dominant position within a substantial part of the Common Market in a way likely to eliminate a competitor is in breach of Article 82, regardless of whether the conduct by the dominant company relates to its exports or to trade within the Common Market, so long as it can be established that the elimination of the competitor would itself have repercussions on the competitive structure of relevant markets within the Community. Whilst the case was also concerned with the detriment to consumers that would flow as the result of the action taken by CSC, the Court placed greatest emphasis on the likely effect on competitive structure of the conduct complained of.

6.2 UNITED BRANDS

The most important early case to come before the European Court under this Article was *United Brands* (European Court 1978),[29] already considered in Chapter 14. This United States multinational exported bananas from its own plantations in South America and had a substantial proportion of the banana market in the Community. The majority of bananas were shipped in the company's own fleet to Rotterdam where they were resold to national distributors in the various Member States, who purchased bananas on a 'free on rail basis' from Rotterdam at prices which varied significantly. United Brands held a substantial market share, amounting to some 40 to 45 per cent in each of the four geographic markets in issue: Germany, Benelux, Ireland, and Denmark. Its dominance in these markets was even greater than might have been expected simply as the result of its market share. The conduct of which the Commission complained involved several separate practices. The first two were:

(a) the prohibition against resale by distributors of green, i.e. unripe, bananas; and

(b) the refusal of supplies on certain occasions to a Danish distributor which had offended United Brands by promoting a competitive brand of banana.

The facts established by the Commission showed that United Brands' policy was to try to sell its product at prices which, both by their absolute level and by their variation as between Member States, sought to extract the highest possible profit from all these countries. Its distributors were left with a relatively small margin for resale which nevertheless had to be accepted because of the market strength possessed by United Brands.

The Court had little difficulty in establishing abusive conduct. The prohibition against trade in green bananas had the effect of an export ban. The bananas arrived in the green, unripened form in Rotterdam, and only ripened at the time and at the speed required by ripeners in order to bring them into the right conditions of sale to suit local markets. In a

---

[28] Whilst the later *ABG* case (pp.300–1) established that regular customers have a right to equitable treatment from a supplier with a dominant market position, it left unclear the rights of occasional customers. A dominant company appears to have no obligation to supply an undertaking with which it had never previously dealt, even an actual or potential competitor, except in the case of access to essential facilities (see pp.316–21).

[29] Ch. 14, pp.268–9, Case 27/76 [1978] ECR 207: 1 CMLR 429.

freer market, the various distributors might well have exchanged supplies with each other in the face of the varying demands of different national markets. The limiting of such resales of unripened bananas meant that in practice the short periods between the attainment of ripeness and the subsequent onset of decay ensured that no exchange of supplies was possible. The Court acknowledged that a restriction of this kind, if imposed simply to maintain a certain quality level, would have been justifiable. However, a complete restriction on the transfer of all green bananas went far beyond such a legitimate aim, because its real purpose was clearly to weaken the bargaining position of the distributors with United Brands.

The second commercial practice found to violate Article 82 was a refusal to continue to supply Olesen, a Danish distributor. The alleged basis for this was that Olesen had been active in promoting sales of competitors' fruit. The Court found that the reaction of United Brands to Olesen's conduct was out of proportion to its alleged 'disloyalty', and ruled that it was not permissible for an undertaking with a dominant position to cut off supplies to a long-standing distributor, so long as its orders placed on the supplier had remained within the normal range.[30]

We have already met the case of *Hugin*,[31] in which a small firm in South East England had sought spare parts for repairing Hugin cash machines, and the action under Article 82 by the Commission failed only because there was no evidence that the refusal by Hugin to supply them had an effect on trade between Member States (the only geographical area affected was a relatively small radius around London). Subject to this qualification it will normally be abusive for spare parts to be refused by the maker of original equipment unless too long a period has passed for it to be commercially reasonable for these to be available (as emphasized in *Volvo/Veng*).[32]

6.3 TYING PRACTICES

Not all refusals to provide goods or services are however unconditional. The refusal may be conditional upon the provision by the dominant company in addition of other goods which are 'tied' to the main supply; the customer who refuses to accept the proposed tie-in will be told however that the 'tying' product is unavailable.

The essence of tying is that the supplier holds a dominant position in a 'tying' product, usually in short supply, which enables him to impose on his customer an obligation to acquire the second product, 'the tied product', at a price often above current market price, even though it is available elsewhere on better terms. There are numerous cases on this practice in United States antitrust law, where the practice is prohibited under Section 3 of the Clayton Act. There are only a few exceptional circumstances in which it can be justified as normal business practice, for example where for technical reasons the tying product, perhaps a piece of equipment, will only work properly if used in association with another

---

[30] An interesting issue with which the Court did not deal is whether it would have been abusive conduct for United Brands to have insisted on the distribution of fruit through exclusive dealers or distributors: in practice exclusivity was unlikely to have been accepted by dealers and distributors in perishable products, whose handling raised many problems not encountered in selling consumer products with a reasonable or indefinite shelf life.

[31] Ch. 14, p.271.   [32] But see also Pelikan/Kyocera, 1995 Annual Report, para. 87.

item.[33] Generally, however, tying arrangements are struck down under US antitrust law, though a 'rule of reason' approach is applied to 'technological tying' when a novel product is involved. A related practice is 'full-line forcing', when the supplier refuses to supply a customer except with its full range of a particular product, e.g. a range of perfumes or paints. A quite separate practice is that of offering to sell two items together to a purchaser for a total price less than that paid for the items purchased separately, known as 'mixed bundling', which was one of the main issues in the *GE/Honeywell* merger case (see Chapter 18, fn. 55).

Example (*d*) in Article 82 refers to the making of contracts 'subject to acceptance by the other parties of supplementary obligations which, by their nature or according to commercial usage, have no connection with the subjects of such contracts'. It was established in *Tetrapak (No. 2)*[34] that, even in cases where the two products are closely associated, this alone will not constitute a 'natural link' justifying tying practices. Tetrapak had argued that if the product formed part of what could be regarded commercially as a 'integrated service' which customers acquired from both the filling machinery and the requisite cartons for aseptic milk products, no breach of 82(*d*) occurred. The European Court, however, confirming the ruling of the Court of First Instance, held that so long as there existed independent manufacturers who specialized in the manufacture of non-aseptic cartons, and so long as there was no intellectual property reasons preventing such manufacturers from starting to make aseptic cartons, Tetrapak had no right to treat the manufacturing equipment and the cartons as an integrated service.

Tying cases under Article 82 may also involve reliance by the owner of the 'tying' product on intellectual property rights. These cases are considered in the next section. Tying, of course, can and often does occur without the supplier having to rely on intellectual property rights, though the practice is considerably more commercially effective if based on such a foundation, particularly where the intellectual property right has a substantial life, for example a copyright.

A variant of the simple refusal to deal involves the imposition on the customers of the dominant company of onerous conditions, such as exclusivity. An example of this which is a minor case but nevertheless significant, was the refusal of *Deutsche Bahn*[35] in late 2000 to respond to the request of a smaller German rail company, GVG and its partner (Swedish State Railway) for the loan of an engine suitable for operating a new rail service from Berlin to Malmo, in circumstances where Deutsche Bahn had ample engines available for loan and there was no other source of suitable traction so that without Deutsche Bahn's assistance the new service could not operate. Moreover even if the engine could be made available, Deutsche Bahn were insisting that GVG should hire Deutsche Bahn's own staff for operation of the entire service, although GVG had its own qualified staff available. The Commission issued a statement of objections with regard to Deutsche Bahn's refusal, although it was anticipated that the dispute would be settled.

Another example occurring in a different context is where Nordion,[36] a Canadian company, was the only company apart from a Belgian company (IRE) able to supply the world market for Molybdenum 99, a source of the material needed for radiopharmaceutical

---

[33] As in, e.g. *US* v. *Jerrold Electronics* and *Dehydrating Process Co.* v. *A.O. Smith Corporation*, described in A.D. Neale and D.G. Goyder, *The Antitrust Laws of the USA*, 3rd edn. (Cambridge University Press, 1981), pp.279–80. See also *US* v. *Microsoft*, 253 F. 3d 34 DC Circ. 2001.

[34] Ch. 14, fn. 12.

[35] Annual Report (1998) at para. 74: [1998] 5 CLMR 142. [36] IP/01/1415 15 October 2001.

material used in nuclear medicine. Nordion had contracts to supply a number of European purchasers, but insisted they entered into requirements contracts preventing them from purchasing the material from IRE or other sources. IRE complained to the Commission and after investigation Nordion agreed that the requirements contract was abusive and that it would not enforce its exclusivity clauses. Exclusivity was also the issue in the case involving ice cream freezer cabinets which arose from the attempt by Masterfoods, a subsidiary of Mars, to contest the practice of Unilever and its subsidiary Van den Bergh Foods to lease out freezer cabinets in Ireland only on condition that they were used exclusively for Unilever icecream. The Commission ruled[37] that the use of such exclusivity clauses by a dominant company was abusive though, a decision is now on appeal to the Court of First Instance.

6.4 TREATMENT OF OCCASIONAL CUSTOMERS

Use of the Article is relatively straightforward when the recipient of the abusive behaviour or treatment is a well established customer, either as part of a distribution network (as in *United Brands*) or by way of a series of individual transactions (as in the *Commercial Solvents* case). Useful pointers on the permitted response of a dominant company to the requirements of customers falling within neither of these categories is found in the *ABG* case, considered by the European Court in 1978.[38] This case arose as the result of oil shortages during the crisis period that started in November 1973. The Commission decided that BP had breached Article 82 by substantially reducing supplies of petrol during this period to a Dutch independent central buying organization, ABG. The Commission relied on the evidence that whilst BP had reduced its supplies at this time to all its customers in The Netherlands, the percentage reduction to ABG was of the order of 73 per cent while the average reduction for its other customers was only about 12.7 per cent. The result of this apparent discrimination was that ABG had to buy its remaining needs on the open market or through the official marketing scheme established for the crisis period by the Dutch government. The Commission defined abuse in this context as 'any action which reduces supplies to comparable purchasers in different ways without objective justification, and thereby puts certain of them at a competitive disadvantage to others, especially when such action can result in change in structures of the particular market'. The Commission pointed out that BP had not supplied any objective reasons for the proportionately greater reduction in supplies to ABG and, after taking into account the extent, regularity, and continuity of commercial relationships between the parties, the conduct was ruled abusive.

The European Court, however, took a radically different view of the commercial relationship between BP and ABG. Accepting the findings of the Advocate General, it held that ABG was far from a regular customer, either by way of long-term contractual obligations or by reason of having made regular spot purchases. On the contrary, ABG was simply an occasional customer and BP was able to show that it had, owing to a reduction in its own crude oil supplies from Libya and Kuwait, reduced its contractual commitment to ABG twelve months before the oil crisis. It had actually requested ABG in future to obtain the greater part of its crude oil from other sources, though BP remained willing to refine this crude oil. Temporarily, in the earlier part of 1973, BP had 'lent' ABG some crude oil to be repaid at a

---

[37] [1998] 5 CMLR 530 on appeal as Case T-65/98.

[38] Reported as *British Petroleum* v. *Commission* Case 77/77 [1978] ECR 1513: 3 CMLR 174. The Commission's decision is reported at [1977] OJ L117/1: [1977] 2 CMLR D1, as *ABG* v. *Esso and Others*.

later date. The Court ruled that it was clearly justifiable to remove these figures from the total oil sales between the parties; once this had been done, the percentage reductions in supplies to ABG during the crisis period became too small to justify any finding of abuse by BP of its market position. Nevertheless, in spite of the reversal of the Commission's decision on the particular facts, the duty of the dominant supplier to deal equitably with its regular customers is now clearly established, even though individual application of this rule will clearly raise difficulties in individual cases.

6.5 COMMERCIAL JUSTIFICATION AND PROPORTIONALITY

There is, however, one good defence to a claim for refusal to deal: reasonable commercial justification. The best known example is that involving a customer with a poor credit record. The supplier may refuse to supply simply because it does not believe that it will be paid for further deliveries, or it may seek through its refusal to apply pressure on the debtor to make partial alternative payment for earlier supplies. In the English High Court case of *Leyland Daf* v. *Automotive Products*[39] a refusal by Automotive Products to make further supplies to Leyland Daf, even though it would take Leyland Daf six to eight months to find an alternative supplier because of stringent product liability requirements in the motor industry, was held to be justified by the Court of Appeal on this basis because of the substantial debt already outstanding from Leyland Daf.

The argument of commercial justification becomes relevant of course in Article 82 cases other than those of refusal to deal, though it is often described in the language of 'proportionality'. This concept[40] originally came into prominence as a principle of German law under which State departments, or organizations, were required not to impose obligation on citizens except to the extent necessary for the attainment of a worthwhile public benefit. It has been widened as a general principle of Community law to apply to undertakings, whose response to competitive pressures should be limited to steps that are appropriate and commercially necessary in the circumstances. Thus claims that restrictive clauses such as tying or exclusivity are needed in order to comply with health or safety obligations as in *Hilti* or *Tetrapak (No. 2)*, have generally been rejected by the Commission and Community Courts as disproportionate to the defendant's situation.

7. ABUSES BY INDIVIDUAL OWNERS OF INTELLECTUAL PROPERTY RIGHTS

7.1 THE EARLY CASES: THE IBM SETTLEMENT

The first ever case to reach the Court on the interpretation of Article 82 came in 1968 under an Article 234 reference from a Dutch court, the *Parke, Davis* v. *Probel* case,[41] and concerned the rights of an individual patent owner. Parke, Davis was the owner of a Dutch drug patent for an antibiotic process called chloramphenicol and sought to use its ownership of this patent to exclude from Holland drugs which had been produced in Italy, where patent

---

[39] [1993] BCC 389: [1994] BCLC 245.

[40] T.C. Hartley, *The Foundations of European Community Law*, 4th edn. (Oxford University Press, 1998), pp.148–9.

[41] Case 24/67 [1968] ECR 55: CMLR 47. See also Ch. 13, pp.249–52.

protection was not then available for drugs or medicine. In so far as the Court's judgment reveals, Parke, Davis had had nothing to do with the production or marketing of the drugs in Italy. Such a normal use of patent protection under national law was held by the Court to be a right protected by Article 30, and by itself could not constitute abuse; abuse necessarily involved an element of impropriety in the way in which the patent right was exercised. Such impropriety could not be said to occur simply because Parke, Davis utilized its patent rights to exclude from Holland drugs which it had neither placed on the market in Italy nor allowed to be manufactured there by a third party. The mere fact that prices were higher in Holland for this particular drug than on the Italian market had no effect on the legal position; indeed, the likely reason for the ability of the Italian manufacturer to undercut the price charged in Holland was that the cost of the research and development of the drug had been incurred largely by Parke, Davis rather than the potential importers. The Court did, however, leave open an important issue, namely the extent to which the existence of the higher price level in one Member State might in some cases be relevant in determining the existence on other occasions of improper exploitation of market power.

Whilst, of course, it is decisions of the European Court and Court of First Instance which carry the greatest authority in this area, an important pointer for the future application of this aspect of the Article by the Commission was found in a case which never reached a formal decision. This was the widely publicized settlement involving International Business Machines (IBM) (Commission 1984). IBM was originally challenged with four practices claimed to be in violation of Article 82, though two of these charges were later withdrawn after IBM modified its marketing policies. The charges which were the subject of the final settlement involved: (a) IBM's practice of including the main memory function in the price of a central processing unit and refusing to supply it separately, a practice known as 'memory bundling'; and (b) its policy of not disclosing important information about the interface of IBM computer systems until they had actually been marketed, thereby placing at a disadvantage the manufacturers of equipment that would have been compatible with the IBM hardware, who were unable to obtain the necessary 'interface disclosure'. The terms of settlement were that the Commission suspended its proceedings under Article 82 in return for an undertaking by IBM to amend its practices relating both to memory bundling and interface disclosure. The Commission retained the right to reopen legal proceedings against IBM should the relevant undertakings not prove in its view satisfactory; IBM agreed to observe the terms of the undertaking at least until 1990, and to give twelve months' notice of any intention to terminate the settlement.

IBM were alleged to have obtained market dominance in large mainframe computers and in the submarket of the IBM Systems 370; the issue of 'memory bundling' ultimately appeared to be less important than that of interface disclosure, because by the time of settlement memory no longer formed a large part of the central processing unit. IBM indicated that it was willing to offer the EEC System-370 with no main memory capacity, or at least only with the capacity required for reasonable tests to be carried out. The more difficult issue of interface disclosure began with an allegation by the Commission as to the foreclosure from competition of independent manufacturers of peripheral equipment that would be compatible with IBM computers; this original complaint was later extended to alleged non-disclosure of the IBM System-370 source code permitting a company to design and prepare software programs that could work in conjunction with IBM software, and also to practices adopted regarding its communications standard known as Systems Network

Architecture (SNA). The Commission had alleged in particular that the non-disclosure of interface information relating to such architecture could conceivably have adverse effects on the data communication industry's efforts to develop its own standard computer networking procedures, since such non-disclosure would prevent other brands of computer equipment from being able to be combined in a simple communications system with IBM products.

Under the terms of the complex settlement, IBM agreed to make interface information available within 120 days following the announcement of a new System-370 product intended for sale within the Community, and to make source code interface information available to competitors as soon after the announcement of a new product as the interface had been technically proved. IBM would also disclose adequate information to competitors to enable them to interconnect with System-370, using SNA, once the relevant format and protocols were stable. However, the undertakings did not extend to interfaces between two distinct products of a subsystem, from which the design of the products could be detected.

This highly complex and technically demanding inquiry[42] may have been satisfactorily resolved from the viewpoint of the Commission and of IBM, for the completion of any litigation to resolve the case would probably have taken several years and a disproportionate amount of the resources of DG Comp. It is clear that the Commission will place great importance on any activity of a dominant company which involves foreclosure of competitors from a particular market, either by insisting that two related products can only be purchased together, e.g. the CPU and its memory, or in cases of what is often called 'implicit tying', where smaller firms within an industry have adapted their products to those of the dominant firm and subsequently suffer a commercial disadvantage when the dominant firm redesigns its products so that competitors' complementary products cease to be compatible.

The undertaking remained in force until 1995 and seems to have been regarded by the Commission as a success. It enabled competitors of IBM entitled to receive interface information under its terms to give credible assurances to their own customers that their product would continue to be compatible with System-370 until at least 1990 (and in fact for a further five years). The making of the settlement in 1984, as opposed to the entering into litigation continuing for many years after that date, gave the required assurance at a much earlier time than would otherwise have been the case. The Commission believes that the incentive provided to IBM to improve its own products after 1984 was not reduced by the existence of its obligations under the undertaking.

If implicit tying is likely to lead to an allegation of abusive conduct, it seems to indicate that companies with a dominant position may not only have a negative obligation to refrain from action that places their smaller competitors at a disadvantage in this way, but that their dominant position imports a responsibility for maintaining a competitive market structure regardless of whether that commercial practice can be shown to have other justifications. This argument seems to be particularly relevant to the issue of non-disclosure of interface information relating to SNA, which was considered likely to restrict the development of markets for communication and area networks. However, its use, may well be valuable to the

---

[42] The *14th Annual Report* (1984) contains details of the decision at pp.77–9. A detailed assessment of the operation of the settlement in the period 1984 to 1995 is found at DG Comp Competition Policy Newsletter (1998) No. 3, pp.7–11.

Commission in future in other areas of advanced technology where a powerful company appears likely to be able, if left unchecked, to use its technical superiority to dampen the level of competition in its chosen markets.

7.2 MICROSOFT

Microsoft as the leading manufacturer and developer of computer software and operating systems has not surprisingly found itself the subject of a number of complaints to the Commission. During the mid-90s it received a complaint from competitors that Microsoft's licensing practices unfairly prevented competitors from the market for personal computer operating systems software. After an investigation the Commission found that through its pricing policy, rebates, and software pricing policies, Microsoft had effectively foreclosed competitors from the European market for the operating software in personal computers. In particular, it had complained about the use by Microsoft of licences which required payment for royalty on every computer produced by a manufacturer or in a particular model series, regardless of whether it had pre-installed Microsoft software. It was claimed that in practice this provision compelled computer manufacturers to acquire all their software from Microsoft. Moreover, the requirement by Microsoft of minimum royalties, regardless of the actual use of their product, was also claimed to be abusive. The investigation was carried out jointly with the US authorities and finally resulted in contemporaneous settlements under both US and EC law.[43] The undertaking given by Microsoft, which would run for just over six years, prevented it from entering into licence agreements for more than a year, from imposing minimum commitments on licensees, and from imposing licences calculating royalties on 'per processor' basis. Existing licences contrary to the provisions were to be terminated if the licensees so wished.

In addition to claims of excessive pricing, price discrimination and exclusivity clauses, a number of complaints of abusive conduct were brought later by competitors in circumstances that bore some resemblance to the *IBM* case. Sun, a manufacturer of servers for computers, both those that operated systems for large installations and for use by smaller installations, claimed that Microsoft had designed its technology so as to prevent the systems produced by Sun from having the optimal interface with those customers who had Microsoft servers. Sun also claimed that Microsoft discriminated in the amount of interface information that it supplied, to its disadvantage. The Commission issued a Statement of Objections and to this were later added further claims that Microsoft had tied the provision of a new media player to its existing operating system without making it available for other manufacturers to incorporate in their systems. These proceedings are still active and may have been delayed by the lengthy Sherman Act monopolization litigation in the USA taking place between Microsoft and the US Federal Anti-trust authorities which did not conclude until the autumn of 2002. It will be interesting to see if the eventual resolution of the outstanding proceedings between the European Commission and Microsoft, is by way of a settlement and series of undertakings on the model of the IBM undertakings, given that the issues are considerably more complex in the *Microsoft* case and go well beyond the issue of interface.

---

[43] [1994] 5 CMLR 143. Undertakings were also obtained in a similar case from Digital. See also [1998] 4 CMLR 4.

7.3 REFUSAL TO SUPPLY SPARE PARTS

The right of the owner of patent or other intellectual property right in a particular jurisdiction to exercise it simply by excluding goods that infringed his territorial monopoly had been clearly confirmed in *Parke, Davis* v. *Probel* as not constituting an abuse. By analogy it appeared almost certain that such an owner would be entitled also to refuse to license his property to third parties. In *Volvo* v. *Eric Veng*[44] and its companion case *Renault* v. *Maxicar*[45] (two similar cases decided on the same day in October 1988) this principle was accepted but subject to a qualification so substantial as to considerably reduce its value. The Court agreed that the owners of protected design, in these cases for car body panels, had the right to prevent third parties from manufacturing, selling, or importing products which infringed the design and that this right to prevent third parties from entering the market comprised the very subject-matter of the exclusive right which national law had granted. Therefore, if Volvo and Renault were obliged as a matter of law to grant third parties a licence to supply products (even in return for reasonable royalties) then this would in effect deprive them of the substance of those exclusive rights. Hence a refusal to grant licences could not in itself constitute an abuse.

The qualification which the Court then stated reflected the underlying relationship between car makers on one hand and car owners on the other, who will need to have them maintained and repaired from time to time. The Court stated that any manufacturer who arbitrarily refused to supply spare parts to independent repairers, or fixed prices of spare parts at an unfair level, or made a decision to stop producing spare parts for particular models, even though many cars of that model were still in circulation, would commit an abuse of the dominant position which each manufacturer necessarily has in respect of many kinds of spare parts for its range of vehicles. The Court seems to be saying that there are situations where the relationship between the manufacturer-owner of intellectual property rights and the seller of the product which it has manufactured is such that the rights themselves cannot be used in a way which effectively reduces the value of the product supplied. However, the Court's final comment, reminiscent of the judgment in *Parke, Davis*, was that the mere fact that prices charged for spare parts by such manufacturers which enjoyed national protective rights for their designs were higher than those charged by independent producers did not necessarily indicate abuse, since the higher prices might be necessary to provide 'a return on the amounts invested in order to perfect the protected design'.

7.4 THE *MAGILL* SAGA

The line of reasoning adopted in the earlier cases was taken a stage further in the subsequent Court of First Instance and European Court decisions in *Magill* v. *Radio Telefis Eireann (RTE)*.[46] Here the intellectual property right concerned was the copyright in the compilation of weekly radio and television schedules. RTE, the Irish radio and television authority, had consistently refused to license Magill, an organization which wished to publish a weekly magazine containing these schedules. Basing its refusal on the grounds of copyright, it was only prepared to license the publication of 24-hour schedules in newspapers (and 48 hours

---

[44] Case 238/87 [1988] ECR 6211: [1989] 4 CMLR 122.
[45] Case 53/87 [1988] ECR 6039: [1990] 4 CMLR 265.   [46] See Ch. 14, fn. 10.

at weekends) with some additional provision at public holidays. Magill claimed that this refusal to license the weekly programme details was an abuse of the monopoly which RTE held in them by virtue of its copyright. The Court of First Instance, largely adopting the reasoning of the Commission but after extensive citation of the earlier case law of the Court of Justice (both from cases concerning Article 82 and those involved with Articles 28 to 30 of the Treaty), confirmed that decision. After defining the relevant product market as RTE's own weekly programme listings and also the guide in which it published them (which of course had a monopoly) it pointed out that only weekly guides, with comprehensive listing for seven days, enabled viewers and listeners to decide in advance which programmes they wished to follow, and to arrange their leisure and domestic activities accordingly. Moreover, the existence of a demand for comprehensive weekly guides was shown by the fact that they were provided in nearly all other Member States irrespective of other available sources of programme information. RTE clearly had a monopoly in the listings themselves and in the right to reproduce and market them as it thought fit through its RTE guide. Third parties like Magill who wished to publish a general television magazine were in a position of economic dependence upon RTE, which could hinder the emergence of any effective competition.

The most interesting section of the decision, however, concerned the definition of abusive conduct. The Court of First Instance drew attention to the extensive case law, which balanced the need for free movement of goods against the protection of subject-matter of intellectual property rights, including copyright. It pointed out that the cases showed that the principle of the supremacy of Community law, particularly concerning such fundamental principles as free movement of goods and competition, normally prevailed over any rule of national intellectual property law contrary to those principles. It referred to the cases of *Volvo* and *Renault*, drawing an analogy between the hypothetical refusal there to supply spare parts to independent repairers or to provide parts at all for cars still in current use, and RTE's actual refusal to license a weekly magazine when there was a clear demand for it. By this action RTE was preventing the emergence on the market of a new product, namely a general television magazine, likely to compete with its own programme magazine. Copyright was being used in the programme listings which RTE produced as part of its broadcasting activities in order to secure a monopoly in the derivative market of weekly television guides, and the offer to provide information for brief periods only did not meet that need.

The Court of First Instance found that preventing the production and marketing of a new product for which there is a potential consumer demand and excluding competition from the market simply to secure a monopoly went well beyond the essential function of copyright as permitted under Community law. RTE's refusal to authorize such publications was justified neither by the specific needs of the broadcasting sector nor of the technical requirements of producing magazines containing the schedules.

When the appeal eventually reached the European Court in 1995, very considerable interest in the final outcome of the case had arisen, particularly in the basis upon which the ultimate finding would be made. Interest was heightened by the publication of the long and scholarly opinion of Gulmann A-G, who took the view that no breach of Article 82 had been committed. He accepted that, in certain special circumstances, the rights of owners of intellectual property have to be balanced against the interests of free competition (as indeed in many cases against the interests of the free movement of goods under Article 30) and the Court had to balance the 'essential function' of intellectual property rights against the other interests to arrive at a solution. In his view, however, the fact that a balance had to be struck did not mean that those interests had to be given equal weight. In his view the balance must always be in favour of intellectual property rights. 'The starting point set out in the Treaty is that intellectual property rights can be exercised even if that leads to obstacles to trade or restrictions of competition. Consequently if exercise of a given intellectual property right is necessary in order for that right to be able to fulfil its essential function, that exercise is not affected by the Treaty rules'.[47] In his view no such special circumstances existed in this case which would justify the removal of the copyright protection in the programme schedules, especially as any product which compulsory licensing would permit would be in direct competition with the programme guide published by RTE. He also distinguished the existing case law prohibiting refusal to supply to a competitor who wished to use a product on a derivative market, e.g. spare parts which the very design of the original car or other machinery made essential, with the different facts of this case where the refusal was to grant a licence to a competitor seeking merely to compete in a secondary market.

When the European Court decision appeared some months later it gave rise to considerable disappointment. This was not so much with the outcome of the case, in favour of the plaintiff, Magill, but with the fact that it concurred with almost the entire decision of the Court of First Instance without adding much detail or further analysis. It also made scarcely any reference to the main points of the Advocate General. Disappointment was also caused by its perceived failure to enunciate a clear doctrinal basis for refusals to license intellectual property rights, an issue of importance in many industrial sectors, notably pharmaceuticals and software.

The European Court in finding in favour of Magill placed weight on two main factors. The first was that there was no actual or potential substitute for the product (a comprehensive guide showing all programmes during the week) for which there was a substantial consumer demand, not currently being met by any broadcasting authority. The second reason was that there was no commercial or technical justification for the refusal to license which entitled the owners of the programme information to grant licences. It is notable that the European Court stressed that the material sought was essentially 'information' rather than intellectual property, the copyright protection arising almost accidentally or incidentally, rather than forming an essential part of the owners' business.

This decision is highly contentious. Interestingly, two powerful additional arguments justifying the Commission's decision were not referred to by the Court. The first is that in considering the concept of abuse, the normal practice to be found within Member States may be of considerable relevance. Here the facts found were that in all Member States, apart from the United Kingdom and Ireland, competing publications containing a full week's programmes of television and radio were commonly found. The fact that these publications existed not only proved that they represented a separate product market for which there was substantial demand, but also illustrated that there could be no overwhelming commercial or technical reason for refusing listeners and viewers the opportunity of planning their activities at least a week ahead. In other words, within the concept of abuse can be included an element of departure from norms of commercial conduct commonly found throughout the Community.

The second distinguishing feature of *RTE* v. *Magill* is that the copyright in the programme

---

[47] Para. 80 of the Advocate General's Opinion.

material only arose in the first place because of the existence of the statutory privilege or monopoly conferred on RTE to act as a broadcasting authority. It could therefore have been appropriately argued that RTE had, not only a right to prepare programme schedules in which it had copyright, but a duty to publicize in every reasonable manner the details of the programmes broadcast pursuant to this monopoly. In other words, the existence of a copyright obtained simply in order to enable the proper performance of a public function may be treated more severely by the Court than a copyright voluntarily acquired by the expenditure of creative effort. This point was not expressly taken by the Court, but may nevertheless have played an important part in its thinking.

7.5 SOFTWARE LICENSING: THE EFFECTS OF *MAGILL*

It has been suggested that this decision may have far-reaching consequences in other sectors since it could be used as a justification for requiring owners of a wide variety of intellectual property rights in, for example, software to grant licences on reasonable terms if it can be shown that there is an existing demand for the material covered by the licences and no convincing technical or commercial reason for refusing to grant it on reasonable terms. It could therefore be used to remove from the owners of a variety of intellectual property rights even that limited protection from obligations to grant licences of relevant material to the extent that the *Renault* and *Volvo* cases had appeared to provide. The special features present in the *Magill* case, however, suggest that the Court will not be keen to apply such principles freely to other types of copyright such as computer programs or patents where similar factors may be absent.

Of course, the recitals to the Software Directive 91/250[48] confirm that its terms are without prejudice to the application of Article 82 when a dominant supplier refuses to provide information necessary for the interoperability of equipment, as in the *IBM* case. Moreover, Article 6 of the Directive allows a person authorized or licensed to use a program to 'decompile' it to allow communication with another program which the licensee has already created. However, this right of decompilation, which is achieved through reverse engineering, may not be used so as unreasonably to prejudice the legitimate interests of that program's owner, nor so as to conflict with his normal exploitation of his program. In the past, however, such an owner was free to refuse to license software to persons whom he suspects may seek to carry out 'decompilation'; following *Magill* (until it is reversed or distinguished in later cases) such a refusal on those grounds alone may be considerably harder to maintain. On the other hand, whilst second-hand cars cannot be operated without the availability of a full range of spare parts, and a television service without adequate published programme schedules is of limited value, the potential range and function of new software programs that licensees may wish to produce to communicate with (and expand the use of) their existing software is unlimited. The analogy with *Magill* may therefore not be straightforward.

Much anxiety has been expressed during and since *Magill* by the owners of intellectual property such as patented drugs or software that the decision might be to make it difficult for owners to refuse requests for licences. Thus the owners of a new patent for, say, a

---

[48] [1991] OJ L122/42. Decompilation can only apply when the owner of the program fails to disclose required interface information.

revoluntionary drug to combat Aids might suddenly find itself besieged with requests for licences to manufacture the product all around the world, or the owners of a valuable software program who wish to exploit it themselves, might be prevented from doing so by being forced into widespread licensing. However, it appears that the Commission has treated the *Magill* judgment as having limited application, not requiring widespread compulsory licensing. Owners of intellectual property rights are normally entitled to decide whether to license or not. Merely to reach a negative decision is not to commit a breach of Article 82. A breach only occurs if there is no commercial justification for or explanation of the refusal, and moreover, the object or result of the refusal is to give the intellectual property rights owner some advantage in a derivative market' which goes beyond the proper protection of 'essential function', as indicated in *Ladbroke* (see Section 9.3).

7.6   IMS HEALTH

A sequel to the *Magill* saga has been the *IMS Health*[49] case which is still pending, but where actions for interim measures have already produced an important ruling from the President of the CFI. Pharmaceutical companies require for their business a large amount of sales information at a local level. Because of data protection legislation in Germany this cannot be provided for groups of less than three pharmacies but needs aggregation at a local level into a number of units each covering at least four or five pharmacies. The system developed in Germany over a number of years, by co-operation between pharmaceutical companies and IMS, is currently known as the '1860 brick structure', under which the country is divided into that number of zones of equivalent size. Originally there were far fewer separate bricks in the system but by the joint efforts of all parties a more detailed system was gradually refined. Rivals to IMS unsuccessfully sought alternative methods for breaking down sales data in Germany and having failed, then sought licences from IMS to use its copyright in the 1860 brick structure. When IMS refused, these rivals complained to the Commission which, following an investigation, granted their request for interim measures under which IMS would have been forced to give immediate licence of the 1860 brick system, in return for royalties set by an independent expert if the parties should fail to agree.

IMS appealed the interim measures decision of the Commission to the President of the CFI, who overruled the Commission's order in a judgment that contained a number of significant comments on the interpretation of *Magill* and whose decision was subsequently upheld by the President of the ECJ. The main ground for his decision was that the granting of interim measures requiring the granting of a licence by IMS would be more likely to cause 'serious and irreparable harm' to IMS, whereas the disadvantage to the complainants of not receiving an immediate licence was lesser. But in the course of his judgment, Judge Vesterdorf, without reaching a final decision on the merits of the case (which was still before the Commission), expressed serious doubts as to whether the *Magill* judgment necessarily meant that IMS would be required under Article 82 to grant compulsory licences in such circumstances. It seemed arguable that the 'exceptional circumstances' of *Magill* did not exist in the present case since IMS were not unilaterally preventing the creation of a market,

---

[49] [2002] 4 CMLR 58 (the President of the CFI's decision on interim measures) and 111 (the Commission's prior decision on interim measures).

but were operating a system which had by through co-operation with the pharmaceutical industry become a *de facto* industry standard.[50] Judge Vesterdorf of the CFI emphasized the need for the plaintiff to show damage to competition, rather than mainly to competitors.

7.7 *TETRAPAK (NO. 1)*

The abuse of power provided by intellectual property rights was also a central theme in other major cases, namely *Hilti*[51] (European Court 1994) and *Tetrapak (No. 1)*[52] (Court of First Instance 1991). The facts in *Hilti* were essentially unremarkable; Hilti attempted to use its intellectual property rights, patent and copyright respectively in nail guns and cartridge strips (into which the nails were fixed before firing) in order to discourage other companies from manufacturing or buying the nails (which enjoyed no such protection) from third parties. Its methods included tying the sale of the nails to the purchase of the cartridges and upon sales of cartridges made without correspondingly large purchase of nails to reduce the discounts provided. The Commission and Community Courts rejected Hilti's argument that it was primarily concerned to prevent damage to users of its guns and cartridges by the use of nails from other sources. There was no evidence that the use of non-Hilti nails had led to accidents, and a complete absence of any current written complaints from Hilti about the quality of nails produced by competitors for use with Hilti's guns and cartridges.

The facts of the *Tetrapak (No. 1)* judgment by the Court of First Instance were altogether more unusual, and the decision is a landmark in the development of case law on abuse.[53] Milk can be provided for household consumption in two main ways. It can be sold fresh, normally in familiar 'gable-shaped' cartons, or it can come as UHT milk, which is aseptic (after sterilization by hydrogen peroxide) and normally sold in 'brick-shaped' cartons. Consumers find it much easier to open the gable-shaped carton and for some years Liquipak, a United States company, had been trying to develop technology to produce machinery for manufacturing gable-shaped cartons in which UHT milk could be sold (thus eliminating the need for brick-shaped cartons). It had collaborated with, and had as its Community licensee, a Norwegian company, Elopak, and with this company it had carried out numerous trials in the development of the new product which it believed had been brought to the point of commercial full-scale development. In doing so it had had the help of an exclusive patent licence from the British Technology Group, BTG, granted in 1981 but in terms which complied with the subsequent Patent Block Exemption (Regulation 2349/84) introduced in 1984. By 1986 Elopak believed it was in a position to challenge Tetrapak, which had at that time some 90 per cent of the Community market in both the machinery for manufacturing the cartons and the cartons themselves.

In that same year, however, Tetrapak acquired the Liquipak group of companies and with them the exclusive licence for developing the gable-shaped aseptic milk carton and necessary filling machinery. Elopak raised a complaint under Article 82 with the Commission and

[50] The detailed arguments of the protagonists can be found in F. Fine, 'NDC/IMS: A logical application of the Essential Facilities doctrine' [2002] 23 ECLR 457–468, responding to an article by John Temple Lang referred to at fn. 75 of this chapter.

[51] See fn. 6, Ch. 14.

[52] *Tetrapak (No. 1)*, Case T-51/89 [1990] ECR II-309: [1991] 4 CMLR 334.

[53] It is noteworthy that in its first major case on this issue the Court took the opportunity to lay down broad principles of the relationship between Arts 81 and 82 rather than deciding the case on relatively narrow technical grounds.

after proceedings had been instituted against Tetrapak, Tetrapak abandoned any claim to exclusivity under the licence, which would have meant that BTG could license other would-be entrants (had it wished to do so) to the market for gable-shaped aseptic milk cartons. In spite of this, the Commission continued with the case because it raised important issues of principle. Tetrapak's acquisition of Liquipak had left only one other active competitor capable of producing aseptic filling machinery and cartons, enjoying only 10 per cent of the market; moreover, the technology of this company, PKL, was inferior to that of Tetrapak since it could only supply individually flattened blanks, and not cartons produced in continuous rolls. The market for the filling machinery was limited: dairies did not change their machines often as they had a life of at least ten years; moreover, milk was not a growing market. All these factors meant that the barriers to entry by new competitors were high.

The issue raised by the actions of Tetrapak was whether the acquisition of the exclusive licence previously owned by its main competitor could constitute an abuse; Tetrapak argued that this could not be so because the agreement itself benefited from an existing block exemption under Regulation 2349/84. It is clear from the Court's decision that the mere existence of the block exemption covering the licence agreement did not automatically prevent abuse. In his lengthy review of the earlier cases on abuse Advocate General Kirschner pointed out that undertakings with a dominant position were entitled to act in a profit-orientated way in order to expand their business activities. They were not required to act contrary to economic sense or their own legitimate interests. On the other hand, commercial steps which might be open to undertakings without a dominant position were, when effected by a dominant company, to be treated as abuse of its power; nor was it necessary to an Article 82 finding for the dominant company to have used that market power in order to obtain the benefit of the acquisition or licence agreement concerned. He referred back to the judgment in *Hoffmann-La Roche*,[54] and pointed to the concept of proportionality underlying the various kinds of abuse dealt with in earlier cases including *United Brands*,[55] *BRT* v. *SABAM*,[56] and other performing rights cases. In *Tetrapak (No. 1)*, a company with some 90 per cent of the market in the aseptic filling machines and the cartons made to be used with them acquired an exclusive licence from its main potential competitor endeavouring to break into that market. The effect of the acquisition of the Liquipak group was that the alternative technology protected by that patent was denied not only to Liquipak but to all Tetrapak's potential competitors. The acquisition of this exclusive licence was a disproportionate method of carrying on business since the acquisition of a non-exclusive licence would also have enabled Tetrapak to use its patented process to improve its own products, but without impeding access by competitors to the market over which Tetrapak enjoyed so dominant a position.

The Court speedily made clear that the principles laid down in *Parke, Davis*, as later qualified in the *Renault/Volvo* cases, would not help Tetrapak. A distinction was drawn between the development of technology in those cases by an individual company which it was then entitled to protect or refuse to license (other than in exceptional circumstances),

---

[54] Case 85/76 [1979] ECR 461, 520: 3 CMLR 211, 274, popularly called the *Vitamins* case.

[55] Case 27/76 [1978] ECR 207: 1 CMLR 429.

[56] Case 127/73 [1974] ECR 51 (the Court's judgment dealing with the direct effect in national Courts of Art. 82) and 313 (the Court's judgment dealing with the issue of whether SABAM was exploiting its dominant position as a copyright authority in Belgium): [1974] 2 CMLR 238 is a consolidated report of both judgments.

and the acquisition in this case by Tetrapak of technology developed by others. The Court, dealing briefly with the concept of abuse because during the hearing of the case Tetrapak had withdrawn their appeal against the Commission's decision on this aspect (though not on other aspects)[57] of the case, found that the mere fact that an undertaking in a dominant position acquired an exclusive licence did not *per se* constitute abuse; on the other hand, in the specific circumstances of the acquisition the exclusivity of the licence acquired had not only strengthened Tetrapak's already considerable domination of the market but also had the effect of preventing, or at the very least considerably delaying, the entry of new competitors into the market.

8. ABUSES BY COLLECTIVE OWNERS OF INTELLECTUAL PROPERTY RIGHTS

8.1 RESTRICTIVE RULES OF COLLECTING SOCIETIES

The application of Article 82 to performing rights societies within the Community raises some novel issues, and cases decided by the Court of Justice have illustrated the potential flexibility of the Article as applied to situations outside normal industrial and commercial markets. The role of performing rights societies, found in most Member States, is to collect and administer very large numbers of copyrights for music to be publicly performed, representing the creative work of composers and librettists, so as to enable the licensing of these works (often by way of a block licence) to all those undertakings which may require their use. These may range from broadcasting authorities and cable TV companies on one hand to individual proprietors of businesses such as discothèques and public halls on the other. Performing rights societies have two advantages; they enable the owners of the individual copyrights (which are often assigned to music publishers for exploitation) to obtain and monitor a greater number of performances of his work, with a corresponding increase in income, while enabling those paying the licence fees to obtain by a single payment a far greater range of copyright material than would be possible if individual negotiations were required for each copyright.

Nevertheless, performing rights societies have on occasion sought to introduce into their rules restrictions going beyond those reasonably necessary for the proper protection and promotion of their members' interests. Such restrictions have been challenged under the provisions of Article 82, involving performing rights societies and similar undertakings in Germany, France, and Belgium. The leading case is *BRT* v. *SABAM*[58] (European Court 1974). Two Belgian radio employees decided to prove that even a 'nonsense song' could become a hit, and wrote a song entitled 'Asparagus Beans', assigning the copyright to Belgian Radio and Television (BRT). BRT then arranged for it to be recorded and for the discs to be sold. SABAM claimed rights in the song on the basis that under its standard form of agreement it

---

[57] The Court's important ruling on the relationship between Arts 81and 82 is considered in detail in Ch. 16.

[58] Case 127/73: [1974] ECR 51 313: 2 CMLR 238. Public interest issues arising in the operation of collective societies are considered in the MMC Reports on *Collective Licensing* (Cm. 530) (1988) and the *Performing Rights Society* (Cm. 314) (1996).

obtained rights over the work of its former members (who included the BRT employees who had written the song) for five years after they had ceased to be members. BRT claimed that SABAM's claim was invalid because SABAM was a *de facto* monopoly, and the five-year restriction went so far beyond its reasonable requirements as to constitute an abuse of its dominant position. An Article 234 reference by a Belgian Court resulted in a ruling from the European Court that any undertaking entrusted with the exploitation of copyrights was likely to hold a dominant position, and that if it imposed on its members obligations not absolutely requisite for the attainment of its legitimate objects, it would be in breach of Article 82. Protection could not be afforded to that organization by reason of Article 86(2) since the responsibilities taken on by SABAM had not been assigned to it by the State, but merely involved the management of private interests, namely intellectual property rights protected by Belgian law. However, the extent to which the validity of any contract in dispute before a national court was thereby affected was for the national Court to decide.

Cases had already been heard and decided by the Commission in connection with the rules of such organizations. In 1971, *GEMA (No. 1)* involved a challenge to the complex set of rules relating to the German Performing Rights Society. The Commission decided that in a number of respects the rules violated Article 82; they discriminated against nationals of other Member States, who were denied credit for royalties which they received from similar associations in the Community, when their status and eligibility for ordinary membership in GEMA were being considered.[59] Moreover, foreign nationals were unable to become members of GEMA's council, nor could music publishing houses outside Germany be admitted to membership. The rules also required higher royalties on records imported or reimported from other Member States than on records produced in Germany.

GEMA was also found to have imposed over-wide obligations on its individual members, requiring, *inter alia*, assignments of their rights in all categories of creative work, and for the whole world; it was made extremely difficult to withdraw from the association because membership had to be for a minimum period of six years. GEMA was therefore required to amend its rules and practices to remove the discriminatory and over-wide provisions.[60]

Subsequently, *Greenwich Film Productions* v. *SACEM*[61] raised further issues arising out of a dispute between the French Performing Rights Society (SACEM) and the producers of a film for which two members of SACEM had composed music. Under the terms of their membership, the copyrights in their work had been assigned to SACEM, though some performances would take place in territories over which SACEM had no direct jurisdiction, outside the Common Market. SACEM sued Greenwich for the royalties in respect of these performances, and Greenwich put forward Article 82 as the ground for non-payment. The issue before the Court was whether Article 82 could apply to the performance in non-EC countries of contracts entered into within the territory of a Member State by parties within the jurisdiction of that State. On an earlier occasion, SACEM had had to alter its rules to

---

[59] This was a more favourable category of membership than the extraordinary membership normally accorded to foreign nationals: [1971] CMLR D35.

[60] In a later Commission decision ([1982] 2 CMLR 482), there has been further review of the GEMA rules, and a negative clearance granted to an amendment aimed at preventing broadcasting companies from obtaining unfair advantages through special royalty-sharing arrangements with composers in return for 'song-plugging'. The Commission emphasized that practices which might in other contexts be an abuse of a dominant position would not necessarily be so if 'indispensable to carrying out the essential purposes of a collecting society'.

[61] Case 22/79 [1979] ECR 3275: [1980] 1 CMLR 629.

comply with Commission requirement that it reduce the restrictions which it imposed, on the same basis as the findings in *GEMA (No. 1)*. SACEM had therefore already eliminated from its rules discrimination against nationals of other Member States and reduced the period for which a member had to bind himself or herself to SACEM.

The results of the case proved unsatisfactory to the composers as well as to the Commission. The Court held that if Article 82 abuses were found, it was for French Courts to decide to what extent the interests of the composers would be affected. The rules of the association were still in breach of Article 82, and the fact that such an abuse affected only the performance in non-member countries of contracts entered into in the territory of a Member State would not preclude the application of that Article. In the event, however, the French Cour de Cassation avoided any application of the ruling by the European Court to the particular case, claiming that the original membership of the two composers in SACEM antedated the application of Article 82 to the case, so that no effect on trade between Member States could be considered attributable to the conduct of SACEM. This unsatisfactory ruling (ignoring the direct effect in national law of Article 82 which was in force at the date when both composers joined SACEM) offers an example, fortunately rare, of a national court ruling which paid scant attention to the terms of the decisions of the European Court.

Article 82 has also been applied[62] to an organization established in Germany for the protection of copyright in order to manage the rights of performers to royalties in respect of visual or sound recordings of their performances which are then shared on an equitable basis with the manufacturers of these recordings. This type of right is normally called 'secondary exploitation' and is, of course, quite separate from the primary exploitation of the copyright in the music and words of the individual works. The defendant, GVL, was the only organization of its kind in Germany, and until November 1980 refused to conclude agreements with performers who were not resident in Germany. The relevant market was found by the Commission and Court to be the commercial management of the secondary exploitation rights of performers, and for this the Court ruled that residence was not a relevant factor. Therefore, the refusal of GVL to act for foreign performers was itself an abuse of their *de facto* monopoly position. Although no fine was imposed because GVL's internal decision had been reversed before the date of the Commission's decision, a valuable ruling had been obtained; in view of the express provisions of Article 7 of the Treaty forbidding discrimination on the grounds of nationality, however, the decision itself caused no surprise.

8.2 EXCESSIVE CHARGES

The question of the level of charges made by such organizations reached the European Court in four linked cases[63] involving the rules of SACEM, referred under Article 234 from French courts. In the first three cases SACEM sought payment of royalties from French discothèques in the Poitiers region which had refused to take out a licence from it; in the other case a disco owner sued Tournier as managing director of SACEM in respect of alleged

---

[62] In *GVL* v. *Commission* Case 7/82 [1983] ECR 483: 3 CMLR 645.
[63] The cases were *Ministère Public* v. *Tournier* Case 395/87: [1989] ECR 2521: [1991] 4 CMLR 248; SACEM v. *Lucazeau* Case 110/88; *SACEM* v. *Debelle* Case 241/88; *SACEM* v. *Soumagnac* Case 242/88: all at [1989] ECR 2811: [1991] 4 CMLR 248.

unfair trading practices under French law. Since 1978 there has been a long-running dispute between SACEM and a large number of French discothèque owners who thought that its rates were too high, discriminated unfairly between categories of discothèque, and refused without objective justification licences for the only category of music in which they were really interested, dance music of predominantly Anglo-American origin such as rock. As it was an Article 234 reference the Court was not asked to resolve the specific disputes between the parties but simply to reply to those questions which the French courts had raised. These questioned the compatibility of the practices of SACEM with respect to this kind of musical material, in the light of its undoubted dominance as a performing rights society within France and the various complaints about the manner in which this was carried out which the cases had raised.

In one aspect of the case the Court's ruling would have disappointed the discothèque owners. It found that SACEM's refusal to grant them licences simply for the foreign reper-toire likely to be preferred by its patrons would not be a restriction of competition unless providing access to part only of the repertoire (at presumably reduced royalties) could also entirely safeguard the interests of composers without increasing the costs of managing and monitoring the use of such copyright works. In other ways, the Court judgment was more favourable to the discothèque owners. It pointed out that if an undertaking such as SACEM imposed special fees for its services which were appreciably higher than those in other Member States, that difference might indicate an abuse of SACEM's dominant position. The burden of proof would then be on SACEM to justify that difference by showing that there were objective differences between its position and that of equivalent organizations in other Member States. The Court mentioned that the level of operating expenses in SACEM appeared particularly high and wondered if this was attributable to lack of competition. However, it refused to rule on whether the amount charged to discothèques themselves, as compared to the rates charged to other large-scale users of recorded music such as TV and radio stations, were unfair discrimination, leaving that awkward question to the national court. The Court decision followed the spirit, though not all the detail, of Jacobs A-G's opinion; he emphasized the particularly dominant position of this kind of organization which had no need to fear competition from foreign performing rights societies and no likelihood of substantial regulation of its affairs by public authority, so that it had near absolute freedom of action, coupled with a clear inequality of bargaining power between it and discothèques which were completely dependent upon it.

The general attitude of the Court in such cases has been robust. It has swept aside a number of the arguments raised by the societies, including protests that they are not 'under-takings', and that the writing of songs and music is a cultural rather than economic activity, and that individual composers or publishers are therefore not entitled to the protection of Article 82. The Court has also refused to allow the rules of such societies to limit the free transfer of copyright items between Member States which have been placed in commercial circulation in a single Member State. Articles 28 to 30 do, of course, also here come into the reckoning as illustrated by the case of *Musik-Vertrieb Membran and K-tel International v. GEMA*[64] (European Court 1982). This involved the question of whether the German

---

[64] Cases 55 and 57/81 [1982] ECR 147: 2 CMLR 44. This case follows closely the earlier precedents of the Court in respect of patents and trade marks. See Ch. 13 at pp.249–53. The distinction between this and *EMI Electrola* v. *Patricia* Case 341/87 [1989] ECR 79: 2 CMLR 413 is that in the latter case the owner of the copyright had not given consent to the marketing of the records.

collecting society which owned the copyright in musical works reproduced on gramophone records was entitled to claim from a parallel importer a fee equal to the royalties ordinarily paid for marketing such records in Germany, less the lower royalties already paid in the United Kingdom, where the records were originally put into circulation by the copyright owner. The Court gave a negative answer emphasizing that sound recordings, even if incorporated in copyright material, are covered by the system of free movement of goods, so that it was contrary to Article 28 for the owner of the copyright in the records to rely on copyright legislation to prevent the import of a product lawfully marketed in another Member State by the owner or with his consent.

8.3 THE COMMISSION'S RELUCTANCE TO INTERVENE

It should also be emphasized that the Commission has not in recent years shown itself enthusiastic about seeking to adjudge the conduct of collective societies against the standards of Article 82 and, particularly since *Automec (No. 2)*, has shown a willingness to return cases for assessment of their individual merits to national courts and competition authorities. In *Tremblay* v. *Commission*[65] and in the *Tournier* group of cases the continuing differences between the French discothèque owners and SACEM (mentioned above) were once again brought to the Commission, but on this occasion the European Court and the Court of First Instance supported the refusal of the Commission to deal further with the individual claims, since they only affected France and had no particular relevance to the functioning of the Common Market. The main interest of the complainant in this case was the recovery of damages that it may have incurred, and a decision of the Commission on such issues would not be binding on the national court or national competition authorities. The Court of First Instance adopted a similar attitude to the Commission's approach in *Koelman* v. *Commission*[66] where a claim by a Dutch composer that the rules of Dutch collecting society BUMA were in breach of Article 81 were found to be rules on which the Commission need not adjudicate, given that Koelman had suffered no financial or personal loss as a result of BUMA's activities.

Nevertheless the inherent nature of collecting societies, required to balance the interests of their many members with there very different priorities and circumstances, means that their rules and operations will always be the subject of complaint. This in turn leads the Commission necessarily to keep their operations under constant review, even if no formal proceedings have been begun. In many cases too the inevitably international nature of their operations will mean that the Commission may be unable to delegate responsibility for the investigations to national competition authorities.

9. REFUSAL OF ACCESS TO ESSENTIAL FACILITIES

9.1 THE 'HARBOUR' CASES

It is a characteristic of Article 82 that it can be applied in a variety of new situations to deal with apparently novel kinds of abuse. The development of the doctrine of 'essential facilities' illustrates this well. 'Refusal to deal' and 'discriminatory dealing' have been well

---

[65] Case C-91/95P [1996] ECR I-5547: [1997] 4 CMLR 211 and Case T-224/95: [1998] 4 CMLR 427.
[66] Case T-575/93 [1996] ECR II-1: 4 CMLR 636: Case C-59/96P (on appeal to ECJ 1997 ECR I-4809).

established examples of abuse for some time and a new category of abusive conduct has now been established which involves a combination of these practices. Essentially the conduct involved is the refusal by an undertaking, which owns or controls a facility or an infrastructure to which competitors require access in order to provide a service to their customers, to allow that access. Alternatively, the abuse may involve allowing access only on such unfavourable and discriminatory terms that it places new or existing competitors at a competitive disadvantage so that they cannot compete effectively.

This essential facility might be a port, harbour, or airport, a national telecommunications network, or a grid for electricity or gas. It might be an electronic system, such as a computer reservation system for airlines, a banking system enabling electronic transfer of funds, or a television network. For a variety of reasons, often connected with its strategic location or formal legislative protection, competitors may regard the particular facility as essential to their commercial needs and will complain to the Commission if they believe that the company controlling the facility is deliberately making it difficult or impossible for them to share it. There is substantial case law in this area; probably the earliest example is *Telemarketing (CBEM v. CLT & IPB)*.[67] IPB sold advertising time on Luxembourg television. It refused to accept advertisements that contained a telephone number from which further information could be obtained by potential customers unless the agency's own number was used. Under an Article 234 reference the European Court ruled:

> if telemarketing activities constitute a separate market from that of the chosen advertising medium, although closely associated with it, and if those activities mainly consist in making available to advertisers the telephone lines and team of telephonists of the telemarketing undertaking, to subject the sale of broadcasting time to the condition that the telephone lines of an advertising agent belonging to the same group as the television station should be used, amounts in practice to a refusal to supply the service of that station to any other telemarketing undertaking.

Essentially the practice amounted to a refusal to supply except on terms which amounted to 'tying', a practice already discussed at pages 298–300.

The development of the doctrine was accelerated by a group of cases involving passenger ferries and their need to use particular harbours within the Community. The first two cases involved the port of Holyhead in Wales, the others, ports in Denmark and France. The first case was *B & I Line v. Sealink Harbours*.[68] Both parties used Holyhead as the base for their Holyhead–Dublin ferry routes, but Sealink were also, through a subsidiary, the owner of the harbour. Unusually, B & I complained of an abuse affecting its business that involved physical interference with its use of the harbour. Schedules for the Sealink ferries were altered so that the Sealink ships passed close by B & I's ferry terminal on their way to the Sealink berths in the inner harbour. Because of the narrowness of the channel, the passing of these Sealink ships caused vertical and horizontal turbulence, such that the B & I linkspan for vehicles and passengers had to be disconnected and its loading period to be interrupted and shortened. The particular complaint of B & I was that Sealink had changed its schedules deliberately to cause more disruption to B & I. For its part, Sealink claimed that the plaintiffs could alter the stern shape of their ferry so that it would suffer less disruption from the passage of the Sealink ferries, and that they were already aware of the problem when they moved to their existing terminal.

---

[67] Case 311/84 [1985] ECR 3261: [1986] 2 CMLR 558.   [68] [1992] 5 CMLR 255.

The Commission ruled that the port of Holyhead was a substantial part of the Common Market and that Sealink had a dominant position there as owner of the port. The port controlled an important corridor for ferry services between Ireland and the United Kingdom. The Commission also ruled that Sealink as the dominant company must not change its schedules to put B & I at a disadvantage, because the physical limitations of the port and the narrowness of its channel meant that B & I's loading and unloading activities of would be affected by Sealink's choice of schedules. By way of interim order the defendants were told to resume their original schedule.

The next case[69] involved the same defendants, Sealink, but a different plaintiff, Sea Containers, also operating out of Holyhead. On this occasion the Commission refused interim measures because the defendants were regarded as having provided sufficient offers of additional slot times to allow the plaintiffs to run a viable service. The activities complained of here were not physical movements of ships, but the loss of commercial access to suitable berths, causing financial loss. Sea Containers also complained that Sealink had developed the port so as to reduce its current capacity and thereby Sea Containers' ability to make a success of their use of it. Sea Containers were particularly worried about delay caused to its proposed introduction of a fast catamaran to the harbour. Although in the event no order was made, the Commission was clearly prepared to develop the doctrine of essential facilities raised in the previous case involving the same harbour. It stated that any dominant company providing an essential facility to competitors which abuses that facility, and refuses access without objective justification, or grants access only on terms less favourable than those which it provides its own services, breaches Article 82. The background to the case was that both parties were trying to introduce the first 'fast cat' wave-piercing catamaran service on the route to Ireland. The Commission believed that Sealink were not negotiating in good faith and had failed to set up adequate procedures for handling its responsibilities as harbour operators towards other users.

In the third case[70] roles are reversed: we find Stena Sealink as the plaintiff in a case involving the refusal by the Danish State railways (DSB) either to allow Stena to build a new private commercial port near Rodby in Denmark, or to operate from the existing port. Rodby-Puttgarden is apparently the best route for ferry crossings between Denmark and Germany and is so commercially attractive that it is used by some 70 per cent of passengers and 88 per cent of lorries between Denmark and Germany. Rodby Harbour was operated by DSB which also ran the ferry jointly with the German railways. Because of the State involvement an Article 86 case was brought in respect of DSB's practices. The Commission ruled that an undertaking owning or managing a port facility from which it provides a ferry service may not, without objective justification, refuse to grant facilities or access to a shipowner seeking to operate in competition on the same route. The case clearly marked a further advance in the doctrine since it was now applied not only to discriminatory treatment for existing customers of a port, but to potential customers who sought entry and were refused access. Clearly the right of access could not unconditional, since there might be

---

[69] *Sea Containers* v. *Stena Sealink* [1994] OJ L15/8. The Commission held that Liverpool was not an effective alternative base for passenger ferry services to Ireland but Sea Containers eventually in 1998 opened its 'fast cat' service from Liverpool, which had better motorway access than Holyhead even if the sea crossing to Ireland was longer.

[70] *Stena* v. *DSB* [1994] OJ L55/52.

circumstances in which it would be unreasonable to expect the owner of the harbour to provide access, for example if it was already full or if there were genuine technical reasons why the new applicant could not be admitted. However, in the view of the Commission, this was not the case at Rodby.

The final case[71] of this quartet involved an Irish ferry line seeking to operate a route from Cork and Rosslare to Roscoff in Brittany, a port controlled by the local Chamber of Commerce, which held a minority interest in Brittany Ferries operating on the same routes between Ireland and Brittany. Roscoff to Cork was undoubtedly the most convenient route and Roscoff had the best harbour facilities at the French end. The Irish line had tried Brest as an alternative and found it unsatisfactory. A special factor here was that the Roscoff Chamber of Commerce had encouraged the Irish line to believe that facilities would be available for ferries in the 1995 summer season but subsequently changed their mind. On this occasion interim measures were ordered for the 1995 summer season, since otherwise the plaintiffs would have found themselves in a very awkward position, being unable to convey the passengers who had already booked in anticipation of a Roscoff service.

9.2 OTHER CATEGORIES OF ESSENTIAL FACILITIES

The Commission has been involved in other such cases connected with essential facilities in the transport sector. Thus in *Aer Lingus/British Midland Airways*,[72] Aer Lingus was in competition on the Dublin–London route with British Midland. Aer Lingus was dominant on the route and decided not to 'interline' with British Midland. Interlining is a standard practice approved by IATA by which airlines agree to accept each other's tickets and receive a compensating proportion of revenue. The Commission ruled that for a new airline seeking to compete on a route, interlining is in practice essential since its absence forces a new entrant either to operate infrequent flights, or to offer frequent flights attracting passengers but accepting that initial passenger utilization of its aircraft will be low. The Commission did not order an indefinite obligation on Aer Lingus to interline but a period of two years; this was considered as sufficient for British Midland to acquire sufficient passenger loading to be able to survive without interlining, if Aer Lingus then decided not to continue with it.

In a decision[73] involving the German Railway Authority, the Deutsche Bahn (DB), DB was found to have discriminated against container cargo being transported through the Benelux Countries to ports there by charging lower freight rates in respect of containers forwarded by it to German ports. Operators of the cargo services through the Benelux countries could not provide rail services but had to obtain them from the German authorities. The Commission held that DB had used its dominant position on the rail transport market to impose higher prices than would otherwise have prevailed, on a discriminatory basis, in order to promote its own combined rail and shipping services as against those of other transport operators who could not provide rail services.

---

[71] *Irish Continental Group v. CCI Morlaix* [1995] 5 CMLR 177.   [72] [1992] OJ L96/34.

[73] *Maritime Container Network* [1994] OJ L104/34: an appeal to the CFI was rejected (Case T-229/94 [1997] ECR II-1689: [1998] 4 CMLR 220).

9.3 THE TIDE TURNS: *BRONNER*

This trend of cases came however to an end with the *Ladbroke Tierce*[74] case. This involved a complaint by Ladbroke which already held a substantial share of the horserace betting market in Belgium but claimed that its operations were being obstructed by the refusal of the racecourse operators' association to allow it radio and television commentaries on race meetings in its betting shops. The CFI held that the provisions of these services were not an essential facility since it was not an essential part of the betting business (nor was their refusal preventing the introduction of a new product or service); and moreover that the racecourse operators were not themselves engaged in competition with Ladbrokes as in running a betting business. Soon after followed the more important case of *Oscar Bronner*.[75] Here for the first time the doctrine of essential facilities was before the European Court and subject to a full analysis by Jacobs A-G, whose opinion was subsequently substantially followed by the Court. In Austria Mediaprint was a publisher of daily papers with a market share of some 46.8 per cent. Bronner meanwhile published a single newspaper with a share of national circulation of 3.6 per cent. Bronner claimed that access to Mediaprint's countrywide home delivery system was the only method available to it of ensuring nationwide punctual house delivery (since postal delivery was not viewed by it as an adequate alternative). Mediaprint justified its refusal to grant access to its system to Bronner on grounds that its home delivery service had been established only with its considerable investment, had little spare capacity to incorporate new publications, and moreover that Bronner did have a choice of other methods to obtain national circulation.

Jacobs A-G stressed the importance of not extending the doctrine in an undesirably wide manner. He emphasized the principle that in general it is pro-competitive (and in the consumer interest) to allow a company to retain for its own use facilities which it has developed for its own business. Otherwise, its incentive to invest in efficient facilities is reduced. The purpose of Article 82 is not to protect the position of individual competitors but to prevent the distortion of competition. To allow the doctrine of essential facilities to lead to the granting of access to such facilities might assist short-term 'static' competition but might well change the 'dynamic' long-term competition in a detrimental way through the removal of appropriate incentives to invest. Moreover, in the current case Bronner had other alternative methods of distribution even if it were uneconomic for it to set up a rival home distribution service. He feared that too broad a definition of the doctrine would leave both the Commission and courts involved in widespread regulation of prices and conditions.

In a relatively short judgment the ECJ agreed with the substance of the Advocate General's opinion. Newspapers could be distributed by post or through sales in shops and kiosks, and it was for Bronner to prove that (as it had not) it was not economically viable for a rival home delivery scheme to be set up with a circulation comparable to that of the Mediaprint system. In response to the questions raised by the Austrian Court under Article 234, the Court ruled that national courts should decide cases of this kind on the basis that the exceptional circumstances of the *Magill* case were not present.

---

[74] Case T-504/93 [1997] ECR II-923: 5 CMLR 309.

[75] Case C-7/97 [1998] ECR I-7791 [1999]: 4 CMLR 112. The case should be read in conjunction with the authoritative earlier analysis of the issues set out by John Temple Lang in *Defining Legitimate Competition: Companies' Duties to Supply Competitors and Access to Essential Facilities*, Fordham Corporate Law Institute (1994), pp.245–313, to which I acknowledge my debt. See also Bergman, Case note [2000] 21 ECLR pp.59–63.

10. OTHER FORMS OF ABUSIVE CONDUCT

10.1 ACQUISITIONS BY DOMINANT COMPANIES

Apart from the principal forms of abuse there are a number of other miscellaneous examples which have been the subject of Commission decisions (formal and informal) and which illustrate the inherent flexibility and wide range of application of the Article.

The first example has to be the well-known case of *Continental Can*, the facts of which are set out in Chapter 17.[76] At the time of the case there was no European Community Merger Regulation (ECMR) in existence, but nevertheless the Commission became concerned that in some circumstances a company with existing dominance could further abuse it, not by any of those abuses involving pricing or refusals to deal, but simply by acquiring other undertakings in the same market. This would enable it to have additional market power and leverage over its competitors. There was no need for the Commission to prove, said the European Court, that the increase in dominance brought about by the merger would necessarily lead, as a matter of causation, to any particular abuse being introduced; an increase in market share alone would be sufficient in these circumstances to constitute abuse.

This approach may well today seem unduly harsh, given the substantive criteria laid down in the Merger Regulation in Article 2, requiring that the dominance of the merged undertaking must not only have been created or strengthened by that particular transaction but have the result of 'significantly impeding' competition in the Common Market. The decision is however a reminder that, had no merger regulation ever been adopted, Article 82 might well have been developed through Commission and Court jurisprudence along lines possibly even more stringent than those contained in the Merger Regulation, even if this is now an argument that is of hypothetical rather than practical significance.

Nor is the reach of Article 82 limited to the acquisition of majority control. It is clear from the *BAT/Reynolds*[77] case (also dealt with in Chapter 17) that the abuse may consist of the acquisition even of minority control provided it gives the acquirers some influence on the commercial policy of the target. The existence of well-established systems of both Community and Member State merger control make it unlikely that a practice Article 82 will be used in the context of acquisitions.

10.2 IMPOSITION OF UNREASONABLE TERMS

Article 82(a) states that the imposition of unreasonable terms and conditions, whether directly or indirectly, is an abuse. This has been of particular relevance to the Commission's approach to national schemes for encouraging the recycling of packaging waste. The 2001 Annual Report sets out some of the principles which it has applied in recent cases, notably that of the *German Green Dot Scheme (DSD)*.[78] Under German laws, DSD operated a

---

[76] At pp.336–7.   [77] At pp.338–9.

[78] [2001] 5 CMLR 609. This case is now under appeal to the CFI. In *Alsatel* (fn. 18, Ch. 14) the terms of the rental agreement for telephone equipment was likewise held abusive because of the penalty imposed on the hirer, if it sought to extend the equipment, was excessive.

nation-wide collection scheme, under which undertakings paid DSD a licence fee and were thereby authorized to place a 'green dot' on their packaging. DSD then agreed to collect this on its behalf. DSD held 82 per cent of the national market for organisations authorized to carry out such services in return for a fee. The term of the licence fee required payment to DSD for every package bearing the green dot and was not limited to those packages which were actually collected by DSD. This restriction meant that existing barriers to entry to market were raised even higher, and provided a disincentive to licensees to make their own disposal arrangements for part at least of their packaging waste. No commercial justification was shown for the clause and DSD was required by the Commission to replace these arrangements with a contract under which the fee was calculated by reference to packaging waste actually collected by DSD.

10.3 NATIONALITY DISCRIMINATION

Discrimination on the grounds of nationality is of course forbidden under Article 12 (formerly Article 6) of the Treaty but may also be treated as an abusive practice under the Article 82. The *GVL* case has already been referred to in the section on collecting societies, as an example of discrimination on grounds of nationality by the German collecting society. In *1998 Football World Cup*[79] a notional fine of 1000 Euros was imposed on the French organizers of ticketing arrangements for the World Cup, for giving preference in the allocation of tickets to those members of the public able to provide an address in France, and for imposing unfair conditions on football supporters in other EEA countries, under which their applications for tickets could only be made through their own national associations (which had far fewer tickets to distribute). Likewise in the *Corsica Ferries*[80] case tariffs set for the pilot service provided to ships had favoured those provided for ships of a particular nationality, a tendency also common to the numerous cases already referred to in Section 4.4 with regard to landing fees at airports in certain Member States.

10.4 ABUSE OF LEGAL PROCEEDINGS

In the *Hilti* case it was held that a dominant company which sought to obtain in respect of a licence required to be granted under national patent law requirements, a royalty six times that finally awarded by an independent expert was itself abusive. Moreover, even the bringing of legal proceedings can itself in certain situations be abusive. In *ITT Promedia* v. *Commission*,[81] the Court of First Instance 1998, the Court upheld the Commission ruling, following a dispute in Belgium over the right to publish telephone directories, that the bringing of legal proceedings could be abusive. In this case Belgacom had originally held a State monopoly for their publication but this had been abolished by statute in 1994. ITT Promedia decided to enter the market and sued Belgacom for failing to provide it with subscriber data needed for compilation of its directory. This claim was settled but Belgacom then issued counter proceedings in connection with an earlier agreement with ITT for the supply of other subscriber data to Belgacom. ITT Promedia complained to the Commission that

---

[79] [2000] 4 CMLR 963.
[80] Case C-18/93 [1994] ECR I-1783 ('*the Corsica Ferries (No. 1)* case'). See Ch. 22, p.485.
[81] Case T-111/96 [1998] 5 CMLR 491.

Belgacom by its counter-claim was seeking to abuse its dominant position so as to drive ITT from the Belgian market. The Commission and the Court of First Instance both rejected ITT's claim but stated the bringing of litigation could be abusive if:

(i) the legal action could not reasonably be characterized as an attempt to establish the bona fide rights of the dominant company; and

(ii) if it had been conceived in the framework of a plan whose goal was to eliminate competition to the dominant company.

16

ARTICLE 82: ITS RELATIONSHIP WITH ARTICLE 81

1. THEIR COMMON FEATURES AND DIFFERENCES

1.1 SIX DISTINCTIONS BETWEEN THE ARTICLES

The case law of the European Court and of the Court of First Instance has clarified the meanings of both these Articles in their application to a wealth of differing circumstances and sectors. The great majority of cases have been concerned with one rather than both Articles, but in some decisions the relationship of the Articles to each other has been a central feature.

No account of EC competition law should disregard the important interaction between these two Articles. At first sight the possibility that such interaction could be significant might seem remote. Although their drafting has some shared characteristics, their individual scope and purpose appear to be mutually exclusive; whereas Article 81 prohibits agreements or concerted practices between two or more undertakings, the primary target under Article 82 is action by a single undertaking abusing its market dominance, without the need to prove any agreement or concerted practice involving another undertaking. One of the main problems encountered by the Commission in enforcing Article 81 is proving the existence of the relevant agreement or concerted practice between two or more undertakings in the absence of unequivocal written evidence. This problem of identification does not arise under Article 82.

Five further important distinctions between the Articles should be noted:

(*a*) Since it is necessary under the terms of Article 82 to establish that the abuse occurred in a market comprising a substantial part of the Common Market, the chief difficulty in such cases (rather than proof of an agreement or concerted practice) is to define accurately the relevant geographic and product markets to which the dominance applies. Such dominance must be either over the entire Common Market or over a single Member State or group of Member States, or possibly a substantial part of a single Member State. By contrast, under Article 81, although the Commission must still carry out economic analysis to identify the markets where the agreements or practices have their effect, their delineation is normally less critical to the outcome of the case, especially where they have as their *object* the restriction of competition, as opposed to *effects* cases.

(*b*) Article 82 provides no sanctions of voidness for illegality against the prohibited conduct, for there is no equivalent of Article 81(2). On the other hand, since Article 82 is directly enforceable in the courts of Member States (confirmed by the 1974 European Court decision in *Belgian Radio and Television* v. *SABAM*[1]) the offending clauses in any contractual provision imposed by way of abuse may be declared void and unenforceable by national courts against contracting parties. Moreover, *Magill*[2] shows that a compulsory licence may be ordered against the dominant company found to have abused its position by refusal to grant one. In *Tetrapak (No. 2)*[3] sweeping remedies were allowed to its customers: the company was required to supply any of them through the Tetrapak subsidiary which the customer chose and at the price made available generally. This was combined with a prohibition against Tetrapak refusing orders from dealers and a requirement upon it that carton discounts be granted solely on the basis of quantities ordered.

(*c*) Since the prohibited action is an 'abuse' of existing market power, logically there can be no exceptions of the kind available under the 'four conditions' contained in Article 81(3). If the dominant company wishes to raise arguments of the kind considered by DG Comp when reviewing the application of these four conditions, it will have to do so by contesting the Commission's claims that the acts which it admits to performing are an 'abuse', and establishing that they are no more than the normal use of its economic strength within the boundaries of legitimate competition, or justified on other grounds. Whilst there is a right in at least refusal to deal cases to rely on 'commercial justification' as a defence, this is considerably more limited in scope than the exemptions made available under Article 81(3). The same would be true of any attempt by a dominant company to rely on the doctrine of proportionality to defend a response to strategic moves by a non-dominant competitor.

(*d*) Whilst a finding of a breach of Article 81 will necessarily involve some restriction of competition, a breach of Article 82 can occur when the abuse of dominance is simply 'exploitative', i.e. an advantage obtained for the dominant company at the expense of the consumer without any effect on the competitive process or the structure of the market in which the dominant company operates.

(*e*) Under Article 81, with an agreement or concerted practice either an 'object' to restrict competition or an appreciable 'effect' on competition must be shown. By contrast, if a dominant enterprise is alleged to have committed abuse the focus normally is on the action of that dominant company (whether it affects the structure of competition in the market or is exploitative of consumers), whether or not the dominant company showed intent to restrict competition by its actions or otherwise to breach the Article.

---

[1] Case 127/73 [1974] ECR 51 (the Court's judgment dealing with the direct effect in national courts of Art. 82) and 313 (the Court's judgment dealing with the issue of whether SABAM was exploiting its dominant position as a copyright authority in Belgium): [1974] 2 CMLR 238 is a consolidated report of both judgments.

[2] Ch. 15, pp.305–8.

[3] See fn. 22, Ch. 14. The availability of damages as a remedy under Arts 81 and 82 is considered in Ch. 21.

1.2 THREE SIMILARITIES BETWEEN THE ARTICLES

Notwithstanding these basic differences between the two Articles, their similarities in both language and position within the overall scheme of the Treaty are significant. Article 83 (which provides the legal basis for Regulation 17/62) requires the Council to adopt regulations or directives to give effect to the principles set out in both Articles. Article 84, dealing with the interim obligations of Member States pending adoption of such Regulation, also refers to both Articles. Moreover, Article 85 obliged the Commission as soon as it took up its duties to ensure the application of the principles laid down in both Articles. Regulation 17 therefore applies to both Articles, and although exemption is not available from Article 82, it is in principle possible (though rare) to lodge details of a specific practice or practices, especially if embodied in written documents, in order to seek a negative clearance. Such a negative clearance is, of course, simply a confirmation that Article 82 does not apply. As the same procedural powers are available to the Commission in Article 82 cases as in Article 81 cases, its powers to conduct investigations under Article 14 of Regulation 17/62 and the range of sanctions available, including penalties, fines, and termination of prohibited conduct, are the same.

Three other important substantive similarities should be noted:

(*a*) In both cases the conduct challenged must be such as to 'affect trade between Member States'. There may be marginal differences in the application of this condition between the two Articles. In the *Bodson*[4] case the European Court stressed that the national court investigating this element should actively take into account the effect on imports of the allegedly abusive conduct, a point not so clearly made in earlier Article 82 Court cases.

(*b*) The examples of abusive conduct given in 82(*a*) to (*d*) include examples identical, or at least very similar, to those referred to under Article 81 as the subject matter of prohibited agreements or concerted practices. Only (*c*) in Article 81 ('the sharing of markets or sources of supply') is omitted from Article 82, since for that 'sharing' two or more undertakings must be involved. The types of conduct referred to are simply examples; the width of the definition of those agreements or concerted practices which have as their object or effect the prevention, restriction, or distortion of competition on one hand, and the definition of abusive conduct on the other, is not limited in either case by the nature of the examples set out. In *Gottrup Klim* v. *DLG*[5] the European Court held that the test for whether a provision in the rules of an agricultural co-operative prohibiting its members from participating in other co-operatives in direct competition with it was in breach of Article 81(1) or Article 82 (if it had a dominant position) was the same, namely whether it was limited to what was necessary to ensure that the co-operative could function properly.

(*c*) The scope of Article 82 is not limited to abuses by single corporate groups. It can be utilized in the case of abuse 'by one or more undertakings' so that, as with Article 81, relationships between undertakings may concern the Commission in both cases, although normally these are more important in Article 81 cases. It was emphasized in

---

[4] *Bodson* v. *Pompes Funèbres Générales* Case 30/87 [1988] ECR 2479: [1989] 4 CMLR 984.
[5] Case C-250/92 [1994] ECR I-5641: [1996] 4 CMLR 191.

the judgment of the European Court in *Compagnie Maritime Belge*[6] that the same conduct or practices engaged in by more than one undertaking can both involve a breach of Article 81 and of Article 82; the language of the court was as follows 'it is clear from the very wording of Article [81] and Article [82] that the same practices may give rise to an infringement of both provisions. Simultaneous application of Articles [81] and [82] of the Treaty cannot be ruled out 'a priori'. Fennelly A-G in his opinion had reached the same conclusion in different words 'Articles [81] and [82] do not exist in watertight compartments'.

1.3 ISSUES OF EXCLUSIVITY INVOLVING BOTH ARTICLES

Cases involving exclusivity obligations can raise closely linked issues involving both Articles. In *Almelo*[7] the European Court had to advise a Dutch Court under Article 234 on a contract between SEP, a consortium of electrical generators, and Almelo, a local distributor, under which Almelo was required to obtain all its electricity from SEP and was banned from importing it from sources outside The Netherlands. The Court ruled that both Article 81 and 82 applied to the exclusivity requirements imposed on Almelo by the agreement, given the dominant position of SEP in the Dutch market for electricity generation.

The two Articles were also well entwined in the *Masterfoods* saga (considered also in Chapter 20). The exclusivity in this case related to the supply by Unilever (through its Irish subsidiary Van den Bergh Foods), of ice-cream freezer cabinets to small retail outlets in Ireland. These outlets only normally have room for a single freezer so that it was not practical for them to have freezers for other makes of impulse ice cream. A new entrant to the Irish market, Mars, through its subsidiary, Masterfoods, challenged the agreements under both Articles. The Irish Supreme Court held in favour of Van den Bergh, but Mars appealed in respect of both Articles to the Irish Supreme Court and also referred the dispute to the Commission. After considerable delay, whilst the Commission sought to resolve the dispute by negotiation, a Commission decision[8] was eventually issued in 1998 which held that the exclusive supply arrangements for these ice-cream freezers in Ireland constituted a breach of both Articles. This decision was then taken by Van den Bergh on appeal to the Court of First Instance, whose decision on the merits is still awaited. In the meantime the European Court has laid down in a separate case[9] that the current appeal by Masterfoods to the Irish Supreme Court must be suspended, to allow the completion of the Community proceedings and to avoid the risk of conflicting outcomes from the national and Community legal process.

2. CASE LAW ON THEIR RELATIONSHIP

2.1 *CONTINENTAL CAN* AND *ITALIAN FLAT GLASS*—COLLECTIVE DOMINANCE EMERGES AS A CONCEPT

The first opportunity for the European Court to comment on the relationship between the Articles came in the *Continental Can* case. As the summary of the case in Chapter 17

---

[6] Ch. 15, fn. 11 and pp.287–8.   [7] Case C-393/92 [1994] ECR I-1477.
[8] [1998] 5 CMLR 530 on appeal as T-65/98.   [9] Case C-344/98 [2001] 4 CMLR 449.

indicates,[10] the Court emphasized that both Articles had been included in the Treaty for the same reason: to ensure that both Article 2, and Article 3(1)(g) could be implemented. They should be interpreted in a purposive way to ensure that the implementation of one Article did not frustrate the purposes of the other. The important result of the approach in this case was to provide the Commission with jurisdiction over those mergers entered into by companies already holding a dominant position. This jurisdiction did not prove of great value to the Commission in practice and, as explained in Chapter 17, has now been rendered less important by the introduction of the Merger Regulation 4064/89, effective from September 1990. The long-term result of the *Continental Can* case, however, has been to make it more likely that Article 81 and Article 82 will be treated as two parts of a whole (or as two sides of the same coin) rather than as largely unrelated.

Whilst in the great majority of cases proceedings brought by the European Commission, or by parties in national Courts, relate to one or other of the Articles, Article 82 does expressly refer to the possibility of abuses being practised by more than one undertaking, often referred to as 'joint' or 'collective' dominance. If this occurs, and there is also some form of agreement or concerted practice between the parties, then as already mentioned there could be a breach of both Articles. In the majority of cases where the Commission have alleged a horizontal cartel against a group of companies with an aggregate market share of a sufficient level for market dominance to be alleged, the Commission has not sought to raise Article 82 arguments, contenting itself with proceedings under Article 81. However, in the *Italian Flat Glass*[11] case, the Commission sought to show that it was legally possible to link agreements and concerted practices referred to under Article 81 to the joint abuse of dominant position referred to in Article 82. It undoubtedly felt that a decision in its favour in this area would provide an important weapon to enable it to deal with oligopolistic markets, which always present the greatest problem for competition authorities. Oligopolists often manage to adjust their relationships with competitors to mutual advantage without the need to enter into agreements or concerted practices. To bring them collectively within the scope of Article 82 for the purposes of imposing a fine or preventing abusive conduct is a much more difficult substantive task for the Commission.

Against this background the facts in *Italian Glass* might at first sight have appeared to provide an encouraging scenario. Three companies supplied glass in Italy, both to the car industry (its primary customer) and to non-automotive users, principally the construction and furnishing industries. These three major companies between them held 95 per cent of the car industry glass market and 79 per cent of the non-automotive market, and it was alleged that the arrangements they had made for the exchange of different categories of product were of such scope and permanence as to constitute 'structural' links rather than merely concerted practices of the kind normally found in Article 81 cases. The Commission imposed fines on three companies under Article 81, but also made a separate finding that the companies were in breach of Article 82 'by abusing their collective dominant position through conduct whereby they deprived customers of the opportunity of getting suppliers to compete on prices and terms of sale, and whereby they limited outlets through the setting of quotas for automotive glass'. The Court of First Instance,[12] however, found a number of errors in the way in which the Commission had handled the case, in particular that it had

---

[10] See Ch. 17, pp.336–7.   [11] [1990] 4 CMLR 535.
[12] Cases T-68, 77, 78/89 [1992] ECR II-1403: 5 CMLR 302.

given insufficient weight to the activities and market power of wholesalers in the non-automotive sector. On the main substantive issue under Article 81 the Court found on the evidence that one of the three companies, Vernante Pennitalia, had not acted in breach of Article 81 though two other companies had done so. However, it overruled the Article 82 finding against all three companies. The key passage in this part of the judgment reads as follows:

There is nothing in principle to prevent two or more independent economic entities from being, on a specific market, *united by such economic links* that, by virtue of that fact, together they hold a dominant position vis-à-vis the other operators on the same market. This could be the case, for example, where two or more independent undertakings jointly have, through agreements or licences, a technological lead affording them the power to behave to an appreciable extent independently of their competitors, their customers and ultimately of their consumers. However, it should be pointed out that for the purposes of establishing an infringement of Article [82], it is not sufficient . . . to 'recycle' the facts constituting an infringement of Article [81], deducing from them the finding that the parties to an agreement or to an unlawful practice jointly hold a substantial share of the market, that by virtue of that fact alone they hold a collectively dominant position, and that their unlawful behaviour constitutes an abuse of that collectively dominant position.[13]

2.2 THE *CMB* CASE—THE DEVELOPMENT OF COLLECTIVE DOMINANCE

Legal commentators then spent considerable time and ingenuity in seeking to interpret the phrase 'united by such economic links'. It is important to bear in mind that the example given by the Court of First Instance of undertakings having a technological lead in a particular market as the results of agreements or licences between them was clearly not meant to be exhaustive. Some light on the proper interpretation of this phrase was later shed by the subsequent European Court decision in *Compagnie Maritime Belge.*[14] Under the provisions of Council Regulation 4056/86, shipping lines are allowed a block exemption for certain activities of their liner conferences in respect of services to or from Community ports. The regulation allows agreements concerning matters such as rate-fixing, coordination of time-tables, allocation of sailings between members, regulation of carrying capacities for individual members, and allocation of cargo or revenue between members. Nevertheless, under Article 8, if the conduct of a conference benefiting from these exemptions has effects which are incompatible with Article 82, the Commission is expressly authorized to withdraw the benefit of the block exemption from those members of the conference. Action was taken by the Commission against three liner shipping conferences, operating routes between Continental North Sea ports such as Rotterdam, and West Africa on the grounds of activities which were not covered by the Regulation. These included entering into loyalty contracts outside the scope of the Regulation with shippers and with other conferences. Members of the conferences were found by the Commission to have collectively abused their dominant position by:

(i)   attempting to enforce agreements under which members of the conference had exclusive rights to ship goods on the route to Zaire;

---

[13] Paras 358, 360.   [14] Ch. 14, fn. 13.

(ii)   making loyalty agreements with certain customers in return for lower shipping rates (a form of exclusive rebate); and

(iii)   introducing a system of 'fighting ships' targeted at particular competitors seeking to enter the market.

These actions had been separately identified from breaches of Article 81; in the Court's view the Commission was correct to treat them under Article 82 as examples of collective dominance by the members of the conference. The Commission was also right, in the Court's view, to find that the members of the conference held a dominant position collectively as a result of their combined market share of more than 90 per cent, strengthened by other circumstances such as the support for the arrangements received from the government of Zaire, the length of time the route had been operated by the conference, and its large size, especially in relation to the size of its competitors. The members of CEWAL used their legitimate links within the framework of the authorized liner conference to participate jointly in activities which went far beyond its legitimate goals; they were thus able to present a common front to any would-be competitors and organize actions in practice equivalent to the unilateral action of a single dominant firm.

In dealing with the Article 82 issues, the Court placed particular emphasis on abuses (ii) and (iii). These contracts provided for substantial rebates where a shipper used members of the conference for 100 per cent of their shipping requirements. If shippers did not meet this obligation, their name was put on a 'blacklist' and they received less favourable service. The members of the conference argued that loyalty arrangements are permitted specifically under Regulation 4056/86, but the Court ruled that the loyalty agreements made were not within the framework of the Regulation, and could be imposed on customers because of the high market share of CEWAL and the lack of a choice of less restrictive discount and bonus schemes.

The final finding of abuse involved the procedure of designating specific sailings by CEWAL members closest to the sailings of competitors as 'fighting ships', involving the joint setting of freight rates for these to match or under-cut the new entrants, with the sharing of any resultant trading loss or earnings between members of the conference. The Court observed that the main purpose of the 'fighting ship' system had been to remove CEWAL's only competitor on the relevant market, and this was ruled a disproportionate response to the conduct of the new entrant, even though without having achieved its objective.

This *CMB* decision seems to make clear that the agreement linking the collectively dominant parties can itself be legitimate, authorized by Community legislation, and not necessarily subject to attack under Article 81, in contrast to the allegedly anti-competitive agreements between the three Italian companies in the *Flat Glass* case which were the basis for the claim in that case of collective dominance. In view of the terms of Article 8 of Regulation 4056/86 this is not a particularly surprising finding.

More surprising, perhaps, is the emphasis placed by the Court of First Instance, though not emphasized by the European Court on the appeal, on the duty of proportionality on the shipping companies in respect of their 'fighting ships' scheme. Some commentators have suggested that to introduce the concept of proportionality into Article 82 is potentially dangerous, since it places the dominant company in a dilemma as to whether a particular commercial reaction to a specific competitive threat will be deemed 'proportionate'. It is said that to argue that a penal provision such as Article 82 should only apply when undertakings can clearly be shown to have acted in breach of normal competitive principles measured objectively, and that the duty to act proportionately imposes too heavy a burden upon them. The weakness in this argument is that, notwithstanding the use of the word 'objective' in *Hoffman-La Roche*, there is inevitably an important element of 'drawing the line' in assessing many aspects of potentially abusive conduct considered under the various sections of Chapter 15, for example in the essential facilities cases. It may be that the phrase 'proportionate' is less appropriate to the assessment of actions of commercial undertakings given that the doctrine derives originally from German law where its application was to legislation. If the term were changed to 'reasonable reaction' to competitor activities, this may provide a better test in a commercial context, though it is unlikely that the outcome of particular cases would be altered on this semantic basis alone.

3. THE INFLUENCE OF MERGER DECISIONS ON THE CONCEPT OF COLLECTIVE DOMINANCE

The development of the concept of collective dominance has however been significantly influenced in recent years by court judgments in merger cases, rather than those specifically dealing with Article 82. Given the language of Article 2 of the Merger Regulation, there seems no reason to doubt that the legal principles underlying collective dominance in these two quite different categories of case are nevertheless the same. Jurisprudence of the Court of First Instance, in dealing with appeals under the Merger Regulation from Commission Merger decisions, is equally applicable in Article 82 cases.[15]

The leading cases on collective dominance under the Merger Regulation are *Kali & Salz*,[16] *Gencor*,[17] and *Airtours*;[18] details of the facts of the cases can be found in Chapter 17 and 18. The *Gencor* decision emphasized the width of the concept, which was not necessarily dependent upon the existence either of economic links between the parties of a structural nature or commercial agreements of any kind, a point later confirmed in *Compagnie Maritime Belge* at a slightly later date. The essential core of this concept was held to be 'the relationship of interdependence existing between the parties to a tight oligopoly within which, in a market with the appropriate characteristics, in particular in terms of market concentration, transparency and product homogeneity, those parties are in a position to anticipate one another's behaviour and are therefore strongly encouraged to align their conduct in the market'.

The Commission's success in the *Gencor* case however was not repeated in *Airtours*. Here the Court of First Instance rejected an attempt by the Commission to broaden the concept of collective dominance so as to cover any situation of an oligopolistic nature, when it would be rational for the major participants in the relevant market (in this case the shorthaul foreign package holiday market in the United Kingdom) individually to restrict the supply of such holidays. In a decision which annulled the Commission's block on the merger, the

---

[15] Though proposed changes by the Commission to the definition of 'dominance' in Art. 2 of the ECMR may change this. See Ch. 18, p.395.

[16] Cases C-68/94 and 30/95 ECR I-1375: [1998] 4 CMLR 829.

[17] Case T-102/96 [1999] ECR II-753: 4 CMLR 971.   [18] Case T-342/99 [2002] 5 CMLR 317.

Court laid down that there had to be three elements present if collective dominance was to be established by the Commission:

(i)   each member of a dominant oligopoly must have the ability to know the other members are behaving so as to be able to monitor sufficiently, precisely, and quickly whether they are adopting a common policy (whether this involves price rises or capacity reductions), which means that there has to be enough transparency for this in the market;

(ii) there must be an incentive to maintain tacit coordination between all the members of the oligopoly over a reasonable period of time, which means in turn that there must be an awareness by each member that any departure from the common policy by one member will provoke retaliation from the others, usually by matching any price cuts or capacity increases; and

(iii) it must be established that the 'foreseeable reaction' of current and future competitors, as well as those of consumers, would not jeopardize the results expected from the common policy.

The outcome of the *Airtours* case may force an amendment not only to its approach in merger cases but also to the Commission's 1998 Notice on access agreements in the telecommunications market. The Notice states that for collective dominance to apply it is sufficient if the undertakings have the kind of independence which often comes about in oligopolistic situations, without the need for any other economic links, such as co-operation agreements. After *Airtours* this statement is unquestionably too broad and requires the qualifications laid down by the Court of First Instance in that case.

4. COLLECTIVE DOMINANCE IN A VERTICAL RELATIONSHIP

Normally in a case of alleged collective dominance the undertakings will be in competition with each other and in a horizontal relationship. In *Irish Sugar*,[19] however, the Court of First Instance confirmed that that there is no inherent reason why collective dominance cannot exist between undertakings even when the relationship is vertical, as for example, between a patentee and its licensees or between a supplier and its distributors. Irish Sugar had itself for several years had a distributor, SDL, which was a wholly owned subsidiary of SDH. Irish Sugar held 51 per cent of the shares in SDH for several years before later acquiring the remaining 49 per cent from its owners. Over the period between 1985 and 1990, half the board of SDH were representatives of Irish Sugar but the other half represented the minority shareholders in SDH. The Irish Sugar chief executive and several of its board members were amongst those who sat on the SDL board. SDL worked closely with Irish Sugar; it was given responsibility for technical services and consumer promotions and marketing whilst the supply obligations were the responsibility of Irish Sugar. Commercial policy including the important topic of pricing and discounts was shared between the parties and SDL undertook that it would purchase all its sugar, subject only to availability, from Irish Sugar. The

---

[19]   Case C-497/99 R [2001]: 5 CMLR 1082.

Court of First Instance made the finding of abuse only against Irish Sugar although both it and SDL were held to have been collectively dominant. It is however an unsatisfactory case because of the facts cited by the Commission; it is possible that Irish Sugar actually controlled SDL at all relevant times (even when holding only 51 per cent of the shares in SDH), a situation to which the 'group economic entity' concept should have applied.

5. THE RELEVANCE OF INDIVIDUAL OR BLOCK EXEMPTIONS TO ARTICLE 82

The mere existence of an agreement which *prima facie* falls within the prohibition of 81(1) but which has received exemption and to which a dominant company is party is clearly not going to be allowed to prevent the utilization of Article 82 by the Commission. This issue arose in the earlier *Tetrapak (No.1)*[20] case, where the Court of First Instance had to decide whether to confirm a Commission decision which raised the question, namely what should happen where the dominant company had entered into an agreement subject to Article 81(1) but within the terms of a later block exemption regulation that effectively removed the prohibition. The resolution of this potential conflict between Articles 81 and 82 was ultimately the only issue before the Court, other matters dealt with in the decision of the Commission relating to the existence of dominance and relevant markets having been conceded by Tetrapak during the hearing.

Tetrapak's argument ran along the following lines. Whilst it was admittedly dominant in relevant markets, namely the production of machinery for filling aseptic UHT milk cartons and the cartons themselves, by acquiring the benefit of an exclusive licence in favour of its competitor Liquipak through take-over it had not breached Article 82 because the agreement was in terms permitted by the then Patent Block Exemption Reg. 2349/84. Such an exemption was a 'positive' action of the Commission in terms of the *Walt Wilhem*[21] judgment, and should not, therefore, lead to any liability under Article 82, since the Commission had in its discretion the alternative remedy of withdrawing the exemption under the terms of the block exemption regulation.

The Court of First Instance nevertheless upheld the Commission's decision that the acquisition of the licence was a breach of Article 82. It pointed out that the withdrawal of the block exemption could only operate in a prospective way, not in respect of the past. The two Articles were independent legal instruments which, within the overall scheme of the Treaty, addressed different situations. The acquisition by a company with a dominant position of an exclusive licence was not *per se* an Article 82 abuse, but the circumstances of the acquisition and the effect it might have on the structure of competition in the relevant market must be taken into account. The Court supported the Commission's conclusion that in this case the acquisition of the particular licence for the packaging of the aseptic milk containers not only strengthened Tetrapak's substantial existing dominance but prevented or at least delayed the entry of new competition into the market. The take-over of Liquipak was simply the means by which Tetrapak had acquired the Liquipak licences and the mere fact that the licences

---

[20] Case T-51/89 [1990] ECR II-309: [1991] 4 CMLR 334. The facts are more fully set out in Ch. 16, pp.310–12.
[21] Case 14/68 [1969] ECR 1: CMLR 100.

themselves had received a block exemption could not render inapplicable the prohibition of Article 82. The Court also pointed out that block exemptions are merely secondary legislation, being a specific application of the grounds for exemption set out in Article 81(3) to particular categories of agreement; by contrast, Article 82 is primary legislation in the Treaty, which takes precedence over such secondary legislation.

The position would differ if an individual exemption had been granted to a particular licence agreement because, if exemption had been sought for an individual agreement in this way, the Commission would have to take account of the particular circumstances in which it was made. The second negative condition of 81(3) itself refers to the requirement that the parties to such individual agreements shall not be afforded by it the 'possibility' even of eliminating competition for a substantial part of the relevant products. Unless these circumstances had altered by the time an Article 82 allegation was later made the earlier findings of the Commission would be relevant and taken into account. By contrast, with a block exemption there is by definition no case-by-case examination of the circumstances of the parties to those agreements and no positive assessment of the overall market situation. The benefit of block exemption is therefore different from any form of negative clearance from Article 82, which had a binding effect upon the Commission; it is not automatically held back from companies which have a dominant position, and therefore cannot take into account in advance their position on relevant markets in respect of any particular agreement.

17

MERGERS (1)

1. EVENTS LEADING TO THE MERGER REGULATION

1.1 THE NEED FOR MERGER CONTROL

Competition authorities tend to regard control over mergers and acquisitions by large and powerful companies as one of their most important concerns. Such authorities are concerned not only with the conduct of undertakings but also with the possible effects on market structures, and especially on the degree of concentration (and consequent increase in market power) which mergers may bring about in particular product and geographic markets. They naturally prefer, therefore, that such mergers are not allowed to occur without careful scrutiny of their likely effects on the competitive process: preferably before they occur, rather than afterwards. In the absence, however, of any rules for ensuring such scrutiny, two possibly undesirable consequences may occur. Undertakings which are prevented from making anti-competitive agreements with each other by the prohibition contained in Article 81(1) may simply determine that, to achieve the objectives of such agreements, they will merge their business operations into a single unit, thereby avoiding the reach of that Article: they may also, by their merger, increase the market power of their combined undertaking in a particular product or geographic market and thus reduce the scope for competition within it. Any competition authority, therefore, with inadequate substantive and procedural control over major merger proposals operates under a severe disadvantage.

Nevertheless, there seems little doubt that those responsible for drafting Articles 81 and 82 did not intend that this should give control over mergers to the Commission. Neither the actual wording of the Article nor the evidence of those who participated in the negotiations leading up to the Treaty or in its early administration support any contrary argument. Nevertheless, concern within DG Comp over this apparent gap in its powers was felt even during its first decade of active operation when, as we have seen, it had a variety of other pressing problems to which prior attention had to be given, in particular those relating to vertical agreements. In a memorandum in 1966[1] it admitted that the concentration of undertakings following transfer of shares or assets was not covered by Article 81. Article 81 ceases to apply once the integration of two or more undertakings has gone beyond the stage of temporary assistance and co-operation to a stage of full-scale merger where both policy

---

[1] 'Le problème de la concentration dans le Marché Commun', *Etudes CEE* (Series Concurrence No. 3, 24 (1966)). As a statement of principle this has now been overruled by the *Philip Morris* decision (fn. 6) and inevitably, therefore, this part of Ch. 17 deals with Art. 81 as well as with Art. 82. The position under the ECSE Treaty was, of course, different (see Ch. 3, p.21).

direction and management have been centralized in a single body. The possible utilization, therefore, of Article 82 in a suitable merger case was not overlooked by the Commission and, in spite of considerable doubts even within DG Comp itself, an opportunity occurred in the early 1970s. It was then decided to seek a ruling from the European Court that Article 82 did enable the Commission to issue a decision prohibiting a merger where the merger itself strengthened pre-existing dominance in a particular market.

1.2 *CONTINENTAL CAN* AND ITS CONSEQUENCES

The case chosen for this purpose was *Continental Can*.[2] The United States company of that name had acquired an 85.8 per cent holding in a German company, SLW of Brunswick. In the following year, Continental Can formed a Delaware corporation known as Europemballage Corporation which opened an office in Brussels and soon afterwards, with financial help from its parent, acquired 91.7 per cent of the shares of a Dutch company, TDV. SLW was the largest producer in Germany of packaging and metal closures whilst TDV was a leading manufacturer of packing material in Benelux. In its decision[3] prohibiting acquisition by SLW of TDV, the Commission stated that it took into account not only the market share which the Continental Can group would as the result of the mergers control in Germany and Benelux, but also the group's advantages over its competitors resulting from its size and economic, financial, and technological importance. In the view of the Commission, all these factors gave the company room for independent action, conferring on it, at least on the German market, a dominant position for lightweight containers for preserved meats, fish, and shellfish as well as on the market for metal closures.

The Court held in a relatively brief judgment that the factual evidence failed to support the Commission's conclusion that Continental Can held a dominant position in the German market. In simply assigning tin cans for fish and tin cans for meat to separate markets and assuming that a high market share within each area involved market power, the Commission had failed to consider the possibility and ability of producers shifting from the manufacture of one product to another, e.g. from fish cans to meat cans or vice versa. It also failed to consider whether large buyers would decide to manufacture their own cans if the price of Continental's cans was too high. The Commission had not prepared adequate evidence relating to the suitability of other types of containers or the probable entry by other companies into the markets if Continental Can utilized their market dominance to raise prices. Its market analysis was simply insufficient to support its conclusion.

Nevertheless, whilst the Commission suffered a defeat on the facts, on the main issue of principle it gained a surprising victory. The Court of Justice chose to interpret Article 82 in a purposive way to give effect to the spirit of the Treaty of Rome and to ensure consistency between Articles 81 and 82. The Court referred to the then terms of Article 3(*f*) and concluded that, as the result of it providing for the institution of a 'system' to protect competition within the Common Market from distortion, there was an underlying principle to be found there that competition must not be eliminated. Its existence was also supported by the principles in Article 2 relating to the harmonious development of economic activities.

---

[2] *Europemballage and Continental Can* v. *Commission* Case 6/72 [1973] ECR 215: CMLR 199. On the question of the basis for the Commission's jurisdiction over this case, see Ch. 23, pp.498–9.
[3] [1972] CMLR D11.

Articles 81 to 82 had, therefore, been included in order to preserve the principles set out in these two Articles. It was not to be supposed (said the Court) that the Treaty should in Article 81 prohibit certain agreements, decisions, and concerted practices that might restrict but would not eliminate competition, while at the same time allowing Article 82 to permit already dominant undertakings, simply by making further acquisitions, to strengthen their position to the extent that any serious possibility of competition in the relevant market would be eliminated. Such a diversity of legal treatment could open a breach in the whole structure of competition law that would jeopardize the proper functioning of the Common Market. Articles 81 and 82 had to be interpreted in a manner which reflected the fact that they were both inserted to achieve the same ends, those set out in Articles 2 and 3(f).[4]

The Court went on to say that Article 82 applied not only to practices directly prejudicing consumers, but also to those that prejudiced consumers indirectly through interference in the structure of markets. It referred to the risk that, if individual undertakings obtained a sufficiently powerful position in markets, all those who remained would become dependent on the dominant undertaking with regard to their market behaviour. There was no need for the Commission to show any cause or connection between the dominant position and the abuse of it. An increase in market share might alone be sufficient to constitute an abuse.

There is perhaps no better example of the difference between the approach adopted by the European Court to the interpretation of the Treaty of Rome and that which would have been adopted by any English Court than this decision, whose outcome was a surprise to many, although received gratefully by the Commission. Unfortunately, though the Commission won the victory relating to the applicability of Article 82 to mergers by companies already holding a dominant position which, therefore, gave it in principle better standing for the future on such issues, the task of winning the subsequent campaign to obtain effective substantive and procedural control over mergers proved more difficult.

The relationship between the *Continental Can* decision and the scope and content of the first draft of the Merger Regulation issued some few months after the decision of the Court (at the request of Member States) was therefore more psychological than substantive. A Council Regulation was essential to merger control, because the use of Article 82 simply on the basis of the *Continental Can* decision would not have provided the Commission with the desired ability to control the creation of a new dominant position as opposed to the ability to prevent an undertaking with an existing dominant position from strengthening it still further, as under the rather unusual facts of *Continental Can*. Such a Regulation was also essential to make pre-notification of major mergers mandatory, so that any necessary powers of the Commission could be exercised before the merger took place rather than being employed in the always more difficult and sensitive task of unscrambling it after completion. Moreover, interim measures (subsequently adopted in some Article 81 and 82 cases) are no real substitute for a regulation containing full procedural powers to control mergers, equivalent to those provided by Regulation 17/62 for other competition cases.

1.3 EARLY DRAFTS OF THE MERGER REGULATION

The original 1973 draft that appeared shortly after *Continental Can* provided a basic scheme of control, though significantly it refers not to Article 82 but to Article 308 of the Treaty as

---

[4] Now 3(1)(g) since the Treaty of Maastricht.

the authority for its enactment.[5] The lengthy recitals refer to the importance of preventing concentration in markets within the Community. For this reason, prior notification of major mergers over a specified threshold was essential. The only mergers to be excluded from its control would be those between undertakings with a joint turnover of less than two hundred million units of account and where the market share of goods or services affected would in no Member State exceed 25 per cent. This was, of course, an extremely low threshold. Article 1 of the Regulations, drawn in terms strongly reminiscent of Article 81, stated that control would apply over all transactions that had the direct or indirect effect of conferring power on the combined undertaking to hinder effective competition. It is also provided that consideration should be given to exempting those mergers 'indispensable to the attainment of an objective which is given priority treatment in the common interest of the Community'. The threshold for compulsory notification was set at one thousand million units of account, calculated on the joint turnover of the undertakings, unless the target undertaking had a turnover of less than thirty million units of account. Decisions had to be rendered within a time limit of 12 months and were subject to review by the Court, just as any other decision of the Commission. The Regulation would apply to both agreed and contested mergers, since it applied to 'transactions' as well as to 'agreements'.

With hindsight, the scope of the proposed new Regulation was undoubtedly too broad. It would have brought within its scope a very large number of mergers, far more than the staff of DG Comp (either in 1973 or even in their increased numbers of later years) could have dealt with within the time limits proposed, save perhaps on what would have been a demonstrably inadequate basis. In any case, political opposition by Member States in the Council ensured that the original 1973 Regulation was not adopted. Subsequent realization within the Commission that the scope of the draft Regulations would need to be modified so as to affect only a smaller proportion of mergers led to new drafts of the Regulations being put forward to the Council in 1982, 1984, and 1986, but even these initially failed to overcome the political deadlock. Important changes in later drafts included a reference to the fact that competition had to be shown to be limited at Community level (rather than Member State level) before the Commission could intervene. Unless the market share in the goods or services covered by the merger exceeded 20 per cent either in the entire Common Market or in a substantial part of it, the merger was to be deemed compatible with the provisions of the Treaty, it being presumed that the merger was incapable of hindering effective competition. The joint turnover jurisdictional threshold was raised from 200 million to 500 million, and subsequently to 750 million ECU.

1.4 THE *PHILIP MORRIS* CASE

Commissioner Sutherland, responsible at the time for competition policy, indicated publicly on a number of occasions from 1985 onwards that failure by Member States to break the deadlock would leave the Commission no alternative but to rely on Articles 81 and 82 for the purposes of merger control. Whilst initial reactions by Member States to this suggestion

---

[5] Article 308 reads: 'If action by the Community should prove necessary to attain . . . one of the objectives of the Community and this Treaty has not provided the necessary powers, the Council shall, acting unanimously on a proposal from the Commission and after consulting the Assembly, take the appropriate measures'.

were sceptical, given the many substantive and procedural difficulties involved, the sub-sequent effect of the *Philip Morris*[6] judgment of the European Court in November 1987 brought home to them the realization that control based on a new Regulation might be far better than reliance on the unpredictable consequences of that case.

The case involved an agreement by Philip Morris to acquire a 30 per cent interest in its competitor, cigarette manufacturer Rothmans, from its South African owners, Rembrandt, though the voting rights to be obtained by Philip Morris were limited to 24.9 per cent. Both groups kept the right of first refusal should the other wish to sell, and there were other arrangements to ensure that Philip Morris had neither board representation nor managerial influence over Rothmans. The Commission had given exemption to these proposals, and the Court upheld its decision in the face of a challenge by two other tobacco companies, BAT and R.J. Reynolds. It ruled that the acquisition of an equity interest in a competitor did not of itself restrict competition, but might serve as an instrument to that end. Article 81 would then become applicable to the relevant agreement.

The central section of the Court's judgment on this legal issue read as follows:

That will be true in particular where, by the acquisition of a shareholding or through subsidiary clauses in the agreement, the investing company obtains legal or *de facto* control of the commercial conduct of the other company or where the agreement provides for commercial co-operation between the companies or creates a structure likely to be used for such co-operation. That may also be the case where the agreement gives the investing company the possibility of reinforcing its position at a later stage and taking effective control of the other company.[7]

1.5 FINAL NEGOTIATIONS FOR THE REGULATION

The decision, though welcome to the Commission, nevertheless left many problems for it. These included the effect of Article 81(2) on the agreement, the lack of time limits or jurisdictional thresholds, and uncertainty as to the exact range of mergers affected. However, perhaps the most important outcome of the case from the Commission's viewpoint was its effect in concentrating the minds of the more unwilling Member States, now fearful of the use of the *Philip Morris* precedent to attack mergers under Article 81, on the terms of the draft Regulation.

In March 1988 a new draft Regulation was therefore presented to the Council, which for the first time included some of the main features of the Merger Regulation that would ultimately be adopted. The criteria for assessment also included for the first time language familiar from both Articles 81 and 82 of 'compatibility' with the Common Market. A merger that gave rise to or strengthened a dominant position in the Common Market or a substantial part of it would not be regarded as compatible. A long list of factors relating to the competitive structure of relevant markets was set out for consideration in connection with the assessment of compatibility. The new thresholds for world turnover were one thousand million ECU with a minimum of fifty million ECU Community turnover for the target company.

These new proposals seemed to break the deadlock, and the arrival of Sir Leon Brittan as

---

[6] *BAT and R. J. Reynolds* v. *Commission and Philip Morris* Cases 142 and 156/84 [1987] ECR 4487: [1988] 4 CMLR 24.

[7] Paras 38–39.

the new Commissioner with responsibility, *inter alia*, for competition brought new impetus. Early in 1989 the Commission responded to Member State criticisms by raising the thresholds for jurisdiction considerably, namely to five billion ECU for aggregate world turnover and to two hundred and fifty million ECU aggregate Community turnover for each of at least two companies involved (with the intention that both figures should be reduced later after experience of the operation of the Regulation). In addition, the exception for mergers between undertakings both having a substantial proportion of their Community turnover in the same Member State was reduced from three-quarters to two-thirds.

When France took over the presidency of the Council at the end of June 1989, it made clear that it regarded agreement on the final text of the Regulation as being a high priority; the succeeding six months of its presidency saw the final difficult stage of the negotiations edge forward to completion. An important difference lay between those Member States that wanted the criteria expressly limited to competition issues (especially Germany and the United Kingdom) and those, such as France, which wanted social and industrial policy issues to remain among the criteria that could be applied. Both Germany and the United Kingdom also sought to keep the right of national competition authorities to retain jurisdiction in those cases where major national interests and markets were involved. On the other hand, the majority of Member States, as well as industrial and commercial interests within them, were attracted by the possibility of a 'one-stop shop' for large-scale mergers with a Community dimension.

2. MERGER REGULATION 4064/89: THE COMMISSION'S JURISDICTION OVER CONCENTRATIONS WITH A COMMUNITY DIMENSION

2.1 THE REGULATION: ITS JURISDICTIONAL SCOPE

Agreement on the text of the Regulation was finally reached at a Council meeting on 21 December 1989, following last-minute concessions by nearly all Member States. The resulting text is contained in Council Regulation 406/489, though a number of other relevant notices have also been published by the Council and the Commission on its interpretation and application. The Regulation[8] came into effect some nine months later, on 21 September 1990. Its recitals are naturally extensive; after pointing out the inadequacy of Articles 81 and 82 to protect the system of undistorted competition envisaged in the Treaty, and the consequent need to introduce a new Regulation based not only on Article 83 but also and principally on Article 308, it restates the essential principle behind the new instrument: that any concentration with a Community dimension creating or strengthening a position as a result of which effective competition in the Common Market or a substantial part of it is

---

[8] The Regulation is referred to below on some occasions for convenience as ECMR. Some important changes to the original text of the Regulation in 4064/89 were made by Reg. 1310/97, which came into effect on 1 March 1998, and references to ECMR normally refer to the Regulation as so amended, unless the context makes clear otherwise. All the cases decided under ECMR can be found on the DG Comp website under 'Mergers-Cases' in both alphabetical and numerical order.

significantly impeded is to be declared incompatible with the Common Market. Jurisdiction over such concentrations is to rest exclusively with the Commission, save for some narrowly defined exceptions to be found in Articles 9, 21(3), and 22(3), which are discussed below.

The Commission has jurisdiction over a range of concentrations which are of a very substantial size and which take wider effect than simply within an individual Member State. It is therefore not normally concerned with companies of a relatively small turnover within the Community; on the other hand if large multinationals, even those whose primary activities are, say, in Japan or the United States, have sufficient turnover within more than one Member State, their acquisitions or joint ventures may fall within the jurisdiction of ECMR, even if at first sight they have little material connection with the Community. This objective is ensured by the minimum jurisdictional figures first proposed in early 1989 and finally adopted:

(i)   at least five billion ECU[9] (£3.6 billion) combined world-wide turnover for all the undertakings, and

(ii) at least two hundred and fifty million ECU (£180 million) Community turnover for at least two undertakings involved, but

(iii) *no* jurisdiction if this Community turnover for each of the participants is achieved as to at least two-thirds from the same Member State.

Article 1 lays down this basic jurisdictional principle, supported by Article 5, which contains necessarily detailed provisions to allow the calculations to be made in individual cases. Turnover for ordinary trading companies is defined so as to cover all sales of goods and services but excluding value added tax and sales tax; for insurance companies and banks different methods of calculation relating to insurance premiums and banking income were provided. To the turnover of both the bidding and the target company are to be added the turnover of its parent and its subsidiary companies forming part of the same group. However, if the acquisition is simply of part of a company's business, for example where a division manufacturing a particular product is being sold rather than the entire company, then the relevant turnover in calculating the seller's world-wide and EC turnover is only that of the division being sold, not the entire company (Article 5(2)). In joint ventures, however, extremely small transactions may be caught since in all cases the turnover of both parents is relevant. In order to prevent the artificial splitting up of a major purchase into a series of transactions each of which remains below the jurisdictional threshold, the Commission may aggregate all transactions made between the parties over a two-year period.

It was originally intended that jurisdictional thresholds would be revised in 1993, but this did not occur. In 1997 the Council of Ministers reached agreement on further extensions to the jurisdictional thresholds; the main objective was to bring within them some concentrations involving undertakings with a reasonably large turnover in at least three Member States but whose aggregate world and Community turnover fell below the original thresholds. Under Article 1(*b*) of Regulation 1310/97 (effective from 1 March 1998) the requirements for a concentration with a Community dimension are met if:

(*a*) the combined aggregate worldwide turnover of all the undertakings concerned is more than 2,500 million ECU;

[9] References to 'ECUs' should be treated as if they now read 'Euros'.

(b) in each of at least three Member States, the combined aggregate turnover of all the undertakings concerned is more than 100 million ECU;

(c) in each of at least three Member States included for the purpose of point (b), the turnover of at least two of the undertakings concerned is more than 25 million ECU each; and

(d) the aggregate Community-wide turnover of each of at least two of the undertakings concerned is more than 100 million ECU

unless each of the undertakings concerned achieves more than two-thirds of its aggregate Community-wide turnover within a single Member State.

Provided that the combined world turnover of five thousand million ECU can be estab-lished, the next task is to assess the Community turnover for the undertakings concerned. Here the requirement is that at least two of the undertakings concerned have a turnover in the Community of at least 250 million ECU (approximately 175 million pounds sterling). If three companies are involved in the transaction, then effectively the undertaking with the smallest Community turnover can be ignored. If this level of turnover has been achieved in the financial year relevant to the transaction, then the Community turnover requirement will be satisfied unless each of the two companies has its main business focus and turnover in the same Member State (when clearly that Member State would have the prior right to assess the validity of the transaction). The technical legal requirement is that the two relevant companies should not achieve more than two-thirds each of their aggre-gate Community-wide turnover within one Member State. For example, suppose that two large chemical companies, R and S, situated in France and England respectively wish to merge, each having a Community turnover of 3,000 million ECU. If R sells at least three-quarters of its turnover, i.e. 2,250 million ECU, in France and 750 million in England, whilst S sells only half (1,500 million ECU) of its turnover in France and the other half (1,500 million ECU) in England, there will be a Community dimension to the transaction. This is because, whilst R does achieve more than two-thirds of its aggregate Community turnover in France, the same cannot be said of S, which only sells half of its turnover in France and the other half in England. If the Community turnover requirements are not met then the concentration in question will not have a Community dimension, however large the aggregate world turnover of the undertakings. It is, nevertheless, important to realize that undertakings may fall within the ECMR on the basis of their turnover even if they have minimal or even no assets within the Community (as in *Gencor/Lonrho*[10] and *Boeing/McDonnell Douglas*[11]).

2.2 THE IDENTIFICATION OF RELEVANT TURNOVER

Before going on, in section 3 of this chapter, to consider the definition of 'control' and 'decisive influence' it is sensible first to understand the correct approach for deciding which undertakings, of those involved in particular transactions, should have their turn-over taken into account for the purpose of the calculation of the thresholds set out in Article 1. The choice of turnover as a criterion for jurisdiction would seem at first sight to

---

[10] Case IV/M619 [1996] 4 CMLR 742. On appeal Case T-102/96 [1999] ECR II-753: 4 CMLR 971.
[11] Case IV/M877 [1997] OJ L336/16.

present fewer problems than the alternatives of market share percentages or asset values. Unlike market shares, figures of turnover are found in the published accounts of public companies, which are in most cases the undertakings involved in transactions potentially subject to the Merger Regulation. Compared to market share calculations, their assessment is straightforward; the definition of turnover is defined in Article 5(1) of the ECMR as 'the amounts derived by the undertakings concerned in the previous financial year from the sale of products and provision of services falling within the undertaking's ordinary activities'.

Nevertheless, in determining whether a particular transaction is a concentration of Community dimension because the turnover thresholds are met, it may sometimes be less than obvious how to identify the undertakings which are relevant for this purpose. The Commission has published a Notice[12] on 'the concept of the undertaking' which provides detailed guidance on this issue. Sometimes such identification may be quite simple. Thus:

(i)   if A acquires the whole of the assets or share capital of B, A and B alone are the relevant undertakings whose turnover is taken into account;

(ii)   if either A or B is a member of a corporate group (as defined in Article 5(4) of ECMR), the other companies in that group will be treated as part of that undertaking; and

(iii) if A and B merge to form a separate undertaking, C, then A and B are the relevant undertakings.

The Notice then goes on to consider more complex situations.[13] It stresses that it is the concept of 'acquiring control' that determines which undertakings are to be taken into account. It is necessary to look at both the 'acquiring' and 'acquired' side of the transaction; on the 'acquiring' side, one or more companies may be obtaining sole or joint control of the assets of subsidiaries of the target and normally the turnover of all these undertakings will be included in the calculation of thresholds. On the 'acquired' side by contrast the seller of such assets or subsidiary companies will not be included, apart from the actual turnover of the businesses sold, provided that after the sale it has no continuing links with the newly merged entity.

Further complexities may arise if an existing joint venture acquires control of another undertaking, or where changes of shareholding occur in an undertaking so that sole control becomes joint control, or vice versa. If B is acquired by an existing joint venture, XY, only the turnover of XY and B will be relevant, provided that XY itself is a full-function joint venture, with sufficient financial and other resources to carry on business on a lasting basis. On the other hand if XY is regarded by the Commission as simply a vehicle for the acquisition of B by X and Y (so that XY has itself no existing commercial character or identity) it is the turnover of X and Y (and their respective corporate groups) which will be aggregated with that of B.[14]

Where the transaction involves changes in the shareholdings held by separate undertakings in an existing joint venture company, as when a joint venture moves from joint control to sole control, the relevant undertakings will be the acquiring shareholder and the joint venture itself, but not the selling company.

---

[12] (1986) OJ C66/14.   [13] Para. 7 ff.   [14] Paras 26–28.

Other situations where the identification of the relevant undertakings may present difficulty include that where the number of shareholders in a joint venture is reduced by only
some of them selling their holdings, whilst the remainder are reduced to the status of
minority shareholders without having any element of decisive influence, either individually
or collectively. In this situation it is likely that this latter category will no longer be considered as relevant to the turnover calculations. In every case however the Commission will
analyse not only the legal rights of the parties, but also the actual way in which those rights
have been exercised. When a joint venture is split up between its members or demerged, the
turnover taken into account will be that of the individual members and of the parts of
the joint venture business that each will be acquiring.[15]

The Notice finally deals with a number of other situations where corporate control may
pass but where the identification of the relevant undertakings may be difficult. These
include an exchange of assets, when a swap is arranged between two undertakings. Even if
the transactions are regarded by the parties as interdependent, they will be treated for the
purpose of the Regulation not as a single concentration, but as two separate transactions: for
each of them the acquiring company and the acquired companies or assets will be relevant.
Even the acquisition of control by individuals may sometimes fall within the scope of the
Regulation, provided that the individual concerned has sufficient economic activity of his
own to effect a lasting change in the structure of the undertaking acquired.

2.3 ARTICLES 5(3) AND 5(4)

A separate Notice issued at the same time deals with the calculation of turnover in cases
that are less than straightforward. The Notice supplements the basic provisions contained in
Articles 1 and 5 of the ECMR. The Notice points out in its initial section that the thresholds
are purely quantitative and based on turnover calculation only, rather than market share,
because the aim is to provide 'a simple and objective mechanism' that can be easily handled
by the companies involved so as to determine whether a transaction is of Community
dimension and, therefore, notifiable. Its purpose is to measure the economic strength of the
undertakings concerned as reflected in turnover figures, regardless of the sector or sectors
where the turnover was achieved and whether those sectors will themselves be affected by
the transaction in question. Clearly it is important to exclude from these figures any
intra-group turnover

An amended Article 5(3) sets out special rules to apply if the undertakings are financial,
such as banks or insurance companies. Replacing the original rules, which were based on the
assets of such institutions and the proportion of their loans made within the Community,
are new rules which focus on turnover. In the case of banks, this is primarily the income
received by way of interest, dividends, commissions, and net profits on their financial operations. In the case of insurance companies, it is the aggregate of their premiums received and
reinsurance premiums paid out. Many detailed problems can arise on the calculation of
turnover and the current Notice deals with a wide range of these, including the following
issues:

— geographical allocation when goods are sold or services provided. In the majority of
  cases the place of sale is attributed to the place where the customer is located because,

[15] paras 46–48.

in most circumstances, that is where the turnover is generated and where competition with alternative suppliers takes place. Thus, for example, in the case of the sale of packaged holidays, competition for the sale of such holidays through travel agents takes place locally, even though the holidays may be enjoyed in a number of distant locations. The essential point is that the turnover is earned locally and that is where the turnover is to be counted;

— adjustment for divestments or acquisitions since the date of the relevant audited accounts have been prepared;

— aggregate calculations when successive acquisitions have taken place within a two-year period; and

— adjustments for exchange rate variations.

In applying these rules to calculate turnover it is important to remember that under Article 5(4) aggregation applies not simply to the companies directly involved in the transaction but to all those companies which they control or by whom they are controlled. The relevant definition of control is found in Article 5(4) and includes:

(a) the undertaking concerned;

(b) those undertakings in which the undertaking concerned directly or indirectly:

— owns more than half the capital or business assets; or

— has the power to exercise more than half the voting rights;

— has the power to appoint more than half the members of the supervisory board, the administrative board or bodies legally representing the undertakings; or

— has the right to manage the undertaking's affairs;

(c) those undertakings in which the undertaking concerned has the rights or powers listed in (b); and those undertakings in which an undertaking as referred to in (c) has the rights or powers listed in (b); and those undertakings in which two or more undertakings have the rights or powers listed in (b).

As a result of the very specific wording of Article 5(4) problems may arise in cases when an undertaking has the *de facto* ability to exercise control over another company in spite of the fact that it does not hold a shareholding above 50 per cent. Its acquisition of less than a 50 per cent holding may have conferred *de facto* control and, in this case, under Article 3, a '*concentration*' may have been deemed to have occurred. It is not necessarily the case, however, that the same answer will be reached under Article 5(4) for determining whether the turnover of the acquiring company in this case is also to be included in the calculation made for assessing relevant turnover.

The problem arose in an early case under the Merger Regulation (*Arjomari/Wiggins Teape*).[16] Arjomari had a 39 per cent shareholding in Wiggins Teape and the remaining shares were widely dispersed. The major shareholder in Arjomari itself was another company, GSL, but its holding was less than 50 per cent. In turn a third company owned a large but not a majority shareholding in GSL. A Community dimension for the case in respect of world turnover calculations would only exist if all of the three companies were each deemed to form part of the relevant acquiring group.

---

[16] Case IV/M25 [1991] 4 CMLR 854.

The Commission placed weight on the fourth ground for qualification under Article 5(4)(*b*), namely that the undertaking 'has the right to manage the undertaking's affairs'. It took the pragmatic view that, whereas the first three examples given under (*b*) gave legal control of the business of the company, there must also be under the fourth heading the right to include companies which, without having this legal right of control, nevertheless *de facto* could be proved in the past to have shown the ability to manage the affairs of that undertaking. The Commission, therefore, examined the voting record at past annual general meetings and found that in practice the voting rights actually exercised, for example by GSL, fell short of 50 per cent by a small fraction. As it could not be shown, therefore, that *de facto* it had the ability, for example, to appoint the members of the board of Arjomari, it could not be considered under Article 5(4). Had it been shown that in practice it had exercised more than 50 per cent of the votes cast then, regardless of its actual shareholding, it would have been considered to have qualified under the fourth heading of Article 5(4)(*b*). Since GSL itself could not qualify, the third party holding the substantial share interest in GSL equally could not qualify. By contrast, in *Eridania/ISI*,[17] an almost equivalent shareholding held in Eridania by Ferruzzi was shown in practice to confer the ability to control Eridania, given the large discrepancy between the Ferruzzi shareholding and the very small shareholdings held by all other members. Even, therefore, in what is supposed to be the purely objective assessment of turnover, the Commission will have to exercise an element of judgment in difficult cases.

By the same token, if the undertaking making the bid for another company does not have a sufficient shareholding in it to maintain an absolute majority at shareholder meetings, it may nevertheless qualify if it has contracts with other companies giving it the right to manage them. In the *Accor/Wagon-Lits*[18] case, Accor had management contracts in a number of relatively small companies owning hotels. The owners of these companies entered into contracts with Accor under which Accor managed the hotels under their own trading names on a long term basis. The Commission decided that the owners of these hotels had virtually withdrawn from management and merely exercised the proprietary rights of shareholders. Accor was, therefore, allowed to include the turnover of these companies in calculating whether it had achieved sufficient turnover to be of Community dimension (which it was apparently anxious to do), and the jurisdiction of the Commission was held to be established.

3. THE MEANING OF A 'CONCENTRATION'

3.1 THE MEANING OF 'CONTROL'

It is an essential element of any scheme of merger control that an exact definition of that particular transaction which gives jurisdiction shall be given, hence the importance under the ECMR of defining a 'concentration'. The term covers the case where two separate undertakings merge into a single body, and also the more common situation (at least in the United Kingdom) where one person or undertaking acquires 'direct or indirect control' of the whole or part of another. This basic definition is found in Article 3(1). 'Control' is

---

[17] Case IV/M62 [1991] 4 CMLR 663.   [18] [1992] OJ L204/1: Case IV/M126 [1993] 5 CMLR M13.

defined as 'rights, contracts or any other means which either separately or jointly . . . *confer the possibility of exercising decisive influence on an undertaking*' (emphasis added) whether this occurs through share ownership, voting or management agreements, or through any other form of rights operating on the undertaking. Also to be considered is the extent to which the acquiring company has rights which affect the commercial strategy and detailed financial management of the company acquired, as opposed to those rights which relate simply to proprietary protection of its investment. It could include an acquisition either of 100 per cent of the shares of a target company or a lesser percentage sufficient in practice to enable such '*decisive influence*' to be exercised. It can also cover cross-shareholdings, cross-directorships and a variety of other means of exercising control.

3.2 THE MEANING OF 'CONCENTRATIVE' JOINT VENTURES

Originally only those joint ventures falling within the definition of 'concentrative' were covered by ECMR, being those which performed on a lasting basis all the functions of an 'autonomous economic entity' and which did not have as their object or effect the coordination of the economic activities of their parents. Subsequent amendment of the ECMR (as explained in successive Interface Notices by the Commission) has considerably widened this definition; it now applies to all 'full-function' joint ventures, even those where there is an element of coordination of the activities of the parents. Reference, therefore, to 'concentration' includes all full-function joint ventures that have a Community dimension. It is, however, important to be aware that, under Article 2(4) of ECMR, when there is an element of coordination this is appraised under the criteria of Article 81(1) and (3), taking into account in particular the activities retained by the parent companies in the same or related markets as those in which the joint venture operates, as well as the degree to which this coordination could allow the possibility of eliminating competition in relevant markets (see Chapter 19 at pp.408–10) for the treatment of joint ventures under the ECMR.

3.3 THE MEANING OF 'DECISIVE INFLUENCE'

The definition of '*decisive influence*' has arisen as a problem for the Commission in a number of decided cases. What is clear is that it will not be necessary for the bidder to acquire full legal control of the target in order to obtain '*decisive influence*'. An acquisition of a minority shareholding may be sufficient and the test is less demanding than that required under Article 5(4), already considered in the context of deciding which companies' turnovers are to be included. In *Eridania/ISI*,[19] Eridania increased its shareholding in ISI to 65 per cent by purchasing 15 per cent from another shareholder, a sugar beet growers' cooperative, Finbieticola, which retained 35 per cent. The Commission decided that before the transaction had occurred Eridania exercised joint control with Finbieticola because the ISI board of directors, on which Eridania had no absolute majority, exercised a number of important rights, including the appointment of a managing director and the making of decisions on the sale of plants and on plant closures. After the transfer, the rights retained by Finbieticola had been considerably reduced and merely enabled it to veto major changes to the structure of the company, such as the issue of new capital or a transfer of its head office.

---

[19] See fn. 17 above.

It was held, therefore, that, as a result of the 15 per cent transfer of shares, Eridania had now acquired sole control in place of the previous joint control with Finbieticola. The transaction was, therefore notifiable.

We have already discussed the *Arjomari/Wiggins Teape*[20] case in connection with the definition of Article 5(4)(b). The case is also relevant to the assessment of '*decisive influence*'. Here the 39 per cent shareholding that Arjomari had obtained in Wiggins Teape was considered by the Commission sufficient to constitute sole control over Wiggins Teape because there were no other shareholders which individually owned more than 4 per cent of the share capital. In practice, therefore, this 39 per cent holding was considered more than sufficient to give Arjomari *de facto* control over the operations of Wiggins Teape, even though a shareholding of 45.19 per cent held in Arjomari by Groupe Saint Louis, as explained above, was deemed insufficient to constitute 'control' for the purposes of Article 5(4), in the absence of showing that such control had actually been exercised at past general meetings.

3.4 JOINT CONTROL

Under the Regulation concentrations may also occur in other situations; one example is where joint control has been created by the transaction. This is illustrated by the *MBB/Aerospatiale*[21] case where Aerospatiale and MBB formed a joint venture to carry out their helicopter businesses which was held by the Commission to give them joint control. Aerospatiale received 60 per cent of the equity and MBB 40 per cent. Under the terms of the relevant agreement all strategic decisions for the joint venture required the unanimous consent of both partners at the supervisory board level. Management of the joint venture was to be exercised by two managing directors acting on a basis of unanimity. Where joint control is obtained the shareholdings of both parties can be aggregated in looking at total turnover, for the purposes of determining whether the concentration has a 'Community dimension'.

It is clear that where two firms each hold 50 per cent in their target company they will have joint control if it. It does not necessarily follow that three or more undertakings acquiring a target will themselves *all* be deemed to acquire joint control. The Commission will only accept the existence of joint control where there is no likelihood that 'shifting alliances' may change the identity of those who jointly control the target. Joint control will normally only be admitted to exist if under the terms of the shareholders' agreement major strategic decisions are subject to veto rights. For example, in the *Paribas/MTH/MBU*[22] case both Paribas and MTH acquired a 40 per cent interest in MBU, a newly-created joint venture. Both Paribas and MTH had a veto over decisions made in shareholders' meetings in spite of the fact that each held only a minority interest in the company. Although the theoretical possibility of changing alliances existed, the veto rights were held sufficient by the Commission to establish joint control. A similar decision was arrived at in the *Volvo/Renault*[23] trucks and buses merger where the parties each acquired a 45 per cent holding in each other, a strong situation of common interest which together with other factors led to a *de facto* permanent common control situation, thus effectively establishing a single economic entity between the two parties. It is also sufficient to establish a '*concentration*' if the

---

[20] See fn. 16 above.
[22] [1991] OJ C277/18, Case IV/M50.
[21] Case IV/M17 [1992] 4 CMLR M70.
[23] Case IV/M4 [1991] 4 CMLR 297.

bidder is an existing joint controller which acquires a further holding in the target company bringing it from 50 per cent to a higher percentage, as in the *ICI/Tioxide*[24] case (where ICI increased its shareholding from 50 per cent to 100 per cent).

Article 3(5), however, provides for certain situations in which a concentration is not deemed to arise, namely:

(*a*) where the acquisition of the 'decisive influence' is purely temporary and obtained by an undertaking with a view to immediate disposal, with the disposal itself taking place within a year of acquisition, or some reasonably short extension if disposal was not possible within the original period set;

(*b*) where a liquidator or receiver acquires control of a company; or

(*c*) in special cases involving financial holding companies engaged in reconstruction.

In 1998 the Commission published a revised Notice in which it provided guidance on its approach to the interpretation of the many difficult issues that can arise in defining whether a concentration has come into existence. This emphasizes that in this process qualitative rather than merely quantitative criteria have to be taken into account, in considering both legal and factual issues.

3.5 THE ISSUE OF PHYSICAL LOCATION

In *Gencor/Lonrho*,[25] the Court of First Instance held that a 'concentration with a Community dimension' does not necessarily have to be one where the undertakings concerned are resident or established in the European Community or have their production assets located there. The test of jurisdiction is one of turnover, i.e. sales carried out within the Common Market, applying the jurisdictional principles laid down in the *Woodpulp* case. Application of the Regulation is justified under public international law when it is foreseeable that a proposed concentration will have an immediate and substantial effect on the Community.

4. NOTIFICATION OF CONCENTRATIONS

4.1 THE TASK OF NOTIFICATION

The Regulation is administered by a division of the Directorate General ('DG Comp') for Competition of the European Commission in Brussels, known as the Merger Task Force (MTF), headed by a director responsible to the Director General of DG Comp, who in turn reports to the Commissioner for Competition. The members of the MTF are Commission officials drawn from the Member States (and sometimes from third countries) with specialist legal, economic, and accountancy qualifications and experience, as well as experience in the administration of competition cases. Whilst the majority are career EC employees, some are national experts seconded for two or three years from their Member States' competition authorities. The Merger Task Force is responsible both for pre-notification negotiations and for dealing with all matters arising following notification of a particular concentration. It is

---

[24] Case IV/M73 [1991] 4 CMLR 792.   [25] Case T-102/96 [1999] ECR II-753: 4 CMLR 971.

organized into a number of divisions which take responsibility for the investigation of individual cases, though the final decision is always that of the Commission itself.

Notification involves provision to the MTF of a substantial quantity of information about the transaction contained in the document known as Form CO, whose outline and structure can be found as an appendix to Regulation 447/98. This document will include details of the method proposed for effecting the concentration, of the relevant corporate groups, their recent accounts, and a full explanation of their ownership and control and of any existing relevant link between the parties. A full analysis of all the 'affected markets', including both product and geographic dimensions, will also be needed together with detailed assessment of the market shares held by the parties and information as to actual or potential barriers to entry. 'Affected markets' are defined as relevant product markets, where the individual or combined market shares of the parties amount to 15 per cent or more for parties in a horizontal relationship and to 25 per cent or more in a vertical relationship. Further information will be needed in appropriate cases on matters such as the degree of vertical integration; distribution systems; research and development expenditure; and the existence of co-operation agreements and the licensing of patents and know-how may also be relevant.

4.2 THE NEED FOR PRE-NOTIFICATION

In the pre-notification stage the Merger Task Force will receive inquiries from undertakings and their professional representatives as to whether a particular transaction (probably not yet finally agreed) does fall within the scope of the Regulation and, if so, what kind of information will be required by the Commission in order to carry out its first stage inquiry both into jurisdiction and, if satisfied on this, into merits. The officials of the Merger Task Force may well then express a preliminary non-binding view on whether the transaction does or does not fall within the jurisdiction of ECMR, and any likely problems that are anticipated with it. At this stage time is not running against the parties but both the parties and the Merger Task Force will be aware that once notification has become mandatory there is then only a short period in which the first phase investigation has to be carried out and a decision reached whether to clear it at that point or pass the case on to the 'second phase'. The Best Practice Guidelines (available on the website of DG Comp under the heading 'Mergers', though an amended draft set of Guidelines was put forward for consultation in December 2002) state that even in straightforward cases it is appropriate to have pre-notification contact with the Task Force, in particular to reduce the risk of lodging an incomplete Form CO. A draft Form CO is often shown to the Commission at this stage to ensure that its requirements in the case are being fully met. The Commission is becoming more inclined to reject a Form CO if it believes that the information contained in it is incomplete or misleading.

4.3 SIMPLE CASES

For relatively small-scale agreements which nevertheless meet the requirements of the thresholds for jurisdiction, there is a provision for short-form notification in paragraph C of Form CO. This applies where a joint venture has no, or minimal, actual, or foreseen activities within the Community, and where joint control of an undertaking is acquired by two or more companies where:

(i)   the turnover for a joint venture or the turnover of the activities contributed by the parents is less than Euro 100 million; and

(ii) where the total value of assets transferred to the joint venture is less than Euro 100 million in the same territory.

In addition the Commission has now adopted a simplified procedure for handling the most straightforward cases, covering both those that benefit from short-form notification and also some others.

Article 4 of the ECMR deals with prior notification and requires the formal notification on Form CO to be lodged within one week of the conclusion of the agreement, or announcement of the public bid, or acquisition of the controlling interest. In practice it is often possible to agree with the Merger Task Force some flexibility in relation to this dead-line. Once notification has been made and jurisdiction established, the Commission has to publish in the Official Journal the fact of the notification indicating the names of the parties and the nature of the concentration. The possible outcomes following notification are dealt with under Article 6. Article 6(1)(a) provides for the possibility that the concentration notified does not for some reason fall within the scope of the Regulation at all; for example it may be that the turnover on either the world or EC basis is insufficient. Another alternative is under Article 6(1)(b) where jurisdiction of the Commission is satisfied, but where the merits of the case notified '*do not raise serious doubts as to its compatibility with the Common Market*'. In this case the case proceeds to clearance at the end of the first stage and is not further examined. Only approximately 5 per cent of notified cases proceed to the second phase under Article 6(1)(c). The content of Form CO is considered further in Section 2 of the next chapter.

5. CRITERIA FOR ASSESSMENT OF A CONCENTRATION

5.1 COMPATIBILITY OF CONCENTRATIONS WITH THE COMMON MARKET: ARTICLE 2(1)

An important feature of ECMR is that the basis on which concentrations are assessed is not identical with that applied to either agreements falling within Article 81(1); or cases of abuse of dominant position falling within Article 82. After deciding whether a particular transac-tion falls within the Regulation, the substantive criteria for assessing that transaction become crucial. As mentioned, the formula chosen in Article 2 has been whether the con-centration is 'compatible' with the Common Market. Criteria of this kind can be defined either in a broad manner, including not only competition issues but also social and indus-trial policy, or they can be more specific and limited to particular issues, for example the effect on competition in the relevant product and geographic markets. Contrary to what may have been expected, the Regulation in its final form does not reflect a compromise between the two approaches; the criteria are firmly based on competition issues, even though Article 2 does apparently contain a suggestion that other factors might be taken into account in a particularly evenly balanced case. The Article sets out the rules to be applied by the Commission by way of three separate subclauses whose relationship to each other is not immediately obvious. Article 2(1) lists several factors to be considered in deciding upon 'compatibility':

— the need to maintain and develop effective competition within the Common Market in view of, among other things, market structures and actual (or potential) competition from other undertakings;

— the economic and financial power and market position of the parties and also of their suppliers and consumers (and their access to alternative supplies);

— legal and other barriers to entry;

— trends of supply and demand in relevant markets; and

— development of technical and economic progress, provided that it is to consumers' advantage and does not form an obstacle to competition.

5.2 ARTICLE 2(2) AND (3)

Formal Commission decisions under Articles 81 and 82 concern agreements already made and implemented and abuses of dominant position that have already occurred. The focus of concern for the Commission under Article 81 is not only the formal content of an agreement but the way in which it has actually operated; under Article 82 the focus is on the effect of the practices by the alleged dominant company over a period of time in the past. By contrast, assessment of concentrations under ECMR necessarily looks to the future, seeking to answer the question 'what effect will this transaction have, if implemented, on competition in the relevant geographical and product/services sector?'. The language of Article 2, which provides the legal criteria for assessment, is similar to that of Article 82, in referring to concentrations which 'create or strengthen a dominant position'; but in its application by the Commission, the fact that the focus is on the future effect of the concentration, rather than on the imposition of penalties for past misconduct, means that the approach under Article 2 inevitably differs in a number of respects from that adopted under Article 82. Underlying the approach of the Commission under the ECMR is the importance of identifying those cases, probably only a small percentage of the total number notified to it, whose implementation might result in serious damage to competition in the relevant market.[26] Sometimes the result of the Commission's examination may lead to a total prohibition of the transaction; in a greater number, conditions may be imposed on the transaction which substantially reduce the adverse consequences. Clearly an advantage of the existence of the ECMR is the removal of the need to consider the use of Article 82 in subsequent cases, if the Commission in exercising its merger control jurisdiction has been able to prevent the creation or strengthening of companies with dominant positions who might subsequently act in an abusive manner.

Article 2(2) and (3) read as follows:

2(2) A concentration which does not create or strengthen a dominant position as a result of which effective competition would be significantly impeded in the Common Market or in a substantial part of it shall be declared compatible with the Common Market.

---

[26] By contrast, if the target company's market share would, absent the concentration, fall into the hands of the bidder anyway, a 'failing company' finding by the Commission may be justified. *France* v. *Commission (Kali and Salz)*, Cases C-68/94 and 30/95 [1998] ECR I-1375: 4 CMLR 829.

(3) A concentration which creates or strengthens a dominant position as a result of which effective competition would be significantly impeded in the Common Market or in a substantial part of it shall be declared incompatible with the Common Market.

Whilst the Article as a whole emphasizes the assessment of competition and structural issues, Article 2(1) provides a reminder to the Commission that in its analysis it should not overlook the many other factors to be taken into account in making its overall assessment, not all of which are purely structural. Article 2 in subclauses (2) and (3) provides the formal legal framework within which the final decision has to be made. However, the approach adopted by the Commission in its application of Article 2 has not been characterized by formal textual analysis.

5.3 THE APPLICATION OF THE CRITERIA

Since the ECMR came into force and up to 31 March 2003 over 2,000 cases have been decided under it by the Commission, of which just over 100 (5 per cent) went into the second phase. Of these twenty received a blocking decision (three of which were later annulled by the Court of First Instance), whilst sixty-two received conditional clearance. In addition ninety-eight of those cleared at the first phase were also made subject to conditions. The build up of notifications of concentrations with a Community Dimension has been impressive; until 1995 the annual total was less than 100, this had risen to 235 in 1998 and then to well over 300 in both 2000 and 2001, reducing slightly thereafter as mergers and acquisition activity slackened worldwide.

It is therefore the second phase cases that tell us most about the application of these criteria, and a number of these cases are referred to in the course of this and the next chapter. For detailed analysis of their application, however, reference should be made to one or more of the specialist text books listed in the Bibliography. Mention should be made that the application of the dominance test set out in Article 2 has recently come in for considerable criticism; and amendment of the dominance test or the alternative criterion of a 'substantial lessening of competition' have been widely advocated as more appropriate. This important issue is discussed both in Section 7 of the next chapter and also in Chapter 25.

6. DEFINITION OF THE RELEVANT PRODUCT OR SERVICE MARKET

6.1 THE COMMISSION'S GENERAL APPROACH

The Commission had, prior to 1990, considerable experience of market analysis in Article 82 cases. The number of cases reaching it, however, under the ECMR and the short time-limits in which decisions have to be prepared have forced on it the development of a more methodical approach to market definition. The Commission is generally regarded as having evolved a more methodical approach to market definition under these pressures than had been the case under Articles 81 and 82. There are many sectors, for example those for petroleum products, pharmaceuticals, and banking, in which the Commission has developed considerable expertise and precedent in its market analysis.

The Regulation itself contains no guidance to the Commission on how it is to approach the task of defining relevant markets, though it has, of course, the benefit both of its own earlier decisions under Articles 81 and 82 and of a number of relevant ECJ decisions. Given the importance of market definition in merger cases it is perhaps surprising that the regulation itself gives no directions as to how this is to be done, though the Commission's general Notice on Market Definition (published in 1997) states the general approach of the Commission in this respect to all cases under Articles 81 and 82, as well as under ECMR. If, for example, in a particular case the combined shares of the target and bidder under one definition of the product market were to be 70 per cent but under another definition 30 per cent, a finding of dominance is obviously far more likely in the first than the second situation. The Commission will normally seek to apply the SSNIP test wherever possible, which is explained in paras 15 to 17 of the Notice. The parties will have completed Form CO (section 6) which asks them to identify 'affected markets' in both a product and geographic sense, but their choice will not be binding on the Commission. Often it is the parties who are seeking for a broader market definition in which the combined market shares will be lower, while the MTF seeks a narrower market in order that market shares can be established which are substantial.

There are many cases where the Commission does not need to make a detailed analysis of the markets and choose between possible alternatives, because it can reach a decision that a clearance can be given to the concentration, even on the assumption that the narrowest possible market definition (giving the highest possible market share) will not raise any problems; an example is the *PepsiCo/General Mills*[27] case. In the great majority of cases, however, a decision on the relevant market will be needed. Easy generalizations about the approach of the Commission to the definition are of limited value; experience of cases to date, however, coupled with the Commission's greater degree of consistency, does show the importance of the following factors:

(i)   the Commission has proceeded normally to adopt narrow product market definitions (for the reasons stated above), while the parties have striven for acceptance of broader markets; though there have been some cases where it has defined markets narrowly and concluded as a result that there was not an overlap between the parties' commercial activities; and

(ii) the Commission is, however, quite prepared in making this assessment to take into account all factors that, in a commercial sense, may render other products interchangeable or substitutable by the consumer.

6.2 ISSUES OF SUBSTITUTABILITY

At this stage the emphasis is on the 'demand side' approach to the substitutability of products. The Commission will look at the essential physical characteristics of products, their prices and their intended use. It will also look at the circumstances in which they are marketed and the nature of the buyer. For example, in *Magneti Marelli/CEAC*,[28] the starter batteries used both as original equipment for new cars and those used as replacements in used cars were identical but were, nevertheless, adjudged to be in separate markets. This was

[27] Case IV/M232 [1992] OJ C-228/6.   [28] Case IV/M43 [1992] 4 CMLR M61.

not only because of the price differences between them, but also because of the fact that the manufacturers were required to supply very large numbers of batteries on a just-in-time basis to car manufacturers under stringent conditions, which differed very much from supplying a wide range of dealers and garages with a variety of replacement batteries for stock for resale to motorists from time to time. A similar decision was reached in *Knorr-Bremse/Allied Signal*[29] where the original equipment market for air brake systems was held distinct from the supply of such products in the after-market.

In *Aerospatiale-Alenia/De Havilland,*[30] an analysis of this kind is applied to the turbo-prop commuter aircraft market. The parties had argued that all aircraft with between twenty to seventy seats constituted the same product market. The MTF, however, analysed the different end uses to which such turbo-prop airliners were put, and came to the conclusion that there were three categories of plane which were essentially purchased by different categories of buyer. After taking evidence from a number of customers for the aircraft, it became clear that for different types of route aircraft with different seat capacity were required. This information enabled the Commission to find that there were actually three sub-markets for purchase, namely those aircraft with twenty to thirty-nine seats, those with forty to fifty-nine seats and those with sixty seats or over respectively. Similar emphasis on customer requirements can be found in a more recent case involving buses manufactured in Germany, *Mercedes Benz-Kässbohrer.*[31] Here the Commission found that the total bus market in Germany is composed of three types of bus; city buses for local use, inter-city buses, and touring coaches. It is important to note, however, that this finding did not stop the Commission, at a later stage in its examination of the transaction, from looking at the degree of substitutability on the supply side which enable the bus manufacturers to switch with relative ease from the manufacture of one bus type to another.

The end use of products is clearly relevant and physical differences between the products which mean that different end uses are possible, are likely to lead to the establishment of separate markets. This issue arose, for example, in *Renault/Volvo,*[32] where the Commission found that trucks of over sixteen tons were a distinct market from those of a smaller size because only the larger category could be used for long-distance haulage.

Whilst the substitutability of particular products by other products is always relevant, the Commission will normally focus on the ability of manufacturers to switch to alternative products when it comes to deal with the assessment of dominance (see Section 8 below). The Commission's practice is not invariably consistent. For example, in *du Pont/ICI,*[33] the Commission defined the market by reference to the end-use applications for the intermediate product nylon fibre and by reference to the requirements of the purchasers of that particular product. It found that nylon fibres for carpets, on the one hand, are not substitutable by nylon fibres used for textile and other industrial applications on the other. The Commission found no competitive overlap between the two markets; it, therefore, focused only on the nylon fibres used for carpet manufacture. The proposed merger gave rise to serious doubts as to compatibility in that specific market alone. It was also suggested that polypropylene fibres were a substitute for nylon fibres for carpet manufacturers but, after examining the evidence from such customers, the Commission found that they cannot

---

[29] Case IV/M377 [1993] 5 CMLR 535.   [30] Case IV/M53 [1992] 4 CMLR M2.
[31] Case IV/M477 [1995] 4 CMLR 600.   [32] See fn. 50.
[33] Case IV/M214 [1995] 5 CMLR M41.

generally switch between the two types of fibres merely as a result of variations in the price ratio between them. Moreover, examining price trends over a period of time showed the Commission that the prices for nylon fibres did not in practice influence prices for the polypropylene fibres.

In some major second-phase cases where there was adequate time for examination of both sides of the relevant market, the Commission has brought both the demand and the supply into the product market analysis. One example is *Nestlé/Perrier*,[34] where a variety of soft drinks were established as not being in practice recognizable by French consumers as substitutes for bottled water. In another case involving consumer products, *Proctor & Gamble/VPS*,[35] the Commission was faced by an argument by P&G that in the feminine hygiene markets sanitary towels and tampons constituted a single product market. The Commission, however, made a finding based on a variety of demand-and supply-side factors that the two products represented separate products. Their conclusion was based primarily on an assessment of differences with regard to the use of the products, consumer preferences (including factors such as comfort, security, and morality) and detailed study of the relevant price movements and usage patterns, coupled with the views of retailers involved in the markets.

Even in the first-phase cases, detailed examination of consumer demand characteristics may be required. *SKB/Block Drug*[36] involved the proposed acquisition by a major pharmaceutical company of a smaller undertaking specializing in the sale of toothpaste for users with sensitive teeth. The combined market shares for this specialist product in the United Kingdom were substantial, but were far lower if toothpaste were regarded as a single general relevant market. On the supply side, it was clear that manufacturers could switch production easily between different types of toothpaste, and that many brands, aimed at a range of different user priorities, shared a common range of ingredients. Many users with sensitive teeth did not purchase the specialist product aimed at them, preferring brands or types which offered 'total care', i.e. a range of features. Given all these factors, the Commission rules at the end of the first phase that there was only a single general market in the United Kingdom, and cleared the merger.

Of course market definition problems are not limited to consumer products. An example of a non-consumer product was the potash market considered in *Kali und Salz/MDK*.[37] Potash is a mineral fertilizer used either by itself or in combination with other plant nutrients to form a compound fertilizer. It is available either as a powder used for mixing with other nutrients or in a granulated form used primarily for direct agricultural application. Whereas the granulated form is usually purchased by farmers, purchasers of the powder form are the producers of compound fertilizers. The granulated form is also 10 per cent more expensive than the other form.

On the supply-side potash producers were able to produce both the standard powder and the granulated product and it was not difficult for them in their factories to change the balance of output of the two products. There was, therefore, a high degree of supply-side substitutability and, based on this evidence, the Commission concluded that the relevant

---

[34] Case IV/M190 [1993] 4 CMLR M17.   [35] Case IV/M430 [1995] 5 CMLR 146.

[36] Cases Comp/M 2192 (decisions of 11 January 2001).

[37] [1994] 4 CMLR 526; [1994] OJ L186/38, Case IV/M 308. See also Ch. 18, p.366, for the result of the appeal to the ECJ in this case which did not, however, affect the market definition.

product market was the entire market for agricultural application, including both the granulated form sold to the farmer and the powder sold to the producers of compound fertilizers. The Commission did not, however, extend its finding to include all forms of compound fertiliser incorporating potash, because of the limited substitutability between them in respect of the different crops and soil conditions for which they were appropriate.

The Commission will normally pay considerable attention to industry customer and practice in assessing such markets. Nevertheless it is prepared on occasion to depart from conventional industry analysis or official classification. In *Ciba-Geigy/Sandoz*,[38] it declined to follow the World Health Organization's 'Anatomical Therapeutic Classification' of pharmaceutical drugs; instead in its market analysis it gave principal emphasis, in the case of over-the-counter drugs, to the requirements of patients and, in the case of prescription drugs, to the views of prescribing doctors. A transaction that involves undertakings active in a large number of separate product or service markets may require analysis by the Commission of the competitive situation in all of these, and the pharmaceutical industry has provided some complex investigations of this kind (for example the *Glaxo/SKB*[39] case).

A market definition is reached by the Commission in the context of the facts of the case found at the time when its investigation is being carried out. Since these facts may change subsequently the CFI has confirmed in *Coca-Cola* v. *Commission*[40] that a market definition by the Commission in an earlier case is not binding on the Commission in a subsequent case.

The Commission's Annual Report on Competition Policy is a useful source of information on the experience of the Commission in analysing the major cases of a particular year. For example, the 1998 Annual Report reviews the approach taken to market definition in the provision of large scale accounting services dealt with in the *Pricewaterhouse/Coopers and Lybrand*[41] case, and its finding that a separate market existed for the supply of accounting services and statutory accounts for very large multinational firms. Their requirements for a global network of offices and staff with the necessary broad experience meant that effectively only one of the big six accounting firms would be acceptable to them. Its 1999 Annual Report emphasized that market definition may itself be influenced by changes in commercial practice, often brought about by the changing requirements of customers. For example, whereas in the past the Commission had regarded *standard* mail services and *express* mail services as having distinctly separate characteristics, it had now recognized that there had been a certain shifting and blurring of the boundaries between them, in that even users of the standard postal services now had certain delivery guarantees available.

The recent case of *Tetra/Sidel*[42] shows that the Commission may intervene to block a merger even if the parties are technically operating in different product markets. Here, Tetra Laval was the market leader in carton packaging, where it had a world market share of some 80 per cent, whilst Sidel was the world leader in the PET (plastic) packaging market, with some 60 per cent. The Commission felt that these two markets, though separate, were closely related and likely to converge in the next few years. The effect, therefore, of the merger would be to reduce the likelihood of Sidel being able to increase the share of PET packaging

---

[38] Case IV/M737 (1997) OJ L201/1.   [39] Case IV/M1846 (decision of 8 May 2000).

[40] Cases T-125 and 127/97 [2000] ECR II-1733: 5 CMLR 467.

[41] Case IV/M1016 [1999] 4 CMLR 665.

[42] Comp M/2416 (original Commission decision): [2002] 5 CMLR 1182 (CFI decision on appeal).

for fruit juices and dairy products in substitution for cartons; this in turn would increase Tetra's ability to control developments in both markets and to increase prices to consumers. This decision, however, was annulled by the CFI in October 2000, and is discussed in the following Chapter 18 (p.393).

7. DEFINITION OF THE RELEVANT GEOGRAPHIC MARKET

7.1 THE COMMISSION'S GENERAL APPROACH

In parallel with establishing the relevant product market it is necessary for the Commission to identify the relevant geographic market. The range of possibilities is that a single Member State (or even a region within a Member State) is the geographical market or perhaps two or more Member States; another alternative is the European Community as a whole and, for some costly and highly technical products, the market may now be worldwide (for example, in *Aerospatiale/Alenia/De Havilland*,[43] where the market was found to be commuter aircraft manufactured worldwide). The Commission's Notice on Market Definition (1997) already mentioned is a valuable source of information in explaining its approach to this task.

With consumer products the geographic market chosen as relevant has often been individual Member States because the basis for distribution is often national, and the imperfections of the Single Market have meant that it is often necessary for a single manufacturer to treat individual Member States as separate markets. Differing local specification requirements corresponding to local consumer wishes and the existence of different legislation prescribing requirements for the goods may also be relevant. As Sir Leon Brittan explained in an address to the Centre for European Policy Studies in Brussels in October 1991 in discussing the *Magneti/Marelli/CEAC*[44] case on car batteries:

no legislation exists preventing the import and sale of batteries into France. Thus, one might expect the geographic reference to be wider than a single Member State. However, when the Commission examined this problem it discovered that due to the existence of consumer brand loyalty and the lack of a cross-border distribution and marketing infrastructure imports would not be likely to enter France in response to an increase in demand, more likely the price would increase. The market was thus considered national. Many Community markets have developed on national lines for hundreds of years. Manufacturing, marketing, and purchasing patterns were national in scope. The removal of regulatory barriers does not in itself create a true single market overnight. The establishment of a true Common Market in business terms with major cross-border distribution and marketing infrastructure occurs gradually. The Commission recognizes and accepts this.

7.2 THE RANGE OF POSSIBLE GEOGRAPHICAL MARKETS

In *American Cyanamid/Shell*,[45] the parties had claimed that the relevant geographic market for the herbicides dealt with them by them was Community-wide. In favour of this argument they cited:

---

[43] See [1991] OJ L 334/42: Case IV/M053 [1992] 4 CMLR M2.   [44] See fn. 28.
[45] Case IV/M354 [1993] OJ C273/6.

(a) centralized production facilities for manufacturing active chemical ingredients and a tendency to the creation of centralized formulating facilities to produce the finished product;

(b) the presence of a large number of medium multi-nationals in this market throughout the EC;

(c) the use of international brand names rather than national names; and

(d) low transport costs relative to the high value of the products.

The Commission, nevertheless, found that the markets were still national. It pointed out that, although manufacturing is centralized, marketing and distribution operations in the herbicide industry are still generally organized on a national basis. In addition, the range of products sold and their individual chemical formulations varied in accordance with the different crop patterns for each country. Moreover, the existing scheme of regulation for the industry encouraged a national approach to marketing because each Member State used its own certification standards. Although there was a Community regulatory regime covering the marketing of plant protection products, classification of products, labelling and packaging, this would only promote Community-wide trading in the long term.

In *Mannesmann/Hoesch*,[46] the Commission found that the market for steel gasline pipes was limited to Germany because the conditions of competition there were different from other Member States. There was only a low level of imports (less than 10 per cent), an absence of harmonization of technical standards, and a purchasing policy of German customers in favour of German products; all this indicated to the MTF that the relevant geographic market for these pipes was Germany alone. Similar considerations apply in the vehicle-building industry as illustrated both by *Mercedes/Kässbohrer*[47] mentioned above and by *Volvo/Renault*,[48] where one of the reasons for considering the markets for buses to be national was the existence of local specification requirements differing substantially between Member States.

Another factor is the existence of other barriers to entry for companies wishing to penetrate national markets. Some of these can exist within a single Member State, such as the basic ratio of value to cost of transport. Goods that have a heavy weight or significant volume in relation to their value will not normally be economic to transport large distances, whether across national boundaries or within a single country. In the Community, of course, there is the additional problem in some cases of language under which expense may be incurred in preparing labelling, instructions and in organizing after-sales service across borders. In *Viag/Continental Can*,[49] a case involving two companies manufacturing cans and glass bottles, the Commission held that since these products had only a small value and take up a great deal of space they cannot economically be shipped for more than 200 kilometres, especially as in many cases deliveries have to be 'just in time', thus giving a great advantage to local suppliers. As a result, the Commission concluded that the market was not one of the whole Community but one of a number of regional geographic markets containing shipping distances not exceeding 200 kilometres.

[46] Case IV/M222 [1992] 5 CMLR 117. [47] See fn. 31. [48] See fn. 23.
[49] Case IV/M081.

Both parties in *Volvo/Scania*[50] were Swedish-based manufacturers of trucks and various types of bus and coach with a combined market share in Sweden of between 50 per cent and 90 per cent. Their combined market share for trucks over 16 tonnes was over 90 per cent. The parties claimed that the appropriate geographic market was not just Sweden, but either Scandinavia as a whole or, even possibly, the whole EC. The Commission, however, placed much weight on the barriers to entry that existed for any manufacturer seeking to enter the Swedish market, in particular the difficulty of establishing an adequate after-sales network. It was influenced by the fact that no other major manufacturer had been able to gain a substantial market share for such vehicles in Sweden over a considerable number of years. The relevant geographic markets were therefore national ones, such as Sweden, Finland, and Denmark.

Operating in favour of expanding the geographic market definition are the harmonization of national legislation and introduction of Community legislation under which the barriers to cross-border entry are gradually broken down. An example is the public procurement Directive referred to in *Mercedes/Kässbohrer*. Also relevant is the *Alcatel/Telettra*[51] case. There the merger involved the acquisition by Alcatel of a controlling interest in Telettra. Both companies were involved in the supply of telecommunications equipment in the Spanish market. The acquisition resulted in an aggregate market share of 80 per cent for both microwave and line transmissions. Moreover, the Spanish telecommunications operator, Telefónica, had a strong position in the Spanish market as a monopolist; it also had a minority shareholding in both companies and a known policy at that time of purchasing only from local suppliers. Notwithstanding these factors, the merger was cleared, largely because of assurances received from Telefónica that not only would it cease to hold any share interest in any of the companies, but would abandon its previous preference for local purchasing and would treat foreign suppliers equally. This was a decision taken in the knowledge that the Commission was itself in the process of seeking to liberalize the telecommunications equipment market throughout the Community. Had this general policy trend not been in evidence, the merger might well have been prohibited. It was only against the background of these changing conditions that the Commission regarded the high market shares of the two parties as no longer representing market dominance, because they would be counterbalanced by the power of a monopolistic purchaser willing to acquire its supplies from both local and foreign sources.

Some of the complexities that can arise in the analysis of the geographic market are well illustrated by *Totalfina/Elf Acquitane*.[52] This involved a bid by one French oil company for another, and both were involved in the sale of a number of different petroleum products. The Commission identified these as including: petrol, motorway fuel sales, aviation fuel sales, domestic heating oil, liquid petroleum gas, sulphur, ethylene, and the transport of refined products by pipeline. In some cases, the whole of France was regarded as the relevant area, in others regional markets of various different configurations were identified, whilst for others they were drawn even more narrowly.

Finally, consumer preference itself remains in some markets a powerful argument for treating the market as national. Perhaps the best available example of this is *Nestlé/Perrier*.[53] Here Nestlé and Perrier between them were dominant in bottled source water in France and owned a number of the leading brands. Their total market share was some 60 per cent and

---

[50] Case Comp/M1672 [2001] OJ L143/74.   [51] Case IV/M0422: [1991] 4 CMLR 778.
[52] Case Comp/M1628 and 1647: [2001] 5 CMLR 682.
[53] Case IV/M190 [1993] 4 CMLR M17: [1992] OJ L356/1.

their main competitor was BSN with some 22 per cent, the remainder of the market being shared by a number of small companies. There were no legislative barriers to entry to the French market if foreign manufacturers wished to enter it; it appeared that on a number of occasions in the past such attempts had been made but always unsuccessfully. A relevant factor was that the great majority of sales were made to large supermarkets or hypermarkets, which were very aware of the loyalty of their customers to the well-known brands owned by the leading French companies. In their view it was unlikely that the French customers would switch to foreign brands because of their deep-seated and long-standing preference for the local product from French springs.

It should not be supposed, however, that in the majority of cases the Commission's decision would be in favour of national markets. For high-technology products and those with a very high capital cost, reflecting substantial amounts of research and development expenditure, it is quite likely that markets will be at least Community-wide, if not world-wide. Such markets will be found for example in communications, computers and large scale transport; see for example the *Aerospatiale*[54] and *Boeing/McDonnell Douglas*[55] cases and *Digital/Phillips*.[56] In some 70 per cent of all its cases, however, the Commission has not needed to reach a firm decision on market definition, because the outcome of the case will, in its view, be unaffected by it.

8. THE DEFINITION OF DOMINANCE

8.1 DOMINANCE BY A SINGLE COMPANY

Once the product and geographic markets relevant to the merger have been determined, the degree of dominance which it will confer in those markets has next to be considered. The concept of dominance is familiar from Article 82 and the definitions contained in the *United Brands*[57] and *Hoffmann-La Roche*[58] cases continue to apply, though their application to individual cases may pose difficulty. The essential element of dominance is the ability to behave independently of its competitors, customers and consumers; in other words to be largely free from the pressures imposed by competition as to price, quality and conditions of business. A degree of dominance cannot be measured, as with a thermometer, in any particular market, but has to be assessed in the light of several factors. The principal factors involved in merger cases are:

(i)   The aggregate of the *market shares* which the combined undertakings will have, provided that these are of a relatively durable nature rather than merely temporary. Just as when assessing the relevant market itself, the concept of dominance has to strike a balance between existing facts and likely future developments. Future developments that are not likely during the next two or three years are too remote to be considered. It is clear from the recitals to the Regulation that a combined share of less than 25 per cent raises no presumption of dominance, but rather a presumption

---

[54] See fn. 43.   [55] [1997] OJ L336/16: Case IV/M877 [1997] 5 CMLR 270.
[56] Case IV/M129 [1991] 4 CMLR 737.
[57] Case 27/76 [1978] ECR 207: 1 CMLR 429.
[58] Case 85/76 [1979] ECR 461: 3 CMLR 211.

of non-dominance. Between 25 per cent and, say, 40 per cent the presumption is relatively low,[59] but once past 40 per cent the presumption increases gradually until once up to, say, 65 per cent or 70 per cent it may be difficult to refute unless the circumstances are extremely unusual as, for example, in *Alcatel*.[60]

(ii) The relationship of the market share of the merging undertaking to those of other competitors will clearly be relevant. If, for example, the merging companies have 40 per cent and 20 per cent respectively and no other company has more than 5 per cent, the gap itself in market share will make it far easier for the combined entity to operate free of the pressures of competition. On the other hand, if there was a competitor in that market also with a 20 per cent share, genuine competition could at least be anticipated from that source to the two merging companies. That fact alone might not be sufficient to enable the concentration to be cleared; other factors would have to be examined relating to the respective strengths of the undertakings, such as their individual product range, the quality of their research and development in a technical industry, the strength of the customer base and the way in which market shares had developed in the past. Also relevant would be the strength of the various buyers in the relevant markets.

(iii) It is clear that certain sectors are likely to be characterized by *volatility of market share*, whereas others, perhaps the more traditional industries, may show a marked degree of stability. In an industry subject to innovation and where R & D plays an important part in the competitive struggle, market shares are likely to vary and are a less certain indicator of market power, as the trend data will show. On the other hand, a case such as *Tetra Pak/Alfa-Laval*[61] is an example of an acquiring company with a market share exceeding 90 per cent maintained consistently for a considerable number of years in the sale of aseptic carton-packaging machines for milk, supported by a wide range of technological advantages over all its competitors.

(iv) Commercial strengths of various kinds can in general play an important part in buttressing the benefits of substantial market share. Intellectual property rights may, as in the *Tetra Pak* case, be relevant since, if they cover a wide range of the necessary technology for entry into the industry, licences may not be available from the dominant company, or may be available only on disadvantageous terms. Such a company as market leader for a number of years may also be skilled at making aggressive use of its patent rights to discourage competition. In consumer products the ownership of well-known trade marks may also play an important role in giving a strong market position. Other factors to be taken into account in the analysis of commercial strengths include:

(a) the forecast of likely product demand and changing patterns of raw material supply and product development in the industry, the time and cost required to enter the market, including the time required for testing and licensing of new products, and the possibility of the need to incur high initial start-up costs;

---

[59] But in the *Rewe/Meinl* case (Case IV/M1221, a decision of 3 February 1999) the bidder's market share in the Austrian food retail market was only 37 per cent but, nevertheless, dominance was found as a result of the particular features of that market, e.g. the bidder's strong position in major urban centres and in Eastern Austria.

[60] See fn. 51.   [61] Case IV/M68 [1992] 4 CMLR M81.

(*b*) whether there are over-capacities in neighbouring geographic and product markets;

(*c*) whether the market is in general over-or under-supplied;

(*d*) the development of Community harmonization of technical standards, and Directives on public procurement mentioned above: and

(*e*) whether the undertakings concerned hold a 'portfolio' of a substantial number of brands in the same geographic market.

8.2 THE 'EFFICIENCIES' DEFENCE

A factor not specifically mentioned in Article 2 is that of efficiencies. Parties to mergers often put forward, as one of their principal arguments, that the merger will bring about important efficiency gains that the parties could not realize on their own, whether through economies of scale or scope or through improvements in geographical coverage, distribution systems or research and development. The Commission has consistently opposed attempts to include such considerations within Article 2, in a number of major cases including *Aerospatiale* and *Kässbohrer/Mercedes Benz*, and even when efficiencies have been acknowledged as a likely outcome, they have been rejected as a defence because of the failure by the parties to show that they will be passed on to the consumers (as in *Accor/Wagon-Lits*). The Green Paper published by the Commission on Merger Review (discussed in Section 7 in the next chapter) nevertheless acknowledged, perhaps reflecting trends in this direction in US antitrust law, that efficiencies should nevertheless be considered and invited comments on this issue.

8.3 *GE/HONEYWELL* AND THE ISSUE OF 'BUNDLING'

The most recent major case involving the analysis of dominance has been *GE/Honeywell*.[62] This merger involving two major US corporations had already been cleared by the US Department of Justice, with very limited conditions attached. The bid involved the takeover by GE, a leading manufacturer of large commercial and regional aircraft engines, of Honeywell, a leader in the production of flight management systems, jet engine starters, marine gas turbines, and other avionic products. The Commission's concern related principally to the future ability of the combined enterprise to strengthen its dominance by its ability to 'bundle', that is to offer discounts to its airline customers, which would provide a major incentive to purchasers of GE aero engines to link these with purchases of avionic products from Honeywell. In addition, the Commission feared that GE's aircraft-financing subsidiary, GECAS, would impose its 'GE only' policy on customers seeking to lease new planes. The merger was therefore blocked, though that decision is on appeal to the CFI.

8.4 CONCLUSIONS ON THE INTERPRETATION OF SINGLE FIRM DOMINANCE

In conclusion, therefore, proving dominance under the Merger Regulation can be difficult for the Commission, since it requires the prediction of future developments from the

---

[62] Case Comp/M2220 (decision of 3 July 2001): DG Comp Competition Policy Newsletter 2001, No. 3, pp.5–13. It is an appeal to the CFI.

starting point of a present situation where some of the facts may be undisputed but others may be controversial. The test applied is essentially one based on a combination of economic theory and past experience. The burden of proof is upon the Commission and not upon the parties and, if the Commission does provide evidence which, on the basis of the test stated above, would reasonably allow a conclusion of dominance, it is for the parties then to show that in the particular case this conclusion can be challenged, e.g. as in the *Alcatel*[63] case. Although in the *AKZO*[64] case the ECJ indicated that in an Article 82 case a market share of 50 per cent raises a rebuttable presumption of an existing dominant position, the Commission has not sought to rely on that principle in merger cases.

8.5 THE 'FAILING COMPANY' DEFENCE

If, however, an undertaking being acquired would go out of business apart from the acquisition, it has normally been assumed that clearance would be given to the transaction, even if the consequence was that the acquirer remained in, or would establish, a dominant position as a result. In *Kali und Salz*,[65] three conditions were laid down for the clearance of such acquisitions:

— that, in the absence of the acquisition, the target (failing company) would become insolvent in the near future;

— that there was no other potential acquirer whose substitution would have been less harmful to competition; and

— that the market share of the target would in any case have gone to the acquirer upon its disappearance from the market. This is known generally as the 'failing firm defence'.

In *BASF/Pantochin/Eurodiol*,[66] however, the Commission stated that the third of these conditions could be ignored if, in the absence of the acquisition, the plant capacity of the insolvent undertaking would have been lost from the market, especially if (as in this case) the loss would have also had serious environmental consequences and supply shortages leading to immediate higher prices.

8.6 DOMINANCE BY MORE THAN ONE COMPANY (COLLECTIVE DOMINANCE): THE ISSUES

There are a number of national competition law systems in the EC, including both Germany and the United Kingdom, under which mergers can be prevented or subjected to conditions either if they are seen to enable single undertakings to acquire an undue degree of market power, or if the outcome of the transaction will be to place two or more companies in a position of collective dominance. Article 82 expressly provides that it can apply when 'one or more' undertakings have a dominant position; the terms of the ECMR, however, do not contain explicit wording of this kind. Clearly the absence of such a provision could have been an embarrassment to the Commission, given that there are a number of important

---

[63] See fn. 51.   [64] Case F-62/86 [1991] ECR I-3359 [1993]: 5 CMLR 215.
[65] Cases C-68/94 and 30/95 [1998] ECR I-1375: 4 CMLR 829.
[66] Case Comp/M2314 [2002] OJ L132/45.

product markets in Member States and in the Community with notably oligopolistic features and which could be rendered even less competitive if further concentration took place which allowed or facilitated coordination between the leading players in the relevant markets.

The Commission's willingness to face this challenge head on was not surprising. The broad terms of Article 2(1) contain adequate support for intervening in such cases as it included the phrases: 'the need to maintain and develop effective competition in view of the structure of all the markets concerned . . .'; and 'the market position of the undertakings concerned and their economic and financial power . . .'.

The first indication of the Commission's willingness to interpret 'dominance' to include collective dominance is found in *Alcatel/AEG-KABEL*,[67] though the doctrine was not actually utilized to block or restrict the terms of the concentration in that case. The most important early precedent in this respect was *Nestlé/Perrier*,[68] in 1992. The relevant facts here, already mentioned in Section 7, p.361, were that Nestlé and Perrier had between them some 60 per cent of the French bottled mineral water market, whilst BSN had 22 per cent and the remainder of the market was shared by a number of much smaller companies with far more limited access to the relevant springs from which the water had (under French law) to be obtained. Nestlé sought to acquire Perrier and was willing in view of its large market share to give up the Volvic brand to BSN, which would have brought their market shares more in line, but still in aggregate leaving these two large companies with a share of 82 per cent. The decision reads:

Para. 120. 'The reduction from three to two suppliers (duopoly) is not amere cosmetic change in the market structure . . . the reduction from three to only two national suppliers would make anti-competitive parallel behaviour leading to collective abuses much easier'.

Para. 121. The mineral water suppliers in France have developed instruments of transparency facilitating a tacit co-ordination of pricing policies . . .

Para. 123. Their reciprocal dependency thus creates a strong common interest and incentive to maximise profits by engaging in anti-competitive parallel behaviour. This situation of common interest is further reinforced by the fact that Nestlé and BSN are similar in size and nature, both active in the wider food industry and already co-operate in some sectors of that industry'. Having made these findings as to the nature of the market, the conclusion which the Commission reached (in para. 131) was that 'the market structure resulting from the merger . . . would create a duopolistic dominant position on the French bottled water market which would significantly impede effective competition and would be very likely to cause a considerable harm to consumers'.

The remedy adopted was to require Nestlé to divest itself of a major brand, not to BSN, as had been proposed by Nestlé, but to a third party, so as to weaken the duopoly power of the two major companies.

The facts in this case were clearly strong enough to provide an ideal base for establishment of a collective dominance doctrine. It has been used subsequently in a number of cases, although it has not always had the result of leading to the blocking of the resulting concentration. An example of a case where it was considered is *Pilkington/SIV*[69] in 1993. This

---

[67] Case IV/M165 [1992] OJ C6/23.   [68] See fn. 34.   [69] Case IV/M358 [1994] OJ L 158/24.

concentration consolidated the position of Pilkington as the second largest company in the European float glass market, the other participants, apart from the market leader St Gobain, being considerably smaller. Although the Commission acknowledged that the industry had been subject to a number of cartels in the past, it ultimately cleared the concentration on the basis of the differing sizes and market shares of the remaining enterprises and the existence of chronic excess capacity, as well as the anticipated 'maverick' aggression expected from Guardian, one of the smaller companies. The Commission argued that chronic excess capacity made collusion less likely because of the high profits that could be earned from cutting price to win marginal additional sales.

8.7 COLLECTIVE DOMINANCE: *KALI UND SALZ*

A serious challenge to the Commission's application in merger cases of the principles of collective dominance was raised before the ECJ in an appeal by France and a French company against the Commission's 1994 decision in *Kali und Salz/MDK*[70] In that second-phase case, the Commission had attached several conditions to its clearance of the merger of the two companies which, between them, would control the entire German market for agricultural potash, and would also have a 23 per cent share of this market in the rest of the Community. It was claimed by the Commission that the merged companies' trading links with the French company (which held 37 per cent of the EC market outside Germany) would lead to oligopolistic collective dominance in that market; for this reason the severance of those trading links was made a condition for clearance of the concentration.

The ECJ had to deal with two main issues. First, whether the Commission was legally entitled to rely on the 'collective dominance' principle under Article 2 as a relevant criterion for assessment of the consequences of the merger. The Court, notwithstanding an opinion by Advocate General Tesauro that the ECMR did not give it such a right, gave an affirmative answer, doubtless strongly influenced by the policy need to provide the Commission with authority over such cases. Such authority was already possessed by a number of national competition authorities, including Germany and the United Kingdom.

The second issue was whether, in the circumstances of this particular case, the Commission had been correct in its determination that the transaction would lead to a situation of collective dominance. The Court laid down four elements which the Commission would have to establish in order to justify such a finding. These were: sufficiently substantial existing market shares for the parties, of a stable character; a sufficient increase in total market share as the result of the merger itself; conditions present in the market, including barriers to entry, which would be likely to encourage mutual interdependence; and existence of structural links between the parties. On the facts of this case, the Court ruled that the structural links that did exist had insufficient influence on the competitive conduct of the parties to bring about collective dominance.

8.8 COLLECTIVE DOMINANCE: *GENCOR* AND *AIRTOURS*

The right of the Commission to take such 'collective dominance' arguments into account has been further confirmed by the *Gencor/Lonrho*[71] case decided by the Court of First

---

[70] See fn. 65.
[71] See fn. 10. For the Court's assessment of the extraterritorial issues, see Ch. 23, p.503.

Instance in March 1999. Gencor held 46.5 per cent of Implats which carried out the activities of the Gencor Group in platinum mining in South Africa. Lonrho similarly held some 73 per cent of a company called LPD, engaged in the same business. The merger proposal would have given Implats a control over LPD and left the platinum market to be supplied only by this group and by one major rival, Amplats. The Court of First Instance upheld the decision of the Commission that this concentration would have led to collective dominance for these two large companies in the world's platinum and rhodium markets. In an important development however the Court stressed that structural links between the parties did not have to be shown; it was enough if 'the relationship of interdependence was existing between the parties to a tight oligopoly within which in a market with the appropriate characteristics . . . these parties were in a position to anticipate one another's behaviour and, therefore, were strongly encouraged to align the conduct in the market'. In other words, the issue was whether the characteristics of the market were conducive to tacit coordination of their activities.

In September 1999, in *Airtours/First Choice*,[72] after a second-phase proceeding the proposal by Airtours to take over First Choice was blocked unconditionally on the ground that the merger would have left the three largest travel companies in the United Kingdom holding 80 per cent of the short-haul package holiday market, a structure which would have enabled them to act in a collectively dominant manner. Airtours, however, successfully appealed against this decision to the CFI on the grounds that the Commission analysis of this market was faulty. In its judgment the CFI severely criticized the quality of the Commission's economic reasoning and laid down that, before a finding of collective dominance could be made, three conditions had to be established:

— sufficient market transparency for each undertaking to be aware precisely and quickly of the way in which each other's market conduct was evolving;

— the situation of tacit coordination must be reinforced by the presence of long-term incentives on the parties not to provoke retaliation by departing from their current policies; and

— the results expected from these common policies must not be at risk from foreseeable reactions from competitors or consumers.

Collective dominance as a feature of merger analysis by the Commission does not of course limit itself to pricing. It can also extend to coordination over capacity, since an industry where it was possible to keep tight control over the building of new production facilities or the provision of additional services would be likely to be one where price levels could be maintained at a higher level than would be the case if such coordination on capacity did not occur. This issue arose in *UPM-Kymmene/Heindl* and *Norske Skog/Parenco/Walsum*.[73] Heindl was a German company which sold its manufacturing assets (producing paper for magazines and newspapers) to two Swedish companies, UPM and Norske Skog. Whilst the market shares of the companies were all below 15 per cent it was suggested that the newly merged companies could tacitly coordinate with the other major manufacturers in these markets in the building of new plants, both by delaying capital investment and by the allocation of building new capacity between them over time, possibly on a rota basis. An

---

[72] Case T-342/99 [2002] 5 CMLR 317.   [73] Case Comp/M2499 [2002] 5 CMLR 1309.

analysis of the paper manufacturing business however convinced the Commission that such coordination was highly unlikely. Each individual plant would necessarily represent a major investment; and the company entitled under such arrangements to come in first with such an investment would have a large commercial advantage over its rivals. Moreover, any participant which desired to break ranks and increase its capacity prematurely would find that effective retaliation by the other companies would be difficult, as the capacity increase for the industry as a whole would be irreversible (unlike a price cut). The only punishment possible in the longer term would be retaliatory increases in capacity which in turn would tend to bring prices down further. The transactions were therefore cleared.

9. THE ATTACK ON DOMINANCE AS A CRITERION FOR ASSESSING MERGERS

9.1 THE CHOICE: 'DOMINANCE SIGNIFICANTLY IMPEDING COMPETITION' OR 'A SUBSTANTIAL LESSENING OF COMPETITION'?

The original reason for the choice of dominance as the criterion was that it had already become a familiar concept under Article 82 and thus the subject of a number of Community Court decisions. Moreover, since in Article 2 the additional requirement had been added that this dominant position should significantly impede competition, it seemed an adequate basis for the assessment of any kind of concentration falling within the scope of the Regulation. On the other hand, it was not the test applied in any other important jurisdiction at that date. The USA has since 1914, in the Clayton Act, adopted the criterion of prohibiting mergers where their effect might be 'substantially to lessen competition'; and this wording had been adopted with minor variations in Australia, Canada, and South Africa and, most recently, in the United Kingdom under the terms of the 2002 Enterprise Act. Nevertheless, the majority of Member States had followed the lead of the Community in adopting the dominance test for national merger control.

This debate over the suitability of the criterion adopted was sparked into life by the Commission's publication of a Green Paper on the review of the Regulation in December 2001, on which extensive consultation then took place both with Member States, industrial and commercial concerns, and many law firms with experience in this area. The Green Paper itself took a conservative approach, stating that the experience of the Commission in applying the test had not revealed 'major loopholes' in its application and pointing out that there were many similarities between the two types of criterion and that the same outcome normally occurred whichever criterion was applied to the same facts. The only concession which the Commission did make in respect to its support for the status quo was an admission that, in a merger between the second and third largest undertakings in the market where neither would have dominance (in view of the relative strength of the largest undertaking) these undertakings might nevertheless be able to raise prices by exercise of their market power following their merger. In this situation the 'substantial lessening of competition' test would clearly be applicable whilst by contrast the test of dominance would not, unless collective dominance could be proved.

9.2 THE DEFINITION OF COLLECTIVE DOMINANCE IN *AIRTOURS*

The weakness in the Commission's position however was then dramatically illustrated by the subsequent (June 2002) *Airtours* ruling of the CFI, and the criticisms of the Commission's approach by the CFI in its judgment. The CFI focused on two principal weaknesses in the Commission's decision. First of these was that its definition of collective dominance was so general that it could be applied to any market regarded as oligopolistic regardless: (i) both of the degree to which the parties had the incentive and ability to practice tacit coordination on output or price as well as the ability to retaliate effectively against any undertaking which decided to cheat; and (ii) of the ability of consumers to react against such moves. The second criticism was that the Commission's analysis of the relevant market was itself faulty, since the required factors needed in a finding of collective dominance was not supported by the evidence in respect of barriers to entry, transparency, volatility of market share, and levels of demand for the package holidays concerned.

The present dominance test is capable of application in two situations, neither of which could be established on the evidence in *Airtours*. These are:

(a) Where there is a *unilateral* effect of the merger, that is the effect simply of A having acquired B leading to an increase in prices or reduction in output, without reference to the ability of other undertakings in the market to coordinate their reactions and future commercial strategy as a result of the merger.

(b) Where the effect of the merger is to enable such a coordinated reaction by undertakings, in circumstances where it can be shown that they will then have collective dominance with the merged undertaking, usually referred to as '*coordinated* effects'.

The dominance test does not however apply to a third situation, where say the second and third largest undertakings in the market merge but there is no likelihood of *coordinated* effects as a result of the merger, but where the small numbers of players remaining in the market means that it will nevertheless lead to undesirable consequences such as price rises for consumers. By contrast the 'substantial lessening of competition' test can be applied to this situation in a relatively straightforward manner. The package of proposals put forward by the Commission in December 2002 sought to re-establish the credibility of the dominance criterion by an amendment of Article 2 so as to enable this third situation also to be covered.

An important consequence of the proposed change would also be to separate the definition of dominance found in the Regulation from that contained in Article 82. This would have the benefit of separating the application of the Merger Regulation in, for example, later cases of collective dominance from any future jurisprudence of the Community Courts on the same concept under the different circumstances of Article 82.

The outcome of this debate is discussed in Section 7 of the following chapter on 'The Future of the Regulation', and in Part III.

18

MERGERS (2)

1. REFERRALS OF CONCENTRATIONS BACK TO MEMBER STATES: ECMR ARTICLES 9 AND 21(3)

1.1 THE 'ONE-STOP SHOP'

It is clear that one of the principal reasons for the acceptance by Member States of the ECMR was the value placed by both the Commission and by business interests throughout the Community on the concept of the 'one-stop shop' for larger concentrations having both a substantial world and Community turnover. No longer would it be necessary to take a case in these circumstances for approval to several national authorities within the European Community; the decision of the Commission, and the Commission alone, would be decisive. Article 21(1), therefore, provides that only the European Commission may take decisions in respect of concentrations that have a Community dimension. Nevertheless, when the final terms of ECMR were being negotiated in 1989, several Member States emphasized the rights of continuing involvement of Member States in certain situations where the particular concentration could have an impact on their economy or on a local market.

We thus find that there are two major exceptions to the 'one-stop shop' rule incorporated in the final form of the Regulation, notably in Article 9 and in Article 21(3) respectively. A further exception to the basic allocation of cases between the Community and Member States is found in Article 22(3), but on this occasion however, it works in favour of the Commission since a Member State may cede jurisdiction when it would otherwise possess it at the national level.

1.2 THE FIRST EXCEPTION — ARTICLE 9

First in importance in this context is Article 9(1), 'referral to the competent authorities of the Member States'. Under this a Member State may request the Commission to grant back to it jurisdiction over a concentration which would otherwise have a Community dimension. It was originally known as 'the German clause', because it was included at the particular request of Germany. The decision to refer back is that of the Commission itself (subject to appeal to the Court of First Instance), and it is clear from cases already decided that the Commission may decide to deal itself with some aspects of the case while referring others back to the Member State, normally those parts of it which have an impact on the 'distinct market' in the Member State. Moreover, the Commission maintains close control of the final outcome of the case under the remaining provisions of Article 9.

To date fifty-three requests have been accepted under this Article, twenty-two as a whole and thirty-one in part only. The greatest number of requests have been made by Germany, the United Kingdom, and France.

The United Kingdom was the first successful applicant under this Article in the *Tarmac/ Steetly*[1] case, in early 1992. This involved a proposed joint venture of a concentrative nature between these two UK companies which would have effectively pooled their building material activities, including bricks, clay roofing tiles, concrete and masonry products. The aggregate world and EC turnover of the parties meant that the case had a Community dimension, but the United Kingdom successfully sought a reference back under Article 9(3) for specific 'distinct markets'. These were:

(i)   the manufacture and sale of bricks in the North East and South West of England; and

(ii)   the manufacture of clay tiles throughout Great Britain.

Following this request the Commission produced two decisions: The first accepted the UK request and set out an assessment in detail of local markets in Great Britain, confirming that there would be a particular local problem in both the North East and South West of the country because the combined aggregate market share of Tarmac and Steetly was 80 per cent or more with little potential for new entry, particularly given the cost of transporting such heavy goods as bricks from other parts of the United Kingdom. Jurisdiction was also ceded with regard to tiles but here the market to be investigated was national because, as lighter products, they could be transferred widely throughout the country. Again there was a significant entry barrier to this market: the need to own adequate clay reserves in order to take part in tile manufacture. The second Commission decision of the same date dealt with the remaining products covered by the joint venture, namely concrete blocks, structural concrete products, and masonry products. The Commission concluded that in respect of these markets the merger was compatible with the Common Market.

The amendments to the ECMR, effective under Council Regulation 1310/97 from 1 March 1998, included some relaxation of the conditions attached to the ability of a Member State to obtain such a reference back. Under Articles 9(2)(*b*) and (3), a Member State is now entitled to make such a request in respect of a 'distinct market' within that Member State which does not constitute a 'substantial part' of the common market; once satisfied that the merger will have an effect on that 'distinct market', the Commission is required to make the reference, back, i.e. without the discretion to retain the case for itself that it has in all other circumstances. In late 2002 further proposals for simplification of these arrangements were put forward by the Commission (see Section 7 of this chapter).

There is some indication that the Commission is becoming more liberal in its application of this Article. In recent years, its Annual Reports record that references back have been made to the competition authorities of France, Italy, Germany, The Netherlands, United Kingdom, Spain, and Denmark. The United Kingdom was, however, denied its request in 1999 to take back the concentration involving Electricité de France's bid for London

---

[1] Case IV/M75 [1992] 4 CMLR 343.

Electricity,[2] largely on the basis that the regulatory control which the UK wished to exercise over the combined company could already be exercised under existing statutory powers. A more unusual case, involving the United Kingdom, was the 1999 *Airtours/First Choice* travel services merger.[3] Here, the Office of Fair Trading decided against requesting an Article 9 reference back on the ground of lack of sufficient effect of the merger on competition in the UK travel agent business, but the Commission, believing the case raised collective domin-ance issues, nevertheless, instituted a second-phase investigation, which led to a 'blocking' decision eventually annulled by the CFI.

This 'split' will normally be on a geographical basis, but can be more complex. Thus in *Shell/DEA*[4] and *BP/E.on*[5] a reference back in both these parallel cases was made to the German BKA of downstream retail petroleum markets in Germany while the Commission conducted a phase two examination of broader upstream markets, such as the supply of ethylene to a number of West European markets.

1.3 THE SECOND EXCEPTION — ARTICLE 21(3)

Article 21(3) presents a different focus on the exceptions to the 'one-stop shop'. Here the emphasis is on the nature of a 'legitimate interest' entitling Member States to intervene, whereas under Article 9(3) the emphasis is on the competition in the distinct local market in the Member State which the concentration would affect. Under Article 21(3):

Member States may take appropriate measures to protect legitimate interests other than those taken into consideration by this Regulation and compatible with the general principles and other provi-sions of Community law. Public security, plurality of the media and prudential rules shall be regarded as legitimate interests . . . Any other public interest must be communicated to the Com-mission by the Member State concerned and shall be recognised by the Commission after an assessment of its compatibility with the general principles and other provisions of Community law before the measures referred to above may be taken . . .

The effect of this provision is primarily negative, providing no new rights for Member States, but accepting the recognition in Community law of their powers to intervene in certain aspects of concentrations that affect them on grounds other than those covered by the ECMR, without according to them any power to authorize concentrations which the Commission may have itself prohibited under the ECMR. A case showing that 'legitimate interest' additional to those specifically mentioned may be accepted by the European Com-mission is that of *Lyonnaise/Northumbrian Water*.[6] The European Commission accepted in March 1995, at the request of the United Kingdom, that the UK system established for the regulation of the water industry did represent such a national legitimate interest. Following privatization of the water and sewerage industry in the United Kingdom in 1989, legislation made mergers between water enterprises above a certain size automatically referable to Competition Commission for assessment. The criterion, which the Competition

---

[2] Case IV/M1346 (decision of 27 January 1999).   [3] Discussed in Ch. 17, pp.367 and 369.

[4] Case Comp/M2389, decision of 20 December 2001.

[5] Case Comp/M2533, decision of 20 December 2001.

[6] Case IV/M567 [1995] 4 CMLR 614. At the time of the case the relevant UK competition authority was the 'Monopolies and Mergers Commission' which was renamed the 'Competition Commission' by the 1998 Competition Act with effect from 1 April 1999.

Commission is required to apply in such cases, is whether the water regulator (the Director General of Water Services) can continue to make comparisons between different water enterprises (each of which has a regional or local monopoly) in maintaining the principle of 'comparative competition' to maintain competitive pressures on them in lieu of actual competition. The regulator uses these principles for a number of purposes, in particular to obtain comparative data on operating and capital costs to enable quinquennial price reviews for each water (or water and sewerage) authority.

The EC decision in March 1995 went beyond simple recognition of this legitimate interest and contained suggestions to the United Kingdom as to how it was to carry out its assessment of the legitimate interest. The decision included a direction to the UK authorities on the following lines:

the control exercised by the UK authorities is aimed at ensuring that the number of independently controlled water companies is sufficient to allow the Director General of Water Services to exercise his regulatory functions . . . in order not to go beyond the interest pursued by the UK regulatory legislation other issues in relation to mergers between water companies can only be taken into account to the extent that they affect the control regime set out above . . .

In the event the UK Competition Commission prepared a report on the *Lyonnaise/Northumbrian* merger which made a finding that the merger could be expected to operate against the public interest, in that it would prejudice the principle of comparative competition, but recommending that remedies by way of price reductions and other conditions be imposed if the merger was allowed to proceed. Following negotiations terms for reducing prices and other conditions were agreed between the parties, the water regulator and the Secretary of State, and were accepted by the European Commission which then proceeded to give a formal clearance under Article 6(1)(*b*).

In 1999 a dispute arose under this Article between the Commission and Portugal, which had tried to block a proposed merger in the banking sector (*BSCH-Champalimaud*).[7] The Commission itself adopted decisions against the Portuguese measures, referring to the exclusive jurisdiction it possessed under Article 21 and on the basis that the 'prudential' grounds, stated by Portugal to justify its actions, were unjustifiable and, in any case, had not been notified to the Commission. Subsequently, revised terms of the merger were agreed and Portugal withdrew its opposition.

1.4 ARTICLE 296—DEFENCE CASES

For completeness there should also be mentioned those merger cases involving military equipment dealt with by Member States under Article 296 of the Treaty of Rome. Strictly such cases are not 'referred back by the Commission', because the terms of this Article provide that the Member State is entitled to take 'measures' to protect its national jurisdiction in defence-related matters, which the Treaty and ECMR do not control. Among the principal cases decided under this heading were the *General Electric Company/British Aerospace/VSEL*[8] in 1995. The two competing bidders were each seeking to acquire VSEL,

---

[7] Cases M1680, 1724, and, later, 1799.

[8] Case IV/M529 [1994], Case IV/M528 OJ C368/23; [1994] OJ C348/6. The relevant Monopolies and Mergers Commission reports are CM2851 (*British Aerospace/VSEL*) and CM2852 *GEC/VSEL*, both published in 1995.

builders of the UK Trident submarines. The UK Government, relying on Article 296, not-withstanding that both bids fell within the turnover threshold of ECMR, instructed the companies not to notify the military aspect of their bids to Brussels. A notification to the Commission was, therefore, made solely of the non-military aspects of the bid, which were relatively minor and were soon cleared. In fact the non-military aspects of VSEL's business, mainly the production of equipment for oil and gas rigs, represented only about 2.5 per cent of its total business. The UK authorities then took over the preparation of the report into the two bids as to the military aspects; and the Competition Commission's reports were pub-lished in May 1995 clearing the British Aerospace bid but recommending by a four to two majority that the GEC bid should not be permitted. Exercising his statutory discretion, however, the Secretary of State ultimately accepted the minority report in the GEC merger which was, therefore, allowed, and the GEC bid ultimately prevailed.

In a 1999 sequel to these cases, the Commission gave a first phase clearance[9] to proposals to merge the non-military business of Marconi Electronic Systems (part of GEC) with British Aerospace finding, in this case, the relevant market to be worldwide. With regard to the military business of the companies, the Commission confirmed again that Article 296 applied. In 2001 although the joint venture between European Aeronautic Defence and Space Company and Nortel Networks[10] was cleared by the Commission under its normal procedures the UK, because of concern over defence and security aspects of the case, exer-cised its powers under this Article to obtain behavioural undertakings from the parties relating to the confidentiality of sensitive information and the development of certain defence technology.

1.5 THE PROVISION FOR 'REVERSE REFERRAL'—ARTICLE 22(3)

A quite different role is played by Article 22(3), which reads:

> if the Commission finds, at the request of one or more Member State, that a concentration . . . that has no Community dimension . . . creates or strengthens a dominant position as a result of which effective competition would be significantly impeded within the territory of a Member State concerned it may, in so far as a concentration affects trade between Member States, adopt the decisions provided for in Article 8.

This 'reverse referral' can be useful to a Member State, which for any reason prefers that a case normally falling within its national jurisdiction under the rules of ECMR, is actually dealt with by the Commission in Brussels. It may be because the resources, or the substan-tive legal provisions of the local competition authority, are thought to be inadequate or inappropriate or, alternatively, because the issues affected are believed by the Member State to be primarily of Community interest. Once the reference back has been made, the Commission will proceed to deal with the case in the normal manner as if it was a second-phase investigation into a concentration with a Community dimension. The Commission is, however, under Article 22(5) allowed to take only 'the measures strictly necessary to maintain or restore effective competition within the territory of the Member State' once its decision has been made that the concentration is incompatible with the Common Market.

---

[9] Case IV/M1438 (decision of 25 June 1999).   [10] Case Comp/M2546 (decision of 10 October 2001).

The trend under Article 81(1) has in recent years following the *Automec (No. 2)*[11] case been towards allocating more responsibility to national competition authorities, within first the framework of the 1997 Notice on Co-operation and more recently the modernization programme. With mergers however there has been some movement at least in the opposite direction. Member States without well-established merger control procedures or institutions have utilized the provisions of this Article to request the Commission to handle several important recent cases: these have included *British Airways/Dan Air*[12] (referred by Belgium), *RTL/Veronica/Endemol*[13] (referred by The Netherlands), *Kesko/Tuko*[14] (referred by Finland), and *Blokker/Toys 'R' Us*[15] (also referred by The Netherlands). Each of the last three cases resulted in an outright prohibition of the proposed concentration; in the *Kesko* and *Endemol* cases the Commission's decisions were upheld by the CFI, which approved both its substantive and procedural findings. Since, however, all Member States now have national merger control authorities to review concentrations that do not have a Community dimension, references by individual Member States to the Commission in the future are unlikely.

Since March 1998, however, the ECMR allows such a reference to be made jointly by more than one Member State, and the first such joint references were made in 2002. In *Promatech/Sulzer*[16] concerns over the Western European market for rapier weaving machines led to a second-phase inquiry which led to undertakings being given by the parties for the disposal of businesses in Italy and Switzerland; the reference in this case was by no fewer than seven Member States. By contrast in *GE Engine Services/Unison Industries*[17] clearance was given for a merger in the US aeroengines business after only a first-phase inquiry.

2. ECMR INVESTIGATORY PROCEDURES AND POWERS

2.1 TIME LIMITS

Time is an important element in all competition cases. The decisions which competition authorities, such as the Commission, have to take often involve examination of activities and agreements of undertakings stretching back over a considerable number of years. It may take such authorities themselves some years to reach decisions in complex cartel and monopoly cases under Articles 81 and 82, and appeals to the Court of First Instance and the European Court of Justice often then follow. The Article 82 case of *Magill*[18] took some ten years to resolve, from the first complaint to the Commission to the final ECJ decision.

For mergers, which often raise difficult competition law issues, this kind of timescale is completely unrealistic. Such transactions are particularly sensitive to even short delays.

---

[11] Case T-24/90 [1992] ECR II-2223: [1992] 5 CMLR 431.
[12] Case T-3/93 [1994] ECR II-121.
[13] Case IV/M343 on appeal Case T-221/95[1999] 5 CMLR 611: [1999] ECR II-1299.
[14] Case T-22/97[1999] ECR II-3775:[2000] 4 CMLR 335.
[15] Case IV/M890 [1998] OJ L316/1.
[16] Comp/M2698 (decision of 24 July 2002).
[17] Comp/M2738 (decision of 17 April 2002).
[18] [1989] 4 CMLR 757 (Commission decision); [1995] Case 214/91 ECR I-743: 4 CMLR 718 (ECJ decision).

Volatility of stock exchange prices and the difficult personal and corporate relationships that may prevail between bidder and target mean that, in many cases, delay of even a few months may be fatal to the completion of the transaction. Time-limits in national merger control systems are, therefore, normally quite strict and, in the case of the Commission, the original time limits suggested as far back as 1973 of twelve months for the Commission to handle a case have now been reduced to, at most, five months for even the longest investigation.[19] Since many of the transactions now reaching the Merger Task Force are so complex, requiring the analysis of numerous products or service markets often in highly technical areas (such as energy, telecommunications or electronic equipment), the task of the Commission in completing its decisions within the mandatory time limits is onerous. Because of the longer time likely to be taken in pre-notification discussions in such cases, the total period for resolving them may well exceed considerably the official periods for the first- and second-phase cases provided for in the ECMR.

2.2 THE FRAMEWORK OF A COMMISSION INVESTIGATION

The procedural rules governing the investigation were originally set out in Regulation 2367/90, later replaced by Regulation 3384/94 and since 21 March 1998 in its turn by Regulation 447/98. Regulation 447/98 is not a complete rewriting of the old rules, but it has introduced a number of features as a result of the experience of the Commission, especially in connection with the problems arising when it sought to impose conditions on a concentration. This may often arise where the parties to a concentration have themselves instituted suggestions for qualifying the original merger plan once they are aware of the likely basis of opposition from the Commission to particular aspects of the concentration.

The structure of Regulation 447/98 is as follows: the recitals state that the Regulation has been modified to make it consistent with the substantive amendments to the Regulation introduced by Regulation 1310/97. In particular, it seeks to place greater emphasis on the parties' and third parties' additional rights of information and right to a hearing before the Commission. Articles 1 to 5 deal with notifications by the parties, who start the time limits running when the relevant Form CO is lodged. In certain cases a 'short-form notice' may be lodged. If a notification of an agreement is regarded by the Commission as not falling for any reason within the jurisdiction of the ECMR, notification is then treated as an application to the Commission under Regulation 17/62. Articles 6 to 10 set out details of the time limits authorized by Regulation 10 of ECMR. The first phase cannot last longer than one month after notification, though this is extended to six weeks in cases where the parties put forward commitments amending their original proposals. The second phase is limited to an additional four months. Articles 11 to 17 deal with the hearing of the parties and of third parties with a legitimate interest in the outcome of the case. A distinction is drawn between:

(i)   parties submitting the notification, always including the bidding company or companies;

(ii)   other involved parties, that is parties to the concentration other than those notifying such as, for example, the seller of a business or an undertaking which is a target of a hostile bid; and

---

[19] But note that the Commission's proposals for reform of the ECMR in December 2002 include suggestions for some further extensions of time in the more difficult cases. See Section 7.

(iii) third parties with a sufficient interest; they may include customers, suppliers, and competitors, or members of relevant management or union organizations.

Articles 14 and 15 provide for oral hearings with the notifying parties to be held in private to supplement the written submissions normally filed. Involved parties and third parties are likewise able not only to make their views known in writing, but also to have a hearing if the Hearing Officer of the Commission thinks that their contribution is likely to be of sufficient importance.

2.3 MODIFICATION BY THE PARTIES OF THE ORIGINAL CONCENTRATION PLAN

Article 18 is significant, since it contains provisions to cover the situation where the parties seek to modify the original concentration plan. A number of cases have occurred, for example *du Pont/ICI*,[20] where the amendments offered to the original scheme had arrived with the MTF so late in the second phase that the Commission had very great difficulty in coping with a proper analysis of its effects during the remaining few weeks of the four months permitted for the second phase. Article 18 now requires any amendment put forward to the Commission by the parties to be submitted within not more than 'three months of the date on which proceedings were initiated', i.e. of the start of the second phase. An extension of this time limit will only be given by the Commission in 'exceptional circumstances'.[21] Formal provision is made for conditions to be imposed as part of a first phase case, provided that the details have been submitted to the Commission not less than three weeks after notification. In such a case, the time limit for a first phase inquiry is extended to six weeks. Articles 20 to 25 complete the Regulation by dealing with a number of technical matters, such as method of transmission of documents, the acknowledgement of receipt of documents and the definition of working days.

2.4 FORM CO

Attached to Regulation 447/98 is Form CO with appendices. This is a complex form which cannot be completed 'off-the-cuff' but requires considerable legal, financial and economic input and, in all likelihood, the assistance of specialist consultants. Among the requirements of this form are:

— Section 1

Extensive background information as to the parties and their representatives.

— Section 2

Details of the concentration, its timing, method, structure, and a list of market sectors involved in the concentration together with financial details for turnover in each Member State as well as Community-wide and worldwide turnover.

— Section 3

Ownership and control of the undertakings involved.

---

[20] Case IV/M214 [1995] 5 CMLR M41.
[21] An extension was granted in Case IV/M 1439 *Telia/Telenor* [2001] 5 CMLR 1226.

— Section 4

Personal and financial links and previous acquisitions of the parties.

— Section 5

Copies of all relevant documentation including public bids, reports and accounts, analysis of markets, etc.

— Section 6

This, perhaps the most demanding, requires market definitions of both product and geographic markets, from which the market power of the new entity arising from the concentration is to be assessed, as already discussed in our treatment of product and geographic market definition.

— Sections 7 and 8

These require further details of many aspects of these markets, including market share, price levels, market entry, demand, research and development, trade associations, and general conditions.

In practice it is essential in all cases to hold pre-notification discussions with the officials of the Commission, who are quite prepared to express preliminary views on the likely main issues that will arise as a result of the notification of the concentration, and may even be prepared to indicate whether the concentration plan as originally proposed will be acceptable or not. 'Best Practice Guidelines' have been published on the DG Comp website. Notification will be required within one week of the conclusion of the agreement or the announcement of a public bid, or the acquisition of a controlling interest (Article 4(1) of ECMR), although in practice the strictness of this deadline may be waived. The mention of these various alternatives indicates the Commission's awareness that 'decisive influence' can be obtained in a number of different ways; some with the agreement of the target and some in a hostile manner. The parties making the acquisition are those that make the notification in one of the official languages of the European Union; the accurate completion of all parts of Form CO which the Commission has not agreed to waive in the particular case is of great importance, since there are fines and penalties for incorrect completion, and the form is likely to play a considerable role in the presentation of the bidder's case. For concentrations where no significant competition issues are raised, a simplified procedure has been introduced for which a much smaller amount of data has to be provided. The officials dealing with the individual cases are mainly drawn from Directorate B, usually referred to as the 'Merger Task Force' or 'MTF', though in Chapter 25, some likely organizational changes affecting the MTF are discussed.

Pre-notification discussion with the MTF is of particular importance in merger cases because:

— it enables the parties to the proposed concentration to become aware at an early stage of the likely concerns of the MTF;

— it may enable the parties to such circumstances to adjust their proposals in a way that will facilitate its clearance at first phase;

— it may enable the Commission to waive the need for the parties to complete certain sections of Form CO which may be irrelevant to a particular case; and

— it will reduce the risk of the Commission returning the notification of Form CO as incomplete (which is now occurring more often).

2.5 THE INQUIRY PROCESS: POWERS OF THE COMMISSION

During the concentration's examination, the first phase of the transaction is suspended, effectively a 'freeze' to prevent either side taking unfair advantage during the investigation. The only exception is contained in Article 7(3) under which a public bid which has been properly notified to the Commission under Article 4 can be completed, provided that in the meantime the bidder does not exercise the voting rights attached to the securities acquired, or does so only to protect the full value of the investment made on the basis of a derogation granted by the Commission. Once the official notification has been made, the MTF team allocated to the case begin an intensive three weeks of analysis of the information provided, while also seeking information from a wide variety of other sources, including suppliers, customers, trade associations, and public authorities. Consultations will also take place widely within the Commission itself and with Member States. Quick visits or surveys may be made in relevant parts of the Community to obtain information, and urgent information requests under Article 11 of ECMR sent out to interested parties. As already stated, the outcome of the enquiry may be one of three alternatives, either:

(a) that the concentration for some reason does not fall within the scope of the Regulation, e.g. because it is not a full-function joint venture or, although a 'concentration', its turnover falls below the required thresholds under Article 1; or

(b) that the concentration is regarded as compatible with the Common Market at the end of the first phase; or

(c) that the concentration raises serious doubts as to its compatibility with the Common Market and so has to be passed on to phase two.

2.6 THE SIMPLIFIED PROCEDURE

The far greater number of concentrations with a Community dimension which are now being notified led to the publication in July 2000 of a Notice setting out the simplified procedure dealing with cases which do not raise competition concerns. The categories of cases which are eligible for this treatment (and which now amount to some 25 per cent of all cases) are as follows:

(i)   When the acquisition involves joint control of a joint venture and the assets and turnover of the joint venture are less than €100 million within the EEA territory.

(ii) When the transaction is between parties not engaged in business activities in the same product or geographical market or related upstream or downstream markets.

(iii) Even when the parties do not meet the conditions of (ii), if the total market share of the parties is less than 15 per cent for horizontal and 25 per cent for vertical relationships.

2.7 POWER TO IMPOSE CONDITIONS AND OBLIGATIONS—ARTICLE 8(2)

During even a first phase enquiry, the parties are free to put forward proposals for eliminating competition problems raised by the concentration which would otherwise lead to a second phase detailed enquiry. Such proposals have, under Article 18 of Regulation 447/98, to be notified to the Commission within three weeks from the original date of notification, so as to give the Commission an opportunity to analyse the proposals put forward and ensure that they actually meet the relevant competition problems, and thus eliminate the 'serious doubts' which would otherwise lead to a second phase enquiry. Usually a first phase undertaking, or conditions of this kind, involves a relatively simple divestment of part of the business of the bidder or target, such as occurred in *Owen-Illinois/BTR Packaging*.[22]

The power of the Commission to attach conditions and obligations to a decision following a second-phase investigation is contained in Article 8(2). The requirement of this Article is that the conditions and obligations have to ensure that the undertakings involved comply with the commitments that they have made to the Commission when modifying their original concentration plan, so as to render the concentration compatible with the Common Market. The parties must put forward any proposals not later than the end of the third month of the second-phase inquiry. The decision at the end of the second phase also deals with ancillary restrictions directly related and necessary to implementation of the concentration (dealt with in Section 4 of this chapter). Article 8(3) ECMR entitles the Commission following a second-phase decision investigation to state that the concentration is incompatible with the Common Market, without reference to any conditions. There have so far been twenty cases in this category,[23] and in other cases the likelihood of such a decision has led to the withdrawal of the notification. Article 10 contains the relevant time limits for the first and second phases which cannot be extended provided that the information supplied by the parties is complete. The only exception is contained in Article 10(5) under which a judgment of the Court of Justice or Court of First Instance annulling the whole or part of the Commission decision, as in *Kali und Salz*,[24] enables the periods laid down in the Regulation (one month—phase one, four months—phase two) to start again.

2.8 THE ADMINISTRATIVE POWERS OF THE COMMISSION

The Commission has the same powers in investigating concentrations as it does under Regulation 17/62 for Article 81 and 82 cases, including the ability to ask Member State competition authorities to carry out investigatory tasks and to carry out 'dawn raids' themselves. This power, however, is only rarely used in merger cases. Commission officials are entitled under Article 13(1) of ECMR:

(i)   to examine the books and business records of the parties;

(ii) to take or demand copies of, or extracts from, these books and business records;

(iii) to ask for oral explanations on the spot; and

(iv) to enter premises for the purposes of their investigation.

Failure to notify a concentration with a Community dimension can lead to the imposition of a fine as can the provision of incomplete or misleading information in Form CO. In June 2002, Deutsche BP was fined €35,000 for unintentionally but negligently supplying

---

[22] Case IV/M1109 (decision of 21 April 1998).

[23] Although three of these decisions have subsequently been annulled by the CFI. See Section 6, pp.392–3.

[24] Cases C-68/94 and 30/95 [1998] ECR I-1375: 4 CMLR 829.

incomplete information relating to an acquisition. Obstruction by parties of the Commission's attempt to seek information can be penalized under Articles 14 and 15 by fines and periodic penalty payments. Professional secrecy is protected under Article 17, under which the Commission and the competent authorities of the Member States and their relevant officials are prevented from disclosing information that is within the category of professional secrecy; information obtained from investigations relating to a particular concentration is not available for the use of any other investigation which the Commission or a Member State may wish to carry out.

There are important rights of defence under Article 18 of ECMR and the Commission is required to give those concerned, including the parties to the concentration, the opportunity of making known their views on the statement of objections which the Commission will provide if it has serious doubts as to whether concentration is compatible. This requirement is supplemented by the further provisions of procedural Regulation 447/98, in particular Articles 14 to 17. The combined effect of this procedural Regulation and the ECMR is that in broad terms third parties and the parties concerned have the same rights of hearing and access to relevant documents as under Regulation 17/62 for Article 81 and 82 cases. The provisions relating, however, to the Advisory Committee differ somewhat in the case of concentrations since, under Article 19 of ECMR, the Advisory Committee is entitled to recommend publication of its opinion once the draft decision has been presented to it (a freedom not given to the Advisory Committee in handling draft decisions under Articles 81 and 82). There are a number of occasions when the Advisory Committee has thought fit to publish its opinions and, on occasion, both the majority and minority opinions, e.g. in *Varta/Bosch*.[25]

2.9 THE BLOCKING OF MERGERS

In some cases, the outcome of the Commission investigation is a total prohibition of the Concentration. Such a decision will reflect the Commission's view that the effect of the merger will be to give the merged entity a degree of dominance in relevant markets that, to use the language of the Regulation, 'will significantly impede effective competition'. In some cases, there may simply be no remedy to the competition problems raised that is acceptable to the parties. *Volvo/Scania*[26] represents one of those cases; Volvo offered a number of commitments, including the opening up of its dealer network in Sweden for heavy lorries to third parties, but none was regarded by the Commission as adequate.

In other cases, there may have been a greater possibility of suitable conditions being agreed, but the parties may have failed to submit their proposals at a suitably early stage or have failed to meet the strict time limits required under the Regulation. Thus, in *GE/ Honeywell*,[27] the Commission would have been willing to clear the merger had GE been prepared to dispose of a sufficiently large percentage of its shares in its aircraft leasing subsidiary, GECAS, to an independent purchaser, but GE failed to agree such proposals within the time limits of the second phase. The merger was, therefore, blocked. It is important to be aware that the total number of mergers so far blocked by the Commission

---

[25] Case IV/M012 [1992] 5 CMLR M1.   [26] Case Comp/M1672 [2001] OJ L143/74.

[27] Case Comp/M2220 (decision of 3 July 2001). See DG Comp Competition Policy Newsletter (2001) No. 3, pp.5–13.

represent a tiny percentage of the cases falling within the Regulation, and that over 90 per cent of all concentrations notified to the Commission are cleared unconditionally.

3. REMEDIES — CONDITIONS AND OBLIGATIONS IMPOSED AS THE PRICE OF CLEARANCE

3.1 THE PURPOSE OF REMEDIES

As we have seen in the previous chapter, the outcome of a merger notification to the Commission is not necessarily that the transaction is either blocked or cleared in its entirety. In between 5 per cent and 10 per cent of all cases notified, the result is a clearance subject to conditions and obligations agreed between the Commission and the parties to the merger. Some of the most important and high profile cases dealt with by the Commission over the last twelve years have been resolved in this way; and those who advise the parties in any case other than the most straightforward have to keep the possibility of such an outcome, at the end of either the first or second phase, in mind right from the early stages of the pre-notification procedure.

Regulation 1310/97, which amended the original Merger Regulation 4064/89, refers in its recital 8 to the powers of the Commission to accept commitments from the parties in the first and/or second phases of the procedure, which will consist of 'conditions' and 'obligations'. It is important to understand the Commission cannot impose these on the parties without their agreement. During both first and second phases, the parties may decide that they should put forward certain suggestions to the Commission, which they believe will enable the substantive criteria contained in Article 2 to be met, by reducing the impact of the merger on the competitive state of the relevant markets. Negotiations will then take place over both the principle and the detail of the proposals; if the Commission is not satisfied that the proposals go far enough, it may request the parties' agreement to more stringent terms.

Although the Commission, therefore, cannot impose a remedy consisting of particular conditions and obligations on the parties, it has two important means at its disposal under the Regulation for putting pressure on them. At the first phase, it can threaten the parties with a full-scale second phase investigation under Article 6(1)(c), rather than simply dealing with them under Article 6(1)(b). Beyond that, once the case has actually entered the second phase, the threat can be that a blocking decision will be reached, unless the parties come up with an adequate package of proposals to meet the perceived problems in some or all of the affected markets.

Over the period in which the Regulation has been operative, there has been extensive case law which illustrates how the Commission will exercise its discretion in such situations. Moreover, its experience has been summarised in a Notice published on 2 March 2001,[28] which also draws on the experience of US anti-trust authorities.

A fundamental principle underlies the whole subject of remedies. This is that the package of remedies agreed must, by their combined effect, eliminate the creation or strengthening of the dominant position identified by the Commission, so that conditions of effective

---

[28] [2001] OJ C68/3.

competition will be maintained on a lasting basis in the relevant markets. The Commission, in applying this principle, will necessarily have to examine every aspect of the merger, including the structure and special characteristics of the relevant markets.

3.2 STRUCTURAL AND BEHAVIOURAL REMEDIES—THE CASE LAW

It was originally thought that the Regulation only empowered the Commission to accept *structural* remedies from the parties, involving the disposal by the bidder or target undertaking of part of its existing business activities or divisions, such as factories, distribution networks, research and development laboratories, or intellectual property rights, including patents and trade marks. Remedies involving restrictions of a *behavioural* nature were not thought permissible. This limitation, however, was removed by the Court of First Instance in *Gencor* v. *Lonrho*;[29] it confirmed the Commission's belief that it was inappropriate in the context of Article 2 merely to require undertakings to abstain from abusing a dominant position, but ruled that, in certain circumstances, behavioural undertakings might prove, either in combination with structural remedies or even on their own, the most effective way of preventing the creation or strengthening of a dominant position. An important difference between the two types of remedy is that a structural remedy is of immediate effect and should not be capable of being reversed in the future, while a behavioural remedy will normally operate only for a fixed period of time (often three or five years) and can be varied or terminated as the result of a major change of circumstances.

An example of a case where behavioural conditions were imposed is *Boeing/McDonnell Douglas*.[30] The Commission found that the takeover by Boeing of one of its main rivals in aircraft manufacture on the world market would strengthen its existing dominant position. It proved impossible to find third parties of sufficient commercial stature to acquire the McDonnell Douglas business, so that finally the conditions agreed by Boeing involved not disposals, but acceptance that, *inter alia*:

— it would guarantee customer support to all purchasers of McDonnell Douglas' aircraft of the same quality as that given to its own customers;

— it would not discriminate against purchasers of McDonnell Douglas' aircraft if they later decided to purchase other aircraft from third parties;

— it would not enter into any additional exclusive arrangements with airlines for a ten year period, nor enforce certain existing exclusive agreements; and

— it would license certain patents to third parties on a non-exclusive basis.

Nestlé/Ralston Purina,[31] by contrast, provides an example of a remedy package that includes both structural and behavioural elements, in a case involving petfood markets in several Member States. Nestlé, the bidder, was required as a condition for clearance to grant an exclusive licence for a long period to a third party for its 'Friskies' brand in Spain, as well as to dispose of a production site near Barcelona. If, however, this proved impossible, it had as an alternative to divest Ralston Purina's 50 per cent interest in a joint venture in Spain. In

---

[29] Case T-102/96 [1999] ECR II-753: 4 CMLR 971.
[30] Case IV/M877: [1997] OJ L336/16: 5 CMLR 270.
[31] Case Comp/M2337 (decision of 27 July 2001).

Italy and Greece it had to grant exclusive licences of its rights under the 'Chow' brand. In *Pernod Richard/Diageo*,[32] the conditions agreed also included the disposal of certain brands acquired by these two bidders from the purchase of the wines and spirits business worldwide of Seagram; brands of rum and whisky had to be transferred to purchasers because of the bidders' dominant position in Iceland and other national markets.

It is important to be aware of the difference between 'conditions' and 'obligations' within a 'remedy package':

— A 'condition' is of primary importance, since it is the (or one of the) measures required to ensure the maintenance, after the merger, of effective competition. If it is breached, the original decision no longer stands and heavy fines (up to 10 per cent of turnover) can be imposed, under Regulation 447/98, Article 14(2).

— An 'obligation', by contrast, represents the steps which the parties are obliged to take in order to implement the conditions agreed, including often the appointment of a trustee to supervise divestiture of assets. If an obligation is not complied with, the undertaking concerned can be punished by a periodic penalty, under Regulation 447/98, Article 15, but such a breach does not involve the revocation of the Commission decision.

Once the parties have reached agreement with the Commission officials as to the remedies in their case, the Commission will proceed to 'market test' them by asking Member States, competitors, and other interested parties if they believe that they are adequate to restore effective competition. Such consultation may even extend in some cases to foreign competition authorities, for example in the USA and Canada, with whom the European Community has a formal Treaty of Co-operation (see Chapter 23, pp.505–6).

3.3 DIVESTITURE — A STRUCTURAL REMEDY

The Commission's wide experience to date has enabled it to produce for the parties in cases involving structural remedies a model form of commitment, which they are required to follow as closely as possible. In addition to the principal conditions, it will contain a number of detailed obligations, whose aim is to ensure that disposals are promptly and effectively carried out, as the price of clearance for the transaction.

The buyer of the assets being disposed of cannot be freely chosen by the parties to the merger. The Commission will insist in the decision that it has to approve the buyer as suitable, being a viable existing or potential competitor; independent of the parties; with appropriate financial resources and expertise; and whose purchase will not itself raise ECMR issues (if the transaction is of a Community dimension). In some recent cases, the Commission has gone even further, insisting that the buyer of the assets must be identified before the merger can be cleared and must also have signed a legally binding contract to acquire them. This is known as the 'upfront buyer' condition (as, for example, in the case of *Robert Bosch/ Rexroth*).[33]

---

[32] Case Comp/M2268 (decision of 8 May 2001).
[33] Case Comp/M2060 (decision of 13 December 2000).

3.4 OTHER FORMS OF STRUCTURAL REMEDIES

Remedies are not, however, limited to the sale of assets to third parties. They may also involve the licensing of technology, the guarantee of products supplied to third parties, or of access to key infrastructure, or the termination of existing exclusive contractual arrangements. They must be capable of being implemented effectively within a short period, without the later need of additional monitoring by the Commission, and must be described by the parties to the Commission in sufficient detail to ensure that their impact can be fully assessed.

Whilst the more common remedy involved disposal of one or more of the target businesses, the Commission may judge it more appropriate in some cases for one or more of the businesses owned by the bidder to be disposed of as, for example, happened in *Exxon/Mobil*[34] and *Bayer/Aventis*.[35] The divestiture may even include businesses where there is no apparent competitive concern, so as to ensure that the buyer acquires a viable package of assets that can compete with the merged undertakings.

If the original proposals of the parties turn out to be impractical within the short timescale permitted (which may be a period of a few months and rarely exceeds a year), they may in default be required to divest another valuable business or business asset in its place (known as the 'crown jewels' solution).

In the event of a remedy involving divestiture, the parties will have to agree to maintain the viability of the business pending its sale, and to refrain from any steps which could make it less attractive to a purchaser. A trustee will have to be appointed to manage the business pending sale and supervise its disposal. If initial attempts to effect the sale fail, the appointed trustee will be placed under considerable pressure to complete the sale within the time limit, either by lowering the price or by adding attractive additional assets to the original business being disposed of.

The Commission has on rare occasions agreed to modify the original conditions imposed, if the parties can show that every effort has been made to carry them out, e.g. to dispose of part of the business acquired to a non-competitor. In *Pirelli Edizone/Telecom Italia*,[36] the sale of the Blu mobile telephone company to a number of competing mobile operators was ultimately agreed to, even though the original conditions had required disposal to a purchaser not already in the mobile telephone business, it having been shown that no such purchaser was available.

4. ANCILLARY RESTRAINTS

4.1 THE CONCEPT

The doctrine under Community law of ancillary restraint refers to restrictive clauses whose presence is, in a commercial sense, essential to the particular transaction to which they are connected and without which that transaction would probably not take place at all. A very common type of ancillary restrain is the restrictive covenant which, on a sale and purchase

---

[34] Case IV/M1383 (decision of 29 September 1999).
[35] Case Comp/M2547 (decision of 17 April 2002).
[36] Case Comp/M2574 (decision of 29 September 2001).

of a business, binds the vendor not to compete with the purchaser for a number of years so that the purchaser will obtain the full value of the goodwill and assets for which he is paying. It is clear that the terms of the restrictive covenant in this situation have to be reasonable in the light of the overall transaction and this will affect its scope, its geographical coverage, and the period of time for which it is applicable. In the general context of a sale it must also be necessary in a commercial sense for adequate protection of the purchaser.

It may be that restrictions contained in transactions which qualify as concentrations within the terms of the ECMR may technically be outside the reach of Article 81(1). Since, however, the ECMR itself disapplies Regulation 17/62 in respect of such concentrations, there needs to be a provision for negative clearance for such clauses in merger cases. For this reason Articles 6(1)(b) and 8(2) of ECMR in their last sentences provide that the decision declaring the concentration compatible shall also cover restrictions directly related and necessary to the implementation of the concentration.

4.2 THE 2001 NOTICE

In July 2001, the Commission published a new Notice replacing its original Notice of 1990. It contains an important policy change, that the Commission will not in future assess ancillary restraints in the course of its substantive decisions, so that the parties will have to make their own assessment of such restraints, with any dispute being resolved by national courts. The Commission states that the terms of the ECMR do not place it under a legal obligation to assess such restraints.[37]

In making their assessment, the parties can, of course, make use of the guidance which the new Notice provides. The main principles stated in the Notice include that:

(i)   the duration of non-competition clauses in favour of the purchaser are generally limited to two years in cases involving the transfer of goodwill alone, and to three years where know-how is also protected;

(ii)   the geographical scope for such clauses is generally limited to the territories where the vendor offered goods or services immediately before the transfer, unless the vendor had already invested in other territories with a view to immediate entry;

(iii) non-solicitation and confidentiality clauses are to be assessed in the same way as non-competition clauses though, in some cases, confidentiality clauses may be accepted for longer than three years;

(iv)   non-competition clauses between the parents of a joint venture and the joint venture can be justified as a general rule for up to five years, though the Notice emphasizes that any such clause providing for a period exceeding three years needs justification in the particular circumstances of the case; and

(v)   licences of intellectual property rights (including know-how), purchase and supply agreements (normally for a maximum of three years) and service and distribution agreements would also be allowed to extend where necessary to cover the transitional period of a new joint venture from dependency to autonomy.

---

[37] It appears however from the subsequent CFI decision in Case T-251/50 *Lagardère/Canal+* of 20 November 2002 that this may be legally incorrect, in view of the mandatory language of Art. 6(1)(b) ECMR.

Contractual provisions which do not constitute ancillary restraints and which infringe Article 81(1) may be capable of benefiting from block exemptions, such as Regulation 2790/99.

4.3 NON-COMPETE CLAUSES

The first example of an ancillary restraint is a non-competition clause which protects the goodwill acquired by the purchaser. The Notice stresses that it is the purchaser which requires such protection and that it is rare that a vendor can reasonably seek to impose any similar restriction on its purchasers. In all cases, however, such clauses must be limited to a duration, geographic area, and the subject matter which are necessary for the protection of the party receiving their benefit.

As stated above, the period of two years is normally the most allowed for transfers of goodwill alone, extended by a further year if know-how is also transferred. In some cases, however, there may be reasons why there is special loyalty between the vendor and its customers and, in these circumstances, sometimes these limits can be extended. The vendor's covenants can bind its subsidiaries and agents, but cannot bind third parties, such as distributors and resellers.

An example of where the parties sought to impose non-compete clauses with excessive coverage was *Tesco/Catteau*.[38] The Commission here objected to the unlimited geographic scope of a non-compete agreement given by the Catteau family on the sale to Tesco of certain supermarket businesses on the Continent, and limited those obligations to specific defined regions in France and Belgium. Moreover, in the same agreement, the members of the Catteau family bound by the restrictions included not only the named principals and vendors but also other members of their family, not all of whom were necessarily shareholders in the relevant company. The Commission also refused to recognize non-compete obligations unlimited in time, holding that a maximum term of three years would be reasonable in the light of Tesco's lack of experience in these continental markets and the fact that no technical know-how, and only limited commercial know-how, were being transferred to them by the Catteau family.

4.4 INTELLECTUAL PROPERTY RIGHT LICENCES

The second example of an ancillary restrain is that of licences for intellectual property rights and know-how. In a number of concentrations, and particularly in full-function joint ventures, an important issue may be the transfer of intellectual property rights by the parents to the joint venture. The parent companies, however, may not be willing to assign these rights absolutely since they may need to retain them for their own trading purposes. The parent companies may, therefore, only be prepared to grant licences to the purchaser of the joint venture to use these rights for the specific respects for which the joint venture has been set up, or relating to the business that the purchaser proposes to carry on utilizing the assets sold.

Such licences are normally regarded as ancillary to the purchase agreement and the Notice indicates that simple or non-exclusive licences of intellectual property rights are normally

---

[38] Case IV/M301 [1993] 4 CMLR 238.

acceptable as necessary and ancillary and can be limited as stated above to certain fields of use. On the whole, territorial restrictions will not normally be looked on with favour though field of use restrictions in non-exclusive licences may be acceptable. Restrictions in licence agreements going beyond this do not obtain the benefit of the negative clearance provisions and they should be assessed on their merits under Article 81(3). They may benefit from the block exemption for Technology Transfer Agreements (Regulation No. 240/96). Similar principles are applied to licences governing trade marks, business names, and similar rights. On occasion vendors may wish to retain control of IPRs for activities other than those being transferred and to provide appropriate licences to enable the purchaser to have the full benefit of the assets being transferred. Alternatively, if the IPRs are to be transferred with the business, it may be reasonable to require the purchaser to licence these back to the vendor to allow the vendor to continue activities outside the scope of the transfer.

4.5 PURCHASE AND SUPPLY AGREEMENTS

The third category of ancillary agreement is purchase and supply agreements. The Notice points out the sale of a business or undertaking may cause problems to the new owner, since the business transferred may find the transfer causes a disruption of its normal sources of supply or the distribution of its product. It is often, therefore, necessary to maintain, at least for a transitional period, links between the vendor and purchaser of the business under which raw materials continue to be supplied by the vendor to the purchaser. The legitimate aim of such obligations to ensure continuity of supply of such products is recognized and accepted provided that it is not made a permanent feature. The Commission does not, however, look with favour on general clauses governing exclusive purchase or exclusive supply, because such exclusivity is not normally necessary to permit the implementation of the concentration. Alternative and less restrictive methods for ensuring reasonable supplies to the purchasing company for its new asset acquired will have to be considered. The arrangements must in any case only be enforced for a reasonably limited period, normally no more than three years. Insofar as a vertical agreement between the parties is not ancillary and infringes Article 81(1), it may be eligible for exemption under Article 81(3) and, in particular, the block exemption conferred by Regulation 2790/99.

Examples of ancillary supply agreements can be found in *ICL/Nokia*,[39] where a provision was treated as ancillary that the vendor (Nokia) and the business transferred by it to ICL would make available to each other any supplies required in the course of their trading for one year. A similar provision was approved in the *Courtaulds/Snia*[40] joint venture whereby the parent companies agreed to supply their joint venture with some products on a non-exclusive basis essential to the activities taken over. The Commission, however, rejected the original proposed duration of the supply agreement, because it regarded it as excessive in the context of the replacement of the original dependent relationship with the parent companies by the new joint venture.

Finally, it should be noted that in some full-function joint venture cases examined under the ECMR rather than under Article 81, the Commission appears to take a more generous view of non-competitive covenants in concentrations than in Article 81 cases. The Notice itself is brief in its treatment of such cases, merely stating that, to the extent that the

---

[39] Case IV/M105 [1991] 4 CMLR 817.   [40] Case IV/M113 [1992] 4 CMLR 349.

prohibition of the parents from competing with the joint venture aims at expressing the reality of the lasting withdrawal of the parents from the market assigned to the joint venture, it will be recognized as an integral part of the concentration. The decisions themselves, however, show that the Commission's general approach will be generous to the parties and will not always strictly apply the normal rules as to proportionality and ancillary nature, which the other provisions of the Notice seem to indicate will be applicable, at least in concentrations that do not constitute joint ventures. Even non-competition clauses given by the parents without limitation of time, apart from the duration of the joint venture itself, will be on occasions regarded as ancillary and, therefore, acceptable.

5. THE RELATIONSHIP BETWEEN ECMR AND ARTICLES 81 AND 82

Articles 81 and 82 were effective from the coming into force of the Treaty of Rome on 1 January 1958, and have played a key role in the development of the Community as central pillars of the Community's constitutional structure. Later regulations, such as the ECMR, have no legal status to nullify or amend these Articles. Nevertheless, whilst this cardinal principle has to be maintained, it is important to be aware of the practical differences in the application of these Articles which the adoption of ECMR has brought about.

Before adoption of the ECMR in December 1989 both Articles 81 and Article 82 had been applied to concentrations, albeit in limited circumstances as described in the previous chapter. No procedural regulations were, however, ever adopted by the Commission or Council to support the application of these Articles in this way. It was the inadequacy, therefore, of these two Articles to provide an effective system of merger control that led ultimately to the adoption of the ECMR which states, in Article 22(2), that Regulation 17/62 has no application to concentrations as defined in Article 3. Moreover, a Notice published simultaneously with the promulgation of the Regulation (ECMR) on behalf of the Commission stated that the Commission would not normally apply the Articles to concentrations except by means of the ECMR.

Articles 81 and 82 do, however, also have direct effect in national Courts. The question, therefore, has been asked whether they can be used to block concentrations in those courts. It would seem that the doctrine of *'provisional validity'* in the *Nouvelles Frontières*[41] case makes this impractical under Article 81, since agreements to acquire share interests remain valid until a court decision striking them down as void under Article 81. In the absence of any relevant implementing regulations this would not appear possible. The position under Article 82, however, is different since there is no provision for exemption equivalent to Article 81(3) and, therefore, the Article can be implemented immediately in national courts without the need for specific Community legislation. In principle, therefore, it seems that a party could challenge a concentration not having a Community dimension in a national court under this Article. The ECJ judgment of *Ahmed Saeed*[42] lends support to this view. The national court judge may well hesitate to enter into the merits of the concentration which is

---

[41] Case 209/84 [1986] ECR 1425: 3 CMLR 173.
[42] Case 66/86 [1989] ECR 803: [1990] 4 CMLR 102.

challenged given the complexities of such an assessment and it would require a strong case, perhaps one involving the very high market shares found in the *Continental Can* case, before any national Court is likely to intervene on the plaintiff's behalf.

6. APPEALS TO THE CFI AND ECJ

6.1 COMPETITION LAW APPEALS IN GENERAL

The Court of First Instance and European Court of Justice have both dealt extensively with competition cases arising under Articles 81 and 82. These cases reach them by one of two main routes:

(i)   by way of appeal against a Commission decision and/or against a fine imposed for a breach of one or more of these Articles. Such cases reach the Court of First Instance initially under Article 230 which allows an appeal from the Commission in the following circumstances:

   (*a*) lack of competence or authority;

   (*b*) infringement of an essential procedural requirement;

   (*c*) infringement of the terms of the Treaty or any rule of law relating to its application; or

   (*d*) misuse of powers.

   A further appeal can take place, on a point of law only, to the ECJ. Examples of such cases would be those brought on appeal from decisions under Article 82 by the Commission, such as *Magill*.[43]

(ii)   By way of request from a national court for a preliminary ruling under Article 234 of the Treaty, as for example in the *Delimitis*[44] and the *Hag*[45] cases.

Article 230 of the Treaty clearly applies to decisions by the Commission under the ECMR and Regulation 4064/89 recognizes the rights of the parties in this respect. Article 21(1) states that 'subject to review by the Court of Justice, the Commission shall have sole jurisdiction to take the decisions provided for in this Regulation'. Article 16 furthermore provides that the Court of Justice has unlimited jurisdiction to review decisions when the Commission has fixed a fine or periodic penalty payments under Articles 14 and 15 of the Regulation.

It is not only actual parties to merger decisions who are entitled to appeal. As under Article 230(2) of the Treaty a person may also appeal in respect of a decision which, 'although in the form of a regulation . . . addressed to another person, is of direct and individual concern to the third party'. A third party with a legitimate interest may also bring an action before the CFI, as for example in *Kayserberg* v. *Commission*.[46] The third party must

---

[43]   See fn. 18.

[44]   Case C-234/89 [1991] ECR I-935: [1992] 5 CMLR 210.

[45]   *Van Zuylen* v. *Hag* (*'Hag 1'*) Case 192/73 [1974] ECR 731: 2 CMLR 127; *CNL-Sucal* v. *Hag* (*'Hag 2'*) Case 10/89 [1990] ECR I-3711: 3 CMLR 571.

[46]   Case T-290/94 [1997] ECR II-2137: [1998] 4 CMLR 336.

then show that the relevant decision is capable of affecting its interests by bringing about a specific change in his legal position. Finally, the appellant has to show that it is 'individually concerned'. This means that the decision must be shown to have affected it by reason of its own particular characteristics which distinguish it from all other persons.

6.2 APPEALS UNDER THE PROVISIONS OF ECMR

The early cases involving appeals to the Courts in Luxembourg involved third parties. In the first case employees of Perrier challenged the substantive decision of the Commission in July 1992 in *Nestlé/Perrier*.[47] The employees were concerned that the acquisition would result in a loss of several hundred jobs and they asked the Court to suspend the Commission's decision. The Court ruled that the employees were entitled to raise an appeal but it refused to grant them an order for interim measures suspending implementation of the decision. The Court noted that under Recital 13 of the Merger Regulation the Commission was required to engage in an appraisal of the merits of a concentration within the general framework of the achievement of the fundamental objectives referred to in Article 2 of the Treaty, including that of strengthening the Community's economic and social cohesion referred to in Article 130(*a*).

The first ruling by the CFI came in the *Zunis Holding*[48] case in October 1993 where shareholders in a target company, the subject of a Commission decision in November 1991 *(Mediobanca/Generali)*,[49] complained about the Commission's finding that the acquisition of shares by Mediobanca up to a total percentage of 12.84 per cent did not constitute a concentration within the meaning of Article 3 of the ECMR. The applicant shareholders tried to obtain an order from the Court that the Commission should re-open proceedings on the basis of late and new information about secret shareholder agreements, which the applicants suggested rendered the influence of Mediobanca greater than had been thought appropriate by the Commission itself. The Court found that, since the Commission's decision did not place any of the applicants as minority shareholders in Generali in a position different to any other shareholder, they were not individually concerned by the decision.

Appeals were brought to the Court of First Instance by Air France against two decisions of the Commission in respect of the acquisitions of British Airways of Dan Air and of TAT European Airways.[50] In the first case, the Commission ruled that the acquisition was outside the scope of the Regulation because the turnover did not reach the required figure. The Commission's decision had not been taken formally after a full first stage enquiry but given informally. It was, nevertheless, held to be an action with legal affect because of the effect it had on the position of the parties. Air France was held entitled to appeal to the CFI because the decision given was of direct and individual concern to it as a competitor in the relevant market; it lost, however, on the merits of the case.

The number and importance of appeals against merger decisions to the CFI is now on the increase. As we have already noted, in *Gencor*,[51] both substantive and procedural issues were

[47] See Ch. 17, fn. 53.
[48] [1993] Case T-83/92 ECR II-1169. On appeal to ECJ, Case C-480/93 P [1996] ECR I-1: 5 CMLR 219.
[49] Case IV/M159 [1994] 4 CMLR M1.
[50] Cases T-2 and 3/93 [1994] ECR II-121, 323.
[51] See fn. 29.

raised, including the right of the Commission to exercise jurisdiction when the parties have no assets within the Community. In the *Coca-Cola* v. *Commission* case[52] Coca-Cola sought not to have the Commission's decision annulled (as it had found in favour of the concentration in which it was involved), but to have certain findings of the Commission overruled, which it believed could be prejudicial to it in future cases. These included a finding that CCSB held a dominant position in the British market for cola drinks, but the CFI held such a finding was unappealable in that, as the concentration in question had been unconditionally cleared, it had no legal effect on the appellant.

The first major substantive appeal against a Commission decision under ECMR was in the *Kali und Salz* case (discussed at p.366). Here, both the French Government and a French company had challenged the decision; whilst the French company simply challenged only the conditions attached, the government attacked the whole decision. The Court's decision in March 1998 clearly showed that it was prepared to examine the detailed reasoning of the Commission and its interpretation of the provisions of the ECMR. The outcome of the Court's decision was the complete annulment of the decision, not simply the removal of the conditions; the Court stated that, if the decision itself was annulled, the conditions attached to it were also invalid. In the event, the Commission finally issued a fresh decision to clear the concentration, even though it was impossible after the passage of four years to reinstate the original commercial relationship of the parties.

It is noteworthy that in this case the ECJ had been prepared to grant interim orders to the parties to preserve the status quo. For example, another of these conditions was that K&S was required to withdraw from an export cartel set up in Vienna for exports outside the Community, in which both SCPA and K&S had 25 per cent. At the request of SCPA the President of the Court of First Instance suspended the withdrawal of K&S from the export cartel because neither of the other shareholders in the cartel organization was willing to buy out the K&S shares, which would automatically dissolve under its provisions upon notice of termination by any one of the shareholders, unless one of the other shareholders was willing to acquire the shares of the withdrawing party. Such an imposed dissolution was felt to be unfair on SCPA until its substantive hearing against the merits of the decision had been heard.

6.3 THE *AIRTOURS* APPEAL

Perhaps however the most important judgment rendered so far by the CFI in dealing with an appeal from the Commission in a merger case was the *Airtours* case in June 2002. As already described in the previous chapter (at p.367) the CFI annulled this decision blocking the merger, and in doing so used language that was severely critical both of the Commission's procedure and of its substantive assessment of the alleged collective dominance situation created by the merger. This decision alone would have been likely to cause a radical change by the Commission in the way in which it handled those Notifications which raise difficult and important issues under Article 2, but just over four months later it was to suffer two further defeats.

---

[52] Cases T-125 & 127/97 *Coca Cola Company* v. *Commission* [2000] ECR II-1733: 5 CMLR 467.

6.4 THE EXPEDITED APPEAL PROCEDURE OF THE CFI: *SCHNEIDER* AND *TETRA*

The CFI has now introduced a system for hearing appeals (not limited to competition cases) on an expedited basis, adopting written procedures but with a full oral hearing. This itself is likely to increase the number of appeals brought. Whilst the *Airtours* decision had been dealt with under the normal procedure (and therefore took nearly three years), both *Schneider/ Legrand* and *Tetra/Sidel* in autumn 2002 were dealt with under the new procedure. In *Schneider*[53] the Commission's analysis of the many national markets in Europe for electrical equipment was found inadequate except for that dealing with the French market; and in respect of that national market its decision was adjudged procedurally unfair, since it differed from the statement of objections in its description of the impact which the combination of the businesses of the two parties would have. In *Tetra/Sidel*[54] the decision of the Commission was based on a theory of leverage; Tetra had a strong position in the manufacture of cartons and carton packaging machinery whilst Sidel manufactured plastic (PET) bottles as well as the machinery used for shaping the raw plastic forms into bottle shapes. There was some limited overlap between the products (milk, fruit juice, and tea and coffee drinks) that could be sold in either form of container. The Commission's decision had been based on its perception that Tetra would be likely to use its dominance in the carton business to discourage packagers from shifting from the use of cartons to that of plastic bottles for their requirements and would be practising 'mixed bundling' by offering discounts to such packagers on their future carton purchases, on condition that they also acquired their plastic bottle machinery from Sidel rather than from other manufacturers. Whilst the CFI confirmed in its decision that the Regulation could be applied to conglomerate mergers and that leverage from a position of dominance in one market to another related market could be the basis for intervention, it found, on the evidence available to the Commission, that this case had not been proved in that it fell far short of establishing that the consequences of the merger justified an adverse decision.

It is therefore likely in future that more decisions will be given under the expedited procedure on appeals from the Commission. Not all of the appeals, however, will necessarily be held under the expedited procedure which might be inappropriate in the more complex cases. The benefit of the expedited procedure, however, is that a judgment can be produced within eight to ten months from the original Commission decision rather than the two to three year period previously experienced. A number of formal appeals against adverse Commission decisions (including one by the parties to *GE/Honeywell*[55]) are still being dealt with under the normal procedure. Moreover, although the majority of these cases involve appeals by the parties against Commission decisions blocking a merger or imposing onerous conditions upon them, others have been brought by third parties objecting to the decision of the Commission to clear a concentration or to attack conditions considered too lenient.

---

[53] Case T-310/01 decision of 22 October 2002. See DG Comp Competition Policy Newsletter (2002) No. 3, pp.7–12 on the expedited appeal process.

[54] Case T-5/02: [2002] 5 CMLR 1182. The Commission is appealing this decision to the ECJ.

[55] Ch. 17, fn. 62, and see R. Reynolds and J. Ordover, 'Archimedean Leveraging and the GE/Honeywell Transaction' [2002] 70 ALJ 171–198.

7. THE FUTURE OF THE REGULATION

7.1 INITIAL STEPS TOWARDS REFORM

Block exemptions enacted by the Commission or Council under Article 81(3), apart from Reg. 4056/86 on maritime transport, have a finite life and therefore have to be reviewed as this comes to an end; in contrast the ECMR has no expiry date but continues indefinitely until it is changed or (a most unlikely outcome) terminated. Although staff resources of the MTF have been steadily increased since 1990, and the prospect of substantial further increases has been recently announced, it still has great difficulty in coping with its caseload within the mandatory time limits. Many of the cases involve major multinationals and a large number of relevant product and service markets of considerable complexity. Even to establish the relevant facts and issues is hard enough, but to apply the ECMR criteria in a fair and consistent way to such a large number of cases, whilst fully complying with the procedural requirements of the Regulation, has proved almost too onerous a responsibility.

A number of measures had been taken by the Commission, to cope with this situation, and they included:

— a new simplified procedure for routine phase-1 cases;

— added emphasis on the pre-notification procedures, including the publication of 'Best Practice' principles; and

— a tendency to declare notifications incomplete (often as a tactical device to give further time for the Commission to consider difficult cases).

Perhaps the most significant consequence of the pressures of the caseload on Commission officials has been the increasing tendency to encourage, at an early stage in the case, offers of concessions and obligations, even before the Commission had itself fully identified the competitive issues which the case presented. This happened often when the parties were seeking to obtain a phase-1 clearance and hoping that by offering early concessions, they would avoid being required to undergo a phase-2 inquiry. Moreover, the Commission was still concerned that its jurisdiction is still inadequate, in that a large number of concentrations with important cross-border effects did not meet the turnover requirements of Article 1 and, therefore, had to be referred to one or more national competition authorities.

7.2 THE 2002 CRISIS

The pressure for reform has been further increased as the result of the three successive adverse judgments of the CFI between June and October 2002, mentioned above, which not only annulled blocking decisions of the Commission but, as already mentioned, contained severe criticisms of both procedural and substantive aspects of its work. Commissioner Monti and the new Director General of DG Comp, Philip Lowe, have been forced by such events to accelerate the process of reform already set in train by the Commission's Green Paper published in December 2001.

The areas where the Green Paper itself had already indicated the possibility of change included:

— the amendment of Article 1(3) thresholds to include all cases where the parties have to obtain clearances from at least three Member States' authorities;

— the replacement of the existing criterion of dominance in Article 2 by the test of whether the merger will lead to a 'substantial lessening of competition';

— greater flexibility in the use of both Article 9 and Article 22(3); and

— procedural improvements which could allow the parties or the Commission on occasion to 'stop the clock' and thus allow more time for analysis of appropriate remedies.

In a major speech in Brussels on 7 November 2002, soon after the last of the three adverse CFI rulings, Commissioner Monti announced that he would shortly be submitting a package of reforms to the Regulation to the full Commission.

7.3 THE REVIEW PROPOSALS

Five weeks later there were therefore published: (i) major amendments to the Regulation; (ii) details of important procedural and organizational changes within DG Comp; and (iii) a Notice on the appraisal of horizontal mergers under the Regulation.[56]

The major changes proposed through the Regulation itself were as follows:

— Article 2 containing the substantive criteria for the assessment of concentrations should be amended; after paragraph (1) listing the matters which the Commission should take into account in making its appraisal, a new paragraph (2) defines a dominant position (by one or more undertakings) 'for the purpose of this Regulation' as where 'they hold the economic power to influence appreciably and sustainably the parameters of competition, in particular, prices, production, quality of output, distribution or innovation, or appreciably to foreclose competition'. The determination of 'dominance' in future under Article 82 cases would no longer, therefore, necessarily impact on the more specific meaning to be given to the word in the Merger Regulation.

— Article 4 dealing with the notification of a concentration with Community dimension to the Commission should be amended, so as to provide an opportunity for parties to request that it should be referred for examination rather by a Member State; the Member State then has ten days in which to express either agreement or disagreement with the request. The Commission then in turn has twenty working days in which to decide whether to retain the case or pass it to the Member State concerned.

— Article 4 also deals with the situation where a concentration not of Community dimension, but affecting more than one Member State, is the subject of a request by the parties that it nevertheless be examined by the Commission; and if all Member States concerned (or at least three Member States) agree to this the Commission would then take exclusive jurisdiction in the case. Negotiations over these matters can take place at a pre-notification stage.

— The procedural requirements for putting both Articles 9 and 22(3) into effect would also be simplified in other ways.

---

[56] [2003] 4 CMLR 230–35.

— The rules governing notification of a concentration are to be relaxed, so as to allow it to be done either before or after a full agreement has been entered into between the parties or a public bid made.

— Additional time would be allowed under both phase-1 and phase-2 for the Commission to reach its decision. In Phase 1 the normal period for the procedure would be twenty-five working days, and this period can be extended up to a total of thirty-five working days in those cases where remedies are being offered by the parties. In phase-2 the normal period would be ninety working days, with a further automatic extension of fifteen working days if remedies are being offered by the parties. Moreover a further extension of up to twenty working days could be taken, if the parties request it within fifteen working days of the opening of the phase-2 inquiry. Thereafter it is only the Commission which could initiate this further extension, provided that the parties also agree.

— The Commission's decision would (contrary to the terms of the Notice which it issued in 2001) be deemed to cover ancillary restrictions on the parties imposed as part of the agreement between them.

7.4 PROCEDURAL CHANGES

The internal organization and working procedures of DG Comp are to be revised and new checks and balances introduced in order to strengthen the economic analysis and fact finding processes which had been severely criticized by the Court of First Instance. These changes would include:

— the creation of the post of a 'Chief Competition Economist' within DG Comp, with a team of economists working for him who will be involved in all major cases;

— the appointment in such cases of a 'peer review' panel of experienced officials, to review provisional conclusions of the investigating team and providing a necessary 'fresh pair of eyes';

— allowing companies involved an earlier opportunity to have access to the file and to review third party submissions made to the Commission in connection with the case;

— the holding of regular 'state of play' meetings between the Commission and the parties during the process, so that these parties are kept fully aware of the progress of investigation and the thinking of the Commission on the merits of the case; and

— the publication of a revised and expanded guidelines on 'Best Practices' in the conduct of such cases.

7.5 NOTICE ON THE APPRAISAL OF HORIZONTAL MERGERS

The Notice is a substantial document of just under 100 paragraphs embodying the experience of the Commission in the many horizontal merger cases it has examined since the Regulation came into force in 1990 and also the case law of the Community Courts. It examines a number of aspects of such cases including:

— the likelihood of anti-competitive effects caused by the merger;

— the relevance of 'buyer power' as a countervailing force to the increased economic power of the parties to the merger;

— the likelihood of new entry and of efficiencies resulting from the merger; and

— the conditions for a 'failing firm' defence.

It points out that such mergers may significantly impede effective competition in one or more of three ways:

— by creating or strengthening an already powerful market position, by enabling price increases by the dominant undertaking, without constraint from existing competitors or customers;

— by eliminating competitive constraints in an oligopolistic market on the leading players, with similar results by way of increased prices (these first two outcomes are normally referred to as 'unilateral effects'); and

— by changing the nature of competition in an oligopolistic market by making it easier for sellers (whether or not they previously did so) to coordinate their conduct (this is normally referred to as a 'coordinated effect').

The Notice examines also certain factors that may need to enter the consideration of the extent of the economic power that the merged undertakings may have or acquire including:

— economies of scale or scope;

— privileged access to supplies of raw material, etc.;

— highly developed distribution and sales networks; and

— access on a privileged basis to capital or relevant technology.

It also reviews in detail the nature of oligopolistic markets and the way in which they may react to mergers by leading players within them, utilizing in particular the terms of the judgment of the Court of First Instance in *Airtours*. A review of the likely effects of all these changes to the operation of the Merger Regulation is contained in the final chapter of this book.

19

JOINT VENTURES AND HORIZONTAL CO-OPERATION AGREEMENTS

1. INTRODUCTION

1.1 WHY JOINT VENTURES ARE FORMED

There are many situations in which a business undertaking, looking at possible developments of its future commercial activities, will decide that it needs a partner (or even more than one) to share in a particular project. Whilst the natural desire to 'go it alone' may be strong, it often has to acknowledge that the development of existing products (let alone the research and development required) may demand investment too great for its own resources. It may, for example, have adequate personnel but inadequate finance; alternatively, whilst finance may be no problem its staff may lack the required expertise. This is particularly likely in areas of quickly developing high technology such as electronics, computers, media, and telecommunications in which an increasing number of undertakings are now involved. The sheer pace of technical and technological development, coupled with an increasing liberalization of many markets throughout the European Union, means that even companies with a powerful position as incumbent national operators in their own home telecommunications market now find that they have to seek partners for developing new services and for finding customers for them on a cross-border basis.

  The task of choosing such a partner is never easy but will necessarily involve careful consideration of the known abilities and resources of the undertakings which themselves might be expected to be their chief rivals in this new field. Such undertakings may be actual competitors already or merely potential competitors. The undertaking being considered for partnership may not be a competitor, actual or potential, but may have expertise in a totally different area which may offer possibilities for combination in the creation of novel products or services. The degree of co-operation proposed may be quite limited, e.g. the operation of joint purchasing arrangements or shared laboratory work, or alternatively may be very extensive, e.g. a proposed merger of the parties' entire interests in a particular field with a consequential need to give up their individual business in that market in favour of the new joint enterprise. A national telecommunications operator may have in place an existing communication network, through which it is seeking to provide not only conventional voice telephony services, but also a range of new services, which may include video conferencing and business data transmission, as well as the provision of digital television services or cable or satellite services. Its potential partner or partners may have customers and expertise in all these areas but, as newcomers, lack access to a sufficient communication network. A joint venture may be the natural outcome from such a situation; indeed a high proportion of all new ventures coming before the European Commission involve telecommunications, often linked to Internet, cable, and satellite services.

What will be required in each case is a structure that is adequate and appropriate to support the task that the joint venture will fulfil. In each case, there would seem at least to be the need for:

— the creation of either a separate legal undertaking, or at least a recognizable joint committee or informal organization clearly identifiable as separate from its parents;

— the transfer by the parents to the new undertaking of personnel and assets (often including intellectual property rights);

— the allocation by formal decision to the new undertaking of responsibility for carrying out its allotted functions; and

— effective joint control by the parents of the joint venture.

1.2 CONTROL OF A JOINT VENTURE

Shared control of a joint venture by its parents can be achieved in a number of ways and this will vary according to the circumstances of the individual case. It may be based on retention of ownership or rights to the use of some or all of the assets of the joint venture such as plant, machine tools, patents, trademarks, and know-how. It is often found in the constitution of the joint venture including the composition of its board of directors or managing committee. It may also be contained in contracts between the joint venture's parents and the joint venture itself as to the running of the business, e.g. the terms of licence agreements for intellectual property rights retained by the parents but licensed to the joint venture.

The essence of joint control is that the parent companies must agree on decisions concerning the activities of the joint venture because of their respective rights of ownership in the joint venture or because the terms of contracts or other provisions in its constitution. If one of the parent companies alone can decide on the commercial activities and strategy of the joint venture then there is no joint control and control will remain in the one company which has the dominant influence.

In the majority of situations joint control is based on the terms of the agreement between the parent companies, as will be illustrated by a number of the cases considered in this chapter. The constitution of the joint venture will contain the provisions required by each party to ensure that they retain sufficient legal rights to ensure that co-operation is required between them over its business strategy. It is important however to distinguish decisions taken by the joint ventures as *shareholders* as compared with those taken to carry out the *managerial* and *commercial aims* of the joint venture. The latter decisions are taken by the governing body, normally the board of directors, of the joint venture. It is at this level that one looks for involvement by the parent companies if the requirement of joint control is to be satisfied. The possession simply of powers referable to the rights of shareholders, e.g. as to the issue of new shares or ultimate closure of the business, do not alone give sufficient control to constitute joint control. If therefore there are several participants in a joint venture it may be that only some of them will, by virtue of their larger shareholding or other rights conferred on them by the joint venture agreement, be considered to have the necessary elements of joint control required by the ECMR.

1.3 THE DISTINCTION BETWEEN JOINT VENTURES THAT ARE CONCENTRATIONS AND THOSE THAT ARE NOT

Having established the essential elements of a joint venture, it is next important to understand when a joint venture is treated as a 'concentration' and therefore potentially subject to the substantive and procedural provisions and timetables of the ECMR, as already described in detail in Chapters 17 and 18. The detailed requirements for a 'concentration' are set out in the next section of this chapter but, in broad terms, require that:

(a) parent companies are acquiring joint control of the joint venture; and

(b) the aggregate turnover of the parent company for the joint venture reaches the thresholds for world and EC turnover, set out in Article 1; and

(c) that the joint venture itself is 'full-function', performing on a lasting basis all the functions of an autonomous economic entity.

If a joint venture satisfies (a) in respect of the required element of joint control, but fails to satisfy both the requirements of (b) and (c), it will not be regarded as a 'concentration'. It will however be potentially within the scope of Article 81(1), provided that it falls within the specific conditions set out in that Article, as well as subject possibly to provisions of national competition law. Those joint ventures however which raise no competition issues will of course fall outside the scope of both Article 81(1) and national competition law.

The treatment of joint ventures under EC competition law has changed over the years. At the beginning, all joint ventures which might affect trade between Member States, and which had as their object or effect restriction of competition within the Common Market, were subject to Articles 81(1) and (3); however, the treatment of such joint ventures changed when the ECMR came into force in September 1990 and, for the first time, brought within its definition of 'concentration' certain categories of joint ventures.

Originally, the only joint ventures that were treated as 'concentrations', and therefore within the scope of ECMR, were those known as 'concentrative' joint ventures, which (as a *positive* matter) performed on a lasting basis all the functions of an autonomous economic entity and, as a *negative* matter, did not give rise to coordination of the competitive behaviour of the parents amongst themselves, or between the parents and the joint venture.

For a variety of reasons, the parties to such agreements and their lawyers often sought to frame joint venture agreements and arrangements in ways that could be brought within the definition of 'concentrative' rather than 'co-operative'; over the early years during which the Merger Regulation operated the Commission moved in favour of broadening the definition given to the concentrative joint venture. The influence however of the Merger Regulation on the definition and characterization of joint ventures has also had its effects on the treatment by DG Comp of co-operative joint ventures.

Even this more liberal approach adopted by the Commission left many full-function joint ventures unable to qualify to be dealt with under the terms of ECMR, but still subject to

Article 81 and its more protracted timescale for assessment. This situation has from 1 March 1998 been changed by Council Regulation 1310/97 amending Article 3(2) of 4064/89, to the effect that *all* full-function joint ventures are now dealt with under the procedural rules and timescale of ECMR. This procedure will mean that, in all cases that would previously have been regarded as 'co-operative' because of the scope that they might have had for the coordination of the activities of the parent companies, the Commission will have a dual test to apply:

(i)   the criteria as to *market dominance* laid down in Article 2(1) of ECMR for assessing *full-function joint ventures*, which are the same as those applicable for the assessment of concentrations where a single bidder is acquiring 'decisive control' over the target; and

(ii) the test of whether *the particular joint venture* has as its object or effect the co-ordination of the competitive behaviour of undertakings that remain independent, under *the criteria of Article 81(1) and (3)*, which are imported into the ECMR by its Article 2(4), albeit in a slightly amended form.

2. THE DEFINITION OF JOINT VENTURES WHICH ARE CONCENTRATIONS UNDER THE MERGER REGULATION

2.1 ECMR ARTICLE 3(1) AND (2): DEFINITION OF A CONCENTRATION

As explained in Chapter 17, it was after many years of negotiation that the terms of the ECMR were finally agreed by Member States and came into force in September 1990. The new regulation provided not only a different substantive test for the assessment of concentrations which adopted the criteria of 'dominance' set out in Article 2, but provided a more streamlined procedure and timeframe for the assessment of individual cases (currently set out in Regulation 447/98), than under Regulation 17/62 for Articles 81 and 82. From the start, it was the intention of the ECMR that certain joint ventures would be able to benefit from the new and speedier procedures of ECMR and would no longer be subject to the procedural regime for Articles 81(1) and (3).

The term 'joint venture' covers a wide range of activities, from the kind of market-sharing and price-fixing arrangements closely akin to a cartel at one extreme to an agreement at the other to merge completely the activities of the participants in a particular product or service whilst the parent companies cease to operate in that market themselves. While the former still require to be analysed under Article 81(1) and (3), the latter would more appropriately be treated as a concentration. It was necessary for the ECMR to set out the criteria for deciding which joint ventures would in future be treated under the criteria appropriate to those of ECMR, which in turn would lead to a more favourable procedure and timescale being available for their assessment. There had always been complaints that the time taken for assessment of joint ventures under Article 81 by the officials in DG Comp was unpredictable and too lengthy; the arrival of the ECMR with its apparently preferential treatment for the 'concentrative' category of joint venture further strengthened the claim by industry for reforms in the treatment even for those joint ventures not covered by the definition of a 'concentration'.

Originally, therefore, to be treated as concentrative and within the ECMR, a joint venture had to meet not only the world and EC turnover requirements contained in Articles 1 and 5, but also had to be:

— legally under joint control of two or more parties;

— formed on a lasting basis to carry out all the functions of an autonomous economic entity (the *positive* condition);

— but not having as its object or effect the coordination of activity, either between its parent companies or between the parent companies and the joint venture (the *negative* condition).

Any joint venture unable to meet both the positive and negative conditions would be described not as 'concentrative', but as 'co-operative' and would fall within the jurisdiction of Article 81 and of Regulation 17/62 with its considerably longer and more unpredictable procedures and time limits. Between 1990 and 1998, the interpretation and application of the negative condition, in particular, caused considerable difficulties both to the Commission itself and also to the parties to such joint ventures. In Commission 'Interface Notices' published in 1990 and in 1994, attempts were made to clarify the distinction; professional legal skills became increasingly utilized to frame joint ventures in such a way as to emphasize the 'concentrative' elements and to downplay the 'coordinating' effects or objectives. The procedures and timetable of ECMR were regarded as so much superior to those operated by the Commission under Article 81 that such efforts were regarded as necessary; in many cases, however, they were not successful in convincing the Commission that a particular joint venture should indeed be treated as a concentration.

2.2 THE EFFECT OF REGULATION 1310/97

The definition of a 'concentration' for the purposes of ECMR was however changed in important respects by Regulation 1310/97, which came into effect on 1 March 1998. This eliminated the 'negative' condition referred to above and expanded the classification of joint ventures falling under the ECMR by limiting the requirements to those of joint control and the 'positive' requirement of full-function. The revised text of Article 3(2) of ECMR reflecting this major policy change now simply reads as follows:

The creation of a joint venture performing on a lasting basis all the functions of an autonomous economic entity, shall constitute a concentration within the meaning of paragraph 1(b) of Article 3.

New Notices were published in 1998 providing guidance as to the Commission's approach to the amended Article 3(2) of the ECMR and its effect on these two requirements. Definition of joint control is dealt with in the Notice on the concept of a concentration[1] whilst the definition of a full-function joint venture is found in a separate Notice[2] dealing separately with this issue. It should always be remembered however that a Commission Notice has no

---

[1] [1998] OJ C66/5.   [2] [1998] OJ 66/1.

legislative force and represents simply guidance as to the current practice of the Commission (rather than hard law), which can on occasion be overruled by decisions of a Community court. On occasion, the Commission has even been known to depart from the approach of its own Notice.

2.3 JOINT CONTROL

In many cases joint control of the joint venture is based not upon shareholding alone but upon the detailed terms of shareholder's agreement between the companies; a majority shareholder may extend to one or more minority shareholders a contractual right to take part in the control of the joint venture. If two undertakings each hold half of the equity of a joint venture, even without further agreement between them, both will be obliged perman-ently to co-operate so as to avoid reciprocal blocking votes on decisions affecting the joint venture's commercial activities. The same would apply to joint ventures with three or more parents if each of them had a right of veto relating to strategic decisions on the business policy of the joint venture. A joint venture with a complex structure may alternatively find itself controlled by a substantial number of undertakings that between them control a majority of the capital or hold together the requisite voting rights. In such cases joint control could only be presumed if the convergence of their economic interests support the notion of a common policy of the parent companies towards the operation of the joint venture.

Paragraphs 21 to 24 and 34 of the 1998 Notice on the concept of 'concentration' provides some guidance as to the notion of joint control:

21. Joint control may exist even where there is no equality between the two parent companies in votes or in representation in decision-making bodies or where there are more than two parent companies. This is the case where minority shareholders have additional rights which allow them to veto decisions which are essential for the strategic commercial behaviour of the joint venture. These veto rights may be set out in the statute of the joint venture or conferred by agreement between its parent companies. The veto rights themselves may operate by means of a specific quorum required for decisions taken in the shareholders' meeting or in the board of directors to the extent that the parent companies are represented in this board. It is also possible that strategic decisions are subject to approval by a body, e.g. supervisory board, where the minority shareholders are represented and form part of the quorum needed for such decisions.

22. These veto rights must be related to strategic decisions on the business policy of the joint venture. They must go beyond the veto rights normally accorded to minority shareholders in order to protect their financial interests as investors in the joint venture. This normal protection of the rights of minority shareholders is related to decisions on the essence of the joint venture, such as changes in the statute, increase or decrease of the capital or liquidation. A veto right, for example, which prevents the sale or winding up of the joint venture, does not confer joint control on the minority shareholder concerned.

23. In contrast, veto rights which confer joint control typically include decisions and issues such as the budget, the business plan, major investments or the appointment of senior management. The acquisition of joint control, however, does not require that the acquirer has the power to exercise decisive influence on the day-to-day running of an undertaking. The crucial element is that the veto rights are sufficient to enable the parent companies to exercise such influence in relation to the strategic business behaviour of the joint venture. Moreover, it is not necessary to establish that an acquirer of joint control of the joint venture will actually make use of its decisive

influence. The possibility to use this influence and, hence, the mere existence of the veto rights, is sufficient.

24. In order to acquire joint control, it is not necessary for a minority shareholder to have all the veto rights mentioned above. It may be sufficient that some, or even one such right, exists. Whether or not this is the case depends upon the precise content of the veto right itself and also the importance of this right in the context of the specific business of the joint venture . . .

34. In the case where a new joint venture is established, as opposed to the acquisition of minority shareholdings in a pre-existing company, there is a higher probability that the parent companies are carrying out a deliberate common policy. This is true in particular where each parent company provides a contribution to the joint venture which is vital for its operation (e.g. specific technologies, local know-how or supply agreements). In these circumstances, the parent companies may be able to operate the joint venture with full co-operation only with each other's agreement on the most important strategic decisions, even if there is no express provision of any veto rights. The greater the number of parent companies involved in such a joint venture, however, the more remote is the likelihood of this situation occurring.

The Notice also includes additional comments on the significance on the nature of the business plan of the joint venture, over which the parties are given a veto right.[3] The more specific such a plan is about the measures to be taken in order to achieve the aims of the joint venture, the more significant are the veto rights in establishing the existence of joint control. This is often the most important issue which the Commission has to resolve in analysing such cases.

2.4 PERFORMANCE OF THE 'POSITIVE CONDITION': FULL-FUNCTION JOINT VENTURES

To qualify as a concentration, the joint venture must be performing on a lasting basis all the functions of an autonomous economic entity, i.e. be capable of performing all the same functions (e.g. research and development, manufacturing, sales, etc) that other independent undertakings in the same market would be carrying out. The 1998 Notice on the concept of full-function joint ventures provides guidance as to how the Commission will assess this 'positive condition', but it is important to be clear that the Notice does not give guidance as to the way in which the substantive provisions of the joint venture and their effect on competition should be assessed; the Notice is concerned solely with the categorization of the individual joint venture in order to decide whether it is to be dealt with under the ECMR or under Article 81.

The approach of the Commission to the interpretation of this 'positive condition' is set out in paragraphs 11 to 15 of this Notice, as follows:

11. Article 3(2) provides that the joint venture must perform, on a lasting basis, all the functions of an autonomous economic entity. Joint ventures which satisfy this requirement bring about a lasting change in the structure of the undertakings concerned. They are referred to in this Notice as 'full-function' joint ventures.

12. Essentially this means that the joint venture must operate on a market, performing the functions normally carried out by undertakings operating on the same market. In order to do so the joint venture must have a management dedicated to its day-to-day operations and access to sufficient resources including finance, staff and assets (tangible and intangible) in order to conduct on a lasting basis its business activities within the area provided for in the joint venture agreement.

---

[3] Para. 26.

13. A joint venture is not full-function if it only takes over one specific function within the parent companies' business activities without access to the market. This is the case, for example, for joint ventures limited to research and development or production. Such joint ventures are auxiliary to their parent companies' products and, therefore, acts principally as a sales agency. However, the fact that a joint venture makes use of the distribution network or outlet of one or more of its parent companies normally will not disqualify it as 'full-function', as long as the parent companies are acting only as agents of the joint venture.

14. The strong presence of the parent companies in upstream or downstream markets is a factor to be taken into consideration in assessing the full-function character of a joint venture where this presence leads to substantial sales or purchases between the parent companies and the joint venture. The fact that the joint venture relies almost entirely on sales to its parent companies or purchases from them only for an initial start-up period does not normally affect the full-function character of the joint venture. Such a start-up period may be necessary in order to establish the joint venture on a market. It will normally not exceed a period of three years, depending on the specific conditions of the market in question.

Where sales from the joint venture to the parent companies are intended to be made on a lasting basis, the essential question is whether, regardless of these sales, the joint venture is geared to play an active role on the market. In this respect the relative proportion of these sales compared with the total production of the joint venture is an important factor. Another factor is whether sales to the parent companies are made on the basis of normal commercial conditions.

In relation to purchases made by the joint venture from its parent companies, the full-function character of the joint venture is questionable in particular where little value is added to the products or services concerned at the level of the joint venture itself. In such a situation, the joint venture may be closer to a joint sales agency. However, in contrast to this situation where a joint venture is active in a trade market and performs the normal functions of a trading company in such a market, it normally will not be an auxiliary sales agency but a full-function joint venture. A trade market is characterized by the existence of companies which specialize in the selling and distribution of products without being vertically integrated in addition to those which are integrated, and where different sources of supply are available for the products in question. In addition, many trade markets may require operators to invest in specific facilities such as outlets, stockholding, warehouses, depots, transport fleets and sales personnel. In order to constitute a full-function joint venture in a trade market, an undertaking must have the necessary facilities and be likely to obtain a substantial proportion of its supplies not only from its parent companies but also from other competing sources.

15. Furthermore, the joint venture must be intended to operate on a lasting basis. The fact that the parent companies commit to the joint venture the resources described above normally demonstrates that this is the case. In addition, agreements setting up a joint venture often provide for certain contingencies, for example, the failure of the joint venture or fundamental disagreement as between the parent companies. This may be achieved by the incorporation of provisions for the eventual dissolution of the joint venture itself or the possibility for one or more parent companies to withdraw from the joint venture. This kind of provision does not prevent the joint venture from being considered as operating on a lasting basis. The same is normally true where the agreement specifies a period for the duration of the joint venture where this period is sufficiently long in order to bring about a lasting change in the structure of the undertakings concerned, or where the agreement provides for the possible continuation of the joint venture beyond this period. By contrast, the joint venture will not be considered to operate on a lasting basis where it is established for a short finite duration. This would be the case, for example, where a joint venture is established in order to construct a specific project such as a power plant, but it will not be involved in the operation of the plant once its construction has been completed.

2.5 THE ABOLITION OF THE 'NEGATIVE CONDITION'

The abolition from 1998 of the negative requirement of 'no coordination between the parties to the joint venture' has greatly simplified the characterization of joint ventures, i.e. whether they are concentrations or not. However, this does not mean that the Commission will ignore the issue of coordination when deciding as a substantive matter whether to grant a clearance to the transaction. In its substantive analysis, the Commission will consider not only whether the concentration itself creates or strengthens a dominant position (under Article 2(1)), but will also examine the issue of coordination. A new Article 2(4) has been added to ECMR by Regulation 1310/97 which reads:

To the extent that the creation of a joint venture constituting a concentration pursuant to Article 3 has as its object or effect the co-ordination of the competitive behaviour of undertakings that remain independent, such co-ordination shall be appraised in accordance with the criteria of Article 81(1) and (3) of the Treaty, with a view to establishing whether or not the operation is compatible with the common market.

In making this appraisal, the Commission shall take into account in particular:

— whether two or more parent companies retain to a significant extent activities in the same market as the joint venture or in a market which is downstream or upstream from that of the joint venture or in a neighbouring market closely related to this market;

— whether the co-ordination which is the direct consequence of the creation of the joint venture affords the undertakings concerned the possibility of eliminating competition in respect of a substantial part of the products or services in question.

3. JOINT VENTURES WHICH ARE CONCENTRATIONS: THEIR TREATMENT UNDER ECMR

3.1 ARTICLES 2(1) TO (3): THE APPLICATION OF THE NORMAL ECMR CRITERIA TO JOINT VENTURES

In recent years approximately three hundred concentrations have been annually notified to the Commission on Form CO and, of these, approximately half are joint ventures. Under the provisions of Article 6(1), the Commission has in each case to examine the notification to see if the transaction in question falls within the scope of the regulation. If the joint venture, once the criteria set out before have been applied, can be classified as a concentration and the appropriate turnover of the parties under Article 1 and Article 5 reaches Community dimension, the Commission implements its 'first-phase' proceeding. If for any reason a notification cannot be classified as a concentration of Community dimension, the application will be rejected, although it may be considered under Article 81 and possibly under national competition law.

First-phase proceedings normally last a month, though in some circumstances they can be extended by a further two weeks. By the end of this period, the Commission will have determined whether the case raises serious doubts as to its compatibility with the Common Market (Article 6(2)). If serious doubts have not been raised, the concentration will be declared 'compatible' and cleared; this may be on the basis that it has not raised any competitive issues at all even though, because of the combined turnover of the parties calculated under Article 1, the transaction had to go through the process of notification to the Commission under ECMR. Alternatively, the Commission may have granted clearance after the first phase examination in return for commitments by the parties to amend or remove particularly clauses in the joint venture agreement which are regarded as unnecessarily restrictive of competition. Commitments would not only relate to clauses in the agreement, but might require divestiture of assets in order to eliminate the problem of creating or strengthening a dominant position.

If serious doubts are raised, the joint venture will be passed into the second phase under Article 6(1)(c) and will be dealt with like any other concentration by way of further detailed examination. A recent example of the way in which such cases are dealt with is *Smith & Nephew/Beiersdorf*.[4] The Commission found that the proposed 50/50 joint venture would involve a substantial horizontal overlap between the parties' respective products in bandages and other wound care items. In particular, there were overlaps in several national markets in the EC for a number of such products. To remove the concerns of the Commission, the parties agreed to divest themselves of some trademarks and business activities in these Member States to third parties. The Commission was also concerned initially with possible 'spillover effects' from the joint venture into other markets in which both companies were engaged, but after detailed investigation concluded that the risk was minimal.

Postal services specializing in outbound cross-border mail was the sector involved in another recent complex case, *TPO/TPG/SPPL*.[5] The parties were the national postal operators of the United Kingdom, The Netherlands, and Singapore. After close examination of the markets for this service in each of these three jurisdictions, the outcome was an unconditional clearance in respect of the United Kingdom because of the existence of sufficient competition there and the existence of only modest entry barriers and full transparency of pricing. By contrast, the Dutch market was regarded as uncompetitive and TPG (the Dutch national postal operator) was required to dispose of its subsidiary already engaged in such services, so that the joint venture could be allowed to proceed in The Netherlands for the other two participants alone.

It is important to emphasize that the criteria which are applied under the ECMR to the concentrative aspect of joint ventures are no different to those which are applying to all other 'concentrations with a Community dimension' under the Regulation. The relevant product or service markets for the joint venture will be analysed and findings made as to the markets in which the parent companies already operate and those in which the joint venture is intended to operate. These markets may be the same as those in which the parents operate, or may be related, or may occasionally be totally distinct, though this is unusual. Thus, for example, in the *Shell/BASF*[6] joint venture case, an analysis was made of the complex arrangements to be made under which the joint venture would operate in Western Europe in the polyethylene business on behalf of both of its parent companies, Shell and BASF. The joint venture was to operate a number of factories previously operated by the parents, would receive supplies of raw material from both of them and would in turn utilize the production from the factories to supply a number of those other factories which the parent companies

---

[4] Case JV/54 (decision of 30 January 2001).   [5] Case Comp/M 1915 (decision of 30 March 2001).
[6] [1998] OJ C81/5. Case IV /M1041 (decision of 23 December 1997).

would retain. The arrangements for a joint venture are often very complex; this places major pressure upon both the parties and the Commission to ensure that the full investigation of the case is carried out within the appropriate time limit applicable under the Merger Regulation.

In *Shell/BASF* the markets for various categories of polyethylene produced by the two parent companies was analysed by the Commission, which reached the conclusion that, because there was a high degree of supply side substitutability between the various companies producing the basic product and the number of other major companies with shares in the relevant markets, the creation of the joint venture would not give the parties a dominant position in them, nor in the related markets of polyethylene technology.

The examination, therefore, of a joint venture between X and Y which qualifies as a concentration under ECMR takes place in exactly the same way under Article 2(1) to 2(3) as an examination of an acquisition by X of Y, in terms of the effect that the concentration is likely to have in creating or strengthening a dominant position in relevant markets. In addition, however, a joint venture may also (in certain cases only) be subject to the special rules of Article 2(4), which relate to the possibility of the concentration having as its object or effect the coordination by the parties their future activities in the same or related markets.

3.2 ARTICLE 2(4): THE APPLICATION OF THE SPECIAL RULES APPLICABLE TO COORDINATION BETWEEN THE PARTIES TO JOINT VENTURES

In many cases of joint ventures that are concentrations, the problem of the coordination of the commercial activities of the parent companies, through the operation of the joint venture, will not be regarded as significant. If, however, the Commission find that a concentration does raise such issues, the application of Article 2(4) will come into play and officials of the Directorate General for Competition familiar with the relevant sectors will seek to apply the principles of Article 81(1) and 81(3) to it.

Article 2(4) applies to the subsequent assessment of the join venture in the following circumstances:

— When a joint venture performs all the functions of an independent economic entity;
— When either its object or effect is, *inter alia*, to coordinate the competitive behaviour between undertakings that remain independent.

Whilst there is no decision yet of the Commission blocking a joint venture because of the degree to which it enabled coordination of a competitive behaviour of the parent companies without meeting the four-fold requirements of Article 81(3), it is the task of the Commission in such cases to apply all the conditions contained in Articles 81(1) and 81(3) to the particular case.

In particular, the Commission will have to consider whether, as a matter of fact, two or more parent companies continue to trade to a significant extent in either:

— the same markets as those in which the joint venture will be operative;
— an upstream market;
— a downstream market; or
— a neighbouring market, which is closely related.

For example, if the proposed joint venture was to operate an oil refinery, the investigation by the Commission would examine whether the parent companies were retaining commercial activities, *inter alia*:

— in the oil refining business itself;

— in the oil exploration or tanker business;

— in the retail fuel business (service stations);

— in, for example, chemical manufacturing where certain processes and products similar to those in the oil industry might also be utilized.

As a matter of prediction, the Commission will have to assess whether it would be possible for the parents to utilize the joint venture to eliminate competition in respect of a substantial part of the role of the products or services, i.e. in any of the possible markets considered above. The possibility may be provided either by the actual terms of the joint venture agreement or as the result of the existing commercial strengths and experience of the parties and their existing alliances; alternatively, a combination of these factors may lead to such a conclusion that coordination is likely. Having established whether the coordination is a possible consequence of the establishment of the joint venture, the Commission next has to seek to predict whether the coordination which the operation of the joint venture would permit, will itself actually enable such an elimination of competition to which Article 81 refers.

It is important to be clear about the nature of the 'coordination' with which Article 2(4) is concerned. It applies only to coordination involving undertakings 'which remain independent'. If only one of the parent companies is active on the relevant market, the Article does not normally apply even if that market is the one in which the joint venture is to operate; the likelihood of coordination between the joint venture and that parent is taken for granted and is not enough to warrant the application of Article 2(4), as the joint venture is insufficiently 'independent' from that parent. If, by contrast, both parent companies are active on the same market, the consequences of such coordination need not, however, be identical or symmetrical for them for the Article to apply. It is sufficient that there is some degree of effect on the conduct or interrelationship of the parent companies. Moreover, when the Article applies, all the factors relevant to Article 81(1) and (3) can be considered.

3.3 CASE LAW UNDER ARTICLE 2(4)

In a number of cases, mainly involving telecommunications, the Commission has already been required to give careful attention to the application of Article 2(4). Some 20 per cent of joint venture concentration cases, under ECMR, raise issues of coordination and examples of such cases can be found in the Annual Report of the Commission and the regular Commission publication 'Competition Policy Newsletter'. An example was *Telia/Telenor/ Schibsted*.[7] Telia and Telenor were the national telephone authorities in Sweden and Norway, respectively; Shibsted was a Norwegian publishing company. Both Telia and Telenor already competed on the Swedish market for website production and Internet gateway services. The Commission did not contest their submission that the joint venture did not have as its

---

[7] Case JV/1 (decision dated 27 May 1998).

object the coordination of their activities on these markets, but was concerned to examine its effect. The function of the joint venture was to provide website production sites and Internet gateway services in Sweden, so as to provide users with easier access. The joint venture would be controlled as to 40 per cent each by Telia and Shipsted and 20 per cent by Telenor.

The Commission found that two main markets were relevant. The first was the production of websites and here the aggregate share of all the parties was less than 10 per cent. Even if the parent companies were to choose to coordinate such activities, they would still not be able to have a restriction on competition and concerns under Article 2(4) were therefore not relevant here. The second relevant market was the dial-up Internet access market for Swedish consumers; here both Telia and Telenor had present substantial market shares of between 25 per cent and 40 per cent and 10 per cent to 25 per cent, respectively.

The Commission felt, however, that the relevant national markets were growing so fast that these existing percentages were too ephemeral to be of much significance and the growth in the markets would make, notwithstanding any coordination of the parties' conduct, restrictions in competition unlikely. On these grounds, no reason under Article 2(4) for restricting the clearance of the joint venture would be found.

The 1998 Annual Report on Competition Policy[8] identified some important issues which have arisen in these cases. These included:

— the relative size of the product or service market involved (both for the joint venture itself and for the parent companies). In general, the smaller the intended market for the joint venture, the less likely the incentive for parent companies to coordinate their commercial activities in the same or related markets;

— the nature of the markets, for example the degree to which their technical content or 'leading edge' characteristics mean that the joint venture will, on the one hand, be independent or, on the other hand, require constant support and technological input from both parents;

— the relationship between the parent companies and whether there are existing joint ventures or other significant commercial links between them; on the other hand, a mere close relationship already existing between the parents does not mean that the newly created joint venture will not also have a separate role and be pro-competitive in its effect.

4. ARTICLE 81 AND JOINT VENTURES WHICH ARE NOT CONCENTRATIONS

4.1 INTRODUCTION

Prior to the ECMR the Commission could only deal with joint ventures as agreements under the provisions of Article 81. In each case, it had to apply the normal rules explained in detail in Chapters 6 to 8 inclusive, and ask in respect of the joint venture agreement whether:

— there was an agreement between one or more undertakings;

---

[8] Pp.77–8.

— whether it might affect trade between Member States; and
— whether it had as its object or effect the prevention or restriction of competition within the Common Market.

If Article 81(1) was applicable, then Article 81(3) also had to be considered as the participants might well wish to argue, in order to obtain an exemption, that the benefits to be expected from the joint venture will outweigh any restrictions on competition that it may involve. The parties to the joint venture would therefore have had to satisfy the Commission under Article 81(3) that it:

— contributed to improving the production or distribution of goods or to the promotion of technical or economic progress;
— whilst allowing consumers a fair share of the resulting benefit whilst not;
— imposing on the undertakings concerned restrictions not indispensable to the attainment of these objectives; nor
— affording such undertakings the possibility of eliminating competition in respect of a substantial part of the products in question.

The Commission soon came to recognize from its cases that there are almost an infinite number of ways in which two or more undertakings can choose to co-operate with each other. As already mentioned, at one end of the spectrum the degree of co-operation may be very limited, e.g. an agreement to share transport or storage facilities or to run a common training course to provide employees with relevant skills or qualifications; at the other end of the spectrum the degree of co-operation may be so considerable and close that it virtually takes on the character of a cartel, e.g. by the exchange of current commercial data on prices and customers leading to a partial or total elimination of competition between the parties. Alternatively the closer co-operation required between A and B may take the form of the establishment by them of a third undertaking, C, in which are vested activities which A and B no longer wish to carry out for themselves. They are thus able to withdraw from that particular market whilst the integration of their interests in the provision of the particular goods or services is irretrievably committed to the new entity, their joint venture.

Between these extremes lie a variety of different forms of co-operation which involve to a greater or lesser degree a commitment to each other, but would involve more than the mere sharing of facilities, whilst still falling short of a full integration of their assets and interests in a particular product or service market.

4.2 APPLICATION OF ARTICLE 81(1) TO JOINT VENTURES: BASIC PRINCIPLES

In making its assessment, the Commission would have to ask on each occasion a number of questions:

— whether the parents themselves were in actual or potential competition with each other;
— whether the parents operated in the same market as the joint venture, or in upstream, downstream, or related markets;

— what functions was the joint venture intended to perform; were they limited, e.g. sales and marketing alone, or research and development alone, or covering a wide range of objectives similar to those of an independent company (of course, in the latter case, the joint venture might qualify as a 'concentration' under the ECMR rather than be subject to Article 81);

— what freedom of action was left to the parent companies and whether they retain the right to compete fully with the joint venture or, more normally, would agree with each other to respect the proposed exclusive jurisdiction of the joint venture in a particular market and not to compete with it;

— what restrictions would be placed on the joint venture as to its right to grant licences of any intellectual property which it might itself develop in the course of its work to third parties.

The first official reaction of the Commission to the handling of such joint venture issues was the publication in July 1968 of a Notice on co-operation between undertakings.[9] This sought to describe the categories of co-operative agreements or joint ventures which it stated should not be regarded as restricting competition under the terms of Article 81(1). They included a range of the more limited categories of co-operation.

Unlike a Regulation, a Notice does not create legal rights or obligations, but simply contains the current policy views of the Commission which may well be subject to change at a later date, as has proved the case with a number of the Commission's Notices. The purpose of this particular Notice was to make clear that certain categories of co-operation having a relatively minor effect on competition were *prima facie* deemed not to fall within the terms of Article 8(1). However, it became clear that the Commission would take a cautious attitude to arrangements which involved co-operation going beyond the categories listed in the Notice. In the great majority of decisions adopted by the Commission in the 1960s and 1970s it tended to apply Article 81(1) in a broad manner to the particular agreement, but would then exempt the agreement in question under Article 81(3). This policy choice had the advantage that, through individual case examination, it provided detailed knowledge to the Commission of the workings and operation of joint ventures. Exemption would in accordance with Regulation 17/62, Article 8(1), be for a limited period only and could have conditions attached, e.g. the parties could be required to notify the Commission on an annual basis of the turnover figures for the joint venture and of the occasions on which, for example, it had refused to make supplies of products or to grant licences of technology which it had developed.

4.3 APPLICATION OF ARTICLE 81(3) TO JOINT VENTURES: BASIC PRINCIPLES

Throughout the 1970s and 1980s the Commission was gradually developing its technique of analysis of the often complex contractual arrangements entered into by the parents of the joint venture. On many occasions the parties to joint ventures would not have notified them to the Commission, being satisfied that they had no appreciable effect on competition, nor effect on trade between Member States, or possibly being prepared to take the risks of non-

[9] [1968] CMLR D 45.

notification, even though not fully satisfied on these matters. On the occasions when agreements were notified to the Commission, it would almost always continue (certainly up to the end of the 1980s) to claim that Article 81(1) was being infringed, even though it would then go on to grant exemption under Article 81(3), on some occasions after requiring certain restrictions to be taken out of the joint venture agreement.

In determining whether the joint venture satisfied the positive conditions of Article 81(3) that it made a contribution to the production or distribution of goods or to promoting technical economic progress, a number of possible factors were taken into account. Of obvious significance would be the ability of the joint venture to develop a new product, such as a drug, which neither of the parent companies had the resources themselves to develop within a realistic timescale. Such considerations might now (though not in earlier years) enable the Commission to grant the joint venture a negative clearance on the grounds that it could not be said realistically to restrict competition. In the sectors where technology was of prime importance such as communications, satellites, computers, or the media, the ability to provide new products and develop new technology responding to demand by customers for new services, often on a worldwide basis, was taken into account. The improvement of quality, the ability to realize scale economies, and the enhancement of standards of safety were also likely to be taken into account.

The second condition of Article 81(3) requires that from the production or distribution improvement or the technical or economic progress users will derive 'a fair share of the resulting benefit'. A criticism sometimes made of the Commission has been that it has not in all cases gone analytically enough into the question of whether users will actually benefit. The Commission has tended rather to make the assumption that, if the first condition as to improvements or progress is satisfied, competition will itself automatically ensure that the benefit will pass through to consumers. In some cases the benefit is not simply a reduction in price or improvement in quality but the creation of a product or service not previously available (e.g. in *Beecham/Parke, Davis*,[10] the potential benefit was the availability of a new drug to prevent damage to blood circulation not previously available on the market).

Turning to the negative conditions under Article 81(3) the first is that the restriction 'does not impose on the undertakings restrictions not indispensable to the attainment of these objectives'. This condition, although expressed negatively, could have equally well been expressed positively, i.e. whether the restriction is one which is essential (indispensable) to the attainment of the commercial objectives of the joint venture. In general the Commission has been fairly liberal in its interpretation of this condition, in that it has only opposed restrictions proposed by the parties when it appeared that these went well beyond the needs of the parties to protect their legitimate interests within the framework of the joint venture. In other words the restriction will only be deleted (or even in extreme cases cause the exemption to be refused) if it is more than a logical and reasonable consequence of the particular relationships into which the parties are entering. If, by contrast, the restriction is seen to be designed to give the parties a more secure position protected from competition than existed before, they will be challenged to justify it.

On occasion the Commission has asked therefore whether the joint venture could have been achieved in a simpler and less restrictive way, e.g. by a licensing agreement rather than by the formation of a subsidiary company accompanied by a number of restrictions on the

---

[10] [1979] OJ L70/11: [1979] 2 CMLR 157.

parents from competing with that company. *BP/Kellogg*[11] was a good example of the need for quite broad restrictions to protect the interests of the parties if they have each committed themselves to the joint venture as the way in which they would in future promote a particular aspect of their business. The parties will be allowed to protect themselves to a proportionate extent against any breaking of the essential logic of that relationship. An area, however, in which the Commission is particularly quick to intervene—if they feel restrictions are being extended too far—is when it is sought to limit the freedom of action of the parties following the termination of the joint venture. A non-competition clause between the parents is usually considered to be indispensable, as it is unreasonable to expect that the parents should allow the joint venture to compete with the parents themselves or that the parents themselves should, in spite of the new relationship between them, compete with each other in the same sector and in competition with their own created joint venture. Of course, in those cases where negative clearance was appropriate, i.e. where the joint venture had no appreciable effect on competition, such clauses would not in themselves lead to a finding that Article 81(1) and (3) were applicable, since such restrictions would be treated as ancillary to the joint venture, as clauses whose presence was commercially essential if the joint venture was to proceed at all.

The Commission is not however normally prepared to agree a long period in which, after the termination of the joint venture, the parents seek to prevent direct competition between them. Clearly there may need to be a transitional period when the existing arrangements are run down, resources allocated to the joint venture are re-transferred and fresh licensing arrangements made to permit an orderly return to the status quo. Quite often then the grant of exclusive intellectual property rights under license by the parties to each other may be justified, though in some other cases the Commission may prefer the rights to be non-exclusive. The Commission's attitude will turn very much on the circumstances of the particular case, especially the degree of competition in the relevant markets.

The final condition for an Article 81(3) exemption is that the parties should not be able to eliminate competition for a substantial part of the products (goods or services) in question. The Commission will carry out analysis of the relevant market conditions which include both the market shares of the parties in Member States and the community as a whole in the light of the respective market shares of their competitors. For example, in *Mitchell Cotts/Sofiltra*,[12] it was clear that whilst Sofiltra were strong on the French air filter market (having more than half) it was very weak in the United Kingdom, whereas with Mitchell Cotts the reverse was the case, even though its market share in the United Kingdom was considerably lower than that of Sofiltra in France. The Commission is always concerned that, after the joint venture has come into full operation, the use of it by the parents should not provide them with a mechanism for reducing or eliminating competition for a substantial part at least of the products. Collaboration therefore across a very large geographic market will prove harder to justify than if limited to a particular Member State or small group of Member States.

Clearly this condition overlaps to some extent with the assessment at the earlier stage of whether the agreement has as its object or effect the restriction of competition in the Common Market. The difference is that at the first stage the Commission is looking broadly at the overall effect of the agreement, whereas at this second stage in examining the

---

[11] [1986] 2 CMLR 619.   [12] [1987] OJ L41/31: [1988] 4 CMLR 111.

application of Article 81(3) it is more concerned with the detail of the restrictive clauses and their effects on the markets concerned. The characteristics and strength of other companies involved in the relevant markets will be important; if the competition faced by the joint venture is severe and its creation seems a logical commercial response to the competition which the parents would face, without giving them a dominant position in that market, the likelihood of an exemption is greater.

In looking at the early application by the Commission of Article 81(3) to joint venture cases, two particular features should be noted. First, the general unwillingness of the Commission to accept that Article 81(1) did not apply at all. The second, which to some degree counterbalanced the first, was that it was rare for a joint venture to be refused an exemption under Article 81(3); in most cases the control imposed by the Commission in this respect did not extend beyond the required amendment of certain restrictive clauses to reduce the effect on competition or to limit their effect to what is regarded as indispensable in the reasonable interests of the parties.

In the second half of the 1980s, rather than starting from the presumption in all cases that almost any joint venture notified to the Commission was likely to have a sufficient effect on competition to fall within the terms of Article 81(1), it began to issue decisions in which the fact that the parties' current commercial activities and their actual and potential resources were in such different sectors meant that their joint venture fell outside Article 81(1) altogether. Such a conclusion, of course, relieves the Commission from the task of having to analyse the individual restrictions contained in the joint venture agreement since they did not need to be individually examined against the requirements of Article 81(3).

Probably the first case in which this can be noted was *Optical Fibres* in 1986[13] and a similar approach is found later in the *Odin*[14] case of 1990. On the other hand, an earlier case, *ICI/Wasag*[15] illustrated the point that there can be joint ventures whose effect on competition in particular markets is potentially so serious that they have to be prohibited, rather than merely required to alter the most anti-competitive clauses in the joint venture agreement.

4.4 THE IMPACT OF THE MERGER REGULATION: PROCEDURAL CHANGES IN THE HANDLING OF CO-OPERATIVE JOINT VENTURES FROM 1990

The implementation of the ECMR from September 1990 had the effect that many of the kind of joint ventures previously considered under the terms of Article 81 were now dealt with rather under the time limits substantive criteria and procedures of ECMR. A clear preference of industry and commerce for procedures that could be completed at most within five months and, in many cases, within four weeks caused pressure to be placed on the other departments and divisions within DG Comp for a less protracted procedure under Article 81. Towards the end of 1992, procedural changes were introduced by the Commission on a voluntary administrative basis. They are now set out in Regulation 3385/94 which came into effect on 1 March 1995 and which also contains the revised Form A/B on which notifications have to be made. Under this Regulation there are provisions for the more speedy handling of structural joint ventures that do not fall within the definition of a

---

[13] [1986] OJ L236/30.   [14] [1990] OJ L209/15: [1991] 4 CMLR 832.   [15] [1979] 1 CMLR 403.

concentration under ECMR. The introduction to Form A/B refers to a period of two months from notification within which the Commission will inform the parties of its initial analysis of the joint venture and of the probable duration of the administrative proceedings for its consideration. Where the parties wish to take advantage of this 'fast track' procedure they must provide more information than is usual in a Form A/B. In such cases, Form A/B has therefore, gained close resemblance to Form CO which has to be completed by parties seeking clearance for their concentration under ECMR.

The Commission frequently publishes in the Official Journal a summary of structural joint venture notifications under Article 81 once they have been received, in order that public comment can be obtained at the beginning. Such notices however are only issued if the parties concerned agree. The fact that the Commission is setting itself more demanding targets for handling such cases is no guarantee in any particular case that 'letters of comfort' will be issued within the two month period; in many cases the complexities of the issue may still require a further extended period of time for the terms of the agreement to be analysed. Nevertheless the Commission undoubtedly wished to reduce the large timescale discrepancies between the consideration of two forms of joint venture, i.e. between the Article 81 and the ECMR procedures, and will not wish in any case that the period for examination of such non-concentrative joint ventures is unnecessarily prolonged. The new arrangements in place for handling all full-function joint ventures within the framework of the ECMR have been motivated by such considerations.

4.5 THE COMMISSION 2001 NOTICE: NEW GUIDELINES FOR HORIZONTAL CO-OPERATION AGREEMENTS

In 1993 the Commission had published a substantial notice setting out its assessment of joint ventures under Article 81 based on its experience up to that time. Since then, however, that Notice has been rendered largely out of date. The definition of those joint ventures which are now classified as concentrations has been broadened by Regulation 1310/97 from 1 March 1998 and moreover, the Commission's own approach to co-operation joint ventures has itself undergone change, leading to a more liberal treatment of this category of agreement.

For these reasons a more recent set of guidelines which came into effect on 1 January 2001, is now the most authoritative source of guidance as to the way in which the Commission will treat a variety of categories of joint venture which do not fall within the jurisdiction of the ECMR. These new guidelines replace both the 1968[16] and 1993 Notices.

A horizontal agreement is one that is made between undertakings at the same level in a particular market, often either actual or potential competitors with each other. The intended scope of the guidelines to all joint ventures that potentially generate efficiency gains means that they apply not only to the specialization and research and development agreements described in the next section, but also to exclusive purchase and selling agreements as well as to a variety of other co-operative arrangements. Agreements on industry standards and on environmental control are also included.

The new Guidelines are intended to provide guidance for the assessment of horizontal co-operation agreements under Article 81. This co-operation can take a number of forms;

[16] See fn. 9.

research and development, joint production, joint purchasing, joint selling (referred to in the Guidelines as 'commercialisation agreements'), standardization, and environmental agreements. The Commission accepts that since such agreements can generate economic benefit, or alternatively lead to competition problems, it should provide a legal framework for their balanced assessment which will itself be based to a greater extent than previously on economic criteria as well as on the existing case law of the European Court and the Court of First Instance. Not all horizontal agreements are of course covered, only those that potentially can produce efficiency gains. They do, however, cover vertical agreements made between competitors. Nor do they seek to cover more complex arrangements covering a number of different areas and methods of operation, nor specific sectors such as agriculture or transport, where special considerations may have to be taken into account.

At the outset there are a number of examples given of agreements that will normally fall outside Article 81(1) altogether. These include those between undertakings which are not competitors with each other, or have no effect on relevant competition, or which involve the undertaking of a project which neither party could individually carry out. In determining whether competition would be effected, the Commission will look at the nature of the market, and the likely effect of the co-operation on prices, quality, or variety of goods or services. Also of concern will be the extent to which the agreement would allow a high degree of common costs to the parties when they combine to manufacture or purchase jointly either an important intermediate product or items which will form a high proportion of the input costs of the final product.

Certain categories of agreement will however almost always fall within Article 81(1). These include those that restrict competition between the parties by price fixing, output limitation, or sharing of customers or markets, all of which are regarded as a direct interference in the competitive process, damaging to customers because they are compelled to pay higher prices or are restricted from access to a full range of choice. In cases that fall on the borderline, important considerations for the Commission will be the existing market share of the parties in relevant markets, entry barriers, buyers' countervailing power and the nature of the product themselves.

The case of *European Night Services*[17] illustrates the importance placed by the Court of First Instance on the accuracy of the Commission's analysis of such factors. In this case, four railways authorities from different Member States had formed a joint venture (*European Night Services*) to provide overnight passenger rail services between the United Kingdom and the continent through the Channel Tunnel. The Commission in its decision had found that the agreement underlying the joint venture had an effect on competition, sufficiently appreciable to bring it within Article 81(1). It had granted an eight year exemption under Article 81(3) subject to the imposition of a number of conditions requiring, *inter alia*, the shareholders to provide 'equivalent services on the same terms' to any other international grouping of railway undertakings.

The CFI, however, annulled the decision finding that the Commission had overstated the market share of ENS in transport services between the UK and the continent in which it was competing with air, coach, ferry, and car transport. Its total share of business and leisure services in all forms of transport was only 7.4 per cent. In the circumstances of the case this

[17] Cases T-374–5, 384 and 388/94, [1998] ECR II-3141: 5 CMLR 718.

could not be deemed to have an appreciable effect on competition in that market, so that Article 81(1) did not apply.

In cases where Article 81(1) does apply the Guidelines then direct the attention of the parties to the content of Article 81(3) and the four conditions which it contains which have to be satisfied. Economic benefits have to be weighed against the degree to which competition is restricted by the agreement and the market power of the participants. Interestingly reference is made to the relevance of efficiency gains, which have of course to be shared with customers and cannot in any case justify the elimination of competition to any major extent.

4.6 JOINT PURCHASING AND JOINT SELLING

Arrangements for *joint purchasing*, if made between SMEs, are nearly always regarded as pro-competitive. They often have both a horizontal and vertical element covering both the arrangements between purchasers and those with their suppliers. Since joint purchasers can themselves become independent sellers in downstream markets both the purchasing and the downstream market have to be analysed. The Commission will ask whether the joint purchasers are competitors in one or more selling markets and if they can achieve market power by coordinating their conduct, which may lead to restriction of competition. If they are however active in different downstream markets fewer problems will be raised. The issue of whether the potentially lower prices that can be obtained by joint purchasing will be passed on to purchasers in that downstream market will also be considered.

Joint selling arrangements are looked on with some suspicion under the Guidelines because it is felt by the Commission, on the basis of considerable case law experience, that it is likely to lead to the fixing of common prices by the parties. There may be cases where the parties could not afford to enter a particular market or sector without the reduction of costs that the agreement may make possible; but the fear of the Commission is that inevitably such arrangements lead to coordination on pricing, not only of the goods or services covered by the joint selling agreement, but in respect also of sales outside the scope of the agreement. Other risks encountered are the exchange of information between the parties which may lead itself to a reduction of competition between them and the possibility that common costs enabled by the agreement may influence pricing coordination even if no direct breach of Article 81 occurs. For these reasons examples of individual exemption for joint selling agreements are rare. The Commission has recently issued a Statement of Objections to the English Football Association Premier League in connection with its joint selling of the TV and other media rights to Premier League matches.[18]

4.7 STANDARDIZATION AND ENVIRONMENTAL AGREEMENTS

Agreements on *standards* are also dealt with in the Guidelines. These are defined as agreements having as their primary objective the definition of technical or quality requirements with which current or future products, production processes or methods may comply. Some of these will clearly fall outside Article 81(1), for example where the agreement is voluntary and operates transparently, or is part of a wider agreement to ensure product compatibility, as for example when they are the result of coordination by recognized standards authorities operating in a non-discriminatory manner.

---

[18] See [2003] 4 CMLR 209–211.

Borderline cases will be those where the parties have joint control over production or innovation and thereby restrict their own ability to produce individual products. If they lose part or all of their freedom to develop alternative standards or the ability to test their own products for compliance, high market shares, however, are not necessarily relevant. Article 81(1) is sure to apply however if the standard is being used as a means aimed at excluding actual potential competition, for example when a trade association sets a standard and then applies pressure to third parties not to market products which fail to comply with it.

In its applications to such agreements of Article 81(3), the Commission will take a positive approach to those which promote economic penetration within the Common Market, provided that the information needed to develop the standard is made available to all those wishing to enter the market and if an appreciable part of the industry is involved. standards clauses should not however have the effect of limiting innovation and should always be applied in a non-discriminatory manner.

The Guidelines also apply to *environmental agreements* under which undertakings combine to achieve pollution control or other environmental objectives (which may include standards or authorized processes). These will normally be sympathetically regarded, if no precise individual obligations are placed on parties or if the obligation upon them is merely to attain an industry-wide environmental target. Borderline examples are those which cover an industry at national and Community level, and also appreciably restrict the parties' ability to decide on the characteristics of their own products or the processes by which they are manufactured. Any grant of special status or exclusivity will be scrutinized very carefully by the Commission and of course any suspicion that the agreement serves as a cover to disguise cartel activity will lead to a full-scale investigation followed, if proved, by the imposition of fines on its members.

5. JOINT VENTURES WHICH ARE NOT CONCENTRATIONS: BLOCK EXEMPTIONS FOR SPECIALIZATION AND R & D AGREEMENTS

5.1 INTRODUCTION

Two categories of joint venture have received special treatment from the Commission, to which, on the basis of its early case law experience, it was able to apply block exemptions covering at least some of the simpler varieties of agreement within these categories, which do not normally present a serious threat to competition. These categories are:

(a) specialization agreements; and

(b) Research and development agreements.

The particular features of each of these are described below, together with some relevant cases and the relevant block exemptions (Reg. Nos 2658 and 2659/2000), which came into force from 1 January 2001. The new Guidelines on horizontal co-operation agreements also deal with these categories of agreement.

5.2 SPECIALIZATION AGREEMENTS: EARLY CASE LAW

A specialization agreement is essentially an allocation of the products to be produced by the parties, so that each can specialize in manufacturing part of a range of goods. Thus, for example, in the case of two motor manufacturers, one might agree to limit its activities to cars of 2,000cc and less and the other to cars of an engine capacity above that level. This allocation is normally combined with close technical co-operation and a mutual obligation to supply each other with the specialized products produced, so that each can sell the full range in those territories allocated for distribution, often on an exclusive basis. This kind of agreement may lead to a reduction in the number of producers of a particular model or type of product, but may enable both companies to realize the benefit of longer production runs and better use of their manufacturing capacity, leading in turn to a reduction of the fixed costs for each product, and thus the final price to the consumer. It may well also have the advantage of improving product quality, as the result of the combination of technical co-operation and specialization.

There is, of course, a wide range of detailed provisions to be tailored to meet the facts of each particular commercial situation. An example of the kind of agreement approved by the Commission in its early years which may serve as a useful model for the kind of co-operation which we are describing is the *Jaz/Peter* case (Commission 1969).[19] Jaz was a French company specializing in electric clocks and alarm clocks, whilst Peter was a German company specializing in large mechanical alarm clocks. Under the arrangements, each agreed to supply the other with its special range of products and spare parts and not to supply any other customers. Each agreed that the other would be entitled to sell the few range of combined products in its own territory, Jaz in France and Peter in Germany. Each agreed not to buy from third parties any clocks or watches of the type covered by the agreement. The effect of these arrangements was to allow each of the two companies to manufacture in much larger quantities than before the range of clocks in which they special-ized, and still to sell the whole range of clocks and watches in its own territory. The increase in production led to a reduction in costs but the agreement did not involve itself with pricing restrictions, the choice of prices being left to the individual companies.

Clearly there was a restraint on competition involved by the agreement. A purchaser in France could not now choose between goods supplied by Jaz or Peter, since in France Jaz was the only distributor for the entire range of clocks, and Peter the only distributor for this range in Germany. On the other hand, the fact that both companies could produce a greater volume of clocks meant that prices could be and were reduced during the period of the agreement. The exchange of technical information between the parties also proved of mutual benefit; the Commission also found that none of the restrictions went beyond the level that was required to support the specialization agreement. When the parties applied for renewal of the exemption in 1977, they were able to show that Jaz had quadrupled its production of pendulum and electric alarm clocks, and that Peter had increased its produc-tion of large mechanical alarm clocks by two and a half times. Not surprisingly, a further exemption was granted. An important element in the Commission's decision was that customers had at all times an adequate choice of such clocks made by competing manu-facturers; even such an apparently beneficial element of co-operation could have been dangerous without substantial competition in the relevant markets, as required by the second negative condition in Article 81(3).

---

[19] [1970] CMLR 129.

A slightly different form of specialization is where the parties combine, not to split a product range between them, but to allocate responsibility for the production and development of individual components for a product they wish to produce jointly. *ACEC/Berliet*[20] is one of the earliest examples (Commission 1968). ACEC, a Belgian company specializing in electric transmissions, had developed a low-weight and high-yield model particularly useful in commercial vehicles and buses. They entered into a collaborative arrangement with Berliet, a French company, which had experience in the manufacture and selling of buses. Responsibilities were divided on the basis that they would co-operate for ten years in the joint development of a bus which would have the ACEC transmission, but the basic structure of the Berliet bus. When a prototype had been made, ACEC would deliver its transmission equipment in France only to Berliet, and Berliet would purchase only electric transmissions made by ACEC, though remaining free to sell its products incorporating such transmissions anywhere in the world. ACEC would deal with Berliet on a 'most favoured client' basis and would guarantee performance by the transmission and continued availability of spare parts.

Restrictions on competition were clearly inherent in the arrangement, as third parties engaged in the manufacture of electric transmissions were no longer able to sell them to Berliet; nor were some bus manufacturers now able to buy the ACEC transmission. However, the restrictions which ACEC and Berliet had accepted were, in the view of the Commission, reasonable, given the commitment which each had entered into with the other.

If successful, the specialization would permit the manufacture of buses in longer production runs, giving a reasonable chance of producing a new model that simplified the mechanical construction and would give better performance and comfort to its users. Though the outcome of the technical research could not be predicted with certainty, the fact that it was being carried out on a collaborative basis by two specialist companies increased the chances of a useful outcome; there was a sufficient degree of probability that the results would be successful to justify the collaboration and the restraints ancillary to it. ACEC remained free throughout to make contracts with other bus manufacturers outside France, and such buses would be able to compete with those produced by the joint venture. Formal exemption was therefore granted by the Commission.

In *Prym/Beka*,[21] Prym was a German company with over 4,000 employees which decided that its capacity for production of sewing needles was inadequate; it made an agreement with a much smaller company in Belgium, Beka, employing only 350 people, that Prym would no longer make sewing needles and would transfer the relevant parts of its plant and equipment to Beka, provided that Beka guaranteed to supply all Prym's requirements. Prym would take a 25 per cent interest in the share capital of Beka and would agree not to purchase its needles elsewhere, unless Beka proved unable to supply its requirements. Originally the agreement also contained market-sharing restrictions, both by definition of end-users and on a geographical basis, but the Commission insisted that the exemption was conditional on the removal of these restrictions. The advantages of the specialization agreements were that the Belgian plant could be more intensively used, increasing by at least 50 per cent its production of needles, whose unit cost was substantially reduced. Though this was not a true specialization agreement (since Prym itself was not allocated a specific product in whose manufacture it would specialize) the effect of the new arrangements for

---

[20] [1968] CMLR D35.   [21] [1973] CMLR D250.

centralizing production at Beka's factory had many of the same advantages and was therefore accepted within 85(3), subject to the deletion of the clauses dealing with the allocation of markets.

A more unusual case involved the allocation of markets in the nuclear industry: *United Reprocessors*.[22] An agreement was made between three undertakings, in the UK (British Nuclear Fuels), France (the Commissariat à l'Energie Atomique), and Germany (KEWA). The agreement notified involved setting up a joint subsidiary company to cover the market of the reprocessing of nuclear fuels. It was agreed that they would not invest in any other business for this purpose and would allocate all their reprocessing work between the three companies. Other restrictions were also accepted including an obligation on KEWA not to build a new reprocessing plant until the throughput of the French and United Kingdom plants reached certain levels. In granting an exemption, the Commission held that the coordination of capital investment between the three companies would ensure that uneconomic plants would not be set up, and would enable the companies to wait until market conditions were more favourable, as well as reducing costs through increasing the production of the existing reprocessing plant. Dealing with a product as delicate and dangerous as nuclear waste, it was seen as essential by the Commission that the reprocessing service should be firmly established. Benefits arose for consumers because the proposed improved stability of the reprocessing service should result in lower electricity costs. The Commission, however, insisted that it should be closely involved in periodically reviewing the arrangements in order to ensure that consumers continued to receive their proportionate share of resulting savings. It also insisted on participating in the monitoring of the throughput of the reprocessing work of the French and United Kingdom plants.

The terms of the decision suggest that the Commission had major doubts about the effect on competition of such an arrangement, and that only the combination of the stringent conditions and the fact that this was a particularly sensitive industry in which to insist on completely free competition justified an exemption. The Commission indeed acknowledged in its decision that for a period competition would actually be reduced.

In recent years, the number of specialization agreements receiving individual exemptions has fallen, although there has been no shortage of notifications involving other kinds of joint venture proposals. The specialization agreements that still come before the Commission seem to fall into two categories. One category deals with industries of particularly advanced technology, where the investment costs are particularly high, and where a substantial element of research and development is involved. *Bayer/Gist-Brocades*[23] (Commission 1975) was an example. Both Bayer, a German company, and Gist-Brocades, a Dutch company, were large drug manufacturers; each produced raw penicillin and intermediate penicillin products for processing into ampicillins and other semi-synthetic products. In order to increase overall production, a specialization agreement was entered into under which Gist-Brocades would specialize in the production of raw penicillin, whilst Bayer would concentrate on intermediate products. The majority of the raw penicillin to be produced by Gist-Brocades would then be forwarded to Bayer for processing into intermediate products, although Gist-Brocades would retain some of the raw penicillin for traditional penicillin

[22] [1976] 2 CMLR D1: cf. KEWA [1976] 2 CMLR D15, a similar decision granting exemption to a joint subsidiary set up to reprocess nuclear fuels in Germany by four companies and which would itself be one of the shareholders in United Reprocessors.

[23] [1976]1 CMLR D98. A subsequent extension of the exemption was granted until 1995.

preparations. Both companies kept the freedom to carry out their own research and development, subject to an obligation to exchange information; various non-exclusive licences for the use of specific chemical processes relating to the production of penicillin were also granted. Although the companies were both large, with substantial financial resources and knowledge of the market, the Commission agreed that production could be carried out more economically as the result of the specialization.

Exemption was granted but with one important amendment. The individual factories were to have been transferred to joint subsidiary companies in which both parties would have a 50 per cent interest and an equal number of directors. Inevitably this would have led not only to joint research, but to joint control over the production and total investment in the individual plants. The Commission felt that this would restrict competition between the companies beyond what was essential to the specialization proposals. The proposal to form joint subsidiaries was therefore abandoned, each company administering the arrangements through their existing corporate structure. Having thus eliminated the restrictions that appeared too wide to be indispensable to the arrangement, the Commission ruled that the exemption could be granted. The specialization agreement would increase availability on world markets of both raw penicillin and intermediate products. The Commission fixed an eight-year period for the exemption but attached conditions, so that it could continue to check the results of co-operation on the competitive process in the relevant markets.

The second variety of specialization agreement, now more commonly found, was brought about by the economic recession of the 1970s and early 1980s. The more generous treatment afforded to crisis cartels at that time illustrates the concern of the Commission in such situations not to be seen to take too rigid a line, and to be accommodating where there was a genuine long-term substantial fall in demand and consequent excess production capacity. An alternative to a crisis cartel is an agreement whereby 'swaps' are made between major companies enabling them to eliminate production capacity they no longer require and to specialize in those fields where they remain strong. The process is illustrated by *Imperial Chemical Industries/British Petroleum Chemicals*[24] (Commission 1984). Both ICI and BPC had manufacturing plants producing PVC (polyvinylchloride) and low-density polyethylene (LDPE). Arrangements were made under which ICI disposed of its modern LDPE production plant in the UK and all related technical information and patents to BPC, whilst in return BPC sold its most modern UK production plant for PVC and related technical information to ICI. The notified agreement related simply to a swap of individual plants enabling ICI in the future to specialize in PVC and BPC in LDPE, neither continuing in the production process of the other product.

As a result of the agreement, BPC and ICI were each able to increase the capacity and the usage of their more modern plant thereby reducing unit costs, always an essential feature in specialization agreements. In the long run, a more healthy industrial structure was likely to be promoted, and although in the short term, the agreement would not improve competition, the Commission was satisfied that in the longer term effective competition would be maintained and consumers not deprived of a range of choice.

[24] [1985] 2 CMLR 330.

5.3 INTRODUCTION OF BLOCK EXEMPTION REGULATION 417/85 AND ITS SUCCESSOR NO. 2658/2000

As the result of the Commission's experience gained in this area it felt able to introduce a block exemption for certain agreements of this kind. Regulation 417/85, as later amended by Regulation 151/93, applied to a variety of specialization agreements including both the type seen in *Jaz/Peter* and in *ACEC/Berliet*. In its reliance on market share thresholds, the Regulation anticipated the approach later to be adopted by the Block Exemption Regulation for Vertical Restraints (2790/99) of maximum market share percentages, though the percentage actually adopted by the two regulations were criticized subsequently for being too low.

The 1985 block exemption was available when the products in question together with other products manufactured by the undertakings which are regarded as equivalent by reason of their characteristic, price and intended use did not represent more than 20 per cent of the market either in the Common Market or a substantial part of it. Moreover, the aggregate turnover of the participating undertakings could not exceed Euros 1 billion. These figures applied when the parties engaged in specialization simply for the purpose of manufacture, but if the parties (or a third party on their behalf) were also responsible for distribution the maximum market share figures applicable were only ten per cent though the maximum aggregate turnover figure itself was not reduced. This block exemption was replaced from the end of 2000 by the new Block Exemption 2658/2000.[25]

By contrast, the single most important change found in the new block exemption is that the maximum turnover requirement has been removed. A market share threshold, however, still remains at the comparatively low figure of 20 per cent, even though transitional relief is given if the share remains at a figure no higher than 25 per cent for two years, or no higher than 30 per cent for one year.

The scope of the block exemption is now wider. Previously it was limited to reciprocal obligations not to manufacture products nor to have them manufactured by other parties or to manufacture products or have them manufactured only jointly. Under the new text the exemption applied not only to such reciprocal specialization but also to unilateral specialization (often known as 'outsourcing agreements') under which one party agrees to cease production of particular items whilst a competitor agrees to supply it to them. Joint production arrangements are also covered by the exemption, which extends, moreover, to ancillary clauses required for the commercial implementation of the agreement, but without constituting its primary purpose, such as the assignment or licensing of intellectual property rights.

The reason that cross-supply clauses are required to be included in such agreements is that these should prevent them being utilized as a means of partitioning territorial markets for the product in breach of Article 81; exclusive purchase and supply clauses are also permitted, in order to facilitate the use of the exemption for outsourcing agreements (Article 2). The parties may set limits to the agreed amount of products and may set the capacity and production volumes of a production joint venture (Article 4). Prices of the products so produced can also be fixed, provided that the joint venture is also responsible for distribution. Joint distribution is allowed, or distribution by a third party so long as it is not a competitor in the relevant market.

---

[25] [2000] OJ L 304/3: [2001] 4 CMLR 800.

The period of the block exemption is ten years from 1 January 2001, subject to a transitional period covering its first year during which those agreements which do not fall within its term but satisfied the conditions for exemption contained in Regulation 417/85 remain exempted. The benefit of the block exemption can be withdrawn by the Commission if it believes that a particular agreement is having effects incompatible with Article 81(3), especially if:

— the agreement is not yielding significant results in terms of rationalization or consumers are not receiving a fair share of its benefits; or

— the products which are the subject of the specialization arrangements are not subject to sufficient competition.

There is no long list of permitted 'white' clauses, and the list of 'black' clauses is short, referring merely to any agreements which, directly or indirectly, had as their object or effect:

— the fixing of prices;

— the limitation of output; or

— the allocation of customers or markets.

5.4 SPECIALIZATION AGREEMENTS: THE GUIDELINES

There are some twenty-five paragraphs in the Guidelines on specialization agreements and these focus on agreements mainly which are not within the scope of the new block exemption. The section also considers a range of joint production agreements. As always the first task of the Commission is of the assessment of the relevant market and the strength of the parties within it relative to the specialization agreement. If the parties are not competitors (or even if they are, but co-operation with competitors is the only commercially justifiable way of launching a new product), then Article 81(1) is unlikely to apply. Borderline cases are those where the market share of the parties exceeds the threshold contained in the block exemption, but where their market power is still restricted; for example, where the concentration ratios of the market are low and there are no existing links between a significant number of competitors. Any specialization agreement, however, that involves agreement by the parties on output directly related to the joint production, or sets prices for them, is likely to fall within the scope of Article 81(1). A number of case studies provide further illustrations of the approach of the Commission to this type of agreement, as with each other category of agreement considered in the Guidelines.

5.5 RESEARCH AND DEVELOPMENT AGREEMENTS: THE 1968 NOTICE ON CO-OPERATION BETWEEN ENTERPRISES

Not all joint ventures fall neatly into a distinct category. Nevertheless, research and development agreements form a distinct group which can be recognized without difficulty; the main purpose of such agreements is to arrange for the carrying out of a number of functions, all of which are essential steps in the lengthy process from the first creative step of the inventor to the delivery of a finished product to customers at a competitive price. They are more common, and more important in their economic and commercial effects, than specialization agreements.

The development of a new product actually begins with basic research carried out in a laboratory or workshop, often taking years rather than months to complete. If the research proceeds successfully, the next stage is to apply its findings to the development of a product that could be saleable, either in competition with existing products serving the same function or as a novel product without immediate competitors. Once development has been completed which, especially in high technology areas, may take several more years, the remaining stages follow a pattern. Production facilities are first set up and manufacturing commenced, coupled with the setting up of distribution systems and suitable promotion, especially for a consumer product. Once the product is on the market, backup arrangements are necessary to provide service and support for guarantee claims, whether the product is a consumer or a capital item.

The Notice on Co-Operation between Enterprises in 1968[26] was initially thought to exempt many research and development agreements from Article 81 altogether. The Notice proved a disappointment, limiting its scope to assist only a narrow group of research and development agreements. It accepted as being outside Article 81 agreements providing simply for exchange of experience and results on the basis of information without any restriction against the undertakings carrying out their own research and development. Agreements of such a pure and limited nature are, however, rare. If there is no right to mutual access to the results, or if the practical exploitation of its results is covered by the agreement, then a restraint on competition may occur. Whilst it is possible to have an arrangement under which there are major and minor participants in the research project, who may receive access to the results in proportion to the degree of their participation in the research work, a restraint of competition again arises if some of the participating enterprises are unable to exploit the results, either totally or to an extent that is not proportionate with their participation. Moreover, if there is any restriction on granting licences to third parties, competition is again likely to be affected, though it is permissible to require a majority decision of the participants for the grant of any individual licence.

5.6 EARLY CASE LAW ON R & D AGREEMENTS

From this Notice alone, one might have assumed that an agreement which imposed no restrictions on the parties' research and development activities would not normally be in breach of Article 81(1). *Henkel-Colgate*[27] (Commission 1971) showed that such an assumption would be fallacious. The two companies involved were both important in the detergent market, Colgate holding some 10 per cent of the EC market and Henkel nearly three times that amount. In three of the Member States their combined market share was over 50 per cent, but they had major competitors, notably Unilever and Proctor & Gamble. The proposed jointly owned company was to be limited to research and development, and not involved with distribution and marketing. It was apparent that in this particular industry the 'cutting edge' of competition lay principally in the ability to improve the technical quality of the product, which, of course, had the effect of placing great importance on their capabilities for research and development. The practical effect of the agreement was to eliminate the likelihood that the firms concerned would carry out their own research, since each party was almost bound to encourage the joint subsidiary to exploit any successful progress which it

---

[26] See fn. 9.   [27] [1972] OJ L14/14.

might make on its own. Any successful results from the collaboration would improve the competitive position of the two parties jointly, whilst eliminating competition in this area between themselves.

In view of the size and strength of both Henkel and Colgate, an unfavourable reaction from the Commission was not unexpected but, perhaps surprisingly, an exemption was given to the agreement limited to research and development on the basis that it might enable technical and economic progress and contained no restrictions that were not indispensable to the arrangements proposed. The proceeds of the collaboration would be available to both on payment of a royalty not to exceed 2 per cent of the net price of the product and on a non-exclusive basis. Licences to use the information could only be granted if both parties agreed, but this limitation was felt to be an inherent consequence of the setting up of the joint research organization for the benefit of the two participants. In order, however, to prevent the joint research from leading to further integrated activities between such substantial companies (such as market-sharing or arrangements over production and sales policies), the Commission imposed stringent conditions on the exemption granted. These included an obligation to pass full information to DG Comp on their policy relating to the licensing of patents and know-how resulting from the joint research, and the provision of information about changes in the shareholding in the joint venture or in other links between the two companies.

Continuing experience with such research and development agreements gradually illustrated to the Commission that, although in nearly all cases it was eventually possible to grant exemption to the agreement, it was often necessary to impose detailed conditions on their operation. This required the Commission to become involved in monitoring the agreements between the parties. In many other cases under Article 81(3), however, once the Commission had rendered a favourable decision it was not concerned with the details of its operation, unless it received complaints that the agreement was not being carried out in accordance with its notified terms.

The need for joint research into long-term problems too difficult for individual companies to undertake was also illustrated in the *Beecham/Parke, Davis* agreement[28] (Commission 1979). Here the parties proposed to carry out joint research into drugs to prevent the impairment of blood circulation, none being available at the time. The time-scale for the work was considered to be at least a decade. Testing alone would be extremely lengthy, and neither company thought it worthwhile to undertake the required investment alone. A joint research programme was set up, to be followed if successful by a development programme. The development programme was expected to last five years before any marketing would be possible. The arrangements involved cross-licensing arrangements for patents on a non-exclusive royalty-free basis, and neither party was prevented from carrying out its own research. The parties agreed that they would exchange information relating to any improvements in manufacturing processes for a term of ten years after the product was marketed. Marketing would be carried out by each party individually.

Exemption was granted for ten years, and the Commission indicated that a conclusive element in this decision was the fact that the new product was to be 'pharmacologically and therapeutically different from all known medicine' so that it was not an issue of improving production of existing products but of creating a new product. Even for companies as large

---

[28] See fn. 10.

as Beecham and Parke, Davis such research and development would stand a better chance of proceeding if carried out on a joint basis. Moreover, both parties remained free to use the results of the research and development independently and could grant licences to third parties without obtaining the prior consent of the other party. Deleted from the arrangements was an obligation to pay royalties for cross-licences since the burden of royalty payments proposed would have been a considerable disincentive for the parties to compete with each other.

It has, however, also always been a major concern of the Commission to prevent the use of an apparently harmless research and development agreement from becoming a market-sharing arrangement. This concern arose in the case of *Carbon Gas Technology*[29] (Commission 1983), which involved a joint venture between three companies, Deutsche BP, Deutsche Babcock, and a German company, PCV, for developing coal gasification. The possible conversion of coal into gas had major industrial and economic significance for Europe in view of its dependence on imported oil. This venture limited to research and development appeared to have important strategic consequences for the European Community and was approved, but only subject to strict conditions. The commercial logic of the venture was that PCV specialized in basic process technology and the manufacture of the equipment required for conversion; Deutsche Babcock were the specialists in constructing large-scale plant in which such equipment should be placed; whilst BP's expertise was in refining oil, with a technology similar to that of gasification. The co-operation between these three large companies would effect considerable savings of both time and money, and it was likely that any technical advances made in improving the process would ensure a share of the benefit for consumers, given the active competition with other fuels.

The parties accepted restrictions on their activity by agreeing to refrain from competition with a joint venture, which meant that in practice they would not compete with each other. If any of them withdrew from the joint venture for a period of five years they agreed not to disclose any know-how that had belonged to the joint venture, whether the know-how originated from the parent company or from the joint venture itself. The exemption was granted on condition that all licensing agreements between the joint venture and its parents were submitted to DG Comp for approval, to prevent them from being used for market-sharing arrangements for sale of the equipment or plant for coal gasification within the Common Market. This was considered a real possibility given the individual strength and contacts of the three companies in their specialized fields.

5.7 INTRODUCTION OF BLOCK EXEMPTION REGULATION 418/85 AND ITS SUCCESSOR 2659/2000

It was noteworthy that, although the enactment by the Council of Regulation 2821/71 had given the Commission the power to issue a block exemption for research and development agreements, legal and political difficulties prevented this until a draft was finally published in early 1984, which after amendment was adopted as Regulation 418/85, effective from 1 March 1985. Its content is much more highly detailed than the equivalent block exemption for specialization agreements already mentioned which came into force on the same day. It provided only a limited exemption for a very basic type of research and development

---

[29] [1984] 2 CMLR 275.

agreement, which might well not infringe Article 81(1) in any case; it was often found inadequate for more ambitious schemes especially if linked with distribution of the resulting product. It was generally regarded by lawyers as having too narrow a basis to be of much value to proposed research and development joint ventures. It was replaced from the end of 2000 by the new Block Exemption 2659/2000.[30]

The most important changes that the new block exemption brings are as follows:

— The thresholds for the aggregate market shares of the parties (previously 20 per cent except where joint distribution was included, in which case it was 10 per cent only) has been raised to 25 per cent with no separate lower threshold for joint distribution.
— Where a production joint venture is established, production targets may be set.
— Where a distribution joint venture is established, sales targets and prices may be set.
— No framework agreement has to be entered into between parties defining the scope of the research and development and the field in which it is to be carried out.

The content of this exemption is rather more complicated than that of the specialization block exemption, and a summary of its individual articles may therefore be helpful. It applies to the following categories of research and development agreements:

— Joint research and development of products or processes and joint exploitation of their results.
— Joint exploitation of the results of research and development previously carried out by prior agreement between the same undertakings.
— Simple joint research and development without subsequent joint exploitation.

In addition, ancillary clauses directly related to the main agreement and necessary for their implementation, such as an obligation not to carry out independently, or with third parties, research and development in the same field during the term of the agreement, are exempted (Article 1).

If the agreement is simply for joint research and development each party must be free thereafter to exploit the results, and all parties must have access to the results of the work. Any joint exploitation must relate to results protected by intellectual property rights which substantially contribute to technical or economic progress and which are decisive for the resulting manufacturing of products or application or processes (Article 2).

The period of exemption for non-competing manufacturers is the period of the research and development and for subsequent joint exploitation for seven years from the time when the contract products are first put on the market within the Common Market; if, however, the parties are in competition the threshold already mentioned of 25 per cent must not be exceeded, nor can an agreement even between non-competitors continue to enjoy exemption after the end of the initial seven year joint exploitation period if their combined market share has itself come to exceed 25 per cent. There is limited transitional relief in Article 6 to qualify the market share rules. A market share of over 25 per cent but only up to 30 per cent can have a two year relief following the year in which the threshold was first exceeded, whilst a share of over 30 per cent can have a transitional period of one year, provided that the aggregate of these two reliefs cannot extend beyond a total of two.

---

[30] [2000] OJ L304/7: [2001] 4 CMLR 808.

Article 5 contains the important 'black list' of research and development agreements which do not enjoy the benefit of the block exemption. The equivalent article in the previous block exemption 418/85 (Article 6) had applied where the parties had, by the agreement, been restricted from certain acts or required not to do certain things; in the new block exemption the criterion is the object of the parties in making the agreement, including:

— limiting the output or sales of the parties;

— fixing prices;

— restricting the parties from entering into research and development in unconnected fields during the agreement or after its expiration in the same or connected fields;

— no-challenge clauses;

— restrictions on passive sales for the contract products in territories reserved for other parties; and

— the requirement not to grant licences to third parties to manufacture the contract products or apply the contract processes in cases where exploitation by the parties themselves does not take place.

Though, as already stated, the parties do have the right to set production targets, sales targets and fixed prices in cases of joint production and distribution respectively.

The new regulation gives the Commission wider powers of withdrawal of the block exemption. No fewer than five examples are given of situations where the effects of research and development agreements may be incompatible with the conditions laid down in Article 81(3), namely:

— where the existence of the agreement substantially restricts the scope for research and development by third parties, because of limited research capacity elsewhere;

— because its existence substantially restricts access of third parties to the market for the contract products;

— because without objectively valid reason the parties do not exploit the results of their research and development;

— where the contract products are not subject to effective competition in the Common Market; and

— because the existence of the agreement would eliminate effective competition in research and development in a particular market.

5.8 R & D AGREEMENTS: THE GUIDELINES

As with the Guidelines to specialization agreements referred to above, the Guidelines here are also set out as a supplement to the Block Exemption. A wide range of agreements is covered including those providing for full research and development co-operation, for joint improvement of the existing technology, the development of new products, the outsourcing of some research and development activities, and the commercialization of research and development already carried out. The only universal requirement is that the 'centre of gravity' of the co-operation lies in research and development. The Commission accepts that such agreements can bring about a wide range of technical or economic progress referred to in the first condition of Article 81(3) by leading to, for example, quicker development of products, cross-fertilization of ideas and experience, cost reductions, and the encouragement of lively SMEs. A corresponding disadvantage which such agreements might bring about might be restrictive effects on output, innovation, or price.

Importance is placed on the identification of the likely effect of the co-operation. This could range from the making of minor improvements to an existing product, or the creation of a new product which might in time come to be regarded as a substitute for an existing product, to the development of an entirely new product such as a vaccine to cure a previously untreatable disease. There will in addition to the market for the product being developed be a market for the relevant intellectual property technology. It may prove necessary for the Commission to analyse the degree of present and potential competition in this market also. It will also be important to identify relevant 'research and development poles' that is particular clusters of investment in the industry directed towards developing a new product for technology. If there are a number of these then horizontal co-operation in research and development is less likely to have an anti-competitive effect.

Many research and development agreements will fall outside Article 81(1) especially if they are entered into by undertakings not themselves competitors or if they are mainly carried out through outsourcing, or only involve pure research activities. There is however more risk of Article 81(1) applying if the research and development is likely to be mainly directed to the launch of a new product, if the parties are existing competitors or if exclusivity of access is given to the results of the co-operation, unless the other party to the agreement is itself an academic body or research organization.

6. RECENT TRENDS IN JOINT VENTURE PROPOSALS

6.1 THE CHANGING BACKGROUND

One of the main changes in recent years has been the increase in the number of joint ventures notified to the Commission both under the ECMR and under Article 81 from those sectors of the economy where technological development is moving forward at speed. It has been particularly noticeable in the telecommunications sector. Whilst the Commission has itself been seeking through the use of directives under Article 86(3) of the Treaty to liberalize national markets for fixed line and mobile telephony, as well as the market for corporate telecommunications services of all kinds and other forms of advanced data communication, it has also been using its jurisdiction over proposed joint ventures under both ECMR and Article 81 to the same ends. National telephone operators in the Community have been forming alliances with one or more other foreign operators so as to be able to put together both national and international services of a 'seamless' nature, meeting current demands from international business for integrated services. In bringing in so-called 'global partners' to give their operations a fully international dimension, their motives are partly defensive, i.e. to protect their own market shares in national markets, but in part aggressive, seeking a share of the potentially profitable 'value-added' services which many large corporate groups are now seeking to obtain. Such alliances which are normally of a non-concentrative nature are not always long-lasting and may shift as commercial pressures and opportunities fluctuate. Nevertheless, it is essential for the Commission to be able to control the basis on which they are drawn up and to eliminate restrictions from them which do not fall within the proper scope of Article 81(3) as applied to individual exemptions.

In paragraph 55 of the 1995 Annual Report of the Competition Directorate, the Commission stated that 'the application of the basic competition rules to these alliances has become one of the major challenges for EU competition policy in recent years. The Commission must ensure that the current restructuring process will lead to competitive and growth-oriented market structures; its policy aimed at liberalizing telecommunications is generating new services and products at competitive prices for consumers, reducing costs for the industry and creating new jobs'. However, it states that these efforts would serve little purpose if new and restrictive agreements, practices, or market structures were allowed to develop which prevented competition from emerging on liberalized markets or, equally, if telephone operating companies could engage in abusive behaviour aimed at preserving their dominant position in individual markets.

6.2 TELECOMMUNICATIONS JOINT VENTURES: SOME CASE LAW

An example was the ATLAS joint venture between the national telephone operators of France and Germany, *France Telecom (FT)* and *Deutsche Telekom (DT)*.[31] Their joint venture was owned by the two parties in equal shares in order to enable them jointly to provide sophisticated communication packages, comprising both voice data communication and also rather less complex 'packet switching' data services for smaller customers, including for example point of sale information for retail chains or transfer systems for banks operating cash machine networks. The potential markets for such services are very large and the fact that both participants retained a vital monopoly of their domestic telecommunications markets and infrastructure, and were seeking through the joint venture further to extend their control over national markets, made it seem initially that an exemption under Article 81(3) might be difficult to obtain.

The Commission granted exemption, but in such a way as to use the leverage of the exemption request to forward its own policy priorities on the two governments concerned, thus enabling liberalization of French and German telecommunications markets to occur more quickly than would otherwise be the case. Conditions imposed on the parties under the exemption decision include:

(a) Applicable only to the formation of ATLAS and the appointment of FT and DT as reciprocal exclusive distributors in their own territory, an exemption period limited to five years from the date on which French and German governments grant the first licences in their countries for the construction or ownership of alternative infra-structures for liberalized telecommunication services.

(b) For the inclusion in the joint venture of the national public switched data network of FT and DT, an exemption period expiring on the same date as (a), but not starting until the date on which both countries first fully liberalized all their telecommunication services (which under existing directives occurred on 1 January 1998).

(c) A guarantee of open access to domestic public switched data networks of both companies even after integration into ATLAS on a non-discriminatory and 'transparent'

---

[31] [1996] OJ L239/29, [1997] OJ L47/8: [1997] 4 CMLR 89.

basis to all service providers, including the implementation of any new standardized interconnection standard.

(*d*) Non-discriminatory treatment of third party competitors in respect of the availability of facilities related services such as interconnection rights.

(*e*) Arms' length dealing between the joint venture and its parent companies, to be externally audited.

(*f*) Separate service contracts for the services to be provided by FT and DT in acting as exclusive distributors for ATLAS and for providing their own services, identifying prices and rebates.

FT and DT were to remain potential competitors of ATLAS and to receive important research development licences from ATLAS. The Commission's view was that the benefits of those joint ventures on such terms would include the provision of better technology at an earlier date. The opportunity of building a 'seamless' trans-European network, including better link-ups between the public switched networks of the parties and their other networks should also in its view enable better technical harmonization for Member States which would also be of benefit to consumers. It is felt that the parties to the joint venture would face substantial competition in all their markets if the liberalization occurred as scheduled within the shape of the directives. The joint venture, however, could not proceed unless all these conditions were satisfied.

Closely linked to the ATLAS exemption was that for *Phoenix*[32] (later renamed Global One) under which FT and DT also acquired a ten per cent interest each in Sprint, a major US telecom operator, so as to be able to provide telecommunications and data services worldwide. A number of the initial restrictions initially placed on the parties in both cases were cut down so as to minimize the risk that the joint venture's strong starting position would enable it to weaken competition from its competitors. The Global One joint venture exemption was granted for a term of seven years from the date of coming into effect of the condition of (*b*) above. A number of other similar joint ventures in the telecommunications sector have also been approved and several joint ventures between major airlines for code-sharing and other forms of co-operation have also been notified and cleared with conditions.

6.3 B2B EXCHANGES

The most recent form of joint venture, and one that is coming to have an increasingly important effect, is that involving the 'electronic exchange' or the 'business to business' (B2B) Internet screen marketplaces. Not all these Internet exchanges, of course, are joint ventures, and of those that are some will be concentrations covered by the Merger Regulation, because they are full-function and come within Article 3(2) of that Regulation. Others, however, will fall under the jurisdiction of Article 81(1), and are likely to take one of two main forms.

The first of these is proprietary, when the market place for buying and selling in a given sector of the economy is established jointly by leading participants in that sector. A recent

---

[32] [1996] OJ L239/57: [1997] 4 CMLR 147.

example considered by the Commission is *My Aircraft.Com*,[33] which although categorized as a concentration because of its full-function nature, could easily have been structured as a joint venture within the scope of Article 81. It had been established by two major US companies, Honeywell and United Technologies, to provide an electronic marketplace for companies involved in the manufacturing and selling of aerospace products and services and to supply management functions for all participants in that industry. It would have to compete with other similar exchanges in the same sector. Giving its first decision and affirmation in this e-commerce area, the Commission indicated that it expected to have to consider a large number of such cases in the future, under both the Merger Regulation and Article 81.

The second form is that of the independent trading exchange, run by an independent undertaking and not causing any 'concentration' to occur, which is open to a wide variety of participants on the basis of the rules which are laid down. They can be used for a number of purposes, including:

— the provision of secure sites where buying and selling can take place of products or commodities on a routine basis, probably integrated with the IT management systems of the participants;

— the provision of information in connection with a particular sector, and the provision of other services such as risk management or quality certification; and

— the provision of auction and exchange services for the participants.

The Commission is well aware of both the pro- and anti-competitive risks of such exchanges and is trying through public consultation and other means to apply established principles of Community competition law to this new phenomenon.[34] The increased price transparency of such exchanges can, in principle, assist the competitive process, but equally it has the potential for increasing collusion between the parties, especially as 'cheating' on price agreements can with such exchanges be easily detected by other participants.

7. THE EFFECT OF THE MODERNIZATION PROPOSALS ON JOINT VENTURES

The White Paper published by the European Commission in April 1999 contained radical proposals under which the notification and exemption system provided for under Regulation 17/62 would be replaced by a new system. Under these proposals, the EC notification system, established for so many years, will be abolished and Article 81(1) and (3) enforced in the future primarily by national competition authorities and national courts, leaving the Commission only to deal with major cases affecting a number of Member States, such as large-scale European cartels.

The proposals in the White Paper do not directly affect the operation of the ECMR and its treatment of joint ventures that are 'concentrations'. Those joint ventures which fall into that definition, under the revised Article 3(2), will continue to be dealt with in the same way

---

[33] Commission Press Statement IP/00/912 of 7 August 2000.
[34] DG Comp Competition Policy Newsletter (2001), No. 3, pp.14–16.

as explained in Sections 2 and 3 of this chapter. The proposals, if implemented, could however have serious consequences for those joint ventures which are not concentrations and are at present dealt with under Article 81. Instead of being able to satisfy the Commission that the relevant joint venture is either outside Article 81(1) or benefits from an individual exemption under Article 81(3), parties will have to make their own judgment as to whether the terms of the joint venture do or do not fit into these categories, without any certainty that ultimately a national court or competition authority, or even the Commission itself, will be of the same opinion. In other words, an important element of legal certainty which the present imperfect system of notification under Article 81 provides will be lost.

As the White Paper acknowledged (in paragraph 79), the position of joint ventures often involves substantial investment and far-reaching integration by the parties and the existence of the compulsory prior notification scheme is clearly more satisfactory for the parties than the need for self-assessment and the continuing risk of a later adverse decision by a national court or competition authority. If the joint venture has already been in existence for some years before such a decision is taken, it may indeed be difficult to amend the original proposals in a satisfactory way and substantial investment will have been made on the basis that the joint venture was fully legal.

Joint ventures which have already received a formal individual exemption from the Commission under Article 81(3) will be able to continue to benefit from its terms until its period expires; those however for which only a comfort letter has been given, either in the form of a negative clearance or exemption, will in principle be liable to challenge in national courts by parties seeking to hold them void under Article 81(2). The new framework for the modernization programme however is the subject of more detailed consideration in the next two chapters, and in Chapter 25.

20

COMMUNITY LAW
AND NATIONAL LAW:
CHANGING RELATIONSHIPS

1. INTRODUCTION: THE ORIGINAL DIVISION
OF RESPONSIBILITY

1.1 THE NEED FOR MEMBER STATE PARTICIPATION IN COMMUNITY COMPETITION POLICY

The previous chapters in this book have explained the emergence of Community competition law as a mature and far-reaching body of rules, affecting businesses of all kinds in practically every sector of the economy. The task of enforcing these rules effectively in a Community of fifteen Member States, with up to ten new members likely to be admitted in 2004, is far beyond the ability of the Commission and Community Courts alone, even if they were granted substantial new resources. It is therefore vital to identify how Member States themselves can play a full and effective role in the application of the competition rules, not only of national law but those of the Community. Competition rules are applied both by national courts and by national competition authorities, though the context of their application differs, as do the resources available to these institutions in the various Member States.

To understand the relationship of Community and national law in this area, it is necessary first to appreciate the original structure of the Treaty and relevant secondary legislation on this issue, and then to see the development of relevant legal principles through case law, leading in recent years towards a major decentralization of the application of Articles 81 and 82. Two major factors can be identified as having contributed to this movement. The first is the accretion of additional responsibilities to DG Comp as a result of new legislation and other developments. These comprise the European Community Merger Regulation and the heavy case-load that this has brought, including a large number of joint ventures, and the Article 86 jurisdiction, including the need to issue directives in many sectors formerly dominated by State controlled enterprises and State aid. A second important factor is the creation and growth in recent years of national competition authorities in all Member States, and their greater ability and willingness to work in co-operation with the officials of the Commission in resolving cases that have both Community and national significance.

The radical White Paper produced by the Commission in April 1999 proposed a modernization programme under which responsibility for enforcing the provisions of Article 81 and

Article 82 would in future be shared more equally between the Commission, which would lose its monopoly for the granting of individual exemption under Article 81(3), and the competition authorities of Member States linked in a close network for the exchange of information and the coordination of their activities with each other and the Commission. National courts too would be able under the new arrangements to play a more significant role, as we shall examine in the following chapter. These proposals, after extensive consultation, were converted into legislation by Regulation 1/2003 which replaces from 1 May 2004 the longstanding Regulation 17/62 which has played such an important role in the development of Community competition policy.

1.2 THE TERMS OF THE TREATY OF ROME

Before examining the detailed provisions of the Regulation it is important to understand how the original division of responsibility operated, as between the Commission and national competition authorities. It was never the case that responsibility for enforcing Articles 81 and 82 lay with the institutions of the Community alone. The inadequate resources of the Commission in general, and of DG Comp in particular, especially in the early years, would have made this impractical, quite apart from any other considerations. In any case the relevant provisions of the Treaty embodied the principle that the competition policy originally referred to in Article 3(f) was to be jointly implemented with Member States, both national courts and competition authorities playing an important role in its enforcement alongside the Commission. Whilst the primary role of such national competition authorities was to enforce their own domestic competition laws, their other responsibility would be to help the Commission to ensure that Community law on this subject was effectively and uniformly enforced.

That this was the original scheme of the Treaty is clearly shown by the terms of Article 83(2)(e). In referring to the regulations or directives to be adopted by the Council 'to give effect to the principles set out in Articles [81] and [82]' this mentions the areas in which in particular such regulations or directives shall operate, including those necessary 'to determine the relationship between national laws and the provisions contained in this Section or adopted pursuant to this Article'.[1] The exact pattern of co-operation could not be foreseen at that early stage; working out the consequences for the Common Market of the terms of Article 81, let alone Article 82, would take at least a decade, as we saw in Part I above.

Since the provisions of the Treaty relating to competition applied only to activities which 'affect trade between Member States', Member States remained free to enact legislation to cover purely domestic issues.[2] In fact, when the Treaty came into force in 1958 limited legislation existed in Member States, ranging from the relatively sophisticated but untried (Germany) to the non-existent. Over the intervening forty-five years all Member States have established national competition authorities, whose primary task is the application of national competition law to local cases outside the scope of Articles 81 and 82, but which must also co-operate on a procedural level with DG Comp on a range of Community cases.

---

[1] The 'Section' referred to original Arts 85 to 90 inclusive, (now Arts 81 to 86) the 'Article' to original Art. 87 (now Art. 83).

[2] Though the scope of such domestic legislation would in time be restricted by the wide interpretation given by the European Court to that very phrase. See Ch. 7, Section 1.

Many of these national competition authorities have already taken the necessary powers to apply both these Articles within their national boundaries, in recognition of the need to decentralize their application, the remainder (including the United Kingdom) will have to do so before the modernizing Regulation comes into force. This development has also been aided by the choice in many Member States of a structure for national competition law which is either identical to that of the Community or at least contains many similar features. In Part 3 of this chapter the main features of national competition authorities are reviewed.

At the time of the signature of the Treaty, however, all these developments lay in the future. Articles 84 and 85 laid down basic ground rules to govern the immediate future until the adoption of Regulations within the scope of Article 83 by the Council. During this interim period, Member States were free to apply both Articles 81 and 82, including the exemption provisions of 81(3), whilst for its part the Commission was entitled to apply the Treaty provisions in this area 'in co-operation with the competent authorities in the Member States, who shall give it their assistance'. The terms of Regulation 17/62, however, ensured that the control of the development of Article 81 would rest firmly with the Commission, for the terms of its Article 9(1) provided that 'subject to review of its decision by the Court of Justice, the Commission shall have sole power to declare Article 81(1) inapplicable pursuant to Article 81(3) of the Treaty'. This key right to grant individual exemption under Article 81(3) was to be the monopoly of the Commission. No national court nor national competition authority was to share it. The importance of a consistent application of 81(3) was considered too vital to be weakened in any way by sharing its application with Member States, many of whom had limited experience of the operation of competition law, or were believed to be insufficiently committed at this early stage to the principles of competition in their national markets. So far as the application of Articles 81(1) and 82 were concerned, national courts and competition authorities were allowed to initiate action against an undertaking provided that the Commission itself had not formally initiated proceedings under Regulation 17. However, in the details of procedural arrangements a considerable degree of co-operation with national authorities was preserved.

1.3 REGULATION 17/62 AND THE NEED FOR CO-OPERATION

Article 10 referred to the contact required between DG Comp and the 'competent authorities' of Member States. They are entitled to receive copies of applications for notification and exemption and the main supporting documents. Article 10(2) set out the principle that administrative procedures shall be carried out in close and constant liaison with these competent authorities, and paragraph (3) provided for the creation of an Advisory Committee on restrictive practices and monopolies to provide the forum in which national authorities may express their views on the procedure. As mentioned in Chapter 4, this is the forum in which Member States become involved in the individual decisions, the views of the Advisory Committee being influential though not decisive. DG Comp preferred naturally to receive the blessing of at least a majority of the Advisory Committee to a proposed decision. If there was substantial opposition within the Committee, the proposals might then have to be taken back for reconsideration in either major or minor respects. However, when DG Comp was convinced that its approach to a particular case was correct, it sometimes persevered in taking a proposed decision to the full Commission even if the vote or opinion of the Advisory Committee had been adverse.

The necessary consequence of such involvement for Member States in the decision-making process of the Commission has been an obligation to co-operate with the administrative and investigatory procedures of the Commission. Articles 11 to 14 of the Regulation contained a number of provisions setting out how this help was to be provided. Thus:

(*a*) Under Article 11(1) the Commission could obtain 'all necessary information' from both governments and competent authorities of Member States as well as from undertakings and associations within those Member States. This was an essential power enabling the Commission to inform itself about the facts and issues relating to a particular complaint or pending case.

(*b*) Article 13(1) provided that the competent authorities of Member States may be asked to conduct investigations which the Commission itself could conduct, including the examination of books and business records, the making of extracts, and the requiring of oral explanations 'on the spot' of the contents of these documents. This power was not much used.

(*c*) Article 14 gave the Commission necessary powers to carry out its own investigations, but with the help of the competent authority which was entitled to (and normally does) escort the Commission officials on their investigations. In the United Kingdom this authority is the Office of Fair Trading. Member States were required under Article 14(6) to give all necessary assistance to the officials authorized by the Commission to make such investigations.

These investigations often involved physical inspection of the books and files of undertakings and could be arranged in advance on a voluntary basis (under Article 14(2)) or sprung as a surprise by way of a 'dawn raid' following a formal decision of the Commission to that effect under Article 14(3).

1.4 EUROPEAN COURT CASE LAW ON 'DAWN RAIDS'

The exact nature of the Commission's powers under Article 14 was the subject of several cases in the European Court of Justice involving the chemical industry. In the *Hoechst*[3] and *Dow*[4] cases the rights of the Commission to carry out searches necessary for the particular stated objectives of its own decision were examined. If the national undertaking seeks physically to bar access to the Commission, its officials cannot use force to obtain entry to business premises without a national court order. The national court must make an order in favour of the Commission if satisfied that the necessary causal link exists between the proposed investigation and its stated objective. In the *Solvay* and *Orkem*[5] cases the Court drew a distinction between the making of factual and objective enquiries from undertakings in the course of such an investigation (which is allowed) and the asking of questions to which replies may force those undertakings to make statements which necessarily admit a breach of the law (not permitted). It was therefore inherent in Regulation 17 that the competent national authorities were to some extent involved in the administrative, fact-finding, and investigatory processes as well as in the decision-making of the Commission.

---

[3] Cases 46/87 and 277/88 [1989] ECR 2859: [1991] 4 CMLR 410.
[4] Cases 85, 97–99/87 [1989] ECR 3137, 3165: [1991] 4 CMLR 410.
[5] Cases 374/87 and 27/88 [1989] ECR 3283, 3355: [1991] 4 CMLR 502.

In a much more recent case (*Roquette*)[6] the European Court has confirmed that national courts are entitled to verify that any coercive measures, such as forcible entry, which the Commission may seek under Article 14 are not 'arbitrary or disproportionate', but is not entitled to demand evidence from the Commission's file as to the grounds for its suspicions that a breach of Article 81 or 82 may have occurred. The Commission must provide the national court with a detailed description of the essential features of a suspected infringement and the involvement of the undertaking against which such coercive measures are sought. It must also indicate the exact matters to which its investigations relate and the need for the particular search. If the national court remains unconvinced by the Commission's evidence, it cannot simply dismiss it as 'arbitrary' or 'disproportionate' but must give the Commission a further opportunity to produce support for its case.

1.5 OTHER MEANS OF MEMBER STATE INVOLVEMENT

Member States are also involved, through the Advisory Committee, in reviewing proposed drafts of new Regulations, including those putting forward proposals for new block exemptions. They have a chance to express their views on these after entering into consultations over the terms of the draft documents with a wide variety of national interested parties and pressure groups. Views of Member States are also made known to the Commission through a number of other formal and informal channels. As a result, although Member States do not customarily initiate individual policies or issue their own suggested drafts for Regulations or for block exemptions, they do have an important role and exercise influence in the framing of policies culminating in both actual decisions and new Regulations. It would therefore be unfair to suggest that the Regulations eventually issued by the Commission, following this lengthy process of consultation, involve some kind of diktat on Member States imposed from above.

2. ARTICLE 81(3) AND THE ISSUE OF SUPREMACY

2.1 THE *WALT WILHELM* CASE AND ITS THREE RULES

The Commission, with the enactment of Regulation 17/62, had firmly established its exclusive right to grant individual exemptions under Article 81(3), in addition to its right under the Treaty, once authorized by the Council, to issue category (block) exemptions. It also had its preferred, but not exclusive, position with regard to the exercise of jurisdiction over Article 81(1) and Article 82. Clearly a Commission decision that a particular agreement fell outside Article 81(1) was binding on national courts and authorities by way of negative clearance; a decision that such an agreement was within the prohibition of Article 81(1) was likewise binding on national courts and authorities, but the difficult question on the issue of supremacy arose in another situation. Was an agreement exempted by the Commission under Article 81(3) capable of prohibition by national law, or did the grant of an exemption by reason of the primacy of Community Law preclude the possibility of prohibition by national law? In general it was clear that agreements must satisfy both Article 81 and

---

[6] Case C-94/00, a decision of the ECJ dated 22 October 2002: [2003] 4 CMLR 46.

national law (the 'double barrier') but this might not be so where the Commission had granted an exemption. Because of the very wide interpretation placed by the early European Court decisions on the concept of 'trade between Member States', this question took on increasing importance; not many agreements of commercial significance, it seemed, would on the basis of such cases be outside the range of Community law, and it thus became important that the European Court of Justice provided an authoritative ruling.

Article 234 of the Treaty provides the appropriate means of obtaining a preliminary ruling on issues of Community law arising in cases being heard in national courts. Its purpose, and a very necessary one, is to ensure that Community law is interpreted in a like manner in all Member States. It was through a preliminary ruling under this Article that a Berlin Court obtained guidance in early 1969 on the relationship between national law and Community law, in the context of parallel investigations being carried out by both the Commission and the German cartel authority (Bundeskartellamt). In recent years, as resources and abilities of national competition authorities have increased, and there has occurred the expansion and refinement of national competition laws substantially based on the principles and language of Articles 81 and 82, so has the willingness and ability of these authorities to work more closely with the Commission. This in turn has made possible the creation of the network of national competition authorities which, as we shall see in the next section of this chapter, forms an essential part of the modernization programme. But all this was far in the future at the time of the *Walt Wilhelm* case.

The background to the case[7] was that certain major manufacturers of aniline dyes had entered into discussions over price increases for their product in circumstances which led to strong suspicion that an agreement had actually been concluded between them as to the timing and level of future increases. Investigations carried out by the Commission led eventually to the bringing of the *Dyestuffs*[8] case. In the meantime, the Bundeskartellamt had begun its own investigation of agreements in which German companies had apparently been involved, and Wilhelm was one of the directors of Bayer involved in this investigation. His claim was that the Bundeskartellamt should desist from carrying out its own investigation whilst DG Comp was carrying out investigations for the Commission into the same matters. The Kammergericht in Berlin referred to the European Court of Justice the issue of whether the Bundeskartellamt could continue with its investigations, or whether under Community law it was required to suspend them pending completion of the investigation being carried out by DG Comp.

The Court pointed out that Community and national laws considered cartels and restrictive agreements from a different point of view; whilst Article 81 regarded them in the light of the obstacles which they would present to trade between Member States, national legislation had its own individual priorities and considerations; though there might be some overlap and interdependence between the two separate investigations, there was no reason in principle why the same agreements could not be the object of two separate parallel proceedings. However, to ensure that the general aims of the Treaty were respected, such simultaneous investigation could only be allowed on the national level if three conditions were satisfied:

(*a*) the national application of the law must not prejudice the full and uniform

---

[7] *Walt Wilhelm* v. *Bundeskartellamt* Case 14/68 [1969] ECR 1: CMLR 100.

[8] *ICI* v. *Commission* Case 48/69 [1972] ECR 619: CMLR 557; several related cases are also reported in [1972] ECR.

application of Community rules, or of the full effect of the measures adopted in the implementation of those rules ('the uniformity rule');

(b) to ensure in any conflict between Community and national rules that the Community law takes precedence (to protect the effectiveness of the Treaty), Member States should not introduce or retain any measures which would prejudice this aim (the 'practical effectiveness rule'); and

(c) individual Member States must take appropriate measures to avoid any risk that a national decision on an issue of competition law might conflict with Commission proceedings still in progress (the 'parallel proceedings' rule).

Whilst these principles gave a clear answer to the Berlin Court as to the proper procedure in the *Walt Wilhelm* case, their application to other circumstances of potential conflict was far from clear, as commentators then noted.[9] As already stated, if the agreement or practice is forbidden by Article 81(1), then the requirements of both uniformity and practical effectiveness underline the impossibility of allowing national law to provide an exemption for it.

In the converse case, where the agreement or concerted practice is outside the scope of Article 81(1) perhaps because it has insufficient effect on trade between Member States, the national authority is clearly free to intervene if it wishes to invoke national law with regard to the domestic effects of the agreement or practice. The intervention in such circumstances is in an area where the Commission either has no jurisdiction under the Treaty or has elected on policy grounds not to exercise any jurisdiction. With regard to the problem of conflict between parallel national community investigation and proceedings, the Commission stated as early as its *4th Annual Report*[10] that the onus was firmly on the national authorities to avoid the risk of conflict, an obligation that could be complied with so long as the national authorities had early consultations with the Commission or even suspended proceedings whilst the Commission investigation was completed.

Whilst acknowledging that the principles in the *Walt Wilhelm* decision provided an answer to the relatively simple situations so far described, the Report also acknowledged that the Court's decision failed to provide answers to the more difficult issue, the status of an agreement granted exemption by the Commission under Article 81(3) when a national authority nevertheless wished to declare it illegal in whole or part. The Commission in its *4th Annual Report* purported to read into the *Wilhelm* decision a rejection by the Court of the argument that exemption by the Commission withdraws only the Community barrier to a restrictive agreement under Article 81(1), leaving unimpaired the national authority's power to prohibit such agreement under its own law (the 'double barrier' theory). However, such rejection can only be found, if at all, implicitly in the Court decision and is not expressly stated in it.

It was clear therefore that there were two situations for which the *Wilhelm* case provided incomplete guidance. First, where the Commission had given an individual exemption to an agreement or concerted practice which a national authority in a Member State wishes either to reject completely or to make subject to some restriction or condition. The second

---

[9] Including K. Markert, 'Some Legal and Administrative Problems of the Co-Existence of Community and National Competition Law in the EEC' [1974] 11 CMLR 92.

[10] (1974) pp.27–31.

problem arose when there is a Regulation in force containing a block exemption for particular forms of agreement, from which the Member State wishes to derogate.

To provide an answer in these situations, it is necessary, whilst bearing in mind the terms of the judgment of the European Court in *Wilhelm*, also to consider the inherent nature of the exemption process for individuals and groups respectively. Although the 'four conditions' to be applied by the Commission are in principle identical for both individual and block exemptions, they are applied in a different way. On one hand, if the exemption flows from an individual decision (which is properly described as administrative or possibly quasi-judicial) it is given on the basis of the particular facts disclosed in the course of the Commission's administrative procedure, rather than from a 'legislative' decision that a particular category or class of agreement both having certain 'plus' (or 'white') features and lacking certain defined anti-competitive 'minus' (or 'black') elements should be exempt. In the latter case, the facts of the individual cases benefiting from the block exemption will never need to be disclosed to DG Comp, since the very concept of the block exemption, emphasized by the recitals to the enabling Council Regulation 19/65, is to provide a legislative solution to the 'mass problem' by excluding the need to notify a large number of separate agreements.[11]

In the *Walt Wilhelm* case the Court refused to accept the argument of the Advocate General that the application of a stricter national law to an individual agreement, possibly overruling the effect of an exemption given by the Commission under Article 81(3), did not prejudice Community law because each system was concerned essentially with the same objectives. Whilst the reasons for its refusal to follow him are not explicitly stated in its judgment, the main difference in the approach of the Court is found in this key section:

Article [81] of the EEC Treaty applies to all the undertakings in the Community whose behaviour it governs either by prohibitions or by means of exemptions granted—subject to conditions which it specifies—in favour of agreements which contribute to improving the production or distribution of products or to promoting technical or economic progress. While the Treaty's primary object is to eliminate by this means the obstacles to the free movement of goods within the Common Market and to confirm and safeguard the unity of that market, it also permits the Community authorities to carry out certain positive, though indirect, action with a view to promoting a harmonious development of economic activities within the whole Community, in accordance with Article 2 of the Treaty.[12]

This passage clearly gives the Community both a positive and a negative function in carrying out its responsibilities. It is hard to see how the grant of an individual exemption by the Commission should not be treated as such a 'positive' act, grounded on both the investigation of the relevant circumstances affecting a particular agreement, and the finding that on balance its preservation is desirable in the public interest of the Community. To quote an early commentary on this issue:

signature of the Treaty by the Member States implies their acceptance of competition policy (as formulated and implemented by the Community authorities) as one of the means of achieving the aims set out in Article 2 of the Treaty and that accordingly the positive aspects of the policy must be

---

[11] See also the *Tetrapak (No. 1)* judgment of the Court of First Instance discussed in Ch. 15, pp.310–12, for comment on the difference between block and individual exemptions under Art. 81(3).

[12] [1969] ECR I-14: CMLR 100, 119.

given the same weight as its negative aspects. Balance must be struck between too little competition at the expense of the consumer and too much competition leading in certain circumstances to inefficiency. If it is right that the Commission's actions should not be frustrated by the application of incompatible national legislation in relation to the former, it must also be right that the Commission should have an equally free hand in relation to the latter. The driver must have the use of the accelerator as well as the brake.[13]

A separate distinction has been suggested between exemptions granted purely for 'public policy reasons', when the Commission's decisions would have to be respected by national courts and authorities, and other cases, when a national authority or court would be free to impose further requirements. It is difficult to see how this distinction could be applied even to individual exemptions, where one has the advantage of a specific finding as to the relevant facts, as it will be hard to distinguish those cases where the public policy element is so great that the exemption should be respected by national courts. In every case where an exemption is granted, the fact that the agreement or practice must comply with all the four conditions contained in Article 81(3) makes it difficult to deny that an element of public policy enters into this assessment. Public policy must enter into an assessment as to whether, for example, an agreement contributes to improving the production or distribution of goods or the promotion of technical or economic progress, but is also likely to be relevant to the assessment of whether consumers receive a fair share of the resulting benefit. An important element in the opinion of Advocate General Roemer is the statement that:

If national authorities thwart the Community exemption through the application of a national rule of prohibition, they no more threaten the objectives of the Treaty than do the parties to that agreement when they refrain from applying it, which can occur at any time. This conclusion applies as a general rule because in principle cartels cannot be considered as instruments of the organisation of the Common Market.[14]

This is surely misleading. If an individual agreement is no longer applied by the parties to it, this has no precedential value, nor does it affect any other agreement between the same or any other parties. On the other hand, an individual exemption has value as a precedent and may affect other persons and Courts in Member States which may take it into consideration in future cases, as well as the parties to the agreement. It reflects a 'positive' policy of the Commission under the Treaty; it is difficult to see how the status of a block exemption cannot equally be described as 'positive' and 'an act of policy' within the spirit of Articles 2 and 3(1)(g) of the Treaty. Indeed, the involvement of Member States in the legislative process leading up to the enactment of block exemptions by way of Regulation is, as we have seen, substantial even though they do not control the final terms in which they are produced. National competition authorities, and Member States themselves, should not therefore be entitled to disregard their terms merely because they prefer a different and stricter solution for their national legislative purposes.

---

[13] D. Barounos, D. Hall, and J. R. James, *EEC Antitrust Law: Principles and Practice* (Butterworths, 1975), pp.142–3.
[14] [1969] ECR I-23: [1969] CMLR 100, 110.

2.2 THE *BMW* AND *VOLKSWAGEN* CASES

It had been hoped that the case of *BMW* v. *ALD Autoleasing*[15] in 1995 would provide the European Court with an opportunity to remove any remaining doubts on this issue. BMW in Germany had sought to prevent its official dealers from selling cars to leasing companies outside their own exclusive territories, issuing a circular ordering them to discontinue such sales to companies like ALD which had established a substantial leasing business throughout Germany. ALD challenged the circular alleging, that it was in breach of Article 81(1) and not within the permitted set of contractual restrictions allowed by Regulation 123/85. The Bundesgerichtof referred the case to the European Court on two issues: first on the application of the terms of Regulation 123/85 to BMW's prohibition on its dealers from making such sales to leasing companies outside their territory, and secondly, if such a restriction was permitted by the exemptions contained in 123/85, whether the German courts could prohibit the practice under national rules against supply boycotts. In his opinion Tesauro A-G came down firmly on the side of the supremacy of Community law, stating that 'to reconcile the primacy of Community law with the possibility of prohibiting an agreement which had been exempted by and under Community law seems to me a desperate undertaking, even a diabolic one'. Unfortunately the European Court, after agreeing with the opinion of the Advocate General that the proposed ban by BMW on its dealers selling to leasing companies was not protected by Regulation 123/85, gave no ruling on the possible conflict between a Community exemption under that Regulation and a German prohibition of the same practice under national law.

In the companion case of *Bundeskartellamt* v. *Volkswagen* the Advocate General (though not the Court) considered whether a negative clearance by the Commission of an agreement under Article 81(1) left a Member State free to restrict or prohibit that agreement. He suggested that this might depend on the basis for the grant of negative clearance; if clearance was granted after a finding that the agreement contained no appreciable restriction of competition, after balancing the various relevant circumstances, then the Member State should not act against that judgment by the Commission. On the other hand, if the negative clearance had been granted simply because the agreement did not affect trade between Member States, then the Member State was entitled to act in regard to the agreement as a case where the Commission had disclaimed any jurisdiction over it.

2.3 THE NEW REGULATION RESOLVES THE ISSUE

The outcome of this long and important debate has however now been resolved, not by any decision of a Community Court, but by the new Regulation 1/2003[16] that replaces Regulation 17/62 from 1 May 2004. The most important single Article in this new Regulation is Article 3, which establishes the supremacy of Community competition law whilst still allowing a limited degree of freedom to national competition authorities in the application of their national law.

---

[15] Case C-70/93 [1995] ECR I-3439: [1996] 4 CMLR 478. In a parallel case *Bundeskartellamt* v. *Volkswagen* similar issues arose, and the European Court's judgment was in similar terms: Case 266/93: [1995] ECR I-3477: [1996] 4 CMLR 505. Whilst the cases dealt with block exemptions, it had been hoped that the Court's judgment would be sufficiently broad to deal with the issue of individual exemptions, too.

[16] [2003] OJ L1/1.

Under its original terms as set out in early drafts the supremacy of Community law in this context was absolute; the text proposed at this time read simply:

Where an agreement, a decision by an association of undertakings or a concerted practice within the meaning of Article 81 of the Treaty or the abuse of a dominant position within the meaning of Article 82 may affect trade between Member States, Community competition law shall apply to the exclusion of national competition laws.

The sweeping nature of this proposal raised numerous objections from Member States. The Commission soon acknowledged that it would be satisfied with a less absolute provision provided that the essential core of the text conferring supremacy on Community law remained intact. After long negotiations the final text adopted makes clear that national competition authorities still retain some freedom to apply their own competition laws alongside Articles 81 and 82. Thus the text of the new Article 3 as finally adopted reads:

1. Where the competition authorities of the Member States or national courts apply national competition law to agreements, decisions of associations of undertakings or concerted practices within the meaning of Article 81(1) of the Treaty which may affect trade between Member States within the meaning of that provision, they shall also apply Article 81 of the Treaty to such agreements, decisions or concerted practices. Where the competition authorities of the Member States or national courts apply national competition law to any abuse prohibited by Article 82 of the Treaty, they shall also apply Article 82 of the Treaty.

2. The application of national competition law may not lead to the prohibition of agreements, decisions by associations of undertakings or concerted practices which may affect trade between Member States but which do not restrict competition within the meaning of Article 81(1) of the Treaty, or which fulfil the conditions of Article 81(3) of the Treaty or which are covered by a Regulation for the application of Article 81(3) of the Treaty. Member States shall not under this Regulation be precluded from adopting and applying on their territory stricter national laws which prohibit or sanction unilateral conduct engaged in by undertakings.

3. Without prejudice to general principles and other provisions of Community law, paragraphs 1 and 2 do not apply when the competition authorities and the courts of the Member States apply national merger control laws nor do they preclude the application of provisions of national law that predominantly pursue an objective different from that pursued by Articles 81 and 82 of the Treaty.

The effect of these rules (which apply also to national courts as explained in the following chapter) is as follows:

(i)   A national competition authority which applies national competition law to an agreement, decision or concerted practice 'which may affect trade between Member States' must also at the same time apply Article 81 (paragraph 1). If dealing with abuse of a dominant position, it must also apply to Article 82.

(ii) In the course of such application national competition authorities may not prohibit under national law agreements, decisions or practices that will either fall outside Article 81(1) or meet the requirements of Article 81(3) whether by individual or block exemption (paragraph 2).

(iii) National competition authorities may however apply national competition law, and paras 1 and 2 do not apply even if national law is stricter than the corresponding Community law, in the case of (a) unilateral conduct engaged in by undertakings, and (*b*) in the application of national merger control law, and (*c*) in applying national law that predominantly pursues a different objective from those of Articles 81 and 82, provided in all cases that the application of national law is itself not in breach of general principles of Community law.

This compromise seems to protect the right of national competition authorities to adopt sanctions under national law for unilateral acts or practices by undertakings which Community rules might not be able to reach, because of the fact that Article 82 applies only to dominant companies. For example, let us suppose that a market investigation by the Competition Commission in the United Kingdom under the Enterprise Act 2002 produces a finding that several companies in a particular sector, for example brewing, have separately adopted practices relating to, for example, exclusive supply or refusal to deal with particular wholesalers, but where none of the brewers can be legally characterized as individually dominant and between whom no agreement or concerted practice can be shown. Under the Enterprise Act the Commission would then be able to impose sanctions against these non-dominant companies individually, not by way of fines (as might have been appropriate following proceedings by the Office of Fair Trading) under the United Kingdom Competition Act Chapter 1 or Chapter 2 (equivalent to Articles 81 and 82) but by way of a varied range of remedies which may be of a different kind (as listed in Schedule 8 of the Enterprise Act). Moreover, measures taken primarily by way of consumer protection in such a case or any other (either under the Competition Act or Enterprise Act) would also be permitted under the terms of this Article.

3. NATIONAL COMPETITION AUTHORITIES AND COMMUNITY LAW

3.1 THE DEBATE ON NATIONAL COMPETITION AUTHORITY PARTICIPATION

The original role envisaged under Regulation 17/62 for the national competition authorities of the Six was very limited, especially as only one Member State at that time, Germany, could be described as having an effective authority with both a full substantive law and the resources to enforce it. Through the Advisory Committee established under that Regulation the Member States could render some help to the Commission in enforcing its Community rules. But it was certainly not anticipated initially they would play an active part themselves in enforcing Community competition law both because of lack of resources and of the legal powers under national law for the enforcement of such rules at a time when their own national laws were only gradually emerging.

Gradually however over the last decade of the twentieth century and with the expansion of the Community from its original membership of six to fifteen Member States the landscape has changed. Not only did the Commission begin to find that national competition authorities were now more willing and able to help it enforce competition policy but it realised that its own resources were more than fully stretched in dealing with major Community-wide cases, particularly cartels, and that maintenance of its monopoly over the grant of individual exemptions (both formal and informal) under Article 81(3) was no longer sensible or indeed possible. The Commission had taken on substantial new responsibilities under the Merger Regulation, including the review of many major joint ventures, an increased caseload under State aid, and more work under Article 86 including the preparation of directives under Article 86(3) in order to liberalize sectors formerly dominated by national monopolies in transport, telecommunications, and energy. The decision in *Automec (No. 2)*[17] had enabled it to give priority to cases with a high Community interest and to consider the allocation of responsibility for dealing with cases not in that category to national competition authorities with the necessary powers.

In an article surveying these developments, a former Director General of DG Comp, Claus Dieter Ehlermann, stated his surprise that the debate on fuller use of national competition authorities for Community law enforcement did not begin until the early 1990s.[18] In this article he describes the steps taken by the Commission after *Automec (No. 2)* to seek greater participation by national competition authorities and to establish ground rules for their extension of jurisdiction. The working party chaired by Jean Dubois in 1994 led to a number of comments in the 1994 *Annual Report*[19] of the Commission as to how it was hoped this decentralization would proceed, as follows:

The [Dubois] Report applies three criteria to identify the cases that might be dealt with by a national authority. First, their effects must be located mainly within a single Member State. However, if an agreement or practice implemented mainly in a Member State raises a question of Community interest, the Commission will initiate proceedings on the basis of Article 9(3) of Regulation 17/62. Secondly, the case must involve infringements of Article [81(1)] that probably do not satisfy the criteria of Article [81(3)]. The case may also involve infringements of Article 82, which are often detected following a complaint. Thirdly, protection at national level must be effective. Such effectiveness depends on various factors; the prime requirement is that there must be adequate legislation. Adequate legislation means legislation that is satisfactory from the point of view of the substantive competition rules. It should be noted in this respect that some national legislations do not provide for the possibility of their competition authorities applying Articles [81] and [82] of the Treaty directly, and that some national legislations are based on concepts of competition other than those Articles. However, national legislation should also provide for effective investigatory powers and for the possibility of effectively penalizing infringements of the competition rules. Yet a legislative arsenal is not sufficient; there must also be the will and means of using it. Each national authority must, therefore, not only have rules of substance and procedure, but also the necessary human and material resources. In addition one must not overlook the possibility of conflicts of interest, particularly in cases involving public enterprises.

3.2 THE 1997 NOTICE ON CO-OPERATION

As part of the same process, the Commission published a Notice at the end of 1997[20] on co-operation with such authorities, intended to operate in parallel with the equivalent 1993 Notice on co-operation with national courts. The 1997 Notice emphasized again the special nature of the role played by competition authorities, primarily concerned with monitoring and enforcing the law rather than resolving disputes between individuals and undertakings,

---

[17] Case T-24/90 [1992] ECR II-2223: 5 CMLR 431.

[18] 'Implementation of EC Competition Law by National Antitrust Authorities', [1996] 17 ECLR 88–95. See also P. Marsden [1997] 17 ECLR pp.234–241. For a later view, see C.-D. Ehlermann [2000] 37 CMLR 537–590.

[19] Pp.38–9.   [20] [1997] OJ C313/3.

without the constraints that courts are necessarily under from the fact that the conduct and timing of cases are controlled not by them but by the parties. The Commission believed that the competition authorities of Member States were often better placed to deal with cases with a Community element than the courts. They often have the ability to acquire detailed and precise knowledge of relevant markets, especially those with distinctive national features, and to carry out investigation, particularly where the impact of the practices or agreements is largely within their own territory. Nevertheless, there would always be a large number of cases for which the Commission would continue to take jurisdiction, either because of the degree of Community interest or because of the importance of the economic or legal issues raised.

3.3 THE MODERNIZATION WHITE PAPER OF 1999

The Commission was by now well aware that reform would have to take a more fundamental character. Senior officials met therefore during 1998 and 1999 on a regular basis, but in some secrecy, to debate the future of the Directorate General for Competition within the Commission, and in particular the need for it to adapt in order to meet the challenge of the likely major enlargement in 2004. The outcome of the deliberations of this working group turned out to be far more radical than had been anticipated. The White Paper setting out its detailed proposals that was published in April 1999 sparked off a lively debate in industrial, commercial, political, legal, and administrative circles and at all levels about the practicality of the new proposals.

The central theme of the White Paper was that, while the monopoly over the granting of individual exemptions granted to the Commission by Regulation 17/62 had been appropriate in its day, it was no longer possible for the Commission to operate it under its present and likely future workload. Even with increased resources, which were by no means guaranteed, it would not be able to operate such a centralized system of control. It would be necessary for it rather to focus on those tasks to which priority had to be given, namely the investigation and enforcement of sanctions against widespread cartels and abuses of dominant position within the Community, whilst sharing with national competition authorities and courts the application of cases under Articles 81 and 82. The Commission had of course contributed to its own predicament by the wide interpretation which it had applied to Article 81(1) and to the very small number of formal decisions which it had proved able to issue each year. But the notification system which Regulation 17/62 had adopted would in any event have ultimately proved unsatisfactory, even if the Commission had been granted greater resources and had not been given the extra responsibilities mentioned above, in particular the application of the Merger Regulation.

The White Paper acknowledged that a consequence of Regulation 17/62 had been an over-emphasis on the legal content of agreements, without sufficient attention being paid to their economic effect, or to the market power of the undertakings concerned. It argued that, whilst the removal of the availability of individual notification by the Commission would to some degree reduce legal certainty for undertakings entering into such agreements, this could be minimized by the fact that there had been four decades of Community experience in the application of Articles 81 and 82, and that case law had clarified many aspects of these Articles. Moreover, the current range of block exemptions starting with Regulation 2790/99 with its emphasis on market share thresholds and limited 'black' lists of forbidden clauses provided a much greater degree of certainty than their earlier counterparts. The regular practice of the issue by the Commission of extensive guidelines could also play an important role in assisting undertakings; the possibility of issuing additional block exemptions was also to be considered.

In place of the notification system, the new system proposed would be that of 'exception légale' under which the application of paragraphs (1) and (3) of Article 81 would be combined, so that agreements, decisions and concerted practices would either be 'valid' (having applied both paras (1) and (3)), or 'void' under para. (2), because they fell within para. (1) without being able to benefit from the provisions of para. (3)). This change would allow the application of Article 81 in its entirety both by national competition authorities and national courts, without having any longer to suspend investigation or judgment, while the Commission decided whether an exemption should be granted.

On the whole the reception of these unexpectedly far reaching proposals was favourable; it was recognised that the Commission had made a real attempt to face the problems that it confronted and its past inadequacies, and had sought to produce a blueprint for the future which offered a genuine prospect of a more effective way of applying competition policy. After considerable debate in the Community institutions and elsewhere it was finally agreed at a Council meeting on 26 November 2002 that the new Regulation embodying these proposals should come into force on 1 May 2004, thus allowing some seventeen months for preparation of the necessary ancillary Commission Notices and guidelines, and for the further strengthening of the existing network between the Commission and national competition authorities. This date was also chosen so as to coincide with the likely date[21] for the admission of a large number of new members, whom it was obviously sensible to admit simultaneously with the introduction of the new rules.

4. THE NEW ROLE FOR NATIONAL COMPETITION AUTHORITIES

4.1 INTRODUCTION

The new role for national competition authorities therefore comes fully into operation in a relatively short time. The new Regulation itself confers far greater responsibilities and jurisdiction on these authorities than could ever have been anticipated in the early days of the Treaty of Rome. To understand their place in the new order, it is necessary both to examine the way in which such authorities are currently organized under national law, and the functions which they will perform under the terms of the new Regulation.

It would perhaps have been convenient at this point to include detailed descriptions of the competition authorities in each of the Member States, setting out the national legislation governing their activities and the separate individual bodies found in each of them, upon which the task of administering the national law falls.[22] At present however change is taking

---

[21] In December 2002 the terms of admission of ten new Member States had been agreed at the Copenhagen meeting of Heads of Member States, subject to ratification by the individual new entrants.

[22] There are numerous sources of information about the current National Competition legislation and national competition authorities on the websites both of the Commission and of the individual authorities, some of which provide English language versions of their legislation. Also useful are the 'National Reports'

place, of a widespread nature, in the laws of nearly all Member States, mainly in response to the adoption by the Council of the new Regulation and the impact of the modernization programme. Such a lengthy description would risk being out of date even before it was published. What therefore seems more relevant is to explain the organization, first of the United Kingdom's own competition law authorities as set up under the 1998 Competition Act and the 2002 Enterprise Act, and then to indicate in general terms the constituent elements common to the national competition authorities of the other Member States.

4.2 UNITED KINGDOM COMPETITION AUTHORITIES

For many years after the United Kingdom joined the Community in 1973, the structure of UK Competition Law and its component authorities remained largely unchanged. The Director General of Fair Trading was responsible for maintaining a register of restrictive agreements under the Restrictive Trade Practices Acts 1976 and 1977 which might then be called before the Restrictive Practice Court for an assessment of whether they should be declared unenforceable as in breach of that law. Mergers and sectoral references, known as 'monopoly references', were made by the Secretary of State or by the Director General of Fair Trading in cases considered appropriate to the Monopolies and Mergers Commission under the 1973 Fair Trading Act. If the MMC after investigation found adverse effects to the public interest in such a case they would make a report to this effect to the Secretary of State for Trade and Industry on an advisory basis and the Secretary of State could then, in conjunction with the Office of Fair Trading, determine appropriate remedies. A Competition Act of 1980 allowed investigation of anti-competitive practices by individual undertakings but proved in practice ineffective.

Such legislative inactivity in national competition law for over twenty years came to an end eventually with the election of a Labour Government in 1997; since then both substantive and procedural changes have been substantial. The effect has been to bring UK substantive law into a much closer relationship with Community competition law and policy, and to bring about elimination in most cases of ministerial rights to intervene. This had involved giving greater responsibilities to both the Office of Fair Trading and the Competition Commission which from 1 April 1999 replaced the Monopolies and Mergers Commission, though performing the same functions. A Competition Appeal Tribunal has been established which deals with appeals both from the Office of Fair Trading under the terms of the Competition Act and with judicial review applications in respect of decisions of the Competition Commission in merger and market investigation cases heard under the Enterprise Act.

The combined effect of the two Acts can be summarized as follows. Chapter 1 and Chapter 2 of the Competition Act reproduce the precise terms of Articles 81 and 82 and authorize the Office of Fair Trading to impose fines for undertakings found in breach. Appeal lies against any such finding or against the fine imposed to the Tribunal which

contained in the 'News Section' of *European Competition Law Review* and *Competition Laws in the EU, its Member States and Switzerland*, edited by F. Vogelaar and others (Kluwer, 2000, Vol.1; 2002, Vol. 2). This work seeks to include in one text all aspects of the competition law of the Member States, but acknowledges that change is so rapid that 'it is like shooting at a moving target'.

is a separate body, and has already rendered a number of important decisions in appeal cases.[23] Appeals can be brought to the Tribunal only by the parties to the decision or by a third party with a 'sufficient interest' in the view of the Tribunal. Moreover, monetary claims can also be made to the Tribunal by those who have suffered financial loss as a result of any infringement of either Chapter 1 or Chapter 2 of the Act or of Article 81 or 82. All such actions for monetary compensation are described generally as 'follow on actions'. Claims for compensation can also be brought by groups of consumers through specific bodies which represent them, again once a decision has been given confirming a breach of either the United Kingdom or EC competition law not still subject to appeal. From the Tribunal itself in all cases appeal lies to the Court of Appeal on points of law only. Criminal proceedings can also be brought against individuals who dishonestly enter into cartel agreements, leading to a range of penalties including both fines and imprisonment.

The Office of Fair Trading not only investigates alleged breaches of Chapters 1 and 2 of the Competition Act, but also determines whether particular mergers or market investigations should be referred to the Competition Commission for examination. These cases are no longer governed by the Fair Trading Act 1973, in which the criterion applied had in principle always been 'the public interest' as defined by Section 84 of that Act, although the effect on competition had normally been the prime element in the assessment. Under the Enterprise Act, however, the criterion is whether the merger will lead to a 'substantially lessening of competition' or in a market investigation, whether there are features of that sector which restrict competition. One of the most important provisions of the Act is the removal of the power of the Secretary of State to make decisions in mergers and market investigation cases. Henceforth, the decision to make a reference will be that of the Office of Fair Trading, now a body corporate, of which the present Director General is both chairman and chief executive, and the decision of the Competition Commission, in such cases, will normally be final. The Secretary of State retains the right of decision only in cases involving a special 'public interest' such as national security or defence, or where Parliament has specifically approved a particular public interest as relevant to the case. In such cases the Competition Commission will, in most respects, render a report but this will not be determinative and will simply be advisory to the Minister, as was previously the case under the Fair Trading Act (except in those cases where no public interest finding had been made, when the Competition Commission's report had always been determinative).

Appeals from decisions of the Office of Fair Trading under the Competition Act or the Competition Commission under the Enterprise Act in respect of mergers or market investigations all go to the Tribunal. In the case of the Competition Act it is a full rehearing of the case, but in the case of appeals on mergers or market investigations under the Enterprise Act, it is of more limited scope by way of judicial review, with appeal of matters of law in all cases from the Tribunal to the Court of Appeal. The jurisdiction of the Tribunal extends to England and Wales, Scotland, and Northern Ireland.

---

[23] These are reported in the Competition Appeal Reports (Comp AR). See 'The First Two Years of the Competition Commission Appeal Tribunal', Jephcott, CYELS Vol. 4 (2001), pp.217–241. The Tribunal and the courts in dealing with cases under the Competition Act are required by s. 60 to apply the Treaty of Rome and the principles and case law laid down by the ECJ and CFI, to ensure consistency with EC law. They must also 'have regard' to any relevant decision or statement of the Commission.

The competition laws of the United Kingdom are thus administered by a number of different bodies each with its separate function, as follows:

(i)   The *political* function of the Secretary of State for Trade and Industry, who under the new regime introduced by the two Acts referred to above has a considerably reduced role, since he makes decisions only in special 'public interest' cases.

(ii)   The *administrative* or *executive* function performed by the Office of Fair Trading, which investigates complaints from third parties or on its own account, and can render decisions imposing fines and banning agreements and practices under the Competition Act, Chapter 1 and Chapter 2, equivalent to Articles 81 and 82, and which also makes references to the Competition Commission in respect of mergers and market investigations.

(iii) The *decision-making body* in merger and market investigation cases, the Competition Commission.

(iv)   The *specialist appellate* body, the Competition Appeal Tribunal, with its dual role of hearing appeals by way of full rehearing from decisions of the Office of Fair Trading under the Competition Act and also by way of judicial review from the Competition Commission under the Enterprise Act, dealing with both procedural and substantive issues in respect of merger and market investigation references.

(v)   *The Courts of First Instance*, which retain jurisdiction in competition cases, though subject to transfer to the Competition Appeal Tribunal on some occasions, under provisions of the Enterprise Act (see Chapter 21, Section 4.3).

(vi)   The *higher courts of law*, namely the Court of Appeal and the House of Lords, which will hear appeals on points of law arising from decisions of the Competition Appeal Tribunal.

4.3 NATIONAL COMPETITION AUTHORITIES IN OTHER MEMBER STATES

Whilst there is obviously considerable variation in detail between the legislative provisions operating in each Member State and between the institutions that each have established to apply national competition law, nevertheless a common pattern can be seen in each of the Member States, which is required by the nature of the subject matter of competition law cases. It is possible to identify six common elements in the law of these Member States which correspond in broad terms, though not in detail, to the structure of the UK system. Thus within each Member State we can find:

(*a*) A *comprehensive law or laws* setting out the substantive and procedural rules. These will be closely modelled in both structure and language on Articles 81 and 82, although in some Member States there are additional or supplementary rules extending the scope of national law beyond these Articles. These statutes will have been amended on a number of occasions and will be undergoing further change as a result of the Modernization Regulation No. 1/2003.

   The oldest of these laws is the law against Restraint of Competition in Germany which came into effect in its original form on the same day as the Treaty of Rome itself, on 1 January 1958. Member States (and, also, the UK) who do not yet have the power under national law to apply Articles 81 and 82 as part of their domestic law will have to amend their statutes in order to comply with Article 3 of the new Regulation as mentioned above. In some cases, for example in Finland and Germany, the definition of an agreement subject to prohibition is more extensive and detailed than that set out in Article 81, and the prohibition of vertical agreements may be drawn up on the basis of abuse. In Germany and Austria, the definition of 'dominance' is rather more specific in terms of market share than that contained in Article 82. In some cases, including Sweden, Finland, and Ireland the right to claim damages for breach of the competition rules is expressly preserved in the governing statute. In four countries, Germany, France, Austria, and Ireland, criminal sanctions of imprisonment can be imposed on individuals concerned, in addition to the fines to be imposed upon undertakings (in all Member States) and individuals (in some Member States). A number of Member States have adopted national block exemptions parallel to those of the Community, and one or two have even added additional block exemptions to national legislation (such as that adopted in Sweden for the benefit of retail co-operatives).

(b) An *administrative body* equivalent to the Office of Fair Trading in the United Kingdom often named as the 'Competition Authority' or 'Competition Commission' which has primary responsibility in the Member State for carrying out national competition policy. It will carry out investigations into suspected breaches and will have powers to make 'dawn raids' on undertakings and to obtain information from third parties. It will have close links on a day-to-day basis with the European Commission and will exchange a large amount of information with them on pending cases. It will normally appoint its national representative on the Advisory Committee in Brussels. It may also have power itself to impose decisions involving fines and prohibition orders against undertakings for breach of national law or for breach of Article 81 or 82; alternatively (in some or all cases) it may have to pass the case on to another body, which alone has the required authority to make binding decisions.

(c) The *decision making body* which in some jurisdictions may be the same as, and in others may be quite separate from, the administrative body referred to under (b). Thus, for example, in Austria, in some cases the Federal Competition Agency, and in other cases the Federal Anti-Trust Prosecutor, bring prosecutions before the Cartel Court which can then alone issue binding decisions on undertakings. In Belgium, whilst the Competition Service can carry out investigations, only the Competition Council can impose fines. In Finland the Market Court imposes fines which are proposed to it by the Competition Authority and similar arrangements prevail in Sweden; whilst the Swedish competition authority can impose injunctions against infringement of national law, only the Stockholm District Court can impose a fine. In Germany on the other hand the Federal Cartel Office (the Bundeskartellamt) is both the administrative and decision making body and a similar situation prevails in The Netherlands, Italy, and Greece. It seems that only in Luxembourg are decisions in all competition cases are made by the Minister of the Economy following the report from the Commission on restrictive commercial practices. This however is likely to change prior to the implementation of the modernization programme. In Portugal fines are normally imposed by the Competition Council, although the main administrative authority (the Directorate General for Trade and Competition) can make decisions and impose fines in a limited range of cases such as refusal to deal.

(*d*) The *appellate body*; in nearly all Member States the rulings of either the administrative body or the decision making authority in competition cases can be appealed to a court or tribunal which has specialized experience in such cases. Whilst in the United Kingdom such appeal is to the Competition Appeal Tribunal, this is unusual; in most cases the appeal is to one of the regular courts. Thus, in The Netherlands the appellate court is the Rotterdam District Court, in Sweden the Stockholm District Court and above it the Market Court, and in Finland it is the Market Court and the Supreme Administrative Court. In France we find this role reserved for the Paris Court of Appeals (and for appeals from the Minister of Economics, as in merger cases, to the Conseil d'État). In Germany the specialist court of appeal is now the Federal Court in Dusseldorf, in Greece it is the Athens Administrative Court of Appeal, and in Austria the Vienna Court of Appeal. There is normally in all Member States a further right of appeal on points of law to higher courts, and requests can be made to the European Court of Justice under Article 234 for opinions on matters of either EC law or on matters of national law which are identical to those arising under Community law (as in the *Oscar Bronner*[24] case).

(*e*) There is often a further body established with solely *advisory powers* which is responsible for preparing reports on the operation of national competition laws and procedures, which are then forwarded to the heads of competition authorities and to the responsible minister in the national government. Not many Member States possess this type of body but those that exist by their reports can have important influence on the development of national law. In Germany the Monopolies Commission plays this role and in Austria the Competition Commission. It is possible that in time other Member States may also find this type of body useful for carrying out reviews of national substantive and procedural law.

(*f*) *Political institutions.* In some Member States the responsible minister with political responsibility for the administration of national competition law may retain powers to intervene in some cases, or indeed in all cases (as in Luxembourg), in other countries he is only entitled to intervene in a limited range of cases. Thus in Germany the Minister for Economic Affairs has the right to intervene to overrule a merger decision of the Bundeskartellamt on grounds of national interest but has only done so on a handful of occasions during the last forty-five years. In France it is the Minister of Finance that makes all decisions in merger cases (though not in other competition cases) where the role of the Conseil de la Concurrence (Competition Commission) is solely consultative. In Portugal a number of important decisions are also made by the Minister but they are still subject to appeal to the Supreme Administrative Court. By contrast in Sweden there is no ministerial right to intervene in competition cases and in The Netherlands the original right of ministers to give instructions in individual cases contained in the 1998 Act has subsequently been abolished, to give full operating independence to the Dutch Competition Authority.

---

[24] Case C-7/97 [1998] ECR I-7791; [1999] 4 CMLR 112.

5. NATIONAL COMPETITION AUTHORITIES AND THE MODERNIZATION PROGRAMME—THE NEW ERA

5.1 INTRODUCTION

The main principles which underlie the Regulation and the modernization programme have already been discussed, but the radical nature of the new functions which the programme confers on such authorities can only be fully appreciated in the context of an examination of the detailed terms of the Regulation. It is the responsibility of Member States to designate those bodies[25] (which could either be administrative or judicial in nature or with a combination of these functions) which are to be its competition authorities, as indeed they have had to do in the past under Regulation 17/62.

The terms of the Regulation need to be read against the background of lengthy recitals which lay out its main principles. These include:

— the importance of ensuring that national competition authorities can apply Articles 81 and 82 in their entirety, including for the first time cases arising under Article 81(3) and that they also do so in all cases where trade between Member States is affected;

— the consequent need for a network joining all such authorities and the Commission through which a high level of co-operation can be maintained and sufficiently detailed information exchanged;

— the retention of the Commission's right (after consultation with the Member State affected) to intervene and take over cases in which an authority is already acting;

— the right of a national competition authority to suspend an investigation into a case if it discovers that another Member State's authority is already dealing with it;

— the general principle that a national authority should suspend investigations into a case if it discovers that the authority in another Member State is already dealing with it;

— the general principle that authorities should avoid decision that are in conflict with those of the Commission or other national authorities; and

— the option for authorities to assist other Member States' authorities by carrying out investigations on their own territory and on their behalf.

5.2 THE CONTENT OF REGULATION 1/2003

Article 1 of the Regulation is the replacement for Article 1 of Regulation 17/62 but differs from it in the important respect that the whole of Article 81, as well as Article 82, now becomes of direct effect and that no 'prior decision' of the Commission is required for the application of Article 81(3).

Article 2 confirms that the original burden of proof that Article 81(1) or Article 82 apply

---

[25] On the question of the 'designation' of national competition authorities see C. Kerse, *EC Antitrust Procedure*, 4th edn. (Sweet & Maxwell, 1998), Ch. 5, pp.202–16.

remains with the Commission or other competition authority seeking to enforce the prohibition but that the undertaking which seeks to show that Article 81(3) is available to exempt
its agreement has itself that burden of proof.

Article 3 contains the rules of supremacy as between national and Community law
described in the previous section of this chapter. This enables national authorities to apply
national law of a different or stricter character in three cases; namely in merger control, in
control of unilateral conduct by undertakings, which do not individually hold a dominant
position, and in applying national law with a predominantly different objective such as
consumer protection or environmental protection laws. The decisions which a national
competition authority can take are specified in *Article 5*, namely those:

— requiring an infringement to be ended;

— ordering interim measures;

— accepting commitments;

— imposing fines and penalties; and

— determining that no grounds for action exist.

Articles 11 and 12 deal with the vital issue of the co-operation required from authorities
throughout the network and commits both the Commission and the authorities to apply the
competition rules of the Community in close co-operation. To some extent the necessary
close connection between these bodies has already been developed, especially in recent years
but the Regulation requires even further co-operation. The network operates not only
between national authorities, but also between the many competition officials who work for
those authorities and are in regular contact with each other through electronic and other
means of communication. It is anticipated that each of the authorities participating, and the
Commission itself, will keep each other fully informed of important general developments
and particular cases. The authority must give the Commission at least thirty days' notice of
the adoption of any infringement decision, the acceptance of a commitment from an undertaking or the withdrawal from such undertaking of a block exemption sending copies of the
relevant documentation. While this is compulsory, the authority may also, at its option,
supply the same information to the authorities of other Member States with whom they are
entitled to exchange information on cases of mutual interest. Moreover the authorities are
free to consult the Commission at any time on any case involving the application of Community law. Ultimately Article 11(6) allows the Commission to take over a case, a power
unlikely to be used lightly and only when after full consultation it looks as if a Member State
may be in danger of producing a result in conflict with well established principles of
Community law.

The exchange of information which underpins the network is covered by Article 12. *The
Spanish Banks* decision, which dealt with the interpretation of Article 20 of Regulation 17/
62, made it clear that information provided by the Commission to national authorities
could not be used for cases under national law but only as a starting point for the authority
to commence its own investigations. The terms of Article 3 will considerably reduce the
difficulties caused to authorities and the Commission by that judgment, since in many cases
the national authority will be applying both national law and Community law in parallel,
where Article 12(2) provides that confidential information from the Commission can be
utilized. Only in cases where an authority is applying national law alone will it have to carry

out its own investigations and obtain its own evidence, without being able to rely on evidence from the Commission.

A number of national authorities apply sanctions not only upon undertakings but also on individuals, usually directors or employees who have been involved in the cartels or other prohibited restrictive practices. In these cases confidential information from elsewhere can only be used in evidence to impose sanctions (of fine or imprisonment) on individuals if both the transmitting and receiving authority have sanctions of a similar type. If not, the information can only be used if it has been collected in a way which respects the same levels of protection of the rights of defence of the individual as is the standard for the recipient authority and only for the application of fines, not for imprisonment.[26]

National authorities have duties of course not only to the Commission but also to competition authorities of other Member States and also to their own national courts. *Article 13* outlines the rights of an authority to suspend or reject proceedings in a case because another Member State is already dealing with it. This however is an optional, not a mandatory, obligation. It is possible that situations may arise where both Member States are keen to continue with their respective investigations and it may be necessary for consultation to take place, officially or unofficially, through the network to avoid conflicting decisions being rendered by two authorities. Article 16(2) provides that authorities cannot take decisions that run counter to existing Commission decisions but this does not apply to conflicts between two authorities of Member States. *Article 15* provides the authorities with the opportunity of assisting their own national courts in competition cases though their involvement is limited to the presentation of written observations, though these may be oral, with the court's consent.

The power of the Commission to carry out its own investigations has been extended under *Articles 17 to 21* and national authorities already have an obligation to provide necessary information to the Commission to enable it to carry out its duties, and to assist it with its dawn raids, if necessary obtaining the required court orders from national courts. Obtaining the court order will be mandatory in the case of searches of domestic premises as opposed to the more normal practice of searching business premises. A fresh power conferred on national authorities by *Article 22* is to carry out within their own territory investigations for other authorities in order to establish whether there has been an infringement of Articles 81 or 82.

Finally *Article 29(2)* entitles authorities to withdraw the benefit of Commission block exemptions in its territory, if it discovers that agreements which have enjoyed the benefits of such exemption have effects in the territory (or part of it) which have all the characteristics of a distinct geographic market. This of course is an additional power to that contained already in Regulation 2790/99 for national authorities and Member States.

5.3 THE JOINT DECLARATION

Alongside the Regulation, a Joint Declaration by the Council and Commission in December 2002 on the functioning of national competition authorities has considerable importance.

---

[26] A number of national competition authorities including the UK now have statutory powers to disclose information to other foreign authorities on a mutual basis, where the case is sufficiently serious. See Enterprise Act, ss. 243 and 244.

This was adopted at the same time as the Regulation and is intended to provide authorities with supplementary guidance on how to operate in co-operation with both the Commission and other such authorities. It contains just twenty-four short paragraphs, but should prove of practical value to officials as they seek to operate the new system from May 2004 onwards.

The Joint Declaration emphasizes that it is political in nature, not legally binding as the Regulation itself, but containing the common understanding shared by all Member States and the Commission as to the way in which the network should operate. The Joint Declaration too will have to be supplemented before 2004 by a further Notice from the Commission dealing with questions of its detailed operation. Member States accept that their own authorities may operate with different systems of enforcement, but that they are all independent from each other and entitled to mutual respect; all will have full legal authority to apply Articles 81 and 82.

The Commission itself is responsible for ensuring that the Treaty and the Regulations made under it are observed by all authorities but will exercise its powers with utmost regard for the essentially co-operative nature of the network. It will itself normally deal with cases if more than three Member States are substantially affected. In other cases individual authorities can assert jurisdiction if the agreement or practice primarily affects that jurisdiction and if moreover that Member State is in a position to gather the necessary evidence, bringing infringement to an end and applying effective sanctions. If more than one authority is potentially involved, case allocation will be discussed between them and if appropriate one Member State nominated as the lead authority. If the same case is investigated by more than one authority, one of them will normally take a formal decision whilst the others stay their proceedings, or alternatively both will deal with the case in close co-operation.

There may be circumstances in which the Commission will nevertheless wish to exercise its powers under Article 11(6) of the Regulation to take over a case, but it will only do so if:

— network members envisage that there will be conflicting decisions in the same case or decisions in conflict with existing case law (either of the Commission or of Community Courts); or

— members are unduly protracting proceedings; or

— a similar problem has arisen in several Member States and there is need for a Commission decision in order to clarify the competition policy of the Community.

The Commission, nevertheless, in cases not covered by Article 11(6) will not normally adopt a decision itself in conflict with a decision of a national competition authority, provided it has been kept fully informed of the case under the provisions of Article 11(3) and (4).

21

NATIONAL COURTS AND THE DIRECT APPLICATION OF COMMUNITY LAW

1. INTRODUCTION AND EARLY CASE LAW

1.1 *HASSELBLAD* AND *BRT* v. *SABAM*

The enforcement of Community competition law was clearly not to be left solely to the institutions of the Community itself; the terms of the Treaty, the wide variety of relevant issues arising in different parts of the Community, and the limited resources of the Commission in general and DG Comp in particular all favoured the greatest possible involvement by national courts in enforcing Articles 81 and 82. The Commission had from its earliest days encouraged Member States' courts to receive hospitably private actions of this kind, hoping that, as in the United States, the burden of public enforcement could be lightened by the increased use of private actions. The Court and Commission had not hesitated to state in their decisions that enforcement of competition policy is not simply a matter of public law but also of private law enforcement. However, implementation of these developments has taken much longer than was originally hoped.

A major factor in the slow development of private litigation in this area has been the easy availability of an alternative remedy, namely the complaint to DG Comp which, at first sight, appeared to have many attractive features. The Commission for many years showed a willingness to give priority to the handling of complaints, even in fairly trivial matters, over certain of its other responsibilities; the wide powers of investigation and discovery under Regulation 17 and the apparent cheapness of involving its services (not to mention the relevant informality with which it could be done) all seemed to undertakings and their lawyers good reasons for approaching the Commission rather than instituting litigation in national courts. The Commission also had the advantage that, if it offered an administrative remedy, this would be applicable throughout the Community rather than merely in the Member State where court action had been started.[1] Formal decisions by the Commission as the result of its investigation of the complaint would be accepted and respected by all national courts within the Community, although the informal

---

[1] Though UK Courts on occasion claim jurisdiction in intellectual property cases to give judgments which have effects outside their own territorial jurisdiction: see for example *Pearce* v. *Ove Arup* [1997] FSR 641 and *Coin Controls* v. *Suzo* [1997] FSR 660.

'comfort letters' to which the Commission had increasingly been resorting were less satisfactory.

The Court of Appeal underlined the importance of the complaint procedure in the *Hasselblad* case.[2] It ruled on a point of law, albeit only by a majority of two to one, that the public interest in ensuring that the Commission was not frustrated in its duty of enforcing the provisions of Articles 81 and 82 was sufficient to provide a defence of 'public interest' against a claim for defamation brought by a party which had been the subject of a complaint, here Hasselblad. The Master of the Rolls referred to the risk that if an action in defamation could be brought in the United Kingdom in connection with the subject matter of a complaint, the substance of that complaint might have to be simultaneously considered by, on one hand, the Commission and the European Court of Justice and, on the other hand, by the UK courts. The increasing volume of the Commission's work meant that its perceived obligation to give priority to complaints was beginning to become an embarrassment. The importance to it, therefore, of the 1992 *Automec (No. 2)*[3] judgment was considerable. Automec was an Italian motor dealer which BMW refused to continue to supply following the expiration of its contract; it raised a complaint against BMW to the Commission under Article 82. The Court of First Instance upheld the right of the Commission to give different degrees of priority to cases in the light of the degree of 'Community interest' that the case presented. Here the Italian Court was already involved in a case brought by Automec against BMW which involved the contractual relationship between the parties within the framework of the then block exemption for motor dealing (Reg. No. 123/85). The Court of First Instance ruled that the Commission was acting within its powers in saying that the dispute between the parties was best resolved by the Italian Court, which in any case could make a reference under Article 234 of the Treaty if any issue of Community law arose. The Court therefore upheld the Commission's decision to refuse to conduct a full investigation into the complaint on the ground that the case did not have the required degree of Community interest. This has provided it with a great element of discretion in determining whether to intervene in cases that may not have a sufficient element of 'Community interest'.

Some advantages could still be obtained by undertakings bringing the matter before the national courts: after all, the Commission was unable to award an ex parte injunction, nor could it award compensation to the complainant (nor legal costs) or consider claims under related heads, such as unfair competition or breach of copyright, at the same time as the main substantive complaint under Article 81 or 82. The foundation for private actions in national courts was laid by the important European Court case of *Belgian Radio and Television* v. *SABAM*[4] which established two important principles. The first was the direct applicability, and therefore enforceability, in national courts of both Articles 81 and 82. Whilst the direct application of the Treaty had been confirmed in a number of earlier cases,

---

[2] *Hasselblad (GB)* v. *Orbinson* [1985] 1 All ER 173: 2 WLR 1: QB 475.

[3] Case T-24/90 [1992] ECR II-2223: 5 CMLR 431. The Commission was given further guidance on its rights in *BEMIM* v. *Commission* Case T-114/92 [1995] ECR II-147: [1996] 4 CMLR 305 and in Case T-5/93 *Tremblay* [1995] ECR II-185: [1996] 4 CMLR 305 by the Court of First Instance, upheld in the latter case by the Court of Justice, Case C-91/95P [1996] ECR I-5547 : [1997] 4 CMLR 211.

[4] Case 123/73 [1974] ECR 51, 313: 2 CMLR 238.

in particular the European Court case of *Van Gend en Loos*[5] in 1963, this application of Articles 81 and 82 was confirmed for the first time in unequivocal terms here, as well as the obligation of the national courts to enforce their provisions.

However, the legal position was also affected by the provisions of Article 9(3) of Regulation 17, which stated that 'authorities' of Member States have jurisdiction and competence to apply Articles 81(1) and 82[6] so long as the Commission had not 'initiated any procedure' under that Regulation. It was originally thought that this expression meant not only all legislative and executive agencies but also all courts and judicial bodies. This view was later shown to be incorrect: in the *BRT* v. *SABAM* case the meaning of the latter words was limited to courts 'especially entrusted to apply domestic competition law or to ensure its application by domestic authorities'.[7] This would, for example, include the tribunal set up under UK competition legislation, the Competition Appeal Tribunal, to hear appeals from the decisions of the Office of Fair Trading and Competition Commission.

1.2 *DELIMITIS* AND *MASTERFOODS*

The rights of national courts in applying Community law were then considered in detail in the *Delimitis*[8] case, the facts of which were discussed in Chapter 10. The chief issue in this dispute between a brewery and its trade customer was whether the exclusive purchasing block exemption then in force covered the exact terms of the arrangements between them. The German Court in the Article 234 reference had also raised a number of questions as to how it should exercise its jurisdiction over the parties in the application of Article 81. In an impressively clear judgment, substantially assisted by the opinion of Van Gerven A-G, the following principles were laid down:

(i) that the national Court could interpret and apply a block exemption (such as 1984/83) but must do so in a strict rather than a flexible manner;

(ii) that the Commission and national courts shared the competence to apply Articles [81(1)] and [82], and could therefore declare an agreement void under Article [81(2)] if it was clearly in breach of 81(1) and unlikely to obtain any Commission individual exemption (taking into account both the previous decisions of the Commission and the terms of relevant block exemptions);

(iii) that the Commission had exclusive jurisdiction to grant exemption under Article 81(3), and national courts could not do so; and

(iv) if a national Court believed that the contract in dispute might be the subject of an individual exemption from the Commission, it could suspend the proceedings or adopt interim measures to protect the interests of the parties. The national court could, in this situation, seek information and assistance from the Commission, which was itself bound under Article [10] of the Treaty with a duty of sincere

---

[5] Case 26/62 [1963] ECR 1: CMLR 105. This case involved, not a competition law point, but the issue of whether the Dutch Government's imposition of an increased rate of import duty on ureaformaldehyde in breach of Art. 12 of the Treaty of Rome could be challenged in the Dutch courts by an undertaking claiming to have been prejudiced by the tax.

[6] But not Art. 81(3).

[7] C.S. Kerse, *EC Antitrust Procedure*, 4th edn. (Sweet & Maxwell, 1998), Ch. 5.

[8] Case 234/89 [1991] ECR I-935: [1992] 5 CMLR 210.

co-operation with the national court. Alternatively, the national court could make a reference under Article [234].

That the process of national litigation could be frustrated to a major degree by parties seeking a decision on Article 81 or 82 issued from the Commission in the course of that litigation, was later dramatically shown by the *Masterfoods*[9] case, which is a landmark decision. Here Irish proceedings between Masterfoods (as plaintiffs) and HB Ice Cream (as defendants) were on appeal from the High Court to the Supreme Court but under a ruling from the ECJ under Article 234 had to be suspended while a Commission decision on the same issue (to the opposite effect from the Irish High Court decision) was appealed by HB Ice Cream to the CFI. This ruling was not surprising since it reflected the supremacy rules contained in *Walt Wilhelm* and *Delimitis*, but it emphasized the difficulty of seeking simultaneously to encourage undertakings to resolve competition law disputes in national courts, whilst retaining the monopoly of the Commission in determining the grant of individual exemptions under Article 81(3).

1.3 THE 1993 NOTICE ON CO-OPERATION WITH NATIONAL COURTS

Following *Delimitis* and in the light of the greater freedom accorded to it in choosing the priority of complaints for investigation under *Automec (No. 2)* the Commission had felt that it was important to issue a general Notice indicating how in its view such co-operation should take place and spelling out the principles from *Delimitis* in more detail. The 1993 Notice on Co-operation with National Courts[10] not only therefore set out the division of responsibility from that case but also provides some guidance to national courts on how they should handle a variety of different situations that might arise. The Treaty did not intend to create new remedies in national courts to ensure observance of Community competition law, but it must be possible for every type of action available under national law to be available also to enforce Community law with direct effect, and subject to the same conditions of admissibility of evidence and procedure. Parties to competition cases in the national courts should have a right to obtain injunctions to prevent infringement of their interests under Community competition rules and a right to compensation for infringements of those rights, when these are also available under national law.

The Commission acknowledged in its Notice that its own resources were inadequate to carry out its many responsibilities and that it was having to give priority to cases of particular political, economic, or legal significance to the Community. Other cases it would prefer dealt with by national courts, which had the advantage of being able, unlike the Commission, to award damages and costs to injured parties and to hear simultaneously claims under both national and Community law. In reaching their decision national courts should always take into account prior decisions or statements of the Commission, though mere administrative letters to parties known as 'comfort letters', were clearly not binding on the courts.[11]

---

[9] Case C-344/98 [2001] 4 CMLR 449. For commentary on this important case, see L Kjølbye, Casenote [2002] 39 *CML Rev* 175–184 and S. O'Keefe, 'First Among Equals: the Commission and the National Courts as enforcers of EC Competition Law' [2001]. 26 ELR 301–311.

[10] [1993] OJ C39/6.

[11] The Perfume Cases (*Procureur de la République* v. *Giry and Others*), Cases 253/78, 37 and 99/79: [1980] ECR 2327, 2481, 2511: [1981] 2 CMLR 99, 143, 164.

When the possibility of individual exemption arose, the national court must act with care, and must normally suspend its proceedings until the Commission had either granted exemption or indicated that it would not do so. To assist national courts further the Commission indicated that it would be willing to provide factual information about relevant market studies and economic data in its possession or about the progress of cases pending before it. It said that it would also try to give priority to those decisions where the outcome of a dispute in a national court depended on it; advice on points of law might also be made available, if requested, though these would in no sense be binding on the national court.

1.4 THE BASIS FOR PRIVATE DAMAGES CLAIMS

The issue of whether an undertaking financially damaged by an agreement or concerted practices entered into in breach of Article 81(1) or by practices prohibited by Article 82 could recover damages in UK courts took some time however to resolve. The Commission itself had often expressed the wish that its public enforcement of the Articles, limited in scope by its overall lack of resources, should be supplemented by private actions brought by litigants in national courts. It referred to the requirements of Article 10 imposing the general obligation of co-operation on Member States in ensuring fulfilment of Treaty obligations, including those arising from the decision of Community institutions including Community courts.

The traditional approach of English courts was to say *ubi remedium, ibi jus*, in other words to look for an existing procedural 'pigeon hole' into which a new category of substantive claim can be fitted rather than to accept the new substantive claim in its own right. Since UK courts, unlike those of the United States, are generally unfamiliar with the concept of awarding damages for the breach of economic laws embodying principles similar to those of Article 81 and 82, the search to find a suitable *remedium*, or cause of action, has proved troublesome. Community law has undoubtedly laid down the *jus*, but places the onus on the Member State to determine how the *remedium* is provided in its own courts.

Three principal suggestions were put forward for the basis of such action, in the course of an extensive debate. First, that the action should be in the form of a claim for wrongful interference in contractual relationships. Second, that it was a new form of tort, the solution preferred by Lord Denning in early cases, which is not covered by any existing cause of action. The third suggestion is an action for breach of statutory duty, the statute being the 1972 European Communities Act under which the Treaty of Rome became part of United Kingdom law. The relevant sections would be sections 2(1) and 3, under whose combined effect the UK courts are required not only to give legal effect to the Treaties, as interpreted by the Courts in Luxembourg, but also to provide for the enforcement of 'remedies and procedures' without further enactment in the United Kingdom so as to give legal effect to them.

This last solution seems in principle the most satisfactory, subject to one technical difficulty, discussed below, namely that under UK law the civil right of action for a statutory breach is not normally available if the statute in question provides an alternative remedy, for example a fine or penalty. However, this argument should not prevail over the express terms of Community case law; in practical terms, whether the right of action is for breach of statutory duty (in the traditional sense) or for breach of the Treaty provisions incorporated in UK law by the 1972 Act may not make a great difference.

1.5 THE *GARDEN COTTAGE* CASE

This issue was discussed by the House of Lords in 1983 in *Garden Cottage Foods Ltd.* v. *Milk Marketing Board*,[12] although strictly it did not form part of the ratio of the case. The Board had a statutory function to sell milk, butter, and cheese. Garden Cottage had been buying butter from the Board since 1980 and had resold most of it to a Dutch purchaser. In March 1982 a new distribution policy was introduced under which Garden Cottage was no longer able to buy direct from the Board but had to buy from one of four distributors approved by the Board. The result of the introduction of these four preferred distributors was to reduce Garden Cottage's profits on the resale of butter, as it would have difficulties in competing with the prices that the four preferred distributors, with their privileged position as direct purchasers from the Board, could quote to customers. Proceedings were started against the Board on the ground that the refusal to supply Garden Cottage with butter in bulk was an abuse of the Board's dominant position. At first instance, Parker J refused to grant any interim relief, such as an injunction, pending trial, as he thought that it would be difficult to frame the terms of an injunction against the Board, and that in any case damages might provide an adequate remedy for Garden Cottage.

The Court of Appeal, however, allowed the appeal by Garden Cottage and granted an interim injunction against the Board preventing it from confining its sale of bulk butter to any particular category of persons and also from discriminating between their different customers save than in accordance with normal practice. In addition to allowing the application for the injunction, Lords Justices Denning and May indicated that they would be in favour of allowing a claim for damages in such circumstances, whilst Shaw LJ expressed doubts. Faced with so important a decision against it, the Board not surprisingly decided to appeal and achieved some success. The House of Lords decided by four votes to one that the injunction granted by the Court of Appeal should be discharged. Lord Diplock for the majority emphasized that in principle the Court of Appeal should not interfere with a trial judge's decision on an application for interlocutory relief unless the judge had reached a decision that was clearly wrong on the facts or law, or where fresh evidence or a change in circumstances had emerged. In the view of the majority, none of these situations applied to the present case so that the original order by Parker J refusing the injunction should be restored. Lord Wilberforce disagreed, being in favour of allowing the injunction to maintain the status quo, which he considered would be more just, and indicated that in his view damages would not be a complete remedy for Garden Cottage, as it would be out of the butter market for a considerable period of time.

In the course of the hearing, the House of Lords entered into a general discussion of the rights of parties in United Kingdom courts under Articles 81 and 82. None of the courts below nor the House of Lords found any difficulty in accepting the principle laid down in *BRT* v. *SABAM* that under these Articles individuals had direct enforceable rights in national courts. The plaintiffs' claim could be categorized in English law probably as a breach of a statutory duty 'imposed not only for the purpose of promoting the general economic prosperity of the Common Market but also for the benefit of private individuals to whom loss or damage is caused by a breach of that duty'. However, the legal question then before

---

[12] [1983] 3 WLR 143: 2 All ER 770: 3 CMLR 43: [1984] AC 130. The Court of Appeal hearing is reported at [1982] All ER 292: QB 1114.

the House of Lords was whether to interfere in an existing grant of an injunction on an interim application. The question of whether damages would be payable if Garden Cottage were successful in their case strictly did not arise as an issue. Nevertheless, the majority of the House saw no reason why damages should not be granted for a breach of Article 82 as a breach of statutory duty, although it did not reach a final decision on this issue. Lord Wilberforce, however, had considerable doubts; whilst he agreed that Community rights had to be enforced in national courts, he felt that a complainant under these Articles was not necessarily entitled to compensation so that the grant of damages by a national court might enlarge, rather than merely enforce, the rights of a claimant.[13]

2. REMEDIES AVAILABLE IN THE UK COURTS BEFORE *CREHAN*

2.1 PROGRESS AT THE ECJ: *FRANCOVICH* AND *BRASSERIE DU PÊCHEUR*

The prospects of UK courts enforcing private claims to damages in competition law cases was however soon to be considerably enhanced by developments in Community law in cases dealing with other issues. The well-known European Court cases of *Francovich* v. *Italy* and *Brasserie du Pêcheur*[14] arose as a result of breaches by Member States, Italy and Germany respectively, of their obligations under Community law. The Court judgments in these cases laid down rules under Community law setting out the circumstances in which national courts should award damages against Member States to private litigants who had been injured by such breaches. These were as follows:

(i)   when the defendant Member State has infringed a rule of Community law intended to confer specific rights to the plaintiff (whether an individual or undertaking); and

(ii) when the defendant Member State's breach is sufficiently serious; and

(iii) when the plaintiff can show direct causation between the Member State breach and its own financial loss.

These three principles were to be implemented by national courts, which were instructed to ensure also that the legal conditions for making such claims were not less favourable than those governing similar domestic cases, nor so restrictive as to make it impossible or excessively difficult to make a successful claim.

These cases did not however directly address the question of whether by parity of reasoning damages could also be claimed for a breach of Community competition law, by a plaintiff that could show financial loss caused by such a breach by a third party rather than

---

[13] It is clear that, if damages would not be an adequate remedy for a breach of Arts 81 or 82, an injunction may be granted: *Cutsforth* v. *Mansfield Inns* [1986] I All ER 577.

[14] *Francovich:* Cases C-6 and 9/90 [1991] ECR I-5357 [1993] 2 CMLR 66. *Brasserie du* Pêcheur v. *Germany* Case 46/93 [1996] ECR I-1029: 1 CMLR 889, AER (EC) 301. For a detailed analysis of the pre-*Crehan* position, see *European Competition Law Annual* 2001, C.-D. Ehlermann and I. Atanasiu, eds. (Hart Publishing, 2002), especially W. van Gerven pp.53–89.

by a Member State. Van Gerven A-G soon afterwards gave strong support to this principle in his opinion in *Banks* v. *British Coal Corporation*,[15] citing earlier European Court jurisprudence. Unfortunately however the Court ruled in that case that the claim for damages was based on Articles of the ECSC Treaty (which required a prior Commission decision on whether a breach of law had occurred); these Articles were not directly effective, so that the *Francovich* principle did not apply. Decisive case law authority on the extent of those rights under UK law therefore was still lacking.

2.2 LATER HIGH COURT CASES

The influence of the trend of these Community cases on the English judiciary was however noticeable in an important case arising on the issue of whether plaintiffs in competition private law actions could rely on prior findings in Community proceedings. In *Iberian* v. *BPB*[16] Spanish importers of plasterboard into the UK complained that their business had in the late 1980s been damaged by practices of BPB which had been found by the Commission (upheld on appeal to both the Court of First Instance and the European Court) to be in breach of Article 86 and led to a fine. The practices consisted primarily of granting special discounts to builders' merchants in the United Kingdom and Northern Ireland who agreed to deal exclusively with BPB and not to buy imported Spanish board. BPB claimed that for the purpose of civil proceedings in the United Kingdom the plaintiffs would have to prove afresh all the relevant facts of the case without being able to place any reliance on the previous findings of the Commission or the Community Courts. The plaintiffs argued that this would make it in practice almost impossible for any plaintiffs to recover civil damages especially as the various Community proceedings had taken nearly a decade. Laddie J upheld the plaintiffs' arguments largely on the grounds of policy, stating that English courts should respect the decision of Community institutions in order to ensure consistency of treatment and avoid the risk of conflicting decisions from the Community and national courts and authorities.

In many of the cases coming before the UK courts at this time, plaintiffs who had entered into standard form contracts (often in the beer supply business) sought to defend against actions by their brewery landlord for payment of arrears of rent of their licensed premises, or in respect of beer supplied, by counter-claiming for damages, on the grounds that the tenancy agreement was itself in breach of Article 81 because of the restrictions imposed on them by its terms, principally from obtaining cheaper supplies of beer on the open market. In all these cases the traditional view of the High Court was maintained, namely that the parties to a contract which is illegal (for so agreements in breach of Article 81 were characterized) were not entitled to recover damages, regardless of whether they had any element of bargaining power on their side or had been forced into the acceptance of an onerous contract in standard form. *Gibbs Mew* v. *Gemmell*[17] may serve as a typical example. Gibbs

---

[15] Case C-128/92 [1994] ECR I-1209: 5 CMLR 30.

[16] [1996] 2 CMLR 601: [1997] EurLR 1. Following the decision by Laddie J on the interlocutory issues, the substantive claim by Iberian under Art. 82 was settled. See also Ch. 15, fn. 20. It has been suggested that the UK Courts might have taken a different attitude if the Commission decision had not been appealed to and upheld by a Community Court. However, such an attitude would appear to be not only in breach of Art. 10 but also inconsistent with the respect which the UK courts are required to give to findings of fact made by the UK Office of Fair Trading in rendering decisions under the Competition Act 1998.

[17] EurLR 588.

Mew, a small brewer, had bought some pubs from Centric, a small company. One of the tenants, Gemmell, was in arrears with his rent and was sued by Gibbs Mew. Gemmell's defence was that the lease was not covered by the current block exemption for exclusive purchasing (No. 1984/83) and counterclaimed for damages in restitution of the sums he had paid for beer. Gibbs Mew had obtained summary judgment in the High Court and to overturn it Gemmell had to persuade the Court of Appeal that one of his claims under Article 81 was arguable, not necessarily at that stage that it was right. On the critical issue of whether Gemmell was entitled to sue as a co-contractor, the Court ruled that he had no such right. Article 81 was directly effective but was designed primarily to protect third party competitors. It was irrelevant that in block exemptions the Commission might pursue wider policy objectives of redressing inequalities in bargaining power; the grounds for exemption under Article 81(3) could not define the scope of Article 81(1) and, as the contract was illegal, neither party was entitled to recover damages from the other.

A further difficulty which was raised by the Courts in the case of plaintiffs seeking to enforce a Community right for damages was the ruling in *Passmore* v. *Morland*[18] that, since Article 81(1) is phrased as a 'effects based' prohibition, the prohibition itself can be made to 'vanish' if there is a change in circumstances. The actual change of circumstances in this case was that the tenancy agreement originally made by Passmore, the tenant, with a multiple pub owner, Inntrepreneur, was subsequently assigned over by the latter to Morland, a much smaller brewery. The Court of Appeal held that even if the terms of the original tenancy had been in breach of Article 81 the prohibition vanished once the effects of the agreement changed, as a result of the assignment to a new owner with a far lesser degree of market power vis a vis the tenant as well as in the beer market generally. The assessment of an agreement under Article 81(1) therefore is not a 'once for all' affair but one which depends on the circumstances at the time when the plaintiff's claim is brought.

3. REMEDIES AVAILABLE IN THE UK COURTS AFTER *CREHAN*

3.1 THE *CREHAN* JUDGMENT IN THE ECJ

In a number of previous beer supply actions, High Court judges had refused to make references to the European Court under Article 234 on the issue of whether co-contractors, such as Messrs Gemmell or Passmore, were under Community law entitled to damages from their brewery landlord, notwithstanding the strict rule of illegality that prevailed under UK law. Finally however such a reference was made in *Crehan* v. *Courage*[19] with results that were to have a major impact on the ability of plaintiffs to bring private actions for damages for breach of competition law in the UK and indeed other Member States.

The facts in *Crehan* were broadly similar to those in the earlier two cases. Crehan was a tenant under a lease with Courage, a large brewer, and owed it substantial sums for beer supplied. He claimed that his contract obliged him to buy beer exclusively from Courage and

---

[18] [1999] 1 CMLR 1129; 1 EurLR 501. The decision is not without criticism. See G. Cumming [2000] 21 ECLR 261–66 and Preece [2000] 21 ECLR 433–36.

[19] Case C-453/99 [2001] 5 CMLR 1058.

that this prevented him from purchasing any quantities on the open market at a lower price. He alleged also that Courage sold its beer at lower prices to independent pub tenants than to tied tenants like himself, and therefore claimed damages against Courage. It was likely that the particular restriction in this lease did infringe Article 81(1) and an earlier notification for individual exemption for this and other similar restrictions in Courage agreements had been withdrawn. The case therefore directly raised the question of whether Crehan was barred from suing Courage simply because he was a party to the contract prohibited by Article 81 rather than a third party damaged by such a contract.

In a relatively short and clear judgment the European Court had no difficulty in deciding in favour of the tenant's right to sue, notwithstanding the fact that he was a co-contractor with Courage. Its findings were:

(a) that a party to a contract liable to restrict or distort competition within the meaning of Article 81(1) can rely on the breach of the Article to obtain relief from the other contracting party;

(b) that Article 81 precludes a rule of national law under which a party to a contract in breach of Article 81 is barred from claiming damages for loss caused by performance of that contract, on the sole ground that he is a party to the contract himself; but that nevertheless

(c) national law may bar him from claiming damages if he bore 'significant responsibility' for the distortion of competition contained in the contract.

The Court stated that the principal reason for the decision was the importance in its view of ensuring the 'full effectiveness' of Article 81. If individuals could not claim damages in such situations, the practical effect of the Article would be put at risk and it was necessary to provide effective protection for plaintiffs in respect of their rights under the Treaty.

The Court also laid down criteria which would be relevant to the assessment of 'serious responsibility'. National courts should take into account:

— the economic and legal context in which the parties had made the contract;

— the respective bargaining power and conduct of the parties;

— whether the plaintiff found himself in a markedly weaker position than the other party, such as seriously to compromise or even eliminate his freedom to negotiate the terms of trade and his capacity to avoid the loss or reduce it to any extent; and

— in the case of a network of similar contracts, a party contracting with a person controlling the network cannot be held to have 'significant responsibility' for the contract, especially if the contract terms were imposed on him by the controller.

3.2 THE US CASES RELEVANT TO *CREHAN*

It is significant that in its ruling the Court is being consistent with the equivalent United States authority, the Supreme Court decision in *Perma Life Mufflers*[20] where it was ruled that a plaintiff who was a co-contractor was entitled to claim treble damages under the Sherman Act from the other party to the contract. In this case where contractual

---

[20] *Perma Life Mufflers* v. *International Parts Corp* 392 US 134 [1968].

restrictions had been placed on a franchisee of car exhaust systems, the contract had included a requirement on it to purchase all specified products from the other party, to operate only from approved locations and to sell at prices fixed by the franchisor without any right to sell competing products. The justification set out in the 6–3 majority opinion given by Mr Justice White in that case was the importance of ensuring that the principles of the Sherman Act were respected, even if the plaintiff and defendant were both parties to the contract.

Left unanswered in the *Crehan* case however were two issues which will inevitably arise once action for damages for breach of Articles 81 and 82 become commonplace. These are the 'passing on defence' and the 'indirect purchaser' issues. In many cases, if there has been a price fixing agreement between A and B, purchaser C may have had to pay a higher price to A and/or B for goods covered by that agreement than he would have done had that cartel not existed. On the other hand C may simply have increased the price he charges to D to whom he resells the products, which may have been sold either as he purchased them from A or B or having had value added in some way. In this situation the question arises, can A and B be sued by either C or D?

Under the US case law, C is still entitled to sue A and B even if he has 'passed on' a higher price to D. The only exception would be when his contract with D had been made on a 'cost plus' basis, where by definition he will have suffered no loss (the *Hanover Shoe* decision). On the other hand as a logical consequence of *Hanover Shoe*, D as merely an 'indirect' purchaser from A or B is not entitled to sue either of them (this being decided by the well-known *Illinois Brick* case).[21] The justification given by the Supreme Court for the *Hanover Shoe* decision is that to allow the 'passing on' defence would be to give anti-trust offenders an opportunity to retain their unlawful profits and to considerably increase the burden on plaintiffs seeking compensation by forcing them to produce a detailed analysis of their business accounts showing their purchases, sales, prices and profits. The decision in *Illinois Brick* is simply the logical consequence of *Hanover Shoe*; if the 'passing off' defence is not allowed to the wrongdoer then it would be unfair that indirect purchasers could recover from him in addition to the direct purchaser, leading to the situation where multiple damages will be paid, which have already (under US law) been subject to trebling!

It is however far from certain that UK courts will follow the US case law precedents. Their normal approach to damage claims of all kinds is to require the plaintiff to show both a cause of action (here 'an illegal contract') and a causal link between the defendant's wrongful act and the plaintiff's losses. If no loss can be shown by the direct purchaser, it is likely however, that the UK courts, having declined to make a finding in his favour, would in contrast be willing to accept suits by indirect purchasers, provided they can show that they have incurred loss; but this is likely whether or not the 'passing off' defence itself is permitted by UK courts.[22]

---

[21] *Hanover Shoe v. United Shoe Machinery Corp* 392 US 481 [1968]. *Illinois Brick Co v. State of Illinois* 431 US 720 [1968].

[22] A. Jones and D. Beard, 'Co-Contractors, Damages and Art. 81: the ECJ finally speaks', [2002], 23 ECLR 246.

4. THE IMPACT OF THE MODERNIZATION PROPOSALS ON NATIONAL COURTS

4.1 THE RECITALS OF REGULATION NO. 1/2003

Notwithstanding the outcome of the *Crehan* v. *Courage* litigation however, the use of national courts as the forum for the resolution of competition law cases between private parties, would still have remained considerably restricted by the combined effect of the *Delimitis* and *Masterfoods* judgments already referred to. The effect of these cases was that the national courts could not rule in any case already in the hands of the Commission (other than to raise issues arising under Article 234) nor assess the application of Article 81(3) to the merits. As a result a number of private actions that had been brought in UK courts had to be suspended while the assessment of Article 81(3), in respect of the agreement in dispute, was carried out by the Commission; this normally would have the result of delaying a substantial resolution of the case by years rather than months. Leading examples of this were *MTV Europe* v. *BMG Records*[23] and *Williams* v. *Welsh RFC*.[24]

This situation could only be altered if the Commission were to yield up its monopoly over the granting of individual exemptions under Article 81(3) and this required a radical reorganization of the entire framework and balance of power between the Commission on the one hand and national courts on the other. Nevertheless, the modernization proposals put forward by the Commission in its White Paper in April 1999, and subsequently implemented by Regulation No. 1/2003 to take effect in May 2004, would at last bring about this important change. The effect of the Regulation is that national courts will henceforward be able, alongside national competition authorities, to have a more important role than before in applying the content not only of their own national law but also of Articles 81 and 82 in their entirety.[25] Agreements will be reviewed as a whole by national courts on the basis of 'exception légale' which means that they will be concerned only with the issue, namely: is the agreement valid or void under Article 81? In answering that question the court will of course have to consider both whether the agreement falls within the scope of Article 81(1) and if so whether it can benefit from the terms of Article 81(3).

A number of the recitals and clauses in the new Regulation directly affect national courts. Recital 3 acknowledges that the limitations which Regulation 17/62 placed on the courts have hampered the application of Commission competition rules and Recital 4 records the need for the courts to be able to apply 81(3) directly to the dispute before them. Recital 7 refers to the essential part played by the courts in being able to award damages to the 'victims of infringement'. Recitals 21, 22 and 27 emphasize three obligations which the new system will place upon them, namely:

— to co-operate with the Commission and to be able to ask it for information or

---

[23] [1997] EurLR 100: 1 CMLR 867.

[24] [1999] EurLR 195. See also J. Groning, 'National Judges in a Modernised Community Law System'; in *European Competition Law Annual 2000; The Modernisation of EC Antitrust Law* (Hart Publishing, 2001), pp. 580–92.

[25] For confirmation of this in the context of Spanish Court proceedings, see C. Fernandez and P. Gonsalez Espejo [2002] 23 ECLR 163–171.

opinions on points of Community law whilst keeping both it and national competition authorities 'sufficiently and well informed' of their proceedings (recital 21);

— to avoid conflicts with the proceedings and decisions of the Commission and other national competition authorities (recital 22); and

— to ask for additional information from the Commission if required in connection with requests by it to enter private homes in order to search for business records (recital 27).

4.2 THE RELEVANT ARTICLES OF REGULATION 1/2003

The Regulation itself spells out the new responsibilities and powers of national courts which are bound by Article 3 dealing with the supremacy of Community law; this Article however allows both national courts and competition authorities an element of freedom in connection with unilateral conduct engaged in by undertakings (whether or not dominant) and also in connection with the application of legislation that predominantly pursues objectives different from that covered by Articles 81 and 82. National courts will be able to apply Articles 81(1) and 81(3) together as confirmed by Article 6. No longer will cases have to be suspended merely because one of the parties has notified the agreement in dispute to the Commission; the court will now have full jurisdiction to determine whether the agreement complies with Article 81 as a whole. The limitations contained in *Delimitis* therefore no longer apply. The effect of the *Masterfoods* judgments however remains important and Article 16(1) emphasizes this by stating that:

When national courts rule on agreements, decisions or practices under Articles 81 or 82 of the Treaty which are already the subject of a Commission decision, they cannot take decisions running counter to the decision adopted by the Commission. They must also avoid giving decisions which would conflict with a decision contemplated by the Commission in proceedings it has initiated. To that effect, the national court may assess whether it is necessary to stay its proceedings. This obligation is without prejudice to the rights and obligations of Articles 234 of the Treaty.

In these new circumstances it is essential for the courts to be in close touch with the Commission as well as with their own national competition authorities (Article 15). They may, under paragraph (1) of Article 15, ask the Commission to send them information or to offer its opinion on questions relating to the application of Community competition rules to the case before it. Member States must under paragraph (2) of the same Article ensure that copies of any written judgment of national courts, relating to Articles 81 or 82, are forwarded to the Commission, once the parties themselves have received the full written judgment. The national court must accept participation in competition cases from both national competition authorities and the Commission, by means of written submission in any case and with its specific consent by way of oral presentation; relevant documents must be forwarded by the court to these parties if necessary and relevant to the assessment of the case. The court itself may be designated by a Member State as a 'competition authority', this being likely when it hears appeals on such cases from national competition authorities.

4.3 THE COMBINED EFFECT OF *CREHAN* AND OF THE NEW REGULATION

The combined effect of the new Regulation and of the *Crehan* decision, means that in future national courts in Member States will have jurisdiction in the following situations:

(i)   to apply Article 81(1) by declaratory judgments and to state that the agreement is outside its scope or within it (*Delimitis*);

(ii) in parallel to apply Article 81(3) dealing with all the four conditions and leading to a decision by the Court that the agreement or certain restrictions within it is/are void or that it is wholly or partially (as a result of severance) valid under the Article. (Regulation No. 1/2003, Article 6).

(iii) To apply Article 82 (the position is unchanged since the Article has direct effect (*BRT* v. *Sabam* and *Delimitis*));

(iv) to award an injunction to restrain a breach of competition law or to prohibit an act or practice in breach (*Crehan: Cutsforth* v. *Mansfield Inns*);

(v)   to give an interim injunction (normally an inherent power of the court);

(vi) to award damages to parties injured financially as a result of breach of competition rules whether or not they are co-contractors, except where the plaintiff has 'significant responsibility' for the restriction in breach of the rules (*Crehan*).

As already explained in the previous chapter however the power to award damages will in the United Kingdom be shared between the High Court and the Competition Appeal Tribunal (CAT) as a result of provisions in the Enterprise Act 2002.[26] Under these, in cases in which there has already been a decision of either the Office of Fair Trading or the Competition Appeal Tribunal that a breach of a Chapter 1 or Chapter 2 prohibition has occurred, or where there is a decision of the European Commission (no longer subject to appeal) that Article 81 or 82 has been infringed, the injured party can bring a claim for damages to the CAT for an award of a sum of money in compensation. This right applies retrospectively even to claims arising before the Enterprise Act came into effect. Moreover under section 16 of the Enterprise Act the Lord Chancellor can make rules, by secondary legislation, which will entitle the High Court to transfer to the CAT part of any case which relates to competition infringement issues and can later retransfer such matters to the High Court. The principle underlining this provision is that the CAT should be allowed in appropriate cases, where it is likely to be more familiar with the background to the case, to assess what, if any, damages should be paid for the competition law infringement, and to relieve the High Court Judge dealing with the case of that responsibility.

It would be simplistic to assume that such an extensive new jurisdiction of the national courts can come into existence without a number of problems. In Part 3 a review of some of these likely problems will be made including the need for specialized judges and tribunal members, the application of Article 81(3) to cases involving complex issues outside the normal competition issues, and the lack of judicial 'architecture' and appellate structures to enable conflicts between the Commission and national courts to be resolved.

---

[26] Sections 18 and 19 permitting monetary claims to the Tribunal both by individuals or undertakings or by consumer bodies on behalf of groups of consumers.

22

MEMBER STATES AND EC COMPETITION RULES

1. ARTICLES 81 AND 82: OBLIGATIONS AS MEMBER STATES

Although the provisions of the Treaty can have direct application to persons and undertakings, the majority of the Articles of the Treaty of Rome are directed towards Member States, either stating principles which they are required to observe, or laying down specific tasks for performance by them. By contrast, Articles 81 and 82, which lay down the main principles of competition law, are not directed primarily towards the Member States, but to individual undertakings and associations of undertakings.

If the activities of Member States were confined simply to the exercise of the traditional powers of governments,[1] such as the conduct of foreign affairs and defence, and the implementation of education, housing, and social policies, then their involvement with Articles 81 and 82 might indeed be limited. In fact, however, all Member States are also involved in a wide variety of both industrial and commercial activities, often in direct or indirect competition with private undertakings; moreover Member States also finance in part or whole the operations of many public undertakings, bodies, authorities, and utilities which have many dealings with other undertakings, even if not directly in competition with them. These activities might include the grant of a monopoly by statute for the public supply of gas, water, electricity, or telephone services, the provision of pilotage or marine environmental services, and television or radio transmission.

The framers of the Treaty anticipated the problems that would arise if the public undertakings of Member States and commercial undertakings in which they might become involved were not made subject to the common rules of competition. Thus, Articles 81 to 89, which comprise the first Chapter of Part 3 entitled the 'Policy of the Community', have a substantial effect on the activities of governments of all Member States; a number of leading European Court and Court of First Instance decisions have dealt with the extent to which the administrative and legislative activities of Member States are subject to them. The approach of the Court has been founded on the basic framework of the Treaty, in particular Article 10, which emphasizes the obligation of Member States to take all appropriate measures to ensure fulfilment of their Treaty obligations which include, under Article 3(1)(g),

---

[1] Insofar, of course, as the Treaty of Rome or successor treaties have not placed them wholly or partly in the hands of Community institutions.

support for 'a system ensuring that competition in the internal market is not distorted': they must also accept obligations which result from action taken under the Treaty by the institutions of the Community, including actions taken against undertakings under Articles 81 and 82. The second part of Article 10 places on them a positive obligation to facilitate the achievements of the Commission's tasks, and a requirement to abstain from any measures which could jeopardize the attainment of Treaty objectives. The Treaty on European Union adopted at Maastricht contains a further requirement that under Article 4(1) the activities of Member States shall include an obligation 'to support the general economic policies in the Community, in accordance with the principle of an open market economy with free competition'.

It would, therefore, have been reasonable to expect Member States to refrain from legislative or administrative policies that offered undertakings a means of escaping their obligations under the competition rules. On the whole this has been the case, but we shall see that certain exceptions exist to this general principle.

2. NATIONAL LAWS AFFECTING PRICE-FIXING: SOME LEADING CASES

2.1 THE FIRST RULE: MEMBER STATES MUST NOT LEGISLATE TO CREATE OR PROTECT AGREEMENTS OR GIVE PRIVILEGES IN BREACH OF ARTICLES 81 OR 82

In dealing with national legislation that might conflict with the competition rules of the Treaty, and in particular with Articles 10, 81, and 82, the case law of the Community Courts has made it clear that in such cases there are two aspects to be considered, which are quite distinct. The first is whether the Member State has itself by its own legislative or administrative measures, or by a combination of them, breached its obligations under Article 10 in a way that might have rendered ineffective the competition rules applicable to undertakings; this could have been by requiring or favouring the adoption of agreements, decisions or concerted practices contrary to Article 81 or by reinforcing their effect, or depriving its own national legislation of its official character by delegating to private traders responsibility for decisions affecting economic markets or by granting them privileges that would lead to a breach of Article 82. This principle was established in *Inno* v. *ATAB*[2] (European Court 1977), an Article 234 reference from the Belgian Court of Cassation concerning the validity of a Belgian statute which required retailers to sell cigarettes and tobacco only at the official price. The official price was the price notified to the authorities for purposes of the assessment of excise duty, together with value added tax. The statute had the effect of preventing retailers from competing with each other on price and would have enabled their trade association to take advantage of its dominance in the Belgian market which, under the protection of such legislation, it would have little difficulty in exploiting and abusing. The

---

[2] Case 13/77 [1977] ECR 2115: [1978] 1 CMLR 283. See J. Temple Lang, 'The duties of co-operation of national authorities and courts under Art. 10' [1998]: 23 EurLR 109 and [2001] 26 EurLR 84 and H. Schepel 'Delegation of Regulatory Powers to Private Parties under EC Competition Law, [2002] 39 CMLR 31–51. See also the opinion of Jacobs A-G in Case C-198/01 *C.I.F.* v. *Autorita Garante della Concorrenza del Mercato* (30 January 2003).

European Court of Justice referred back to the principles embodied in Articles [3(1)(g)] and [10] of the Treaty, and from their combined effect found no difficulty in reading into the Treaty an implied duty on Member States not to adopt or maintain in force any measure which could deprive Article 82 of its effectiveness. The Court also stated that Member States should not enact measures enabling private undertakings to escape from the constraints imposed by the competitive scheme of the Treaty; it added that any national measure which had the effect of facilitating the abuse of a dominant position capable of affecting trade between Member States would generally be incompatible with Articles 28 and 30.

The freedom of Member States to enact legislation reducing or eliminating price competition was the central issue in a later case[3] (*Leclerc Books*) under Article 234, where a French court sought a ruling of the European Court of Justice on whether the Treaty prohibited the establishment of a system within a Member State to control the price at which books, whether locally published or imported, could be sold only at a price of not more than 5 per cent below the official price named by the publisher or importer. The French Government was held to be entitled to enact resale price maintenance legislation for books published in France so long as no Community sectoral policy had been adopted relating to the pricing of books, and so long as the legislation did not conflict with other provisions of the Treaty, notably Articles 28 and 30. On the basis of these latter articles, however, the Court ruled that price restrictions imposed on books imported into France would be illegal, since they would rank as being of 'equivalent effect' on imports; the only exception would be if it were established that the original exports of the books had been for the sole purpose of circumventing the legislation by subsequent reimportation.[4] The argument of the French government that the legislation in its entirety was indispensable to protect both specialist book shops and books as a cultural medium against the likely reduction in variety and availability of books if unrestricted price competition was allowed failed to convince the Court, and the exceptions contained in Article 30 were held not to apply here so as to effect any qualification to the prohibitions in Article 28.

National legislation was also considered in two cases by the European Court in which, although the legislation did not actually require anti-competitive conduct in breach of these Articles, it nevertheless provided considerable support for private agreements of such a kind. Both cases were Article 234 references from Belgian courts. The first was the *Flemish Travel Agents* case[5] where a Royal Decree required travel agents not to depart from official tariffs and not to share commissions with their customers. Standard forms of agreement between such travel agencies and tour organizers were ruled by the Court to constitute a breach of Article 81. Under the Decree, a travel agent which complained of 'cheating' by other travel agents could obtain an injunction against them and ask for their operating licences to be withdrawn. The judgment of the Court was unequivocal, that Belgium was in breach of Article 81. The second case, *Van Eycke* v. *ASPA*,[6] led to a less clear-cut answer. Here the Royal Decree provided that the holders of deposits in savings accounts were only entitled to tax

---

[3] Case 229/83 [1985] ECR 1: 2 CMLR 286.

[4] The issue of whether the reimportation was genuine or artificial, i.e. simply to avoid the effects of the French law, would be for the national court to decide. Its companion case is *Leclerc Petrol* Case 231/83 [1985] ECR 305: 2 CMLR 524, officially *Cullet* v. *Leclerc*. See also Case C-9/99 *Échirolles Distribution* [2000] ECR I-8207.

[5] Its full title is *VZW Vereniging van Vlaamse Reisebureaus* v. *VZW Sociale dienst van de Plaatselijke en Gewestelijke Overheidsdiensten* Case 311/85 [1987] ECR 3801: [1989] 4 CMLR 213.

[6] Case 267/86 [1988] ECR 4769: [1990] 4 CMLR 330.

relief on the income if interest rates did not exceed 7 per cent. Mr Van Eycke alleged that the decree merely confirmed an existing restrictive agreement between the banks. The Court ruled that in such a case the central issue was whether the legislation merely confirmed the method of restricting interest rates which the interbank arrangements had set out, or whether it went further. Finding ambiguity in the evidence on this issue, the Court referred it back to the national court.

The issue of the enactment by Member States of legislation reducing or eliminating price competition also arose in the air transport sector. As noted in Chapter 7 (at pp.107–8), the European Court decided in *Nouvelles Frontières*[7] that Member States and the Commission remained free, in the absence of any Community rules, to adjudicate under the terms of Articles 84 and 85 respectively on the admissibility of agreements and practices and the abuse of dominant position. In these circumstances it was uncertain whether Member States were entitled to continue to create and enforce domestic legislation covering such matters as tariffs, charter flights, discount fares, and the general terms and conditions upon which air travel was provided to other countries within the Community. It could have been argued, by analogy with *Leclerc Books*, that until a Common Community policy on air transport had been adopted by the Council, Member States retained jurisdiction in this area, even if the effect might be to permit agreements or practices by individual undertakings which were inconsistent with the provisions of Articles 81 and 82. Since the adoption of a number of Community regulations dealing with air transport, this issue is less important, apart from the continued absence of Community jurisdiction over routes from or to destinations outside it.[8]

It is clear however that a Member State does retain the freedom to determine the prices to be charged for particular goods and services, if it does so as manifestly an exercise of governmental authority in a sector where this power has not been removed from it as the result of Community legislation, as for example by the regulations forming the Common Agricultural Policy. In *Cullet* v. *Leclerc*, France had fixed maximum prices for retail sales of petrol, but this was not adjudged a breach of Article 10 by the Court of Justice; there was no attempt to achieve this result by delegating the responsibility for fixing prices to suppliers or retailers of the product by means of industrywide agreements.

The national legislation introduced may have had an impact on the relevant professional or trade bodies which is simply too limited to allow a conclusion that the State has thereby delegated to them the task of fixing prices or terms of business. Examples of such legislation can be found in two recent Italian cases. In *Conte* v. *Rossi*[9] architects were allowed to set their fees for professional services and have them endorsed as appropriate by their association in cases where they had to sue for their recovery. When Conte was sued by Rosso for her fees he claimed that the endorsement given by her association represented a 'decision' prohibited by Article 81. The Court of Justice however ruled that this was not so; the endorsement only had legal effect if the debtor failed to dispute it and was in any case not binding upon the local court.

In *Arduino*[10] the tariff in issue was that of members of the Italian Bar, which set both maximum and minimum fee levels for their services. But again it was clear that the legislation fell short of allowing the Bar to adopt a 'decision' that would bind their members. The

---

[7] *Ministère Public* v. *Asjes*, Cases 209–213/84 [1986] 3 CMLR 173.
[8] See Ch. 7, pp.108–9.
[9] Case C-221/99 [2002] 4 CMLR 269.   [10] Case C-35/99 [2002] 4 CMLR 866.

legislation did not contain either procedural arrangements or substantive requirements capable of ensuring that the Bar was exercising an authority fully delegated to it by the State; any draft tariff produced by the Bar had to be approved by the Minister for Justice, who himself after consulting two public bodies could then amend the draft. Moreover the local court in assessing such fees was also allowed to depart from the tariff, in exceptional circumstances.

Moreover, if the government measure simply consists of a prohibition of a particular practice, and in its self-contained form has no requirement of any agreement or practice to be entered into, then again there can be no breach of Article 10, as in the case of *Meng*,[11] where German law had forbidden the sharing of commission by insurance brokers with their clients. If however there is some real link between national legislation and the subsequent autonomous conduct of the undertaking in then entering into a related agreement or practice relating to prices or conditions of business, Article 81 may have been breached; if so, anyone suffering financial loss may have a claim under the principle of *Francovich* discussed in the previous chapter, so long as the breach of Community law is regarded as sufficiently serious.

2.2 THE SECOND RULE: UNDERTAKINGS DO NOT ESCAPE ARTICLES 81 OR 82 MERELY BECAUSE OF STATE ACTION AFFECTING THEIR MARKETS

The second aspect of the rule relates to the undertakings themselves, and whether they have acted with sufficient autonomy to have themselves breached Article 81 or whether the terms of the legislation relating to their conduct left insufficient freedom to them for their actions to be characterized as independent.

Undertakings cannot claim that Articles 81 and 82 do not apply to them simply because national legislation or executive action has reduced the degree of competition within the market. The leading cases, like *Inno/ATAB*, dealt with the cigarette and tobacco markets, in Belgium and Holland respectively. In *Fedetab*[12] (European Court 1980) the Belgian legislation imposing strict price control at the retail level considerably reduced the scope for competition. Excise duty in fact comprised some 70 per cent of the price of an average packet of cigarettes. In this situation, the legislation laid down strict requirements for the affixing to every packet of the exact price upon which the relevant duty had been calculated in order to reduce the scope for fraud. These laws, of course, also considerably reduced the scope for competition but the European Court ruled that competition could have remained in three important areas, namely profit margins for both wholesalers and retailers, rebates, and terms and conditions of supply including credit terms. These were all areas where in a competitive market variations would have been anticipated, as particular undertakings sought to increase their market share by improving the terms offered to their more favoured customers, but which under the rules of the relevant trade association had been suppressed so as to exclude the element of uncertainty which such competition would have brought. Fedetab's appeal against the decision of the Commission that its recommendation to members as to standard terms of business and prices to be charged contravened Article 81(1) was therefore rejected.

---

[11] Case C-2/91 [1993] ECR I-5751.   [12] Case 209/78 [1980] ECR 3125: [1981] 3 CMLR 134.

To similar effect was the Court's decision in the later *SSI*[13] case (1985) relating to Dutch legislation, along similar lines but involving not only regulations relating to excise taxes but the permitted level of price increases by Dutch manufacturers and restraints on their profits. Once again, while the Court accepted that this legislation had considerably affected the climate of competition, it held that its terms did not prevent all aspects of competition between those engaged in the trade. Competition would still have been possible (had the relevant trade associations not prevented it) on such promotional matters as giving additional discounts or rebates, and providing more favourable terms and conditions of sale. A decision finding breaches of Article 81(1) by the association of Dutch tobacco dealers was therefore also upheld.

It will be comparatively rare for government involvement through legislation or administrative action to be so all-pervasive as to eliminate the possibility of competitive activity to such an extent that Articles 81 and 82 can no longer have any application. The only case in which this has been found to occur was the *Sugar Cartel* case[14] (European Court 1975) where the Italian government limited competition with regard to imports into Italy of sugar in no fewer than four major respects. There is no other recorded case in which all these conditions have applied, and it seems unlikely that defendants will be allowed to rely on this precedent save in the most unusual circumstances. Even though in the SSI case the Dutch authorities had held formal consultations with the cigarette industry on its agreed objectives, including the guarantee of substantial tax revenue for government and stable income for retailers, the Dutch government had not gone to the extent of suggesting to undertakings that they should support those objectives by anti-competitive arrangements.

In the majority of cases, as we have seen, the defence of State compulsion (as in *Fedetab*, for example) has been dismissed on the ground that the State action left sufficient 'breathing space' in which the undertakings could operate without being required to act in contravention of Articles 81 or 82. However, if the State action was sufficiently compelling and allowing no room for manoeuvre, it would provide a defence to the undertaking, against both Commission proceedings and any private action by an injured third party.[15]

It can also be said with confidence that if Member State governments merely encourage undertakings to establish prices and regulate industry by methods reducing or eliminating competition, this is no defence if the legislation is permissive rather than strictly mandatory. Nor will it be any defence to show that there is governmental ratification for the implementation of schemes to regulate prices and other industry conditions that were originally agreed between the undertakings themselves. Justification for this statement can be found in the twin French cases of *Pabst and Richarz KG* v. *BNIA*[16] (Commission 1976) and *BNIC* v. *Clair*[17] (European Court 1985).

---

[13] Cases 240–242, 260–262, 268–269/82 [1985] ECR 3381: [1987] 3 CMLR 661.

[14] Case 40/73 [1975] ECR 1663: [1976] 1 CMLR 295. Details of this case are set out in Ch. 7, pp.144–5.

[15] There is, however, an argument based on European Court decisions in other fields that an undertaking which seeks to rely on State action as a defence against a claim of anti-competitive behaviour must itself take the risk that the State was not authorized by Community law to compel such action.

[16] [1976] 2 CMLR D63. The Commission's comment on this case in the *6th Annual Report* (1976), p.68, was that it showed 'where associations or undertakings entrusted with certain statutory powers act beyond their powers and take measures to regulate the market, the object or effect of which is to promote the uniform conduct of its members, they cannot evade the rules of competition and hold the State responsible for their actions'.

[17] Case 123/83 [1985] ECR 391: 2 CMLR 430.

In the first, the *Armagnac* case, this famous brandy was produced under the auspices of the trade association BNIA, whose function was to regulate the affairs of the industry and in particular to regulate the quality and control and the terms upon which it was sold, as well as providing technical and research assistance to the growers. The association had a chairman appointed by the French Ministry of Agriculture, twelve delegates representing producers and co-operatives, and another twelve representing wholesalers, distillers, and brokers. All sales of armagnac were graded from 0 to 5, the most expensive variety being grade 5, VSOP Napoleon at least five years old. Forty per cent of industry production was sold in France, and 60 per cent was exported either in bottles or in bulk. The majority of exports were in bulk, and the association had authority to issue certificates of age for these. The association effectively controlled all movements of bulk armagnac and was fully informed of the stocks of various ages and grades held by the members of the association.

Concern had apparently been felt that some German importers had sold the brandy under a false trade description, claiming lower grades to be grade 5. The association, purporting to deal with this abuse, imposed a ban upon bulk deliveries of grades 4 and 5. German importers, who had become used to receiving bulk deliveries of the higher grade, complained to the Commission that this restriction was in breach of Article 81. It was claimed that, whatever the alleged justification for the interference by the association in trading practices, its effect would be artificially to reduce the supply and increase the price of the higher grades of brandy. The Commission ruled that the decision of the association was a breach of Article 81; it pointed out that the effect of the ban on bulk supplies was far in excess of the measures that would have been necessary to carry out the quality protection obligations assigned to BNIA by the relevant French decrees. The objective of BNIA's decision appeared rather to be to restrict competition within the Common Market and to increase the price of the highest grades by reducing their availability on the German market. The Commission ruled that other administrative and legal means to stop unfair practices or false trade designations were available, and those should have been applied in a way that was proportionate to the disclosed problem, rather than by the exercise of powers to prevent altogether bulk deliveries of the two highest grades.

In 1982 the Commission ruled that similar practices fixing the price of cognac by a similar professional association responsible for that industry was likewise in breach of Article 81, this being confirmed by the 1985 European Court decision in the *BNIC/Clair* case. Here, the association also had the function of acting as a joint trade organization between the various interests in the cognac industry. It provided technical details and information as to the supply and demand for the products, it supervised maintenance of industry standards, and subject to government supervision was entitled to implement rules for the marketing of cognac, including prices and terms of payment.

A committee representing the various interests in the trade, similar to that in the armagnac industry, decided prices and conditions of sale. A committee decision had to be approved by a three-quarters majority of the members of the association, who included delegates of wine growers, dealers, brokers, workers, and technicians. Once the rules had thus been adopted, the association was entitled to apply to the French Minister of Agriculture to extend the agreement compulsorily for a specified period to all members of the trade, whether or not they were participants in the joint trade organization. Once the ministerial decree had been made, any contract failing to comply with it would be void. In the relevant year, a minimum price of wines for distillation into cognac had been fixed, but

Clair had made contracts for sale to various growers at prices below those allowed. BNIC claimed that this agreement was void; Clair responded by arguing that the price-fixing was contrary to Articles 81 and 82. The French court before whom the case came made an Article 234 application to the European Court to determine whether this form of price-fixing was covered by Article 81(1).

The European Court answered in the affirmative.[18] The Court ruled that any agreement which had the object or effect of restricting competition by fixing minimum prices for the purchase of a semi-finished product (wine) could affect trade between Member States, even if the semi-finished product was not itself traded between Member States, as long as it formed the basis of a final product (cognac) marketed elsewhere in the EC. The fact that the agreement had been concluded within the framework of a public law, with the 'blessing' of government, could not affect the application of Article 81; nor would the fact that the persons who signed the agreement were themselves largely appointed by a government minister on the nomination of the relevant trade organization be considered relevant.

2.3 MANDATORY TARIFFS FOR SECTORS OF THE ECONOMY

More recently, however, there have been disturbing signs that these principles laid down in earlier cases are being diluted in situations where Member States have laid down mandatory tariffs for particular sectors, after consultation with industry representatives. Such tariffs have been fixed, for example, for German road hauliers and inland waterways and for Italian road hauliers.[19] The common feature of these cases was that the members of the Consultative Committee consulted by the Member State for the implementation of the detailed tariffs were not only industry representatives, the majority being public authority members not engaged in the industry who were required by the national statute to act in the interests of all users, including small and medium-sized businesses (SMEs in Community jargon) and economically weak areas. Nevertheless, the Member State retained a right in all cases to overrule decisions of these committees if it disagreed with their findings. Some concern must be felt at the risk that, notwithstanding these theoretical safeguards in the process leading up to the publication of the mandatory tariff, the interests of members of the industry may in practice predominate, so that the outcome may be remarkably similar to a price cartel for the industry.

In some cases however the element of public interest in the determination of the tariffs may be minimal, and in such cases it is likely that the Court of Justice would rule both that the Member State was in breach of Article 10 and that the undertaking or association was in breach of Article 81. This occurred in relation to custom agents' tariffs in Italy. In

---

[18] In a further Art. 234 case involving the cognac industry the Court predictably ruled that a levy on a French wine-grower for exceeding his production quota was a private arrangement subject to Art. 81. The French government was held in breach of Art. 10 by adopting and extending to non-members of the relevant trade association the burden of such production levies and restrictions: *BNIC* v. *Aubert* Case 136/86 [1987] ECR 4789: [1988] 4 CMLR 331.

[19] *Reiff* Case C-185/91 [1993] ECR I-5801: [1995] 5 CMLR 145. *Germany* v. *Delta* Case C-153/93 [1994] ECR I-2517: [1996] 4 CMLR 21. *Spediporto* v. *SMG* Case C-96/94 [1995] ECR I-2883: 4 CMLR 613. A similar approach was adopted by the Court in *Bassano* Cases C 140–142/94 [1995] ECR I-3257: [1996] 4 CMLR 157 concerned with the granting of licences in an Italian town authorizing the opening of retail shops.

Commission v. *Italy*[20] the Court had held that the law requiring the agents' association to fix their charges was unenforceable, because its terms included little or no 'public interest' in the fixing of the charges; indeed the association was given a freedom to draw up the tariffs and conditions of business in a way damaging to competition between them. In *Commission* v. *CNST*[21] the association was subsequently itself held in breach of Article 81 because the tariff made large increases to the minimum charges previously in force and introduced rules that curtailed the freedom of agents to reduce their costs or to offer reductions in charges to their customers.

2.4 THE *ALUMINIUM CARTEL* CASE

In the light of the above, it will not come as a surprise that mere Governmental encouragement however without any statutory basis provides no defence to a claim under Article 81 or 82, as the *Aluminium Cartel*[22] case shows. The Commission decision, issued in 1984, concerned agreements between major Western producers of aluminium which ensured that during the years 1963 to 1976 all Eastern Bloc source material passed into the hands of the leading Western producers, who prevented their competitors from obtaining the benefits of metal at lower prices, removing a major source of price competition from Western markets. The original scheme for preventing the marketing of Eastern Bloc aluminium in the West, in a way which would reduce the overall level of prices, had been entered into with at least the tacit support of the British government, which had been concerned with the risk that the market price for aluminium would be substantially reduced by Eastern Bloc material at a time when there was no UK law limiting the agreements that could be made with regard to such foreign source material, this being several years before the entry of the United Kingdom into the European Community and its acceptance of the Treaty, including Articles 81 and 82. The Commission held that the encouragement given by the British government did not provide any defence to a charge under Article 81, although it might be a factor reducing the culpability of defendants and therefore relevant to the assessment of whether any fine should be imposed, and if so how large.[23]

3. ARTICLE 86(1) AND (2): PUBLIC UNDERTAKINGS SUBJECT TO THE TREATY RULES ON COMPETITION

3.1 THE PURPOSE OF THESE ARTICLES

It is not only by legislative or executive acts that Member States may become involved in interference with the normal working of competition. Member States are themselves involved in the provision of public services in many ways, either through nationalized industries or public corporations of many kinds. Their right to preserve their own balance

---

[20] Case C-35/96 [1998] ECR I-3851: 5 CMLR 889.
[21] Case T-513/93 [2000] ECR II-1807: 5 CMLR 614.
[22] See Ch. 9, pp.145–7, for a fuller account of the facts of the case.
[23] In the event, no fines were imposed on the participants to the agreement.

of public and private enterprise is specifically retained under Article 295.[24] It is, however, undoubtedly true that if public undertakings were treated by Member States in a more favourable manner than other enterprises, considerable damage could be done to the process of competition in national markets in ways that would affect trade between Member States. For this reason, Article 86 was included in this part of the Treaty; unlike Articles 81 and 82, it is specifically aimed at Member States, but its function is to clarify the application of the competition rules to them, rather than to restrict their application. This Article has a close connection with Article 10. Moreover, Article 86 applies not only to competition rules but to a number of other Treaty obligations of Member States, including the adjustment of State monopolies (Article 31), free movement of labour (Article 39), the right of establishment (Article 43), and freedom of services (Article 49). Therefore Article 86 is normally necessarily applied in connection with another Treaty Article. Undoubtedly, however, its major significance and use, of increasing importance during recent years, has been in connection with breach by public undertakings in Member States of the rules contained in Articles 81 and 82.

Article 86 contains three paragraphs. The first lays down the broad principle:

(1) In the case of public undertaking and undertakings to which Member States grant special or exclusive rights, Member States shall neither enact nor maintain in force any measure contrary to the rules contained in this Treaty, in particular to those rules provided for in Article [12] and Articles [81 to 90].

The second paragraph contains a relatively narrow exemption to the basic principle contained in paragraph (1). Three cumulative conditions have to be satisfied before it comes into operation:

(2)(i) The undertakings concerned must have been entrusted with the 'operation of a service of general economic interest' or 'having the character of a revenue-producing monopoly'.

(ii) The application of the Treaty rules would obstruct the performance in law or fact of the particular tasks assigned to it.

(iii) In any case the development of trade must not be affected (if the exemption were otherwise available) to an extent contrary to the interests of the Community.

The third paragraph, dealt with in section 4 of this chapter, provides the Commission with important powers to issue directives and make decisions relevant to liberalization of particular national markets and to prevent breaches of competition law by Member States.

3.2 PUBLIC UNDERTAKINGS AND UNDERTAKINGS WITH SPECIAL OR EXCLUSIVE RIGHTS

Two categories of undertaking are affected by these rules, namely 'public undertakings' and public, quasi-public, or private undertakings to which 'special or exclusive rights' have been granted. The general rules therefore apply, *inter alia*, to all public bodies which possess an identity independent from that of the Member State itself; this appears to exclude only

---

[24] Article 295 reads 'This Treaty shall in no way prejudice the rules in Member States governing the system of property ownership'.

actual departments or ministries of the government forming an integral part of the executive or administrative function of the State.[25]

Help in interpretation of the meaning of 'public undertaking' in Article 86(1) is obtained from Article 2 of Commission Directive 80/723 of 25 June 1980 on 'transparency of relationships', introduced under the authority of Article 86(3), defining it as follows: 'Any undertaking over which the public authorities may exercise directly or indirectly a dominant influence by virtue of their ownership of it, their financial participation therein or the rules which govern it'.[26] That definition covers a very wide range of bodies, including large-scale nationalized industries responsible for the production and distribution of gas and electricity, national railway authorities, and many other public bodies, large and small, engaged in public economic activity. It includes the provision of services, even if these also involve the sale of goods.

The second category of undertaking mentioned in Article 86(1) is narrower since, although public undertakings could often be described as enjoying 'special' or 'exclusive' rights, the phrase refers to undertakings not actually public but which have nevertheless been granted such special privileges in order to carry out functions regarded as important by Member State governments. This category included bodies authorized to operate State television and broadcasting services.[27] It also covers bodies with rights to prescribe standards for particular sectors, such as agricultural produce, and those responsible for regulating people employed in particular trades or professions. It also covers bodies authorized to run ports, airports, or other public facilities, and private operators of telecommunication services provided that the special rights which they have been granted have been accorded only to a limited number of undertakings. In the United Kingdom, the Drivers and Vehicles Licensing Office in Swansea and Her Majesty's Stationery Office, both now privatized, would qualify, as would bodies with the right to supervize activities in particular sectors (such as the Meat and Livestock Commission) and bodies such as the Law Society or the General Medical Council responsible by statute for regulating particular professions. 'Special rights' have also been defined by Directive 94/46, referred to in the context of the telecommunications industry in section 4 below.

The 1984 European Court decision in *IAZ International Belgium* v. *Commission*[28] concerned a trade association granted such statutory rights by the Belgian government for approving appliances for connection to the public water supply, evidenced by the award of official certificates of conformity. The association, used its rights in a way designed to force all manufacturers and importers of washing machines to become members, by making difficulties in the granting of such certificates to parallel importers and concerns which preferred to import appliances without joining the association. Applying Article 86, the Court held that the association was subject to Article 81 notwithstanding its statutory functions.

---

[25] See A. Pappalardo, 'Measures of the States and Rules of Competition of the EEC Treaty', (1984) *Eleventh Annual Proceedings of Fordham Corporate Law Institute* 515–41.

[26] [1980] OJ L195/35 as later amended by Directive 85/413 [1985] OJ L229 and see also [1993] OJ L254 and [2000] OJ L193/75. See *1994 Annual Report*, p.135.

[27] See, e.g. *BRT* v. *SABAM* Case 127/73 [1974] ECR 313: 2 CMLR 238, and *Sacchi* Case 155/73 [1974] ECR 409: 2 CMLR 177.

[28] Case 96/82 [1983] ECR 3369 [1984] 3 CMLR 276 (also known as *Anseau-Navewa* v. *Commission*).

A similar conclusion was reached in *RTT* v. *GB/INNO*,[29] where the Belgian national telephone company had legal powers to give licence approvals to telephone equipment imported for sale by third parties, but made qualification by them unduly onerous. Their actions were challenged by GB/INNO, a super-market chain, importing cheaper forms of equipment which were in competition with RTT's more expensive equipment. The European Court held that it was a breach of Articles 82 and 86 for an enterprise such as RTT having a dominant position in one market (the operation of a telephone service) to reserve for itself ancillary activities (improvement of equipment) which might enable it to foreclose other competitors from that market, given that any safety or other technical objective could be achieved by the publication of specifications rather than by licensing. Such standards could, moreover, be better enforced by an independent body, rather than by RTT as a national telephone operator.

Merci Convenzionali Porto di Genoa v. *Gabrielli*[30] provided the European Court with a further opportunity to define the types of undertaking caught by Article 86(1). Merci Convenzionali held exclusive rights under Italian law to operate the Port of Genoa and made excessive charges for its monopoly stevedoring services provided to Gabrielli, a company importing steel. The Court held that the port undertaking was one with 'exclusive rights' under 86(1) and that a Member State could not reserve jobs in stevedoring operations carried out by it for Italian nationals alone; such reservation was a breach not only of Article 39 but also of Article 82 since the port was a substantial part of the Common Market and was operated in a manner which was abusive. The abuses included charging excessively high prices and refusing to make use of modern technology in its operations.

Subsequent legislation adopted by the Italian government dealing with the arrangements for the use of temporary labour in the port were also struck down by the Commission as in breach of Articles 82 and 86, since it enabled the port authority to create a monopoly in the supply of such labour to a single undertaking, which would thereby gain an advantage over all its competitors. (*Community* v. *Italy*).[31] Italian legislation was also ruled to infringe these Articles in the *Piloting Tariffs*[32] case where, following an adverse decision by the European Court on the pilotage charges in the port of Genoa in *Corsica Ferries (No. 1)*[33] the amending legislation was also held by the Commission to be discriminatory against non-Italian shipowners.

Although a number of Italian measures have been found illegal, as mentioned above, one of the rare findings of a service qualifying as one of 'general economic interest' was made in *Corsica Ferries (No. 2)*.[34] The services provided were local mooring operations in La Spezia and Genoa. The Court of Justice ruled that the provision of a general mooring service, available at all times and in all conditions, was within this definition, especially as the charges payable had been subjected to widespread consultations with all affected parties and were based on objective local and national criteria. In any case the arrangements were justified under Article 46 of the Treaty on public security grounds.

---

[29] Case C-18/88 [1991] ECR I-5941.

[30] Case C-179/90 [1991] ECR I-5889: [1994] 4 CMLR 422. A similar case involved monopoly stevedoring rights in La Spezia, *Silvano Raso* Case C-163/96 [1998] ECR I-533: 4 CMLR 737.

[31] [1998] 4 CMLR 73.

[32] [1998] 4 CMLR 91.

[33] Case C-18/93 [1994] ECR I-1783.   [34] Case C-266/93: [1998] ECR I-3949: 5 CMLR 402.

3.3 THE LIMITED EXEMPTION IN ARTICLE 86(2)

The exemption from the competition rules contained in Article 86(2) for bodies entrusted with the operation of services of general economic interest or having the character of revenue producing monopolies, has some similarities to Article 81(3); it is, however, a far more difficult exemption to obtain. The three cumulative exemptions listed above have been strictly construed by the Community Courts, and are applicable to a relatively narrow range of bodies. Indeed some bodies falling within 86(1) would not meet the requirements for exemption under 86(2), though it is also possible that some private undertakings which would not fall under 86(1) (as neither 'public' nor having 'special or exclusive rights') might nevertheless qualify for exemption under (2) if carrying out tasks of sufficient 'general economic interest'.

This means that the scope of the exemption is limited to activities of a public undertaking which have a direct relationship with its main statutory functions and are not, for example, simply commercial activities which are ancillary to them. To obtain the benefit of this restricted exemption, however, the undertaking must show that there is an inherent conflict between the task imposed upon the undertaking and the application of the Treaty rules. That this is a substantial burden is clearly illustrated by the *Telespeed (British Telecom)*[35] case decided by the European Court in 1985. The Commission's decision was that British Telecom, at that time 'a public corporation established by statute holding a statutory monopoly on the running of telecommunication systems in the United Kingdom',[36] was abusing a dominant position under the meaning of Article 82. The abuse of its dominant position had occurred through the prohibition against private message-forwarding agencies in the United Kingdom transmitting messages, whose originators and recipients were resident in other countries, through the British network. This could be done at a cheaper rate than sending the messages direct between two other countries. It is interesting that the appeal against the Commission's decision was not brought by British Telecom itself, which accepted the Commission decision, but by the Italian government which obviously regarded it as a precedent relevant to its own public undertakings.

Amongst the arguments raised by the Italian government was that Article 86(2) protected BT in acting to prohibit the activities of such independent agencies, so as to protect the services or general economic interest which BT was required by statute to carry out. The European Court rejected this argument, on the ground that in taking action against the private agencies BT was acting not in an official capacity, but simply in its commercial capacity, like any other undertaking engaged in business. The management of public telecommunications equipment and the placing of that equipment at the disposal of consumers against payment of a fee was inherently a business, not a governmental, activity. The rules under which telex messages were forwarded had been prepared by British Telecom alone and were not laid down by statute. They clearly formed an integral part of its business strategy and activity.

The leading case on the interpretation of the exemption under paragraph 2 is *Corbeau*.[37]

---

[35] Case 41/83 [1985] ECR 873: 2 CMLR 368, reported under the name of *British Telecommunications: Italy v. Commission.*

[36] The quotation is taken from an account of the case at p.96 of the *15th Annual Report* (1985). The case related to practices of British Telecom between 1975 and 1981, before its privatization.

[37] Case C-320/91 [1993] ECR I-2533: [1995] 4 CMLR 621.

Paul Corbeau ran a business in Liège which undertook to collect letters from the sender's home address to be delivered into a local area by the next morning, essentially a 'rapid delivery' service claimed to be superior to that of the normal post. Corbeau was prosecuted under Belgian law which gave the official post office exclusive rights to collect, transport, and deliver all mail in Belgium. The Liège Court sought guidance under Article 234 on the compatibility of this law with Article 86. The European Court ruled that it was contrary to Article 86 for Belgian law to prohibit competitors to the Post Office from providing services that the Post Office did not offer, with additional features such as collection from the sender's address, greater speed or reliability of delivery and distribution, and the possibility of changing the destination of a letter in the course of transit. Creators of such special services should not therefore face prosecution unless it could be shown that their existence would compromise the whole economic basis and equilibrium of the general postal service. Whether Corbeau's service was such a threat to the Belgian postal services was a matter for the national court to decide with the burden of proof firmly on the Post Office. The test laid down here is not very different from that provided in the *Telespeed* case referred to above, though in that case it was absolutely clear that BT's activity in prohibiting the activities of private message-forwarding agencies was not needed to protect the financial equilibrium of a universal telephone service.

3.4 THE GRANT OF EXCLUSIVITY

The necessity for providing exclusivity to a public undertaking was challenged in several other later cases. In *Höfner and Elser* v. *Macrotron*[38] the German legal monopoly for employment recruitment held by an official body was reviewed. Whilst legally only the Bundesanstalt für Arbeit was allowed to act as an employment agency, in practice private bodies competed with it because the official body was clearly unable to cope with the volume of business. The client of a private employment agency refused to pay their charges on the basis that the activities of such an 'unofficial' agency were illegal. The reference under Article 234 to the European Court by the Munich Oberlandesgericht produced a finding that the legal status of the Bundesanstalt für Arbeit did not prevent it being an 'undertaking'; finding jobs for applicants was an economic activity. The fact that this body could not in practice handle the demands in a modern economy for employment services meant that its dominant position, under law, became illegal, nor did it require any special privileges under Article 86(2) in order to carry out its duties. Whilst it was an undertaking with responsibility for the operation of a service of 'general economic interest', the exemption under 86(2) only arose when application of Community competition rules would actually interfere with those responsibilities. Here it was not competition rules that made it impossible for the duties to be carried out, but the inadequacy of the institution, which had encouraged private companies to enter into competition with it.

In two Italian cases involving similar facts (*Job Centre Co-op*[39] and *Carra*[40]) national law had provided that only undertakings registered with the Ministry of Employment were allowed to operate as employment agencies for temporary workers. The Court of Justice

[38] Case C-41/90 [1991] ECR I-1979: [1993] 4 CMLR 306.
[39] Case C-55/96 [1997] ECR I-7119: [1998] 4 CMLR 708.
[40] Case C-258/98 [2000] ECR I-4217: [2002] 4 CMLR 285.

found in both cases on Article 234 references that such a prohibition was in breach of the Article, if it created a situation where public placement offices were manifestly unable to satisfy demand for such services but it was impossible for private agencies to operate. The Court emphasized that national courts should refuse to implement such legislation without waiting for its formal withdrawal.

Exclusivity was also an issue in the *ERT* case.[41] ERT had an exclusive right to broadcast its television programmes in Greece and sought to prevent potential operators from competing with it, in particular DEP and the Mayor of Thessaloniki which had set up a local television station, TV 100. The Court found that the grant of that exclusive right would infringe Article 86 'if those rights are liable to create a situation in which that undertaking is led to infringe Article [82] by virtue of a discriminatory broadcasting policy which favours its own programmes, unless the application of Article [82] frustrates its performance of the particular tasks entrusted for it'. Whereas in *Hofner* the facts showed that the exclusivity itself was an abuse, in ERT no such finding was made; what the Court made clear is that the possibility of abuse is sufficient to infringe Article 86, even if ERT had not taken any active steps to abuse the dominant position which Greek law had given it.

The Court has, however, for its part not in the past been disposed to interpret Article 86(2) broadly, even where the functions performed by the undertaking are central to the proper functioning of the economy of a Member State. In *Züchner* v. *Bayerische Vereins-bank*,[42] Züchner was a customer of this German bank and queried whether it was entitled to agree with all other banks in the Federal Republic of Germany a uniform service charge for transfers of sums of a similar amount to other Member States. The bank argued that by reason of the special nature of the services which banks provide, especially in regard to transfer of capital, they should be considered as undertakings 'entrusted with the operation of services of general economic interest within the meaning of Article 86(2)'. Although the Court accepted that the transfer of funds from one Member State to another normally carried out by banks is an operation which has a public element, it ruled that banks do not come within the classification of Article 86(2), unless in performing such transfers they can be shown to operate a service of general economic interest with which they have been entrusted through measures adopted by government. The Court declined to make such a finding.

The same principle arose in the *Ijsselcentrale*[43] case. Local distributors of electricity in Holland complained to the Commission that an agreement between the four Dutch generators of electricity (all owned by local authorities) and their joint venture SEP violated Article 81. The restrictive clauses in the agreement not only provided for coordination of their activities but prevented imports and exports by any undertaking other than SEP and required the generators to impose similar restrictions on their local distributors, who in practice passed these obligations on to their own customers; these included large industrial concerns who might well have wished to import electricity, for example, from Germany. The Commission ruled that although the supply of electricity was a service of general economic

---

41 Case C-260/89 [1991] ECR I-2925: [1994] 4 CMLR 540.

42 Case 172/80 [1981] ECR 2021: [1982] 1 CMLR 313.

43 [1992] 5 CMLR 154 (the Commission decision) upheld on appeal by the Court of First Instance Case T-16/91 [1992] ECR II-2417: [1997] 4 CMLR 453 and by the European Court (save on one minor ground) Case C-19/93P [1995] ECR I-3319: [1997] 4 CMLR 392.

interest, it could be carried out satisfactorily without the control of import and export required by the agreement; in other words, the restrictions were in the terminology of Article 81(3) 'not indispensable to the attainment of its objectives'.

The mere grant by the State to an organization of exclusive rights does not necessarily mean that there will automatically be a breach of the Article, as is illustrated by *La Crespelle*.[44] Here the French Government had granted to some fifty approved bovine insemination centres throughout France exclusive rights in particular regions of the country. Another unofficial establishment with similar objects opened in the Mayenne area and was sued for damages by the local official centre. The defence to the claim was that the exclusive rights were in breach of Article 86(2). The justification given by the French government for them was that the long term programme for improving the quality of breeding stock would be damaged if the centres (which were non-profit making) had to engage in price competition with other centres and were thereby forced to reduce their extensive research programmes. A procedure did exist for enabling orders from farmers or breeders for semen from outside France to be supplied through the centres. The Court of Justice upheld the legality of the exclusive arrangements under an Article 234 reference.

3.5 SERVICES OF GENERAL ECONOMIC INTEREST—A DEFINITION

In recent years concern has been expressed by a number of Member States, and especially France, that sufficient consideration had not been given in the application of Article 86(2) to the need for a broad and sympathetic definition of the phrase 'services of general economic interest' and their social function. A new Article 16 was introduced into the Treaty by the Treaty of Amsterdam emphasizing that the Community and Member States should each 'take care that such services operate on the basis of principles and conditions which enable them to fulfil their missions'. While the terms of the new Article do not alter the language or legal effect of the phrase, its existence means that in practice that the Commission has now had to adopt a more cautious approach to its interpretation.

This is shown by its Communication on Services of General Interest published on 19 January 2001,[45] which defined them as covering both market and non-market services, which member states have classified as of general interest and subject to specific public service obligations, having an economic nature but not necessarily profit making. The Commission acknowledged that to compile a comprehensive list of these services would be difficult and that Member States should be left to determine their exact scope. States remained free to lay down by way of non-discriminatory legislation standards of security, quality and regularity on all operators. The Commission was at pains to emphasize that in its liberalization programmes it had always sought to maintain their 'public sector obligation' content and that these programmes had themselves often improved the quality and affordability of such services.

While national courts are entitled to apply the first two conditions, the determination of the third issue, whether the development of trade has been affected by the practices to an extent contrary to the interests of the Community, appears to be for the Commission alone to decide. This issue remained in doubt until the *Ahmed Saeed* case, confirmed later by guidelines published in 1991 on the application of EC competition rules to the telecom-

---

[44] Case C-323/93 [1994] ECR I-5077.   [45] [2001] OJ C17/4: 4 CMLR 882.

munications sector. It is clear that the national court can decide that competition rules apply to the organization with a responsibility for general economic services and that it does not need protection from the competition rules to carry these out. However, if the national court believes that protection is required, then it must pass to the Commission the responsibility for determining if the derogation from these rules is likely to affect trade to an extent contrary to the interests of the Community, by showing that trade between Member States in the relevant market had been sufficiently affected: (*Commission v. Netherlands: Commission v. France*).[46]

4. ARTICLE 86(3): DIRECTIVES AND DECISIONS OF THE COMMISSION

4.1 THE INITIAL USE OF SUCH DIRECTIVES: TELECOMMUNICATIONS

This provision has become increasingly important over the last ten years, as the Commission has realized that if Article 86 is to be an effective means of improving the competitiveness of vital sectors of the economies of Member States, then it will need to use its powers to address appropriate directives and decisions to them. The Commission has freedom here to act without the formal consent being required of the Council or any other Community institution, though it uses its power with discretion and only after extensive consultation.

The initial principal use of directives was in telecommunications; the Commission had for some time viewed with concern the practices of Member States in granting special or exclusive rights to national telecommunications organizations in drawing up specification for the installation and operation of terminal equipment such as telephone exchanges. In order to remedy the situation it adopted Directive 88/301 which set out a number of principles for Member States to observe in order to improve the competitive situation applying to this equipment and to bring to an end existing breaches of the Article. The Directive provided that:

(i) Member States should withdraw such exclusive or special rights from their own favoured undertakings relating to telecommunications terminal equipment;

(ii) Member States should ensure that undertakings have the right to import, market, connect, and maintain terminal equipment;

(iii) type approval specifications should be drawn up by bodies independent of the operation of telecommunications network or terminal providers; and

(iv) all contracts for leasing or maintenance of such equipment should be terminable on not more than a year's notice, thus preventing the use of long-term contracts as a means of shutting out new competitors for longer periods.

The validity of this Directive was challenged by France and other Member States. Eventually

---

[46] *Commission v. Netherlands* Case C-157/94 [1997] ECR I-5699: [1998] 2 CMLR 373, *Commission v. France* Case C-159/94 [1997] ECR I-5815: [1998] 2 CMLR 373. M. Ross [2000] 25 EurLR 22–38.

the issue reached the European Court of Justice[47] which upheld the right of the Commission to deal with breaches of Article 86 by such a Directive which specified in a general way the obligation which the Treaty imposed on Member States. It was not necessary, said the Court, for the Commission to utilize Article 226, which applied only when specific infringements of the Treaty had occurred. Nor was it necessary for the Commission to obtain from the Council separate measures under Articles 83 or 95 of the Treaty. Dealing with provisions (i) and (ii) above, it upheld the requirement by the Commission that exclusivity should no longer be permitted for telecommunications operators since restrictions issued for this purpose by Member States would in any case be in breach of Article 28. Point (iii) relating to type approval was also approved. The Court did, however, annul the prohibition in the Directive on special rights (largely because of failure by the Commission to provide an adequate definition of this category) and also those relating to long-term contracts under (iv). The reason for this latter ruling was that the practice of long-term contracts was one adopted by independent undertakings rather than Member States and should, therefore, be dealt with under Article 81 or 82 rather than Article 86. Directive 88/301 was amended by Directive 94/46 in the light of this Court decision so as to incorporate a full definition of 'special rights', namely rights granted to a limited number of undertakings through any legislative, regulatory, or administrative instrument which, within a geographical area:

limits to two or more the number of such undertakings, otherwise than according to objective, proportional and non-discriminatory criteria, or designates, otherwise than according to such criteria, several competing undertakings, or confers on any undertaking or undertakings, otherwise than according to such criteria, any legal or regulatory advantages which substantially affect the ability of any other undertaking to import, market, connect, bring into service, and/or maintain telecommunication terminal equipment in the same geographical area under substantial equivalent conditions.

A related but even more significant Directive (Reg. 90/388) was enacted in 1990 dealing with telecommunications services themselves.[48] This provided for the abolition of monopoly rights in the provision of such services and opened them up to competition; the arrival of digital networks and other technical advances had made possible enormous improvements in the quality, variety, and commercial value of these services, and liberalization of the market was essential if users were to benefit fully from them. It was necessary that each Member State set up an independent authority to carry out the regulatory functions previously dealt with by the national telephone authority. The Directive in its original terms provided that monopoly rights could be retained by Member States in four areas, namely:

(i)   voice telephony services to the general public;

(ii) satellite services;

(iii) mobile telephones; and

(iv) radio and TV broadcasts.

---

[47] *France v. Commission* Case C-202/88 [1991] ECR I-1223: [1992] 5 CMLR 552.

[48] This Directive was also challenged by some Member States, with an identical outcome to that in the earlier case referred to in fn. 47, in Cases C-271, 281, 289/90 [1992] ECR I-5833 (*Spain and Others v. Commission*).

However, these services were brought within the scope of the Directive by amending legislation following the pattern set out in the 1995 Green Paper adopted by the Commission, which set out its general policy towards liberalization of the telecommunications sector. Directive 94/46 brought satellite station equipment and satellite communication services within the scope of both 88/301 and 90/388. A later Directive, 95/51, provided for the abolition of all restrictions on the transmission of telecommunications services on cable TV networks (apart from voice telephony services) from 1 January 1996, making possible the interconnection of all cable TV networks, and national public telephone networks. By Directive 96/2 mobile telephones were also brought within the scope of Directive 90/388, and Member States had thereafter to abolish all special or exclusive rights for incumbent national operators, enabling new entrants to set up rival systems, including access to suitable frequencies on equal terms with the incumbents. By bringing down in this way the cost to the public of mobile services, an important step was taken towards the complete liberalization of voice telephony.

The final and most important liberalization was introduced by the 'Full Competition Directive' (96/19), taking effect from 1 January 1998. By that date any exclusive rights within a Member State for the provision of voice telephony services had to be abolished, and rules introduced to make competition with the incumbent national operators fully effective. For example, interconnection rules had to be transparent and non-discriminatory, and access for new entrants facilitated. Transition periods for adjustment were granted to the smaller Member States with less developed or smaller telephone networks. In 1999 the Services Directive was amended so as to require telecommunications and cable networks owned by the same undertaking to be operated as separate legal bodies.

In 2000 the Commission adopted a consolidating Directive (2887/2000) to take effect from July 2003, which incorporates all the previous directives made under either Article 86(3) or Article 95, followed in 2002 by a Council and Parliamentary package of other measures relating to the regulatory framework for telecommunications, as greater powers are vested in national regulatory authorities to apply the relevant rules within their own territories, which are becoming more closely linked to competition policy, rather than regulatory principles, as the degree of competition in this sector increases. In addition the Electronic Communications Networks and Services (Antitrust) Directive 2002/77 repealing the original 90/388 Services Directive, was adopted by the Commission.[49]

4.2 OTHER RELATED INITIATIVES OF THE COMMISSION

The Commission has not however been solely dependent on Article 86(3) for liberalization of this market, and has also used its opportunities in cases under Articles 81 and 82 and above all under the Merger Regulation to move its policy of liberalization forward. It has taken the initiative in 1998 and 1999 to investigate the charges made by fixed line operators and the interconnection charges between fixed and mobile operators throughout the Community, which resulted in significant price reductions for these services.

It has also opened major sectoral inquiries under Article 12 of Regulation 17/62 (an underused Article but retained in the modernization Regulation No. 1/2003 as Article 17)

---

[49] This Directive also takes effect from 25 July 2003 and applies to all electronic 'networks' and 'services' rather than merely telecommunications 'networks' and 'services'. [2002] 5 CMLR 1142: OJ L249/21.

into local loop unbundling, mobile phone 'roaming charges' and leased lines. The first two are still in progress. The Commission has also brought a large number of infringement actions under the directives against Member States, and recent Annual Reports record significant decisions of the Court of Justice in favour of the Commission in this sector. An important example of such cases was the decision rendered against France in 2001,[50] in which the French rules for financing the universal service elements of its telecommunications system were adjudged unfairly weighted against new entrants and lacking a sufficient degree of transparency and proportionality.

4.3 COUNCIL AND EUROPEAN PARLIAMENT DIRECTIVES— OTHER SECTORS

Directives have also been issued by the Council (rather than the Commission) for both the electricity and gas sectors (96/92 and 98/30 respectively), under which national markets have been opened up for the first time to new suppliers from abroad. In some cases an independent supplier can have third-party access as of right to the national network; in other cases Member States have the option of a 'single-buyer system' under which the national operator retains an effective monopoly for many classes of customer but has to supply them at prices no less favourable to the customer than those available from third parties, whether within or outside the Member State.

In the case of postal services a Directive was issued jointly by the Council and the European Parliament (97/67) requiring certain postal services to be opened to competition for the first time, but accompanied by a Notice from the Commission spelling out in detail the way in which the competition rules should be applied in the sector.

In looking across therefore at the whole range of markets traditionally dominated by national incumbents, including telecommunications, energy, and postal services towards which the Community's liberalization policies have been directed, it is noteworthy that Article 86(3) has played, at an early stage, a leading part in establishing important principles and in putting pressure on Member States to accept the principle of change, even if in recent years the role of Council Directives has become correspondingly greater. In its 2001 Annual Report[51] the Commission has however fired a warning shot towards the Member States; in the context of opposition to its attempts to complete full liberalization in the gas and electricity sectors in the next few years. It mentions that Article 86(3) remains available as a means by which the Commission can advance its policies without first having to obtain Member State approval through the Council, if this should seem the only way forward.

It should be emphasized that Article 86(3) has not given the Commission unlimited general freedom to impose legislation on Member States. The Court of Justice has in the various cases referred to above has made it clear that the Commission is not entitled to impose new obligations, but only to determine the obligations already imposed on Member States by the Treaty with regard to public undertakings or undertakings granted special or exclusive rights. Its power is more limited than the Council's powers to issue directives through normal Community procedures in conjunction with the European Parliament and the Commission. The Commission has therefore used its powers under Article 86(3) sparingly and only where its awareness of the existence of many infringements by Member States

---

[50] Case C-146/00. *Commission* v. *France*: (decision dated 6 December 2001).   [51] Para. 94.

of fundamental rules of the Treaty makes it necessary, to avoid having to bring a large number of infringement proceedings and to provide operators in the sector with the required minimum amount of legal certainty. Such Directives are moreover only introduced after considerable consultation and dialogue with the institutions of the Community, Member States, and other interested parties.

4.4 COMMISSION DECISIONS UNDER ARTICLE 86(3)

The nature of 'decisions' issued under Article 86(3) is quite different from that of directives. Decisions are given in specific cases where a Member State appears to be in breach of the Treaty rules particularly of Articles 81 and 82 or the terms of a Directive under Article 86. Such decisions have affected a number of sectors. The first such decision is recorded in the *15th Annual Report*,[52] declaring a Greek law requiring all public property to be insured with a particular state-owned insurance company to be incompatible with the Treaty. Subsequent *Annual Reports* record several other examples. In December 1993 the Commission, following complaints from shipping lines, issued a decision requiring Denmark to bring to an end a refusal to grant access to port facilities at Rodby in Denmark, or alternatively to construct new facilities for such lines on land adjacent to the existing port so that competitive services between Denmark and Germany could be instituted. Rodby had been owned and managed by the State-owned Danish Railway Company which had exclusive rights to organize rail traffic in that country. The Commission found[53] that there was no objective justification for the refusal of the Danish authorities to provide port facilities either in the existing port or on the adjacent available land in order to strengthen the joint dominance of the Danish and German State railway companies on the existing ferry route from Rodby. This case had elements in common with earlier Article 82 cases on access to essential facilities (see Chapter 15, section 8).

Liberalization to the mobile telephone sector led to infringement proceedings against both Italy and Spain for raising barriers to entry against would-be competitors with the incumbent national operator. A formal decision was taken in the case of Italy[54] for discriminating in favour of Telecom Italia Mobile, the State operator, against Omnitel Pronto Italia by requiring Omnitel to pay a substantial entry fee for their licence although no equivalent payment was required from Telecom Italia. The decision of the Commission provided that Italy must either insist on an equivalent payment from the incumbent operator or adopt corrective measures in favour of Omnitel that would be equivalent in economic terms. In other words, the decision placed the Italian government under an obligation not to undermine the competition introduced by the requirement of other directives to authorize the second mobile telephone operator. In reaching its decision the Commission relied on the European Court's judgment in the 1991 *Terminal Equipment* case on Directive 88/301.[55] In 1996 an equivalent decision was rendered against Spain in respect of the initial licence fee imposed on Airtel Movil as the public operator, Telefonica, had been granted its licence without an initial licence fee.[56]

---

[52] (1985) pp.201–2.   [53] *1993 Annual Report*, p.471.
[54] *1995 Annual Report*, p.54: [1996] 4 CMLR 700.
[55] See fn. 47.   [56] *1996 Annual Report*, p.55.

The landing fees structure at Brussels Zaventem airport also provoked intervention by the Commission.[57] The airport operated a discount system on landing fees based on the minimum number of daily arrivals related to a particular size of aircraft. The effect of the discount structure was that only a carrier based at the airport and having a very large number of arrivals and departures could gain the benefit of these discounts. This rule favoured Sabena which had by far the largest number of movements, but the scale was not cost-related and did not follow the recommendations of the ICAO as to the criteria for assessment of landing fees, which are a significant part of an airline's operating costs. The Commission found that the airport authority was applying dissimilar conditions to other airlines than Sabena, placing the majority of them at a competitive disadvantage in breach of Article 82(c). Since it was a Member State which had established the relevant fee system, this State measure infringed both Article 82 and Article 86. Recent *Annual Reports* continue to record successful action taken against Member States in respect of discriminatory landing fees charged at national airports, including Portugal[58] and France in 1999 and Spain in 2000.

---

[57] [1996] 4 CMLR 232.
[58] [2002] 4 CMLR 31.

23

INTERNATIONAL ASPECTS OF EC COMPETITION LAW

1. INTRODUCTION

This chapter examines the three main ways by which the Community has been able to—and continues to attempt to—surmount the limitations of its territorial legal jurisdiction in order to address foreign anti-competitive activity that has an impact either on competition either in Europe or on the competitiveness of European companies abroad.

The first method involves applying EC competition law in what some might view as an 'extraterritorial' manner, that is, to foreign undertakings themselves, when their actions have an anti-competitive impact in Europe. This is different, of course, from the direct application of the principles contained in Articles 81 and 82 to countries that are members of the EEA. In such situations, this is simply domestic enforcement of the European regime by the governments of those countries, rather than extraterritorial enforcement of EC law by the Community institutions themselves.[1] While the 'effects'-based rationale for extraterritorial enforcement is generally recognized (if not wholly accepted) as a matter of public international law, the European institutions do not generally justify their foreign enforcement activities on this ground. Indeed, they do not describe such enforcement as 'extraterritorial' at all. Rather than reaching out to foreign conduct on the basis that it *affects* trade within the common market, the European institutions have laboured to explain that when they have enforced their law against a particular foreign actor, they have done so on the basis that the foreigner is responsible for conduct that is actually occurring *in* Europe.

The first section of this chapter describes the various legal tests and contortions of reasoning in which the Commission and the Courts have had to engage in order to achieve this result. The section then examines some of the problems that this can cause to arise both for European enforcers and for foreign undertakings engaged in commerce in an increasingly interconnected global economy, particularly where the 'effects' test for jurisdiction appears to be gaining greater acceptance amongst other competition authorities than the

---

[1] The EEA Agreement effective from 1 January 1994 means that the EC Treaties and secondary legislation made by the Council and Commission are also applied in parallel to Norway, Iceland, and Liechtenstein, known as the three EFTA States. The EEA Agreement contains provisions which match as closely as possible the equivalent clauses of the Rome Treaty including those dealing with competition policy. Arts 53 and 54 of the EEA Agreement are the equivalent to Arts 81 and 82 of the Rome Treaty. The EFTA Surveillance Authority is responsible for ensuring the application of the Agreement, subject to the jurisdiction of the EFTA Court, whose website is www.efta.int/docs/Court/information/intro.htf.

test employed by the Community's own institutions. The section also reminds readers of the Commission's own initial preference for justifying its international enforcement activities on the 'effects' test, a preference which is increasingly reasserting itself, particularly in merger cases. The section concludes that, to the extent that unilateral enforcement action against foreign anti-competitive conduct is necessary and feasible, the difficulties that the 'European' tests for jurisdiction present for effective and acceptable enforcement will lead the Community inevitably to rely more on the effects test, rather than their own creative 'European' model.

The second method of addressing foreign conduct with anti-competitive consequences for Europeans grows out of the limitations of the first. No matter which test is used to justify extraterritorial application of laws, purely unilateral enforcement will always be an uphill and lonely struggle against undertakings that will be keen to remain at a distance. The most obvious problem is an evidentiary one though: while it may be clear what anti-competitive harm a foreign activity may do to the common market, the evidence of the activity itself may reside in another country. No matter how powerful they may seem, European Commission officials cannot simply arrive in another sovereign jurisdiction and commence a dawn raid. Nor will faxing information requests to foreign undertakings guarantee as full a response as may be desired, or indeed any response at all.

The only way that the Commission can get the evidence that it requires is by combining forces with the competition authority that is responsible for the undertakings' 'home' jurisdiction, or the jurisdiction where the evidence required is thought to be located. This is why the Community institutions has been building bridges across various political borders so that the Commission can exchange information with, and benefit from the enforcement powers of, the American, Canadian, Japanese, and other governments. Bilateral enforcement efforts based on such international agreements can help authorities to address conduct that harms competition and consumers within their respective jurisdictions. The Council and the Commission have also noted how such enforcement co-operation can help trade.[2] In particular, the European Commission can use 'positive comity' commitments that trigger foreign enforcement activity against foreign conduct which may not be harming competition and consumers in Europe, but may be preventing European undertakings from entering a particular foreign market. At the same time, of course, it is important to note that the American and Canadian authorities can use the same instruments to incite European enforcement action against European undertakings that may be harming American or Canadian exporters or investors.

The second section of this chapter thus examines the main aspects of the bilateral agreements that the Community has signed with its counterparts in other jurisdictions and some of the benefits and limitations of these commitments from the perspectives of both the enforcers and the private sector. In particular, it examines concerns that have been raised by undertakings to ensure that exchanges of information among competition authorities do not jeopardize the confidentiality of business information.

The third method employed by the Community to address foreign anti-competitive activity stems from of the limitations of the first two methods. Unilateral extraterritorial

---

[2] Communication to the Council, submitted by Sir Leon Brittan and Karel Van Miert, 'Towards an International Framework of Competition Rules', COM (96) 296 final, 18 June 1996 (hereinafter, 'Commission Communication').

enforcement and bilateral enforcement co-operation would not be necessary, so goes the argument, if the Community's trading partners would only make sure that they were addressing anti-competitive conduct in their own markets which may also be distorting competition in the common market, or which may be impeding European companies' abilities to access those foreign markets. This is the primary rationale for the Community's quest for a global solution to international restraints of trade and competition. By seeking global commitments to be agreed by all Members of the World Trade Organization, the Community hopes to ensure that its trading partners' own domestic enforcement efforts are more effective. In particular, the Community wants all countries to undertake that in enacting competition 'measures', they will ensure that their laws and enforcement efforts will not discriminate against foreign undertakings, goods or services (or favour their own), and that mechanisms are put in place to guarantee that the many and various authorities will co-operate with one another, even when it may not be in their narrow national interests to do so. The overall goal is for all countries to undertake that in their own markets they have the tools to be able to address anti-competitive activities of an 'international dimension'. Activities that are of particular interest to the Community include both international cartels that harm European consumers and business practices in other countries that impede the ability of European companies to access foreign markets.

The third and final section of this chapter thus examines the various proposals that the Community has made in this regard along with some competition commitments already present on the global stage.

2. EXTRATERRITORIALITY AND THE EFFECTS TEST

2.1 THE PRINCIPLE OF EXTRATERRITORIALITY

By definition, extraterritorial enforcement conjures up images of a law being applied beyond the territorial ambit of its sovereign legitimacy. It is not surprising then that this is tolerated only in the exception, and even then remains tainted by a somewhat pejorative connotation. To counter this, perhaps, the long arm of American antitrust law is only extended into another country's territory when it can be justified objectively. The American authorities and courts thus permit the application of many US laws (including antitrust laws) to foreign actors where the latter's conduct could be seen to have a 'direct, substantial and reasonably foreseeable' effect on US commerce.[3] There are various attractions to this test; for one thing, an action's effects are presumably something that is capable of being determined objectively. The 'directness' and 'substantiality' of that effect ought to be capable of proof through analysis of economic evidence. Resort to legal argument will be required to demonstrate the 'reasonable foreseeability' of such effects, but even then, it will be hard to argue with the facts, and again, economic evidence would be useful to identify which consequences were likely to be foreseen. Some cases of extraterritorial enforcement will be easier to justify than others. In the case of cartel activity at least, price increases will have been the primary

---

[3] Foreign Trade Antitrust Improvements Act of 1982 (7 *Sherman Act*, 15 USC 6a).

rationale for the activity in question. Even if clever defence counsel can credibly deny this, such effects would be hard to deny as being 'reasonably foreseeable' consequences of the activity. It may become more difficult to display the effects with other conduct—such as exclusive purchasing commitments or a particular merger transaction—but this does not mean that the effects test itself is any less relevant or applicable to these situations as well.

Despite the initially appealing logic of the effects test, American legal incursions have been met with blocking statutes in many countries, who simply will not tolerate their citizens—whether corporate or corporeal—being prosecuted or sued under the laws of another government.[4] This is particularly so when the actions occur wholly within the 'home' territory, when they may or may not be illegal under domestic law, or may even have been authorized by the domestic government. While the Community institutions themselves have not erected blocking statutes, they have made clear in the Commission Communication and otherwise their distaste for extraterritorial enforcement. This policy stance has meant that the Commission has had to find other justifications when it has wanted to address foreign conduct with anti-competitive effects within Europe.

The next section examines how the Community has been, for the most part, wary of using extraterritorial enforcement in the true sense of the word. Rather than allow itself to be perceived as reaching out and applying EC law within another sovereign territory, the Community institutions have instead devised various legal tests that seek to bring the conduct and the culprits *within* the ambit of EC law.

The European Commission, Council and Court have all provided various grounds by which EC competition law can be applied to foreign undertakings whose conduct has anti-competitive effects in the common market. As mentioned above, the criteria differ, but the result is the same; by typifying the activity in question as being domestic, the conduct is seen to fall within European legal jurisdiction, and no resort to 'extraterritorial' enforcement is required. Nevertheless, while an eminently neat legal solution may appear to have been devised, the contortions that are required to label some conduct as European and other conduct as not raises problems both for businesses and for enforcers.

2.2 THE GROUP ECONOMIC UNIT DOCTRINE

The most established basis in EC competition law for asserting jurisdiction over foreign companies is the doctrine of the 'group economic unit'.[5] This test attributes to foreign parents responsibility for the anti-competitive activities of a subsidiary that is present and active in Europe and over which they supposedly exert some control; and owing to the supposed control that the parent can exert and should have exerted over the subsidiary, the parents, and other relevant members of the group may be brought within the jurisdiction of European law.

This method of asserting jurisdiction is not of course unproblematic. In its reasoning, the Court has emphasized the corporate structural relationship between the parent and the subsidiary and merely considered the parent's *ability* to control the latter, rather than

---

[4] In Canada, the Foreign Extra-territorial Measures Act, RSC CL F-29 (1985) and in the UK, the Protection of Trading Interests Act, 1980, Ch. 11.

[5] Case 48/69 *ICI* v. *Commission* [1972] ECR 619: CMLR 557, Case C-73/95P *Viho Europe BV* v. *Commission* [1996] ECR I-5457: [1997] 4 CMLR 419.

whether that control was actually exercised. Consequently the facts of each case do not need to be analysed other than to set out the relevant corporate organisation chart, and show where control could and, presumably, should be exercised. In a post-Enron world, it is perhaps natural to seek to attribute corporate responsibility where control is possible, and thus should have been exercised. However, it is still at least arguable that European jurisdiction over foreign undertakings should be based on a role that is more active than that. After all, the European subsidiary is present in Europe, and available to be fined. Where the subsidiary is being wound down, however, or has insufficient assets to satisfy a judgment against it, enforcers will naturally want to seek the controlling mind of the company group, whether or not it actually controlled the anti-competitive conduct in question. Whether the parent should be entitled to rely on a defence that it was not involved in the subsidiary's daily activities and should not therefore be responsible for all of its actions raises difficult issues that would benefit from further clarification by the Commission and the Court.

2.3 THE CONCEPT OF IMPLEMENTATION OF AN AGREEMENT: *DYESTUFFS* AND *WOODPULP* (NO. 1)

Where matters have become rather more confused, however, is with the rejection by the Court of the Commission's use of the effects doctrine itself to justify asserting jurisdiction against foreign cartel members. The conflicting policy interests involved are most clearly displayed by a brief account of the arguments of the various parties, Advocates General, and interested governments in the *Dyestuffs* and *Woodpulp* cases.

ICI was alleged to have assisted in concerted practices relating to price increases for various dyestuffs by giving price instructions to its wholly owned subsidiary incorporated in Belgium, although itself as a parent company demonstrably neither directly present in nor trading with the Community. The arguments relied on by the Commission in support of the imposition of a fine on ICI rested on three separate though related bases: first, that ICI by its actions, notably the giving of such instructions for performance by its subsidiary, had *actually been itself engaged* in the concerted practices, treating the subsidiary company as if it were simply the agent of the parent. The second basis claimed was that ICI was present within the Community *by reason of the corporate control* it was entitled to exercise over its subsidiary (the 'group economic unit' argument). The third ground was that in any case the actions taken by ICI had *produced effects* within the Common Market.

Interestingly, Advocate General Mayras came down in favour of acceptance only of the third argument. He conceded that under international law the Community could exercise jurisdiction outside its territorial bounds, but based its right to take action simply on the effects doctrine, for the application of which he laid down three conditions, namely that the effects must be (*a*) direct and immediate, (*b*) reasonably foreseeable, and (*c*) substantial. It did not extend to enable the Community to implement 'coercive measures or indeed any measure of enquiry, investigation or supervision outside the territorial jurisdiction of the authorities concerned where execution would inevitably infringe the internal sovereignty of the State on whose territory they claim to act'. The Court was careful to avoid either specific acceptance or rejection of the findings of the Advocate General, but based its decision against ICI on the second argument raised, namely that of the 'group economic unit' theory. It said: 'The fact that a subsidiary has separate legal personality is not sufficient to exclude the possibility of imputing its conduct to the parent company . . . In the circumstances, the formal separation between these companies, resulting from their separate legal personality, cannot outweigh the unity of their conduct on the market for the purposes of applying the rules on competition'.[6]

In reaching its decision the Court implicitly rejected the argument of the UK government contained in a well known *aide-mémoire* of October 1969 to the Commission. It is argued that the attribution of the activities of even a wholly owned subsidiary through its parent company involved an unacceptable rejection of its separate corporate status; in the view of the UK government, ICI could not possibly be held liable for the activities even of its wholly owned subsidiary company on the Continent. In other words it rejected the whole 'group economic unit' argument. However, this view had changed by the time of the *Woodpulp* case.

In the *Woodpulp* case, the Commission prosecuted a foreign cartel for raising prices within the Common Market.[7] The accused were producers of bleached sulphate pulp established outside the Community who had entered into price fixing arrangements. The producers were exporting either directly to purchasers within the Community or though branches, subsidiaries, agencies or other establishments in the Community. The Commission established jurisdiction by concluding that 'the *effect* of the agreements and practices on prices announced and/or charged to customers and on resale of pulp within the EEC was . . . not only *substantial* but *intended* and was the primary and direct result of the agreements and practices'.[8] The producers appealed the decision, claiming that it involved an incorrect assessment of the territorial scope of Article 81. The Court did not refer specifically to the effects test in its judgement. Instead it ruled that the conduct infringing Article 81 consisted of two elements, the formation of the agreement and the implementation of it. Wholly ignored was the logical third step: that of the anti-competitive effect. The Court simply stated that 'the producers in this case *implemented* their pricing agreement within the common market. It is immaterial in that respect whether or not they had recourse to subsidiaries, agents, sub-agents, or branches within the Community in order to make their contacts with purchasers within the Community'.[9] In *Woodpulp*, since the cartel agreement had been 'implemented' within the Common Market—through a marketing organisation run by the parties in a Member State—it became a European matter and was thus subject to European competition law.

Of course, the fact that the Court did not expressly reject the effects test means that its application as a legal basis for jurisdiction is still possible. Whether or not there is any significant difference in fact between the two tests is the subject of some debate. Van Gerven A-G, along with other commentators, has found that the two doctrines can 'lead to different

---

[6] [1972] ECR 662–3: CMLR 629. The 'group economic unit' concept was further confirmed soon afterwards in both *Centrafarm BV* v. *Sterling Drug Inc.* Case 15/74 [1974] ECR 1147: 2 CMLR 480, and *Istituto Chemioterapico Italiano and Commercial Solvents Corporation* v. *Commission* Cases 6–7/73 [1974] ECR 223: 1 CMLR 309. Advocate General Warner at ECR 264: 1 CMLR 321, stated that it is difficult but not impossible for a subsidiary to rebut the presumption of *de facto* control by its parent.

[7] Cases C-289, 104, 114, 116–17, 125/85. *Ahlstrom and Others* v. *Commission* [1988] ECR 5193: 4 CMLR 901. See Ch. 7, pp.75–6.

[8] [1985] 3 CMLR 474 (emphasis added).

[9] Cases C-89, 104, 114, 116–17, 125/85. *Ahlstrom and Others* v. *Commission,* [1988] ECR 5243: 4 CMLR 941 (emphasis added).

results in a narrow but significant group of cases'.[10] For example, there are doubts whether the implementation doctrine would establish jurisdiction in cases of direct sales by companies to customers within the Community in the absence of any type of marketing organization, or in respect of refusal to supply or collective boycotts entered into outside the Community by undertakings established outside the Community. However, it is not difficult to imagine cases where different results would occur. For example, the implementation doctrine's insistence on there being some form of activity by the accused parties on the ground in the Community means that a wholly foreign cartel agreement which raises prices, but does so through arms-length sellers, may arguably not be implemented in a sufficiently 'European' manner to attract European jurisdiction. As such, considerable harm may be done to consumers that would be able to be addressed if the effects test were used instead. At the same time, though, the fact that the Commission does not require any proof of anti-competitive effect in order to justify an assertion of jurisdiction means that some conduct that should not be investigated at all may come under DG Comp's magnifying glass. This would happen in the case of business practices that are clearly implemented in the common market, and which may appear to harm competition, but where it no anti-competitive effect in Europe can be proven. A network of vertical restraints, or an export cartel, that may harm foreign competitors or foreign consumers, respectively, are obvious examples. Such conduct would not attract a fine or other remedial measure unless there was evidence of a substantive offence, of course, but it is at least arguable that the Commission is free to assert jurisdiction over any undertakings with operations in Europe without any evidence that their conduct actually has an anti-competitive impact within the common market. Without a requirement of having to prove reasonably foreseeable anti-competitive effects resulting from their conduct, too many companies may be brought within the scope of an initial investigation.

Who is to say that the Court is wrong in not simply using the effects test to justify extraterritorial enforcement? Other competition authorities are also reluctant to admit that they enforce their laws extraterritorially. The American authorities have rarely admitted that they enforce their laws in an 'extraterritorial' manner, even when they are clearly prosecuting foreign undertakings or individuals for foreign activity that has harmful effects in the United States. They focus on the harm to United States commerce. Presumably, such reasoning would bring much of the same type of conduct within the ambit of European law. However, the European Court has preferred to eschew any proof of anti-competitive harm in order to allow the Commission to assert jurisdiction, and instead has preferred to create a legal fiction that focuses on creating the impression that a foreign agreement is actually European. From an enforcement approach this may be a more effective way of addressing harmful effects that occur but are difficult to establish. However, it seems that the chance of either inadequate or inappropriate enforcement is higher under the current Community regime.

---

[10] W. Van Gerven, 'EC Jurisdiction in Antitrust Law Matters: the *Woodpulp* Judgment', 1989 Fordham Corporate Law Institute, pp.451–83; J.P. Griffin, 'Foreign Governmental Reactions to U.S. Assertion of Extra-territorial Jurisdiction' [1998] 19 ECLR pp.64–73

2.4 THE MERGER REGULATION: CONCENTRATIONS WITH A COMMUNITY DIMENSION

The third way of bringing foreign undertakings within European jurisdiction exists through the Merger Regulation.[11] Indeed, as Article 1 makes clear, the Regulation itself will only apply where a concentration has what is defined is a 'Community dimension', in terms of involving the requisite amount of sales within Europe.[12] Article 5(1) goes on to specify that Community turnover consists of 'products sold or services provided to undertakings or consumers in the Community or in a Member State'. As such, unlike the Court's approach in *Woodpulp*, no distinction is made between sales made directly, or made through a branch, agent, subsidiary or distributor within the Community by a foreign undertaking. Defining business activity in this manner avoids any admission that what is really going on is the extraterritorial application of European law to foreign undertakings. After all, their sales are 'in' Europe and thus, the merger's effects are also likely to be there, at least to the extent of those sales.

It is difficult to distinguish the effects test from the turnover test in this regard, and indeed, the Commission has been quite explicit in linking the two concepts. In the *Gencor* case, the Commission blocked a merger between two companies incorporated in South Africa that would have led to 'the creation of a dominant duopoly in the platinum and rhodium markets as a result of which competition would have been significantly impeded in the common market'.[13] The Commission justified exercising its jurisdiction using language usually associated with the effects test stating that 'application of the regulation is justified under public international law when it is foreseeable that a proposed concentration will have an immediate and substantial effect in the Community . . . It is therefore necessary to verify whether the three criteria of immediate, substantial and foreseeable effect are satisfied in this case'.[14] The Court found that the 'concentration would have the direct and immediate effect of creating the conditions in which the abuses were not only possible but economically rational'.[15] The Court concluded that 'it was in fact foreseeable that the effect of creating a dominant duopoly position in a world market would also be to impede competition significantly in the Community an integral part of that market.'[16] The underlying rationale for the turnover tests in the Merger Regulation is indistinguishable from the 'effects' test.

A similar situation arose in the *Boeing/McDonnell-Douglas* case, where the Commission exercised its jurisdiction over a merger between two US corporations on the basis that both parties exceeded the Community turnover requirements.[17] Commissioner Mario Monti commented that the Court had made clear that the Commission's application of EC competition law to foreign undertakings in such cases was in accordance with the principles of public international law where the merger produced direct, substantial, and foreseeable

[11] Council Regulation (EC) 4064/89 of 21 December 1989 on the control of concentrations between undertakings [1989] OJ L395.
[12] See Ch. 17, Section 2.
[13] Case T-102/96 *Gencor Ltd* v. *Commission* (1999) ECR II-753: 4 CMLR 971, at para. 91.
[14] Paras 90, 92.
[15] Para. 94.
[16] Para. 100.
[17] Case IV/M877 [1997] OJ L336/16; [1997] 5 CMLR 270.

effects within the Community.[18] The propriety of the effects test has thus been clearly accepted in the context of merger control.

From this description of the three tests, it might be concluded that the logical way for EC competition policy to develop in this area would be to accept the effects test more fully, at least in order to supplement the 'group economic unit' doctrine and to replace, where inconsistent, the peculiar 'implementation' doctrine.Without a firm statement in this regard from the Community institutions, however, this will have to evolve gradually. The coherence and effectiveness of EC competition law enforcement would, however, benefit from the formal adoption of the effects test sooner rather than later. This is particularly the case as the occasions when the Commission needs to reach beyond its borders increases. When it takes jurisdiction over a merger there is a clear, and effects-based, rationale. For the credibility of EC law within Europe and internationally, both among undertakings and other competition authorities, this approach needs to spread to the non-merger area of EC law enforcement. The Community's credibility amongst other competition authorities is important, not the least because the occasions where the Commission needs the help of such comrades-in-arms in order to address truly foreign conduct far outnumber the situations where it can handle such conduct itself. The next section examines this in more detail.

3. ENFORCEMENT CO-OPERATION THROUGH BILATERAL MEASURES

3.1 THE NEED FOR CO-OPERATION

The Community has recognized that it cannot merely rely on its own legal concepts and procedures to act against foreign business conduct that harms the common market. There are a number of reasons for this. First of all, if such conduct does not harm competition or consumers within Europe, it is difficult to use the 'European' tests to address foreign conduct, even if it may be impeding the ability of European competitors to access and compete in foreign markets. The effects doctrine would be no easier to apply in such cases as well, of course. Finally, extraterritorial enforcement brings with it a great many political 'negative externalities' as it necessarily involves the perception of enforcement activity in another sovereign territory.

This section examines how the Community has tried to address the limitations of unilateral extraterritorial enforcement by developing increasingly detailed enforcement co-operation agreements with foreign governments. To some extent such arrangements merely offer a formal framework within which a great deal of informal co-operation has already been occurring between the European Commission and foreign authorities. To that extent, though, the agreements provide an important imprimatur of legitimacy to such *ad hoc* co-operative enforcement activities, as well as a formal mechanism through which they can be channelled and intensified. The exchange of confidential information about a particular international case is a very important way of ensuring that the best placed authority can effectively address it. Even more important mechanisms, like positive comity for example,

---

[18] M. Monti, 'Co-operation between competition authorities—a vision for the future', The Japan Foundation Conference, Washington DC, 23 June 2000, at p.2, available at www.europa.eu.int.

have been created for authorities to use to request, enforcement action in another State. Positive comity is particularly helpful when it allows the Community to induce another authority to enforce its laws in its own jurisdiction, for example, to address business practices that impede the entry of European competitors, provided that there is a evidence of a competition harm in the market of the requested authority. The next sub-sections examine the main aspects of the agreements that have been signed to date, the benefits they provide, as well as some of their limitations.

3.2 BILATERAL AGREEMENTS MADE BY THE COMMUNITY

To bridge the divide between national competence and international anti-competitive activity, governments have negotiated legal assistance treaties, usually of a bilateral nature. The Community and the US entered into their first antitrust co-operation agreement in 1991.[19] This agreement provides for forms of co-operation that have become fairly standard in most similar accords between other jurisdictions. It contains what are known as passive, or traditional, comity provisions, which permit an active communication of information and a consideration of a trading partner's interests, but do not involve any 'triggering' of enforcement activity in another jurisdiction. This latter action, by contrast, can only arise when a positive comity request is made, and one country asks another to begin enforcement proceedings in its own jurisdiction.

In terms of traditional comity, the 1991 Community/United States Agreement provides that the authorities will notify one another when practices or enforcement activities would affect the other party to the Agreement. The Agreement also contains fairly basic provisions to allow information to be exchanged between the authorities and permitting them to coordinate their enforcement activities in accordance with 'traditional comity', explained in more detail below. However, it is important to note that in complying with such commitments the Agreement cannot be interpreted inconsistently with US or Community legislation. Perhaps most important in this regard are rules which protect the confidentiality of information that is gathered in investigations. The 1991 Agreement also contains certain basic provisions to provide positive comity that are examined in more detail below. In 1998 the Community and United States entered into a separate accord expressly supplementing these positive comity commitments. In particular, they specified the conditions under which the party requesting enforcement action should suspend its own enforcement activities and let the requested party 'take the lead', so to speak.[20] This suspension arrangement was limited, however, to competitor-only complaints dealing with allegations of export restraints, i.e. where the anti-competitive activities at issue do not harm the requesting parties' consumers (or harm them only incidentally) and the primary problem is exclusionary conduct directed at the requested party's competitors.

The Community and Canada also entered into a co-operation agreement in 1999[21] which is broadly similar to the first Community–US accord of 1991 and which provides for reciprocal notification of cases under investigation by either authority, coordination by the

---

[19] [1991] 4 CMLR 823. Following a successful challenge by France to the Commission, on the basis that the Agreement should have been made by the Council (Case C-327/91 [1994] ECR I-3641: 5 CMLR 517. The Agreement was ratified in 1995 by the Council [1995] OJ L 95/45).

[20] [1998] OJ L 173/26: [1999] 4 CMLR 502.   [21] [1999] OJ L 175.

two authorities of their enforcement activities; positive and negative comity provisions and the exchange of information between the parties, while also not affecting either party's confidentiality obligations with respect to such information. Other accords are also being prepared between the Community and Japan, Brazil, Israel, Mexico, South Africa, the Russian Federation, and the Ukraine. Similarly, many EEA countries have signed co-operation agreements with the Commission, which are also designed to ensure that such regimes align their enforcement regimes with European law.[22] Despite the lack of any formal arrangement, the Commission also co-operated informally with many other authorities, in particular Australia and New Zealand. Many of these informal contacts come about as a result of the Commission's participation in regional and multilateral meetings of competition authorities, at the OECD, the International Competition Network (ICN), or the World Trade Organization (WTO).[23]

The closest co-operation relationship to date that the Community has with foreign governments, though, is that with its major trading partner, the US. Indeed, the two parties have begun designing a blueprint for future co-operation by issuing 'best practice guidelines' with respect to their co-operation in merger cases.[24] They have proposed that their investigation timetables run in parallel to increase the effectiveness of co-operation and that merging parties be given the possibility of meeting with them together to discuss timing issues. Companies are encouraged to waive confidentiality so that the authorities can exchange information and allow joint Community/US interviews of the companies involved. Points are designated for when it would be appropriate for direct contacts to occur between senior officials. The best practices guidelines also stress that the outcome of an agency's investigation will not be affected by an undertaking's decision to abide by only some of the agency's recommendations. Therefore companies are still left with the discretion to decide to what extent they co-operate regarding confidentiality waivers, transaction timings, and notification decisions.

3.3 THE PRINCIPLE OF NOTIFICATION

Notification is an essential principle of a co-operation agreement which ensures coordination by providing for the reciprocal notification of competition cases under investigation which might affect the important interests of the government of the other authority. The US–Community agreement provides guidance on the particular situations where these effects and interests may occur, but it is still general enough to cover most enforcement situations. These include cases that are relevant to the enforcement activities of the other party, or involve anti-competitive activities carried out in significant part in the other

---

[22] *2001 Annual Report*, pp.146–7.

[23] OECD Members have agreed a non-binding Hard-core Cartel Recommendation based on the above agreements, which sets out the kind of enforcement co-operation that Members should provide in addressing such practices. The International Competition Network is a network of competition authorities with the aim of improving worldwide co-operation. It does not exercise any rule-making function but serves as a forum to establish best practices to be implemented by individual agencies whether unilaterally, bilaterally or multilaterally. The work of the ICN is considered at the end of this chapter.

[24] 'EU and US issue best practices guidelines concerning bilateral co-operation in merger cases', Brussels 30 October 2002, (IP/01/1591).

party's territory, or involve a merger or acquisition in which one or more of the relevant undertakings is a company incorporated under the laws of the other party, or where the anti-competitive practice involves conduct encouraged or approved by the other party or involves remedies that would require or prohibit conduct in the other party's territory. In practice the number of notifications made under this agreement has risen gradually each year. In 2001, for example, there were eighty-four notifications from the Community to the United States and 37 notifications from the United States to the Community of both merger and non-merger cases.[25]

3.4 TRADITIONAL COMITY

Traditional comity is the 'general principle that a country should take another country's important interests into account in its own law enforcement in return for their doing the same'.[26] While this principle does not provide an obligation to take another country's interests into account, it does help to avoid conflicts about the application of extraterritorial jurisdiction. For example, although the *Boeing/McDonnell Douglas* merger highlighted the different approaches taken by the United States and the Community to merger control (or at least to the exclusive purchasing agreements at the heart of the case itself) and the difficulties of co-operation in the face of such different standards, the Commission did take the US government's concerns relating to important US defence interests into consideration to the extent consistent with Community law, and limited the scope of its own enforcement action accordingly to commercial aircraft.[27] Comity has also played a part in the Department of Justice decisions on the international telecommunications joint ventures between *BT/MCI*[28] and *Sprint/France Telecom/Deutsche Telekom*.[29] It is thought that the Department of Justice would have prohibited the *BT/MCI* transaction if it had not been for the competitive policies and safeguards that were being incorporated into the UK telecommunications regulatory regime, whilst the absence of such safeguards in the *Sprint* case meant that the DOJ imposed more stringent conditions. For example, the substantive requirements imposed on MCI were devised to 'avoid direct US involvement in BT's operation of its telecommunications network in the UK on an ongoing basis, minimizing the potential for conflict with UK authorities'.[30]

3.5 POSITIVE COMITY

This principle applies where undertakings from one party to a co-operation agreement are being harmed by the anti-competitive practices occurring within the territory of another party. As the injured party cannot itself initiate extraterritorial enforcement proceedings

---

[25] Commission Report to the Council and European Parliament for the period 1 January to 31 December 2001, COM [2002] 505 17 September 2002.

[26] M. Janow, *Antitrust Goes Global* (Brookings Institutions, 2000), p.33.

[27] DG Comp Competition Policy Newsletter, Vol. 3 No. 2 Summer 1997, pp.29–31.

[28] [1994] OJ L223/36 [1995] 5 CMLR 285.

[29] Case Comp/M 1741: [1996] OJ L239/57: [1997] 4 CMLR 147.

[30] J. McDavid: *Antitrust Goes Global*, op. cit. p.182.

(because of the absence of evidence of harm to competition in its own market) it has to rely on the other party taking action on its behalf.

The most public informal case of positive comity involved investigations by both the DOJ and the Community of the practices of A.C. Nielsen, a US company that tracks retail sales. Following a complaint by Neilsen competitor IRI, the Department of Justice investigated Nielsen's practices of bundling or tying the terms of contracts in one country with those in other countries. Specifically the authorities were interested in whether Nielsen offered customers more favourable terms in countries where the company had market power as a way of ensuring that the customers would agree to use Nielsen in countries where it faced significant competition. The US notified the Community of the problem and let the latter take the lead in the investigation since the conduct mostly affected Europe and the Commission itself 'showed a firm intention to act'.[31] The Commission subsequently found that Nielsen had indeed implemented various exclusionary practices designed to impede IRI from entering the European market. As a result, Nielsen gave undertakings to the Commission to address the concerns of both the Community and the United States. The two authorities had co-operated extensively throughout the process.

Formal use of the positive comity mechanisms has been limited to the referral in the *SABRE-Amadeus* case.[32] After having started its own investigation, the United States Department of Justice asked the European Commission to investigate possible anti-competitive conduct by Amadeus, the dominant computer reservation system in Europe, which might be preventing the US-based SABRE computer reservation system from competing effectively in certain European Member States. The DOJ justified the referral, and importantly the temporary suspension of its own investigation, by stating that it believed that the Commission was in the best position to investigate the matter. The exclusion of a US competitor was a concern for the United States, but it justified the referral to the Community because European consumers were also affected by the conduct, which took place within the Commission's jurisdiction.[33] The US government's concerns, and those of SABRE, were largely resolved when the European Commission issued a Statement of Objections to member airlines of the Amadeus network, particularly Air France.

3.6 THE ISSUE OF CONFIDENTIALITY

Both the Community/United States and Community/Canada Agreements have a confidentiality provision whereby parties can refuse disclosure of any information if it is prohibited under the law of the party that holds the information or if it would be incompatible with the important interests of the party that holds it. Therefore there is a significant amount of discretion that is left open to the parties as to how far their co-operation extends. This is also a reflection of the importance of such information to the companies involved. They will want to be assured that any information exchanged will not be made known to

---

[31] J. Rill and C. Wilson, and S. Bauers, *Antitrust Goes Global*, op. cit. p.193.
[32] J. Rill, C. Wilson, and S. Bauers, *Antitrust Goes Global*, op. cit. p.195.
[33] J. Rill, C. Wilson, and S. Bauers, *Antitrust Goes Global*, op. cit. p.197.

competitors of the company and will only be used for the purpose, for which it has been exchanged.

In addition, the Community distinguishes between confidential *business* information and confidential *agency* information. Confidential business information is information obtained in the course of an investigation (including business or trade secrets) and cannot be disclosed to the United States unless the relevant company expressly agrees. Confidential agency information relates to the investigation itself (including procedural aspects) and can be disclosed to the United States. The United States on the other hand does not make such a distinction and prohibits the disclosure of *any* information that it holds without the consent of the undertakings involved, except in relation to administrative or judicial actions or proceedings.

Therefore, a waiver of confidentiality is almost always required from parties involved in an Community/United States investigation. Past experience has shown that waivers are more readily given in merger cases where companies involved will co-operate in order to get expedited clearance for their merger.[34] However, reports have also shown that there has also been an increased level of information sharing between the Community and the United States in cartel cases including one company providing a waiver allowing the two authorities to exchange views regarding confidential evidence.[35] These developments are all the more important as the effectiveness of co-operation in cartel cases depends greatly on the ability of the agencies involved to share confidential information.

Particular problems also arise with respect to the differences in the regimes in the EU and Canada. The Community, for example, will restrict disclosure of confidential information to the Canadians in much the same way as it distinguishes between business secrets and other agency information. However, in Canada information is protected if it is held by the Competition Bureau and was obtained under the powers provided by the Competition Act. Information provided voluntarily to the Competition Bureau (including business secrets) is not protected, however. Therefore it would appear that information provided by the Community to Canada could be released or accessed under an Access of Information request under Canadian law, as it was not obtained using Canada's competition law. To try to address this, the Canadian Commissioner for Competition has issued a specific Communication of Confidential Information which states that such shared information would also be covered by Canada's confidentiality provisions. The question for undertakings, of course, is whether this assurance is enough. Companies should also note that confidential information in the hands of the Competition Bureau could be disclosed to the Community where the purpose is to receive reciprocal assistance regarding a Canadian investigation. However, the authority to do this is somewhat ambiguous and as a result the Commissioner has proposed amendments to the Competition Act in order to give formal status to such a disclosure of information.[36]

The OECD has also examined the need for a requirement for comparable downstream

---

[34] M. Monti, 'Co-operation between competition authorities—a vision for the future', The Japan Foundation Conference, Washington DC, 23 June 2000, see fn. 18.

[35] Commission Report to the Council and European Parliament for the period 1 January to 31 December 2001, COM [2002] 505 17 September 2002. See also Commission Press Statement IP/02/1585 of 30 October 2002.

[36] L. Hunter and S. Hutton, 'EU-Canada Co-operation' (2002) *European Antitrust Review*.

protection of information, as a way of reconciling business needs for confidentiality and the authorities' need for information. Downstream protection would assure undertakings involved in investigations that any foreign co-operating agency would have in place comparable protections for shared information through a case-by-case examination and assurance that adequate protection exists for the particular information being sought.[37]

3.7 SUBSTANTIVE DIFFERENCES IN LAW

Another restriction on the utility of positive comity results from substantive differences in the parties' laws. Positive comity—and indeed co-operation itself—can only apply where the anti-competitive conduct is illegal in the jurisdiction of the requested party. The US authorities still approach vertical arrangements in sufficiently different a way from the Community that co-operation may not work when 'westward' (Community to United States) positive comity requests are made about such restrictions. European competition law prohibits arrangements that may significantly restrict competitors' access to a market. US competition law, however, takes further factors into account and requires that the arrangement must substantially lessen competition as well. As such, it is not likely to be the case that the United States will act against vertical restraints—even when expressly requested to do so by the Community—absent evidence that the arrangements substantially lessen competition, despite the fact that they may impede the ability of a European company to enter the US market.[38]

As has been pointed out by one American lawyer, 'it is not realistic to expect one government to prosecute its citizens solely for the benefit of another. We should not expect the principle of positive comity to impact dramatically on the proposition that laws are written and enforced to protect national interests'.[39] Fundamentally, the application of positive comity is dependent on the good will and trust of the parties, factors that do not always come to the fore when their own political and economic interests are affected. However, this self-interest can also induce co-operation, as the reciprocal nature of such agreements tends to make them self-enforcing. This was illustrated in the Community's willingness to co-operate in the *SABRE-Amadeus* matter in order to reap the benefits of such co-operation in subsequent cases. As Alexander Schaub explained, the American request's effect on the dynamic of trans-Atlantic co-operation was: 'important . . . psychologically. We have given our people the instruction to consider this as a priority case because we are aware of the fact that how we handle American positive comity requests will certainly determine largely how the US authorities will handle our future requests'.[40]

The trust implicit in the use of positive comity—particularly when one authority suspends its own enforcement activities—is most likely to work between jurisdictions that have well-developed, mature competition law systems, and a history of international contacts. It

---

[37] OECD Global Forum on Competition—'Information Sharing in Cartel Cases'. [CCNM/GF/COMP/2002], 30 January 2002, available at www.oecd.org.

[38] P. Marsden, *Antitrust Goes Global*, pp.117–136.

[39] J. R. Atwood 'Positive Comity; Is it a positive step?', 1992 Fordham Corporate Law Institute (B. Hawk, ed. 1993), pp.86.

[40] A. Torres, 'E.U. Gives Priority to US Airline Reservation Case' (9 September 1997) citing Alexander Schaub (www.insidetrade.com).

is least likely to work when the requesting party 'does not have the resources, the experience or legal infrastructure to undertake a requested investigation',[41] or, as has been noted above, does not prohibit the particular practices under its own law.

3.8 THE LIMITATIONS OF BILATERAL CO-OPERATION

The inherent limitations of bilateral enforcement co-operation have led the Community to push for wider and deeper commitment from their trading partners. Three limitations stand out in particular. First, the fact that co-operation is subject to various restrictions, and is voluntary in any event, has led the Community to push for binding commitments between governments to help one another battle international anti-competitive practices. Second, the fact that co-operation to date has been primarily of a bilateral nature has meant that enforcers are simply not able to keep up with the increasing prevalence of international anti-competitive activity. Even the development of a wider patchwork of individual agreements among countries would not constitute a web that would be broad enough, or strong enough, to capture all international cartels, let alone other forms of anti-competitive activity. As such, the Community has urged that whatever binding commitments are negotiated be of a multilateral nature, so that they stamp out anti-competitive conduct throughout the world. Third, the fact that countries may have inadequate resources or differing legal regimes means that it will be difficult for their governments to act against anti-competitive conduct, and co-operate in that regard with one another. As such, the Community is pressing for all governments to agree to 'common approaches' that they will take to anti-competitive conduct.

The next and final section reviews some of the Community's proposals for such binding, multilateral rules, examines some existing 'competition' rules of that nature, and evaluates the extent to which they will be able to help induce individual competition authorities to address conduct in their markets which is either harming competition in Europe or impeding the ability of European companies to enter and expand in such foreign markets.

4. PROPOSALS FOR MULTILATERAL MEASURES

4.1 THE COMMUNITY'S APPROACH

The Community has admitted that one of its 'main reasons' for recommending 'the adoption of international rules on competition' has always been 'as part of the Community's strategy on market access: anti-competitive practices are keeping our firms out of third country markets but they cannot, in the absence of proper enforcement measures in those third markets, be tackled effectively without international rules'.[42] The Commission had noted that European companies were not doing as well overseas as their foreign competitors were doing in Europe. As Karel Van Miert has noted in Annex B of the Van Miert Report:

[our] strict competition policy guarantees companies from third countries that access to the

---

[41] M. Janow, *Antitrust Goes Global*, p.41.
[42] Commission Communication, Annex at p.2 (see fn. 2).

Community market will not be compromised as a result of restrictive practices by European companies seeking to protect their traditional markets.

But this guarantee calls for reciprocity! If other countries are less vigilant than we are with regard to the anti-competitive behaviour of their companies, access to their markets for Community products will be blocked.[43]

Strict reciprocity would require that foreign countries adopt the European enforcement model. The Community has not called for this expressly. However, in 1994, Van Miert did commission a 'Group of Experts' to 'consider these issues and contribute towards a European Community approach based largely on *our experience* on the integration of the internal market'.[44] In July 1995, the Experts issued their report, which found that purely domestic competition law enforcement was unable to address all aspects of market-closing business conduct. In addition, they found that international competition law enforcement efforts were being hampered by the non-binding nature of existing agreements, the differences between—and gaps within—existing competition laws, and the fact that many countries did not even have a competition regime at all. On the basis of this report, in June 1996 Brittan and Van Miert issued a joint 'Trade and Competition' Communication from the Commission to the European Council, the Community body responsible for negotiating international treaties.[45] This Commission Communication recommended that WTO Members negotiate a binding agreement to enact, enforce and co-operate in enforcing competition laws, in accordance with common minimum international standards. The Commission has since done a great deal of work in setting out what those standards should look like. Not surprisingly, early proposals had a distinctly European flavour.

During the past few years the Community has produced a detailed set of proposals for global rules on exclusive arrangements. One of its first proposals was ready in 1996, when the European Commission suggested that '[a] common approach to vertical restrictions could be found by concentrating on restrictions that create barriers to market access. The [WTO] . . .. could examine to what extent competition authorities could take into account the international dimension and weigh the effects on domestic competition of market access restrictions'.[46] This suggestion resembles European competition policy's approach of concentrating on arrangements of a 'Community dimension' that restrict trade between Member States. This was no accident, of course. Sir Leon Brittan argued that for 'the next stage in the logical process of opening up world markets to trade and competition . . . what the Community has gone through these last forty years is of considerable relevance to the challenge facing the wider world'.[47] This was to apply to issues of both process and of substance. With respect to procedures, for example, the Van Miert Group of Experts had recommended that WTO rules should comprise 'a list of minimum principles . . . [which]

---

[43] European Commission, *Competition Policy in the New Trade Order: Strengthening International Co-operation and Rules*, Report of the Group of Experts (Luxembourg: OOPEC, July 1995), p.3 (the 'Van Miert Report') (emphasis added).

[44] The Van Miert Report. Annex B, 'Text of letter of convocation'. External experts included Professors Immenga, Jenny, and Petersmann of Germany, France, and Switzerland respectively and Commission experts Ehlermann, Pons, Abbott, Lamoureux, Marchipont, and Jacquemin.

[45] See fn. 2.

[46] Commission Communication at p.11 (emphasis added).

[47] L. Brittan, 'A Framework for International Competition', Address to World Economic Forum, Davos (3 February 1992) in *International Economic Insights*, Issue 3 (March/April 1992), pp.21–22.

should be incorporated into the national law of the participating countries in much the same way as European Directives: each country would have an obligation as to the result to be achieved, but would not be obliged to amend its current legislation if it already contained these principles or if it was open to similar interpretation'.[48] As to the substance of the common rules, the Van Miert Group recommended that in analysing exclusionary arrangements, '[a] "rule of reason" approach is desirable ... Vertical agreements raise ... difficulties since opinions differ as to the conditions under which they are acceptable from a competition perspective'.[49] They did not propose leaving each Member completely free to conduct its own analysis, though. Foreseeing 'disputes over international rules of reason', the Van Miert Group recommended a WTO agreement to 'define minimum standards for national rules of reason and rules of conflicts of jurisdiction'.[50] Their specific proposal was for a formula that would 'prohibit agreements where their restrictive effect on competition is not offset by an advantage for the consumer and/or where they constitute a barrier to market access'.[51] As in European competition law, this would establish a competition offence that had a form of efficiency defence, as well as a separate offence of impeding market access.

4.2 THE US APPROACH

Across the Atlantic, however, the United States approach had been historically against multilateral disciplines on how governments should enforce their competition law. When such rules had been proposed in the 1940s, the US Congress refused to sign up to them, out of a fear that multilateral rules would lead to a watering down of US standards'.[52] When WTO competition rules were being discussed again in the late 1990's, then Assistant Attorney General for Antitrust Joel Klein issued 'A Note of Caution with respect to a WTO Agenda on Competition Policy'.[53] He submitted that the binding nature of WTO commitments would mean that governments would only be able to agree on the most general standards. This would inevitably be far less than was present in the purely hortatory *UNCTAD Set*, or the Model Law programme it was developing, and would not provide any guidance to countries in the early stages of developing a competition law regime.[54] Moreover, fixing such norms in international law might inhibit the policy competition between regimes and the resulting evolution that allows competition policy analysis itself to keep up with the changing nature and effect of business practices. Agreeing minimum standards could even allow

---

[48] The Commission's Experts Group recommended EU law as one of the principles: 'As regards the control of dominant positions, a regime similar to that of Article [82] of the ... Treaty appears appropriate insofar as it focuses on the abusive behaviour of enterprises in a dominant position'. Van Miert Report at p.22.

[49] Van Miert Report at pp.21–22.

[50] Van Miert Report at p.25.

[51] Van Miert Report at pp.21–22 (emphasis added).

[52] D. Wood, 'Remarks on Regulatory Co-operation for Effectiveness and Compliance: Joint Action among Securities, Banking and Antitrust Regulators', 91 Am. Soc'y Int'l L. Proc. 223, at 228.

[53] J. Klein, 'A Note of Caution with respect to a WTO Agenda on Competition Policy', presented at the Royal Institute of International Affairs, Chatham House, London, 18 November, 1996 (available at www.usdoj.gov).

[54] UNCTAD Secretariat, 'Continued Work on the Elaboration of a Model Law or Laws on Restrictive Business Practices', Draft, 21 August 1995 (available at www.unctad.org).

anti-competitive conduct to restrict trade if it enabled countries with lax enforcement regimes to hide behind an inadequate but nevertheless global benchmark. That was a real risk if, as seemed likely, a negotiation of binding rules involved a multilateral barter down to the lowest common denominator.

While American antitrust enforcement moreover would be likely to satisfy a common international standard, there was a concern that its coherence, rigor and the finality of its decisions would be put into question if subjected to international challenge and review by trade officials and diplomats unfamiliar with competition policy. Whether the US government signed up to WTO competition rules or not, Klein argued that a minimalist approach at the global level could well thwart its—and other international—efforts to get other governments to increase their enforcement activities. The way forward, Klein submitted, was through the continued refinement and expansion of enforcement co-operation agreements between governments. Co-operation among enforcers could improve their understanding of each other's laws and enforcement approaches and thereby bring about a convergence of legal positions of both substance and procedure. In the longer term, this would better help to create and support an international code of binding rules of the highest, rather than the lowest, calibre. A virtuous circle could then evolve among competition laws, bilateral co-operation, and multilateral code building.

The DOJ did not prevail, however. At the WTO's first Ministerial Conference to consider the issue, then US Trade Representative, Charlene Barshefsky, announced that the US government was 'willing to go along with others who wish to begin a modest work program in the areas of investment and competition, as part of a balanced overall agenda for the WTO'.[55] WTO Members then accepted the Community's proposals to form a WTO Working Group 'to study issues raised by Members relating to the interaction between trade and competition policy, including anti-competitive practices'.[56]

During the discussions at the Working Group over the past few years, governments have learned a lot from each other's enforcement experience, and are generally supportive of the need for competition rules. The Community has also amended some of its more European-sounding proposals to align them more with generally acceptable 'trade' and 'competition principles. As a result, the current work plan at the WTO is to 'focus on the clarification of: core principles, including transparency, non-discrimination and procedural fairness, and provisions on hard-core cartels; modalities for voluntary co-operation; and support for progressive reinforcement of competition institutions in developing countries through capacity building.[57] These are to a large extent 'motherhood and apple pie' issues about which agreement is possible. Indeed, it is arguable that competition laws and their enforcement are already subject to WTO commitments to be non-discriminatory and transparent.[58] It is beyond the scope of this chapter to consider the ramifications of the proposals being currently considered.[59] However, an examination of some of the existing competition rules at

---

[55] Statement by Ambassador Charlene Barshefsky, 9 December, 1996, WT/MIN (96)/ST/5 (available at www.wto.org/archives/st5.htm).

[56] WTO, Singapore Ministerial Declaration, Conf. Doc. WT/MIN(96)/DEC/W, 13 December 1996 (96–5315), (hereinafter, 'Singapore Declaration'), para. 20 (available at www.wto.org).

[57] WTO, Doha Ministerial Declaration, WT/MIN(01)/DEC/W/1 (14 November 2001) at para. 25 (emphasis added) (available at www.wto.org).

[58] *GATT* Arts. III and *GATS* Article XVII.

[59] For such a consideration, see P. Marsden, *A Competition Policy for the WTO* (Cameron May, 2003).

the WTO may indicate some of the kinds of concerns that might be raised in future negotiations for rules on competition law enforcement itself.

4.3 THE 1996 WTO *REFERENCE PAPER*: PRO-COMPETITIVE REGULATORY PRINCIPLES

Soon after the end of the Uruguay Round of trade negotiations, governments recognized that prohibitions of discrimination in world trade might not be sufficient to ensure that formerly publicly run sectors became competitive. This was particularly the case for the telecommunications markets. As a US government submission explained:

the negotiating parties [accepted] that a grant of *de jure* market access and national treatment was insufficient to grant *de facto* or effective market access, absent commitments by governments to regulate former monopolies in a pro-competitive manner, because such former monopolies have both the ability and the incentive to dictate anti-competitive terms of market entry for new competitors.[60]

A right of general entry had to be provided to new competitors, whether domestic or foreign, through pro-competitive 'asymmetric regulation' of major domestic suppliers.[61] Trade negotiators thus provided a *Reference Paper on Pro-competitive Regulatory Principles* to require that WTO Members ensure that their large incumbents provide sufficient entry points on satisfactory terms so that their competitors could connect to their networks.[62]

The approach in the *Reference Paper* is part competition policy, part regulation.[63] It protects competition by requiring that governments prohibit major suppliers from engaging in anti-competitive practices that frustrate market entry. It promotes competition by requiring that major suppliers provide their competitors with market access, for example, by allowing other firms to connect to their telecommunications networks on non-discriminatory terms and conditions, in a timely manner and upon request.[64] 'Major suppliers' are those with the power to 'materially affect the terms of participation (having regard to price and supply)' due to their control over 'essential facilities' or their 'position' in the market.[65] Examples of anti-competitive practices include 'anti-competitive cross-subsidisation' and 'use' of information obtained from competitors with anti-competitive results'.[66] As the *Reference Paper* imposes regulatory obligations, certain competition policy-related concepts are left undefined, including 'anti-competitive', 'essential facilities', and 'use' of one's position. Furthermore, a supplier can be 'major' without being what competition authorities would consider to be 'dominant'. Each signing Member undertakes to have its regulator, which can be a competition authority, adhere to these commitments.[67] When a Member has made the *Reference Paper* part of its specific commitments under the General

---

[60] Communication from the United States, 'The Impact of Regulatory Practices, State Monopolies, and Exclusive Rights on Competition and International Trade' WT/WGTCP/W/83 (14 August 1998) (hereinafter 'US Communication 83') at 11 (available at www.wto.org).

[61] US Communication 83 at 12.

[62] Negotiating Group on Basic Telecommunications, *WTO Reference Paper on Basic Telecommunications* (24 April 1996) (hereinafter, '*Reference Paper*').

[63] *Reference Paper*, Art. 1.1 and 2.2, respectively.

[64] *Reference Paper*, Art. 2.2.

[65] *Reference Paper*, Definitions.　　　　[66] *Reference Paper*, Art. 1.2.　　　　[67] *Reference Paper*, Art. 2.5.

Agreement on Trade and Services (*GATS*), any failure to adhere to it can be the subject of WTO dispute settlement.

The *Reference Paper* is more detailed than any other binding multilateral 'competition' rules. As such, trade negotiators are seeking to test the applicability of its principles to other formerly 'public' sectors with monopolistic or oligopolistic characteristics, including postal and courier, air transport, and energy as well as non-public sectors such as 'distribution' services. A 'built-in agenda' to this end is firmly in place and discussions are well-advanced.[68]

One of the most important aspects of 'unfinished business' of course, is to determine the meaning of the competition terms that are strewn throughout the *Reference Paper*. Competition law in America, Australia, Canada and even the Community only imposes similar obligations on firms to help their competitors when at least four conditions have been satisfied: first, the firms have been found to be 'dominant', as opposed to being merely 'major'; second, they have been proven to be abusing their dominant position by, for example, refusing to deal with their competitors, and third, this has been proven to have had the effect of lessening competition substantially,[69] or of eliminating it all together.[70] In addition, the preferred model in both Europe and the United States appears to be one where governments only intervene to order the owner of an essential facility to provide its competitors with access to it if, in addition to the above three conditions, it is not possible (or at least not economically feasible) for the competitors to develop a competing facility.[71] Of course, as a matter of logic, if a facility truly is 'essential' for competition to exist, then the elimination of competition is the only logical result of any denial of access to it. In any event, the *Reference Paper* does not require evidence of 'elimination' or 'substantial lessening' of competition. It focuses purely on the denial of access to a facility that is controlled by a supplier that is 'major' either on its own, or with other providers.

It is more than a little unfortunate that the *Reference Paper* set such an obviously regulatory approach that is so different from current practice under the laws of most WTO Members, particularly when the American and European approaches to essential facilities have been converging towards one another and when governments generally have been favouring the use of competition law disciplines rather than regulation. Any one of the four conditions required by the competition law analysis set out above is far more rigorous than the criterion to which Members have committed themselves in the *Reference Paper*. Since the *Reference Paper* influences how Members intervene in their markets, this divergence needs to be resolved sooner rather than later. This is particularly important because of the use of the provisions of the *Reference Paper* in dispute settlement procedures. This is particularly the case since the *Reference Paper*'s provisions are already being relied upon in dispute settlement proceedings.

---

[68] WTO Secretariat, 'Distribution Services—Background Note by the Secretariat' S/C/W/37, 10 June 1998 at 14; Inside US Trade, 'US presses for alternative negotiating methods for *GATS*', (20 August 1999) available at www.wto.org).

[69] US Sherman Act, 15 U.S.C., Section 2; Australian Trade Practices Act 1974 (consolidated), Section 46; Canadian *Competition Act*, R.S.C. 1985, c. C-34, as amended.; Sections 78 and 79. See, e.g. *MCI Communications Corp v. AT&T*, 464 US 891(1983).

[70] *Bronner* v. *MediaPrint* Case C-7/97 [1998] ECR I-7791 [1998]: 4 CMLR 112.

[71] *MCI Communications Corp v. AT&T, Bronner.*

4.4. APPLICATION OF THE *REFERENCE PAPER*— MEXICAN TELECOMS

The US has used the *Reference Paper* already to effect considerable changes to the business environment in Mexico. The case in question arose after an American telecoms provider, Sprint, had partnered with Mexico's largest supplier of telecommunications services, Telmex, to provide mobile telecommunication services in the United States and Mexico. AT&T and MCI had to settle for deals with lesser Mexican players and could not benefit from Telmex's considerably larger network. They called upon the US Trade Representative to help them achieve the kind of access enjoyed by Sprint. The resulting American WTO complaint requested that Telmex be required to provide these US firms with non-discriminatory access as provided for under the *Reference Paper*.[72] After only a few months of the pressure of strained trade relations with the United States, the Mexican telecoms regulator COFETEL issued a set of 'Asymmetric Regulations for Telmex'. These ordered Telmex to provide its long distance competitors with access to its network at cost.[73] The United States then withdrew its WTO complaint.[74]

It is interesting to note that at no point did AT&T, MCI, or the USTR make a public request for the Mexican competition authority to investigate Telmex's activities, and of course they had no incentive to do so. Their allegations would have had to survive a rigorous market analysis and satisfy a competition law standard—that competition in the relevant market had been proven to have been 'diminished, impaired or prevented',[75] before the Mexican competition authority would have intervened. The complainants and the USTR obviously thought that they stood a much better chance of success if Geneva-based trade panellists reviewed their complaint under the pro-competitive rules of the *Reference Paper*. They would not have to find evidence of 'harm to competition' but simply a failure by Mexico to honour its commitment to *promote* competition by increasing foreign entry. From the point of view of international trade policy, the use of this standard, combined with the threat that Mexican products would be barred from the vast American market, makes Mexico's capitulation and imposition of 'asymmetric regulations' on its 'major supplier' was not at all surprising.

As the initial Mexican case was settled through bilateral 'negotiation', WTO dispute settlement panels have not yet had an opportunity to explain what the *Reference Paper*'s pro-competitive regulatory principles actually mean. Given the vagueness of its terms, however, problems of interpretation are likely to arise in any dispute settlement proceeding. To minimize the possibility of regulation being introduced when it is not appropriate, the meaning, application and even the propriety of pro-competitive regulation are matters that have to be decided as a matter of urgency. Being part of the *GATS*, it is natural for the *Reference Paper* to have more to do with promoting 'market access' than with protecting the

---

[72] *Mexico—Measures Affecting Telecommunications Services—Request for Consultations by the United States*, WT/DS204/2 (17 August 2000) (available at www.wto.org).

[73] Inside Trade, 'USTR backs off Mexico WTO threat in wake of telecom company deal' (available at www.insidetrade.com) (1 June 2001).

[74] The battle continues, however. A recent WTO update of dispute settlement cases (WT/DS/OV/7, www.wto.org) reports that '[o]n 13 February 2002, the United States requested the establishment of a new panel. In particular, the United States [is claiming] that Mexico's measures . . . did not prevent Telmex from engaging in anti-competitive practices', WT/DS204/3. At the time of writing, the Panel report is still pending.

[75] *Ley Federal de Competencia Económica*, Diario oficial de la federacion (24 December 1992) Arts 8 and 10.

competitive process. It is closer to entrant-friendly *ex ante* regulation than to competition law, which disciplines anti-competitive behaviour after it has been proven likely to harm competitors or consumers. Of course, a bias towards entry is to be expected in any trade agreement, and should not necessarily be condemned, particularly when it applies to sectors that are controlled by former public monopolies and where mandated access is essential for competition to exit at all. The question most relevant to the development of further 'competition' rules at the WTO, though, is how appropriate the *Reference Paper* is as a template for opening up other sectors. This is particularly the case for those sectors where the role and effect of government regulation is minimal or has long since ceased to operate.

These are all difficult issues that WTO Members, and dispute settlement panellists, will not be able to ignore. It is to be hoped that the Multilateral Competition Agreement that the Community now so ardently seeks from its WTO colleagues will eventually provide a much needed 'competition policy' anchor to help to determine how these existing terms will be interpreted and applied in the telecoms and other sectors.

4.5 THE INTERNATIONAL COMPETITION NETWORK (ICN)

What is more likely to provide such guidance at a much earlier date, however, is the work that competition authorities themselves are doing under the auspices of the ICN, referred to earlier.[76] There will still need to be a binding agreement in place, most likely at the WTO, to ensure that competition principles prevail over mere demands from companies for access to their rival's supply or customer base. Such an accord is likely to take a great deal of time for governments to negotiate, however, and for dispute settlement panellists at the WTO to interpret in any substantive manner. In the meantime, the officials at DG-Comp, at the European Commission, and at over sixty other competition authorities around the world have been meeting to learn from one another's expertise through the virtual network, the ICN. They share experience learned from actual cases and develop 'best practice guidelines' about how they should enforce their laws (in particular, in a non-discriminatory manner) and how they should co-operate with one another to address anti-competitive conduct with international effects.[77] They have addressed topics relating to harmonising procedures and reducing costs and burdens (to both business and governments) associated with multi-jurisdictional merger review. They have begun an international competition law advocacy programme to help explain the importance of competition policy to governments that may be resistant to such arguments, or at least may pay little heed to the policy advice of the competition authority in their jurisdiction. They have examined the substantive analytical framework underpinning merger control analysis, evaluating the propriety and applicability of the three main tests: 'substantial lessening of competition', 'dominance', and 'public interest'.

This exchange of learning should only increase, and when necessary, could be implemented in binding commitments that might form the basis of an accord at the WTO. For the meantime, however, the most pragmatic advances in international enforcement of competition law generally, will likely come from the ICN. They will help competition authorities to understand the concerns that other governments have about extraterritorial enforcement, and its limitations, and should provide a stable but flexible basis for international co-operation at the bilateral, regional, and multilateral levels.

---

[76] See fn. 23.   [77] See www.internationalcompetitionnetwork.org.

PART III

CONCLUSIONS AND PROSPECTS

24

FORTY-FIVE YEARS OF THE TREATY OF ROME

1. THE COMMISSION'S TASK 1958–2003

1.1 THE BASIC PRIORITIES FOR THE COMMISSION

Over the forty-five years since the Treaty of Rome was signed Community competition law has developed into a mature system, and the final part of this work looks back at its development. There is in reality no perfect occasion for such a review since the development and implementation of the law and underlying policy proceeds on a gradual, unpredictable, and frequently interrupted basis. Nevertheless, after such a period both the competition policy of the Community and the institutions responsible for it may be assumed to have reached a point of development when it is both necessary and valuable to provide a general assessment of its achievements, which is provided in this chapter. In the following chapter, we look ahead to changes that may be necessary for the Commission in general and DG Comp in particular to meet their responsibilities and priorities at the start of the twenty-first century.

The framework of the Treaty of Rome (as subsequently amended) sets out the main objectives and tasks of its institutions; these tasks comprise principally the promotion, throughout the Community, of economic growth and expansion, an increase of its stability and living standards, and the maintenance of close relation-ships between Member States. The means whereby the objectives were to be achieved were a number of common policies laid down in Article 3 including, of course, in paragraph (1)(g) 'the institution of a system ensuring that competition in the Common Market is not distorted'. The characteristics of this system would necessarily have included:

(a) the establishment of primary rules, both substantive and procedural, of sufficient width, clarity, and certainty to ensure a reasonable degree of compliance in all economic sectors covered by the policy, which in turn could provide a stable foundation for business development, to apply both to horizontal and to vertical relationships;

(b) the consistent application of competition policy throughout the geographical area of the Community, actively carried out not only by the institutions of the Community but by Member States themselves, to ensure that the implementation of the relevant provisions of the Treaty was both legally consistent and complete;

(c) the even-handed application to both Member States and undertakings within the

Community of the rules comprised in this system, within the framework of the
Treaty and regulations made under it; and

(*d*) acceptance by the Council of Ministers and Member States that the human and
financial resources required for the effective implementation of the system by relevant Community institutions should be adequate for the considerable tasks involved.

1.2 THE CHANGING ECONOMIC BACKGROUND

Any attempt to make a balanced assessment must, of course, take into account not only
periods of success and forward movement but also the problems encountered, both internal
and external. Over this period the Commission has at certain times certainly faced considerable difficulties in both the economic and the political spheres. In particular, the economic
background against which it operates has undergone disruption and substantial change. The
early years of the Six, even up to the start of the 1970s, can be seen in retrospect as a
comparatively calm period, remarkable for steady economic growth through-out much of
the territory of the Community. The continuous growth of both the internal and external
trade of the Community and rising standards of living in its individual Member States
(other than a few clearly identifiable regions such as the southern part of Italy) contributed
to the willingness of governments of Member States to agree readily to the grant of extensive
powers to the Commission in this area of competition policy, both those relating to procedures and to the application of substantive law. Even during the mid-sixties, when the
Council remained largely inactive as the result of political deadlock, the powers already
granted to the Commission and the decisions that towards the end of this time began to
come from the European Court of Justice ensured that, in this area at least, progress continued. At the same time, a relatively relaxed approach was taken by the Community and its
Member States to State aid, which was not regarded initially as having much influence on
the competitive structure of markets within the Community.

All this changed during the early seventies. The sharp increase in oil prices in late 1973 led
to nearly a decade of stagnation in economic growth and an acute increase in mutual
sensitivity between Member States concerned about the effect of government involvement
in sectors such as steel, textiles, and shipbuilding, where the economic consequences of the
new era were most keenly felt. It was also unfortunate, as many commentators have pointed
out, for all Member States, that the expansion of the Community to nine (including the
United Kingdom) and then to ten Member States took place against such a background,
accentuating problems as well as opportunities for the enlarged Common Market. Nevertheless the Community continued to expand, the entry of Spain and Portugal in 1986 bringing
its membership to twelve, and reaching its present level of fifteen with the accession of
Austria, Finland, and Sweden at the start of 1995; Norway, Iceland, and Liechtenstein comprise the current 'EFTA Members' of the European Economic Area (EEA). None of these
three countries are however among the ten which have been invited to join the Community
in May 2004, subject to ratification by each of the invitees.

The development of competition policy continued steadily over the 1980s and 1990s.
Under active Competition Commissioners, Peter Sutherland (for the period 1985–88) Sir
Leon Brittan (1989–92), and Karel van Miert (1993–99), DG Comp was able to place
greater emphasis on the positive aspects of its responsibilities. Special attention was paid to
liberalization of air transport and some progress made in the enactment of both procedural

and substantive regulations within whose framework progress could be made (if slowly) towards a greater freedom for airlines to fix their own fares, without having on all occasions to obtain government approval. Maritime transport was also given a block exemption, and a number of major cases brought against price fixing and other anti-competitive practices within this sector.

Some of the most important changes in the jurisdiction of the Commission occurred at the end of the 1980s. The enactment in 1989 of Merger Regulation 4064/89 filled an important gap, allowing proposed concentrations that might enable dominant positions to be created or strengthened in particular sectors to be prohibited, or at least subjected to conditions which would reduce the likelihood of consequent damage to the competitive process in those markets. Moreover, the approval by the European Court[1] of the use by the Commission of its powers under Article 86(3) to issue Directives, to put pressure on Member States to open up their telecommunications terminal equipment and services market in order to establish a functioning market within the Community for large-scale information technology, was vital. These decisions led in turn to the enactment of a number of Council Directives, particularly in the fields of energy and communication, designed to liberalize national markets traditionally dominated in most Member States by State controlled national operators not subject to adequate outside competition, though there continued to be serious opposition to the full liberalization of the gas and electricity markets, especially from France.

The technological boom in particular in the communications, computer hardware and software, transport, and energy markets throughout the 1990s meant that pressures on the Commission further increased. There were a large number of joint venture proposals which had to be dealt with under either Article 81 or the Merger Regulation, and it became apparent that the original division by category of joint ventures into 'co-operative' (considered under Article 81) and 'concentrative' (considered under the Merger Regulation) was unworkable. New legislation had to be brought in to ensure, from 1 March 1998, that all 'full function' joint ventures could benefit from the fixed timetable of the Merger Regulation. The actual number of mergers with a Community dimension, now including of course all full function joint ventures, also increased to well over 300 a year, of which some five per cent raised serious doubts about their effects on competition in the relevant sectors and needed the more detailed assessment of the second phase procedure.

2. THE COMMISSION'S LEGISLATIVE PROGRAMME

2.1 THE INITIAL CHOICES

One method of following the administrative and policy-making progress of DG Comp, through, *inter alia*, Commission and Court decisions, is by reading the relevant *Annual Reports on Competition Policy*; these are normally published by the Commission in the latter part of each year to cover the previous calendar year's activities. Whilst the Annual Reports are valuable in their coverage of the events of that particular year, the calendar year is itself an artificial period; inevitably, therefore, they include reference to many developments that

[1] See Ch. 22, Section 4.

are incomplete. To gain a better idea of the progress of DG Comp, it is more helpful to read the reports for several years consecutively. Moreover, the *Annual Report on Competition Policy* suffers from the inherent defect of having been written by the very officials whose administrative actions form the principal subject of the report. An objective assessment of their work has normally, therefore, to be left either to writers of textbooks and articles in legal periodicals or to the more ephemeral comment of daily and weekly newspapers. Whilst Annual Reports provide an invaluable record of the tangible legislative and administrative achievements and decisions of a calendar year, they inevitably omit much that is necessary to a full understanding of what actually occurred, in much the same way that the annual report of a public company, whilst truthfully recording the salient features of a single year's trading, may not necessarily give much information about vital changes in management style or boardroom policy. They include the current aspirations of the Commission in a number of directions, but not necessarily all the problems (internal and external) which may obstruct their achievement.

Nevertheless, our review begins with a reference to the aims expressed in the very first Annual Report, published to cover the period to the end of 1971. In listing these, DG Comp had, of course, already had the benefit of over a decade of experience in administering Articles 81 and 82, and chose to give priority to the following issues:

(*a*) the need to take action with special vigour against restrictions on competition and practices jeopardizing the unity of the Common Market notably sharing markets, allocating customers and collective exclusive dealing agreements, and preventing agreements which indirectly resulted in concentrating demand on particular producers;

(*b*) with regard to systems of distribution, any degree of exclusivity permitted must not prevent distributors and consumers from obtaining goods in Member States 'on the terms customary in that State';

(*c*) heavy fines should be expected by those undertakings engaged in restrictions on competition causing serious damage to consumers' interests, and which were clearly forbidden;

(*d*) the Commission would reinforce the competitive position of undertakings by exempting (both by individual decisions and by means of a block regulation) positive forms of co-operation, particularly between small and medium-size businesses; and

(*e*) the Commission did not intend to apply the prohibitions of Article 81 to restrictions on competition which had no appreciable effect on the Common Market.

The extent of the Commission's success in carrying out these aims has been considered in Part II above. In general, within the limits of its resources, the Commission has been reasonably effective. Experience has shown that, while in applying Articles 81 and 82 many difficulties have arisen, the Articles themselves are not flawed nor inadequate as a foundation for the establishment of the necessary system referred to in Article 3(1)(*g*) of the Treaty, save in the area of merger control, for which a special Regulation has proved necessary. These two Articles, however, are merely the framework for the application of the detailed rules of the system and cannot by themselves provide answers to all the questions which arise over their implementation. It is, therefore, to the legislation adopted by both Council and Commission, as well as to the case-law of the Commission and Court, that we must turn for many of these answers.

To have expected DG Comp to administer a competition law in the form contained simply in those two Articles, even as supplemented by Articles 83 to 86, would clearly have been unreasonable, given that responsibility for the development of competition policy was assigned under the terms of the Treaty to the Commission and was not simply to be enforced through national courts or the European Court of Justice.[2] The Commission was, of course, to be subject in making decisions to a right of review by the European Court under Article 230 for the benefit of affected undertakings. This right of review applied primarily to matters of procedure rather than to substantive criteria, though the Court's decisions starting with *Consten-Grundig* soon made it clear that in the course of such review important principles of substantive law would also have to be laid down. Whether competition policy would be a question of 'steering' or merely 'drifting' was very much for the Commission itself; in particular, the key area of interpreting the basis of granting exemption under Article 81(3), whether by way of individual decision or by application to categories of agreement, rested exclusively with it, a Treaty requirement reinforced by the unequivocal terms of Article 9(1) of Regulation 17/62.

2.2. BLOCK EXEMPTIONS—THE ORIGINAL APPROACH

Once the implementation of Regulation 17 had brought about the early problem of mass notification, the major priority for DG Comp had to be the enactment of detailed regulations to lay down the exact criteria for block exemptions. This required analysis of the different kinds of agreement and clauses found within them, which needed to be classified into the categories of 'harmless', 'borderline', and 'harmful', before any form of block exemption could be provided. The adoption of legislation[3] embodying the terms of block exemptions, though sometimes a painfully protracted process, has enabled the Commission to dispense with the need for individual notification of a very large number of agreements, especially those vertical ones dealing with distribution and licensing.

The original approach of the Commission to block exemptions therefore in the field of distribution was relatively simple, as exemplified by the original Regulation 67/67 which applied for just over fifteen years until replaced by Regulations 1983/83 and 1984/83 on exclusive distribution agreements and exclusive purchasing agreements respectively. These in turn were supplemented in 1988 by Regulation 4087/88 on franchising agreements. The tendency in each of these regulations was to extend the white (permitted) list of restrictions which could be included without losing the benefit of the exemption; although the intention of the Commission was to assist suppliers, wholesalers, and retailers to prepare agreements that could benefit from the exemption, it had the unintended consequence of making the

---

[2] This policy differed from the choice made by the US when first enacting the Sherman Act in 1890. It is the decisions of Federal courts over subsequent years that have provided the corpus of legal principles and refinements by which the Act has been interpreted, without the assistance of delegated legislation in the nature of block exemptions that Art. 81 for its part appears to have expressly contemplated (i.e. by its reference to exemption for 'categories' of agreement).

[3] Many senior Commission officials do not accept that block exemption regulations are of legislative character, but are rather just an exposition of the provisions of Art. 81(3) for enforcement purposes. See E. Paulis, *Checks and Balances in the EU Antitrust Enforcement System* (Fordham Corporate Law Institute, 2002), [to be published in late 2003].

regulations far too complex and legalistic. Although there had been a number of ECJ decisions to assist in the assessment of such vertical agreements, a number of 'grey' areas were still left. The 'opposition' procedure was therefore invented to try and provide a procedural mechanism under which the parties could submit to DG Comp clauses containing an element of restriction but which fell neither within the short list of prohibited (black) clauses or the longer permitted 'white' list. Unfortunately use of the opposition procedure was not popular and it became clear to the Commission that a new approach to the drafting of block exemptions might be necessary. Matters were brought to a head by the impending expiry at the end of 1997 of both Regulations 1983/83 and 1984/83. Their life was extended temporarily for two years up to the end of 1999 and a Green Paper on vertical restraints (referred to in Chapter 10) was produced in late 1996 as a consultation document relevant to their replacement. This Green Paper contained, inter alia, the results of a survey by the Commission on the attitude of all those interests involved in the process of distribution towards the existing exemptions, especially in the light of the changing nature of the distribution process.

2.3 BLOCK EXEMPTIONS — THE NEW APPROACH

The new approach of the Commission was indicated in its *1998 Annual Report*[4] as follows:

The general idea is that there should be a single and very broad block exemption regulation covering all vertical restrictions of competition in respect of all intermediate and finished goods and all services. A limited number of restrictions would be excluded, such as price-fixing agreements for example. These would form a 'black list' of clauses that were not exempted by the regulation. The regulation would not seek to list the clauses that were exempted, as is done in the block exemption regulations currently in force, and this would immediately remove the straitjacket effect associated with the present 'white lists', which incite firms to force their agreements into a mould provided by the relevant block exemption regulation.

The wide objective of this wide-ranging and flexible exemption regulation would be to give a measure of freedom and legal certainty to the very many firms that do not possess market power. Within the limits thus mapped out they would not have to be concerned for the validity of their agreements under Community law. To preserve competition on markets, and to confine the benefit of the exemption to firms with no great market power, the regulation would lay down market share thresholds beyond which the block exemption would no longer apply. The fact that these thresholds were exceeded would not mean that the agreements were necessarily unlawful, but only that they would have to be examined for compatibility on an individual basis.

The Commission had had difficulty when consulting about the introduction of a new composite regulation covering the transfer of technology a few years earlier, because of opposition to a proposed market share threshold of 40 per cent, beyond which a licensee holding such a share could not benefit. The ultimate outcome, when the terms of Block Exemption Regulation 240/96 were adopted, was that the 40 per cent threshold was not made an absolute bar against the licensee benefiting from the exemption but was merely a ground upon which the Commission could consider withdrawal of the exemption, if it appeared that such a market share for a licensee was preventing the relevant products from being exposed to effective competition in the licensed territory.

---

[4] See pp.21–22.

No such difficulties were encountered with the introduction of the new distribution Regulation 2790/99 and the Commission's new approach has been regarded as a successful reform. The new Regulation eliminated the special provisions for the beer and petrol sectors that had been contained in Regulation 1984/83. The Commission on principle dislikes sectoral block exemptions unless the characteristics of the sector are so special, and the lobbying power of its members so great, that a tailor-made block exemption is inevitable, as in the case of maritime transport. In the case of the motorcar industry it was inevitable that Regulation 1475/95 (which itself had replaced Regulation 123/85) would be replaced by another Regulation (1400/2002) dealing alone with motor vehicles. The Commission's policy however to increase the commercial independence of motor vehicle distributors throughout the Common Market, and to enhance their ability to accept orders from outside their primary sales areas, has had the effect of making the final terms of the Regulation 1400/2002 even more complex. It has also led the Commission to the publication of very detailed guidelines on the interpretation and application of the regulations. Lengthy published guidelines by the Commission have also been a feature of the other more recent block exemptions.

In providing in 2000 revised versions also of the block exemption regulations (2658 and 2659/2000) covering specialization and research and development the Commission has sought to utilize the same principles as under Regulation 2790/99, even though these two categories are essentially dealing with horizontal agreements between undertakings who may be actual or potential competitors. 'White lists' have again been omitted and market share thresholds for research and development agreements increased to 20 per cent whilst turnover thresholds were eliminated from the specialization agreement. Nevertheless, the drafting by undertakings of such horizontal agreements within the terms of the block exemption remains far less widespread than in the context of vertical agreements where the model of the new regulation has largely been followed, given its greater flexibility.

A common feature of all the recent block exemptions has been greater provision for the withdrawal of the benefits, if the Commission becomes aware that a particular agreement or group of agreements have effects incompatible with Article 81(3), and in particular under Regulation 2790/99 if access to the relevant markets is significantly restricted by the cumulative effects of parallel networks of similar vertical restraints, implemented by competing suppliers or buyers. Member States too have a similar right of withdrawal in respect of agreements operating within them which are found to have the same effect.

3. POSITIVE AND NEGATIVE AIMS OF COMPETITION POLICY

3.1 NEGATIVE AIMS ALONE ARE NOT ENOUGH

The Commission, like all competition authorities, has in recent years become the victim of rising expectations. It is required to give greater weight not only to the well established 'negative' aspects of competition policy but also now in more cases to the 'positive' requirements and aims of such policy. Legislative aims in framing competition policy are usually directed at the prevention of agreements, practices, or mergers, or at the growth of monopoly power or dominance regarded as undesirable, and the early targets for such legislation are normally obvious. Moreover, substantial public support is normally found for this control from which direct consumer benefit is assumed. The Sherman Act in the United States was the earliest example of such legislation, which has now been adopted not only in the Community but in the United Kingdom in the Competition Act 1998 (replacing the earlier Restrictive Trade Practice legislation), and in similar terms in many other jurisdictions across the world. Such legislation provides sanctions on the undertakings involved which may be civil, rendering void and unenforceable agreements that fall within the prohibition, and also in a few jurisdictions, including the USA and now the United Kingdom, may involve criminal penalties for individuals, including both fines and imprisonment.

Once, however, a competition authority has achieved a reasonable degree of success in implementing such forms of negative control, it is usually realized that such control alone may not in the long run satisfy public or political demand for the achievement of tangible results in liberalizing markets previously dominated by State-owned or State-controlled organizations. The aim of the competition authorities then becomes that of combining their negative responsibilities with the positive need to provide a framework within which competition in all its many forms and varieties can be encouraged. It has to be encouraged not only in structural terms, by ensuring that there are sufficient undertakings capable of competing with each other within individual product and geographic markets, especially in new sectors, but also by giving support to the agreements and practices that undertakings desire to enter into in the avowed interests of fostering competition, of developing new products, especially in areas of advanced technology, and of adopting new methods of distribution, for example franchising.

The experience of the Commission has been that it is better to seek to carry out its positive responsibilities by legislation, that is primarily through the introduction of block exemptions as described in the previous section. Through the more recent approach to such legislation as described, under which the parties to both vertical and horizontal arrangements in well-defined categories are encouraged to make their agreements in a way that is consistent with the new legislation, positive policies can be pursued by the Commission in respect of those undertakings at least which have limited market power. Moreover, even those undertakings which are compelled to seek individual approval (formal or informal) for such agreements will tend to do so on the basis that either they are only required to do so because their market share exceeds that of the threshold provided, or because one or more of the clauses sought to be included in the agreement is arguably within the list of prohibited clauses, possibly because of special features of the sectors within which they operate. Such applicants will normally seek to convince the Commission that in all other respects their agreements will follow the pattern laid down by the block exemption and may receive individual exemption on this basis.

Through the provision therefore of a form of legislative template for such agreements the Commission seeks to minimize the need for implementing its policy in respect of at least these categories of agreement by individual review or individual exemption. Given its inevitably limited resources it has preferred to concentrate these on those cases which represent the essentially negative aspect of its Article 81 responsibilities, and normally involve cartels which extend to more than one Member State and require considerable investment and resources in their investigation and punishment. Flagrant breaches of the Treaty of this kind cannot be dealt with by legislative means alone but only by application of resources to individual cases. Experience shows that their investigation will often be very demanding because they will cover an extensive period of time, involve multiple undertakings in a variety of Member States and other jurisdictions, and will need the investigation of voluminous documents and even computer records. Even with the recent success of the Leniency Programme, under which participants in a cartel can seek a reduction in the fines payable or in certain cases complete immunity from fines by confessing at a sufficiently early stage the details of their participation, the workload on the Commission for each case can be enormous. A brief review of the text of any major cartel decision of the Commission, or a judgment on appeal to the CFI, will underline the truth of this statement.

But if the Commission is therefore forced to spend a substantial proportion of its budget and human resources in the pursuit of cartels, and to a rather less extent abuse by dominant companies of their position, why should it not seek to reduce still further its involvement in those routine Article 81 cases which have less 'Community interest'? These may involve not clear breaches of Articles 81 and 82 or contravention of well-established Community law principles, such as resale price maintenance or export bans, but may merely raise more technical issues on the interpretation and application of Article 81(3). Would it not be more sensible to delegate the implementation of Article 81 substantially to Member State national competition authorities and national courts, so as to enable the negative aspects of those cartel cases which do have a Community interest (of which there seem to be a continuing stock) to become the primary focus of its activities? Just as the Commission itself finds that it can often receive major assistance in international cartel cases from the USA and competition authorities within other jurisdictions, inside and outside the Community, could it not receive assistance for Member States also in dealing with those cases which they may be better placed to handle than the Commission itself? Such was the thinking behind the Modernization White Paper of 1999 which has now been accepted as the blueprint for the new system for applying Articles 81 and 82 coming into effect on 1 May 2004.

3.2 NEGATIVE AND POSITIVE POLICY ASPECTS—THE MERGER REGULATION

In an ideal world the implementation of the Merger Regulation would enable both negative and positive objectives to be achieved. The negative aspect is obviously the ability of the Commission to block joint ventures or mergers that clearly fall within the terms of Article 2 because of the damage that they would impose on competitive structures in particular markets. In practice not a large percentage of the concentrations that have a Community dimension are actually blocked by Commission decision; only twenty in the last twelve years, although many more have received restrictive conditions (remedies) attached to their implementation, often involving divestiture of substantial assets, in order to restore markets to a competitive state that would otherwise have been seriously affected by the merger. Many other possible mergers have undoubtedly been deterred by the existence of the Merger Regulation, though their exact number is inherently unknowable. The deterrent or negative effect of the Merger Regulation remains of considerable importance, given an undoubted trend towards oligopoly in many sectors including oil, finance, telecommunications, and in particular the media. The possibility of combining control both over channels of distribution

and the news or entertainment content to be so distributed offers the opportunity for
incumbents to seek to foreclose entry to national markets, and has led to several blocking
decisions under the Merger Regulation in order to prevent situations of this kind arising in
particular Member States.[5]

There is also however an important positive aspect of merger control under the Regulation, in that conditions can be imposed by way of remedies in order to achieve the result of
what may be an improvement in the competitive structure of the relevant sector. The
Commission has drawn attention in its recent Annual Reports to a number of these cases.
An example was the merger proposed between *Telenor* and *Telia*[6] the incumbent telecommunications operators in Norway and Sweden respectively and each others' closest actual
and potential competitors. This finding was based on detailed evidence obtained as to the
operation of these markets, as well as the fact that each had a stronger degree of control over
their network infrastructures than any other competitor in the Nordic area. The pre-merger
level of competition between them was found to be an important constraint on price levels
which benefited other market participants, owing to the non-discrimination provisions in
relevant telecommunications regulations. The effect of the merger would have been to
remove this constraint and to have allowed the merged entity to have controlled a significant
proportion of the whole transmission infrastructure. The merged entity would also have
become to a higher degree than either of the individual parties a necessary contracting party
for all competitors in the Nordic region. Although ultimately the merger did not take place,
the conditions imposed upon it would otherwise have had a positive effect in a number of
television service and other related markets. The companies would have been required to
open up access to the telephone markets in both countries as well as to divest their respective
cable-TV businesses. Moreover, both Telia and Telenor committed themselves to remove all
existing overlaps between them in the field of telecom services; they agreed additionally to
implement a set of measures to promote competition in the provision of the local loop
joining the consumer to its local exchange, an important element in encouraging new entry.

The Commission had a similar task in the *EDF/ENBW* case reported in the Annual Report
of 2001.[7] Here the proposed concentration was between EDF, the French national incumbent electricity company, and a major German electricity supplier, ENBW. EDF had a
dominant position on the French market with a market share of approximately 90 per cent.
ENBW was considered one of the most likely entrants to the French market, strategically
well placed to supply a number of large industrial customers there, since its supply area was
in the southwest of Germany where there is a long common border with France. However,
two of the four Franco-German electricity interconnectors were in the ENBW supply area;
EDF thus by acquiring ENBW would become less exposed to competition in France. The
remedies adopted in the case were more complex than normal, and in particular sought to
address the competition concerns for those French customers for whom ENBW had been
a potential competitor. EDF undertook therefore to provide competitors with access to

[5] For example, *MSG Media Services* Case IV/M469 [1994] OJ L364/1. *Nordic Satellite Distribution* Case IV/
M490 [1995] OJ 5 CMLR 258: [1996] OJ L53/20. *RTL/Endemol/Veronica* Case IV/M553 [1996] OJ L134/32.
[6] Case Comp/M1439 [2000] OJ L40/1: [2001] 4 CMLR 1226.
[7] See pp.67–68, *ENDW/EDF/Cajastur/Hidrocantabrico* Case M2684, [2002] 4 CMLR 1291, had similar
features; here the Commission was able, through the conditions imposed on the parties, to improve the
interconnector capacity for electricity supply from France into Spain and to reduce the relative isolation of
the Spanish electricity market.

generation capacity located in France up to an agreed maximum. It was felt that these detailed arrangements for access to generation capacity would be the most effective means of preserving competition in the French electricity markets after the merger.

4. THE PROBLEM OF RESOURCES

4.1 STAFFING LEVELS OF DG COMP

In assessing the performance of DG Comp over the last forty-five years a relevant factor should be the degree to which adequate resources were provided to it from the Community budget. It is likely that resources allocated for expenditure on public purposes will always be regarded as inadequate by those responsible for administering them as well as by those for whose benefit they are administered; whether the public purpose be health, social security, education, or defence, the same principle holds good. By comparison with such major areas of public expenditure, the sums available for expenditure in enforcing competition policy are indeed small. Nevertheless, problems of inadequate resources still remain for such authorities. Governments in Member States moreover tend to take an ambivalent view towards their own competition authority. On the one hand there is clearly need for the existence of such authorities to deal with clearly anti-competitive agreements, practices, mergers, and monopolistic activities whose termination or prevention can be shown to benefit both the consumer and the general economy. On the other hand, governments are also concerned by the problems which competition authorities may cause, by threatening to challenge or investigate activities which individual ministries may regard as their own responsibility, and where the link between the authorities' intervention on the side of com- petition and consequent benefit is less obvious. This ambivalence is also found within the European Community.

The history of DG Comp does show a steady increase in the manpower provided to it, as the responsibilities placed upon it gradually grew. Thus from a handful of 'A' grade officials in its early years the total had risen after thirty years to 300, including 140 'A' grade officials, and by ten years later (1998) to 450 altogether including some 225 'A' grade officials. The current figure of total employment in DG Comp is around 600 of whom some half are 'A' grade officials. It should be remembered that just under ten per cent of the 'A' grade officials are concerned with State aids rather than competition issues. These numbers overall how- ever are not insignificant, though less than those of some national competition authorities.

On the other hand the history of DG Comp shows also a steady growth in its incremental responsibilities in not only State aids but also in the considerable amount of additional work brought about by the liberalization process under Article 86(3), and during the nineties the heavy workload introduced by the Merger Regulation. Many of the tasks more recently added, in particular a growing number of major cartel cases, are extremely labour intensive, and the resources available in this respect have not always matched the demands placed upon DG Comp. Of the 90 per cent of its staff that deal with competition matters, some sixty are employed in the Merger Task Force and some forty in policy coordination and in the office of the Director-General; the remainder are distributed between the various sec- toral directorates. For a Community of over 380 million people and fifteen Member States, this is still clearly inadequate, let alone the enlarged Community of the future.

4.2 THE UNSOLVED PROBLEM—NOTIFICATION

From necessity therefore the Commission has sought to improve its procedures and over the period these have in many respects improved. The Annual Reports show a continuing consciousness of, and preoccupation with, the importance of minimizing the difficulties and delays inevitably imposed by the institutional structure and bureaucracy of such an organization, not to mention the difficulties caused by the necessity of supporting eleven official languages. The introduction of Regulation 1216/99 has considerably reduced the number of notifications of vertical restrictions; the new form of Regulation 2790/99 has, as already explained in Chapter 10, simplified the legal position and reduced the number of notifications made. The Notice on Agreements of Minor Importance has been further extended in 2001 so as to eliminate the need to notify more of the de minimis category of agreements; the Commission has continued to take a harder line with regard to complaints unless they have a clear Community interest.

Unfortunately, none of these procedural changes, valuable though each may be in its own way, could compensate for the fundamental and unavoidable weakness of the notification system operated by DG Comp. This system remained in outline unchanged from its original structure, even though many detailed improvements have been made and internal time-limits adjusted, mainly as a result of the pressures exerted by the Merger Regulation. The fundamental problem was that at any one time there will be a considerable number of notified agreements sitting in files awaiting decision by the Commission, whose status might remain in doubt for some years whilst the parties probably continued to operate them without any certainty as to the outcome of the notification (though doubtless as the decades pass with a greater feeling of freedom). This of course was not necessarily of concern to all companies which have made a notification; some might well prefer not to hear anything from the Commission for a considerable period (if ever) on the assumption that they would receive a 'comfort letter' in due course and in the meantime can enjoy the benefit of freedom from fines on an indefinite basis: they might even prefer this uncertain status to being granted an exemption limited in time, possibly subject to reporting and other conditions. Other notifying companies might feel that if they later require a ruling, formal or informal, they could then apply sufficient pressure to the Commission to ensure a response. The actual number of pending cases at any one time therefore did not represent an equivalent number of dissatisfied companies unable to place reliance on commercial arrangements they have made and notified. Even so, the size of the backlog of pending cases has and remains a problem for both DG Comp and many of its industrial and commercial clients, in particular those who wished to commit themselves to a substantial investment on the assumption that a particular agreement will not be found void under Article 81(2). With so large a backlog, whose number is annually confirmed by the figures of outstanding cases given in the Annual Report, the criteria for priority remained important, but in practice were rarely disclosed. Clearly, however, the strictly chronological order of notification is not always decisive, and agreements have been known to languish without any real attention for several years.[8]

---

[8] The question of delay in the disposal of cases is the subject of Art 5 of the European Convention on Human Rights, referring to the entitlement 'to a fair and public hearing within a reasonable time'. See *Baustahlgewebe* v. *Commission* Case C-185/95P [1998] ECR I-8417: [1999] 4 CMLR 1203.

4.3 THE HANDLING OF COMPLAINTS

Apart from the responsibilities of preparing draft regulations, notices, and explanatory memoranda, examples of which are referred to in Part II above, the workload of DG Comp arises mainly from three sources: notification of agreements, handling complaints, and 'own initiative' investigations. One of its unsolved problems has always been the difficulty in the allocation of resources devoted respectively to complaints and notifications. Although the backlog of notifications has now been substantially reduced from the levels prevalent in earlier years, largely as a result of the wider application of block exemptions, the figures published in recent Annual Reports show that the number of agreements notified but not dealt with is still obstinately and undesirably high. It is likely that some of these agreements date back many years, and may by now have been abandoned by the parties or overtaken by changes in circumstances. Resources should ideally have been concentrated on eliminating or at least substantially reducing this backlog so that the Commission could operate under a predictable time-scale for its remaining and current notifications. Clearly, however, some of the resources that should have been applied in this way have had in the past to be devoted to handling a wide range of complaints that regularly reach DG Comp from all parts of the Community about alleged agreements or practices, or abuses of dominant position, alleged to be in breach of Article 81 or 82.

The original tradition of DG Comp was that all complaints, even the comparatively trivial, were given priority and dealt with as promptly as possible. Against a background of the substantial growth in its jurisdiction and the need to keep the backlog of cases under control, the *Automec (No. 2)*[9] decision brought welcome relief from this burden. The Court laid stress on the importance of the Commission having the ability to set priorities and to use its discretion to decide those cases which were of principal relevance to the Community. The basis for a rejection of any complaint will be, as in the *Automec (No. 2)* case, that the issues are better dealt with by national courts or competition authority applying either Community law or national law principles and rules. This decision enabled the Commission to begin to decentralize the administration of Article 81(1) and to begin encouraging national courts and competition authorities to deal with cases under Articles 81 and 82.

This change was of course assisted by the fact that during the 1980s and 1990s almost all Member States had either created new competition authorities of their own or had strengthened the powers and resources of their existing authorities. In nearly all cases national laws were closely modelled on or (in the case for example of Italy) as exact models of the Community pattern. The chief problem in the decentralization of the work remained: that of the Commission's monopoly under Article 9 of Regulation 17/62 in the application of Article 81(3) to grant individual exemptions. It was therefore with this problem that the White Paper on modernization produced in April 1999[10] mainly dealt. What is clear from the experience of the Commission is that a notification system can only work effectively when the number of notified agreements are relatively few: control procedures of Regulation 17/62 are not workable even in a small country and are totally unworkable in a modern fully developed economy covering fifteen Member States. Therefore it is far better to use the limited resources of the Commission to investigate those agreements which by their nature

---

[9] Case T-24/90 [1992] ECR II-2223: 5 CMLR 431.   [10] [1999] OJ C132/1: 5 CMLR 208.

are unlikely to be notified because of their potential damage to competition, and to leave the examination of all other agreements to national courts and competition authorities.

Paragraph 24 of the 1999 Annual Reports makes the point that the Commission's monopoly on the application of Article 81(3) blocks decentralized application by both courts and competition authorities and leaves the Commission as the sole real guarantor of compliance with the competition rules. This situation is all the more worrying as around half of all cases handled by the Commission start as notifications. However, notifications no longer bring to the Commission's attention the important competition cases: while the Commission is giving its attention to analysing these notified agreements, it is unable to investigate properly the complaints it receives or to conduct the necessary own-initiative proceedings against the most serious infringements. It is therefore primarily a question of resources that has driven the Commission and the Community generally to the adoption of Regulation 1/2003. In the following chapter we look at some of the likely consequences that may flow from that important step.

5. THE COMMISSION AND THE COMMUNITY COURTS

5.1 THE FIRST THIRTY YEARS (1958 TO 1988)

Regardless of the resources made available to DG Comp as a competition authority, its achievements can be assessed in another way. To every institution such as the Commission, opportunities are often presented by a random conjunction of events, quite separate from its own acts or decisions, enabling unexpected progress to be made in the implementation of its policies. These may be described as 'windows of opportunity'. The structure of the Treaty and the organization of the Commission have meant that from time to time such opportunity has arisen, mainly as the result of rulings both by the CFI and by the ECJ. These cases have arisen either as a result of requests for preliminary rulings by national courts under Article 234, or as a result of requests for review by undertakings of the legality of decisions by the Commission, under Article 230. The Chronological Table at the front of this book illustrates that during the early years of the operation of the Treaty cases came only slowly, so that the first decisions of the Commission are not found until 1964 and the first decisions of the Court under Article 230 do not occur until the *Grundig* case in 1966. Looking at the cases decided in the years immediately after 1966, the Commission's preoccupation with vertical relationships (so often the subject of complaint by a distributor or licensee) is noticeable, especially those dealing with exclusive distribution, whilst only a minority of the decisions relate to cartels, trade associations, and other mainly horizontal relationships. This preoccupation with the vertical arose directly from the early policy choice made in the course of negotiations leading up to the adoption of Regulation 17, that the range of vertical agreements for which in practice notification would be needed would be very wide. Had the mesh of the net for notification been less fine, and fewer notifications thus required in the early stages of the Commission's work, more attention could have been paid at that vital time to horizontal agreements, and particularly to cartels allocating national markets. As it was, not until the end of the 1960s did the Commission and the Court get to grips with substantial horizontal cartels of the type found in the *Dyestuffs* and *Sugar* cases, which of course present much greater evidentiary problems.

The assumption has often been made that this policy choice became inevitable as a result of the *Grundig* case, and that the importance attached by the Court to the principle of unity of the market made it inevitable that DG Comp would choose to concentrate first on vertical rather than horizontal relationships. This viewpoint, however, can be challenged since, notwithstanding the importance of the *Grundig* case, the policy choice to concentrate on vertical agreements was made long before the adoption of the *Grundig* decision by the Commission in 1964. The critical policy choice was inherent in the structure of Regulation 17 itself which, coupled with the wide interpretation initially given by the Commission and the Court to Article 81(1), gave only very limited measures relieving agreements from notification.[11] The chief strength of Regulation 17 lay in the powers of investigation and decision which it conferred upon the Commission, and the fact that it gave Member States both an opportunity and an obligation to co-operate in the system without, however, giving them more than an advisory status in the course of the actual decision-making. The Regulation also confirmed the 'prohibition' rather than the 'abuse' theory, a decision that removed any doubts that might have remained about the initial interpretation of Article 81, but which itself contributed substantially to the width of the jurisdiction taken by the Commission. Much of the Regulation, therefore, represented an opportunity at a crucial early time in the development of policy giving DG Comp a strong procedural base for its future activities. However, the weakness of the Regulation was that it encouraged so many notifications of vertical agreements to DG Comp that it was left unbalanced and overburdened in a way that would affect its approach, not for just the rest of that decade, but for the remainder of the twentieth century.

Nevertheless, during its early years the Commission's chief windows of opportunity came undoubtedly from the Court, which went out of its way to emphasize the importance that Articles 81 and 82 played in the overall scheme of the Treaty by giving broad interpretation in a number of leading cases to the essential elements in those Articles. The extent to which the Court had taken trouble to do this has been pointed out by an authoritative source. After stressing that the application of Article 234 always posed particular difficulties for the Court because of the risk that the findings of the national court were wrong or did not arise from the evidence established, or that the questions put to the European Court might have been inadequately phrased, Lord Slynn (then Advocate General and later the United Kingdom Judge) pointed out some years ago that the Court nevertheless had in a number of ways given great assistance to the Commission in its task. It had treated as a priority from the outset the creation of a single market for Member States rather than focusing on issues of efficiency or even of consumer protection. To quote his words:

It is wholly consistent with this approach that the Court took a broad view of what constitutes a concerted practice . . . that it should treat as part of contractual arrangements what on the face of it could appear to be background or contextual material . . . that it should see one individual contract as part of a network rather than in isolation . . . that it should construe 'undertaking' broadly, 'relevant market' narrowly, often by reference to the nature of the product, of the end uses, or in relation to intraband rather than broader market considerations, that it should accept a narrow geographical base such as that of one or several Member States rather than by taking a broader

[11] Reg. 17, Art. 4(2).

region as the area appropriate for the relevant market; that it should define abuse in terms of its effect on competition rather than by balancing whether the allegedly abusive conduct might contribute to economic efficiency.[12]

The Court also made it clear that it would not intervene on applicants' behalf in the course of Commission investigations unless there were cogent grounds for doing so, nor would it annul Commission decisions on procedural grounds unless there was either a cardinal flaw in the process or a total inadequacy of economic analysis.

One must give credit to DG Comp for taking full advantage in the early years at least of the support which it received from the Court. As can be seen by a study of its individual decisions year by year, it fully utilized the width of interpretation accorded by the Court to the principal elements of Articles 81 and 82. It did not find itself handicapped, as have some national courts, by technical or narrow interpretation of its jurisdiction and powers. Moreover, the Commission did its best to pay attention not only to the words of the Court's decision but also to the rather broader 'signals' which the Court had apparently been trying to send to it as to the general conduct of its cases, *Continental Can* being a good example of a warning in that period that superficial analysis would not be tolerated even if the decision appeared on the facts to be (from the Commission's viewpoint) an obvious one.

5.2 THE PERIOD FROM 1989 ONWARDS

A new relationship however between the Community Courts and the Commission began in 1989. It had been clear for some time before that date that the ECJ was not an appropriate forum for the detailed review of Commission competition decisions, when appeals were brought by undertakings which had been subject to adverse decisions and often fines in addition. Although the jurisdiction of the CFI was not of course limited to competition cases except in its initial first four years, the majority of the Commission decisions against which an appeal was brought to it did involve alleged breaches of Articles 81 and 82. Inevitably the decisions of the Commission themselves were lengthy and involved much detailed factual as well as legal analysis. The many other pressures on the ECJ with its responsibility for not only dealing with disputes between Member States and between Community institutions, and other important constitutional issues arising under the Treaty itself through the mechanism of Article 234, meant that painstaking analysis of the facts of an alleged cartel or the abuse of dominant position imposed unreasonable burdens upon it. What was needed was a rather less formal tribunal sitting in Chambers of not less than three or more than five members, able to involve itself closely in the often intricate details of the Commission's decision. Given the Commission's combined role as prosecutor, judge, and jury in competition cases,[13] it was clearly vital that confidence in the whole process be maintained by the availability of a thorough appellate forum, dealing with the detailed case as one of its essential responsibilities rather than as one of many equally important duties.

---

[12] In an address 'EEC Competition Law from the Perspective of the Court of Justice', *Twelfth Annual Proceedings of Fordham Corporate Law Institute* 383 (1985).

[13] For the purposes of Art 6 of the European Convention of Human Rights the ECJ has held that the Commission itself is not a 'tribunal' (*Van Landewijck* v. *Commission* Cases C-209 to 215, 218/78 [1980] ECR 3125: [1981] 3 CMLR 134; but the fundamental rights of the parties to a Commission decision are preserved by the availability of an appeal to the CFI. See K. Lenaerts and I. Maselis, *Procedural Rights and Issues in the Enforcement of Arts. 81 and 82.* (2000 Fordham Corporate Law Institute), pp.279–363.

Since that date the work of the CFI has not disappointed the hopes of those responsible for its establishment.[14] It has produced a number of notable judgments in competition cases, a large number of which, especially in cartel cases, have substantially upheld the decision of the Commission, even if on a number of occasions also fines have been marginally reduced, mainly on procedural grounds. There have also been some sharp defeats for the Commission where the CFI has not been afraid of expressing its disapproval of the procedures or findings of the Commission in language that is never less than precise and occasionally even savage.

Dealing first with appeals against decisions under Articles 81 and 82, amongst the numerous cases heard, there has been a reasonable number of successful appeals, often on procedural grounds including the well known *PVC, Solvay, SNCF, UIC*, and *Florimex*;[15] more recently in *European Night Services*[16] the Court's decision was notable for its critique of a Commission finding that a joint venture set up to run night services through the European Tunnel by four national railway undertakings with less than 10 per cent of the relevant market share for transport services had a restrictive effect on competition within the Common Market. Another notable judgment overruling the Commission was *Bayer/Adalat* (discussed at Chapter 6, pp.70–1) in which it refused to apply the concept of 'agreement' to the unilateral refusal of supplies by Bayer to its wholesale distributors in France and Spain because of their practice of sending some of these supplies by way of parallel exports into higher price countries such as the United Kingdom. In the *Italian Flat Glass* case the court was also critical of some of the evidence relied upon by the Commission by its attempt to 'recycle' Article 81 evidence in order to utilize it under Article 82 as well. On the other hand it has broadly been supportive of the Commission's approach to, and decisions in, some complex and controversial Article 82 cases such as *Tetrapak (No. 2), Magill, CMB*, and *TACA*.

The CFI also has of course to deal with merger appeals against the Commission's decisions under the Merger Regulation which came into force shortly after the formation of the Court itself. As we have seen in Chapter 18, pp.391–3, the delay inherent in the normal appeal procedure for such cases meant originally that it was rarely worthwhile for dissatisfied undertakings to raise an appeal against a substantive finding of the Commission which had blocked or imposed onerous conditions on a proposed merger. Nevertheless on occasions, when a point of principle has been felt at stake some appeals have been brought. The case of *Gencor*, for example, laid down important principles on the definition of collective dominance under the regulation and on issues of extraterritoriality. Most influential however in recent years was the 2002 judgment in *Airtours*, where the Commission's blocking decision on a proposed merger in the UK foreign package holiday market was held unjustified because of undue reliance on the collective dominance theory, against a background of evidence which in the opinion of the CFI fell far short of proving that such a state of affairs existed. Moreover the language used by the CFI could only be described as severe.

---

14 Johnston A., *Judicial Reform and the Treaty of Nice* [2001] 38 CML *Rev* 499, 503.

15 *PVC* Cases 79, 84–86, 89, 91–92, 94, 96, 98, 102,104/89 [1992] ECR II-315: 4 CMLR 357. *Solvay* Cases T-30–32/91 [1995] ECR II-1775, 1821,1825: [1996] 5 CMLR 91. *SNCF* Cases T-79–80/95 [1996] ECR II-1491: 4 CMLR 334. *UIC* Case T-14/93 [1995] ECR II-1503: [1996] 5 CMLR 40. Upheld on appeal by the *ECJ* Case C 264/95P [1997] 5 CMLR 49. *Florimex* Case T-70–71/92 [1997] 5 CMLR 769. *BEUC* Case T-37/92 [1994] ECR II-285: [1995] 4 CMLR 167.

16 See Ch. 7, p.90.

This particular case had taken nearly three years from the date of the original Commission decision to the date of the CFI judgment. The arrival however of an expedited appeal procedure for cases which did not raise highly complex factual issues meant that three months later, two further cases under this new procedure were handed down, namely the *Schneider/LeGrand* and *Tetra/Laval/Sidel*. The *Schneider* decision in particular had some common features with that of *Airtours* in that the fact finding processes of the Commission were severely criticized, whereas the *Tetra/Laval* case turned more on the question of burden of proof in a case where the adverse finding was principally based on the theory of economic leverage by a dominant company from one market to another. Nevertheless the combined effect of these three judgments (delivered in a space of just over four months) on the morale of the Commission and its Merger Task Force in particular was potent and led directly to the revised proposals made in December 2002 for changes to the Merger Regulation (see Chapter 18, section 7).

The relationship between the ECJ and the Commission is primarily felt in two ways. The first is in the treatment by the ECJ of appeals from the CFI which are of course limited on points of law in competition cases. In this respect the ECJ has in most cases upheld the CFI's judgment on issues of principle, even if on occasion it has placed a different emphasis when making its own findings.[17] The second relationship is the result of Article 234 cases, where one could name by way of example the *Bronner* and *Masterfoods* cases as laying down legal principles providing important assistance to the Commission. In the first case the outcome was a clear signal as to the limits of the doctrine of essential facilities which some commentators had thought had been extended too far in certain earlier Commission decisions. In the second case the Court confirmed the obligation of courts in Member States to suspend proceedings whilst the Commission was itself dealing with the same issue and even while further appeals from its rulings were still possible to Community courts. Moreover, in the context of the Merger Regulation an appeal from a Commission decision unusually was heard directly by the ECJ in *Kali und Salz* as the result of the involvement of France in the case. Here it laid down the important principle that Article 2 of the Merger Regulation did permit the Commission to take into account issues of collective dominance, even though on the facts of the particular case the Commission's conditions imposed on the merger were annulled.

6. THE ACHIEVEMENTS AND FAILURES OF THE COMMISSION: AN ASSESSMENT

6.1 THE RELEVANT BACKGROUND

In this final section we seek to draw up a balance sheet for the Commission, which recognizes both its achievements and its failures. Taking first its achievements, the starting point must be the willingness of the Commission to adapt over the last forty-five years to the changing demands made upon it. The political and economic circumstances in which it operates have changed substantially over this period. The pace of change in recent years has been particularly marked as the nature of the world of business and industry has

---

[17] K. Lenaerts, 'The European Court of First Instance: Ten Years of Interaction with the Court of Justice', in *Liber Amicorum in honour of Lord Slynn: Judicial Review in European Union Law*, (Kluwer 2000), pp.97–116.

altered, under the combined force of globalization and the computer and communications technological revolutions. Pressures on senior officials of DG Comp have increased markedly, both in terms of the time-scale within which decisions, both formal and informal, are expected, and because of the controversial and complex nature of cases before them, particularly those arising under the Merger Regulation. The political drive towards enlargement, which is to culminate in the admission of up to ten new Member States in 2004, has itself increased the pressures on the Commission to find urgently legislative and administrative solutions to enable it to handle adequately the many areas for which it is responsible.

A continuing challenge therefore for the Commission has been to adapt itself to new circumstances, both economic and political, prevailing not only in the Community itself but in the world generally. It may not always have reacted as quickly as its critics would have urged, but it has so far nevertheless shown impressive ability to find solutions to existing problems. Going back to the 1970s, its ability to adapt was shown in its handling of crisis cartels in a number of industries. It showed itself sensitive to the problems of particular sectors and undertakings at a time of economic difficulty following the rise in oil prices: cases such as *Synthetic Fibres*, *URG/KEWA*, and *International Energy Authority*[18] illustrate this flexibility. As we have already noted, its realization that its approach to block exemptions in the 1980s and early 1990s had become too legalistic and negative, when a more liberal and 'effects based' style both of economic analysis and of drafting was more appropriate, led to a marked simplification of the block exemption on vertical restraints in Regulation 2790/99. This trend was enhanced by the introduction of Regulation 1216/99 making retrospective notification possible for vertical agreements.

But of course in drawing up such a balance sheet it is important to remember that it is not only DG Comp itself or even the Commission as a whole that can claim the entire credit (or blame) for achievements or failures. On occasion it is the Council that has played a decisive influence by enacting appropriate legislation to confer additional powers on the Commission when it has received cogent argument that such new powers were required, for example with regard to Regulation 1216/99. On other occasions it is the outcome of Article 234 decisions of the ECJ in cases such as *Masterfoods* or *Crehan* v. *Courage* which have clarified uncertainties or provided a powerful signal to the Commission as to the way in which legal developments should be driven. On the other hand let us give credit to the Commission for having on occasion itself provided the initiative and fresh thinking which has been a decisive factor in advances in policy or increased effectiveness of administration. In some cases it has clearly benefited from the experience of, and co-operation given by competition officials, in the USA and other nations, especially in the handling of cartels and of mergers, where jurisdictions have had a mutual interest in close coordination.

6.2 THE COMMISSION'S GREATER TRANSPARENCY

The first achievement that should be mentioned is the creation of a far greater measure of transparency for the work of DG Comp as a whole. It introduced in 1994 an EC

---

[18] *Synthetic Fibres* [1985] 1 CMLR 787; *KEWA* [1976] 2 CMLR D15; *URG* [1976] 2 CMLR D1; *International Energy Authority* [1984] 2 CMLR 186.

competition policy newsletter published three times a year giving details of recent decisions and policy articles by officials. It has also published a number of guidelines to block exemption regulations and useful guides to procedure. It now also makes full use of modern technology: from the middle of 1996 it has had its own Internet page on the World Wide Web. This contains information on the main aspects of competition policy, including mergers, and a full set of press releases, the full text of current legislative provisions, and of relevant Commission decisions. A full list of comfort letters is provided (though not the individual text) and up to date statistics on merger cases given. Separate sections set out speeches given and articles published by the Competition Commissioner or by the Director-General of DG Comp. Given the large amount of current information often required by those involved in competition cases, this development is a great advance though it would be undesirable if relevant information ceased to be available from the Commission in traditional printed form and could only be found on the Internet.

6.3 THE ACHIEVEMENTS OF THE COMMISSION

Turning to substantive issues the following events and developments seem worthy of mention:

6.3.1 The Switch of Focus away from Vertical Agreements

After primary emphasis had been placed in the early years on the regulation of vertical agreements, both through individual decisions and early block exemptions, the gradual development of the Single Market and the implementation of block exemptions covering a wider range of agreements of a vertical nature made it possible in the late nineties for some resources to be switched, making a more effective challenge to major cartels affecting a number of Member States, of the kind which in the past had not previously been challenged at all or only over a very lengthy period owing to lack of resources.

6.3.2 Cartels

The likelihood of such cartels being discovered has been increased as a result of the implementation first of the original, and now the revised, Leniency Programme, which provides a real incentive for participants to approach the Commission to give them sufficient information enabling it either to carry out an investigation under Article 14(3) of Regulation 17/62, or to find an infringement of Article 81(1) (see Chapter 9, pp.147–9).

Experience in earlier cases had shown the great evidential problem in such cases where there is no 'insider' to provide key information about the workings of a cartel, so that the prosecution can only proceed on the basis of piecing together fragments of documentary information from a number of different sources. Hence, the Leniency Programme is probably the most important factor in enabling the recent remarkable growth in the number of successfully prosecuted cases and the increase in the number of fines, which in 2002 reached nearly one billion euros, a fact proudly commented on by Commissioner Monti at the end of that year, a year which in other respects, (particularly in regard to the Merger Regulation) had been particularly difficult for him personally and the Commission.

6.3.3 Application of Competition Rules to New Sectors

The Commission has been able to apply Article 81(1) and (3) to a large variety of new sectors including the media, communications, sport, and transport as well as to the more traditional range of goods and services with which it had been concerned in its earlier decades. It has not been afraid to apply Article 81(3) to situations even where some novel factors have been brought into account, such as environmental gains, and even where the parties were required to accept considerable restrictions on their freedom, for example, the phasing out of production of certain less efficient models of household goods, such as washing machines and refrigerators, on an industry-wide basis.[19] The Commission has provided extensive published guidelines explaining its underlying reasoning relating both to vertical and horizontal block exemptions, which are of value not only to the parties but also to Commission officials who have to deal with them.

6.3.4 Essential Facilities

It has been able to establish the concept of essential facilities firmly in the jurisprudence of Article 82, applying it in a wide range of situations including harbours, airports, bank payment systems, and computer reservation systems. Notwithstanding the firm signal given by the ECJ in *Bronner*, and the later setback which it received in the 'interim measures' appeals in *IMS* at a later date, it has been able to utilize the concept in a wide variety of situations where dominant companies might otherwise have been able to foreclose access to competitors. This has been particularly valuable in the telecommunications sector, where by both Directives and Decisions under Article 86(3) it has established strong criteria for national competition authorities in terms of the basis for competition in that sector between incumbents and new entrants.

6.3.5 Bilateral and Multilateral Co-operation Agreements

It has created strong bilateral co-operation agreements covering both traditional and positive comity, not only with the USA but with Japan, Canada, Australia, and other important antitrust jurisdictions. This has both provided a good deal of information of value in particular cases, for example, cartels where proceedings had already taken place in the USA and large fines imposed so that Community proceedings could subsequently follow aided by those earlier proceedings; but this also gave valuable psychological support to the Commission, supplementing the work of existing multinational organizations such as OECD and the newly formed organization for co-operation between national competition agencies, the International Competition Network (ICN). (See Chapter 23, pp.504–11).

6.3.6 The Merger Regulation

Under the Merger Regulation the Commission has created an efficient system for handling more than 300 concentrations of Community Dimension each year, which has provided both a firm timetable allowing even the most complex cases to be resolved in less than five months while enabling the clearance of the remaining 95 per cent through shorter and more simplified procedures, even if in some cases a limited range of conditions had to be applied. Because of its widely drawn turnover-based jurisdictional range, the Commission has in

---

[19] CECED [2000] OJ L187/47: 5 CMLR 635. For a fuller exposition of this aspect of the Commission's approach to Art. 81(3), see R. Whish, *Competition Law*, 4th edn. (Butterworth 2001), pp.126–7.

effect become a 'world competition authority', at least in respect of all major companies which do substantial business in the EC as well as elsewhere. Its achievements in this respect remain, notwithstanding the problems that have arisen both with regard to its procedures and its substantive criteria for assessment, which will inevitably lead to major changes in the Regulation, as discussed later in this chapter and in Chapter 25.

6.4 THE FAILURES OF THE COMMISSION

It would however be misleading not also to enumerate alongside these important achievements the areas where success has been partial, elusive or even sometimes totally absent.

6.4.1 The Notification System for Article 81 Under Regulation 17/62

The situation in which the original system of agreements restricting competition was introduced is now so unfamiliar to us, as we look back over more than four decades to its start, that it is important to remember why it was adopted. As explained in Chapter 4, the way in which Article 81 should at its outset be interpreted and applied was far from clear. Many forms of cartel had been regularly entered into by European businessmen prior to the Treaty of Rome without any realization that they were of damaging economic effect; on the contrary their impact on employment and levels of demand for goods and services were often genuinely, if incorrectly, believed to be stabilizing. The Commission could not therefore risk allowing decisions on the application of Article 81(1) and 81(3) to be left to national courts or authorities where these existed. The monopoly over the granting of individual notification enabled by Regulation 17/62 Article 9(3) was the natural method of maintaining the necessary degree of control for the Commission at this critical early stage.

The notification system adopted, neither wholly compulsory nor totally voluntary, had nevertheless some advantages in its initial stage.[20] The absence of time limits meant that the Commission could investigate at its own speed those agreements which were notified to it, and accord priority to those that seemed most relevant. The granting of an individual exemption could be retrospective to the time of notification, and the parties to it would be free from risk of fine, unless a Regulation 17/62, Article 15(6) Notice had been issued, which was rare. Case experience could thus gradually be gathered by officials which would in time entitle them to claim authority from the Council for the preparation and promulgation of the first block exemption.

A solution suitable therefore for the 1960s and 1970s turned out, nevertheless, to be unworkable and ineffective for the far more complex and demanding conditions of the final decades of the twentieth century. The Commission found itself, for both administrative and linguistic reasons, unable to issue more than a few formal decisions under Article 81(3). Although the actual number of such decisions, as recorded by Annual Reports eventually rose from single figures in each year to as many as forty-two in 1998 and sixty-eight in 1999, this still represented less than ten per cent of the total number of cases dealt with in each year. Moreover, each formal decision was itself taking an unreasonably long time to be issued; for example the *1998 Annual Report*[21] records that of the eleven formal decisions

---

[20] W. Wils, 'Notification, Clearance and Exemption in EC Competition Law' (1999) 24 EurLR 139–156.
[21] p.28.

issued in that year the shortest duration was over two years, the longest eight years and the average four years and ten months.

In the vast majority of cases, therefore, parties notified agreements but had to be satisfied with a solution not even referred to in the Regulation, that of the 'comfort letter'. The effect of such an administrative letter from the Commission was simply that, on the information supplied to the Commission, it was prepared to confirm either that Article 81(1) did not apply or that the four conditions of Article 81(3) were satisfied. John Temple Lang, a former Commission official with long experience of its operations, records that the 'comfort letter' procedure, for all its legal shortcomings, 'worked satisfactorily and gave rise to almost no litigation'.[22] Nevertheless the lack of legal certainty and absence of time limits on the Commission for issuing either a formal or an informal ruling led to wide and justifiable criticism. The introduction of Regulations 1215 and 1216/99 which came into force in June 1999 and permitted retrospective exemption for all vertical agreements, as a result of the considerable widening of the terms of Article 4(2) in Regulation 17/62, did ease the position. With hindsight this can be seen to have been an important part of the new approach to be set out shortly afterwards in the modernization White Paper of April in that year. This at last called for the removal of the Commission's monopoly under Article 81(3) in individual cases and of the notification system as a whole. The likely advantages and problems which this new system will bring from 2004 are discussed in the next chapter.

6.4.2 The Treatment of Vertical Agreements

The priority given by the Commission in its early years to distribution systems, which were the subject of the earliest case-law of the European Court and of the first block exemptions is important. After the original attempt to cover both exclusive distribution arrangements and exclusive purchase arrangements by a single block exemption (67/67) the subsequent block exemptions in 1983 were separately drawn for each type of agreement. That for exclusive purchase agreements (1984/83) itself included special rules for both beer and petrol sectors. All these regulations however relied not only on a list of 'black' prohibited clauses, but set out a lengthy list of other restrictions regarded as less significant on a permitted 'white' list, rather than allowing all such clauses to be permitted within the scope of the block exemption other than one of the 'black' listed clauses. This more liberal solution had to wait until Regulation 2790/99 which eliminated not only the 'white' list and sectoral provisions for beer and petrol, but consolidated the previous block exemptions not only for exclusive distribution agreements and exclusive purchasing agreements, but also for franchise agreements previously covered by Regulation 4087/88. Extensive guidelines were also produced for the application of block exemptions which left nevertheless a number of unanswered questions, especially on the precise status of agency agreements and franchise agreements. Regulation 2790/99 also covered the separate category of selective distribution agreements where considerable confusion had previously arisen about the criteria for distinguishing between those agreements that fell outside Article 81(1) altogether and those which fell within it, but might be capable of exemption under Article 81(3) on an individual basis.

The problem of framing an appropriate block exemption for vehicle distribution has

---

[22] J. T. Lang, 'Legal Certainty and Legitimate Expectations as General Principles of Law', in U. Bernitz and J. Nergelius (eds), *General Principles of European Commercial Law* (Kluwer, 2000), pp.163–84 at p.175.

remained a concern for the Commission. Although the current Block Exemption 1400/2002, the third to be adopted, is the one which grants the greatest degree of commercial freedom to dealers and imposes the most restrictions on vehicle manufacturers, nevertheless even this seems unlikely to solve the fundamental problem of imbalance of bargaining position between suppliers and dealers. The creation of a workable single Community market for cars, where consumers have a genuine range of choice for the purchase of different models from manufacturers in different Member States, still seems far off, even though a number of new provisions in the current Regulation provide a greater range of freedom for dealers. Major car manufacturers have long treated their dealers, not as true distributors with freedom of operation in the conduct of their own business, but as quasi-agents with only a limited range of freedom and the likelihood of sanctions if they are too active in extending sales beyond their primary territory in their home State. It may be too early to forecast the failure of Regulation 1400/2002 in this respect but it certainly cannot yet be ranked as one of the achievements of the Commission.

6.4.3 Supply Quotas

Unless the European Court of Justice overturns the decision of the CFI in *Bayer/Adalat*, the Commission will find itself in difficulties in applying Article 81 to the difficult situation of pharmaceutical companies, who seek to distribute their products throughout the Community but find that the lack of price harmonization between different Member States creates a problem: it has led to wide differences of price imposed by national governments, which in turn has led to widespread parallel importing from 'low price' to 'high price' countries. The response by Bayer and other pharmaceutical manufacturers has been essentially unilateral, and there are problems, as the CFI indicated, in seeking to characterize it as a form of implied agreement or consensus with its wholesalers, who have at no time expressed consent to the limitation of supplies which the manufacturers would like to impose upon them, even though there were in *Bayer/Adalat* similar factors to the earlier cases of *Ford* and *Sandoz*, where an agreement was implied because of the underlying basis of the distribution agreement. If the Commission is to make progress in the area it may be only through the invocation of Article 82. Even this may only be possible where the supplier has a particularly strong position in a national market with regard to the individual drug supplied, and on the basis of a redefinition of relevant and narrower product markets.

6.4.4 Article 82

The case law of both Commission and Court in this area is extensive, but nevertheless there is still an unsatisfactory lack of clarity about the key concepts of dominance and abuse. As indicated in Chapter 14, the definition of dominance is one often difficult to apply to the fact of particular markets. The law appears moreover to have moved from a situation where an undertaking either is or is not dominant, taking market share and all other circumstances into account, to one where it may fall either into a category of dominance or of 'super dominance'. In the latter case its obligations not to engage in one of a number of particular practices may depend upon the actual market share which it holds and its relationship to the other members of that market, calculated on what appears to be almost a 'sliding scale'. It appears that the law has moved on quite a long way from the simple rule contained in the *ECS/AKZO* case where the possession of a regular market share of 50 per cent or more was deemed to constitute a presumption of dominance.

Whilst the Commission has been able to bring a number of successful cases in this area, and has generally received broad support from the Community Courts when appeals have been heard, and while the different categories of abuse have grown impressively (as the length of Chapter 15 indicates), nevertheless there remains a broad suspicion that, particularly in cases concerned with pricing, the Commission's analysis of what constitutes abuse is unduly restrictive on dominant undertakings.

Whilst the Commission has not (contrary to fears originally expressed) taken the outcome of the *Magill* decision of the ECJ as a basis for seeking compulsory licensing in a wide variety of situations, it does appear from the outcome of the later interim measure cases in *IMS* that its assessment of *Magill* may nevertheless be broader than that of the ECJ and CFI. It must be acknowledged however that the *IMS* case itself does raise particular difficulties, because of the degree to which the intellectual property rights concerned in the '1860 brick structure' represents the respective contribution of IMS on the one hand and the pharmaceutical industry on the other to its development.

6.4.5 European Community Merger Regulation

As already mentioned, the summer and autumn of 2002 proved painful for the Commission and in particular its officials engaged in the Merger Task Force. For nearly twelve years the application of the Regulation had been regarded as the Commission's greatest success. It had managed to combine the effective administrative handling of the 95 per cent of concentrations that had a Community dimension but could be disposed of relatively simply under the first phase procedure, with the detailed analysis of the remaining five per cent of those cases which raised a real likelihood of creating or strengthening a dominant position, as a result of which effective competition would be significantly impeded. The Merger Task Force had apparently been able, admittedly only through massive efforts, to cope over the nineties with handling an increase from sixty cases in the first year to well over 300 by the end of the century. This total included a number of complex mergers and joint ventures in major sectors such as oil, chemicals, telecoms, finance, and aeronautics. The Commission had only blocked twenty cases over this period, these being the rare group of cases where no remedies of a satisfactory nature could be suggested by the parties that would effectively eliminate the damage to competition that the merger would cause in relevant markets. In many others structural or behavioural conditions, often of a complex nature, had been agreed as conditions for approval. While the application of the rules in certain mergers between major US companies had provoked some controversy and an 'agreement to disagree' over the assessment of the case, overall relationships with the US antitrust authorities continued to be close and co-operation working well on a day-to-day basis. The tone of the tenth anniversary conference held in Brussels in September 2001, if not exactly triumphalist, at least was one of satisfaction at real achievement. Collective dominance had been upheld as a principle applicable to merger cases in *Kali und Salz* and *Gencor* (even if on the facts the Commission had been overruled by the ECJ in the first case) and it was clear that this doctrine would continue to play an important part in future cases. But the Commission was certainly not complacent and in its December 2001 Green Paper had put forward a number of suggestions of further improvements to the operation of the Regulation.

All this was changed however by the publication in June 2002 of the *Airtours* decision by the CFI, followed in late October of that year by the decisions of *Schneider* and *Tetra/Laval/Sidel*. Three blocking decisions were annulled in language highly critical of the

Commission's economic analysis, fact-finding competence, and application of economic theories. Since the decisions are often treated collectively as a wholesale assault on the previously high reputation of the Commission for application of the Merger Regulation, it is important to distinguish between the separate grounds in each case for the annulment of the original decision.

In *Airtours*, the blocking decision had been based on a finding that the UK short-haul foreign package holiday market would, as a result of the proposed merger, create a market collectively dominated by three major undertakings, leading to a reduction in the availability of holidays and an increase in their price. The CFI found that the Commission's analysis was inadequate in a number of respects namely that:

— it failed to provide adequate evidence to support a finding that there was an existing tendency in the sector to collective dominance;

— it did not take account of current and past volatility in the market;

— it underestimated the foreseeable reaction of smaller tour operators, consumers, and hotel operators to any coordination between the three major players; and

— it relied, in some cases, on documentary evidence which had been misinterpreted and misapplied.

In *Schneider*, the two main criticisms related to :

— with regard to the French market (where dominance and effect on competition was clearly established) the Statement of Objections had failed to set out fully the case against the merger, which had only been explained in the decision itself, so that the defendants had not been allowed an adequate opportunity of making their case; and

— in regard to the other national markets, the Commission had failed to do a full analysis of their individual state and the relevant strength of the parties within it.

In *Tetra/Laval/Sidel*, the Commission had relied on a theory of 'leverage', arguing that Tetra's admitted dominance in its main markets (aseptic carton packaging equipment) would allow it to offer juice and milk packagers special terms if they were to agree to purchase their stretched blow moulding machines required for the making of PET bottles from the target company, Sidel, thereby shifting demand away from Sidel's competitors. The court found that the evidence for this was weak and insufficient to justify a blocking decision. In this case, though not in the other two, the Commission has appealed to the ECJ, arguing that the level of the burden of proof imposed on the Commission was too high. In the following chapter the Commission's response to the outcome of these cases will be discussed.

25

THE FUTURE OF EUROPEAN COMPETITION LAW

1. INTRODUCTION

1.1 REFORMS SUGGESTED IN THE THIRD EDITION

All the previous chapters of this edition have dealt with the past development of the competition policy of the Community and with the variety of economic and legal issues with which it has had to contend. These include both procedural and substantive questions, some of long standing and some relatively new on the scene. In this final chapter it is time to anticipate the future progress of competition law and competition policy in Europe, and to seek to identify those current problems for which effective solutions will be required in the next few years.

At this point it is also salutary for the author to look back at the equivalent chapter[1] which closed the previous edition, in order to see whether his analysis five years ago of some of the reforming steps which the Commission and Council might take have actually come to pass. The main reforms identified as necessary in 1998 can be listed as follows:

(i) the clarification of the substantive rules, by publication of more Notices and Guidelines, in support of Regulations conferring block exemptions under Article 81(3), and the prompt withdrawal of the existing Notices when they no longer reflected the current thinking of the Commission or the content of Court decisions;

(ii) a more limited interpretation of the scope of Article 81(1), perhaps by the more liberal application of the 'rule of reason', which could lead to a reduction in the number of cases regarded as having sufficient 'Community interest' so as to require the attention of DG Comp, and thus allowing a greater number to be handled by Member States through their national competition authorities, especially when that authority had received under national law the power to apply Articles 81 and 82;

(iii) the introduction of reasonable time limits for the issue by the Commission of a preliminary assessment of the merits or demerits of all notified agreements, with a view to expediting the notification process generally and reducing the existing backlog of cases;

(iv) a greater selectivity in the choice of cases dealt with by DG Comp, in particular those relating to vertical agreements;

---

[1] Ch. 26, pp.587–604.

(v) the provision of greater assistance to national courts in handling issues arising in disputed cases, particularly when the issue of whether an individual exemption could be granted under Article 81(3) had arisen;

(vi) the need to improve the transparency of procedures and processes generally under the Merger Regulation;

(vii) the continued application of competition law principles not only to undertakings but to Member States under the provisions of Article 10 and Article 86, especially in the context of national price fixing and other sectoral legislation which might interfere with the operation of competition, in particular by discrimination in favour of national undertakings;

(viii) a campaign to bring national competition laws of Member States more into line with those of the Community and to persuade those remaining Member States without powers under domestic law to enforce Articles 81 and 82 to introduce them;

(ix) the maintenance of close working relationships with other Community institutions, in particular the European Parliament and the Economic and Social Committee;

(x) the encouragement of an exchange of staff on a reciprocal basis in order to bring national experts to Brussels from national competition authorities and vice versa, and also the introduction of short exchanges between senior officials in DG Comp and those in responsible positions in industry and commerce; and

(xi) finally, and more ambitiously, the adoption by the Commission of a radical policy of decentralization under which Member States through their national competition authorities would receive authority to deal not only with mergers that did not have a Community dimension, but also with cases under Articles 81 and 82. This should include those where individual exemption was claimed under Article 81(3); here a ruling could be given by a national competition authority if it arose in a case arising before a national court, rather than having the case suspended for a long period while the issue had to be resolved in Brussels by DG Comp.

1.2 THE PROGRESS OF REFORM SINCE 1998

Looking back at this 'menu for change' it is good to record that in many, if not all, respects there has been substantial movement in the same direction as that of these rather optimistic suggestions. Moreover, as the list of achievements at the end of the previous chapter indicates, some important and welcome reforms have indeed taken place that were not included in that list. For example the new approach to the treatment of vertical agreements under Article 81(3) through the revised form of block exemptions starting with 2790/99 has not only introduced a greater degree of legal certainty for undertakings making such distribution arrangements, but has also considerably reduced the number of occasions on which DG Comp has had to be consulted on questions arising in this area. It has not only been the improved clarification of the substantive content of the block exemptions but also their clarity of drafting which has been such a welcome improvement.[2]

---

[2] H. Xanthak, *The Problem of Quality in EU Legislation: What on Earth is Really Wrong?* [2001] 38 CMLR 651–676.

The fact is that the current state of European Competition policy and the approach of DG Comp and the Commission generally towards their responsibilities in this area have changed out of all recognition over the last five years. We are now facing the prospect with effect from May 2004 of three simultaneous changes of major significance which will in due course necessarily alter the shape and effectiveness of the competition policy of the Community in an irrevocable and fundamental manner. In this sense therefore the situation now is completely different from that of five years ago. These major changes have all been referred to in various chapters in Part II but it may be appropriate to recall them at this point:

— the implementation of Regulation 1/2003, replacing Regulation 17/62, as the principal basis for the modernization programme under which the administration of Articles 81 and 82 is being decentralized and in large measure entrusted to national competition authorities and national courts, by the introduction of the principle of 'exception légale' and the removal of the Commission's monopoly of granting individual exemption;

— the introduction of a new revised Merger Regulation containing many important changes in both substance and procedure, and designed to respond to the critics of the Commission's procedures found in particular in the CFI judgments in *Airtours* and *Schneider LeGrand*;

— the enlargement of the Community by the accession of up to ten new Member States, mainly from Eastern Europe.

The remainder of this chapter will therefore deal with likely future developments in European competition law and the implementation of the new system by DG Comp and national competition authorities and national courts, in addition to the other Community institutions. We will consider in order the impact of modernization programmes (Section 2), the future of the Merger Regulation (Section 3), and finally in (Section 4) a number of other new elements that will play an important part in determining the direction of future policy.

2. THE IMPACT OF THE MODERNIZATION PROGRAMME

2.1 THE COMMISSION AS GUARDIAN OF THE TREATY

The starting point in the analysis of this programme has to be the role of the Commission in general and of DG Comp in particular, as the familiar structure of Regulation 17/62 passes into history to be replaced at 1 May 2004 by the new rules and unpredictable consequences of Regulation 1/2003. It is a change to be welcomed and is timely. As a former Head of the Commission's Legal Service has said[3] 'For the Community to have started with the authorization system and to evolve towards a legal exception system would be a natural and historically justified crescendo'. This process will have taken nearly half a century; during this time

---

[3] Giuliano Marenco, 'The Modernization of EC Antitrust Policy', in *European Competition Law Annual 2000*, C.-D. Ehlermann and I. Anastasiu (eds) (Hart Publishing, 2001), p.175. This volume is essential reading for all those interested in the modernization programme of the Commission.

considerable experience has been gathered within the Community how competition policy can be framed, consulted over, and finally put into effect, as a co-operative process between all of the many interested parties, including not only the Commission and its many Directorates General, responsible for different areas of its work, but also the Council and other Community institutions, Member States, and their own competition authorities.

It is however essential, if the new system is to work effectively, that the Commission remains in control at the centre able to initiate both policy consultation and policy implementation. The Treaty of Rome gives to the Commission alone this key right to initiate proposals for legislation; its responsibilities often involve it in mediating between the varying and sometimes conflicting aims of Member States relating to the adoption of these proposals, and finally implementing them alongside existing competition policies of the Community. By contrast the role of the European Parliament is generally to receive and consider proposals sent initially by the Commission to the Council and then passed on by the Council for consideration. In the context moreover of Article 83 of the Treaty the appropriate regulations needed from time to time to give effect to the principles of Articles 81 and 82 are first proposed by the Commission itself and then finally enacted by the Council after consulting the European Parliament. The Commission, which under the terms of Article 211 of the Treaty is responsible, *inter alia*, for exercising the powers conferred on it by the Council for the implementation of Regulations enacted by the Council. It is thus charged with acting in the interests of the Community *as a whole*; its members are to be 'completely independent' in the performance of their duties taking instructions neither from any Member State, government, or any other body.[4]

These principles are fundamental to the proper working of the Community, but in recent years suggestions have been made on occasion that the European Parliament should be given a more proactive role and even a veto on Commission proposals for regulation in the area of competition policy. Such suggestions have been made in the current course of negotiations on the terms of the European Convention. If this were to occur, there is a real risk that short-term political or even nationalistic motives might lead to the European Parliament seeking to interfere in the making of competition policy, including State aid issues, in a way that has never been possible in the past and which would, if introduced, substantially damage the ability of the Commission to implement policy in the interests of the Community as a whole, in the new environment of Regulation 1/2003.

The Joint Statement[5] published by the Council and the Commission in December 2002 at the time when the final terms of that Regulation were adopted by the Council emphasize this principle; paragraph 9 reads:

The Commission, *as the Guardian of the Treaty, has the ultimate but not the sole responsibility for developing policy and safeguarding efficiency and consistency* (emphasis added). Therefore the instruments of the Commission on the one hand and of the national competition authorities of the other hand are not identical. The additional powers the Commission has been granted to fulfil its responsibilities will be exercised with the utmost regard for the co-operative nature of the Network.

---

[4] John Temple Lang, 'How much do the Smaller States Need the European Commission? The Role of the Commission in a changing Europe', [2002] 39 CMLR 315–335.

[5] Council Document No. 15435/02, published 10 December 2002. (Available on Council's electronic document register.) See also DG Comp Competition Policy Newsletter, No. 1, 2003, 'Regulation 1/2003—a modernised application of EC Competition rules', pp.3–8.

2.2 THE EXTENDED POWERS OF THE COMMISSION

The new Regulation therefore, while it contains a deliberate sacrifice by the Commission of its monopoly over the granting of individual exemptions, in some important respects provides it with additional powers needed in order that it may maintain its central influence on policy. These additional powers include:

(i) under Articles 3(1) and 3(2) the right to require national competition authorities, when implementing national competition law equivalent to Articles 81 and 82, also to apply Articles 81 and 82. In this way the long running uncertainty about the rights of such national authorities to apply national law that is stricter than Community law has been removed since it is no longer allowed. As emphasized in Chapter 20 at pp.445–7, there are only three exceptions to this principle:

— the application of stricter national laws which prohibit or sanction unilateral conduct. This would allow, for example, action by the Competition Commission, as one of the national competition authorities of the United Kingdom, following a market investigation of a particular sector under the Enterprise Act 2002, to impose sanctions on undertakings that did not individually have a dominant position within the terms of Article 82, but were nevertheless engaged in forms of anti-competitive practice that reduced the competitive nature of the sector;

— the application of national merger controls; and

— the application of national laws that 'predominantly pursue an objective different from that pursued by Articles 81 and 82', such as consumer or environmental laws;

(ii) the strengthening of the Commission's power of decision, beyond the familiar power contained in Article 3 of Regulation 17/62, to require infringements to be brought to an end under the wider powers now set out in Article 7. This permits the Commission to impose on the undertakings concerned (in addition to any fines or penalties imposed under Articles 23 or 24) 'any behavioural or structural remedies' so long as these are 'proportionate' to the infringements committed and necessary to bring it effectively to an end. The 'structural' remedy, which might involve even divesture of part of the business of undertaking, can however be implemented only in rare cases, where there is no behavioural remedy available or where it would be 'more burdensome' to the undertakings than a structural remedy;

(iii) the right under Article 8 to impose interim measures on parties following the finding of a prima facie case of infringement, which was not contained in Regulation 17 and for which in the past the Commission has been dependent on the case law jurisprudence of the ECJ;

(iv) the right under Article 9 to accept binding commitments from undertakings as part of the settlement of an infringement action by the Commission, when these are regarded as sufficient to meet its concerns. This gives the Commission in effect the legal powers to enter into 'consent decrees' of the kind favoured in the USA following the initiation by antitrust authorities of federal court action, but without necessarily the intervention of Community courts unless an appeal is made to the CFI;

(v) the right, in place of granting individual exemption under Article 9 of Regulation 17/62, to make under Article 10 a general finding of inapplicability of Article 81. This form of decision can be taken either because the conditions of Article 81(1) have not been satisfied or because the conditions of Article 81(3) are satisfied so that Article 81(1) is no longer applicable. But it is important to note that such a decision is not itself a grant of individual exemption and indeed could be made equally well in a case involving Article 82;

(vi) Article 17 incorporates the underused, but potentially important, Article 12 of Regulation 17/62, dealing with the right of the Commission to investigate sectors of the economy, but adds additionally a right to enquire into 'particular types of agreement' across sectors. Until such investigations were launched into aspects of the telecommunications' markets in 1999, this power had only been used on two minor occasions. It is to be hoped that in the future, freed of the burden of handling individual notifications, DG Comp may find resources and opportunities to investigate particular market sectors and types of agreement, as a result of which action could be taken under Articles 81 and 82, and such enquiries may produce important experience and data for DG Comp on the operation of particular markets and type of agreement, which may itself be useful in the future. This is shown by the experience in the United Kingdom of the Monopolies and Mergers Commission and its successor, the Competition Commission, in carrying out enquiries known under its Fair Trading Act jurisdiction as 'monopoly references',[6] which unearthed numerous anti-competitive practices in particular sectors by undertakings, none of whom were necessarily dominant;

(vii) for the first time, under Article 19 the Commission receives the power, for the purpose of collecting information, to interview an individual or the representative of an undertaking who gives consent, to supplement its well established powers under Article 18 to send out written requests for information (the old 'Article 11' requests under Regulation 17/62);

(viii) for the first time also the Commission has gained the right to search not only business premises of undertakings suspected of a 'serious violation' of Article 81 or Article 82 (Article 20), but also the private homes of directors, managers, or other members of staff (Article 21). The Commission must however first obtain a Court Order from the national court and proceed in accordance with the procedural safeguards laid down by the European Court in earlier case law and recently confirmed in the *Roquette* case (see Chapter 20, p.440); and

(ix) it has also received under Article 29 the general power to withdraw the benefit of existing block exemptions from particular agreements if their effect is incompatible with the terms of Article 81(3). This particular power adds to those already set out in recent block exemptions such as Regulation 2790/99. Member States are granted an equivalent power if the effects are felt in the territory or in a part of the territory 'having all the characteristics of a distinct geographic market'.

The position of the Commission therefore has been strengthened by the terms of the

---

[6] Now under the Enterprise Act 2002 known as 'market investigations'.

Regulation notwithstanding the surrender of the monopoly which Article 9(1) of Regulation 17/62 previously conferred. The only power which it sought during the negotiations, but which was not granted, was that to issue under its own authority (rather than under the authority of the Council) new block exemptions. It was felt ultimately by Member States that this would give the Commission too wide a power and would be inconsistent with the spirit of the new co-operative arrangements being made with them.

2.3 PRIORITIES FOR DG COMP

The internal organization of DG Comp will clearly have to be adjusted to fit in with these new arrangements. The whole focus of its work will shift towards proactive enforcement of the competition rules, based on both its own investigations and following the receipt of complaints and away from the largely reactive treatment of individual notifications with which officials had in the past largely been concerned. It will continue to need its sectoral expertise and to maintain its division into sectoral areas that can utilize this past experience. This, however, will need to be combined with a reorganization of the way in which the Merger Task Force itself will be structured, so as to meet the criticisms of the procedures contained in the CFI judgments in *Airtours* and *Schneider LeGrand*. Moreover officials from the new Member States will obviously have to be integrated into a wide range of posts within DG Comp; and ideally national experts from these countries will also be given an opportunity of secondment for two or three year periods, so that they can in time take back to their own national authorities an understanding of the working methods and techniques developed over many years in DG Comp.

An important priority will also be to reduce the backlog of existing cases. Article 34(1) of the new Regulation states that from the date of its application (1 May 2004) all existing notifications and applications will lapse; this means that from that date no further individual exemptions will be granted. This does not mean however that the existing individual exemptions will become automatically null and void, as by Article 34(2) it is confirmed that any 'procedural steps' already taken under Regulation 17/62 and certain block exemption Regulations such as 4056/86 will continue to have effect. All existing individual exemptions will however lapse when their current permitted duration comes to an end. It seems unlikely that DG Comp will wish to be generous in granting new formal exemptions in the transitional period remaining under the old regulation. The status of comfort letters too from 1 May 2004 is dubious. They have of course never had any binding legal effect on national courts, though in some cases their terms have nevertheless been influential. Both national competition authorities and national courts will no doubt in the future feel free to examine them again afresh, when they are put forward by undertakings as grounds for finding that Article 81 or 82 should not apply. In practice they may still have, therefore, some limited value, as indications of at least a Commission view at a particular past date that the relevant agreement or practice either fell outside the terms of either Article, or by reason of Article 81(3) conditions was one to which the sanction of nullity would not apply.

One of the most important divisions of the reformed DG Comp will in future be that responsible for publication of Commission Notices and Guidelines, the need for which will increase. A number of new Notices will be issued prior to the new Regulation coming into force, and after that date both national authorities and courts will continue to be concerned to have available as much published information as possible on the application of their responsibilities. It is only in the exceptional case before a national court that the Commission is likely to be willing to intervene as provided for under the Regulation[7] (by written opinion or even oral presentation); it is therefore primarily on published information, Guidelines, and Notices, that the parties and their legal representatives will have to rely. The practice in the United States of issuing 'Business Review Letters' may have to be replicated in Brussels; the joint statement contains at least one unnumbered but important promise, namely that 'the Commission will from time to time publish opinions on matters where it appears because of the novelty of the subject-matter that this may be helpful'. This possibility is going to be limited to cases where the need for clarification is urgent, for example because major investment under a proposed joint venture within the jurisdiction of Article 81 is dependent upon it and only when the question to be resolved is genuinely novel or important, taking into account all relevant factors. The Commission has also announced that it will be publishing additional Notices before 1 May 2004 on:

— the working of the network (to supplement the Joint Statement of 16 December 2002);

— the exchange of information between the Commission and individual national competition authorities;

— on the handling of complaints;

— on the meaning of 'effect on trade' (which now becomes a key element in the application of Article 3); and

— in the application of Article 81(3).

But it is unlikely that even the issue of all these publications will be sufficient to meet the requirements of Member States and their authorities and courts, when confronted in the early years of the new regime with their fresh responsibilities and the need to deal with difficult questions under Community law.

The Commission will clearly have to make decisions from the outset as to the priorities it will adopt in its new and very different role. Commissioner Monti will undoubtedly be making numerous speeches in the period leading up to the introduction of the Regulation on these policy choices. Clearly enforcement action against major cartels with participants in a number of Member States will continue to have the highest priority; the Commission will be happy that at least some of the resources at present applied in a review of notified agreements can be applied alternatively in this way. There are however still a number also of difficult Community-wide policy issues with which DG Comp will wish to continue to concern itself. An obvious example is the question of supply quotas operated by pharmaceutical companies and the approach to be adopted towards them, whether under Article 81 or 82, once the final outcome of the legal proceedings in *Bayer/Adalat*[8] is known. The revision of Regulation 240/96 on the transfer of technology is another major pending responsibility, which will require attention in order to bring the terms of that block exemption in line with the new approach adopted for vertical restraints and the block exemptions also on specialization and research and development. Even though considerable responsibility in respect of telecommunications will have been devolved also to Member States under

---

[7] Art. 15.
[8] See Ch. 6, pp.70–1

the terms of the Framework Directive with effect from 25 July 2003,[9] the Commission will still wish (as the Directive allows it) to keep a careful eye on the process of liberalization in this and other sectors in the field of energy where problems remain with the attitude of some Member States. There is even a possibility that in some sectors it may again have to issue further Directives under Article 86(3) if progress is found to be thwarted by Member States.

2.4 THE COMMISSION'S RELATIONSHIPS WITH NATIONAL COMPETITION AUTHORITIES

Turning to relationships with national competition authorities, this is an area where many question marks still remain. Over recent years it is quite true that working relationships between such authorities and with the Commission have improved considerably and the habit of working together on cases of mutual interest has become quite normal. Some factors in this improvement have included the harmonization of national laws to incorporate those principles found in Articles 81 and 82 in nearly all Member States, the experience of successful case handling following exchange of information between Brussels and the Member States, as well as improved resources and standards of operation now to be found in the majority of national competition authorities. Important too has been a greater willingness on the part of DG Comp to trust individual authorities to handle cases that previously it might have sought to keep for resolution in Brussels.

The new Regulation and the Joint Statement lay out a framework for the network though its full nature remains undefined, perhaps necessarily so. The network is of course a tangible link based on an electronic communication web between Brussels and the national competition authorities, and between the individual competition authorities themselves. It is also however an intangible relationship between individual national and Commission officials, now that the original perceived subordination of the national authorities to an all-powerful DG Comp no longer applies. This is now replaced by an association, if not of equals, at least of organizations with a reasonable degree of mutual respect for each other's expertise based on the General Principles of the Joint Statement which emphasizes in Articles 5 to 10:

— the position of the national competition authorities as fully competent to apply Articles 81 and 82 and to contribute actively to the development of competition law in practice within the Community;

— their independence from each other, with different national enforcement systems, but with mutual recognition of these as the basis for co-operation;

— the fact that such co-operation takes place on the basis of equality, respect, and solidarity; and

— the need that any information becoming available between DG Comp and one authority shall also be made available and accessible to other members of the network.

The provisions of the new Regulation, even as supplemented by the Joint Statement, do not provide, however, a sufficiently strong or detailed legal basis to guarantee that the new

---

[9] Reg. 2002/21.

system will work. There is still much reliance on 'soft law' through Notices and Guidelines and good intentions, and rather too little on 'hard law', through the provisions of regulations. This is perhaps inevitable at the outset; if there are serious difficulties in consistency of application or in the operations of the network in the early years, further regulations are however likely to be issued, utilizing the experience of first attempts to coordinate activities in so ambitious a way between so many Member States. This after all was the nature of the 'learning curve' of the early development of the application of Article 81 in the1960s and 1970s as explained in Part I; the difference in the first decade of the twenty-first century will be that the pressure of economic and political events will be that much greater and the timescale for reform much shorter.

The Commission of course will possess its ultimate sanction, that contained in Article 11(6) for initiating its own proceedings to implement Articles 7–10, thereby relieving the national competition authorities of their competence in a particular case. It is likely that it will only do so in exceptional circumstances. These might apply if a Member State had blatantly failed to act in a non-discriminatory manner, by favouring the activities of one or more of its undertakings regarded as 'national champions', leading to protests from other Member States. Alternatively it might happen when a Member State had genuinely attempted to bring proceedings under Article 81 or 82 against an undertaking but was obviously unable to collect the evidence required because the relevant conduct was found to be outside its territorial reach. The Joint Statement refers in paragraph 21 to situations where such intervention is envisaged and, while it obviously could not refer explicitly to situations of the kind mentioned above, it has provided the following grounds for possible intervention under this Article:

— when two network members are envisaging conflicting decisions in the same case;
— when a network member envisages a decision that is in conflict with existing Community law;
— when there is undue delay by a Member State in dealing with a case;
— when the national competition authority does not in any case object; and
— when there is a common policy imperative to develop Community competition policy.

Paragraph 19 specifically refers to the Commission being particularly well placed to intervene in cases where at least three Member States are involved in the particular case.

Relationships between DG Comp and national competition authorities are governed principally by four important Articles in Regulation 1/2003 namely:

— Article 3, dealing with supremacy, requiring in practice the parallel application of Articles 81 and 82 alongside national law in the great majority of significant cases.

— Article 11, setting out the co-operation principles of the network on the basis of consultation and the provision of at least thirty days' prior notice of national decisions requiring infringement decisions, the accepting of commitments, or the withdrawal of the benefit of block exemptions.

— Article 12, relating to the exchange of information between national competition authorities to the extent permitted by national law. The *Spanish Banks*[10] principle

---

[10] Case C-67/91 [1992] ECR I-4785.

(insulating the use of Community case information from the application of national law) has been largely replaced by the second sentence of Article 12(2), allowing information exchange between competition authorities and the Commission and between each other to be used for national law cases as well as for Articles 81 and 82 cases, so long as it does not lead to a ' different outcome'.

— Article 13, that if two or more authorities are dealing with the same set of facts following a complaint, or the same agreement, the fact that one is already dealing with it shall be sufficient grounds for the other to suspend proceedings or reject the complaint.

In assessing the future development of the network a number of its features need emphasizing. Whilst each authority will be able to deal with its purely national cases, its limited territorial jurisdiction means that in many cases, when more than one Member State is involved, its decisions will only be of limited effect. This is so, even if it is able, through use of the network, to acquire sufficient evidence to reach a finding on the application of both national and Community law. In many cases therefore only the Commission will be able to issue infringement decisions which will have effect in a number of Member States or throughout the Community. The Community may therefore take up or take over cases involving undertakings in more than one Member State, where that Member State has tried but failed to enforce its judgment against undertakings whose anti-competitive practices in breach of the Treaty may well be taking place across more than one territory. Rather than the national competition authority resenting the need to share its jurisdiction with the Commission, it may well find that the bringing in of the Commission's wider range of powers may be to its advantage in the long run.

If the network develops as intended, DG Comp may itself find that it can learn from the experience of national competition authorities, not only in the way that cases are handled, but also in the application of substantive legal provisions and in connection with particular processes for obtaining information and evidence. This possibility was referred to by Professor Ehlermann[11] as the 'bottom up' approach in which 'the law bubbles up', a familiar phenomenon and one of the great merits of a federal structure such as the United States. While the opposite outcome, that of divergent decisions in different jurisdictions, leading to inconsistency of rules within the enlarged Community, may still be a risk, this is less likely within a framework where individual exemptions are not granted by any authority and notification of such agreements to such an authority affords no protection against the application of the competition rules.

It is important to stress that, although the new Regulation does not expressly prohibit the operation by a national competition authority of a notification system for particular categories of agreements, this is unlikely to be appropriate or necessary. The essence of the new arrangements is that Article 81 is applied (just as Article 82 has been) as a single provision: the outcome of its application will either be that the agreement is null and void as a result of which other sanctions may follow, such as fines, or that the Article does not apply, so that the agreement is enforceable. Neither the Commission nor any national authority will be in the business of granting individual exemptions.

A relatively new complication that has arisen in certain Member States, including the

---

[11] In his Introduction to *European Competition Law Annual 2000: The Modernization of EC Antitrust Policy* (Hart Publishing 2001), pp.xxii.

United Kingdom, is the introduction of criminal sanctions against individuals who participate in hardcore cartels.[12] Whilst there is some evidence from the United States, with its long
experience of the application of severe criminal sanctions including heavy fines and prison
sentences to individual directors and managers of companies found to have participated in
price-fixing or other horizontal cartel activities, that this may be an essential weapon in the
armament of antitrust authorities, it may not however be as effective in the European
context. The United States has the advantage of the Grand Jury investigation procedure and
moreover the availability of contingent fees which facilitates the bringing of related civil
proceedings for treble damages against the undertakings found to have participated in such
activities.[13] It is quite possible also that such enquiries and proceedings may even delay for
considerable periods or frustrate the bringing of proceedings under Articles 81 and 82
against the undertakings involved and the exchange of information between Member States
under the terms of Article 12 of the new Regulation.

2.5 THE COMMISSION'S RELATIONSHIPS WITH NATIONAL COURTS

The third group of institutions affected by the Regulation on modernization are national
courts. The shortest Article in Regulation 1/2003 is Article 6 which states simply that
'national courts shall have the power to apply Articles 81 and 82'. No longer will such courts
be faced with a frustrating inability to apply Article 81(3) in the course of their handling of a
civil case where often a party has made, usually at the last minute, notification of an
agreement which is the subject of the case, so that the court has then to wait until the
Commission has acted, leading almost inevitably to the suspension of the hearing, as
described in Chapter 21. The court will in future by contrast be able to apply both Article
81(1) and 81(3) in parallel and will reach a decision that restrictive clauses in the relevant
agreement are enforceable (either because outside Article 81(1) or saved by 81(3)) or are not
and therefore void; it will then have to go on to consider under national law whether
severance of the remaining clauses can take place so that they remain enforceable.

Courts of course do not have the facility of an existing electronic or other form of
network with the Commission nor with national competition authorities. Courts, unlike
competition authorities, do not choose their cases but have to react in respect of those cases
which reach them as the result of the initiation of suit by plaintiffs. The 1993 Notice on Co-
operation with National Courts[14] published by the Commission did not lead to a substantial
increase in the number of cases in which the Commission became involved in national
courts; indeed there were few such cases. The new Regulation will therefore effectively for
the first time bring the Commission in principle, and possibly in practice, more into the
process of the application of Articles 81 and 82 in national courts. These courts will still of
course be subject to the restriction imposed on them by the *Masterfoods* judgment, whose

---

[12] Section 188, Enterprise Act 2002.

[13] C. Jones, *Private Enforcement of Antitrust Law in the EU, UK and USA*, 1st edn. (Oxford University Press,
1999). An important development recently has been the decision of the United States Court of Appeals for the
District of Columbia in *Empagran* v. *Hoffman-La Roche* on 17 January 2003, holding that non-US purchasers
may recover treble damages under the antitrust laws in US Courts, even if the transactions giving rise to the
damages took place outside the US, and notwithstanding that the parties had no connection with the USA, so
long as the illegal conduct had an effect on US commerce and injured at least one US party.

[14] [1993] OJ C39/6.

effect is reproduced in Article 16 and prevents them from either making decisions that run counter to the decision adopted by the Commission, or which would conflict with the decision contemplated by the Commission in proceedings which it has initiated.

Article 15 of the Regulation seeks to provide a framework within which the new relationship could work. It entitles the court to ask the Commission to transmit information in its possession to the court or to give its opinion on questions concerning the application of Community competition rules; Member States will have to forward to the Commission copies of any written judgments by such courts which apply to either Article 81 or Article 82. National courts must allow national competition authorities to submit observations on the application of these Articles in cases coming before them; oral participation will be much rarer, whether by the Commission itself or by the national competition authority, and requires the specific permission of the court in each case. The national court can in due course be asked to send copies of documents relevant to the case to the national competition authority and the Commission, so that they can prepare submissions to the Court.

In practice, competition issues often arise not as the sole, or even the main, issue between the parties in a particular case but as one of a number of questions with which the court is required to deal. It is clearly a step forward that the court will now be able to reach its finding on that question, without having to provide for the suspension of the whole case (which may be for a considerable period while the issue is considered in Brussels), and which may in turn prevent the other issues between the parties being satisfactorily dealt with. On the other hand considerable concern has been expressed at the burden which this new responsibility may impose upon national courts and national judges. Two types of burden have been especially mentioned; the first is that the application of the conditions in Article 81(3) may require the judge to balance up policy issues involving not only the commercial interests of the parties and the operation of relevant commercial markets but broader social and environmental issues with which it is less familiar. The second possible burden is the sheer complexity and consequent long duration of some competition cases. If for example the agreement under challenge is a multi-party one as for example in the *Premier League*[15] case concerning exclusive television rights to Premier League football matches, the consequence is likely to be (as I expressed it in another place)[16] 'mountains of paper, many volumes of economic analysis and statistics, and endless lever arch files of correspondence and other documents, not to mention an excess of economic experts expounding at great length to perplex the court'.

At that seminar at the European University Institute in Florence in May 2000 many other papers on the likely problems of modernization were presented. It was encouraging to hear from some of the senior judges there that they felt that the problem of handling large-scale competition cases at first instance or on appeal were little more onerous than those that they faced in other subject areas. Nevertheless, the need for specialization will undoubtedly arise, and those Member States which do not yet have a reasonable number of judges with appropriate case law experience and familiarity with economic concepts will certainly need to face up to this need.

Competition issues can come before national courts in a number of ways.[17] One

---

[15] [1999] UKCLR 258.

[16] In *European Competition Law Annual 2000*, referred to in fn. 3.

[17] W. Van Gerven, *European Competition Law Annual 2001* (Hart Publishing, 2003), pp.53–89.

560 CONCLUSIONS AND PROSPECTS

undertaking may sue another for sums alleged due under a contract and the defendant may claim the contract is unenforceable under Article 81(2); this is normally described as a 'nullity' case. Alternatively the claim may be that the defendant should pay damages to the plaintiff because of losses which the plaintiff sustained as the result of a contract made by the defendant either with the plaintiff or with third parties, containing restrictive clauses, a 'damages' claim. Repayment may be sought of sums paid under the alleged illegal contract or of profits made by the defendant as the result of it (a 'restitutionary' claim). The challenge for the national judge will be to identify the point of competition law in the case and indeed he is required to do this even if the parties do not themselves raise it (*Van Schijndel*);[18] he must then utilize the provisions of Article 15 in the Regulation to give himself the best possible chance of resolving it correctly. It is almost certain however that in the early years of the new regime there will be unsatisfactory or inconsistent national court decisions given and indeed conflicts between courts in separate Member States. Problems of 'forum shopping' are also highly probable, as has already occurred for example in the field of patent enforcement litigation within the Community.

Such unsatisfactory outcomes of competition cases may arise for a number of reasons; the court's unfamiliarity with technical economic arguments, a misunderstanding of the Community rules or jurisprudence, or unavailability of crucial documents. Alternatively it may be the failure of a legal representative to put forward the arguments in an appropriate manner, or simply the fact that a small undertaking, faced by a much larger opponent with greater resources may be unable to produce necessary expert or other evidence required. There is some anecdotal indication already however that the likelihood of competition cases in national courts being brought and being dealt with satisfactorily is increasing.

The ECJ gave national courts an important signal in *Crehan* v. *Courage*[19] as explained in Chapter 21 that it regarded these actions as important for the determination of nullity and damage claims, so that public policies underlying competition law should not be frustrated by national technical rules. Whilst there have been many reasons why private damage actions have not become common, now at last there are signs that this situation may be changing subsequent to *Crehan*. In a recent Article 234 reference,[20] *Munoz and Fruticola* v. *Frumar and Redbridge*, the Court ruled that a civil action for damages was possible in a national court if regulatory rules (relating in this case to the labelling of fruit and vegetables) are not enforced by the public authorities in a Member State. Moreover, by way of example, substantial damages have been recovered by undertakings from companies found to have been participants in the vitamins cartel (referred to in Chapter 9); and in Sweden in November 2002, SAS were awarded a very large sum in damages against the Swedish Civil Aviation Administration for discriminatory pricing practices relating to Arlanda Airport.

2.6 THE JUDICIAL ARCHITECTURE OF THE COMMUNITY

The final problem, and one of the more serious ones relating to the future involvement of national courts, is that of providing a system of appellate courts through the provision of

---

[18] Cases C-430/431 of 1993 [1995] ECR I-4705: [1996] 1 CMLR 801.
[19] Case C-453/99 [2001] 5 CMLR 1058: A. Komninis, 'New Proposals for Private Enforcement of EC Competition Law' [2002] 39 CMLR 449–487.
[20] Case C-253/00 [2002] 3 CMLR 734.

appropriate 'judicial architecture'. If one sought an ideal court structure for the Community within which both Articles 230 and 234 could be applied within reasonable time limits to competition law cases as well as to others, there would be a group of three or four regional chambers of the CFI,[21] to which appeals could be brought in competition cases from the highest national courts and, in addition, Article 234 references would need to be made to the CFI in Luxembourg rather than solely to the ECJ.

Prior to the Treaty of Nice, the appellate position was far from such an ideal. No appeal could be brought from any national court in a competition case to any Community court, and Article 234 references could only be made to the ECJ which were taking normally up to twenty-one months, though this was not the fault of the ECJ. There was therefore the risk of major inconsistencies between the way in which civil action in competition matters were dealt with and the outcome of such cases, in the different national jurisdictions. The IGC held at Nice at the end of 2000 however, making use of prior detailed preparatory work carried out by working parties appointed by the Community Courts, led to some significant amendments to the Treaty of Rome in the Treaty of Nice, which corresponded to some of the urgent needs for reform which these working parties had already identified.[22] These included the following:

— a recognition that the CFI is not merely an attachment to the ECJ, but is a court that has its own jurisdiction recognized in the Treaty (Article 220);

— to it the Council may in future annex judicial panels (Article 225A) with a jurisdiction to hear and determine cases at first instance, with an appeal to the CFI. It is likely that Commission staff cases will be the first category to be nominated for hearing by such panels; but the use of such panels could be utilized in the future for other categories of case, including competition cases; and

— the CFI is also to have jurisdiction to hear and determine questions referred for a preliminary ruling under Article 234, in specific areas to be laid down by the Statute of the court.

What this could mean for the future is that, if numerous cases involving competition issues were to require determination under Article 234, these could be referred to the CFI rather than the ECJ, unless under the qualifications contained in Article 225 the case 'required a decision of principle likely to affect the unity or consistency of Community law' so that it would go direct to the ECJ. An appeal would be from the CFI's decision under Article 234 to the ECJ if 'there is a serious risk of the unity or consistency of Community law being affected', although this is less likely.

---

[21] The earliest reference to the possibility of regional chambers of the CFI appears to be J. Weiler and J. Jacqué, *On the Road to European Union: A New Judicial Architecture* [1990] 27 CMLR 185–207.

[22] See A. Johnston, *Judicial Reform and the Treaty of Nice* [2001] 38 CMLR, 499–523, and also *The Future of the European Judicial System*, A. Dashwood and A. Johnston (eds) (Hart Publishing, 2001). The text of the Treaty can be found at [2001] OJ C80/1. A similar debate over the need for specialist Community Courts is also taking place over the need for a Patent Court to apply the Community Patent Convention.

3. THE FUTURE OF THE MERGER REGULATION

3.1 THE NEED FOR TRUST

In Chapter 18 the reasons underlying the presentation in December 2002 of important proposals for the amendment of the Merger Regulation were explained (in Section 7). A Council Regulation will be needed for the amendments to be officially adopted and at the time of writing it is far from clear what their final form will be. It is likely however that not only will there be changes to the substantive criteria for the assessment of concentrations with a Community dimension, but that there will be also amendments to some of its procedural provisions; in addition there will be changes to the internal organization of the Commission and the way in which major cases are handled. These latter changes can be implemented however without altering the Regulation.

What effect will these changes be likely to have on the way in which the Regulation is administered? There is little doubt that the severe shock to the confidence of the Commission which the three annulment judgments in the summer and early autumn of 2002 brought about will have a long term impact on its whole operation. To be effective, a competition authority has to win and retain the trust of its constituency, which is made up of the industrial and commercial undertakings around, not only Europe but the entire world, with whom it has to do business, as well as their professional advisers. Because of the market sensitivity, time constraints, and high public profile of the merger control process, this element of trust is especially important for the Commission. If it can retain it, then it can continue to carry out its responsibilities even if individual major decisions, such as *Boeing/McDonnell Douglas* and *GE/Honeywell*, are controversial. But if it loses it, then to operate the Regulation effectively under all the inevitable pressures that accompany the process becomes very difficult, especially if its own self-confidence is affected.

In looking at the administration of the Regulation, a sense of proportion is of course needed. Of well over two thousand cases already decided less than five per cent have been through the second phase examination reserved for concentrations that raise serious doubts about their compatibility with the Regulation. Of these probably only a dozen or so could be described as controversial in their outcome. Nevertheless, if the procedural process or economic reasoning of the Commission in any such case can be successfully challenged on appeal, it has the immediate potential to damage not only the reputation of the officials closely involved but also the general good name of the Commission.

The likely result of the need for the Commission to regain the trust which it has thus risked losing can be looked at under three heads, which have already been described above as:

— the amendment of the substantive criteria for the assessment of individual cases;

— procedural changes to the Regulation; and

— internal administrative and organizational changes not requiring changes to the Regulation.

3.2 CHANGES TO SUBSTANTIVE CRITERIA IN THE REGULATION

The debate over whether the existing criteria for the assessment of concentrations should remain as set out in Article 2, or be changed in some minor or major respect, was in progress for some time before the *Airtours* decision was issued, and, unlike some of the other proposed reforms, is not merely a reaction to the comments of the CFI in that and the other two annulments of Commission blocking decisions. The main argument of those who sought to replace the dominance test in Article 2 with that of 'a substantial lessening of competition' criterion (often for convenience referred to as the 'SLC test') was that the wording of Article 2 failed to cover the situation where the merger brought about unilateral effects on the relevant market but without any one or more undertakings becoming dominant in that market. The amendment therefore proposed by the Commission in December 2002 sought to broaden the definition of dominance in Article 2 to bridge this gap, by the following language:

For the purpose of this Regulation, (emphasis added) one or more undertakings shall be deemed to be in a dominant position if, with or without coordinating, they hold the economic power to influence appreciably and sustainably the parameters of competition, in particular, prices, production, quality of output, distribution or innovation, or appreciably to foreclose competition.

The weakness of this proposed amendment of the meaning of 'dominance' as the central element of the Article is that it dilutes it, by extending its scope to situations where the market share and influence on the competitive process of the merging parties is well below that of undertakings with paramount[23] market power, which alone would have been caught under the present wording of the Article, whether such power was exercised unilaterally or collectively. It has the same broad coverage in practice as the SLC test, but without the clear focus which that test brings to market analysis, and necessarily involves the Commission in mental and verbal gymnastics in its application. It would be far better for the Commission to acknowledge that the original dominance test is indeed flawed and that its proposed extension of its scope is confusing: the present proposal is likely to make more, rather than fewer, difficulties for undertakings seeking to anticipate whether their particular proposal for a merger is likely to be caught by its terms.[24]

The Commission has stated that one of the principal reasons for remaining with a dominance test is that it does not want to lose the benefit of the case law established by more than two thousand existing decisions under the present wording. But it is in practice quite rare for Commission decisions in merger cases to rely on past precedents, explicitly or even implicitly, save perhaps in relation to market definition when past precedent has some obvious relevance and convenience. Most cases turn on their own facts, and the key primary task for the Commission is to ascertain these in a methodical and complete way, as it signally failed to do in *Schneider LeGrand*. The use of precedent is incidentally far more relevant in Article 81 and 82 cases, in respect of which there are many more CFI and ECJ decisions to be applied.

Another proposal by the Commission is that efficiency arguments will be taken into

---

[23] This phrase is normally applied to undertakings with at least the 50 per cent market share enjoyed by AKZO in *ECS/AKZO*, Case C-62/86 [1991] ECR I-3359: [1993] 5 CMLR 215.

[24] For the contrary view of the Head of the Bundeskartellamt, see U. Böge and E. Muller, 'From the Market Dominance Test to the SLC Test: Are there any reasons for a change?', [2002] 23 ECLR 495–498.

consideration as part of the market analysis. While in principle this seems unobjectionable, the qualifications which attend it seem in practice likely to eliminate any likelihood that they will prove a decisive factor in any case. For the parties will have to show that the efficiencies are specifically secured by the merger (and not by other causes), are sufficiently substantial to deserve attention, are verifiable once the merger occurs, and moreover confer benefits to consumers as well as to the parties. In weighing up the many other factors that may be relevant in horizontal mergers the December 2002 Notice on their appraisal will be a useful reference point for both the Commission and the parties, but it will not be able to outweigh the problems that an unsatisfactory redefinition of dominance in Article 2 will produce.

3.3 CHANGES TO PROCEDURES OF THE COMMISSION IN APPLYING THE REGULATION

Many of the proposals in this category were on the table before the results of the three appeals to the CFI were known, but in its wake they have become yet more necessary. It has been clear for some time that the existing time limits were too short in all cases except the numerous straightforward ones dealt with under the simplified procedure. The pressure on both the Merger Task Force and the parties became especially acute when it was necessary to consider remedies put forward by the parties anxious to resolve problems arising in particular markets affected by the concentration; the Task Force itself had often not had sufficient time to acquire enough knowledge of the way such markets actually operated, while the parties anxious to 'get the deal through' felt under great pressure to come up with proposed remedies, even before the Commission had established to its own satisfaction the objections which it had to the transaction.

The new proposals, which seem likely to be adopted, allow for extra time to be claimed by the parties and by the Commission at both the first and second phases, in particular when remedies have been put forward for consideration and need careful analysis by the Commission, as well as 'market testing' with third parties affected, such as competitors. As much as thirty-five days could be added under the Commission's proposals to the total timeframe in which a second phase case is dealt with. This adjustment is clearly necessary, as the current time limits are inadequate to allow the Commission to deal adequately with a complex case. A particular weakness of the Commission's procedure was illustrated by *Schneider LeGrand*. The numerous national markets in Europe for electrical components of many kinds, in which both parties were important players, had apparently not been analysed in sufficient depth, so that the decision was based not on reliable factual data relating to those individual markets, but on apparent generalizations about European markets in aggregate. One of the difficulties for the Commission is that Article 11 of the Regulation seems to assume that the information gathered by the Commission will be based mainly on that supplied by third parties, whose interests in some cases in providing comprehensive and accurate data may be limited. The Commission does not seem to go out in a sufficiently methodical way to collect its own data, even by the employment of economic consultants or through seeking access at an early stage to information in the possession of national competition authorities. The availability of some extra time for the more difficult cases may possibly help to some degree in this respect, but is not the whole answer.

To be welcomed, however, is the provision for greater flexibility in the procedures which determine when notification has to be made, and in the handling of cases with a Community dimension which may be suitable for passing over (in whole or part) to national competition authorities under Article 9, and cases without a technical Community dimension but with sufficient cross-border effect to justify assessment by the Commission at the request of one or more Member States under Article 22. This latter series of proposals is in line with the whole approach of the modernization programme, to giving greater responsibility to national authorities, so long as the necessary procedures to resolve whether the entire case, or only certain aspects of it, are to be passed over to a Member State, are conducted promptly.

3.4 INTERNAL CHANGES TO COMMISSION PROCEDURE

Some important changes to procedure in the handling of cases, and some administrative reforms regarded as necessary in the light of the criticisms made by the CFI, may actually have as much impact on the future handling of these cases as any amendment of the Regulation itself. It has been recognized that DG Comp lacks economic expertise at the highest level, which may have been one of the contributory causes to the weakness of the analysis of the alleged collective dominance in *Airtours*. The appointment of a Chief Economic Adviser, together with additional economists to provide him with an effective staff, should strengthen its ability to carry out the often complex examination of relevant markets and the impact of the concentration upon them. Moreover these changes should also prove valuable in the more difficult examples of application of Articles 81 and 82. It is also likely that DG Comp will make more use in future of outside economic consultants and of econometric studies in order to satisfy itself that the theories that it chooses to rely upon in complex cases are supported by the facts of the case.

During the course of the inquiry the parties are to be treated to a more regular account of the thinking of the Commission, by 'State of Play' meetings, and given prompter access to third party evidence in order that responses can be made at an earlier stage. A basic weakness in the existing structure of the investigation process has also been recognized; there will be in the future be more opportunity for the draft findings of the inquiry team to be reviewed internally by senior colleagues, and 'peer review' is likely to become the rule rather than the exception for all major cases. Whilst the ideal structure for merger review is that which requires the process of investigation and assessment to be carried out by separate groups or, better still, different bodies and this may yet become the final solution that the Commission is forced eventually to adopt, nevertheless these internal changes may help to reduce substantially the occasions for adverse comment on its performance by the CFI.

It is sometimes suggested that an increase in the involvement and resources of the hearing officers, who report not to DG Comp but to the Competition Commissioner direct, would be an important factor in improving the standard of merger, and also other, Commission decisions. Their functions and responsibilities are set out in a Decision of the Commission of 23 May 2001,[25] and are to ensure that:

— Relevant procedures are correctly carried out and oral hearings are properly conducted;

– Parties to the case are treated fairly, and in particular are allowed early and sufficient access to the file in order to have full knowledge of the case against them;

---

[25] [2001] OJ L162/21.

— In the preparation of draft Commission decisions, due account is taken of all relevant facts, whether favourable or unfavourable to the parties concerned; and

— Any enquiries conducted by the Commission to assess the 'competitive impact' of remedies proposed in any case are sufficiently objective (e.g. in their selection of respondents or in the methodology adopted).

Hearing officers make two reports in each case; the first is an interim report after the oral hearing to the Commissioner, which may contain reference to the need for the Commission to obtain further information or to withdraw certain arguments against the parties. The second is attached to the final draft decision sent to the Commissioners, and is later published.

It is clear that these cumulative powers could enable hearing officers to play an important role in ensuring procedural fairness in the conduct of a case. But it is only in an exceptional case that they would be able to become involved in substantive issues, such as, for example, the assessment of the relevant product or geographic market. Given the number of separate cases with which each hearing officer is likely to be involved, it would not be possible for them, especially in the fast moving process that a major merger case becomes, to play in any significant sense a judicial role. That is not to deny that even the terms of their existing mandate might enable them on occasion to play a wider role than is now normal; but even this would not of itself provide on its own a solution to the problems which the Commission faces in the application of the Merger Regulation.

The effect of the critical decisions of the CFI in merger cases recently will inevitably mean that DG Comp generally will be more cautious in their approach to those cases where a blocking decision or the imposition of onerous conditions are possible. This will be particularly the situation where the identities of the undertakings or their nationality make the outcome of the case one with an inevitably high profile. The knowledge that the scrutiny to be given to any appeal by the CFI will be searching, as evidenced by the judgments in even the expedited cases of *Schneider LeGrand* and *Tetra/Laval/Sidel*, is itself a major incentive for the Commission to ensure that facts are fully investigated and the application of economic theories fully supported by them. Unsuccessful parties will clearly be more willing to appeal than in the past. It is to be hoped however that all these circumstances will not have the undesirable effect of making the Commission fearful of making blocking decisions. That would indeed be an unfortunate outcome of the largely salutary message which the CFI decisions should have given, that a competition authority which has in practice become a world competition authority for merger control cannot have less than world class standards.

4. THE WAY AHEAD

4.1 THE NEW ECONOMY

Quite apart from the introduction of the modernization programme and the changes to which the Merger Regulation will be subject there are other important elements which will play an important part in the future of Community competition policy, and which should receive mention in this final section. Each of them is individually significant enough to deserve more extensive coverage, but in the context of a general textbook a brief reference is all that can be made, and for more detailed coverage reference should be made to the many titles referred to in the Bibliography or to articles referred to in footnotes to the text.

These features can be summarized as continuing changes in the categories of services representing the new economy, the effects of the Internet, the need for more extensive bilateral and multilateral co-operation between competition authorities, and the development of more sophisticated relationships between lawyers and economists engaged in competition cases.

Many traditional product and service markets will continue to exist as in the past, but there will continue to be a growth in the number of new markets in the new economy, which will present increasing difficulties to Commission administrators.[26] Life would be much simpler for them if there were a greater degree of stability in the range of markets, and the predictability of decisions would certainly be greater. We know however that the current pace of technological change is set to continue, and may even accelerate. The characteristics of these markets include the tendency of the most successful undertaking to acquire dominance and a large market share, as the sector 'tips' in its direction and competitors find it hard to match its technical lead. That product or service, too, however, may have a fairly short life, before it is in turn replaced by a more advanced alternative which in turn captures consumer imagination and offers better value. The cost structure of such undertakings will typically be one of high fixed costs and low marginal costs; they normally have to invest heavily to build up networks so as to gain the benefit in time of the network effect. The Commission is of course aware of the need to move beyond the simple rules of *ECS/Akzo* in assessing when prices of such dominant undertakings are excessive or predatory, and have shown willingness to apply the more appropriate criteria of long range incremental costs (LRIC) in such cases.[27]

4.2 THE EFFECT OF THE INTERNET

The impact of the Internet on competition has already both been exaggerated by some commentators and downplayed by others. From the viewpoint of the Commission it has had both positive and problematic effects, and the same has been true for national competition authorities, as the experience of the Bundeskartellamt (BKartA) has shown.[28] On the positive side, it has increased transparency and has put pressure on both buyers and sellers by enabling the creation of electronic markets of both a B2B and B2C character. It can for example remove the need for intermediaries, e.g. travel agents, between the supplier of services, airlines, and their customers; it can transform the nature of distribution as the original distinction between wholesalers and retailers becomes blurred. In the words of the head of the BKartA, the Internet 'has no time for quiet contemplation' nor does it allow patterns of trade or existing economic concepts to stand still.

But it also has the potential for misuse, if linked with exclusivity requirements or other anticompetitive practices in order to control the operation of electronic markets in favour of particular categories of buyer or seller. Moreover, the facility which it provides for the

---

[26] C. Ahlborn, D. Evans, and A Padilla, 'Competition Policy in the New Economy: Is European Competition Law Up To the New Challenge?' [2001] 22 ECLR 156–167.

[27] See Ch. 15, pp.288–9.

[28] U. Böge, *E. Commerce and Competition* in *EU Competition Law and Policy: Developments and Priorities* (Hellenic Competition Commission, 2002), pp.63–76.

instantaneous exchange of information between undertakings could well be utilized to assist the operation of a cartel, though this might itself be a high risk operation because of the difficulty (far greater than in the case of mere paper) of ensuring that e-mails between the participants were permanently deleted before any investigation took place.

4.3 THE INTERNATIONAL DIMENSION

The continuing trend towards globalization will certainly continue and means that co-operation between different jurisdictions will become even more necessary than at present. An even higher proportion of concentrations of Community dimension will involve undertakings with activities extending across many countries, and cartels too, as experience has shown in the last few years, may well be operated with a geographical range wider than in the past. In merger cases of course the parties often have an incentive to waive their rights to prevent competition authorities from disclosing confidential information, whereas in Articles 81 and 82 cases they are far less willing to do so. But even in the latter case considerable help can be provided by way of background information and advice on techniques for obtaining evidence, as well as the coordination of timetables and procedures when cases are proceeding in parallel, which is quite often the situation when proposed mergers are being examined concurrently on both sides of the Atlantic. The forum for the exchange of ideas and co-operation on an international scale that the ICN will provide will become of even greater value in the future, but is, nevertheless, unlikely to lead to agreement on international rules on antitrust of a substantive nature.

4.4 THE NEED FOR A SPECIALIST COMPETITION PROFESSION

The final element of change to be mentioned is the need to develop a new specialist profession, which would combine the training and best characteristics of the competition lawyer and the economist. The growing importance of competition law as a mainstream commercial subject has meant that the large band of highly skilled antitrust lawyers in the USA have now been joined by a smaller, but equally competent, group in the European Community and other jurisdictions around the world. Likewise, there are now far more economists (academics and consultants) with experience of working in the general area of competition and monopoly, who are often called in to help either the authorities or the parties in leading cases. But what has not yet developed is the appearance, as a recognizable group, both of lawyers who are as much at home in discussing the latest econometric techniques and the merits of different kinds of consumer survey as they are with analysing the latest ECJ judgment on the scope of collective dominance, and of economists who likewise are as well equipped to analyse the language of a block exemption as to discuss the cost of capital. There are of course a number of talented and experienced practitioners and academics who, as individuals, have shown the ability to combine the twin disciplines. But the demands of competition law in the twenty-first century including the likely increase in the complexity of markets will require greater numbers of academically alert practitioners and practitioner-academics, who can combine in their training and practice the technical disciplines and analytical abilities of both professions. The evolving history of Community competition law with which this book has been concerned has shown clearly that such a development would be in the interests of the undertakings which are the subject matter of investigation as well as of the competition authorities themselves.

SOURCES OF LAW AND BIBLIOGRAPHY

SOURCES OF LAW

While legal practitioners and officials will be aware of the sources from which detailed information about cases and competition policy can be obtained, students are often unsure where they should best look for this information. The Treaty of Rome is, of course, the essential starting point. It should be studied in one of the annotated editions published by the leading law publishers.[1] The official source of information is the Official Journal, published in all official Community languages, but in English since 1973 only when the United Kingdom became a Member State.[2] The series marked 'L' includes details of actual competition cases decided by the Commission, whilst series 'C' contains details of proposed exemptions for specific cases, negative clearances, and other relevant items of information relating to the work of DG Comp. The complete text of the Regulations issued by the Commission or by the Council is also essential, and the best collection of the material is the *EC Competition Law Handbook*, published annually by Sweet & Maxwell. It contains not only the text of all relevant documents and notices published by the Commission but also extensive lists of the decisions of the Commission and the judgments of the Court of First Instance and of the European Court of Justice.

An important source of official information are the *Annual Reports* of DG Comp, which have been published since 1971 and contain useful summaries of the facts and decisions of complex cases and a review of the work of the Commission in each year. The decisions of the Court of First Instance and the European Court of Justice often have to be read in full detail, and are found either in the official European Court Reports (ECR) or in the Common Market Law Reports (CMLR). The official reports of the Courts in Luxembourg are divided into ECR I for the cases decided by the European Court itself and ECR II for cases of the Court of First Instance.[3] The ECR series is published only slowly, normally at least a year after the case has been decided, but does include the officially approved text of the Advocate-General's opinion in European Court cases and of the Court judgment. By contrast, the decisions reported in CMLR appear with commendable speed on a monthly basis, competition cases being contained in Volumes 4 and 5 for each year. For most practical purposes these are the reports which the student will find most convenient to use in respect of recent cases, and especially when the official language of a case is not English, with the consequential delay in the publication of the official English translation. The most recent decisions of the Commission can be found initially only in the Official Journal until reports become available in CMLR and later (if appealed) in ECR I or II for the European Court and the Court of First Instance

---

[1] It is important to ensure that the copy purchased or consulted is fully up to date, incorporating not only the original treaties, but also the amending Treaties of the Single European Act (1987), the Treaty of Maastricht (1993), the Treaty of Amsterdam (1997), and the Treaty of Nice (2003).

[2] Some special editions of the Official Journal containing English texts of important regulations, directives, and other official notices and publications prior to 1973 were published at the time when the UK joined.

[3] There is also an ECJ website: www.curia.eu.int. Here full texts of Court judgments (ECJ and CFI) can be found on the date they are issued (though not in all languages immediately). The EUR.Lex site is also valuable for a wide range of information and documents, including the official Journal, the Treaties, current legislation, and other documents of public interest: www.europa.eu.int/eur-lex/en/index.html

respectively. Reports of UK and Irish cases involving EC law can, since March 1997, be found in a new series of reports, European Law Reports, cited as Eur. LR. Decisions of the UK Competition Appeal Tribunal are found in the Competition Appeal Reports (Comp.AR).

In recent years DG Comp has made efforts to make its operations better known to the outside world, particularly to those who have to deal with it. It issues numerous press releases dealing with cases settled between the parties and the Commission, and other recent developments. It publishes, often in recognizable bright yellow covers, good general descriptions of the application of Articles 81 and 82 in particular contexts, and of its procedures and method of investigation. It also publishes updated collections of the various Regulations and Notices dealing with the Merger Regulation, as well as substantial memoranda on new block exemptions when these are introduced.

Every four months it brings out an EC Competition Policy Newsletter containing speeches by senior officials as well as articles and case notes by officials of DG Comp, in English and French. This publication is free and can be requested from: EUR-OP, MER 195 (Competition), 2 rue Mercier, L2985 Luxembourg. It can be read on line at
http://www.europa.eu.int/competition/publications/cpn
Moreover since July 1996 DG Comp has been placing much other information on its own website
(http://www.europa.eu.int/competition/index_en.html)
which contains information on its activities including press releases, full texts of current legislation, Acts published in the Official Journal in the previous month, and a list, with references, of Commission decisions and, usually, the text of the decision. The most recent *Annual Report* can be read together with an updated list of other available Community publications on competition. This site has been well prepared and is

of considerable value to those who, for either professional or academic reasons, need to keep in close contact with the operations of DG Comp. It is in fact almost the only place where the full text of first phase merger cases can be found immediately.

Students will also find in their law libraries a variety of textbooks on the topic of European competition law, often of formidable length and scholarship. The Bibliography which follows lists books of various kinds available on many aspects of competition law, whose number has substantially increased over recent years. The date of any publication must always be carefully considered in view of the continuing changes and development of competition policy, and the regular appearance of important new Commission or Court judgments changing the law in major or minor respects. This renders any book published at risk of becoming quickly outdated, whatever its original value. The Bibliography contains details of books which I have found useful in preparing this work and during the course of my teaching. It does not purport to be exhaustive and in particular I have not included a number of books which, whilst useful in their day, have now been rendered virtually obsolete by the passage of time. On the other hand, some listed books published a number of years ago have either been updated or, even if not updated, remain valuable, especially on historical aspects of the subject. The choice of titles is necessarily selective and the non-appearance in the list of any particular title does not constitute any comment upon its worth. Books in the Oxford European Community Law Library to which this book belongs are listed elsewhere.

Finally, there are also a number of excellent specialist periodicals on the subject of European Law which often contain articles on competition law; these include *Common Market Law Review* and *European Law Review,* as well as the long-established *Modern Law Review.* Other periodicals devote themselves exclusively to the subject of EC competition law, principally the *European Competition Law Review*. Undoubtedly the best source of articles, however, written in depth by judges and advocates-general of the Community Courts and practitioners from many jurisdictions as well as senior officials of DG Comp and national competition authorities, is the annual volume containing the proceedings of the Fordham Corporate Law Institute, Fordham University, New York City. The articles in these volumes are prepared for the annual October conference of the Institute, organized for many years by Professor Barry Hawk, and are published annually in the summer following each conference. They combine in unusual measure the qualities of authority and of radical analysis and provide an invaluable source of information and research material, to which I must acknowledge my own indebtedness. Also of great value are the annual publications of the Robert Schuman Centre at the European University Institute, Florence, prepared from the material provided by those attending by invitation each summer at seminars held on major topics in EC competition law.

BIBLIOGRAPHY

1. General Books on EC Law

BEATSON, J. and TRIDIMAS, T. (eds.), *New Directions in European Public Law*, 1st edn. (Hart Publishing, 1997).

BREALEY, M. and HOSKIN, M., *Remedies in EC Law*, 2nd edn. (Sweet & Maxwell, 1998).

BROWN, L. and KENNEDY, T., *The Court of Justice of the European Communities*, 5th edn. (Sweet & Maxwell, 2000).

CAMBRIDGE YEARBOOK OF EUROPEAN LEGAL STUDIES (Oxford University Press annually since 1998).

CRAIG, P. and DE BURCA, G., *EC Law: Text Cases and Materials*, 3rd edn. (Oxford University Press, 2002).

DASHWOOD, A. and JOHNSTON, A. (eds.), *The Future of the Judicial System of the European Union* (Hart Publishing, 2001).

HARTLEY, T.C., *The Foundations of European Community Law*, 5th edn. (Oxford University Press, 2003).

LASOK, K., *Law and Institutions of the European Communities*, 7th edn. (Butterworths, 2001).

LONBAY, J. and BIONDI, A., *Remedies for Breach of EC Law*, 1st edn. (Wiley, 1997).

MATHIJSEN, P., *A Guide to European Union Law*, 7th edn. (Sweet & Maxwell, 1999).

OLIVER, P., *Free Movement of Goods in the EC*, 4th edn. (Sweet & Maxwell, 2002).

RUDDEN, B. and WYATT, D., *EU Treaties and Legislation*, 8th edn. (Oxford University Press, 2002).

STEINER, J., WOODS, L., and TWIGG-FLESNER, C., *Textbook on EC Law*, 8th edn. (Oxford University Press, 2003).

VAUGHAN, D., *Law of the European Community*, (looseleaf) Butterworth, 2 Vols.—first published 1997.

2. Books on EC Competition Law (General)

ALBORS-LLORENS, A., *EC Competition Law and Policy*, 1st edn. (Willan Publishing, 2002).

BELLAMY, C., CHILD, G., and ROTH, P., *Common Market Law of Competition*, 5th edn. 2 Vols. (Sweet & Maxwell, 2001).

BISHOP, S. and WALKER, C., *The Economics of*

EC Competition Law, 2nd edn. (Sweet & Maxwell 2002).

GERBER, D., *Law and Competition in Twentieth Century Europe* (Oxford University Press, 1998).

FAULL, J. and NIKPAY, A., *The EC Law of Competition* (Oxford University Press 1999).

JONES, A. and SUFRIN, B., *EC Competition Law: Text, Cases, and Materials* (Oxford University Press 2001).

JONES, C. and VAN DE WOUDE, M., *EC Competition Law Handbook* (reissued annually) (Sweet & Maxwell).

KORAH, V.L., *An Introductory Guide to EC Competition Law and Practice*, 7th edn. (Hart Publishing, 2000).

—— *Cases and Materials on EC Competition Law*, 2nd edn. (Hart Publishing 2001).

LANE, R., *EC Competition Law*, 1st edn. (Longman, 2000).

LINDSTRUP, G. (ed.), *Butterworth's Competition Law Handbook*, 8th edn. (Butterworths, 2002).

RITTER, L., BROWN, D., and RAWLINSON, F., *European Competition Law; A Practitioners Guide*, 2nd edn. (Kluwer, 2001).

ROBERT SCHUMAN CENTRE, *European University Institute, Florence* (eds. Ehlermann, C.D., and others), annual publication on 'European Competition Law' since 1995, including *The Modernization of EC Antitrust Policy* (2000) (pub. 2001) and *Effective Private Enforcement* (2001) (pub. 2003).

SAUTER, W., *Competition Law and Industrial Policy in the EU* (Oxford University Press, 1997).

WAELBROECK, M., and FRIGNANI, A., *European Competition Law* (Transnational Publishers, New York, 1999).

3. (a) Books on Special Aspects of EC Competition Law

ANDERMAN, S.D., *EC Competition Law and Intellectual Property Rights* (Oxford University Press, 1998).

BLUM, F. and LOGUE, A., *State Monopolies under EC Law* (Wiley, 1998).

BUENDIA SIERRA, J., *Exclusive Rights and State Monopolies under EC Law* (Oxford University Press, 2000).

CAMERON, P., *Competition in Energy Markets* (Oxford University Press, 2002).

COOK, J. and KERSE, C., *EC Merger Control*, 3rd edn. (Sweet & Maxwell, 2000).

CHRISTOU, R., *International Agency Distribution and Licensing Agreements*, 3rd edn. (FT Law and Tax, 1996).

EC Merger Control Reporter (Kluwer—looseleaf).

GOYDER, J., *EC Distribution Law*, 3rd edn. (Palladian Law Publishing, 2000).

JONES, C., *Private Enforcement of Antitrust Law in the EU, UK and USA*, 1st edn. (Oxford University Press, 1999).

KERSE, C.S., *EC Antitrust Procedure*, 4th edn. (Sweet & Maxwell, 1998).

KORAH, V.L. *Technology Transfer Agreements and the EC Competition Rules*, 1st edn. (Oxford University Press, 1996).

—— and O'SULLIVAN, D., *Vertical Agreements: Distribution under the EC Competition Rules* (Hart Publishing, 2002).

LEVY, N., *The Control of Concentrations between Undertakings*, Vol. 5 of 'Competition Law of the European Community' (Matthew Bender, 2002).

NAVARRO, E., FONT, A., FOLGUERA. J., and BRIONES, J., *Merger Control in the EU* (Oxford University Press, 2002).

ORTIZ BLANCO, L., *EC Competition Procedure* 1st edn. (Oxford University Press, 1996).

—— and VAN HOUTTE, B., *EC Competition Law in the Transport Sector*, 1st edn. (Oxford University Press, 1997).

ROWLEY, J. and BAKER, D., *Merger Control: The International Regulation of Mergers and Joint*

Ventures, 3rd edn. 3 Vols. (Sweet & Maxwell, 2000).

VOGELAAR, F., STUYCK, J., and VAN REEKEN, B. (eds.), *Competition Law in the EU, its Member*

States and Switzerland, 2 Vols. (Kluwer, 2000 and 2002).

WESSELING, R., *The Modernization of EC Antitrust Law* (Hart Publishing, 2000).

3. (b) Books on Special Aspects of Subjects Related to EC Competition Law

ANDERSON, D. and DEMETRIOU, M., *References to the European Court*, 2nd edn. (Sweet & Maxwell, 2002).

BERNITZ, U., *European Law in Sweden* (Stockholm University, 2000).

CORNISH, W.R., *Intellectual Property: Patents, Copyright, Trade Marks, and Allied Rights*, 4th edn. (Sweet & Maxwell, 1999).

DE BURCA, D. and SCOTT, J. (eds.), *The EU and WTO: Legal and Constitutional Issues* (Hart Publishing, 2001).

EVENETT, S., LEHMANN, A., and STEEL, B. (eds.), *Antitrust Goes Global* (Brookings Institution, Washington DC, 2000).

GORMLEY, L., *Prohibiting Restrictions on Trade within the EEC* (North-Holland, 1985).

NORBERG, S. (and others), *EEA Law: A Commentary on the EEA Agreement*, 1st edn. (1993, Fritzes, Stockholm).

WEILER, J., SLAUGHTER, A.M., and SWEET, A.S. (eds.), *The European Court and National Courts*, 1st edn. (Hart Publishing, 1998).

4. Books on UK and EC Competition Law

BUTTERWORTHS COMPETITION LAW ENCYCLOPAEDIA—looseleaf, 3 Vols. (eds. FREEMAN, P. and WHISH, R.)

FRAZER, T. and WATERSON, M., *Competition Law and Policy*, 1st edn. (Harvester Wheatsheaf, 1994).

FURSE, M., *Competition Law of the UK and EEC*, 3rd edn. (Oxford University Press, 2002).

GREEN, N. and ROBERTSON, A. (eds.), *The Europeanisation of UK Competition Law* (Hart Publishing, 1999).

LIVINGSTON, D., *Competition Law and Practice*, 1st edn. (FT Law and Tax, 1995).

MIDDLETON, K., *UK and EC Competition*

Documents, 2nd edn. (Oxford University Press, 2002).

RODGER, B. and MACCULLOCH, A., *Competition Law and Policy*, 2nd edn. (Cavendish Publishing, 2001).

SMITH, M., *Competition Law: Enforcement and Procedure* (Butterworths, 2001).

SWEET & MAXWELL, *Encyclopaedia of Competition Law*—looseleaf, 3 Vols. (ed. R. Merkin).

TAYLOR, P., *EC and UK Competition Law and Compliance* (Sweet & Maxwell, 1999).

WHISH, R., *Competition Law*, 4th edn. (Butterworths, 2001).

5. Other Works

AMATO, G., *Antitrust and the Bounds of Power* (Hart Publishing, 1997).

DELL, E., *The Schuman Plan and the British Abdication of Leadership in Europe*, 1st edn. (Oxford University Press, 1995).

DIEBOLD, W., *The Schuman Plan: A Study in Economic Co-operation* (Praeger, 1959).

DUCHÊNE, F., *Jean Monnet: The First Statesman of Interdependence* (Norton, 1994).

GEORGE, S., *An Awkward Partner: Britain in the*

Economic Community, 2nd edn. (Oxford University Press, 1994).

MAYNE, R., *The Recovery of Europe*, 1st edn. (Weidenfeld & Nicholson, 1970).

MONNET, J., *Memoires*, trans. Richard Mayne (Collins, 1978).

PERITZ, R., *Competition Policy in America; History, Rhetoric, Law* (Oxford University Press, 2001).

POSNER, R., *Antitrust Law*, 2nd edn. (University of Chicago Press, 2001).

INDEX

Entries followed by 'early', 'previous', 'current', or 'future' in parentheses refer specifically to that stage of the development of the law.

production and development of components,
allocation of responsibility for 421
provisions of 420
recession, during 423
special category of joint venture, as 419
sub-contracting agreement, notice on 230–1
supply quotas 544
Supremacy of EC Law
the previous debate 440–5
the effect of reg. 1/2003 445–7
Sutherland, Peter 522
Sweden 454, 455

T

technology transfer
block exemption Regulation 240/96 173
black list 236
detail of 234–7
future of 237–8
licences to which not applying 237
market share proposals 234
opposition clause 237
patent and know-how block exemptions,
amalgamation of
previous 230–4
current 235–7
future 237–8
report on operation of 238
trade marks, application to 240–1
travaux preparatoires 233–4
white list 235–6
telecommunications
Article 86(3), Directives and decisions on
490–2, 523
changing background of 431–2
competition policy 4
concentrative joint ventures 409–10
joint ventures, case law 432–3
Mexican Telecoms case 517–18
mobile telephone sector, liberalization of 494
television rights
sports broadcasting, individual exemption
133–4
trade association
cartel as 79
cartels operated by or through
Dutch cases 156–7
information, exchange of 157–9
restrictions on competition 160–2
standards and certification, controlling
159–60
categories of 80–1
constitution 79–80
decisions by
informal 81–2
meaning 67–8, 80–2

non-binding 81–2
definition 78–9
performing rights societies 162
rules of 80
ancillary restrictions 101
special or exclusive rights, with 484
trade between Member States, agreements affecting
affect, meaning 88
analysis of 83
application of Articles 81 and 82 compared 88–9
banking sector 88
commercial activities 90
domestic nature, of 87
early cases on 42–4, 83–5
freedom of trade, threat to 84
industry's original assumptions as to its
meaning 53
need to protect common market 42–4
insufficient 89
networks of 86
original interpretation 83
later developments 87–8
tests as to 84
trade, meaning of 90
trade mark licences
block exemption Regulation 240/96, application
of 240–1
individual exemption 241
trade marks
commercial value 239
common origin, goods of 261–3
Community 247
early cases 239–40
effect of Trade Mark Directive 247–8
effectiveness of EC law, use of rights to defeat
43
exhaustion of rights principle 256, 258–60
horizontal agreements 239–40
markets in which goods sold, right to determine
259
Member State law, harmonization of 247
similar, attempt to prevent use of 263–4
trade unions
undertakings, not 62
Treaty of Paris
Article 65 20–1
Article 66 20–1
Article 67 21
central control, elements of 20
competition rules as compared with those under
Treaty of Rome 27–8
conditions of competition, interference with 21
enforcement provisions 20
expiration of 103
objectives 19
pricing practices, prohibited 22
sanctions 20–1